O9-ABE-591

Journalizing and Posting

GENERAL JOURNAL ③ PAGE 1

DATE		DESCRIPTION	POST. REF.	DEBIT	CREDIT
20–					
June	1	Cash	111	70 0 0 0 00	
		L. A. Cruz, Capital			70 0 0 0 00
		Original investment by			
		Cruz in Cruz Auto Detail.			

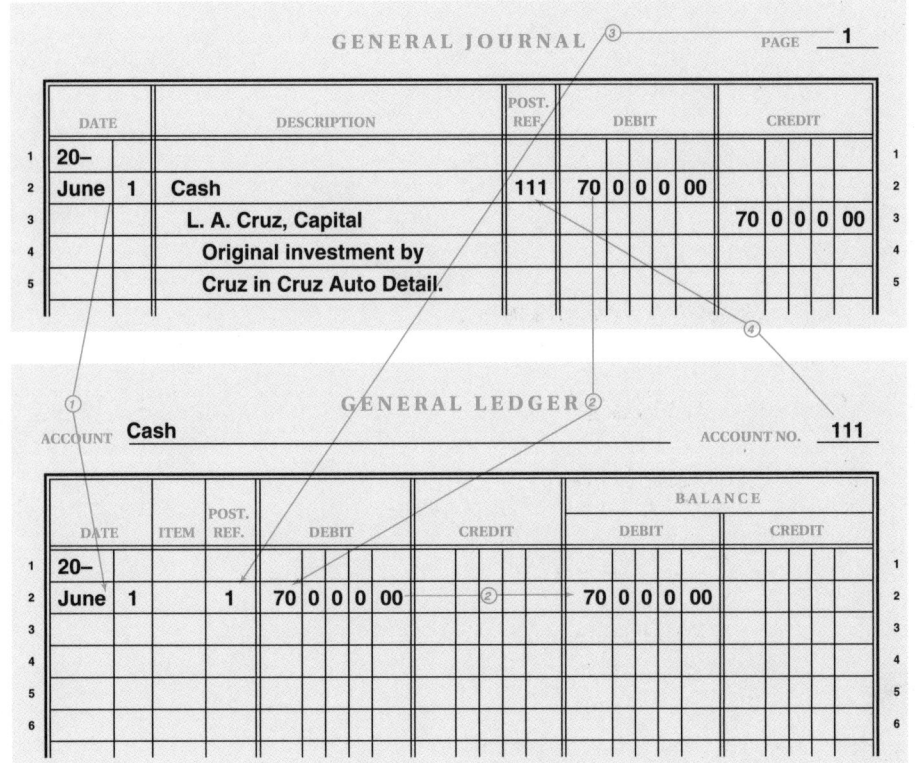

① Date of transaction
② Amount of transaction
③ Page number of the journal
④ Ledger account number

GENERAL LEDGER ②

ACCOUNT Cash ACCOUNT NO. 111

DATE		ITEM	POST. REF.	DEBIT	CREDIT	BALANCE DEBIT	BALANCE CREDIT
20–							
June	1		1	70 0 0 0 00	② →	70 0 0 0 00	

The Work Sheet

Account Name	Trial Balance Debit	Trial Balance Credit	Adjustments Debit	Adjustments Credit	Adjusted Trial Balance Debit	Adjusted Trial Balance Credit	Income Statement Debit	Income Statement Credit	Balance Sheet Debit	Balance Sheet Credit
	Assets →				Assets →				Assets	
		Liabilities →				Liabilities →				Liabilities
		Capital →				Capital →				Capital
	Drawing →				Drawing →				Drawing	
		Revenue →				Revenue →		Revenue		
	Expenses →				Expenses →		Expenses			

Steps in the Closing Process

R Close the Revenue accounts into Income Summary.
E Close the Expenses accounts into Income Summary.
I Close the Income Summary Account into the Capital Account, transferring the net income or net loss to the Capital Account.
D Close the Drawing account into the Capital Account.

College Accounting

DATE DUE

10-24-06	2-1-05
Feb 14, 2007	
2-2-13	
5-27-14	
5/1/17	

DEMCO, INC. 38-2931

College Accounting

SEVENTH EDITION 1–14

Douglas J. McQuaig

WENATCHEE VALLEY COLLEGE

Patricia A. Bille

HIGHLINE COMMUNITY COLLEGE

HOUGHTON MIFFLIN COMPANY BOSTON NEW YORK

[redacted]

NOV 0 1 2004

Senior Accounting Editor: Bonnie Binkert
Associate Sponsoring Editor: Margaret E. Monahan
Editorial Associate: Damaris R. Curran
Senior Project Editor: Chere C. Bemelmans
Editorial Assistant: Elisabeth Kehrer
Senior Production/Design Coordinator: Carol Merrigan
Manufacturing Manager: Florence Cadran
Marketing Manager: Melissa Russell

This book is written to provide accurate and authoritative information concerning the covered topics. It is not meant to take the place of professional advice. The companies and financial information in this book have been created for instructional purposes. No reference to any specific company or person is intended or should be inferred. Any similarity with an existing company is purely coincidental.

Cover design: Rebecca Fagan
Cover image: John Sill

Comments about *College Accounting,* Seventh Edition, can be sent to the authors at the following e-mail address: pbille@uswest.net.

Credits

Introduction
p. 2, Tony Freeman/Photo Edit; p. 4, Michael Newman/Photo Edit; p. 5, Robert Brenner/Photo Edit.

Chapter 1
p. 8, Yvonne Hemser/Gamma Liaison; p. 10, Tony Freeman/Photo Edit; p. 15, Bob Daemmrich/Stock Boston.

Chapter 2
p. 37, S. Dooley/Gamma Liaison; p. 46, Charles Gupton/Stock Boston; p. 51, R. Rathe/Stock Boston.

(Credits continued on page C-1.)

Copyright © 2001 by Houghton Mifflin Company. All rights reserved.

No part of this work may be reproduced or transmitted in any form or by any means, electronic or mechanical, including photocopying and recording, or by any information storage or retrieval system without the prior written permission of Houghton Mifflin Company unless such copying is expressly permitted by federal copyright law. Address inquiries to College Permissions, Houghton Mifflin Company, 222 Berkeley Street, Boston, MA 02116-3764.

Printed in the U.S.A.

Library of Congress Catalog Card No.: 96-76929

ISBN: 0-618-022813

123456789-VH-04 03 02 01 00

This text is sincerely dedicated to the students who will use it.

Every possible effort has been made to produce an understandable, up-to-date, and accurate presentation of the fundamentals of accounting.

This text is intended to be an important element in your course, as well as an invaluable future reference for you in the preparation of your career in business.

Best wishes for your success.

Douglas J. McQuaig

Patricia A. Bille

Contents

Preface

The goals for the Seventh Edition of *College Accounting* are the same as they have been for the previous editions: to provide students with a strong basic knowledge of accounting terms, concepts, and procedures, always taking into consideration students' widely varying objectives, which include:

- preparation for entering the job market in accounting.
- a practical background in accounting for beginning other careers, such as clerical, secretarial, technical, sales, and management positions.
- retraining for career changes.
- preparation and background for more advanced studies in accounting.

Drawing from more than 60 years of combined teaching experience, we have developed an up-to-date, understandable, and teachable basic accounting text. The text is logically organized, liberally illustrated, and paced in a manner that is easy for students to read and understand. Based on extensive reviews, campus visits, and conversations with many accounting instructors and students, we have updated, revised, and improved both the text and the ancillary materials.

The accounting principles described are those endorsed by the Financial Accounting Standards Board.

CHARACTERISTICS OF COLLEGE ACCOUNTING

Focus on the Fundamentals

College Accounting, Seventh Edition presents the fundamentals of accounting in a practical, easy-to-comprehend manner. Great emphasis is placed on developing a firm foundation of fundamental procedures. Appropriate repetition enables students to develop confidence in themselves and to make progress in gradual stages. This repetition is accomplished through extensive use of examples and color-coded illustrations. Color photographs round out the text, which is designed to serve the wide range of student experiences.

Recording business transactions is directly related to the fundamental accounting equation. Each newly introduced transaction is fully illustrated and is supported with T account examples. Comprehensive reviews of T accounts, organized in relation to the fundamental accounting equation, appear in the Student Working Papers with Study Guide to assist as students review material and complete assignments.

Reading Comprehension

College Accounting, Seventh Edition is a very readable text. We write in short sentences and use many illustrations to help students relate the words to the procedures. Each chapter of *College Accounting* has been reviewed by business instructors who teach English as a Second Language courses and English for Special Purposes courses, as well as by students enrolled in these classes. With their assistance and advice, we have taken steps to ensure that the text is accessible to all readers.

Each chapter is limited to the presentation of one major concept, which is amply illustrated with business documents and report forms. As terms are introduced, they are defined thoroughly and are used in subsequent examples. Comprehension is also enhanced through the use of "Remember" and "FYI" statements. These short, marginal notes present a learning hint or a capsule summary of a major point made in preceding paragraphs as well as practical tips or information about the topic. End-of-chapter summaries review each performance objective presented in the chapter using text and illustrations.

Emphasis on Accounting Terminology

We firmly believe that accounting is the language of business and that learning new terminology is an essential part of a first course. Each key term is printed in green and is explained when it is first introduced. The end-of-chapter glossary repeats the definitions of the terms presented in the chapter. In addition, page numbers are included for each glossary term, making it easy for students to refer to a term in the chapter.

Questions, Exercises, and Problems *College Accounting,* Seventh Edition provides a wealth of exercise and problem material that is supported by the Working Papers with Study Guide, offering instructors a wide choice for classroom illustrations and assignments. Each chapter ends with comprehensive review and study material consisting of a review of performance objectives; a glossary; discussion questions; exercises; several components—called Consider and Communicate, What If . . ., Critical Thinking, A Matter of Ethics, and Web Work—that foster problem solving and communication skills; and two sets of comparable A and B problems, progressing from simple to complex in difficulty.

- ***Discussion Questions*** Questions, based on the main points in the text and appropriate for either class discussion or for homework, are included at the end of each chapter.
- ***Exercises*** For practice in applying concepts, exercises are provided with each chapter. Each exercise is described briefly in the margin with a reference to the appropriate performance objective.
- ***Consider and Communicate*** Each Consider and Communicate question requires that students first think about the concepts presented in the chapter. Then they are asked to explain the concepts by applying what they have learned.
- ***What If . . .*** Each What If . . . assignment describes a set of accounting circumstances and asks students to use their knowledge of accounting, life experiences, and common sense to form a verbal or written response. These responses require a slightly higher level of thinking than the more basic Consider and Communicate feature.
- ***Critical Thinking*** Critical Thinking exercises provide an opportunity for students to develop their problem-solving skills and employ their knowledge of accounting to complete a task. The Critical Thinking feature is appropriate for individual or team responses and requires yet a higher level of thinking than the What If . . . feature.
- ***A Matter of Ethics*** In this exercise, a situation is described and students are asked to decide whether the action is ethical. Students are also asked to suggest what implications the described behavior might have. These

exercises are particularly valuable in fostering discussion by the class or in small groups.

- ***Web Work*** New to this edition, these assignments challenge students to browse the Web by suggesting topic-related descriptors in the URL or web address window. Students are further directed to look for certain details and then discuss or write about their discoveries.
- ***Problems*** Each chapter contains four A problems and four B problems. The A and B problems are parallel in content and level of difficulty. They are arranged in order of difficulty, with Problems 1A and 1B in each chapter being the simplest and the last problem in each series being the most comprehensive. Each problem is accompanied by a Check Figure so students can compare their total and correct errors in computation.

PROVEN COLOR-CODED PEDAGOGY

The Seventh Edition of *College Accounting* continues to implement a color-coded pedagogy that helps students recognize and remember key points. The pedagogical use of color also helps students understand the flow of accounting data and identify different types of documents and reports used in accounting. Finally, the use of color in this text helps students identify the performance objectives for each chapter, recognize the performance objectives called for in each exercise and problem, and review material efficiently and effectively.

- **Performance objectives** are highlighted in orange throughout the text. They are listed at the beginning of each chapter and restated alongside the related text discussion. They are referenced by a performance objective number in the chapter summary and in the exercises and problems.
- **Key terms** are printed in green. They are defined in the text and repeated in a glossary at the end of the chapter.
- **Remembers,** highlighted in blue, are learning hints or summaries placed in the margin of the text. These marginal notes often alert students to common procedural pitfalls and help them complete their work successfully.
- **FYIs,** highlighted in purple, are practical tips or information about accounting and business.
- **Tables,** outlined in purple, help students quickly identify material that must be examined as a unit and is not part of running text.

The Seventh Edition's consistent use of color extends to the treatment of accounting forms, financial statements, and documents in the text and end-of-chapter assignments.

- **Source documents,** such as invoices, bank statements, facsimiles, and other material that originates with outside sources, are shown in yellow.
- **Working papers, journals, ledgers, trial balances, and other forms and schedules** used as part of the internal accounting process are shown in green.
- **Financial statements,** including balance sheets, income statements, statements of owner's equity, and statements of cash flows, are shown in blue.

This distinctive treatment differentiates these elements and helps students see where each element belongs in the accounting cycle. Seeing these relationships helps students understand how accountants transform data into useful information.

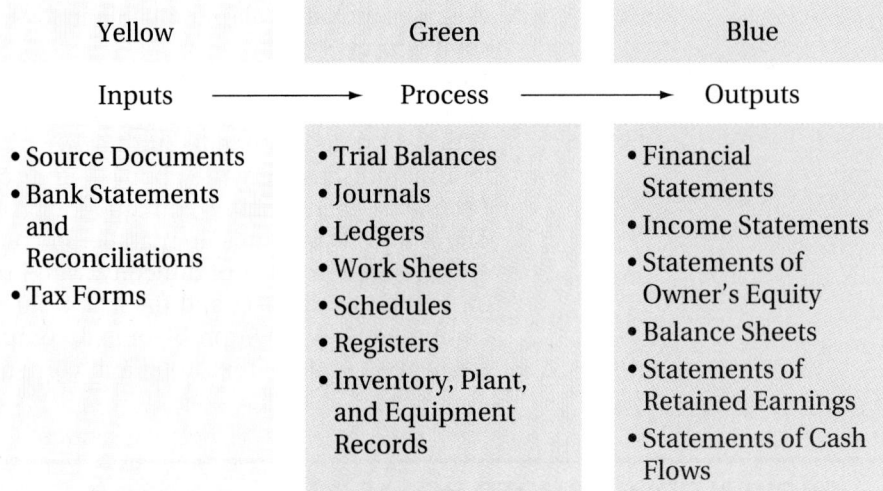

Yellow	Green	Blue
Inputs →	Process →	Outputs
• Source Documents • Bank Statements and Reconciliations • Tax Forms	• Trial Balances • Journals • Ledgers • Work Sheets • Schedules • Registers • Inventory, Plant, and Equipment Records	• Financial Statements • Income Statements • Statements of Owner's Equity • Balance Sheets • Statements of Retained Earnings • Statements of Cash Flows

GUARANTEE OF QUALITY MATERIAL

Successful use of an accounting text depends on more than the interesting and memorable presentation of material by the instructor and the text. The overall quality of the opening windows, examples, illustrations, color photographs, end-of-chapter questions, exercises, and problems, as well as ancillary materials, are critical to learning and retaining the facts and concepts covered in the course. Instructors and students must be assured that these materials are complete, consistent, and accurate.

Together with our publisher, we have taken a multistep approach to ensure quality materials for classroom use. The quality control system begins with in-depth reviews of the original manuscript and concludes with accuracy reviews of page proof by instructors who are actively teaching the course.

CHAPTER COVERAGE

College Accounting, Seventh Edition is designed primarily for use in a one-semester course. The text is divided into parts: Chapters 1–5 cover the full accounting cycle for a sole proprietorship service business. Chapters 6–9 cover the combined journal, bank accounts, and payroll accounting. Chapters 10–14 cover special journals and the full accounting cycle for a merchandising firm.

The following appendices expand content coverage and increase the instructor's options for structuring the course:

- *Appendix A: Methods of Depreciation (after Chapter 4)* This appendix describes methods of depreciation, including the Modified Accelerated Cost Recovery System.
- *Appendix B: Bad Debts (after Chapter 7)* This appendix covers the allowance and specific charge-off methods.
- *Appendix C: Inventory Methods (after Chapter 14)* This appendix describes methods of valuing inventories using weighted-average cost, FIFO, and LIFO.

- *Appendix D: The Statement of Cash Flows (after Chapter 14)* This appendix discusses the indirect method of determining cash flows.
- *Appendix E: Financial Statement Analysis (after Chapter 14)* This appendix describes percentages and ratios used to interpret information in financial statements.

SPECIAL FEATURES AND ENHANCEMENTS FOR THE SEVENTH EDITION TEXT

- ***Complete Revision and Review*** The text and the end-of-chapter assignment materials have been thoroughly revised, updated, and reviewed.
- ***Full-Color Design with Photographs*** The Seventh Edition maintains its exciting full-color design, complete with two or three color photographs and accompanying captions in each chapter. These photographs help students visualize the concepts discussed in the chapter and glimpse them in practice.
- ***Drawings of Concepts*** Many chapters contain pictorial images to appeal to students' varied learning styles and enhance the text, color-coded forms, and rich illustrations.
- ***Transparent Acetate Pages*** New to Chapter 4, Adjusting Entries and the Work Sheet, we have created transparency overlays that allow students to build a work sheet in stages, better visualizing the steps involved in the process.
- ***Windows on the World Wide Web*** New to this edition, these chapter openings provide a hands-on look at many of today's most well known businesses that are active on the Web. Each window first introduces students to the company and then asks a series of questions about the company that relate directly to the chapter topics. We provide web addresses for further investigation of the company. These questions and addresses are designed to prompt discussion, written responses, or additional questions surrounding the chapter.
- ***Extended Examples*** Cruz Auto Detail is integrated throughout Chapters 1–5 to illustrate the completion of the accounting cycle for a sole-proprietorship service business.

  Jackson Electric Supply is featured throughout Chapters 10–14 to illustrate the completion of the accounting cycle for a sole-proprietorship merchandising business using special journals.
- ***Student Annotations*** Additional Remembers and FYIs have been added to this edition. Remembers summarize key concepts for students, and FYIs are brief, interesting pieces of information about current business practice.
- ***Continuous General Ledger Problem*** A continuous general ledger problem featuring Like New, a sole proprietorship that renews furniture, begins in Chapter 3 by opening the accounting books for Like New. Students are required to enter into the software (for example, Peachtree, QuickBooks, or Houghton Mifflin's Windows General Ledger) the company name, company type, as well as the chart of accounts before journalizing and posting the first month's transactions and printing a trial balance. After Chapter 4 (Adjusting Entries and the Work Sheet), students continue with Like New by completing the end-of-the-month adjustments and printing the financial statements. After Chapter 5 (Closing Entries and the Post-Closing Trial Balance), students again work with Like New to close the books for the month and print a post-closing trial balance.

Like New returns after Chapters 10–12 when the owner decides to add a line of merchandise and to introduce special journals for sales, purchases, cash receipts, and cash payments.

- ***Icons*** The following four icons accompany end-of-chapter assignments:

  The first icon indicates exercises designed to enhance students' verbal and written communication skills as well as their group skills.

  The second icon on the left indicates assignments that involve critical thinking, to emphasize the importance of understanding how specific accounting procedures relate to accounting as a whole.

  Problems that can be solved using the Houghton Mifflin Windows General Ledger program are designated by the third icon on the left.

  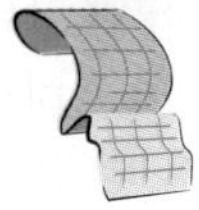

  Problems that can be worked using Spreadsheet Applications for *College Accounting* are identified by the fourth icon on the left.
- ***New Web Assignments*** Web Work exercises provide opportunities for students to do hands-on web browsing and sharpen their oral and written communication skills, as well as their critical thinking skills.
- ***Check Figures*** Check Figures appear alongside every A and B problem in the text.
- ***Cumulative Self-Checks*** Questions (true/false, multiple choice, matching, and completion) and brief application problems follow every two to four chapters. These self-checks let students check their understanding of what they have read in the preceding chapters.
- ***Accounting Cycle Review and Comprehensive Review Problem*** These features give students the opportunity to apply accounting procedures to help them understand the process they have just studied in a series of chapters (1–5) and (7–14).

  In this edition, we have added a second Accounting Cycle Review Problem. Both Problems A and B involve the full accounting cycle, one for Fun World Waterslides and the other for Lakeland Indoor Sailboats, both sole-proprietorship service businesses.

  The Comprehensive Review Problem following Chapter 14 involves the full accounting cycle for Fine Fabrics, a sole-proprietorship merchandising business.

OTHER SPECIAL FEATURES AND ENHANCEMENTS FOR THE SEVENTH EDITION

Supplemental Learning Aids and Instructor's Support Package

Complete descriptions of all of the supplemental learning aids and support materials and of the following new items for students and instructors are included in the Instructor's Resource Manual with Solutions.

For Students

- ***McQuaig/Bille Interactive Learning Center*** The student web site, new to the Seventh Edition, expands the concepts and ideas presented in the text. The site offers interactive chapter quizzes that consist of 10 multiple choice and 10 true/false questions for each chapter, enabling students to test what they've learned and to find out why their answer is right or wrong. Suggested research activities, performance objectives, key terms, and company links are also offered on this site.

- ***Study Materials in the Working Papers with Study Guide*** The Working Papers with Study Guide contains rich discussions of the following topics to assist students in their study of accounting:

  Review of T Account Placement and Representative Transactions
  How to Study Accounting
  How to Solve Accounting Problems
  Ten-Key Skills Review
  Introduction to Spreadsheets
  Review of Business Mathematics
  How to Work a Practice Set
  Suggested Abbreviations for Account Titles

- ***Suggested Homework Check Questions*** Appearing in the Instructor's Resource Manual with Solutions, these questions, keyed to end-of-chapter assignments, provide students with the opportunity to practice the interpretive portion of the accounting process.
- ***Houghton Mifflin Windows General Ledger Software*** To accompany the Seventh Edition, Houghton Mifflin's new generic Windows general ledger program is available for student use. This package offers complete coverage of accounting concepts and procedures in an extremely simple and user-friendly computerized environment. Selected problems from *College Accounting,* Seventh Edition can be solved using this program.
- ***Spreadsheet Applications for* College Accounting** This innovative accounting software lets students solve end-of-chapter problems using Lotus 1-2-3 or Excel spreadsheet software. Students can select from prepared templates and use them to solve end-of-chapter problems accompanied by the spreadsheet icon. Instructions explaining how to convert Lotus templates to Excel and solve the problems are a feature of this program.
- ***Practice Sets*** A complete selection of manual and computerized practice sets is available for use with *College Accounting,* Seventh Edition. A complete listing and description of each practice set and its support package can be found in the Instructor's Resource Manual with Solutions.

  New to the Seventh Edition is the ***Whitewater Kayaks Practice Set.*** The practice set is based on a sole proprietorship and covers a one-month accounting period, enabling the student to acquire experience in dealing with the entire accounting cycle. In addition to a student text to complete the practice set manually, a CD-ROM gives the student the option of completing the practice set electronically using Peachtree 7.0, QuickBooks 2000, or Houghton Mifflin Windows General Ledger Software.

For Instructors

- ***McQuaig/Bille Interactive Learning Center*** The instructor web site, new to the Seventh Edition, offers additional instructor resource material. The site offers an enrichment manual designed to increase instructor options and to expand the flexibility of *College Accounting,* Seventh Edition. Teaching ideas and techniques, solutions to end-of-chapter problems, instructor outlines, performance objectives, and key terms are also offered on this site.
- ***Instructor's Solutions Manual*** to accompany ***Whitewater Kayaks Practice Set*** New to the Seventh Edition, the practice set is based on a sole proprietorship, covering a one-month accounting period, enabling the student to acquire experience in dealing with the entire accounting cycle. In addition to a student text to complete the practice set manually, a CD-ROM gives the student the option of completing the practice set electronically using Peachtree 7.0, QuickBooks 2000, or Houghton Mifflin Windows General Ledger Software.

Content Changes in the Seventh Edition

A complete list of content changes from the Sixth Edition to the Seventh Edition of *College Accounting* can be found in the Transition Guide, located in the Instructor's Resource Manual with Solutions. The following is a brief listing of the most important revisions and changes:

- ***Introduction to Accounting*** We have added the paraprofessional accountant as a section and a key term, and we now discuss the CMA certificate.
- ***Chapter 1 Asset, Liability, Owner's Equity, Revenue, and Expense Accounts*** We rewrote sample transactions to parallel the end-of-chapter problems. We added a section on numbering the chart of accounts when using a computer.
- ***Chapter 2 T Accounts, Debits and Credits, Trial Balance, and Financial Statements*** In Performance Objective 7, we eliminated (c) prepare a balance sheet containing the statement of owner's equity information. We edited the section entitled The T Account Form with Debits and Credits for clarity (in the previous edition, this was called Recording Transactions in T Account Form). This section provides the procedures to follow in the earlier analysis for reference when working with each transaction.
- ***Chapter 4 Adjusting Entries and the Work Sheet*** We included a new section on journalizing adjusting entries.
- ***Chapter 6 Accounting for Professional Enterprises: The Combined Journal (Optional)*** This was Appendix B in the previous edition. We have added three Performance Objectives: Performance Objective 4—Prepare a work sheet for a professional enterprise; Performance Objective 5—Prepare financial statements for a professional enterprise; and Performance Objective 6—Record adjusting and closing entries in a combined journal.
- ***Chapter 8 Employee Earnings and Deductions*** This was Chapter 7 in the previous edition. We have updated the tax rules while adding a new key term: *withholding allowance*. A more precise distinction is now made between allowance and exemptions.
- ***Chapter 9 Employer Taxes, Payments, and Reports*** This was Chapter 8 in the previous edition. We have expanded Objective 8 to include end-of-year adjustments for accrued salaries and wages. Based on advice from our customers and reviewers, we deleted coverage of special deposit schedule rules (including four key terms: *monthly deposit schedule rule, semi-weekly deposit schedule rule, $100,000 one-day rule,* and *$500 rule*). We replaced the example Form 940 with Form 940EZ.
- ***Chapter 12 The Cash Receipts Journal and the Cash Payments Journal*** This was Chapter 11 in the previous edition. We inserted a section on Sales Returns and Allowances and Sales Discounts on an Income Statement.
- ***Chapter 13 Work Sheet and Adjusting Entries*** This was Chapter 12 in the previous edition. We changed the chapter title from Adjusting Entries to Work Sheet and Adjusting Entries and we relocated the expanded chart of accounts to Chapter 14.
- ***Chapter 14 Financial Statements, Closing Entries, and Reversing Entries*** This was Chapter 13 in the previous edition. This chapter now includes the expanded chart of accounts and an explanation on the arrangement of the accounts. We combined the discussion of Other Income with that of Other Expenses.

New

We introduce the following chapter in the Seventh Edition: Chapter 6 Accounting for Professional Enterprises: The Combined Journal (Optional)

SUPPLEMENTARY LEARNING AIDS FOR STUDENTS AND SUPPORT MATERIALS FOR INSTRUCTORS

For the Seventh Edition, we have assembled the most comprehensive package of student and instructor aids to complement a wide variety of teaching styles and course emphases. Detailed descriptions of each element of the support package are available in the Instructor's Resource Manual with Solutions.

For Students

- Working Papers with Study Guide 1–9
- Working Papers with Study Guide 1–14
- Working Papers with Study Guide 15–27
- McQuaig/Bille Interactive Learning Center
- Houghton Mifflin Windows General Ledger Software for Selected Problems
- Spreadsheet Applications for College Accounting
- Accounting Video Workshop
- Small Business Video
- Practice Sets:
  - *Divesports* (after Chapter 3)
  - *Sounds Abound,* Second Edition (after Chapter 5; can be used with Houghton Mifflin's General Ledger Software Program)
  - *Let's Party* (after Chapter 5; can be used with Peachtree 3.5 or 5.0)
  - *Lawson's Supply Center, Inc.* (after Chapters 8 and 9; can be used with Houghton Mifflin's General Ledger Software program)
  - *Crystal Clean Maintenance* (after Chapter 9)
  - *Oak Creek Canyon Jewelers* (after Chapter 9; can be used with Peachtree 3.5 or 5.0)
  - *Rug Bug* (after Chapter 14; can be used with Peachtree 3.5 or 5.0)
  - *Whitewater Kayaks* (after Chapter 14; can be used with Peachtree 7.0, QuickBooks 2000, or Houghton Mifflin's General Ledger Software program)
  - *The Wax Works: A Cumulative Shoebox Practice Set with Business Papers* (after Chapter 14)

For Instructors

- Instructor's Resource Manual with Solutions
- Test Bank
- McQuaig/Bille Interactive Learning Center
- Computerized Test Bank
- Achievement Tests (A and B)
- Teaching and Solutions Transparencies
- Instructor's Guide to Accounting Video Workshop
- Instructor's Solutions Manuals for all practice sets

ACKNOWLEDGMENTS

We sincerely thank the editorial staff of Houghton Mifflin for their continuous support. Also, we thank our many students at Highline Community College for their observations and evaluations.

During the writing of the Seventh Edition, we consulted many users of the text throughout the country. Their constructive suggestions are reflected in the changes that have been made. Unfortunately, space does not permit mention of all those who have contributed to this volume. Some of those, however, who have been supportive and have influenced our efforts, are:

Joseph F. Adamo, CAZENOVIA COLLEGE
Clifford Bellers, WASHTENAW COMMUNITY COLLEGE
Catherine F. Berg, NASSAU COMMUNITY COLLEGE
Kenneth W. Brown, UNIVERSITY OF HOUSTON
Howard Bryan, SANTA ROSA JUNIOR COLLEGE
Theresa Capretta, TOMBALL COLLEGE
Carmela C. Caputo, EMPIRE STATE COLLEGE
Anthony R. Carbone, MASSACHUSETTS BAY COMMUNITY COLLEGE
C. P. Carter, UNIVERSITY OF MASSACHUSETTS–LOWELL
Janet Cassagio, NASSAU COMMUNITY COLLEGE
Michael S. Chaks, RIVERSIDE COMMUNITY COLLEGE
Frank Cress, BUTTE COLLEGE
Dana A. Crismond, MOUNTAIN EMPIRE COMMUNITY COLLEGE
Martha J. Curry, HUSTON-TILLOTSON COLLEGE
Carl Dauber, SOUTHERN OHIO COLLEGE–NORTH EAST
Allan Doyle, PIMA COLLEGE
Carl D. Erickson, INTERNATIONAL BUSINESS COLLEGE
William M. Evans, CERRITOS COLLEGE
Donald E. Foster, TACOMA COMMUNITY COLLEGE
Mary D. Foster, ILLINOIS CENTRAL COLLEGE
Lynne Fowler, HEALD BUSINESS COLLEGE
Walter A. Franklin, PALM BEACH COMMUNITY COLLEGE
Alan P. Fraser, RIO HONDO COLLEGE
William French, ALBUQUERQUE TECHNICAL-VOCATIONAL INSTITUTE
Theresa V. Gann, SAN JACINTO COLLEGE
Marlin Gerber, KALAMAZOO VALLEY COMMUNITY COLLEGE
Helen Gerrard, MIAMI UNIVERSITY–HAMILTON & MIDDLETOWN CAMPUSES
Charles F. Grant, SKYLINE COLLEGE
Harry Gray, INDIANA VOCATIONAL TECHNICAL COLLEGE
Gary Guinn, SKAGIT VALLEY COLLEGE
Julia F. Harrison, COLUMBUS STATE COMMUNITY COLLEGE
Robert Hartzell, COLORADO MOUNTAIN COLLEGE
C. Robert Hellmer, MILWAUKEE AREA TECHNICAL COLLEGE
Donald L. Holloway, LONG BEACH COMMUNITY COLLEGE
Jay S. Hollowell, COMMONWEALTH COLLEGE–VIRGINIA BEACH CAMPUS
Janis Hutchins, LAMAR UNIVERSITY–PORT ARTHUR
Thomas Jackson, CERRITOS COMMUNITY COLLEGE
Eugene Janner, BLINN COLLEGE
Edward H. Julius, CALIFORNIA LUTHERAN UNIVERSITY
James Kahl, LOWER COLUMBIA COLLEGE
Ann P. King, BRANELL INSTITUTE
Bobbie Krapels, MEMPHIS STATE UNIVERSITY

Ronald K. Kulhanek, GREAT LAKES JUNIOR COLLEGE
Joanne M. Landry, MASSASOIT COMMUNITY COLLEGE
Shirley Hsiang-ju Wen Leung, LOS MEDANOS COLLEGE
Ken Liebham, COLUMBIA GORGE COMMUNITY COLLEGE
Loren Long, ELGIN COMMUNITY COLLEGE
Gloria J. Lynch, MT. ALOYSIUS JUNIOR COLLEGE
Ted Lynch, HOCKING COLLEGE
Patricia McDaniel, CENTRAL PIEDMONT COMMUNITY COLLEGE
Shirl Mallory, COOSA VALLEY TECHNICAL INSTITUTE
Elizabeth Barnard Miller, COLUMBUS STATE COMMUNITY COLLEGE
Donald E. Morehead, HENRY FORD COMMUNITY COLLEGE
Robert S. Nash, HENRY FORD COMMUNITY COLLEGE
Jerome P. Neadly, MORTON COLLEGE
Dolores J. Osborn, CENTRAL WASHINGTON UNIVERSITY
Vincent Pelletier, COLLEGE OF DUPAGE
Daniel J. Pike, ROCHESTER INSTITUTE OF TECHNOLOGY
Bernard Piwkiewicz, LANEY COLLEGE
Gray R. Ragsdale, CENTRAL TEXAS COLLEGE
Karen D. Richardson, TARRANT COUNTY JUNIOR COLLEGE–NORTHEAST CAMPUS
Fabiola Rubio, EL PASO COMMUNITY COLLEGE
Paul T. Ryan, JACKSON STATE COMMUNITY COLLEGE
Nelda Shelton, TARRANT COUNTY JUNIOR COLLEGE–SOUTH CAMPUS
Nancy Sheridan, BUCKS COUNTY COMMUNITY COLLEGE
Bill Smith, PORTLAND COMMUNITY COLLEGE
Harold R. Steinhauser, ROCK VALLEY COLLEGE
Nancy Stewart, ODESSA COLLEGE
Joseph Stoffel, WAUBONSEE COMMUNITY COLLEGE
Ron Summers, OKLAHOMA CITY COMMUNITY COLLEGE
Rahmat Ola Tavallali, WALSH COLLEGE
William G. Vendemia, YOUNGSTOWN STATE UNIVERSITY
Russell Vermillion, PRINCE GEORGE'S COMMUNITY COLLEGE
Florence G. Waldman, KILGORE COLLEGE
Martha Walty, SAN JOSE CITY COLLEGE
Dick D. Wasson, SOUTHWESTERN COLLEGE
Jim M. Weglin, NORTH SEATTLE COMMUNITY COLLEGE
Sharon Welch, PIMA COMMUNITY COLLEGE–WEST CAMPUS
Nancy T. Weller, GRAND RAPIDS JUNIOR COLLEGE
Bobby R. Williams, MCLENNAN COMMUNITY COLLEGE

A special note of thanks to the individuals who contributed greatly by reviewing page proofs and checking the end-of-chapter questions, exercises, and problems:

Gregory D. Barnes, CLARION UNIVERSITY
William A Barzen, ST. PETERSBURG JUNIOR COLLEGE–ST. PETERSBURG CAMPUS
Jennifer L. Berry, PARKS JUNIOR COLLEGE–SOUTH
Charles M. Betts, DELAWARE TECHNICAL AND COMMUNITY COLLEGE
Gary R. Bower, COMMUNITY COLLEGE OF RHODE ISLAND
Jay M. Bruns, TAMPA COLLEGE–PINELLAS
Ron Burnette, MACOMB COMMUNITY COLLEGE
Carolyn A. Byrd, ST. PETERSBURG JUNIOR COLLEGE–CLEARWATER CAMPUS
Lee Cannell, EL PASO COMMUNITY COLLEGE
Tim Carse, BARNES BUSINESS COLLEGE, DENVER
Henry Dalehite, HEALD COLLEGE
Mark Dawson, DUQUESNE UNIVERSITY
Steven M. Day, DIXIE COLLEGE

Diana Dewald, MANATEE COMMUNITY COLLEGE
Patricia A. Doherty, BOSTON UNIVERSITY SCHOOL OF MANAGEMENT
Richard Dugger, KILGORE COLLEGE
Nina Edgmand, SALT LAKE COMMUNITY COLLEGE
Hussein Emin, NASSAU COMMUNITY COLLEGE
Harry Gary, INDIANA VOCATIONAL TECHNICAL COLLEGE
Roxanne Gooch, CAMERON UNIVERSITY
Christine Uber Grosse, THUNDERBIRD, THE AMERICAN GRADUATE SCHOOL OF INTERNATIONAL MANAGEMENT
Dennis A. Gutting, ORANGE COUNTY COMMUNITY COLLEGE
Gloria M. Halpern, MONTGOMERY COLLEGE
Joyce Henzel, ROGERS STATE COLLEGE
Carla Hogan, SHORELINE COMMUNITY COLLEGE
Sally E. Huttemann, NATIONAL TECHNICAL INSTITUTE FOR THE DEAF AT ROCHESTER INSTITUTE OF TECHNOLOGY
Thomas L. Jackson, CERRITOS COLLEGE
David G. Jordan, BRYANT & STRATTON BUSINESS INSTITUTE
Jimmy King, MCLENNON COMMUNITY COLLEGE
Jacob V. Lamar, MONROE COLLEGE
Cathy Xanthaky Larson, MIDDLESEX COMMUNITY COLLEGE
Donald MacGilvra, SHORELINE COMMUNITY COLLEGE
George J. McGowan
Gail A. Mestas
Michael F. Monahan
Jenine Moscove, BRANFORD HALL CAREER INSTITUTE
Salah Negm, PRINCE GEORGE'S COMMUNITY COLLEGE
Daniel J. Pike, ROCHESTER INSTITUTE OF TECHNOLOGY
Linda L. Scott, INDIANA VOCATIONAL TECHNICAL COLLEGE
S. Murray Simons, MOUNT IDA COLLEGE
Elaine Simpson, ST. LOUIS COMMUNITY COLLEGE AT FLORISSANT VALLEY
Calvin L. Snyder, POLK COMMUNITY COLLEGE
Marion Taube, UNIVERSITY OF PITTSBURGH
Steven C. Teeter, UTAH VALLEY COMMUNITY COLLEGE
Josephine Vondras, ORANGE COUNTY COMMUNITY COLLEGE
Nicholas Walker, SAN JOAQUIN DELTA COLLEGE
Stan Weikert, COLLEGE OF THE CANYONS
Kay Westerfield, UNIVERSITY OF OREGON
Avalon White, BARTON COUNTY COMMUNITY COLLEGE

As always, we would like to thank our families for their understanding and cooperation. Without their support, this text would never have been written. Heartfelt appreciation is extended to Beverlie McQuaig for her detailed proofreading and good humor. Pertinent suggestions for updating the material were given by Judith McQuaig Britton, C.P.A., of Smith, Bunday, Berman, Britton; John McQuaig, C.P.A., of McQuaig and Welk; and Laurie McQuaig Ramaley, D.C. We also express continued gratitude to Bruce Bille, Tracy Bille-Newkirk, James Newkirk, C.P.A., and Adeline Harris for their encouragement and assistance, and to the memory of Ryan Bille and Wesley Harris for their courage and inspiration.

Douglas J. McQuaig

Patricia A. Bille

College Accounting

Introduction to Accounting

Performance Objectives

After you have completed this introduction to accounting, you will be able to do the following:

1. Define *accounting.*
2. Explain the importance of accounting information.
3. Describe the various career opportunities in accounting.

Accounting is often called the language of business because, when confronted with events of a business nature, all people in society—owners, managers, creditors, employees, attorneys, engineers, and so forth—must use accounting terms and concepts to describe these events. Examples of accounting terms are *net, gross, yield, valuation, accrued, deferred*—the list could go on and on. So it is logical that anyone entering the business world should know enough of its "language" to communicate with others and to understand their communications.

As you acquire a knowledge of accounting, you will gain an understanding of the way businesses operate and the reasoning involved in making business decisions. Even if you are not involved directly in accounting activities, you will certainly need to be sufficiently acquainted with the "language" to be able to understand the meaning of accounting information, how it is compiled, how it can be used, and its limitations.

You may be surprised to find that you are already familiar with many accounting terms. Recalling your personal business activities and relating them to your study of accounting will be very helpful to you. For example, when you purchased this textbook, you exchanged cash or a promise to pay cash for the book. As you will see, this exchange is an accounting event. You are going to recognize many activities and terms as you begin your study of accounting.

DEFINITION OF ACCOUNTING

Objective 1
Define *accounting.*

Accounting is the process of analyzing, classifying, recording, summarizing, and interpreting business transactions in financial or monetary terms. A business transaction is an event that has a direct effect on the operation of an economic unit, is expressed in terms of money, and is recorded. Examples of business transactions are buying or selling goods, renting a building, paying employees, and buying insurance.

The primary purpose of accounting is to provide the financial information needed for the efficient operation of an economic unit. The term **economic unit** includes not only business enterprises but also not-for-profit entities, such as government bodies, churches and synagogues, clubs, and fraternal

Accounting is an important part of all types of businesses. These cruise ships require the same extensive recordkeeping as any large destination resort. The ship is a large floating hotel with guests, employees, management, recreational activities, restaurants, and shops.

organizations. Business enterprises or organizations may be called firms or companies. All of these entities require some type of accounting records. An **accountant** is a person who keeps the financial history of the transactions of an economic unit in written form.

Because it is important that all those who receive accounting reports be able to interpret them, a set of rules or guidelines for the accounting process has been developed. These guidelines or rules are known as **generally accepted accounting principles (GAAP)**.

Bookkeeping and Accounting

There are distinctions between bookkeeping and accounting. The two processes are closely related, but there is no universally accepted line of separation. Generally, bookkeeping involves the systematic recording of business transactions in financial terms. Accounting functions at a higher level. An accountant sets up the system that a bookkeeper uses to record business transactions. An accountant may supervise the work of the bookkeeper and prepare financial statements and tax reports. Although the bookkeeper's work is more routine, it is hard to draw a line where the bookkeeper's work ends and the accountant's begins.

IMPORTANCE OF ACCOUNTING INFORMATION

Objective 2

Explain the importance of accounting information.

Anyone who aspires to a position of leadership in business or government needs a knowledge of accounting. A study of accounting gives a person the necessary background and also gives him or her an understanding of the scope, functions, and policies of an organization. A person may not be doing the accounting work, but he or she will be continually dealing with accounting forms, language, and reports.

Users of Accounting Information

Owners Owners have invested their money or goods in a business organization. They desire information regarding the company's earnings, its prospects for future earnings, and its ability to pay its debts.

Managers Managers and supervisors have to prepare financial reports, understand accounting data contained in reports and budgets, and express future plans in financial terms. People who have management jobs must know how accounting information can be developed in order to evaluate performance in meeting goals.

Creditors Creditors lend money or extend credit to the company for the purchase of goods and services. The company's creditors include suppliers, banks, and other lending institutions, such as loan companies. Creditors are interested in the firm's ability to pay its debts.

Government agencies Taxing authorities verify information submitted by companies concerning a variety of taxes, such as income taxes, sales taxes, and employment taxes. Public utilities, such as electric and gas companies, must provide financial information to regulatory agencies.

Accounting and Technology

Before the invention of calculators and computers, all business transactions were recorded by hand. Now computers perform routine recordkeeping operations and prepare financial reports. Computers are used today in all types of businesses, both large and small. One question often arises: "Is the computer taking over accountants' jobs?" Actually, with the introduction of computers, more jobs have been created to fulfill management's need for more information.

Regardless of whether a business uses a computer, the nature of accounting is the same. The computer is a powerful tool of the accountant. However, as a tool, the computer is only as useful as the ability of the operator. The operator must be skilled to key the correct information into the computer program. Otherwise, as the saying goes, "garbage in, garbage out."

CAREER OPPORTUNITIES IN ACCOUNTING

Objective 3

Describe the various career opportunities in accounting.

To find job opportunities in accounting, all you need to do is read the newspapers' classified advertisements or browse the Internet. Although the jobs listed in these ads require varying amounts of education and experience, most of them are for positions as accounting clerks, general bookkeepers, or accountants. Let's take a look at the requirements and duties of these positions.

Accounting Clerk/Technician

An accounting clerk/technician does routine recording of financial information. The duties of accounting clerks vary with the size of the company. In small businesses, accounting clerks handle most of the recordkeeping functions. In large companies, clerks specialize in one part of the accounting system, such as payroll, accounts receivable, accounts payable, cash, inventory, or purchases. The minimum requirement for most accounting clerk positions is one term or semester of an accounting course.

General Bookkeeper

Many small- and medium-sized companies employ one person to oversee their bookkeeping operations. This person is called a general or full-charge bookkeeper. The general bookkeeper supervises the work of accounting clerks. Requirements for this job vary with the size of the company and the complexity of the accounting system. The minimum requirement for most general bookkeeper jobs is one or two years of accounting as well as experience as an accounting clerk.

Paraprofessional Accountant

To bridge a gap between the general bookkeeper and the professional accountant many firms are hiring **paraprofessional accountants**. They are able to manage the duties of the general bookkeeper as well as many of the duties of a professional accountant under that accountant's supervision. Qualifications generally include a two-year degree or certificate in accounting as well as appropriate prior experience.

Accountant

The term *accountant* describes a fairly broad range of jobs. The accountant may design and manage the entire accounting system for a business. The accountant may also prepare the financial statements and tax returns and perform audits. Many accountants enter the field with a four-year college degree in accounting; however, it is not unusual for accountants to start at entry-level positions and work their way up to management positions. Although accountants are employed in every kind of economic unit, they are classified into one of three categories: public accounting, managerial or private accounting, and not-for-profit accounting. We'll briefly look at these categories.

Accountants are employed in every kind of economic unit. Many start in entry level positions and work their way up to management.

Public Accounting Certified public accountants (CPAs) are independent professionals who provide services to clients for a fee. To become a CPA, a person must have a college degree, pass a rigorous examination, and generally complete a work-experience requirement. Public accountants design accounting systems, prepare tax returns, provide financial advice about business operations, and audit financial statements.

Managerial or Private Accounting Most people who are accountants are employed by private business organizations. These accountants (not necessarily CPAs) manage the accounting system, prepare budgets, determine costs of products, and provide financial information for managers and owners. Accountants have many opportunities to advance into top management positions. The Certified Management Accountant (CMA) exam has become an important partner to the CPA credentials.

Not-for-Profit Accounting Not-for-profit accounting is used for government agencies, hospitals, churches and synagogues, and schools. Accountants for these organizations prepare budgets and maintain records

Organizations that are in business to serve rather than make a profit require accounting procedures, just as do profit-making organizations. The difference is in the mission of the organization—profit or not-for-profit.

sharing is caring
THE SALVATION ARMY
God bless you

of revenues and expenses. It should be noted that some not-for-profit organizations do in fact make a profit; however, the profit is kept in the organization and not distributed. For example, a hospital makes a profit and then reinvests the profit in modern equipment. Local, state, and federal government bodies employ vast numbers of people in accounting positions.

CHAPTER REVIEW

Review of Performance Objectives

1. Define *accounting.*

   Accounting is the process of analyzing, classifying, recording, summarizing, and interpreting business transactions in financial or monetary terms. It is also an information system and the language of business.

2. Explain the importance of accounting information.

   A study of accounting gives a person the necessary background to understand the scope, functions, and policies of an organization.

3. Describe the various career opportunities in accounting.

   Accountants, paraprofessional accountants, bookkeepers, and accounting clerks will find employment opportunities in several areas—in the public sector, the private sector, or not-for-profit organizations.

GLOSSARY

Accountant A person who keeps the financial history of the transactions of an economic unit in written form; sometimes mistakenly called a bookkeeper. (2)

Accounting The process of analyzing, classifying, recording, summarizing, and interpreting business transactions in financial or monetary terms; sometimes mistakenly called bookkeeping. (1)

Economic unit Includes both business enterprises and not-for-profit entities, such as government bodies, churches and synagogues, clubs, and fraternal organizations. (1)

Generally accepted accounting principles (GAAP) The rules or guidelines used for carrying out the accounting process. (2)

Paraprofessional accountant A person who is qualified in accounting to assume the duties of a general bookkeeper as well as some of those of a professional accountant under that accountant's supervision. (4)

Transaction An event directly affecting an economic entity that can be expressed in terms of money and that must be recorded in the accounting records. (1)

1 Asset, Liability, Owner's Equity, Revenue, and Expense Accounts

WINDOWS ON THE WORLD WIDE WEB

Just can't get enough Gap jeans or leather? Then you've already had experience with accounting. When you plunk down $48 for a pair of Gap jeans, to you it's an expense. To the store it's revenue. When you decide to use your MasterCard to buy the matching leather jacket for $198, you've incurred a liability—a promise to pay the credit card company for your purchases at a later date. All those pants and jackets sold at thousands of stores add up. How much revenue do you think Gap earned last year? Was it in millions or billions? What was Gap's equity, which is the difference between assets and liabilities? What are some of Gap's assets, the stores and businesses Gap owns? To find out check **www.gapinc.com/performance/annual_reports/pdf/fin_annual_98.pdf.**

Performance Objectives

After you have completed this chapter, you will be able to do the following:

1. Define and identify *asset, liability,* and *owner's equity* accounts.
2. Record a group of business transactions, in column form, involving changes in assets, liabilities, and owner's equity.
3. Define and identify *revenue* and *expense* accounts.
4. Record a group of business transactions, in column form, involving all five elements of the fundamental accounting equation.

As we stated in the Introduction, accounting is the process of analyzing, classifying, recording, and summarizing business transactions. We now introduce the analyzing, classifying, and recording steps in the accounting process.

ASSETS, LIABILITIES, AND OWNER'S EQUITY

The Fundamental Accounting Equation

Objective 1

Define and identify *asset, liability,* and *owner's equity* accounts.

Assets **are properties or things of value, such as cash, equipment, copyrights, buildings, and land, owned and controlled by an economic unit or business entity.** By the term business entity, we mean that the business is an economic unit in itself, and the assets or properties of the business are

When a company's liabilities are greater than its assets, it may be forced into bankruptcy. The money earned from a going-out-of-business sale is used to pay creditors.

-PUBLIC NOTICE-
GOING OUT
OF BUSINESS
GRAND OPENING
CHURCH ST
ONE

completely separate from the owner's personal assets. However, the owner has a claim on the assets of the business and a responsibility for its debts. **The owner's right, claim, or financial interest is expressed by the word equity in the business.** Another term that could be used is capital. Whenever you see the term owner's equity, it means the owner's right to or investment in the business.

FYI

Other terms for equity are *investment, net worth,* or *proprietorship.*

Assets	=	**Owner's Equity**
Properties or things of value owned by the business		Owner's *right* to or investment in the business

Suppose the total value of the assets is $40,000 and the business entity does not owe any amount against the assets. Then,

Assets	=	**Owner's Equity**
$40,000	=	$40,000

Or suppose the assets consist of a truck that costs $28,000. The owner has invested $10,000 for the truck, and the business entity has borrowed the remainder from the bank, which is a creditor (one to whom money is owed). This business transaction or event can be shown as follows:

Assets	=	**Liabilities**	+	**Owner's Equity**
Items owned		Amounts owed to creditors		Owner's investment
$28,000	=	$18,000	+	$10,000

We have now introduced a new classification, liabilities, which represent debts. They are the amounts that the business entity owes its creditors. The debts may originate because the business bought goods or services on credit, borrowed money, or otherwise created an obligation to pay. The creditors' claims to the assets have priority over the claims of the owner.

An equation expressing the relationship of assets, liabilities, and owner's equity is called the fundamental accounting equation (Assets = Liabilities + Owner's Equity). We'll deal with this equation constantly from now on. If we know two parts of this equation, we can determine the third. Let's look at some examples.

Determine Assets Ms. Jones has $9,000 invested in her travel agency, and the agency owes creditors $2,000; that is, the agency has liabilities of $2,000. Then,

Assets	=	Liabilities	+	Owner's Equity
?	=	$2,000	+	$9,000

We can find the amount of the business's assets by adding the liabilities and the owner's equity:

	$ 2,000	Liabilities
+	9,000	Owner's Equity
	$11,000	Assets

The completed equation now reads

Assets	=	Liabilities	+	Owner's Equity
$11,000	=	$2,000	+	$9,000

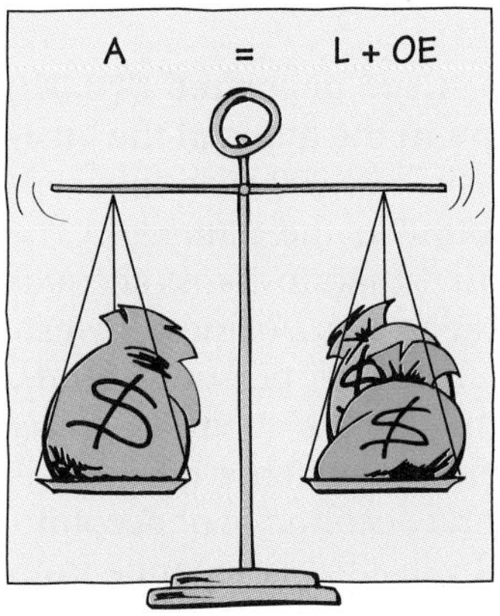
A = L + OE

Like a teeter totter, the equation stays in balance by making equal or offsetting increases and decreases to one side or both sides.

Determine Owner's Equity Mr. Owen owns an auto lube shop. His business has assets of $36,000, and it owes creditors $5,000; that is, it has liabilities of $5,000. Then,

Assets	=	Liabilities	+	Owner's Equity
$36,000	=	$5,000	+	?

We find the owner's equity by subtracting the liabilities from the assets:

	$36,000	Assets
−	5,000	Liabilities
	$31,000	Owner's Equity

The completed equation now reads

Assets	=	Liabilities	+	Owner's Equity
$36,000	=	$5,000	+	$31,000

Determine Liabilities Mr. Cannon's insurance agency has assets of $42,000; his investment (his equity) amounts to $20,000. Then,

Assets	=	Liabilities	+	Owner's Equity
$42,000	=	?	+	$20,000

To find the firm's total liabilities, we subtract the equity from the assets:

	$42,000	Assets
−	20,000	Owner's Equity
	$22,000	Liabilities

The completed equation reads

Assets	=	Liabilities	+	Owner's Equity
$42,000	=	$22,000	+	$20,000

Recording Business Transactions

Objective 2

Record a group of business transactions, in column form, involving changes in assets, liabilities, and owner's equity.

As you know, business transactions are events that have a direct effect on the operations of an economic unit or enterprise and are expressed in terms of money. Each business transaction must be recorded in the accounting records. As business transactions are recorded, the amounts listed under the headings Assets, Liabilities, and Owner's Equity change. However, **the total of one side of the fundamental accounting equation must always equal the total of the other side.** The categories under these three main headings are called accounts.

RYDER
RYDER
RYDER

Assets owned by a business may be as small as its office supplies or as large as its delivery van or building.

Let's look at a group of business transactions. These transactions are typical of those seen in a service or professional type of business. In these transactions, let's assume that L. A. Cruz establishes her own business and calls it Cruz Auto Detail. Cruz Auto Detail is a sole proprietorship, or a one-owner business.

Transaction (a) Cruz deposited $70,000 in a bank account in the name of the business. Cruz deposits $70,000 cash in a separate bank account in the name of Cruz Auto Detail. This separate bank account will help Cruz keep her business investment separate from her personal funds. This is an example of the separate entity concept, according to which a business is treated as a separate economic or accounting entity. The business is independent or stands by itself; it is separate from its owners, creditors, and customers.

The Cash account consists of bank deposits and money on hand. The business now has $70,000 more in cash than before, and Cruz's investment has also increased by $70,000. The account denoted by the owner's name followed by the word *Capital* records the amount of the owner's investment, or equity, in the business. The effect of this transaction on the fundamental accounting equation is as follows:

	Assets	=	Liabilities	+	Owner's Equity
	Items owned		Amounts owed to creditors		Owner's investment
	Cash	=			L. A. Cruz, Capital
(a)	+70,000	=			+70,000

Besides cash, an investment may be in the form of goods, such as equipment. The word *Capital* used under Owner's Equity therefore does not always mean that cash was invested.

Transaction (b) Bought equipment, paying cash, $43,000. Cruz's first task is to get her company ready for business; to do that, she needs the proper equipment. Accordingly, Cruz Auto Detail buys equipment whose cost is $43,000 and pays cash. **It is important to note at this point that Cruz does not invest any new money. She simply exchanges part of the business's cash for equipment.** Because equipment is a new type of property for the firm, a new account, Equipment, is created. Equipment is included under Assets. As a result of this transaction, the accounting equation changes:

	Assets		=	Liabilities	+	Owner's Equity
	Items owned			Amounts owed to creditors		Owner's investment
	Cash	+ Equipment	=			L. A. Cruz, Capital
Initial Investment	70,000		=			70,000
(b)	**−43,000**	**+43,000**				
New balances	27,000 +	43,000	=			70,000
	70,000			70,000		

Transaction (c) Bought equipment on account from Williams Auto Supply, $7,000. Cruz Auto Detail buys equipment costing $7,000 on credit from Williams Auto Supply.

The Equipment account shows an increase because the business owns $7,000 more in equipment. There is also an increase in liabilities because the business now owes $7,000. The liability account **Accounts Payable** is used for short-term liabilities or charge accounts, usually due within thirty days. (The company to which we owe money is called a creditor.) There is now a total of $77,000 on each side of the equals sign. Because Cruz Auto Detail owes money to Williams Auto Supply, Williams Auto Supply is called a creditor of Cruz Auto Detail.

	Assets		=	Liabilities	+	Owner's Equity
	Items owned			Amounts owed to creditors		Owner's investment
	Cash	+ Equipment	=	Accounts Payable	+	L. A. Cruz, Capital
Previous balances	27,000 +	43,000	=			70,000
(c)		**+ 7,000**		**+7,000**		
New balances	27,000 +	50,000	=	7,000	+	70,000
	77,000			77,000		

Observe that the recording of each transaction must yield an equation that is in balance. For example, transaction (b) resulted in a minus $43,000 and a plus $43,000 *on the same side,* with nothing recorded on the other side, and transaction (c) resulted in a $7,000 increase to both sides of the equation. It does not matter whether you change one side or both sides. **The important point is that whenever a transaction is properly recorded, the accounting equation remains in balance.**

Transaction (d) Paid Williams Auto Supply, a creditor, on account, $2,000. Cruz Auto Detail pays $2,000 to Williams Auto Supply, to be applied against the firm's liability of $7,000.

With this payment, cash is being reduced. At the same time, the firm *owes* less than before, so the transaction should be recorded as a reduction in liabilities.

	Assets		=	Liabilities	+	Owner's Equity
	Items owned			Amounts owed to creditors		Owner's investment
	Cash	+ Equipment	=	Accounts Payable	+	L. A. Cruz, Capital
Previous balances	27,000 +	50,000	=	7,000	+	70,000
(d)	−2,000			−2,000		
New balances	25,000 +	50,000	=	5,000	+	70,000
	75,000			75,000		

Transaction (e) Bought supplies on account from Rossi and Company, $800. Cruz Auto Detail buys buffer pads, cleaners, and waxes from Rossi and Company for $800. Pads, cleaners, and waxes are listed under Supplies instead of under Equipment because a detailing company will use these items in a relatively short period of time. Equipment, on the other hand, normally lasts a number of years.

	Assets			=	Liabilities	+	Owner's Equity
	Items owned				Amounts owed to creditors		Owner's investment
	Cash	+ Equip.	+ Supp.	=	Accounts Payable	+	L. A. Cruz, Capital
Previous balances	25,000	+ 50,000		=	5,000	+	70,000
(e)			+800		+800		
New balances	25,000	+ 50,000 +	800	=	5,800	+	70,000
	75,800				75,800		

Accounting, as we said before, is the process of analyzing, classifying, recording, summarizing, and interpreting business transactions in terms of money. Look at the transactions thus far for Cruz Auto Detail and see if you recognize that we have gone through certain steps (in the form of questions). Let's illustrate these steps using transaction **(e)**, bought supplies on account from Rossi and Company.

1. **What accounts are involved?** Supplies and Accounts Payable are involved.
2. **What are the classifications of the accounts involved?** Supplies is an asset and Accounts Payable is a liability.
3. **Are the accounts increased or decreased?** Supplies is increased because Cruz Auto Detail has more supplies than before. Accounts Payable is also increased because Cruz Auto Detail owes more than before.
4. **Is the equation in balance after the transaction has been recorded?** Yes.

Next, we record the transaction. We will stress this step-by-step process throughout the text. This example serves as an introduction to **double-entry accounting**. The "double" element is demonstrated by the fact that each transaction must be recorded in at least two accounts, keeping the accounting equation in balance.

Summary of Transactions

Let's summarize the business transactions of Cruz Auto Detail in column form, identifying each transaction by a letter of the alphabet. To test your understanding of the recording procedure, describe the nature of the transactions that have taken place.

	Assets						=	Liabilities	+	Owner's Equity
	Cash	+	Equip.	+	Supp.		=	Accounts Payable	+	L. A. Cruz, Capital
Transaction (a)	+70,000									+70,000
Transaction (b)	−43,000		+43,000							
Balance	27,000	+	43,000				=			70,000
Transaction (c)			+ 7,000					+7,000		
Balance	27,000	+	50,000				=	7,000	+	70,000
Transaction (d)	− 2,000							−2,000		
Balance	25,000	+	50,000				=	5,000	+	70,000
Transaction (e)					+800			+ 800		
Balance	25,000	+	50,000	+	800		=	5,800	+	70,000
	75,800							75,800		

The following observations apply to all types of business transactions:

1. Every transaction is recorded as an increase and/or decrease in two or more accounts.
2. One side of the equation is always equal to the other side of the equation.

In this chapter we are using a column arrangement as a practical device to show how transactions are recorded. This arrangement is useful for showing increases and decreases in various accounts as a result of the transactions. We also showed new balances after recording each transaction.

REVENUE AND EXPENSE ACCOUNTS

Objective 3

Define and identify *revenue* and *expense* accounts.

Revenues are the amounts earned by a business. Examples of revenues are fees earned for performing services, income from selling merchandise, rent income for the use of property, and interest income for lending money. Revenues may be in the form of cash or credit card receipts. Revenues may also result from credit sales to charge customers, in which case cash will be received at a later time.

Expenses are the costs that relate to earning revenue (or the costs of doing business). Examples of expenses are wages expense for labor performed, rent expense for the use of property, interest expense for the use of money, and advertising expense for the use of various media (for example, newspapers, radio, and direct mail). Expenses may be paid in cash when incurred (that is, immediately) or at a later time. Expenses to be paid at a later time involve Accounts Payable.

Revenues and expenses directly affect owner's equity. **If a business earns revenue, an increase in owner's equity occurs. When a business incurs or pays expenses, owner's equity decreases.** For the present, think of it this way: If the company makes money, the owner's equity is increased. If the company has to pay out money for the costs of doing business, then the owner's equity is decreased. Revenues and expenses fall under the umbrella of owner's equity: Revenue increases owner's equity; expenses decrease owner's equity.

Chart of Accounts

The **chart of accounts** is the official list of accounts *tailor-made* for the business. All the company's transactions must be recorded using the official account titles.

We now present the chart of accounts for Cruz Auto Detail. Some of the accounts are new to you, but they will be explained as we move along. When numbering account titles, the 100s are used for assets, the 200s are used for liabilities, the 300s are used for owner's equity accounts, the 400s are used for revenue accounts, and the 500s are used for expense accounts. You will encounter longer account numbers, but the first digit will usually be the same for any service business. In any case, use the exact account titles listed in the company's chart of accounts. Any changes must be approved by management.

FYI

When setting up and maintaining the chart of accounts on a computer, you may find that you must reserve the 500 accounts for cost accounts (used in a merchandising business). You may need to number expenses as 600s. Read the setup instructions in your software package.

Chart of Accounts

Assets

111 Cash
113 Accounts Receivable
115 Supplies
117 Prepaid Insurance
124 Equipment

Liabilities

221 Accounts Payable

Owner's Equity

311 L. A. Cruz, Capital
312 L. A. Cruz, Drawing

Revenue (increase in Owner's Equity)

411 Income from Services

Expenses (decrease in Owner's Equity)

511 Wages Expense
512 Rent Expense
513 Advertising Expense
514 Utilities Expense

Recording Business Transactions

Objective 4

Record a group of business transactions, in column form, involving all five elements of the fundamental accounting equation.

Soon after the opening of Cruz Auto Detail, the first customers arrive, beginning a flow of revenue for the business. Let's examine more transactions of Cruz Auto Detail for the first month of operations.

Transaction (f) Sold services for cash, $3,520. Cruz Auto Detail receives cash revenue of $3,520 in return for services performed for customers over two weeks. In other words, the company earns $3,520 for services performed for cash customers. Revenue has the effect of increasing owner's equity, but because the company wants to know how much revenue is earned, we set up a special column for revenue. The revenue account for Cruz Auto Detail is called Income from Services. The accounting equation is affected as follows (PB stands for previous balance, and NB stands for new balance).

	Assets			= Liabilities +	Owner's Equity	
	Cash	+ Equipment +	Supplies	Accounts Payable	L. A. Cruz, Capital +	Revenue
PB	25,000 +	50,000 +	800 =	5,800 +	70,000	
(f)	+3,520					+3,520 (Income from Services)
NB	28,520 +	50,000 +	800 =	5,800 +	70,000 +	3,520
	79,320			79,320		

Transaction (g) Paid rent for the month, $900. Shortly after opening the business, Cruz Auto Detail pays the month's rent of $900. Rent is payment for the privilege of occupying a building.

It seems logical that, if revenue is added to owner's equity, then expenses (the opposite of revenue) must be subtracted from owner's equity. To be consistent, a separate column is set up for expenses.

We want to have a running total of the amount of expenses to be subtracted from owner's equity. To keep up this running total, as each new expense is incurred (or comes into being), it must be added to the previous total.

	Assets			= Liabilities +	Owner's Equity		
	Cash	+ Equip. +	Supplies	Accounts Payable	L. A. Cruz, Capital +	Revenue −	Expenses
PB	28,520 +	50,000 +	800 =	5,800 +	70,000 +	3,520	
(g)	−900						+900 (Rent Expense)
NB	27,620 +	50,000 +	800 =	5,800 +	70,000 +	3,520 −	900
	78,420			78,420			

NEW ACCOUNTS
AND
LOANS

Banks and other financial institutions sell their services to other businesses as well as to individuals.

Because the time period represented by the rent payment is one month or less, we record the $900 as an expense. If the payment covered a period longer than one month, we would record the amount under an asset called Prepaid Rent.

Let's review the mental process for formulating the entry by asking:

1. **What are the accounts involved?** In this transaction, they are Cash and Rent Expense.
2. **What are the classifications of the accounts involved?** Cash is an asset, and Rent Expense is an expense.
3. **Are the accounts increased or decreased?** Cash is decreased because after the payment we have less cash than we had before. Rent Expense is increased. Thus there is a $900 reduction in total owner's equity as a result of the expense.
4. **Is the equation in balance after the transaction has been recorded?** Yes.

Transaction (h) Bought insurance for one year, $360. Cruz Auto Detail pays $360 for a one-year liability insurance policy. At the time of payment, the company has not used up the insurance, so it is not yet an expense. As the insurance expires (is used), it will become an expense. **However, because it is paid in advance for a period longer than one month, it has value and is recorded as an asset.**

	Assets				=	Liabilities +	Owner's Equity		
	Cash	+ Equip.	+ Supp.	+ Ppd. Ins.		Accounts Payable	L. A. Cruz, Capital	+ Revenue	− Expenses
PB	27,620	+ 50,000	+ 800		=	5,800	+ 70,000	+ 3,520	− 900
(h)	−360			+360					
NB	27,260	+ 50,000	+ 800	+ 360	=	5,800	+ 70,000	+ 3,520	− 900
	78,420					78,420			

At the end of the year or accounting period, an adjustment will have to be made to take out the expired portion (that is, coverage for the months that have been used up) and record it as an expense. We discuss this adjustment in a later chapter.

Observe that each time a transaction is recorded, the total amount on one side of the equation **remains equal** to the total amount on the other side. As proof of this equality, look at the following computation:

Cash	$27,260	Accounts Payable	$ 5,800
Equipment	50,000	L. A. Cruz, Capital	70,000
		Revenue	3,520
Supplies	800		$79,320
Prepaid Insurance	360	Expenses	− 900
	$78,420		$78,420

Steps in Analyzing Transactions

Now that we have recorded transactions in all five classifications of accounts, let's pause to go through the steps we have followed:

Step 1 Read the transaction to understand what is happening and how it affects the business. For example, the business has more revenue, or has more expenses, or has more cash, or owes less to creditors.

Step 2 Identify the accounts involved and decide whether the accounts are increased or decreased. Look for Cash first; you will quickly recognize if cash is coming in or going out.

Step 3 Decide on the classifications of the accounts involved. For example, Equipment is something the business owns, and it's an asset; Accounts Payable is an amount the business owes, and it's a liability; Rent is an expense.

Step 4 After recording the transaction, make sure the accounting equation is in balance.

Transaction (i) Received a bill from *Valley News* for newspaper advertising, $400. Cruz Auto Detail receives a bill from the *Valley News* for newspaper advertising, $400. Cruz Auto Detail has simply received the bill for advertising; it has not paid any cash. Previously, we described an expense as money to be paid for the cost of doing business. An expense of $400 has now been incurred (or has taken place), and it should be recorded as an increase in expenses (Advertising Expense). Also, since the company owes $400 more than it did before and intends to pay at a later time, this amount should be recorded as an increase in Accounts Payable.

	Assets				=	Liabilities	+	Owner's Equity				
	Cash	+ Equip.	+ Supp.	+ Ppd. Ins.		Accounts Payable		L. A. Cruz, Capital	+	Revenue	−	Expenses
PB	27,260	+ 50,000	+ 800	+ 360	=	5,800	+	70,000	+	3,520	−	900
(i)						+400						+400 (Advertising Expense)
NB	27,260	+ 50,000	+ 800	+ 360	=	6,200	+	70,000	+	3,520	−	1,300
	78,420					78,420						

Transaction (j) Sold services on account to Costello Taxi, $1,050. Cruz Auto Detail signs a contract with Costello Taxi to do detailing on credit. Cruz Auto Detail completes a detailing job and bills Costello Taxi $1,050 for services performed.

A company uses the **Accounts Receivable** account to record the amounts due from charge customers (legal claims against charge customers). Since Cruz Auto Detail's claim against Costello Taxi is $1,050 more than before the transaction took place, it seems logical to add $1,050 to Accounts Receivable. Revenue is earned (recognized) when the service is performed, so there is an increase in revenue. Keep in mind that Accounts Receivable is an asset. An asset is something that is owned, and Cruz Auto Detail owns a claim of $1,050 against Costello Taxi.

	Assets					=	Liabilities	+	Owner's Equity				
	Cash	+ Equip.	+ Supp.	+ Ppd. Ins.	+ Accts. Rec.		Accounts Payable		L. A. Cruz, Capital	+	Revenue	−	Expenses
PB	27,260	+ 50,000	+ 800	+ 360		=	6,200	+	70,000	+	3,520	−	1,300
(j)					+1,050						+1,050 (Income from Services)		
NB	27,260	+ 50,000	+ 800	+ 360	+ 1,050	=	6,200	+	70,000	+	4,570	−	1,300
	79,470						79,470						

When Costello Taxi pays the $1,050 bill in cash, Cruz Auto Detail will record this transaction as an increase in Cash and a decrease in Accounts Receivable. At that time, Cruz Auto Detail will not make an entry in the revenue account, because the revenue was earned and recorded when the service was performed.

Transaction (k) Paid on account to Williams Auto Supply, a creditor, $2,000. Cruz Auto Detail pays $2,000 to Williams Auto Supply, its creditor (the party to whom it owes money), as part payment on account.

	Assets					=	Liabilities	+	Owner's Equity		
	Cash	+ Equip.	+ Supp.	+ Ppd. Ins.	+ Accts. Rec.		Accounts Payable		L. A. Cruz, Capital	+ Revenue	− Expenses
PB	27,260	+ 50,000	+ 800	+ 360	+ 1,050	=	6,200	+	70,000	+ 4,570	− 1,300
(k)	−2,000						−2,000				
NB	25,260	+ 50,000	+ 800	+ 360	+ 1,050	=	4,200	+	70,000	+ 4,570	− 1,300
	77,470						77,470				

Transaction (l) Received and paid a bill from Midwest Power, Inc., $160. Cruz Auto Detail receives a bill from Midwest Power, Inc., for $160. The accounting equation is affected as follows:

	Assets					=	Liabilities	+	Owner's Equity		
	Cash	+ Equip.	+ Supp.	+ Ppd. Ins.	+ Accts. Rec.		Accounts Payable		L. A. Cruz, Capital	+ Revenue	− Expenses
PB	25,260	+ 50,000	+ 800	+ 360	+ 1,050	=	4,200	+	70,000	+ 4,570	− 1,300
(l)	−160										+160 (Utilities Expense)
NB	25,100	+ 50,000	+ 800	+ 360	+ 1,050	=	4,200	+	70,000	+ 4,570	− 1,460
	77,310						77,310				

Transaction (m) Paid on account to *Valley News*, a creditor, $400. Cruz Auto Detail pays $400 to the *Valley News* for advertising. Recall that this bill was recorded as a liability in transaction (i). The equation is as follows:

	Assets					=	Liabilities	+	Owner's Equity		
	Cash	+ Equip.	+ Supp.	+ Ppd. Ins.	+ Accts. Rec.		Accounts Payable		L. A. Cruz, Capital	+ Revenue	− Expenses
PB	25,100	+ 50,000	+ 800	+ 360	+ 1,050	=	4,200	+	70,000	+ 4,570	− 1,460
(m)	−400						−400				
NB	24,700	+ 50,000	+ 800	+ 360	+ 1,050	=	3,800	+	70,000	+ 4,570	− 1,460
	76,910						76,910				

Transaction (n) Paid wages of a part-time employee, $1,400. Cruz Auto Detail pays wages of a part-time employee, $1,400.

	Assets					=	Liabilities	+	Owner's Equity		
	Cash	+ Equip.	+ Supp.	+ Ppd. Ins.	+ Accts. Rec.		Accounts Payable		L. A. Cruz, Capital	+ Revenue	− Expenses
PB	24,700	+ 50,000	+ 800	+ 360	+ 1,050	=	3,800	+	70,000	+ 4,570	− 1,460
(n)	−1,400										+1,400 (Wages Expense)
NB	23,300	+ 50,000	+ 800	+ 360	+ 1,050	=	3,800	+	70,000	+ 4,570	− 2,860
	75,510						75,510				

Transaction (o) Bought equipment from Williams Auto Supply, $1,500, paying $600 in cash and placing the balance on account. Cruz Auto Detail buys additional equipment from Williams Auto Supply for $1,500, paying $600 down, with the remaining $900 on account. Because buying an item on account is the same as buying it on credit, both *on account* and *on credit* are used to describe such transactions.

	Assets						= Liabilities +	Owner's Equity				
	Cash	+ Equip.	+ Supp.	+ Ppd. Ins.	+ Accts. Rec.		Accounts Payable	L. A. Cruz, Capital	+	Revenue	−	Expenses
PB	23,300	+ 50,000	+ 800	+ 360	+ 1,050	=	3,800	+ 70,000	+	4,570	−	2,860
(o)	−600	+1,500					+900					
NB	22,700	+ 51,500	+ 800	+ 360	+ 1,050	=	4,700	+ 70,000	+	4,570	−	2,860
	76,410						76,410					

Cruz Auto Detail lists this $1,500 as an increase in assets. Note that three accounts are involved in this transaction: Cash, because cash was paid out; Equipment, because the company has more equipment than before; and Accounts Payable, because the company owes more than before.

Transaction (p) Received cash on account from Costello Taxi, a customer, $850. Cruz Auto Detail receives $850 from Costello Taxi to apply against the amount billed in transaction (j). Costello Taxi now owes Cruz Auto Detail less than it did, and so Cruz Auto Detail deducts the $850 from Accounts Receivable. An exchange of assets has no effect on the total of the equation.

	Assets						= Liabilities +	Owner's Equity				
	Cash	+ Equip.	+ Supp.	+ Ppd. Ins.	+ Accts. Rec.		Accounts Payable	L. A. Cruz, Capital	+	Revenue	−	Expenses
PB	22,700	+ 51,500	+ 800	+ 360	+ 1,050	=	4,700	+ 70,000	+	4,570	−	2,860
(p)	+850				−850							
NB	23,550	+ 51,500	+ 800	+ 360	+ 200	=	4,700	+ 70,000	+	4,570	−	2,860
	76,410						76,410					

Since Cruz Auto Detail had listed the amount as revenue, it shouldn't be recorded as revenue again. Think of paying income tax on the $850—once is enough.

Transaction (q) Sold services for cash, $2,700. Cruz Auto Detail receives cash revenue of $2,700 in return for services performed for customers for the rest of the month.

	Assets						= Liabilities +	Owner's Equity				
	Cash	+ Equip.	+ Supp.	+ Ppd. Ins.	+ Accts. Rec.		Accounts Payable	L. A. Cruz, Capital	+	Revenue	−	Expenses
PB	23,550	+ 51,500	+ 800	+ 360	+ 200	=	4,700	+ 70,000	+	4,570	−	2,860
(q)	+2,700									+2,700 (Income from Services)		
NB	26,250	+ 51,500	+ 800	+ 360	+ 200	=	4,700	+ 70,000	+	7,270	−	2,860
	79,110						79,110					

Transaction (r) Cruz withdrew cash for personal use, $3,000. At the end of the month, Cruz withdraws $3,000 in cash from the business for her personal living costs. A **withdrawal** is the taking of cash or other assets out of a business by the owner and is treated as a temporary decrease in owner's equity. Withdrawals are different from expenses. Expenses are paid to someone else for the cost of goods or services used in the business. Withdrawals are paid directly to the owner. A withdrawal may consist of cash or other assets.

Because the owner takes cash out of the business, there is a decrease of $3,000 in Cash. This also decreases Capital, because Cruz has reduced her equity. We record $3,000 as a minus under Capital and label it as Drawing.

	Assets									=	**Liabilities**	+	**Owner's Equity**				
	Cash	+	Equip.	+	Supp.	+	Ppd. Ins.	+	Accts. Rec.		Accounts Payable		L. A. Cruz, Capital	+	Revenue	−	Expenses
PB	26,250	+	51,500	+	800	+	360	+	200	=	4,700	+	70,000	+	7,270	−	2,860
(r)	**−3,000**												**−3,000** (Drawing)				
NB	23,250	+	51,500	+	800	+	360	+	200	=	4,700	+	67,000	+	7,270	−	2,860
	76,110										76,110						

Summary of Transactions f Through r

Figure 1 on the opposite page summarizes business transactions f through r of Cruz Auto Detail, with the transactions identified by letter. To test your understanding of the recording procedure, describe the nature of the transactions.

CHAPTER REVIEW

Review of Performance Objectives

1. Define and identify *asset, liability,* and *owner's equity* accounts.

   Assets are cash, properties, or things of value owned by the business. *Liabilities* are amounts the business owes to creditors. *Owner's equity* is the owner's investment or net worth.

2. Record a group of business transactions, in column form, involving changes in assets, liabilities, and owner's equity.

   The accounting equation is stated as assets equals liabilities plus owner's equity. Under the appropriate classification, a separate column is set up for each account. Transactions are recorded by listing amounts as either additions to or deductions from the various accounts. The equation must always remain in balance.

3. Define and identify *revenue* and *expense* accounts.

   Revenue consists of amounts earned by a business, such as fees earned for performing services, income from selling merchandise, rent income for the use of property, and interest earned for lending money. *Expenses* are the costs of earning revenue—that is, of doing business—such as wages expense, rent expense, interest expense, and advertising expense.

4. Record a group of business transactions, in column form, involving all five elements of the fundamental accounting equation.

FIGURE 1

	Assets					=	Liabilities +	Owner's Equity		
	Cash +	Equip. +	Supp. +	Ppd. Ins. +	Accts. Rec.	=	Accounts Payable +	L. A. Cruz, Capital +	Revenue −	Expenses
Bal.	25,000 +	50,000 +	800			=	5,800 +	70,000		
(f)	+3,520								+3,520 (Income from Services)	
Bal.	28,520 +	50,000 +	800			=	5,800 +	70,000 +	3,520	
(g)	−900									+900 (Rent Expense)
Bal.	27,620 +	50,000 +	800			=	5,800 +	70,000 +	3,520 −	900
(h)	−360			+ 360						
Bal.	27,260 +	50,000 +	800 +	360		=	5,800 +	70,000 +	3,520 −	900
(i)							+400			+400 (Advertising Expense)
Bal.	27,260 +	50,000 +	800 +	360		=	6,200 +	70,000 +	3,520 −	1,300
(j)					+ 1,050				+1,050 (Income from Services)	
Bal.	27,260 +	50,000 +	800 +	360 +	1,050	=	6,200 +	70,000 +	4,570 −	1,300
(k)	−2,000						−2,000			
Bal.	25,260 +	50,000 +	800 +	360 +	1,050	=	4,200 +	70,000 +	4,570 −	1,300
(l)	−160									+160 (Utilities Expense)
Bal.	25,100 +	50,000 +	800 +	360 +	1,050	=	4,200 +	70,000 +	4,570 −	1,460
(m)	−400						−400			
Bal.	24,700 +	50,000 +	800 +	360 +	1,050	=	3,800 +	70,000 +	4,570 −	1,460
(n)	−1,400									+1,400 (Wages Expense)
Bal.	23,300 +	50,000 +	800 +	360 +	1,050	=	3,800 +	70,000 +	4,570 −	2,860
(o)	−600	+1,500					+900			
Bal.	22,700 +	51,500 +	800 +	360 +	1,050	=	4,700 +	70,000 +	4,570 −	2,860
(p)	+850				−850					
Bal.	23,550 +	51,500 +	800 +	360 +	200	=	4,700 +	70,000 +	4,570 −	2,860
(q)	+2,700								+ 2,700 (Income from Services)	
Bal.	26,250 +	51,500 +	800 +	360 +	200	=	4,700 +	70,000 +	7,270 −	2,860
(r)	−3,000							−3,000 (Drawing)		
Bal.	23,250 +	51,500 +	800 +	360 +	200	=	4,700 +	67,000 +	7,270 −	2,860

Life Side of Equals Sign	
Cash	$23,250
Equipment	51,500
Supplies	800
Prepaid Insurance	360
Accounts Receivable	200
	$76,110

Right Side of Equals Sign	
Accounts Payable	$ 4,700
L. A. Cruz, Capital	67,000
Revenue	7,270
	$78,970
Expenses	−2,860
	$76,110

The accounting equation has been expanded and appears as follows:

Assets = Liabilities + Owner's Equity (Capital) + Revenue − Expenses

Accounts are classified and listed under each heading. Transactions are recorded by listing amounts as either additions to or deductions from the various accounts. The equation must always remain in balance.

Glossary

Accounts The categories under the Assets, Liabilities, and Owner's Equity headings. (10)

Accounts Payable A liability account used for short-term liabilities or charge accounts, usually due within thirty days. (11)

Accounts Receivable An account used to record the amounts owed by charge customers (legal claims against charge customers). (17)

Assets Cash, properties, and other things of value owned by an economic unit or business entity. (7)

Business entity A business enterprise, separate and distinct from the persons who supply the assets it uses. Property acquired by a business is an asset of the business. The owner is separate from the business and in fact has claims on it and a responsibility for its debts. (7)

Capital The owner's investment, or equity, in an enterprise. (8)

Chart of accounts The official list of account titles to be used to record the transactions of a business. (14)

Creditor One to whom money is owed. (8)

Double-entry accounting The system by which each business transaction is recorded in at least two accounts and the accounting equation is kept in balance. (12)

Equity The value of a right or claim to or financial interest in an asset or group of assets. (8)

Expenses The costs that relate to earning revenue (the costs of doing business); examples are wages, rent, interest, and advertising. They may be paid in cash, immediately or at a future time (accounts payable). (13)

Fundamental accounting equation (Assets = Liabilities + Owner's Equity) An equation expressing the relationship of assets, liabilities, and owner's equity. (8)

Liabilities Debts, or amounts owed to creditors. (8)

Owner's equity The owner's right to or investment in the business. (8)

Revenues The amounts a business earns; examples are fees earned for performing services, sales of merchandise, rent income, and interest income. They may be in the form of cash, credit card receipts, or accounts receivable (charge accounts). (13)

Separate entity concept The concept according to which a business is treated as a separate economic or accounting entity. The business stands by itself, separate from its owners, creditors, and customers. (10)

Sole proprietorship A one-owner business. (10)

Withdrawal The taking of cash or other assets out of a business by the owner for his or her own use. (This is also referred to as *drawing*.) A withdrawal is treated as a temporary decrease in owner's equity. (20)

QUESTIONS, EXERCISES, AND PROBLEMS

Discussion Questions

1. Define assets, liabilities, owner's equity, revenues, and expenses.
2. Explain the separate entity concept.
3. How do Accounts Receivable and Accounts Payable differ?
4. Describe two ways to increase owner's equity and two ways to decrease owner's equity.
5. How will the fundamental accounting equation change if supplies are purchased on account? Explain how this purchase will or will not change the owner's equity.
6. When an owner withdraws cash or goods from the business, why is this considered an increase to the Drawing account and not a wages account?
7. Define *chart of accounts,* and identify the categories of accounts.
8. What account titles might you suggest for the chart of accounts for a pet grooming shop owned by C. D. Tran? List the accounts by account category and include an appropriate account number for each.

Exercises

P.O. 1

Calculate missing items in the accounting equation.

Exercise 1-1 Complete the following equations:

a. Assets of $21,000 = Liabilities of $7,200 + Owner's Equity of $ 13,800
b. Assets of $ 47,000 − Liabilities of $19,000 = Owner's Equity of $28,000
c. Assets of $26,000 − Owner's Equity of $14,200 = Liabilities of $ 11,800

P.O. 1

Calculate missing items in the accounting equation.

Exercise 1-2 Determine the following amounts:

a. The amount of the liabilities of a business that has $58,580 in assets and in which the owner has $34,300 equity. 24,280
b. The equity of the owner of a van that cost $28,000 who owes $6,200 on an installment loan payable to the bank. 21,800
c. The amount of the assets of a business that has $8,730 in liabilities and in which the owner has $21,500 equity. 30,230

P.O. 1

Formulate the accounting equation.

✓**Exercise 1-3** Dr. J. O. Strain is an optometrist. As of December 31, Dr. Strain owned the following property that related to his professional practice, Strain Optical Clinic:

Cash, $1,040
Supplies, $950
Professional Equipment, $30,000
Office Equipment, $6,230

On the same date, he owed the following business creditors:

Borian Supply Company, $2,956
Ramirez Equipment Sales, $3,200

Compute the following amounts in the accounting equation:

Assets $ 38,220 = Liabilities $ 6156 + Owner's Equity $ 32,064

P.O. 1,3

Describe transactions affecting the accounting equation.

Exercise 1-4 Describe a business transaction that will do the following:

a. Increase an asset and increase a liability
b. Decrease an asset and decrease a liability
c. Decrease an asset and increase an expense
d. Increase an asset and increase owner's equity
e. Increase an asset and decrease an asset
f. Increase an asset and increase revenue

P.O. 2

Describe various transactions.

Exercise 1-5 Describe a transaction that resulted in the following entries:

	Assets			= Liabilities +	Owner's Equity
	Cash +	Supplies +	Equipment	Accounts Payable	L. Junko, Capital
(a)	+12,500				+12,500
(b)	−1,800		+1,800		
Bal.	10,700 +	+	1,800 =	+	12,500
(c)		+350		+350	
Bal.	10,700 +	350 +	1,800 =	350 +	12,500
(d)	−1,000		+5,000	+4,000	
Bal.	9,700 +	350 +	6,800 =	4,350 +	12,500
(e)	−1,500			−1,500	
Bal.	8,200 +	350 +	6,800 =	2,850 +	12,500

P.O. 1,3

Classify accounts.

Exercise 1-6 Label the following accounts as asset (A), liability (L), owner's equity (OE), revenue (R), or expense (E):

a. Office Supplies
b. Professional Fees
c. Prepaid Insurance
d. R. L. Osborn, Drawing
e. Accounts Payable
f. Service Income
g. R. L. Osborn, Capital
h. Rent Expense
i. Accounts Receivable
j. Wages Expense

P.O. 4

Describe various transactions.

Exercise 1-7 Describe a transaction that resulted in the following changes in accounts:

a. Rent Expense is increased by $930, and Cash is decreased by $930.
b. Advertising Expense is increased by $237, and Accounts Payable is increased by $237.
c. Accounts Receivable is increased by $226, and Service Income is increased by $226.
d. Cash is decreased by $390, and L. J. Miller, Drawing, is increased by $390.
e. Equipment is increased by $644, Cash is decreased by $200, and Accounts Payable is increased by $444.
f. Cash is increased by $370, and Accounts Receivable is decreased by $370.

P.O. 4

Describe various transactions.

Exercise 1-8 Describe the transactions that are recorded in the following equation.

	Assets			= Liabilities +	Owner's Equity			
	Cash +	Accounts Receivable +	Equipment	Accounts Payable	S. Yamamoto, Capital +	Revenue −	Expenses	
(a)	+18,000		+6,000		+24,000			Put cash & equip into business
(b)	−920						+920 (Rent Expense)	Paid Rent
Bal.	17,080 +	+	6,000 =	+	24,000 +	−	920	
(c)		+2,900				+2,900 (Service Income)		worked for promise
Bal.	17,080 +	2,900 +	6,000 =	+	24,000 +	2,900 −	920	
(d)	−3,000		+12,000	+9,000				Bought equip cash down & credit
Bal.	14,080 +	2,900 +	18,000 =	9,000 +	24,000 +	2,900 −	920	
(e)	−2,400				−2,400 (Drawing)			Paid self
Bal.	11,680 +	2,900 +	18,000 =	9,000 +	21,600 +	2,900 −	920	
	Total	32,580		Total	32,580			

CONSIDER AND COMMUNICATE

If a bookkeeper accidentally increased the Cash account by $450 when it should have been decreased after purchasing equipment for cash, what changes would take place in the equation? What other outcomes might there be in this situation?

WHAT IF . . .

The owner of a business needed cash for personal use, and there was enough cash in the account to cover the check. What if the owner then entered the transaction as a decrease to Cash and an increase to Wages Expense? Describe the effect on the fundamental accounting equation. Is it still in balance? Was this a correct recording of the transaction? If not, how should it have been recorded?

CRITICAL THINKING

Please read the following memorandum and follow the instructions set forth.

MEMORANDUM

TO: Your Name
FROM: Kathy Dunn, Supervisor
DATE: July 31, 20—
SUBJECT: Calculations for Lawrence Co.

Please provide the following ASAP (as soon as possible).

1. The balance of cash in Lawrence Company's checkbook shows $6,290. I need to know if this ties to or matches the Cash account

balance. I do know that total assets amount to $42,770, and Equipment amounts to $34,180. Other noncash assets are Supplies, $800, and Prepaid Insurance, $1,500.
2. C. Lawrence, the owner, wants to know the amount of her owner's equity. I pulled the outstanding bills, which amount to $6,174.
3. Please put the information in a memo addressed to me.
4. Thank you for your prompt response.

PROBLEM SET A

For additional help, see the demonstration problem at the beginning of each chapter in your Working Papers.

P.O. 1,2,3,4

Problem 1-1A In July of this year, B. R. Peters established a business called Sunshine Realty. The account headings are presented below. Transactions completed during the month follow.

Assets			= Liabilities +	Owner's Equity		
Cash +	Office Supplies +	Office Equipment	Accounts Payable	Capital ,	+ Revenue	− Expenses

a. Peters deposited $11,500 in a bank account in the name of the business.
b. Paid the office rent for the current month, $800, Ck. No. 1000 (Rent Expense).
c. Bought office supplies, paying cash, $253, Ck. No. 1001.
d. Bought office equipment on account from Brennan Computers, $3,485.
e. Received a bill from the *Weekly Journal* for advertising, $574 (Advertising Expense).
f. Paid on account to Brennan Computers, a creditor, $900, Ck. No. 1002.
g. Sold services for cash, $4,230 (Service Income).
h. Received and paid the bill for utilities, $296, Ck. No. 1003 (Utilities Expense).
i. Paid on account to the *Weekly Journal,* a creditor, $574, Ck. No. 1004.
j. Paid auto expenses, $341, Ck. No. 1005 (Auto Expense).
k. Peters withdrew cash for personal use, $1,150, Ck. No. 1006 (Drawing).

Check Figure
Left side of equals sign total, $15,154

Instructions

1. In the equation, write the owner's name above the term *Capital.*
2. Record the transactions and the balance after each transaction. Identify the account affected when the transaction involves revenue, expenses, or a withdrawal.
3. Write the account totals from the left side of the equals sign and add them. Write the account totals from the right side of the equals sign and add them. If the two totals are not equal, first check the addition and subtraction. If you still cannot find the error, reanalyze each transaction.

P.O. 1,2,3,4

Problem 1-2A In March, L. P. Sloan, M.D., established the Sloan Sports Medicine Clinic. The clinic's account headings are presented below. Transactions completed during the month of March follow.

Assets				= Liabilities +	Owner's Equity		
Cash +	Supplies +	Professional Equipment +	Office Equipment	Accounts Payable	, Capital	+ Revenue −	Expenses

a. Sloan deposited $25,000 in a bank account in the name of the business.
b. Paid the rent for the month, $1,100, Ck. No. 1000 (Rent Expense).
c. Bought supplies on account from Offices Inc., $850.
d. Bought professional equipment on account from Liu Company, $7,600.
e. Received a bill from the *Weekly Chronicle* for advertising, $585 (Advertising Expense).
f. Paid on account to Liu Company, a creditor, $2,860, Ck. No. 1001.
g. Sold professional services for cash, $5,455 (Professional Fees).
h. Received and paid the bill for utilities, $384, Ck. No. 1002 (Utilities Expense).
i. Paid the salary of the assistant, $1,800, Ck. No. 1003 (Salary Expense).
j. Bought a copy machine on account from Velos Office Equipment, $4,400.
k. Sloan withdrew cash for personal use, $2,500, Ck. No. 1004 (Drawing).

Check Figure
Cash, $21,811

Instructions

1. In the equation, write the owner's name above the term *Capital.*
2. Record the transactions and the balance after each transaction. Identify the account affected when the transaction involves revenue, expenses, or a withdrawal.
3. Write the account totals from the left side of the equals sign and add them. Write the account totals from the right side of the equals sign and add them. If the two totals are not equal, first check the addition and subtraction. If you still cannot find the error, reanalyze each transaction.

P.O. 1,2,3,4

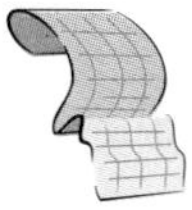

Problem 1-3A P. K. Asher, Attorney at Law, opened her office on October 1. The account headings are presented below. Transactions completed during the month follow.

Assets					= Liabilities +	Owner's Equity		
Cash +	Office Supplies +	Prepaid Insurance +	Office Equipment	+ Library	Accounts Payable	, Capital	+ Revenue −	Expenses

a. Asher deposited $20,000 in a bank account in the name of the business.
b. Bought office equipment on account from Norbert Equipment Company, $12,600.
c. Asher invested her personal law library, which cost $5,800. (Increase the account Library and increase the account P. K. Asher, Capital.)
d. Paid the office rent for the month, $850, Ck. No. 2000 (Rent Expense).
e. Bought office supplies for cash, $773, Ck. No. 2001.
f. Bought insurance for two years, $495, Ck. No. 2002.
g. Sold legal services for cash, $3,248 (Professional Fees).
h. Received and paid the telephone bill, $216, Ck. No. 2003 (Telephone Expense).
i. Paid the salary of the part-time receptionist, $890, Ck. No. 2004 (Salary Expense).
j. Bought gas and oil for the van, paying cash, $105, Ck. No. 2005 (Van Expense).

k. Sold legal services for cash, $2,240 (Professional Fees).
l. Paid on account to Norbert Equipment Company, a creditor, $1,800, Ck. No. 2006.
m. Asher withdrew cash for personal use, $2,150, Ck. No. 2007 (Drawing).

Check Figure
Right side of equals sign total, $37,877

Instructions

1. In the equation, write the owner's name above the term *Capital.*
2. Record the transactions and the balance after each transaction. Identify the account affected when the transaction involves revenue, expenses, or a withdrawal.
3. Write the account totals from the left side of the equals sign and add them. Write the account totals from the right side of the equals sign and add them. If the two totals are not equal, first check the addition and subtraction. If you still cannot find the error, reanalyze each transaction.

P.O. 1,2,3,4

Problem 1-4A R. C. Nye started Nye's Pest Service on May 1 of this year. The account headings are presented below. During May, Nye completed the transactions that follow.

Assets						= Liabilities +	Owner's Equity		
Cash +	Accounts Receivable +	Supplies +	Prepaid Insurance +	Truck +	Equipment	Accounts Payable	Capital ,	+ Revenue	− Expenses

a. Nye deposited $8,000 in a bank account in the name of the business.
b. Bought a used truck from Essen Motors for $15,650, paying $2,100 in cash, and placing the remainder on account.
c. Bought equipment on account from Granger Company, $2,800.
d. Paid the rent for the month, $850, Ck. No. 3001 (Rent Expense).
e. Bought insurance for the truck for the year, $825, Ck. No. 3002, Policy No. 311D.
f. Sold services for cash for the first half of the month, $3,264 (Service Income).
g. Bought supplies for cash, $462, Ck. No. 3003.
h. Sold services on account, $822 (Service Income).
i. Received and paid the bill for utilities, $188, Ck. No. 3004 (Utilities Expense).
j. Received a bill for gas and oil for the truck, $238 (Truck Expense).
k. Sold services for cash for the remainder of the month, $2,784 (Service Income).
l. Nye withdrew cash for personal use, $1,350, Ck. No. 3005.
m. Paid wages to the employees, $2,420, Ck. Nos. 3006–3008 (Wages Expense).

Check Figure
Cash, $5,853

Instructions

1. In the equation, write the owner's name above the term *Capital.*
2. Record the transactions and the balance after each transaction. Identify the account affected when the transaction involves revenue, expenses, or a withdrawal.
3. Write the account totals from the left side of the equals sign and add them. Write the account totals from the right side of the equals sign and add them. If the two totals are not equal, first check the addition and subtraction. If you still cannot find the error, reanalyze each transaction.

PROBLEM SET B

For additional help, see the demonstration problems at the beginning of each chapter in your Working Papers.

P.O. 1,2,3,4

Problem 1-1B On June 1 of this year, R. B. Ayala, Optometrist, established the Ayala Eye Clinic. The clinic's account names are presented below. Transactions completed during the month follow.

Assets			= Liabilities +	Owner's Equity		
Cash +	Office Supplies +	Office Equipment	Accounts Payable	Capital	+ Revenue	− Expenses

a. Ayala deposited $12,000 in a bank account in the name of the business.
b. Paid the office rent for the month, $730, Ck. No. 1001 (Rent Expense).
c. Bought supplies for cash, $652, Ck. No. 1002.
d. Bought office equipment on account from Foster Company, $4,568.
e. Bought office equipment from Wesley Office Supply, $2,950, paying $500 in cash and placing the balance on account, Ck. No. 1003.
f. Sold professional services for cash, $1,540 (Professional Fees).
g. Paid on account to Wesley Office Supply, a creditor, $1,200, Ck. No. 1004.
h. Received and paid the bill for utilities, $242, Ck. No. 1005 (Utilities Expense).
i. Paid the salary of the assistant, $1,230, Ck. No. 1006 (Salary Expense).
j. Sold professional services for cash, $2,528 (Professional Fees).
k. Ayala withdrew cash for personal use, $1,530, Ck. No. 1007 (Drawing).

Check Figure

Left side of equals sign total, $18,154

Instructions

1. In the equation, write the owner's name above the term *Capital.*
2. Record the transactions and the balance after each transaction. Identify the account affected when the transaction involves revenue, expenses, or a withdrawal.
3. Write the account totals from the left side of the equals sign and add them. Write the account totals from the right side of the equals sign and add them. If the two totals are not equal, first check the addition and subtraction. If you still cannot find the error, reanalyze each transaction.

P.O. 1,2,3,4

Problem 1-2B On July 1 of this year, S. E. Taylor, D.C., established the Taylor Chiropractic Clinic. The organization's account headings are presented below. Transactions completed during the month of July follow.

Assets				= Liabilities +	Owner's Equity		
Cash +	Supplies +	Professional Equipment +	Office Equipment	Accounts Payable	Capital	+ Revenue	− Expenses

a. Taylor deposited $16,000 in a bank account in the name of the business.
b. Paid the office rent for the month, $1,000, Ck. No. 2001 (Rent Expense).
c. Bought supplies for cash, $685, Ck. No. 2002.
d. Bought professional equipment on account from Chiropractic Equipment Company, $18,435 (Professional Equipment).

e. Bought office equipment from Dotcom Computers, $3,295, paying $990 in cash and placing the balance on account, Ck. No. 2003.
f. Sold professional services for cash, $1,160 (Professional Fees).
g. Paid on account to Dotcom Computers, a creditor, $900, Ck. No. 2004.
h. Received and paid the bill for utilities, $227, Ck. No. 2005 (Utilities Expense).
i. Paid the salary of the assistant, $1,326, Ck. No. 2006 (Salary Expense).
j. Sold professional services for cash, $1,285 (Professional Fees).
k. Taylor withdrew cash for personal use, $1,600, Ck. No. 2007 (Drawing).

Check Figure
Cash, $11,717

Instructions

1. In the equation, write the owner's name above the term *Capital.*
2. Record the transactions and the balance after each transaction. Identify the account affected when the transaction involves revenue, expenses, or a withdrawal.
3. Write the account totals from the left side of the equals sign and add them. Write the account totals from the right side of the equals sign and add them. If the two totals are not equal, first check the addition and subtraction. If you still cannot find the error, reanalyze each transaction.

P.O. 1,2,3,4

Problem 1-3B A. P. Manley, a graphic artist, opened a studio for her professional practice on August 1. The account headings are presented below. Transactions completed during the month follow.

Assets					= Liabilities +	Owner's Equity		
Cash +	Office Supplies +	Prepaid Insurance +	Office Equipment	+ Library	Accounts Payable	Capital	+ Revenue	− Expenses

a. Manley deposited $15,500 in a bank account in the name of the business.
b. Bought office equipment on account from Specialized Equipment Company, $8,430.
c. Manley invested her personal library, $6,500. (Increase the account Library and increase the account A. P. Manley, Capital.)
d. Paid the rent for the month, $960, Ck. No. 1000 (Rent Expense).
e. Bought office supplies for cash, $836, Ck. No. 1001.
f. Bought insurance for two years, $890, Ck. No. 1002.
g. Sold graphic services for cash, $1,460 (Professional Fees).
h. Paid the salary of the part-time assistant, $800, Ck. No. 1003 (Salary Expense).
i. Received and paid the bill for telephone service, $182, Ck. No. 1004 (Telephone Expense).
j. Paid on account to Specialized Equipment Company, a creditor, $550, Ck. No. 1005.
k. Sold graphic services for cash, $1,548 (Professional Fees).
l. Paid cash for minor repairs to graphics equipment, $68, Ck. No. 1006 (Repair Expense).
m. Manley withdrew cash for personal use, $1,050, Ck. No. 1007 (Drawing).

Check Figure
Right side of equals sign total, $29,828

Instructions

1. In the equation, write the owner's name above the term *Capital.*
2. Record the transactions and the balance after each transaction. Identify the account affected when the transaction involves revenue, expenses, or a withdrawal.

3. Write the account totals from the left side of the equals sign and add them. Write the account totals from the right side of the equals sign and add them. If the two totals are not equal, first check the addition and subtraction. If you still cannot find the error, reanalyze each transaction.

P.O. 1,2,3,4

Problem 1-4B On March 1 of this year, L. P. Duong established Duong's Catering Service. The account headings are presented below. Transactions completed during the month follow.

Assets						= Liabilities +	Owner's Equity		
Cash +	Accounts Receivable +	Supplies +	Prepaid Insurance +	Truck +	Equipment	Accounts Payable	____, Capital	+ Revenue	− Expenses

a. Duong deposited $15,000 in a bank account in the name of the business.
b. Bought a truck from Crandal Motors for $12,580, paying $2,500 in cash and placing the balance on account, Ck. No. 500.
c. Bought catering equipment on account from Castor Company, $2,520.
d. Paid the rent for the month, $695, Ck. No. 501 (Rent Expense).
e. Sold catering services for cash for the first half of the month, $1,810 (Catering Income).
f. Bought insurance for the truck for one year, $686, Ck. No. 502.
g. Bought catering supplies for cash, $285, Ck. No. 503.
h. Received and paid the heating bill, $140, Ck. No. 504 (Utilities Expense).
i. Received a bill from Quick Gas and Lube for gas and oil for the truck, $93 (Truck Expense).
j. Sold catering services on account, $927 (Catering Income).
k. Sold catering services for cash for the remainder of the month, $2,521 (Catering Income).
l. Paid the salary of the assistant, $1,342, Ck. No. 505 (Salary Expense).
m. Duong withdrew cash for personal use, $1,350, Ck. No. 506 (Drawing).

Check Figure
Cash, $12,333

Instructions

1. In the equation, write the owner's name above the term *Capital.*
2. Record the transactions and the balance after each transaction. Identify the account affected when the transaction involves revenue, expenses, or a withdrawal.
3. Write the account totals from the left side of the equals sign and add them. Write the account totals from the right side of the equals sign and add them. If the two totals are not equal, first check the addition and subtraction. If you still cannot find the error, reanalyze each transaction.

2 T Accounts, Debits and Credits, Trial Balance, and Financial Statements

WINDOWS ON THE WORLD WIDE WEB

The entertainment conglomerate, Viacom, sold off parts of its publishing businesses in 1998 for $4.6 billion in cash, yet it still owns MTV, Showtime, and Nickelodeon. How did this sale affect its net income (the difference between earned revenue and incurred expenses)? What would Viacom's balance sheet—assets equal liabilities plus owner's equity—look like? Imagine you had to record Viamcom's sale of the development operations of Virgin Interactive Entertainment Limited for $122.5 million in cash to Electronic Arts Inc. How would you record this transaction in a T account? Check the following web site to review the financial facts and figures for this show business empire:
www.sec.gov/Archives/edgar/data/813828/0001005477-99-001528.txt.

Performance Objectives

After you have completed this chapter, you will be able to do the following:

1. Determine balances of T accounts having entries recorded on both sides of the accounts.
2. Present the fundamental accounting equation with the T account form, and label the plus and minus sides.
3. Present the fundamental accounting equation with the T account form, and label the debit and credit sides.
4. Record directly in T accounts a group of business transactions involving changes in asset, liability, owner's equity, revenue, and expense accounts for a service business.
5. Prepare a trial balance.
6. Prepare (a) an income statement, (b) a statement of owner's equity, and (c) a balance sheet.
7. Prepare (a) an income statement involving more than one revenue account and a net loss, and (b) a statement of owner's equity with an additional investment and either a net income or a net loss.
8. Recognize the effect of transpositions and slides on account balances.

We introduced the fundamental accounting equation as *Assets = Liabilities + Owner's Equity.* We also discussed the recording of transactions involving two new classifications of accounts: *Revenue* and *Expenses.* With the addition of Revenue and Expenses, the fundamental accounting equation was brought up to its full size of five account classifications. There are only five classifications; so, as far as you go in accounting—whether you are dealing with a small, one-owner business or a large corporation—there will be these five major classifications of accounts.

In this chapter, we will record the same transactions in T account form, and we will prove the equality of both sides of the fundamental accounting equation. We will do this by means of a trial balance, which we will discuss later in this chapter.

THE T ACCOUNT FORM

So far, we have recorded business transactions in a column arrangement. For example, the Cash account column in the books of Cruz Auto Detail is shown below.

Cash Account Column

Transaction	**(a)**	70,000
Transaction	**(b)**	−43,000
Balance		27,000
Transaction	**(d)**	−2,000
Balance		25,000
Transaction	**(f)**	+3,520
Balance		28,520
Transaction	**(g)**	−900
Balance		27,620
Transaction	**(h)**	−360
Balance		27,260
Transaction	**(k)**	−2,000
Balance		25,260
Transaction	**(l)**	−160
Balance		25,100
Transaction	**(m)**	−400
Balance		24,700
Transaction	**(n)**	−1,400
Balance		23,300
Transaction	**(o)**	−600
Balance		22,700
Transaction	**(p)**	+850
Balance		23,550
Transaction	**(q)**	+2,700
Balance		26,250
Transaction	**(r)**	−3,000
		23,250

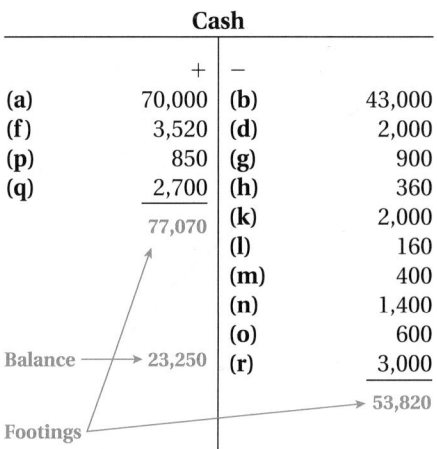

Cash

	+		−
(a)	70,000	**(b)**	43,000
(f)	3,520	**(d)**	2,000
(p)	850	**(g)**	900
(q)	2,700	**(h)**	360
	77,070	**(k)**	2,000
		(l)	160
		(m)	400
		(n)	1,400
		(o)	600
Balance →	23,250	**(r)**	3,000
			53,820
Footings			

As an introduction to the recording of transactions, the column arrangement had the following advantages:

1. In the process of analyzing the transaction, you
   a. Recognized the need to determine which accounts are involved.
   b. Determined the classification of the accounts involved.
   c. Decided whether the transaction resulted in an increase or a decrease in each of these accounts.
2. You further realized that, after each transaction had been recorded, the two sides of the fundamental accounting equation were in balance. In other words, the total of one side of the accounting equation equaled the total of the other side.

Now, instead of recording transactions in a column for each account, we will use a **T account form** for each account. *The T account form has the advantage of providing two sides for each account; one side is used to record increases in the account, and the other side is used to record decreases.*

Objective 1

Determine balances of T accounts having entries recorded on both sides of the accounts.

After we record a group of transactions in a T account, we add both sides and record the totals in small, pencil-written figures called **footings**. Next, we subtract one footing from the other to determine the balance of the account. For the Cash account, shown previously, the balance is $23,250 ($77,070 − $53,820).

We now record the balance on the side of the account having the larger footing, which, with a few minor exceptions, is the plus (+) side. The plus side of a T account is the side that represents the **normal balance** of that account. The normal balance may, however, fall on either the left or the right side of an account, depending on what type of account it is. To review, we presented the T account for Cash; Cash is classified as an asset, and all assets look like the following T account:

Assets	
+	−
Left	Right

However, **not all classifications of accounts have the increase side on the left.**

Recall that we placed revenue and expenses under the "umbrella" of owner's equity. Revenue increases owner's equity, and expenses decrease owner's equity. The T accounts for this situation are as follows:

Owner's Equity

− Left ↓	+ Right ↓
Expenses	**Revenue**
+ Left | − Right	− Left | + Right

Expenses cause a decrease in owner's equity

Revenues cause an increase in owner's equity

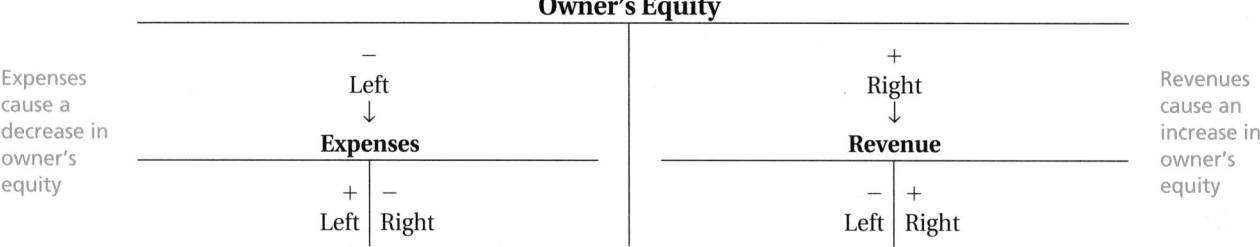

Increases in owner's equity are recorded on the right side of the account. Because revenue increases owner's equity, additions to revenue are also recorded on the right side.

Decreases in owner's equity are recorded on the left side of the account. Because expenses decrease owner's equity, additions to expenses are also recorded on the left side.

Using the five classifications of accounts, the fundamental accounting equation looks like this:

$$\text{Assets} = \text{Liabilities} + \overbrace{\text{Capital} + \text{Revenue} - \text{Expenses}}^{\text{Owner's Equity}}$$

Remember!

The entry for a business transaction may include any combination of pluses and minuses: pluses and pluses, pluses and minuses, or minuses and minuses.

Because revenue and expenses appear separately in the income statement, we will stretch out the equation to include them as separate headings, like this:

Assets = Liabilities + Capital + Revenue − Expenses

We can now restate the equation with the T forms and plus and minus signs for each account classification:

Assets		=	**Liabilities**		+	**Owner's Equity**		+	**Revenue**		−	**Expenses**	
+	−		−	+		−	+		−	+		+	−
Left	Right		Left	Right		Left	Right		Left	Right		Left	Right

Objective 2

Present the fundamental accounting equation with the T account form, and label the plus and minus sides.

Before we go on, let us point out the increase, or plus, side of each account classification. You can recognize these in the accounting equation using T accounts.

Assets	The *left* side is the *increase* side.
Liabilities	The *right* side is the *increase* side.
Owner's Equity	The *right* side is the *increase* side
Revenue	The *right* side is the *increase* side.
Expenses	The *left* side is the *increase* side.

Because revenue is an addition to owner's equity, the placement of the plus and minus signs is the same as for owner's equity. On the other hand, because expenses are treated as deductions from owner's equity, the placement of the plus and minus signs is reversed. We will use this form of the fundamental accounting equation throughout the remainder of the text.

Your accounting background up to this point has taught you to analyze business transactions to determine which accounts are involved and to recognize that each amount should be recorded as either an increase or a decrease in these accounts. Now the recording process becomes a simple matter of knowing which side of the T accounts should be used to record increases and which should be used to record decreases. **Generally, you will not be using the minus side of the revenue and expense accounts, since transactions involving revenue and expense accounts usually result in increases in these accounts.** An exception to this statement is where errors have been made and require correction. Let's now add the last element to the T account before we record the familiar Cruz Auto Detail transactions.

THE T ACCOUNT FORM WITH DEBITS AND CREDITS

Objective 3

Present the fundamental accounting equation with the T account form, and label the debit and credit sides.

The left side of a T account is called the **debit** side; the right side is called the **credit** side. The T accounts representing the accounting equation now contain both the signs and the words *Debit* and *Credit*. There are only five classifications of accounts. These classifications are contained in the fundamental accounting equation:

Assets		=	**Liabilities**		+	**Owner's Equity**		+	**Revenue**		−	**Expenses**	
+	−		−	+		−	+		−	+		+	−
Debit	Credit		Debit	Credit		Debit	Credit		Debit	Credit		Debit	Credit

The following table summarizes debits and credits and how they are affected by increases and decreases. **The critical rule to remember is that the amount placed on the debit side of one or more accounts MUST equal the amount placed on the credit side of another account or accounts.**

Debits Signify		**Credits Signify**	
Increases in	Assets Drawing Expenses	Decreases in	Assets Drawing Expenses
Decreases in	Liabilities Capital Revenue	Increases in	Liabilities Capital Revenue

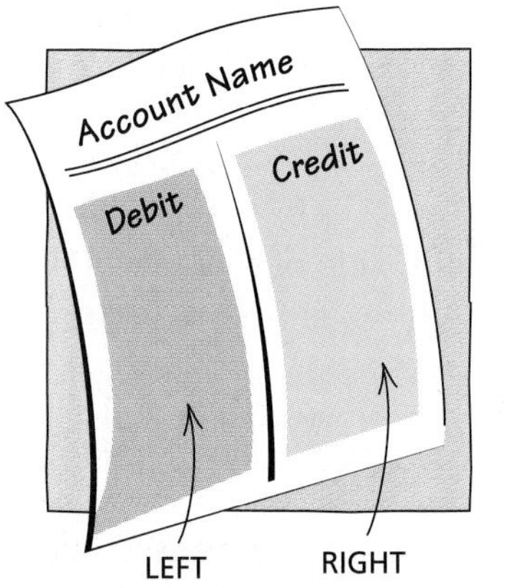

Account Name
Debit
Credit
LEFT
RIGHT

Debit is always the left side of the account, and credit is always the right side of an account. The + or −, however, changes with the type of account.

Before we begin recording, notice the new T account below the Capital account, L. A. Cruz, Drawing. Recall that the Capital account is increased when amounts are invested and decreased when amounts are taken out.

Capital	
−	+
Debit	Credit
	Amounts in

Drawing	
+	−
Debit	Credit
Amounts withdrawn	

We reserve the minus or debit side of the Capital account for permanent withdrawals, those made when the owner decides to reduce the size of the business permanently or when a net loss forces such a reduction. This concept is best illustrated by showing the Drawing T account under the umbrella of the Capital account.

Capital

− Debit	+ Credit

Drawing

+ Debit	− Credit

RECORDING BUSINESS TRANSACTIONS IN T ACCOUNTS

Objective 4

Record directly in T accounts a group of business transactions involving changes in asset, liability, capital, revenue, and expense accounts for a service business.

Our task now is to learn how to record business transactions in the T account form. First, let's review the steps in analyzing a business transaction.

1. **Decide which accounts are involved.**
2. **Classify the accounts involved** (asset, liability, capital, revenue, expense).
3. **Decide if the accounts involved are increased or decreased.**
4. **Decide which accounts are debited and which accounts are credited.**
5. **Check to see if the equation is in balance after the transaction has been recorded.**

For example, let's analyze the first transaction of the Cruz Auto Detail transactions using this five-step process. To formulate the entry, you must be able to visualize the fundamental accounting equation in the form of T accounts. With that in mind, the first transaction is as follows:

In transaction (a), Cruz deposited $70,000 cash in a bank account in the name of the business. This transaction results in an increase to Cash with a debit and an increase in the Capital account with a credit.

1. **Decide which accounts are involved.** The two accounts involved are Cash and L. A. Cruz, Capital.
2. **Classify the accounts involved (asset, liability, capital, revenue, expense).** Cash is an asset and L. A. Cruz, Capital, is an owner's equity account.
3. **Decide if the accounts involved are increased or decreased.** Cash is being deposited in the bank account, an increase to Cash. The owner has invested that cash in the business and has increased L. A. Cruz, Capital.
4. **Write the transaction as a debit to one account (or accounts) and a credit to another account (or accounts).** Since Cash is an asset and Cash is increased, Cash is debited. We now need an offsetting credit. L. A. Cruz, Capital, is an owner's equity account and is increased. L. A. Cruz, Capital, is credited. You now have a debit equal to a credit.
5. **Check:** There is at least one account debited and at least one account credited, *and* the total amount(s) debited equal the total amount(s) credited. **You now have a debit equal to a credit, a $70,000 debit to Cash and a $70,000 credit to L. A. Cruz, Capital.**

Bicycle Repairs
Sales and Hire
PADDY'S
BIKE
SHOP
BICYCLES
FOR
HIRE
BICYCLES FOR HIRE

Stores such as this bike shop classify revenue accounts for each service activity—sales, repairs, and rentals. They may also classify expense accounts separately.

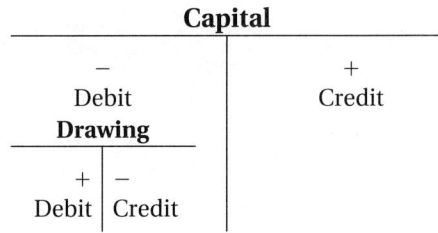

The resulting transaction in T account form follows:

Cash		L. A. Cruz, Capital	
+ Debit	− Credit	− Debit	+ Credit
(a) 70,000			(a) 70,000

In transaction (b), Cruz Auto Detail bought equipment, paying cash, $43,000. This transaction results in an increase to Equipment with a debit and a decrease to Cash with a credit.

Assets		=	Liabilities		+	Owner's Equity		+	Revenue		−	Expenses	
+ Debit	− Credit		− Debit	+ Credit		− Debit	+ Credit		− Debit	+ Credit		+ Debit	− Credit

Cash	
+ Debit	− Credit
	(b) 43,000

Equipment	
+ Debit	− Credit
(b) 43,000	

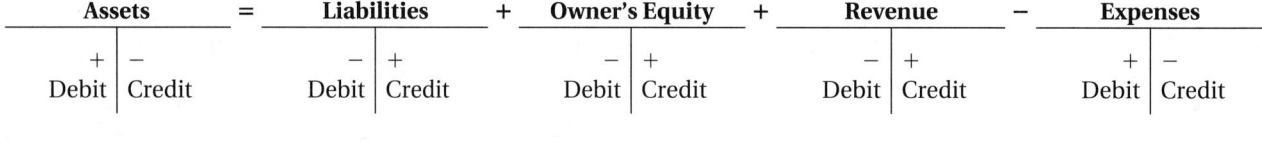

In transaction (c), Cruz Auto Detail bought equipment on account from Williams Auto Supply, $7,000. This transaction results in an increase to Equipment with a debit and an increase to Accounts Payable with a credit and is shown in T accounts as follows:

Assets		=	Liabilities		+	Owner's Equity		+	Revenue		−	Expenses	
+ Debit	− Credit		− Debit	+ Credit		− Debit	+ Credit		− Debit	+ Credit		+ Debit	− Credit
Equipment			**Accounts Payable**										
+ Debit	− Credit		− Debit	+ Credit									
(c) 7,000				(c) 7,000									

In transaction (d), Cruz Auto Detail paid Williams Auto Supply, a creditor, $2,000. This transaction results in a decrease to Cash with a credit and a decrease to Accounts Payable with a debit.

Assets		=	Liabilities		+	Owner's Equity		+	Revenue		−	Expenses	
+ Debit	− Credit		− Debit	+ Credit		− Debit	+ Credit		− Debit	+ Credit		+ Debit	− Credit
Cash			**Accounts Payable**										
+ Debit	− Credit		− Debit	+ Credit									
	(d) 2,000		(d) 2,000										

In transaction (e), Cruz Auto Detail bought supplies on account from Rossi and Company, $800. This transaction results in an increase to Supplies with a debit and an increase to Accounts Payable with a credit.

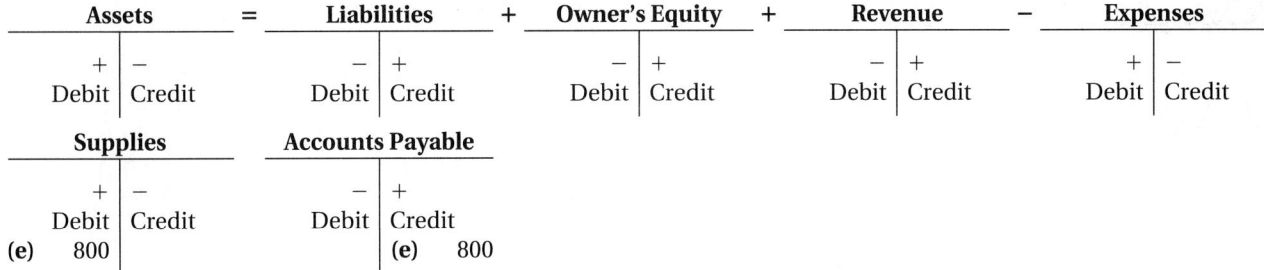

Assets	=	Liabilities	+	Owner's Equity	+	Revenue	−	Expenses
+ Debit | − Credit		− Debit | + Credit		− Debit | + Credit		− Debit | + Credit		+ Debit | − Credit

Supplies

+ Debit	− Credit
(e) 800	

Accounts Payable

− Debit	+ Credit
	(e) 800

Here is a restatement of the accounts after recording transactions (a) through (e). To test your understanding of the process, trace through the recording of each transaction and describe what happened in the transaction. Footings or subtotals (remember, always write the footings smaller than the entries and in pencil) are required to compute the balances of the accounts. The balances are written in the accounts on the side with the larger total.

Assets	=	Liabilities	+	Owner's Equity	+	Revenue	−	Expenses
+ Debit | − Credit		− Debit | + Credit		− Debit | + Credit		− Debit | + Credit		+ Debit | − Credit

Cash

+ Debit	− Credit
(a) 70,000	(b) 43,000
	(d) 2,000
	45,000
Bal. 25,000	

Accounts Receivable

+ Debit	− Credit

Supplies

+ Debit	− Credit
(e) 800	

Equipment

+ Debit	− Credit
(b) 43,000	
(c) 7,000	
50,000	

Accounts Payable

− Debit	+ Credit
(d) 2,000	(c) 7,000
	(e) 800
	7,800
	5,800

L. A. Cruz, Capital

− Debit	+ Credit
	(a) 70,000

L. A. Cruz, Drawing

+ Debit	− Credit

Income from Services

− Debit	+ Credit

Wages Expense

+ Debit	− Credit

Rent Expense

+ Debit	− Credit

Advertising Expense

+ Debit	− Credit

Utilities Expense

+ Debit	− Credit

Remember!

The normal balance of an account classification is on the plus side.

FYI

The T account is not only a learning tool, but will serve you well as a problem-solving device when you need to analyze a transaction prior to recording it—manually or on a computer.

Let's pause to see if the two sides of the equation are equal by listing the balances of the accounts:

Account Name	Accounts with Normal Balances on the Left or Debit Side Assets Drawing Expenses	Accounts with Normal Balances on the Right or Credit Side Liabilities Capital Revenue
Cash	$25,000	
Supplies	800	
Equipment	50,000	
Accounts Payable		5,800
L. A. Cruz, Capital		70,000
	$75,800	$75,800

In transaction (f), Cruz Auto Detail sold services for cash, $3,520. This transaction results in an increase to Cash with a debit and an increase to Income from Services with a credit.

Assets		=	Liabilities		+	Owner's Equity		+	Revenue		−	Expenses	
+ Debit	− Credit		− Debit	+ Credit		− Debit	+ Credit		− Debit	+ Credit		+ Debit	− Credit

Cash	
+ Debit	− Credit
(f) 3,520	

Income from Services	
− Debit	+ Credit
	(f) 3,520

In transaction (g), Cruz Auto Detail paid rent for the month, $900. This transaction results in an increase to Rent Expense with a debit and a decrease to Cash with a credit.

Assets		=	Liabilities		+	Owner's Equity		+	Revenue		−	Expenses	
+ Debit	− Credit		− Debit	+ Credit		− Debit	+ Credit		− Debit	+ Credit		+ Debit	− Credit

Cash	
+ Debit	− Credit
	(g) 900

Rent Expense	
+ Debit	− Credit
(g) 900	

In transaction (h), Cruz Auto Detail bought insurance for one year, $360. This transaction results in an increase to Prepaid Insurance with a debit and a decrease to Cash with a credit.

Assets		=	Liabilities		+	Owner's Equity		+	Revenue		−	Expenses	
+	−		−	+		−	+		−	+		+	−
Debit	Credit		Debit	Credit		Debit	Credit		Debit	Credit		Debit	Credit

Cash

+ Debit	− Credit
	(h) 360

Prepaid Insurance

+ Debit	− Credit
(h) 360	

In transaction (i), Cruz Auto Detail received a bill from the *Valley News* for a newspaper advertisement, $400. This transaction results in an increase to Advertising Expense with a debit and an increase to Accounts Payable with a credit.

Assets		=	Liabilities		+	Owner's Equity		+	Revenue		−	Expenses	
+	−		−	+		−	+		−	+		+	−
Debit	Credit		Debit	Credit		Debit	Credit		Debit	Credit		Debit	Credit

Accounts Payable

− Debit	+ Credit
	(i) 400

Advertising Expense

+ Debit	− Credit
(i) 400	

In transaction (j), Cruz Auto Detail sold services on account to Costello Taxi, $1,050. This transaction results in an increase to Accounts Receivable with a debit and an increase to Income from Services with a credit.

Assets		=	Liabilities		+	Owner's Equity		+	Revenue		−	Expenses	
+	−		−	+		−	+		−	+		+	−
Debit	Credit		Debit	Credit		Debit	Credit		Debit	Credit		Debit	Credit

Accounts Receivable

+ Debit	− Credit
(j) 1,050	

Income from Services

− Debit	+ Credit
	(j) 1,050

In transaction (k), Cruz Auto Detail made a payment to Williams Auto Supply, a creditor, $2,000. This transaction results in a decrease to Cash with a credit and a decrease to Accounts Payable with a debit.

Assets		=	Liabilities		+	Owner's Equity		+	Revenue		−	Expenses	
+	−		−	+		−	+		−	+		+	−
Debit	Credit		Debit	Credit		Debit	Credit		Debit	Credit		Debit	Credit

Cash

+ Debit	− Credit
	(k) 2,000

Accounts Payable

− Debit	+ Credit
(k) 2,000	

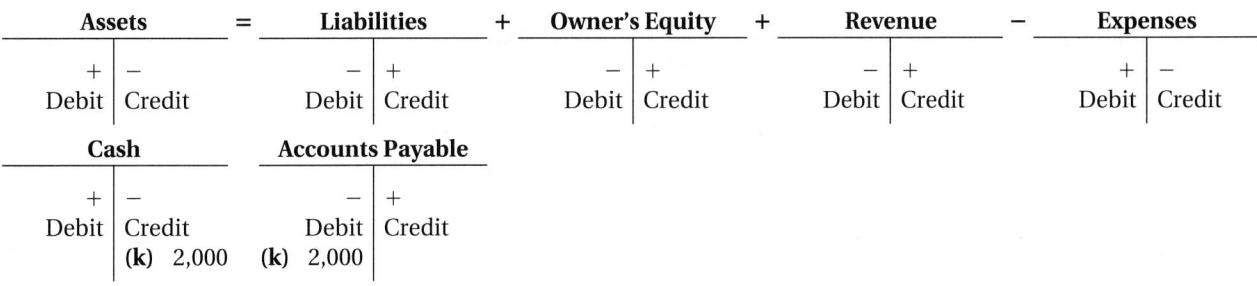

In transaction (l), Cruz Auto Detail received and paid a bill from Midwest Power, Inc., $160. This transaction results in an increase to Utilities Expense with a debit and a decrease to Cash with a credit.

Assets		=	Liabilities		+	Owner's Equity		+	Revenue		−	Expenses	
+	−		−	+		−	+		−	+		+	−
Debit	Credit		Debit	Credit		Debit	Credit		Debit	Credit		Debit	Credit
Cash												**Utilities Expense**	
+	−											+	−
Debit	Credit											Debit	Credit
	(l) 160											**(l)** 160	

In transaction (m), Cruz Auto Detail made a payment on account to *Valley News,* a creditor, $400. This transaction results in a decrease to Accounts Payable with a debit and a decrease to Cash with a credit.

Assets		=	Liabilities		+	Owner's Equity		+	Revenue		−	Expenses	
+	−		−	+		−	+		−	+		+	−
Debit	Credit		Debit	Credit		Debit	Credit		Debit	Credit		Debit	Credit
Cash			**Accounts Payable**										
+	−		−	+									
Debit	Credit		Debit	Credit									
	(m) 400		**(m)** 400										

In transaction (n), Cruz Auto Detail paid wages of a part-time employee, $1,400. This transaction results in an increase to Wages Expense with a debit and a decrease to Cash with a credit.

Assets		=	Liabilities		+	Owner's Equity		+	Revenue		−	Expenses	
+	−		−	+		−	+		−	+		+	−
Debit	Credit		Debit	Credit		Debit	Credit		Debit	Credit		Debit	Credit
Cash												**Wages Expense**	
+	−											+	−
Debit	Credit											Debit	Credit
	(n) 1,400											**(n)** 1,400	

In transaction (o), Cruz Auto Detail bought equipment from Williams Auto Supply, $1,500, paying $600 in cash and placing the balance on account. This is called a **compound entry**; that is, more than one debit or more than one credit is recorded. The transaction results in an increase to Equipment with a debit, a decrease to Cash with a credit, and an increase to Accounts Payable with a credit.

Assets		=	Liabilities		+	Owner's Equity		+	Revenue		−	Expenses	
+	−		−	+		−	+		−	+		+	−
Debit	Credit		Debit	Credit		Debit	Credit		Debit	Credit		Debit	Credit

Cash	
+	−
Debit	Credit
	(o) 600

Accounts Payable	
−	+
Debit	Credit
	(o) 900

Equipment	
+	−
Debit	Credit
(o) 1,500	

In transaction (p), Cruz Auto Detail received cash on account from Costello Taxi, a customer, $850. This transaction results in an increase to Cash with a debit and a decrease to Accounts Receivable with a credit.

Assets		=	Liabilities		+	Owner's Equity		+	Revenue		−	Expenses	
+	−		−	+		−	+		−	+		+	−
Debit	Credit		Debit	Credit		Debit	Credit		Debit	Credit		Debit	Credit

Cash	
+	−
Debit	Credit
(p) 850	

Accounts Receivable	
+	−
Debit	Credit
	(p) 850

In transaction (q), Cruz sold services for cash to customers for the rest of the month, $2,700. This transaction results in an increase to Cash with a debit and an increase to Income from Services with a credit.

Assets		=	Liabilities		+	Owner's Equity		+	Revenue		−	Expenses	
+	−		−	+		−	+		−	+		+	−
Debit	Credit		Debit	Credit		Debit	Credit		Debit	Credit		Debit	Credit

Cash	
+	−
Debit	Credit
(q) 2,700	

Income from Services	
−	+
Debit	Credit
	(q) 2,700

In transaction (r), Cruz withdrew cash for personal use, $3,000. This transaction resulted in an increase to Drawing with a debit and a decrease to Cash with a credit.

Assets		=	Liabilities		+	Owner's Equity		+	Revenue		−	Expenses	
+ Debit	− Credit		− Debit	+ Credit		− Debit	+ Credit		− Debit	+ Credit		+ Debit	− Credit

Cash

+ Debit	− Credit
	(r) 3,000

L. A. Cruz, Drawing

+ Debit	− Credit
(r) 3,000	

Summary of Transactions

The following T accounts show the transactions as they are ordinarily recorded. Footings are shown in color. You will notice that the balance of each account is normally on the plus side. Note that, in recording expenses, you place the entries only on the plus, or debit, side. Also, in recording revenue, you place the entries only on the plus, or credit, side.

FYI

Traditionally, accountants use the abbreviations Dr. for Debit and Cr. for Credit.

Assets		=	Liabilities		+	Owner's Equity		+	Revenue		−	Expenses	
+ Debit	− Credit		− Debit	+ Credit		− Debit	+ Credit		− Debit	+ Credit		+ Debit	− Credit

Cash

+	−
(a) 70,000	(b) 43,000
(f) 3,520	(d) 2,000
(p) 850	(g) 900
(q) 2,700	(h) 360
77,070	(k) 2,000
	(l) 160
	(m) 400
	(n) 1,400
	(o) 600
	(r) 3,000
Bal. 23,250	53,820

Accounts Receivable

+	−
(j) 1,050	(p) 850
Bal. 200	

Supplies

+	−
(e) 800	

Prepaid Insurance

+	−
(h) 360	

Equipment

+	−
(b) 43,000	
(c) 7,000	
(o) 1,500	
Bal. 51,500	

Accounts Payable

−	+
(d) 2,000	(c) 7,000
(k) 2,000	(e) 800
(m) 400	(i) 400
4,400	(o) 900
	9,100
	Bal. 4,700

L. A. Cruz, Capital

−	+
	(a) 70,000

L. A. Cruz, Drawing

+	−
(r) 3,000	

Income from Services

−	+
	(f) 3,520
	(j) 1,050
	(q) 2,700
	Bal. 7,270

Wages Expense

+	−
(n) 1,400	

Rent Expense

+	−
(g) 900	

Advertising Expense

+	−
(i) 400	

Utilities Expense

+	−
(l) 160	

FYI

A memory tool that helps some students to memorize debits and credits in T accounts is the trial balance equation A + D + E = L + C + R.

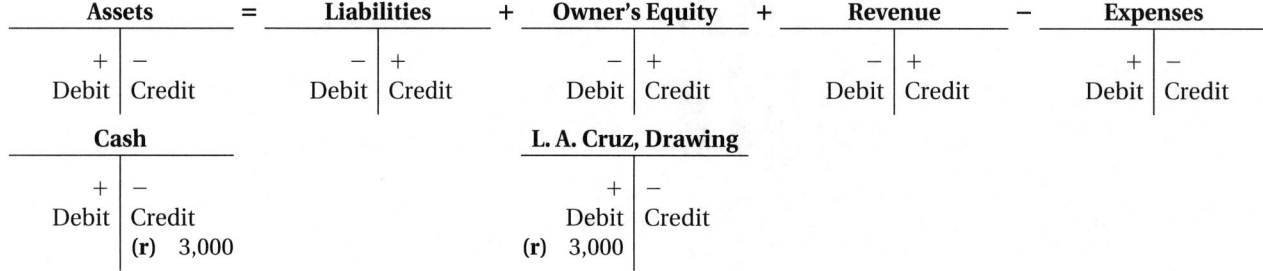

THE TRIAL BALANCE

Objective 5

Prepare a trial balance.

You can now prepare a trial balance by simply recording the balances of the T accounts in two columns. The **trial balance** is a listing of account balances in two columns—one labeled Debit and one labeled Credit—to prove that the total of all the debt balances equals the total of all the credit balances. A trial balance is not considered a financial statement; it is, as the name implies, a trial run by the accountant to prove that the debit balances equal the credit balances. This is evidence of the equality of the two sides of the fundamental accounting equation. The accountant must prove that the accounts are in balance before preparing the company's financial statements.

In preparing a trial balance, shown in Figure 1, record the accounts with balances in the same order as they are listed in the chart of accounts. The balance sheet accounts are listed first, followed by the income statement accounts.

- Assets
- Liabilities
- Owner's Equity
- Revenue
- Expenses

Cruz Auto Detail
Trial Balance
June 30, 20—

Column headings identify information in each column

ACCOUNT NAME	DEBIT	CREDIT
Cash	23,250.00	
Accounts Receivable	200.00	
Supplies	800.00	
Prepaid Insurance	360.00	
Equipment	51,500.00	
Accounts Payable		4,700.00
L. A. Cruz, Capital		70,000.00
L. A. Cruz, Drawing	3,000.00	
Income from Services		7,270.00
Wages Expense	1,400.00	
Rent Expense	900.00	
Advertising Expense	400.00	
Utilities Expense	160.00	
	81,970.00	81,970.00

Accounts listed in order of the chart of accounts

Dollar signs are not used on a trial balance.

Single underline beneath figures to be added

Double underline beneath column totals

FIGURE 1

The normal balance of each account is on its plus side. Remember that when there is more than one entry in an account, we record the totals in footings and subtract one footing from the other to determine the balance. Record this balance on the side of the account with the larger footing. (Here we record the Drawing account balance in the debit column because it has a debit balance. We do not deduct Drawing from the Capital account when we prepare the trial balance.) The following table indicates where each of the account balances would normally be shown in a trial balance.

	Trial Balance	
Account Titles	Left or Debit Balances	Right or Credit Balances
	Assets	
		Liabilities
		Capital
	Drawing	
		Revenue
	Expenses	
Totals	XXXX XX	XXXX XX

MAJOR FINANCIAL STATEMENTS

Remember!

Accounting is defined as the process of analyzing, classifying, recording, and summarizing business transactions.

Earlier we listed *summarizing* as one of the five basic tasks of the accounting process. To accomplish this task, accountants use financial statements. A **financial statement** is a report prepared by accountants to summarize the financial affairs of a business for managers and others, both inside and outside the business.

Note that the headings of all financial statements require three lines:

1. Name of the company (or owner, if there is no company name)
2. Title of the financial statement
3. Period of time covered by the financial statement, or its date

Remember!

The three-line heading of a financial statement answers the questions Who? What? and When?

Also, note that dollar signs are placed at the head of each column and with each total. Single lines (drawn with a ruler) are used to show that the figures above are being added or subtracted. Lines should be drawn across the entire column. A double line is drawn under the final total in a column.

PROJECTED EARNINGS

A business's operating decisions are made from financial statements such as income statements.

The financial statements are all interconnected. The income statement must be prepared first, followed by the statement of owner's equity, and then the balance sheet.

The Income Statement

Objective 6a

Prepare an income statement.

The **income statement** shows total revenue minus total expenses, which yields the net income or net loss. The income statement shows the results of business transactions involving revenue and expense accounts—in other words, how the business has performed—over a period of time, usually a month or a year. When total revenue exceeds total expenses over the period, the result is **net income**, or profit. If the total revenue is less than the total expenses, the result is a **net loss**.

FYI

The income statement is sometimes called the *statement of income and expenses* or *profit and loss statement.*

The income statement in Figure 2 shows the results of the first month of operations for Cruz Auto Detail.

Three-line heading

Cruz Auto Detail
Income Statement
For Month Ended June 30, 20—

① Name of company
② Title of statement
③ Period of time

Revenue:		
Income from Services		$7,270.00
Expenses:		
Wages Expense	$1,400.00	
Rent Expense	900.00	
Advertising Expense	400.00	
Utilities Expense	160.00	
Total Expenses		2,860.00
Net Income		$4,410.00

Colon
Indent
Listed in order of chart of accounts
Indent again
Dollar sign at head of column or to show subtotal or total
Transfer net income figure to statement of owner's equity.
Single underline beneath the final figure
Double underline beneath grand total

FIGURE 2

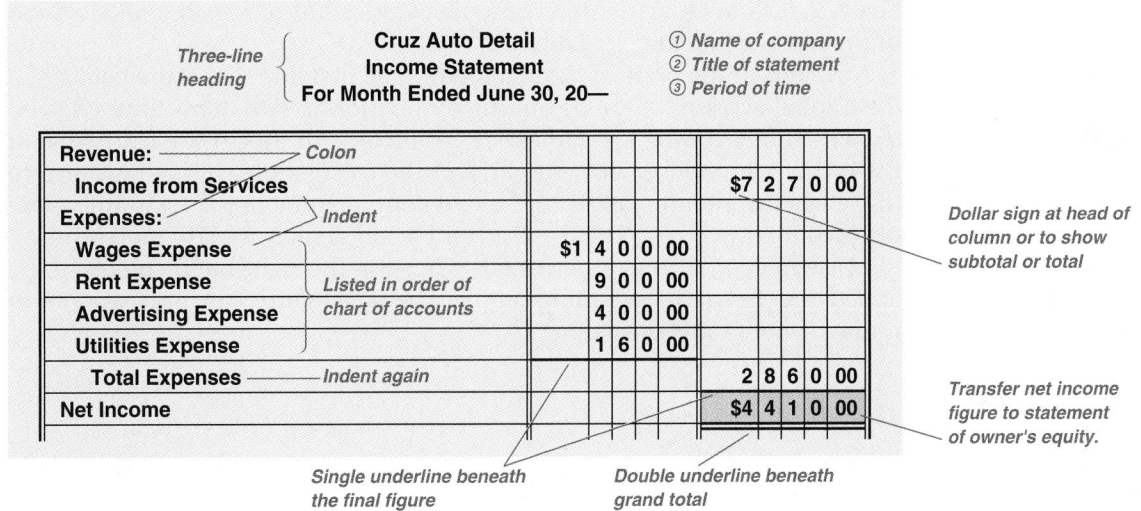

For convenience, the individual expense amounts are recorded in the first amount column. Thus, the total expenses ($2,860) may be subtracted directly from the total revenue ($7,270).

FYI

Compare the third line of the income statement heading with the third line of the balance sheet heading shown in Figure 4.

The income statement covers a period of time, whereas the balance sheet has only one date: the end of the financial period. On the income statement, the revenue for June, less the expenses for June, shows the results of operations—a net income of $4,410. To the accountant, the term *net income* means "clear" income, or profit after all expenses have been deducted. Expenses are usually listed in the same order as in the chart of accounts. Revenue and expense amounts are taken directly from the trial balance.

The Statement of Owner's Equity

Objective 6b

Prepare a statement of owner's equity.

We said that revenue and expenses are connected with owner's equity through the financial statements. Now let's demonstrate this by a statement of owner's equity, shown in Figure 3 (page 48), which the accountant prepares after he or she has determined the net income or net loss on the

Three-line heading:

Cruz Auto Detail
Statement of Owner's Equity
For Month Ended June 30, 20—

① Name of company
② Title of statement
③ Period of time

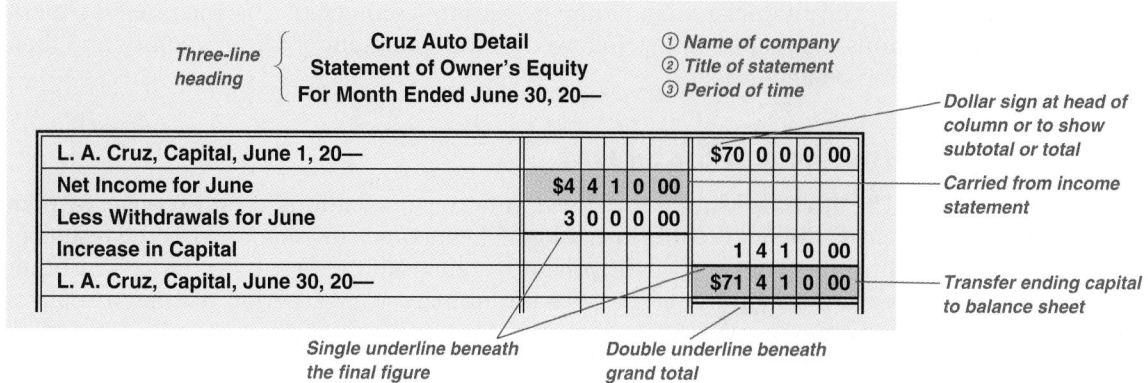

L. A. Cruz, Capital, June 1, 20—		$70 0 0 0 00
Net Income for June	$4 4 1 0 00	
Less Withdrawals for June	3 0 0 0 00	
Increase in Capital		1 4 1 0 00
L. A. Cruz, Capital, June 30, 20—		$71 4 1 0 00

Dollar sign at head of column or to show subtotal or total

Carried from income statement

Transfer ending capital to balance sheet

Single underline beneath the final figure

Double underline beneath grand total

FIGURE 3

income statement. The **statement of owner's equity** shows how—and why—the owner's equity, or Capital account, has changed over a stated period of time (in this case, the month of June). Notice the third line in the heading of Figure 3. It shows that the statement of owner's equity covers the same period of time as the income statement.

Now look at the body of the statement. The first line shows the balance in the Capital account at the beginning of the month. Two items have affected owner's equity during the month: A net income of $4,410 was earned, and the owner withdrew $3,000. To perform the calculations smoothly, move to the left-hand column and list these two items, subtracting withdrawals from net income ($4,410 − $3,000 = $1,410). The difference ($1,410) represents an increase in capital. This difference is placed in the right-hand column to be added directly to the beginning capital. The final figure is the ending amount in the owner's Capital account.

Remember!

The income statement is prepared first, so that net income can be recorded in the statement of owner's equity. The statement of owner's equity is prepared second, so that the ending amount of capital can be recorded in the balance sheet, which is prepared last.

The Balance Sheet

Objective 6c

Prepare a balance sheet.

After preparing the statement of owner's equity, we prepare a balance sheet. The **balance sheet** shows the **financial position**, or the condition of a business's assets offset by claims against them at a point in time. It summarizes the balances of the asset, liability, and owner's equity accounts on a given date (usually the end of a month or year). The balance sheet is, thus, like a snapshot—a picture of the financial condition of the business at that point in time.

The ending capital balance in the balance sheet is taken from the statement of owner's equity. Note that the accounts appear in the same order as in the chart of accounts.

In the **report form** of the balance sheet, the elements in the accounting equation are presented one on top of the other. A balance sheet prepared on June 30 for Cruz Auto Detail in report form would look like Figure 4.

Income Statement Involving More than One Revenue Account and a Net Loss

Objective 7a

Prepare an income statement involving more than one revenue account and a net loss.

When an organization has more than one distinct source of revenue, a separate revenue account is set up for each source. See, for example, the income statement of Rule Miniature Golf presented in Figure 5. Also note that expenses are greater than revenues, resulting in a net loss.

Cruz Auto Detail
Balance Sheet
June 30, 20—

Assets		
Cash	$23 2 5 0 00	
Accounts Receivable	2 0 0 00	
Supplies	8 0 0 00	
Prepaid Insurance	3 6 0 00	
Equipment	51 5 0 0 00	
Total Assets		$76 1 1 0 00
Liabilities		
Accounts Payable		$4 7 0 0 00
Owner's Equity		
L. A. Cruz, Capital		71 4 1 0 00
Total Liabilities and Owner's Equity		$76 1 1 0 00

Carried from statement of owner's equity

FIGURE 4

FIGURE 5

Rule Miniature Golf
Income Statement
For Month Ended September 30, 20—

Revenue:		
Admissions Income	$9 6 2 4 00	
Concessions Income	2 7 1 2 00	
Total Revenue		$12 3 3 6 00
Expenses:		
Wages Expense	4 1 2 3 00	
Advertising Expense	3 1 7 00	
Total Expenses		13 4 7 5 00
Net Loss		1 1 3 9 00

Remember!

The amounts in the left column are used to calculate totals. Amounts in the right column are totals or grand totals.

Statement of Owner's Equity with an Additional Investment and a Net Income

Objective 7b

Prepare a statement of owner's equity with an additional investment and either a net income or a net loss.

Any additional investment by the owner during the period covered by the financial statements should be shown in the statement of owner's equity, since such a statement should show everything that has affected the Capital account from the *beginning* until the *end* of the period covered by the financial statements. For example, assume that the following information is true for the C. P. Walsh Company, which has a net income:

Balance of C. P. Walsh, Capital, on April 1	$87,000
Additional investment by C. P. Walsh on April 12	10,000
Net income for the month (from income statement)	2,600
Total withdrawals for the month	2,100

FIGURE 6

C. P. Walsh Company
Statement of Owner's Equity
For Month Ended April 30, 20—

C. P. Walsh, Capital, April 1, 20—		$87 0 0 0 00
Additional Investment, April 12, 20—		10 0 0 0 00
Total Investment		97 0 0 0 00
Net Income for April	$2 6 0 0 00	
Less Withdrawals for April	2 1 0 0 00	
Increase in Capital		5 0 0 00
C. P. Walsh, Capital, April 30, 20—		$97 5 0 0 00

The statement of owner's equity in Figure 6 shows this information.

The additional investment may be in the form of cash. Or the investment may be in the form of other assets, such as tools, equipment, and similar items. In the case of investments of assets other than cash, the assets should be recorded at their fair market value. **Fair market value** is the present worth of an asset, or the amount that would be received if the asset were sold to an outsider on the open market. Fair market value may differ greatly from the amount the owner originally paid for the asset.

Statement of Owner's Equity with an Additional Investment and a Net Loss

Assume the following for the L. N. Reems Company, which has a net loss:

L. N. Reems, Capital, on Oct. 1	$70,000
Additional investment by L. N. Reems on Oct. 25	6,000
Net loss for the month (from income statement)	250
Total withdrawals for the month	420

The statement of owner's equity in Figure 7 shows this information.

FIGURE 7

L. N. Reems Company
Statement of Owner's Equity
For Month Ended October 31, 20—

L. N. Reems, Capital, October 1, 20—		$70 0 0 0 00
Additional Investment, October 25, 20—		6 0 0 0 00
Total Investment		$76 0 0 0 00
Less: Net Loss for October	$ 2 5 0 00	
Withdrawals for October	4 2 0 00	
Decrease in Capital		6 7 0 00
L. N. Reems, Capital, October 31, 20—		$75 3 3 0 00

FYI

The information normally shown in the statement of owner's equity is sometimes included as part of the owner's equity section of the balance sheet in computerized general ledger systems.

ERRORS EXPOSED BY THE TRIAL BALANCE

Although using a computer greatly reduces the occurrence of addition and subtraction errors, it does not prevent the occurrence of other kinds of errors, such as recording transactions incorrectly.

If the debit and credit columns in a trial balance are not equal, then it is evident that we have made an error. Possible mistakes include the following:

- Making errors in arithmetic, such as errors in adding the trial balance columns or in finding the balances of the accounts.
- Recording only half an entry, such as a debit without a corresponding credit, or vice versa.
- Recording both halves of the entry on the same side, such as two debits rather than a debit and a credit.
- Recording one or more amounts incorrectly.

Procedure for Locating Errors

Suppose that you are in a business situation where you have recorded transactions for a month in the account books, and the accounts do not balance. To save yourself time, you need to have a definite procedure for tracking down the errors. The best method is to do everything in reverse, as follows:

- Look at the pattern of balances to see if a normal balance was placed in the wrong column on the trial balance.
- Re-add the trial balance columns.
- Check the transferring of the figures from the accounts to the trial balance.
- Verify the footings and balances of the accounts.

As an added precaution, form the habit of verifying all addition and subtraction as you go along. You can thus correct many mistakes *before* the time comes to prepare a trial balance.

When the trial balance totals do not balance, the difference might indicate that you forgot to record half of an entry in the accounts. For example, if the difference in the trial balance totals is $20, you may have recorded $20 on the debit side of one account without recording $20 on the credit side of another account.

FYI

Even if debits equal credits, this does not necessarily mean that there were no errors in the recording of the transactions. For example, a transaction may have been forgotten, it may have been included twice, or it may have been written for an incorrect amount.

Another possibility is to divide the difference by 2; this may provide a clue that you accidentally recorded half an entry twice. For example, if the difference in the trial balance is $600, you may have recorded $300 on the debit side of one account and an additional $300 on the debit side of another account. Look for a transaction that involved $300 and then see if you have recorded both a debit and a credit. By knowing which transactions to check, you can save a lot of time.

Transpositions and Slides

Objective 8

Recognize the effect of transpositions and slides on account balances.

If the difference is evenly divisible by 9, the discrepancy may be either a transposition or a slide. A **transposition** means that the digits have been transposed, or switched around, when the numbers were copied from one place to another. For example, one transposition of digits in 916 can be written as 619.

Correct Number	Number Copied	Difference	Difference Divided by 9
916	619	297	$297 \div 9 = 33$

A **slide** is an error in placing the decimal point; in other words, a slide in the decimal point. For example, \$27,000 could be inadvertently written as \$2,700:

Correct Number	Number Copied	Difference	Difference Divided by 9
27,000	2,700	24,300	24,300 ÷ 9 = 2,700

Or the error may be a combination of a transposition and a slide, as when \$450 is written as \$54:

Correct Number	Number Copied	Difference	Difference Divided by 9
450	54	396	396 ÷ 9 = 44

Again, the difference is evenly divisible by 9 (with no remainder).

CHAPTER REVIEW

Review of Performance Objectives

1. Determine balances of T accounts having entries recorded on both sides of the accounts.

   Add the amounts listed on each side of the T account. The totals are called footings. To get the account balance, subtract the total of the smaller side from the total of the larger side. Record the account balance on the larger side.

2. Present the fundamental accounting equation with the T account form, and label the plus and minus sides.

Assets		=	Liabilities		+	Owner's Equity		+	Revenue		−	Expenses	
+	−		−	+		−	+		−	+		+	−
Left	Right		Left	Right		Left	Right		Left	Right		Left	Right

3. Present the fundamental accounting equation with the T account form, and label the debit and credit sides.

Assets		=	Liabilities		+	Owner's Equity		+	Revenue		−	Expenses	
+	−		−	+		−	+		−	+		+	−
Left	Right		Left	Right		Left	Right		Left	Right		Left	Right
Debit	Credit		Debit	Credit		Debit	Credit		Debit	Credit		Debit	Credit

4. Record directly in T accounts a group of business transactions involving changes in asset, liability, capital, revenue, and expense accounts for a service business.

   The transactions are recorded by first recognizing and classifying the accounts involved. Next, decide whether the accounts involved are increased or decreased, and record the amounts as additions or subtractions in the accounts. The equation must always remain in balance.

5. Prepare a trial balance.

   A trial balance is a list of all account balances in two columns—one labeled Debit and one labeled Credit. The trial balance shows that both sides of the accounting equation are equal. The heading consists of the company name, Trial Balance, and the date.

6. Prepare (a) an income statement, (b) a statement of owner's equity, and (c) a balance sheet.

   (a) An income statement shows the results of operations of a business for a period of time. It includes revenue and expense accounts and reports either a net income or a net loss. (b) A statement of owner's equity shows the activity in the owner's equity, or Capital account, for a period of time. It includes the balance in the Capital account at the beginning of the period plus any additional investments and any increase or decrease in capital as the result of a net income (or a net loss) minus (or plus) any withdrawals. (c) A balance sheet shows the financial condition of a business at a point in time. It summarizes the balances of the asset, liability, and owner's equity accounts on a given date.

7. Prepare (a) an income statement involving more than one revenue account and a net loss, and (b) a statement of owner's equity with an additional investment and either a net income or a net loss.

   (a) An income statement containing more than one revenue account requires an additional line for each type of revenue, followed by a total amount of revenue. (b) A statement of owner's equity involving an additional investment requires a line for each additional investment beneath the beginning capital amount, followed by a total amount of investment.

8. Recognize the effect of transpositions and slides on account balances.

   An error in a trial balance may be a transposition or a slide. The clue is whether the difference in account balances or trial balance totals is evenly divisible by 9. With a transposition, some digits have been switched around. With a slide, the decimal point has been recorded in the wrong place.

Glossary

Balance sheet A financial statement showing the financial position of an organization on a given date, such as June 30 or December 31. The balance sheet lists the balances in the asset, liability, and owner's equity capital accounts. (48)

Compound entry A transaction that requires more than one debit or more than one credit to be recorded. (42)

Credit The right side of a T account; to credit is to record an amount on the right side of a T account. Credits represent increases in liability, capital, or revenue accounts and decreases in asset, drawing, or expense accounts. (36)

Debit The left side of a T account; to debit is to record an amount on the left side of a T account. Debits represent increases in asset, drawing, or expense accounts and decreases in liability, capital, or revenue accounts. (36)

Fair market value The present worth of an asset, or the amount that would be received if the asset were sold to an outsider on the open market. (50)

Financial position The resources or assets owned by an organization at a point in time, offset by the claims against those resources and owner's equity; shown on a balance sheet. (48)

Financial statement A report prepared by accountants that summarizes the financial affairs of a business. (46)

Footings The totals of each side of a T account, recorded in small, pencil-written figures. (34)

Income statement A financial statement showing the results of business transactions involving revenue and expense accounts over a period of time. (47)

Net income The result when total revenue exceeds total expenses over a period of time. (47)

Net loss The result when total expenses exceed total revenue over a period of time. (47)

Normal balance The plus side of a T account. (34)

Report form The form of the balance sheet in which assets are placed at the top and liabilities and owner's equity are placed below. (48)

Slide An error in placing the decimal point in a number. (52)

Statement of owner's equity A financial statement showing the activity in the owner's equity Capital account, over the financial period. (48)

T account form A form of account shaped like the letter T in which increases and decreases in the account may be recorded. One side of the T is for entries on the debit or left side. The other side of the T is for entries on the credit or right side. (34)

Transposition An error that involves interchanging, or switching around, digits during the recording of a number. (51)

Trial balance A list of all account balances to prove that the total of all the debit balances equals the total of all the credit balances. (45)

QUESTIONS, EXERCISES, AND PROBLEMS

Discussion Questions

1. Explain the difference between a balance sheet and a trial balance.
2. Does the term *debit* always mean "increase"? Does the term *credit* always mean "decrease"? Explain why.
3. What are footings?
4. Are the three financial statements presented in this chapter connected to each other? If so, how are they connected?
5. Describe a compound entry.
6. In a trial balance, if total debits equal total credits, what does this mean?
7. Give an example of a slide and a transposition. How can you determine whether an error involves a slide or a transposition?
8. What do we mean when we say that revenues and expenses are under the umbrella of owner's equity?

Exercises

P.O. 4

Describe transactions.

Exercise 2-1 During the first month of operation, Sherrard's Auto Supply recorded the following transactions. Describe what has happened in each of the transactions (a) through (k).

Cash

Debit		Credit	
(a)	3,300	(b)	435
(k)	1,125	(c)	98
		(e)	75
		(g)	900
		(i)	92
		(j)	325

Accounts Receivable

Debit		Credit	
(h)	915		

Supplies

Debit		Credit	
(d)	280		

Equipment

Debit		Credit	
(f)	3,850		
(g)	1,835		

Accounts Payable

Debit		Credit	
		(d)	280
		(g)	935

C. S. Sherrard, Capital

Debit		Credit	
		(a)	3,300
		(f)	3,850

C. S. Sherrard, Drawing

Debit		Credit	
(j)	325		

Income from Services

Debit		Credit	
		(h)	915
		(k)	1,125

Rent Expense

Debit		Credit	
(b)	435		

Utilities Expense

Debit		Credit	
(i)	92		

Advertising Expense

Debit		Credit	
(c)	98		

Miscellaneous Expense

Debit		Credit	
(e)	75		

P.O. 1,2,3

Draw T accounts and record the plus and minus signs.

Exercise 2-2 On a sheet of paper, set up the fundamental accounting equation with T accounts under each of the five account classifications, noting plus and minus signs on the appropriate sides of each account. Under each of the five classifications, set up T accounts, again with the correct plus and minus signs and debit and credit, for each of the following accounts of Crystal Shoe Repair.

Cash
Accounts Receivable
Supplies
Equipment
Accounts Payable
K. Chan, Capital
K. Chan, Drawing
Income from Services
Rent Expense
Wages Expense
Utilities Expense
Miscellaneous Expense

P.O. 2,3,4

Record transactions in T accounts.

Exercise 2-3 T. M. Nestler operates Nestler Carpet Cleaners. The company has the following chart of accounts:

Assets

Cash
Accounts Receivable
Supplies
Prepaid Insurance
Cleaning Equipment
Truck
Office Equipment

Liabilities

Accounts Payable

Owner's Equity

T. M. Nestler, Capital
T. M. Nestler, Drawing

Revenue

Income from Services

Expenses

Wages Expense
Truck Expense
Utilities Expense
Advertising Expense

Using the chart of accounts above, record the following transactions in pairs of T accounts. Give the T account to be debited first and the account to be credited to the right. Show debit and credit and plus and minus signs. (Example: Received and paid the bill for the month's rent, $592.)

Rent Expense		Cash	
Dr.	Cr.	Dr.	Cr.
+	–	+	–
592			592

a. Received and paid the electric bill, $87.
b. Bought supplies on account, $238.
c. Paid for insurance for one year, $409.
d. Made a payment on account to a creditor, $605.
e. Received and paid the telephone bill, $47.
f. Sold services on account, $465.
g. Received and paid the gasoline bill for the truck, $109.
h. Received cash on account from customers, $787.
i. Nestler withdrew cash for personal use, $300.

P.O. 4
Classify accounts.

Exercise 2-4 List the classification of each of the following accounts as A (asset), L (liability), OE (owner's equity), R (revenue), or E (expense). Write Debit or Credit to indicate the increase side, the decrease side, and the normal balance side.

"Plus" side

Account	Classification	Increase Side	Decrease Side	Normal Balance Side
0. Cash	A	Debit	Credit	Debit
1. Wages Expense	E	D	C	D
2. Equipment	A	D	C	D
3. K. Coe, Capital	OE	C	D	C
4. Service Revenue	R	C	D	C
5. K. Coe, Drawing	OE	D	C	D
6. Accounts Receivable	A	D	C	D
7. Rent Expense	E	D	C	D
8. Fees Earned	R	C	D	C
9. Accounts Payable	L	C	D	C

P.O. 5
Prepare a corrected trial balance.

Exercise 2-5 Little Ones Day Care, owned by J. L. Little, hired a new bookkeeper who is not entirely familiar with the process of preparing a trial balance. All the accounts have normal balances. Find the errors, and prepare a corrected trial balance for December 31 of this year.

Little Ones Day Care
Trial Balance
December 31, 20—

ACCOUNT NAME	DEBIT	CREDIT
Accounts Receivable		15,500.00
Cash	3,900.00	
Accounts Payable		9,700.00
Equipment	27,000.00	
J. L. Little, Capital		29,200.00
J. L. Little, Drawing		1,700.00
Prepaid Insurance		500.00
Income from Services		34,000.00
Rent Expense		3,500.00
Supplies	1,800.00	
Utilities Expense	3,600.00	
Wages Expense	15,400.00	
	72,900.00	75,200.00

P.O. 5,6,7a
Prepare trial balance and financial statements.

Exercise 2-6 During the first month of operations, Laslo Advertising Agency recorded transactions in T account form. Prepare a trial balance dated March 31 of this year. Prepare an income statement, statement of owner's equity, and balance sheet. *Note:* transaction (a) is original investment; (d) is additional investment.

Cash

(a)	5,100	(c)	350
(e)	3,500	(f)	600
(k)	7,580	(h)	175
		(i)	2,400
		(j)	2,200

Accounts Receivable

(g)	2,600		

Office Supplies

(c)	350		

Equipment

(b)	1,600		
(d)	3,200		

Accounts Payable

		(b)	1,600

O. D. Laslo, Capital

		(a)	5,100
		(d)	3,200

O. D. Laslo, Drawing

(j)	2,200		

Consulting Fees

		(e)	3,500
		(k)	7,580

Advertising Fees

		(g)	2,600

Salary Expense

(i)	2,400		

Rent Expense

(f)	600		

Utilities Expense

(h)	175		

P.O. 8

Determine the effects of errors.

Exercise 2-7

	Amount of Difference	Debit or Credit Column of Trial Balance Understated or Overstated
0. Example: A $282 debit to Accounts Receivable was not recorded.	$282	Debit column understated
a. A $32 debit to Supplies was recorded as $320.	288	Debit over
b. A $255 debit to Accounts Payable was recorded twice.	255	Credit under
c. A $79 debit to Prepaid Insurance was not recorded.	79	Debit under
d. A $63 credit to Cash was not recorded.	63	Debit over
e. A $180 debit to Equipment was recorded twice.	180	Debit over
f. A $54 debit to Supplies was recorded as $45.	9	Debit under

P.O. 8

Determine the effects of errors.

Exercise 2-8 Which of the following errors would cause a trial balance to have unequal totals? As a result of the errors, which accounts are overstated (by how much) or understated (by how much)?

no a. A purchase of office equipment for $380 was recorded as a debit to Office Equipment for $38 and a credit to Cash for $38.

no b. A payment of $140 to a creditor was debited to Accounts Receivable and credited to Cash for $140 each.

no c. A purchase of supplies for $115 was recorded as a debit to Equipment for $115 and a credit to Cash for $115.

yes d. A payment of $86 to a creditor was recorded as a debit to Accounts Payable for $86 and a credit to Cash for $68.

CONSIDER AND COMMUNICATE

You are studying with a study buddy. Your study buddy can't accept that the left side of a T account is a debit and the right side is a credit in every part of the fundamental accounting equation. He just can't let go of his other definitions—he says, "But a credit memo is good, so I should always credit an account when increasing it." How would you respond to this confusion?

CRITICAL THINKING

The bookkeeper has made the following errors in recording transactions:

1. Recorded the entry to buy supplies for cash twice.
2. Did not enter the transaction to record the payment of the rent.
3. Recorded the amount paid for utilities as a debit to Salaries Expense instead of a debit to Utilities Expense.

Instructions

Explain the following things about *each* of these errors:

a. Will the error cause the trial balance to be out of balance?
b. How will this error change the financial statements; for example, will net income be overstated or understated or will assets be understated or overstated?
c. Explain how you would correct each error.

A MATTER OF ETHICS

You had lunch with a friend who is an accounting clerk at a business near your office. During your conversation, your friend discusses the amount of cash the business has in the bank, how sales are not going very well, and the salaries of various employees. Is her revealing these details ethical or unethical?

WEB WORK

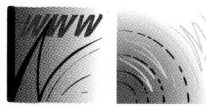

Using an Internet web browser, type in the search box the phrase *accounting practices.* Search for an article or find a home page that will provide you with information about accounting practices or rules. Narrow your search by adding accounting terms to the search box—for example, accounting practices fair market value or accounting practices balance sheet. Discuss or prepare a written response of your findings.

PROBLEM SET A

For additional help, see the demonstration problems at the beginning of each chapter in your Working Papers.

P.O. 2,3,4

Problem 2-1A During February of this year, D. O. Kent established Malcolm Leather Repair. The following asset, liability, and owner's equity accounts are included in the chart of accounts:

Cash	Office Equipment
Supplies	Accounts Payable
Shop Equipment	D. O. Kent, Capital
Store Equipment	

The following transactions occurred during the month of February:

a. Kent deposited $20,000 cash in a bank account in the name of the business.
b. Bought shop equipment for cash, $1,732, Ck. No. 1000.
c. Bought supplies on account from Melor Company, $413.
d. Bought store shelving for $808 from Kohler Hardware; payment is due in thirty days.
e. Bought office equipment from Stegal Office Supply, $399, paying $200 in cash and placing the balance on account, Ck. No. 1001.

f. Paid on account to Kohler Hardware, a creditor, $208, Ck. No. 1002.
g. Kent invested his personal leather working tools in the business with a fair market value of $300.

Check Figure
Cash balance, $17,860

Instructions

1. Write the account classifications (Assets, Liabilities, Owner's Equity, Revenue, Expense) in the fundamental accounting equation, as well as the plus and minus signs and Debit and Credit.
2. Write the account names on the T accounts under the classifications, place the plus and minus signs for each T account, and label the debit and credit sides of the T accounts.
3. Record the amounts in the proper positions in the T accounts. Write the letter next to each entry to identify the transaction.
4. Foot and balance accounts.

P.O. 1,2,3,4,5,7a

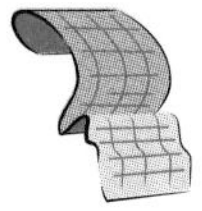

Problem 2-2A L. S. Quillan established the Quillan Copy Service during June of this year. The accountant prepared the following chart of accounts:

Assets
Cash
Supplies
Computer Software
Office Equipment
Electric Sign

Liabilities
Accounts Payable

Owner's Equity
L. S. Quillan, Capital
L. S. Quillan, Drawing

Revenue
Income from Services

Expenses
Advertising Expense
Rent Expense
Utilities Expense
Wages Expense
Miscellaneous Expense

The following transactions occurred during the month of June:

a. Quillan deposited $15,000 cash in a bank account in the name of the business.
b. Bought office equipment for cash, $685, Ck. No. 1001.
c. Bought computer software from Sysco Computer Center, $890, paying $200 in cash and placing the balance on account, Ck. No. 1002.
d. Paid current month's rent, $725, Ck. No. 1003 (Rent Expense).
e. Sold services for cash, $1,048 (Income from Services).
f. Bought an electric sign from Mory Sign Company, $1,325, paying $325 in cash and placing the balance on account, Ck. No. 1004.
g. Received bill from *The Times* for advertising, $434 (Advertising Expense).
h. Bought supplies on account from Jenkins Supply, $1,185.
i. Received and paid the electric bill, $188, Ck. No. 1005.
j. Paid on account to *The Times,* a creditor, $434, Ck. No. 1006.
k. Sold services for cash, $1,272.
l. Paid wages to an employee, $655, Ck. No. 1007.
m. Quillan invested his personal computer (Office Equipment) in the business with a fair market value of $1,200.
n. Quillan withdrew cash for personal use, $750, Ck. No. 1008.
o. Received and paid the bill for city business license, $35, Ck. No. 1009 (Miscellaneous Expense).

Check Figure
Trial balance total, $21,395

Instructions

1. Record the owner's name in the Capital and Drawing T accounts.
2. Correctly place the plus and minus signs for each T account, and label the debit and credit sides of the accounts.
3. Record the transactions in the T accounts. Write the letter of each entry to identify the transaction.
4. Foot the T accounts and show the balances.
5. Prepare a trial balance, with a three-line heading, dated June 30, 20—.

P.O. 1,2,3,4,5,6

Problem 2-3A T. D. Ming, a physical therapist, opened Ming Physical Therapy Clinic. Her accountant provided the following chart of accounts:

Assets

Cash
Accounts Receivable
Office Equipment
Office Furniture

Liabilities

Accounts Payable

Owner's Equity

T. D. Ming, Capital
T. D. Ming, Drawing

Revenue

Professional Fees
Consulting Fees

Expenses

Salary Expense
Rent Expense
Utilities Expense
Miscellaneous Expense

The following transactions occurred during July of this year:

a. Ming deposited $25,000 in a bank account in the name of the business.
b. Bought filing cabinets on account from Mead Office Supply (Office Equipment), $225.
c. Paid cash for chairs and carpets (Office Furniture) for the waiting room, $938, Ck. No. 1000.
d. Bought a photocopier from MJ's Office Equipment, $635, paying $135 in cash, placing the balance on account, Ck. No. 1001.
e. Received and paid the telephone bill, which included installation charges, $127, Ck. No. 1002.
f. Sold professional services on account, $1,723.
g. Ming invested her personal computer, printer, and scanner (Office Equipment) in the business with a fair market value of $2,300 (additional investment).
h. Received and paid the bill for the state physical therapy convention, $365, Ck. No. 1003 (Miscellaneous Expense).
i. Received and paid the electric bill, $84, Ck. No. 1004.
j. Received cash on account from credit customers, $789.
k. Paid on account to Mead Office Supply, a creditor, $155, Ck. No. 1005.
l. Paid the office rent for the current month, $680, Ck. No. 1006.
m. Sold consulting services for cash, $565.
n. Paid the salary of the receptionist, $715, Ck. No. 1007.
o. Ming withdrew cash for personal use, $1,075, Ck. No. 1008.

Check Figure
Net Income, $317

Instructions

1. Record the owner's name in the Capital and Drawing T accounts.
2. Correctly place the plus and minus signs for each T account, and label the debit and credit sides of the accounts.

3. Record the transactions in the T accounts. Write the letter of each entry to identify the transaction.
4. Foot the T accounts and show the balances.
5. Prepare a trial balance as of July 31, 20—.
6. Prepare an income statement for July 31, 20—.
7. Prepare a statement of owner's equity for July 31, 20— (Reminder: Additional investment).
8. Prepare a balance sheet as of July 31, 20—

P.O. 1,2,3,4,5,6,7b

Problem 2-4A On July 1, N. B. Edgar opened Coin-Op Laundry. Edgar's accountant listed the following chart of accounts:

Cash
Supplies
Prepaid Insurance
Equipment
Furniture and Fixtures
Accounts Payable
N. B. Edgar, Capital
N. B. Edgar, Drawing
Laundry Revenue
Wages Expense
Rent Expense
Utilities Expense
Miscellaneous Expense

During July, the following transactions were completed:

a. Edgar deposited $20,000 in a bank account in the name of the business.
b. Bought tables and chairs for cash, $450, Ck. No. 1200.
c. Paid the rent for the current month, $705, Ck. No. 1201.
d. Bought washers and dryers from Eldon Equipment, $17,400, paying $4,000 in cash and placing the balance on account, Ck. No. 1202.
e. Bought laundry supplies on account from Borkal Distributors, $410.
f. Sold services for cash, $862.
g. Bought insurance for one year, $468, Ck. No. 1203.
h. Paid on account to Eldon Equipment, a creditor, $550, Ck. No. 1204.
i. Received and paid the electric bill, $118, Ck. No. 1205.
j. Paid on account to Borkal Distributors, a creditor, $145, Ck. No. 1206.
k. Sold services to customers for cash for the second half of the month, $881.
l. Received and paid the bill for the business license, $45, Ck. No. 1207.
m. Paid wages to an employee, $1,146, Ck. No. 1208.
n. Edgar withdrew cash for personal use, $875, Ck. No. 1209.

Check Figure

Net Loss, $271

Instructions

1. Record the owner's name in the Capital and Drawing T accounts.
2. Correctly place the plus and minus signs for each T account, and label the debit and credit sides of the accounts.
3. Record the transactions in the T accounts. Write the letter of each entry to identify the transaction.
4. Foot the T accounts and show the balances in each account.
5. Prepare a trial balance as of July 31, 20—.
6. Prepare an income statement for July 31, 20—.
7. Prepare a statement of owner's equity for July 31, 20—.
8. Prepare a balance sheet as of July 31, 20—.

PROBLEM SET B

For additional help, see the demonstration problems at the beginning of each chapter in your Working Papers.

P.O. 2,3,4

Problem 2-1B During December of this year, E. B. Romburg established Romburg's Aerobics. The following asset, liability, and owner's equity accounts are included in the chart of accounts:

Cash
Supplies
Exercise Equipment
Office Equipment
Video Equipment
Accounts Payable
E. B. Romburg, Capital

During December, the following transactions occurred:

a. Romburg deposited $28,000 in a bank account in the name of the business.
b. Bought exercise equipment for cash, $6,375, Ck. No. 1001.
c. Bought supplies on account from Hernandez and Company, $632.
d. Bought a printer (Office Equipment) on account from Office Warehouse, $824.
e. Bought exercise equipment on account from Donovan Company, $336.
f. Romburg invested his video equipment with a fair market value of $8,300 in the business.
g. Made a payment to Hernandez and Company, a creditor, $330, Ck. No. 1002.

Check Figure
Balance of Cash, $20,959

Instructions

1. Write the account classifications (Assets, Liabilities, Owner's Equity, Revenue, Expense) in the fundamental accounting equation, as well as the plus and minus signs and Debit and Credit.
2. Write the account names on the T accounts under the classifications, place the plus and minus signs for each T account, and label the debit and credit sides of the T accounts.
3. Record the amounts in the proper positions in the T accounts. Write the letter of each entry to identify the transaction.
4. Foot and balance accounts.

P.O. 1,2,3,4,5

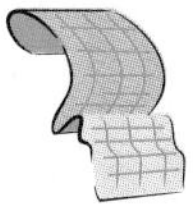

Problem 2-2B S. D. Orren established Orren's Cyber Service during November of this year. The accountant prepared the following chart of accounts:

Assets
Cash
Supplies
Computer Software
Office Equipment
Electric Sign

Liabilities
Accounts Payable

Owner's Equity
S. D. Orren, Capital
S. D. Orren, Drawing

Revenue
Income from Services

Expenses
Advertising Expense
Rent Expense
Utilities Expense
Wages Expense
Miscellaneous Expense

The following transactions occurred during the month:

a. Orren deposited $15,000 in a bank account in the name of the business.
b. Paid the rent for the current month, $630, Ck. No. 2001.
c. Bought office desks and filing cabinets for cash, $930, Ck. No. 2002.
d. Bought a computer and printer (Office Equipment) from Mega Computer Center for use in the business, $4,300, paying $2,500 in cash and placing the balance on account, Ck. No. 2003.
e. Bought an electric sign on account from Sign Works, $1,200.
f. Orren invested her personal computer software with a fair market value of $900 in the business.
g. Received a bill from *Business News* for newspaper advertising, $126.
h. Sold services for cash, $755.
i. Received and paid the electric bill, $158, Ck. No. 2004.
j. Paid on account to *Business News*, a creditor, $126, Ck. No. 2005.
k. Sold services for cash, $1,035.
l. Paid the wages to the employee, $742, Ck. No. 2006.
m. Received and paid the bill for the city business license, $35, Ck. No. 2007.
n. Orren withdrew cash for personal use, $550, Ck. No. 2008.
o. Bought printer paper and letterhead stationery on account from Office Suppliers, $86.

Check Figure
Trial balance total, $20,776

Instructions

1. Record the owner's name in the Capital and Drawing T accounts.
2. Correctly place the plus and minus signs for each T account, and label the debit and credit sides of the accounts.
3. Foot the T accounts and show the balances.
4. Prepare a trial balance with a three-line heading, dated November 30.

P.O. 1,2,3,4,5,6

Problem 2-3B B. D. Lander, an optometrist, opened a clinic in the name of B. D. Lander, O.D. Her accountant prepared the following chart of accounts:

Assets

Cash
Accounts Receivable
Office Equipment
Office Furniture

Liabilities

Accounts Payable

Owner's Equity

B. D. Lander, Capital
B. D. Lander, Drawing

Revenue

Professional Fees
Consulting Fees

Expenses

Salary Expense
Rent Expense
Utilities Expense
Miscellaneous Expense

The following transactions occurred during June of this year:

a. Lander deposited $18,000 in a bank account in the name of the business.
b. Bought a facsimile machine from Marshall's Equipment for $395, paying $100 in cash, and placing the balance on account, Ck. No. 1001.
c. Lander invested her personal office equipment in the business with a fair market value of $8,600 (additional investment).
d. Bought waiting room chairs and tables (Office Furniture), paying cash, $1,132, Ck. No. 1002

e. Bought an intercom system on account from Regal Office Supply (Office Equipment), $356.
f. Received and paid the telephone bill, $84, Ck. No. 1003.
g. Sold consulting fees on account, $1,287.
h. Received and paid the electric bill, $95, Ck. No. 1004.
i. Received and paid the bill for the State Optometric Convention, $250, Ck. No. 1005
j. Sold consulting fees on account, $1,836.
k. Paid on account to Mead Office Supply, a creditor, $165, Ck. No. 1006.
l. Paid the rent for the current month, $640, Ck. No. 1007.
m. Paid salary of the receptionist, $785, Ck. No. 1008.
n. B. D. Lander withdrew cash for personal use, $1,000, Ck. No. 1009.
o. Received $350 on account from patients who were previously billed.

Check Figure

Net Income, $1,269

Instructions

1 Record the owner's name in the Capital and Drawing T accounts.
2. Correctly place the plus and minus signs for each T account, and label the debit and credit sides of the accounts.
3. Record the transactions in the T accounts. Write the letter of each entry to identify the transaction.
4. Foot the T accounts and show the balances.
5. Prepare a trial balance as of June 30, 20—.
6. Prepare an income statement for June 30, 20—.
7. Prepare a statement of owner's equity for June 30, 20— (Reminder: additional investment).
8. Prepare a balance sheet as of June 30, 20—.

P.O. 1,2,3,4,5,6,7b

Problem 2-4B On May 1, C. O. Hobart opened Self-Service Laundry. Hobart's accountant listed the following chart of accounts:

Cash
Supplies
Prepaid Insurance
Equipment
Furniture and Fixtures
Accounts Payable
C. O. Hobart, Capital
C. O. Hobart, Drawing
Laundry Revenue
Wages Expense
Rent Expense
Utilities Expense
Miscellaneous Expense

During May the following transactions were completed:

a. Hobart deposited $20,000 in a bank account in the name of the business.
b. Bought chairs and tables (Furniture and Fixtures) paying cash, $354, Ck. No. 1000.
c. Bought laundry supplies on account from Fenton Supply Company, $248.
d. Paid the rent for the current month, $695, Ck No. 1001.
e. Bought washing machines and dryers from Walder Equipment Company, $11,500; paying $3,500 in cash, and placing the balance on account, Ck. No. 1002.
f. Sold services for cash for the first half of the month, $1,236.

g. Bought insurance for one year, $360, Ck. No. 1003.
h. Paid on account to Walder Equipment Company, a creditor, $500, Ck. No. 1004.
i. Received and paid electric bill, $88, Ck. No. 1005.
j. Sold services for cash for the second half of the month, $727.
k. Paid the wages to the employee, $1,221, Ck. No. 1006.
l. Hobart withdrew cash for his personal use, $940, Ck. No. 1007.
m. Paid on account to Fenton Supply Company, a creditor, $100, Ck. No. 1008.
n. Received bill from the county for sidewalk repair assessment, $120 (Miscellaneous Expense).

Check Figure

Net Loss, $161

Instructions

1. Record the owner's name in the Capital and Drawing T accounts.
2. Correctly place the plus and minus signs for each T account, and label the debit and credit sides of the accounts.
3. Record the transactions in the T accounts. Write the letter of each entry to identify the transaction.
4. Foot the T accounts and show the balances.
5. Prepare a trial balance as of May 31, 20—.
6. Prepare an income statement for May 31, 20—.
7. Prepare a statement of owner's equity for May 31, 20—.
8. Prepare a balance sheet as of May 31, 20—.

3 The General Journal and the General Ledger

WINDOWS ON THE WORLD WIDE WEB

How do you keep track of the money you earn and spend? If you were keeping books for Sean "Puffy" Combs, the rapper, that would be quite a job! How much did Puff Daddy make in 1998? Check out this URL to find out: **http://asylum.aol.com/cgi-bin/news?&loadstory=938811701**.

Pretend you were to record his concert and record sales earnings, as well as his designer clothing purchases, in a general journal and general ledger. Compare his salary with the average salary of an accountant or auditor, which was $40,500 in 1999. When you finish school you may not be earning as much as a popular musician, but wouldn't it be helpful to know what the job you want might pay? Check out the following web site to find out about average salaries of the most popular careers: **http://www.aol.com/webcenters/workplace/career.adp**.

Performance Objectives

After you have completed this chapter, you will be able to do the following:

1. Record a group of transactions pertaining to a service enterprise in a two-column general journal.
2. Post entries from a two-column general journal to general ledger accounts.
3. Prepare a trial balance from the ledger accounts.
4. Correct entries using the ruling method.
5. Correct entries using the correcting entry method.

Recall that *recording* is a step in the definition of accounting. Here we introduce the *journal* as the official record of business transactions. We have recorded business transactions as debits and credits to T accounts. We introduced T accounts because, in the process of formulating debits and credits for business transactions, it's easier to visualize these debits and credits as the plus and minus sides of the T accounts involved. **Formulating the appropriate transaction debits and credits is the most important element in the accounting process.** It represents the very basic foundation of accounting, and all the structure represented by financial statements and other reports is entirely dependent upon it. After determining the debits and credits, the accountant records the transaction in a journal and a ledger.

The initial steps in the accounting process are

1. Record business transactions in a journal.
2. Post entries to accounts in the ledger.
3. Prepare a trial balance.

In this chapter, we present the general journal and the posting procedure.

THE GENERAL JOURNAL

We have seen that an accountant must keep a written record of each transaction. You could record the transactions directly in T accounts; however, only part of the transaction would be listed in each T account. A **journal** is a book in which business transactions are recorded as they happen. In the journal, both the debits and the credits of the entire transaction are recorded in one place. Actually, the journal is a diary for the business, in which you record in day-by-day order all the events involving financial affairs. A journal is called a *book of original entry.* In other words, a transaction is always recorded first in the journal. The process of recording a business transaction in the journal is called **journalizing**. The information about transactions comes from business papers, such as checks, invoices, receipts, letters, and memos. These **source documents** furnish proof (objective evidence) that a transaction has taken place, and they should be identified in the journal entry whenever possible. The basic form of journal is the **two-column general journal**. The term *two-column* refers to the two columns used for debit and credit amounts.

As an example of journalizing business transactions, let's use the transactions for Cruz Auto Detail. The pages of the journal are numbered in consecutive order. This is the first page, and so we write a 1 in the space for the page number. Also, we must write the date of each transaction. Let's begin with the first entry.

Objective 1

Record a group of transactions pertaining to a service enterprise in a two-column general journal.

Transaction (a) June 1: L. A. Cruz deposited $70,000 in a bank account in the name of Cruz Auto Detail.

First, we will show the complete journal entry.

GENERAL JOURNAL PAGE 1

	DATE		DESCRIPTION	POST. REF.	DEBIT	CREDIT	
1	20–						1
2	June	1	Cash		70 0 0 0 00		2
3			L. A. Cruz, Capital			70 0 0 0 00	3
4			Original investment by				4
5			Cruz in Cruz Auto Detail.				5

To explain the entry, we break it down line by line. On the first line at the top of the page, we record the page number where indicated. On line one, we record the year in the left part of the Date column. On the second line, we record the month in the left part of the Date column and the day of the month in the right part of the Date column. We don't have to repeat the year and month until we start a new page, or until the year or month changes.

(Because our illustrations are separated, however, the month may be repeated to eliminate confusion.)

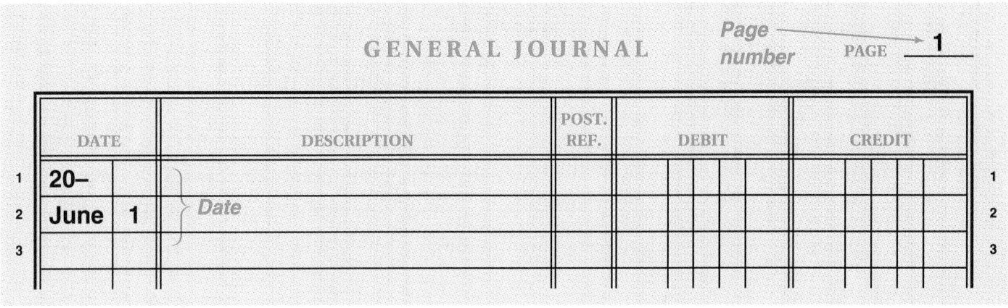
GENERAL JOURNAL
Page number
PAGE 1
DATE
DESCRIPTION
POST. REF.
DEBIT
CREDIT
20–
June 1
Date

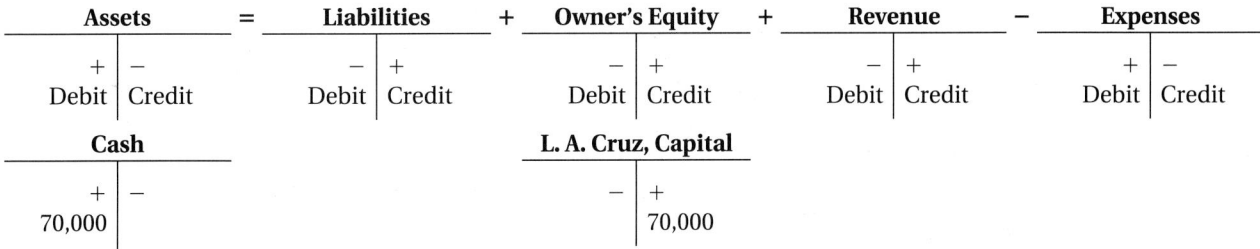

Decide which accounts should be debited and credited. We do this by first deciding which accounts are involved and whether they are increased or decreased. We then visualize the accounts and their plus and minus sides.

Cash is involved in our example. Cash is an asset because it falls within the definition of "things owned." Cash is increased, so we debit Cash.

L. A. Cruz, Capital, is involved. L. A. Cruz, Capital, is an owner's equity account because it represents the owner's investment. L. A. Cruz, Capital, is increased, so we credit L. A. Cruz, Capital. Let's show these entries by referring to our reliable fundamental accounting equation with the accompanying T accounts:

Assets		=	Liabilities		+	Owner's Equity		+	Revenue		−	Expenses	
+	−		−	+		−	+		−	+		+	−
Debit	Credit		Debit	Credit		Debit	Credit		Debit	Credit		Debit	Credit

Cash		L. A. Cruz, Capital	
+	−	−	+
70,000			70,000

You perform this process mentally. If the transaction is more complicated, draw the T accounts on scratch paper. Using T accounts is the accountant's way of drawing a picture of the transaction. You must get into the T account habit; it will be a great help to you in the future.

Always record the debit part of the entry first. Enter the account title—in this case, Cash—in the Description column. Record the amount—$70,000—in the Debit amount column.

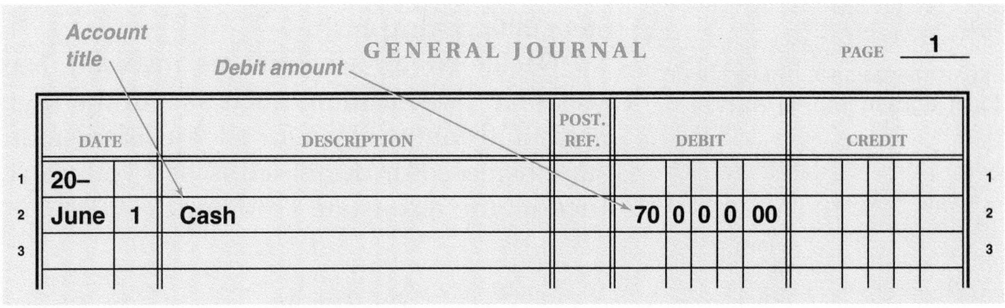
Account title
Debit amount
GENERAL JOURNAL
PAGE 1
DATE
DESCRIPTION
POST. REF.
DEBIT
CREDIT
20–
June 1
Cash
70 0 0 0 00

FYI

Customarily, accountants don't abbreviate account titles.

Next, record the credit part of the entry. Enter the account title—in this case, L. A. Cruz, Capital—on the line below the debit in the Description column, indented about one-half inch. On the same line, write the amount in the Credit column.

GENERAL JOURNAL PAGE 1

Date		Description	Post. Ref.	Debit	Credit
20–					
June	1	Cash		70 0 0 0 00	
		L. A. Cruz, Capital			70 0 0 0 00

Indent the account title that is credited

FYI

The explanation refers to the source document.

You should now write a brief explanation, in which you should refer to business papers, giving such information as check numbers, receipt numbers, or invoice numbers. You may also list names of charge customers or creditors, or terms of payment. Enter the explanation below the credit entry, indented an additional one-half inch.

GENERAL JOURNAL PAGE 1

Date		Description	Post. Ref.	Debit	Credit
20–					
June	1	Cash		70 0 0 0 00	
		L. A. Cruz, Capital			70 0 0 0 00
		Original investment by			
		Cruz in Cruz Auto Detail.			

Indent again for the explanation

Remember!

In the transaction, L. A. Cruz deposited $70,000 in a bank account in the name of Cruz Auto Detail.

For an entry in the general journal to be complete, it must contain (1) the date, (2) a debit entry, (3) a credit entry, and (4) an explanation. To anyone thoroughly familiar with the accounts, the explanation may seem quite obvious. Nevertheless, record the explanation as a required, integral part of the entry. To make the journal entries easier to read, leave one blank line between each transaction in your homework.

Remember!

Like a trial balance, there are no dollar signs in journal entries.

Transaction (b) June 2: Cruz Auto Detail bought equipment costing $43,000, paying cash.

Decide which accounts are involved. Next, determine which of the five possible classifications each part of the transaction applies to. Visualize the plus and minus signs for each classification. Decide whether the accounts are increased or decreased. When you use T accounts to analyze the transaction, the results are as follows:

Equipment	
+	–
Debit	Credit
43,000	

Cash	
+	–
Debit	Credit
	43,000

Now journalize this analysis below the first transaction. Record the day of the month in the Date column. Remember, you do not have to record the month and year again until the month or year changes or you use a new journal page.

GENERAL JOURNAL PAGE 1

	DATE		DESCRIPTION	POST. REF.	DEBIT	CREDIT	
1	20–						1
2	June	1	Cash		70 000 00		2
3			L. A. Cruz, Capital			70 000 00	3
4			Original investment by				4
5			Cruz in Cruz Auto Detail.				5
6							6
7		2	Equipment		43 000 00		7
8			Cash			43 000 00	8
9			Bought equipment for cash.				9

Skip a line between entries in homework

Transaction (c) On June 3, Cruz Auto Detail bought equipment costing $7,000 on credit (on account) from Williams Auto Supply. Again start with the T accounts.

Equipment	
+	−
Debit	Credit
7,000	

Accounts Payable	
−	+
Debit	Credit
	7,000

Remember!

In trying to figure out how a transaction should be recorded, first decide on the accounts involved. Then classify the accounts as A, L, OE, R, or E. Next, ask yourself whether the accounts are increased or decreased, and think of the related accounts with their plus and minus sides. Now the debits and credits of the transaction will fall into place.

After skipping a line in the journal, record the day of the month and then the entry. In journalizing a transaction involving Accounts Payable, always state the name of the creditor in the explanation. Similarly, in journalizing a transaction involving Accounts Receivable, always state the name of the customer who charged the amount in the explanation.

GENERAL JOURNAL PAGE 1

	DATE		DESCRIPTION	POST. REF.	DEBIT	CREDIT	
10							10
11		3	Equipment		7 000 00		11
12			Accounts Payable			7 000 00	12
13			Bought equipment on				13
14			account from Williams Auto				14
15			Supply.				15

When a business buys an asset, the asset should be recorded at the actual cost (the agreed amount of a transaction). This is called the **cost principle**. For example, suppose that the $7,000 that Cruz Auto Detail paid for the equipment from Williams Auto Supply was a bargain price, as Williams Auto Supply had been asking $8,500 for the equipment. The day after Cruz Auto Detail took possession of the equipment, it received an offer of $8,100 from another party, but the offer was declined. Cruz Auto Detail *should record the cost of the equipment as the actual amount paid in the transaction that occurred,* which is $7,000. This is true even though the fair market value may indeed be $8,100.

Transaction (d) On June 4, Cruz Auto Detail pays $2,000 to be applied against the firm's liability of $7,000. Picture the T accounts like this:

Cash	
+	–
Debit	Credit
	2,000

Accounts Payable	
–	+
Debit	Credit
2,000	

In this case, we see that cash is going out, so we record it on the minus side. We now have a credit to Cash and have completed half of the entry. Next, we recognize that Accounts Payable is involved. We ask ourselves, "Do we owe more or less as a result of this transaction?" The answer is "less," so we record it on the minus, or debit, side of the account.

Remember!

Get in the T account habit. Picture the T accounts in your mind, or draw T accounts on paper with their plus and minus signs. The T account habit is a must.

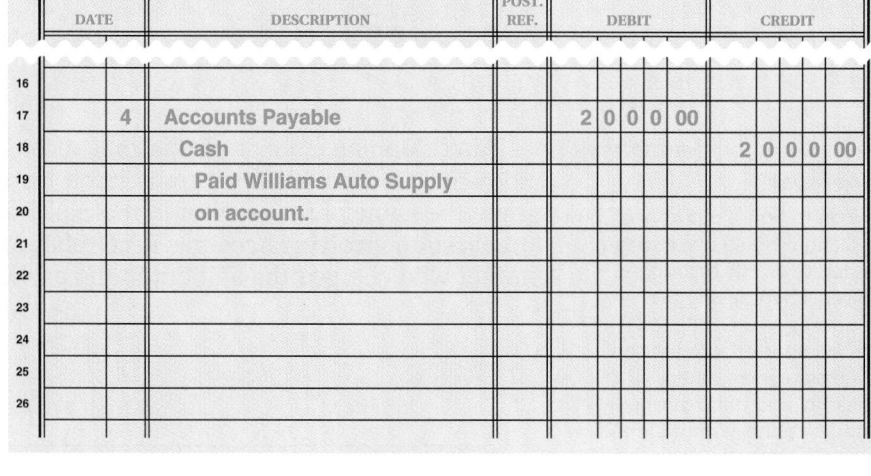

GENERAL JOURNAL PAGE 1

	DATE		DESCRIPTION	POST. REF.	DEBIT	CREDIT	
16							16
17		4	Accounts Payable		2,000.00		17
18			Cash			2,000.00	18
19			Paid Williams Auto Supply				19
20			on account.				20
21							21
22							22
23							23
24							24
25							25
26							26

Now let's list the transactions for June for Cruz Auto Detail with the date of each transaction. The journal entries are illustrated in Figures 1, 2, and 3.

Heavy-duty ladders, spray painting machines, and a truck to carry it all in are part of the equipment used by these house painters.

FIGURE 1

GENERAL JOURNAL PAGE 1

DATE		DESCRIPTION	POST. REF.	DEBIT	CREDIT
20–					
June	1	Cash		70,000.00	
		L. A. Cruz, Capital			70,000.00
		Original investment by			
		Cruz in Cruz Auto Detail.			
	2	Equipment		43,000.00	
		Cash			43,000.00
		Bought equipment for cash.			
	3	Equipment		7,000.00	
		Accounts Payable			7,000.00
		Bought equipment on			
		account from Williams Auto			
		Supply.			
	4	Accounts Payable		2,000.00	
		Cash			2,000.00
		Paid Williams Auto Supply			
		on account.			
	4	Supplies		800.00	
		Accounts Payable			800.00
		Bought buffer pads,			
		cleaners, and waxes on			
		account from Rossi and			
		Company.			
	7	Cash		3,520.00	
		Income from Services			3,520.00
		Cash revenue.			
	8	Rent Expense		900.00	
		Cash			900.00
		For month ended June 30.			

June 1 Cruz invests $70,000 cash in her new business.

2 Buys equipment costing $43,000, paying cash.

3 Buys equipment costing $7,000 on credit from Williams Auto Supply.

4 Pays $2,000 to Williams Auto Supply, to be applied against the firm's liability of $7,000.

4 Buys buffer pads, cleaners, and waxes on account from Rossi and Company, $800.

7 Cash revenue received, $3,520.

8 Pays rent for the month, $900.

FIGURE 2

Remember!

You must enter the year and the month at the top of every page in the journal.

GENERAL JOURNAL PAGE 2

DATE		DESCRIPTION	POST. REF.	DEBIT	CREDIT
20–					
June	10	Prepaid Insurance		360 00	
		Cash			360 00
		Premium for one-year vehicle			
		insurance policy.			
	14	Advertising Expense		400 00	
		Accounts Payable			400 00
		Received bill for advertising			
		from Valley News.			
	15	Accounts Receivable		1050 00	
		Income from Services			1050 00
		Billed Costello Taxi for			
		services performed.			
	15	Accounts Payable		2000 00	
		Cash			2000 00
		Paid Williams Auto Supply			
		on account.			
	18	Utilities Expense		160 00	
		Cash			160 00
		Paid bill for utilities, Midwest			
		Power, Inc.			
	20	Accounts Payable		400 00	
		Cash			400 00
		Paid Valley News in full.			
	24	Wages Expense		1400 00	
		Cash			1400 00
		Paid wages of part-time			
		employee.			

Remember!

Six types of information must be entered in the general journal for each transaction: the date, the title of the account to be debited, the amount of the debit, the title of the account to be credited, the amount of the credit, and the explanation.

June 10 Pays for a one-year vehicle insurance policy, $360.

14 Receives bill for newspaper advertising from *Valley News,* $400.

15 Cruz Auto Detail signed a contract with Costello Taxi to perform detailing work and then bills Costello Taxi $1,050 for services performed.

15 Pays $2,000 to Williams Auto Supply as part payment on account.

18 Receives and pays bill for utilities from Midwest Power, Inc., $160.

20 Pays *Valley News* for advertising, $400 in full. (This bill has been previously recorded.)

24 Pays wages of part-time employee, $1,400.

FIGURE 3

GENERAL JOURNAL — PAGE 3

DATE		DESCRIPTION	POST. REF.	DEBIT	CREDIT
20–					
June	26	Equipment		1,500.00	
		Cash			600.00
		Accounts Payable			900.00
		Bought equipment on			
		account from Williams Auto			
		Supply.			
	30	Cash		850.00	
		Accounts Receivable			850.00
		Received from Costello Taxi			
		to apply on account.			
	30	Cash		2,700.00	
		Income from Services			2,700.00
		Cash revenue.			
	30	L. A. Cruz, Drawing		3,000.00	
		Cash			3,000.00
		Withdrawal for personal use.			

Remember!

Every business transaction requires at least one debit and at least one credit. In a general journal, the debit part of the entry is recorded first. The credit part of the entry is recorded next, followed by a brief explanation of the transaction.

June 26 Buys additional equipment costing $1,500 from Williams Auto Supply, paying $600 down with the remaining $900 on account.

30 Receives $850 from Costello Taxi to apply on amount previously billed.

30 Cash revenue received, $2,700.

30 Cruz withdraws cash for personal use, $3,000.

POSTING TO THE GENERAL LEDGER

You can see that the journal is the *book of original entry.* Each transaction must first be recorded in the journal in full. However, it is difficult to determine the balance of any one account, such as Cash, from the general journal entries. So the **ledger account** has been devised to give us a complete record of the transactions recorded in each individual account. **The general ledger contains all the accounts.** It may be a loose-leaf binder so that you can add or remove pages. The process of transferring information from the journal to the ledger accounts is called **posting**.

FYI

While charts of accounts vary from business to business, the beginning numbers for assets, liabilities, owner's equity, revenues, and expenses are standard for a service business. Some account numbers are much longer than three digits.

The Chart of Accounts

The accounts in the ledger are arranged according to the chart of accounts, which is the official list of the ledger accounts in which transactions of a business are recorded. Assets are listed first, liabilities second, owner's equity

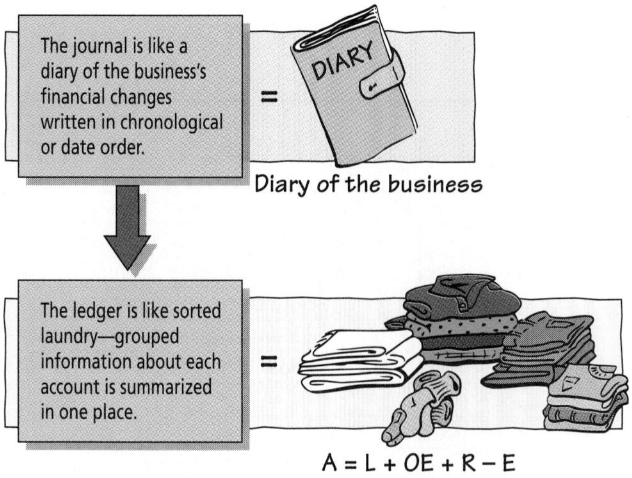
The journal is like a diary of the business's financial changes written in chronological or date order.
=
DIARY
Diary of the business
The ledger is like sorted laundry—grouped information about each account is summarized in one place.
=
A = L + OE + R − E

third, revenue fourth, and expenses fifth. The chart of accounts for Cruz Auto Detail is as follows:

FYI

Notice the space in the account numbers between 117 and 124. Generally, the account numbers from 120 to 129 are reserved for assets that have a length of life of more than one year, such as equipment, buildings, and land. Such space lets you add accounts in any part of the chart of accounts.

FYI

For merchandising businesses selling goods (vs. services), Expenses will start with a 6 because accounts starting with a 5 are reserved for accounts related to the cost of the goods being sold.

Remember!

In recording transactions for a business in the journal, one must use the exact account titles as listed in the company's chart of accounts.

Chart of Accounts

Assets (100–199)

111 Cash
113 Accounts Receivable
115 Supplies
117 Prepaid Insurance
124 Equipment

Liabilities (200–299)

221 Accounts Payable

Owner's Equity (300–399)

311 L. A. Cruz, Capital
312 L. A. Cruz, Drawing

Revenue (400–499)

411 Income from Services

Expenses (500–599)

511 Wages Expense
512 Rent Expense
513 Advertising Expense
514 Utilities Expense

Notice that the arrangement of the chart of accounts consists of the balance sheet accounts followed by the income statement accounts. The numbers preceding the account titles are the **account numbers**. Accounts in the ledger are kept by numbers rather than by pages because it is hard to tell in advance how many pages to reserve for a particular account. When you use the number system, you can add sheets easily. The digits in the account numbers also indicate account *classifications.* For most companies, assets start with 1, liabilities with 2, owner's equity with 3, revenue with 4, and expenses with 5. The second and third digits indicate the positions of the individual accounts within their respective classifications.

The Ledger Account Form (Running Balance Format)

We have been looking at accounts in the simple T account form primarily because T accounts illustrate situations so well. The debit and credit sides are specifically labeled. The T account form is used to solve problems because it is such a good way to picture account activity. However, determining the balance of an account using the T account form is difficult. You must add both columns and subtract the smaller total from the larger. To overcome this disadvantage, accountants generally use the four-column account form with Balance columns in the general ledger. Let's look at the Cash account of Cruz Auto Detail in four-column form (Figure 4) compared with the T account form. *Leave the Post. Ref. column blank for now.*

FIGURE 4

Cash

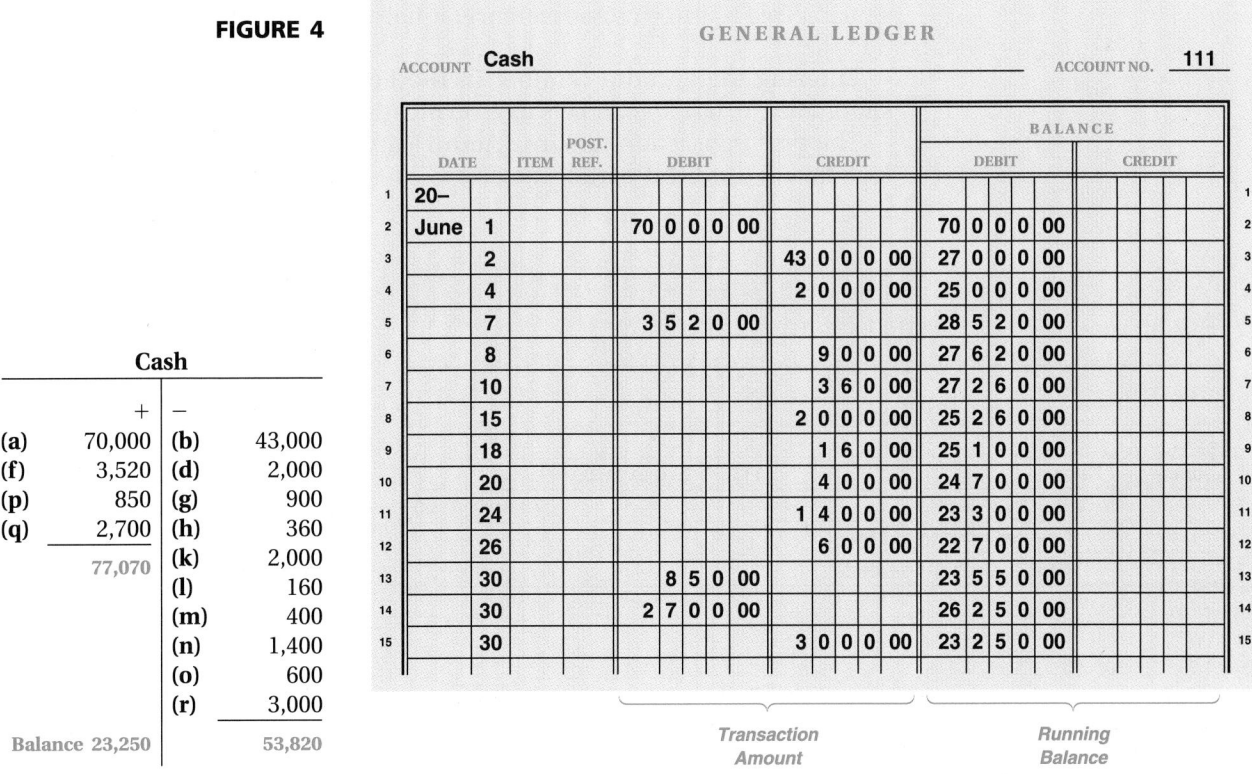

	+		−
(a)	70,000	(b)	43,000
(f)	3,520	(d)	2,000
(p)	850	(g)	900
(q)	2,700	(h)	360
	77,070	(k)	2,000
		(l)	160
		(m)	400
		(n)	1,400
		(o)	600
		(r)	3,000
Balance	23,250		53,820

GENERAL LEDGER

ACCOUNT **Cash** ACCOUNT NO. **111**

DATE		ITEM	POST. REF.	DEBIT	CREDIT	BALANCE DEBIT	BALANCE CREDIT
20–							
June	1			70,000 00		70,000 00	
	2				43,000 00	27,000 00	
	4				2,000 00	25,000 00	
	7			3,520 00		28,520 00	
	8				900 00	27,620 00	
	10				360 00	27,260 00	
	15				2,000 00	25,260 00	
	18				160 00	25,100 00	
	20				400 00	24,700 00	
	24				1,400 00	23,300 00	
	26				600 00	22,700 00	
	30			850 00		23,550 00	
	30			2,700 00		26,250 00	
	30				3,000 00	23,250 00	

Transaction Amount (Debit and Credit columns) *Running Balance* (Balance columns)

Note the calculation of the running balance. In the abbreviated form, it looks like this:

ACCOUNT **Cash** ACCOUNT NO. **111**

DATE		ITEM	POST. REF.	DEBIT	CREDIT	BALANCE DEBIT	BALANCE CREDIT
20–							
June	1			70,000 00		70,000 00	
	2				43,000 00	27,000 00	
	4				2,000 00	25,000 00	

70,000
−43,000
27,000
− 2,000
25,000

The Posting Process

Objective 2

Post entries from a two-column general journal to general ledger accounts.

In the posting process, you must transfer the following information from the journal to the ledger accounts: the *date of the transaction,* the *debit and credit amounts,* and the *page number* of the journal. Post each account separately, using the following steps. Post the debit part of the entry first. After locating the account in the ledger, you need to do the following steps.

1. Write the date of the transaction in the account's Date column.
2. Write the amount of the transaction in the Debit or Credit column and enter the new balance in the Balance columns under Debit or Credit.
3. Write the page number of the journal in the Post. Ref. column of the ledger account. (This is a **cross-reference**; it tells where the amount came from.)
4. Record the ledger account number in the Post. Ref. column of the journal. (This is also a cross-reference; it tells where the amount was posted.)

Entering the account number in the Post. Ref. column of the journal should be the last step. It acts as a verification of the three preceding steps.

The first transaction for Cruz Auto Detail is illustrated in Figure 5. Let's look first at the debit part of the entry.

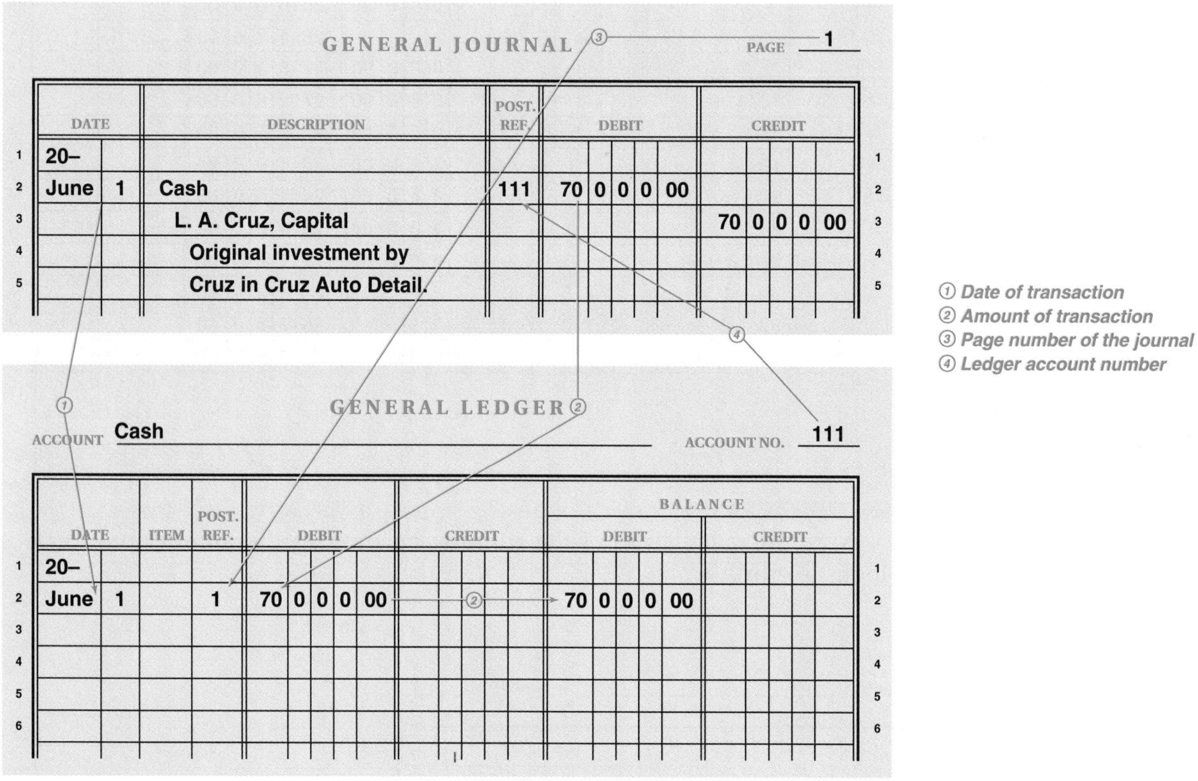
GENERAL JOURNAL
PAGE 1
DATE
DESCRIPTION
POST. REF.
DEBIT
CREDIT
20–
June 1
Cash
111
70 0 0 0 00
L. A. Cruz, Capital
70 0 0 0 00
Original investment by
Cruz in Cruz Auto Detail.
GENERAL LEDGER
ACCOUNT Cash
ACCOUNT NO. 111
DATE
ITEM
POST. REF.
DEBIT
CREDIT
BALANCE
DEBIT
CREDIT
20–
June 1
1
70 0 0 0 00
70 0 0 0 00
① Date of transaction
② Amount of transaction
③ Page number of the journal
④ Ledger account number

FIGURE 5

Next we post the credit part of the entry, as shown in Figure 6.

The accountant usually uses the Item column only at the end of a financial period. The words that may appear in this column are *balance, closing, adjusting,* and *reversing.* We will explain the use of these terms later.

Incidentally, some accountants use running balance–type ledger account forms that have only one balance column. However, we have used the two-balance-column arrangement to show clearly the appropriate balance of an account. For example, in Figure 5, Cash has a $70,000 balance recorded in the Debit column (normal balance). In Figure 6, L. A. Cruz, Capital, has a $70,000 balance recorded in the Credit column (normal balance).

In the recording of the second transaction, shown in Figure 7, see if you can identify in order the four steps in the posting process.

GENERAL JOURNAL — PAGE 1

DATE		DESCRIPTION	POST. REF.	DEBIT	CREDIT
20–					
June	1	Cash	111	70 0 0 0 00	
		L. A. Cruz, Capital	311		70 0 0 0 00
		Original investment by			
		Cruz in Cruz Auto Detail.			

GENERAL LEDGER

ACCOUNT L. A. Cruz, Capital — ACCOUNT NO. 311

DATE		ITEM	POST. REF.	DEBIT	CREDIT	BALANCE DEBIT	BALANCE CREDIT
20–							
June	1		1		70 0 0 0 00		70 0 0 0 00

① Date of transaction
② Amount of transaction
③ Page number of the journal
④ Ledger account number

FIGURE 6

FIGURE 7

GENERAL JOURNAL — PAGE 1

DATE		DESCRIPTION	POST. REF.	DEBIT	CREDIT
	2	Equipment	124	43 0 0 0 00	
		Cash	111		43 0 0 0 00
		Bought equipment for cash.			

GENERAL LEDGER

ACCOUNT Cash — ACCOUNT NO. 111

DATE		ITEM	POST. REF.	DEBIT	CREDIT	BALANCE DEBIT	BALANCE CREDIT
20–							
June	1		1	70 0 0 0 00		70 0 0 0 00	
	2		1		43 0 0 0 00	27 0 0 0 00	

ACCOUNT Equipment — ACCOUNT NO. 124

DATE		ITEM	POST. REF.	DEBIT	CREDIT	BALANCE DEBIT	BALANCE CREDIT
20–							
June	2		1	43 0 0 0 00		43 0 0 0 00	

Remember!

Do not record account numbers in the Post. Ref. column of the journal until the amounts have been posted to the ledger accounts as either debits or credits.

Remember!

Posting is simply transferring or copying exactly the same date and the debits and credits listed in the journal entry from the journal to the ledger.

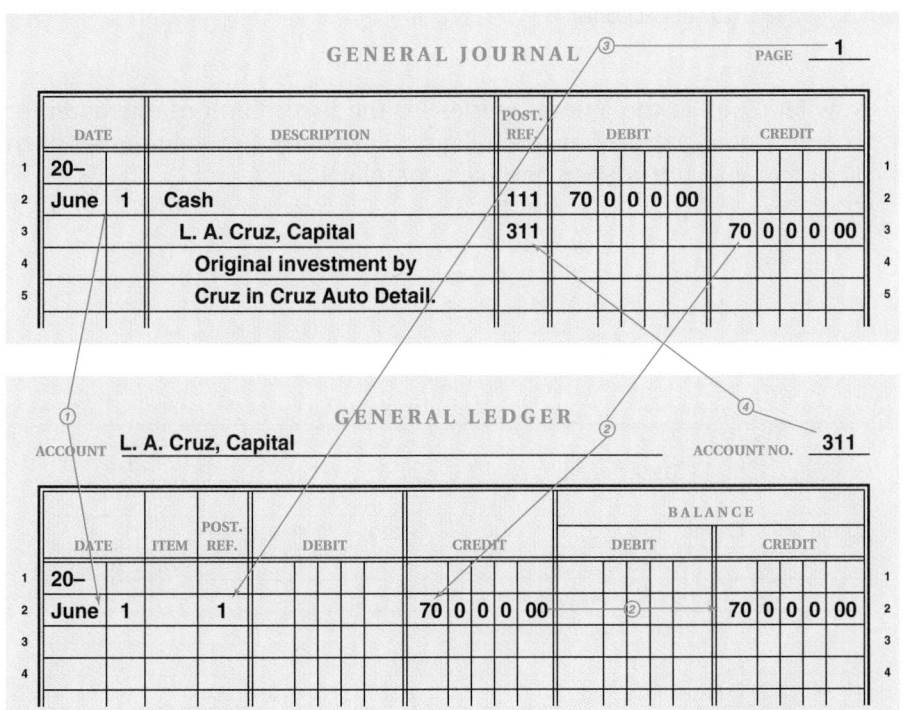

Now let's look at the journal entries for the first month of operation for Cruz Auto Detail. As you can see in Figure 8, the Post. Ref. column has been filled in, because the posting has been completed.

FIGURE 8

GENERAL JOURNAL PAGE 1

DATE		DESCRIPTION	POST. REF.	DEBIT	CREDIT
20–					
June	1	Cash	111	70,000.00	
		L. A. Cruz, Capital	311		70,000.00
		Original investment by			
		Cruz in Cruz Auto Detail.			
	2	Equipment	124	43,000.00	
		Cash	111		43,000.00
		Bought equipment for cash.			
	3	Equipment	124	7,000.00	
		Accounts Payable	221		7,000.00
		Bought equipment on			
		account from Williams Auto			
		Supply.			
	4	Accounts Payable	221	2,000.00	
		Cash	111		2,000.00
		Paid Williams Auto Supply			
		on account.			
	4	Supplies	115	800.00	
		Accounts Payable	221		800.00
		Bought buffer pads,			
		cleaners, and waxes on			
		account from Rossi and			
		Company.			
	7	Cash	111	3,520.00	
		Income from Services	411		3,520.00
		Cash revenue.			
	8	Rent Expense	512	900.00	
		Cash	111		900.00
		For month ended June 30.			

FIGURE 8 (continued)

GENERAL JOURNAL PAGE 2

DATE		DESCRIPTION	POST. REF.	DEBIT	CREDIT
20–					
June	10	Prepaid Insurance	117	360 00	
		Cash	111		360 00
		Premium for one-year vehicle			
		insurance policy.			
	14	Advertising Expense	513	400 00	
		Accounts Payable	221		400 00
		Received bill for advertising			
		from Valley News.			
	15	Accounts Receivable	113	1050 00	
		Income from Services	411		1050 00
		Billed Costello Taxi for			
		services performed.			
	15	Accounts Payable	221	2000 00	
		Cash	111		2000 00
		Paid Williams Auto Supply			
		on account.			
	18	Utilities Expense	514	160 00	
		Cash	111		160 00
		Paid bill for utilities, Midwest			
		Power, Inc.			
	20	Accounts Payable	221	400 00	
		Cash	111		400 00
		Paid Valley News in full.			
	24	Wages Expense	511	1400 00	
		Cash	111		1400 00
		Paid wages of part-time			
		employee.			

GENERAL JOURNAL PAGE 3

DATE		DESCRIPTION	POST. REF.	DEBIT	CREDIT
20–					
June	26	Equipment	124	1500 00	
		Cash	111		600 00
		Accounts Payable	221		900 00
		Bought equipment on			
		account from Williams Auto			
		Supply.			

FIGURE 8 (continued)

	30	Cash	111	850.00	
		Accounts Receivable	113		850.00
		Received from Costello Taxi			
		to apply on account.			
	30	Cash	111	2,700.00	
		Income from Services	411		2,700.00
		Cash revenue.			
	30	L. A. Cruz, Drawing	312	3,000.00	
		Cash	111		3,000.00
		For personal use.			

FYI

Computerized accounting programs also require journal explanations and will generate posting references.

In making journal entries, you will sometimes find that there are not enough lines at the bottom of a page to record the entire entry. In this case, do not split up the entry; instead, record the entire entry on the next journal page. The ledger entries for Cruz Auto Detail are shown in Figure 9.

FIGURE 9

GENERAL LEDGER

ACCOUNT Cash ACCOUNT NO. 111

DATE		ITEM	POST. REF.	DEBIT	CREDIT	BALANCE DEBIT	BALANCE CREDIT
20–							
June	1		1	70,000.00		70,000.00	
	2		1		43,000.00	27,000.00	
	4		1		2,000.00	25,000.00	
	7		1	3,520.00		28,520.00	
	8		1		900.00	27,620.00	
	10		2		360.00	27,260.00	
	15		2		2,000.00	25,260.00	
	18		2		160.00	25,100.00	
	20		2		400.00	24,700.00	
	24		2		1,400.00	23,300.00	
	26		3		600.00	22,700.00	
	30		3	850.00		23,550.00	
	30		3	2,700.00		26,250.00	
	30		3		3,000.00	23,250.00	

ACCOUNT Accounts Receivable ACCOUNT NO. 113

DATE		ITEM	POST. REF.	DEBIT	CREDIT	BALANCE DEBIT	BALANCE CREDIT
20–							
June	15		2	1,050.00		1,050.00	
	30		3		850.00	200.00	

FIGURE 9 (continued)

ACCOUNT **Supplies** ACCOUNT NO. 115

DATE		ITEM	POST. REF.	DEBIT	CREDIT	BALANCE DEBIT	BALANCE CREDIT
20–							
June	4		1	800 00		800 00	

ACCOUNT **Prepaid Insurance** ACCOUNT NO. 117

DATE		ITEM	POST. REF.	DEBIT	CREDIT	BALANCE DEBIT	BALANCE CREDIT
20–							
June	10		2	360 00		360 00	

ACCOUNT **Equipment** ACCOUNT NO. 124

DATE		ITEM	POST. REF.	DEBIT	CREDIT	BALANCE DEBIT	BALANCE CREDIT
20–							
June	2		1	43000 00		43000 00	
	3		1	7000 00		50000 00	
	26		3	1500 00		51500 00	

ACCOUNT **Accounts Payable** ACCOUNT NO. 221

DATE		ITEM	POST. REF.	DEBIT	CREDIT	BALANCE DEBIT	BALANCE CREDIT
20–							
June	3		1		7000 00		7000 00
	4		1	2000 00			5000 00
	4		1		800 00		5800 00
	14		2		400 00		6200 00
	15		2	2000 00			4200 00
	20		2	400 00			3800 00
	26		3		900 00		4700 00

ACCOUNT **L.A. Cruz, Capital** ACCOUNT NO. 311

DATE		ITEM	POST. REF.	DEBIT	CREDIT	BALANCE DEBIT	BALANCE CREDIT
20–							
June	1		1		70000 00		70000 00

FIGURE 9 (continued)

ACCOUNT **L.A. Cruz, Drawing** ACCOUNT NO. **312**

DATE		ITEM	POST. REF.	DEBIT	CREDIT	BALANCE DEBIT	BALANCE CREDIT
20–							
June	30		3	3,000.00		3,000.00	

ACCOUNT **Income from Services** ACCOUNT NO. **411**

DATE		ITEM	POST. REF.	DEBIT	CREDIT	BALANCE DEBIT	BALANCE CREDIT
20–							
June	7		1		3,520.00		3,520.00
	15		2		1,050.00		4,570.00
	30		3		2,700.00		7,270.00

ACCOUNT **Wages Expense** ACCOUNT NO. **511**

DATE		ITEM	POST. REF.	DEBIT	CREDIT	BALANCE DEBIT	BALANCE CREDIT
20–							
June	24		2	1,400.00		1,400.00	

ACCOUNT **Rent Expense** ACCOUNT NO. **512**

DATE		ITEM	POST. REF.	DEBIT	CREDIT	BALANCE DEBIT	BALANCE CREDIT
20–							
June	8		1	900.00		900.00	

ACCOUNT **Advertising Expense** ACCOUNT NO. **513**

DATE		ITEM	POST. REF.	DEBIT	CREDIT	BALANCE DEBIT	BALANCE CREDIT
20–							
June	14		2	400.00		400.00	

ACCOUNT **Utilities Expense** ACCOUNT NO. **514**

DATE		ITEM	POST. REF.	DEBIT	CREDIT	BALANCE DEBIT	BALANCE CREDIT
20–							
June	18		2	160.00		160.00	

Preparation of the Trial Balance

Objective 3

Prepare a trial balance from the ledger accounts.

The trial balance is simply a list of the ledger accounts that have balances. A trial balance is presented in Figure 10.

Remember that the trial balance proves only that the total ledger debit balances equal the total ledger credit balances. Even when the debit and credit balances are equal, other types of errors may slip through—for example,

1. Posting the correct debit or credit amounts to the incorrect account.
2. Neglecting to journalize or post an entire transaction.

FIGURE 10

Cruz Auto Detail
Trial Balance
June 30, 20—

ACCOUNT NAME	DEBIT	CREDIT
Cash	23,250.00	
Accounts Receivable	200.00	
Supplies	800.00	
Prepaid Insurance	360.00	
Equipment	51,500.00	
Accounts Payable		4,700.00
L. A. Cruz, Capital		70,000.00
L. A. Cruz, Drawing	3,000.00	
Income from Services		7,270.00
Wages Expense	1,400.00	
Rent Expense	900.00	
Advertising Expense	400.00	
Utilities Expense	160.00	
	81,970.00	81,970.00

If the temporary balance of an account happens to be zero, insert long dashes through both the Debit Balance and the Credit Balance columns. We'll use another business, the Bessett Company, in this example. Its Accounts Receivable ledger account appears below.

ACCOUNT **Accounts Receivable** ACCOUNT NO. **113**

DATE		ITEM	POST. REF.	DEBIT	CREDIT	BALANCE DEBIT	BALANCE CREDIT
20–							
Oct.	7		96	140.00		140.00	
	19		97	238.00		378.00	
	21		97		140.00	238.00	
	29		98		238.00	—	—
	31		98	162.00		162.00	

Steps in the Accounting Process

1. **Record the transactions of a business in a journal (book of original entry or the day-by-day record of the transactions of a firm).** An entry should be based on some source document or evidence that a transaction has occurred, such as an invoice, a receipt, or a check.
2. **Post entries to the accounts in the ledger.** Transfer the amounts from the journal to the Debit or Credit columns of the specified accounts in the ledger. Use a cross-reference system. Accounts are organized in the ledger according to the account numbers assigned to them in the chart of accounts.
3. **Prepare a trial balance.** Record the balances of the ledger accounts in the appropriate column, Debit or Credit, of the trial balance form. Prove that the total of the debit balances equals the total of the credit balances.

Source Document

A source document can be an invoice, a receipt, a check, etc. We now add an important detail in the recording of a journal entry. This detail consists of listing the related source document number, which is used as a reference for the proof of a transaction. Figure 11 is an example of a source document followed by the journal entry (Figure 12) and ledger accounts (Figure 13). Note how the explanation differs from the one we showed earlier.

FIGURE 11

Williams Auto Supply
220 East Ames Street
Detroit, Michigan 48222

No. 4-962

Sold By: 203 Date: 6/4/20—
Name: Cruz Auto Detail
Address: 1701 East Delaware Street
Detroit, Michigan 48228
Terms: Net 30 days

QUANTITY	DESCRIPTION	UNIT PRICE		AMOUNT	
36	Benton Car Wash, 64 oz	3	72	133	92
12	Benton Car Wax, 64 oz	12	21	146	52
12	Beetle Tire Dressing, 40 oz	5	16	61	92
12	Starr Leather Dressing, 8 oz	9	46	113	52
36	Buffer Pads, 9″	4	59	165	24
24	Beetle Upholstery Cleaner, 20 oz	3	76	90	24
24	Sponges	1	12	26	88
1	Bag Cloths	2	50	2	50
1	Buffer	59	26	59	26
	TOTAL			800	00

Record in the journal (Figure 12). Note how the explanation includes important information from the source document presented earlier.

GENERAL JOURNAL — PAGE 1

DATE		DESCRIPTION	POST. REF.	DEBIT	CREDIT
	4	Supplies	115	800 00	
		Accounts Payable	221		800 00
		Bought buffer pads,			
		cleaners, and waxes			
		from Williams Auto Supply,			
		Inv. No. 4-962.			

FIGURE 12

Post to the ledger (Figure 13).

ACCOUNT Supplies — ACCOUNT NO. 115

DATE		ITEM	POST. REF.	DEBIT	CREDIT	BALANCE DEBIT	BALANCE CREDIT
20–							
June	4		1	800 00		800 00	

ACCOUNT Accounts Payable — ACCOUNT NO. 221

DATE		ITEM	POST. REF.	DEBIT	CREDIT	BALANCE DEBIT	BALANCE CREDIT
20–							
June	3		1		7000 00		7000 00
	4		1	2000 00			5000 00
	4		1		800 00		5800 00

Previous postings (rows June 3 and June 4, $2,000 debit)

FIGURE 13

CORRECTION OF ERRORS

Errors are occasionally made in recording journal entries and posting to the ledger accounts. Never erase them, because it might look as if you were trying to hide something. The method for correcting errors depends on how and when the errors were made. There are two manual methods for correcting errors; they are

1. The ruling method.
2. The correcting entry method.

Ruling Method

Objective 4

Correct entries using the ruling method.

You can use the ruling method to correct an error in the journal before posting or to correct an error in the ledger after an entry has been posted.

Correcting Errors Before Posting Has Taken Place When an error has been made in recording an account title in a journal entry, draw a line through the incorrect account title in the journal entry, and write the correct account title immediately above. Include your initials with the correction. For example, an entry to record payment of $700 rent was incorrectly debited to Salary Expense.

DATE		DESCRIPTION	POST. REF.	DEBIT	CREDIT
20–		Rent Expense			
Mar.	1	~~Salary Expense~~ DJM		700 00	
		Cash			700 00
		Paid rent for the month.			

When an error has been made in recording an amount, draw a line through the incorrect amount in the journal entry, and write the correct amount immediately above. For example, an entry for a $230 payment for office supplies was recorded as $320. Include your initials with the correction.

DATE		DESCRIPTION	POST. REF.	DEBIT	CREDIT
20–				pb 230 00	
Apr.	6	Office Supplies		~~320 00~~	pb 230 00
		Cash			~~320 00~~
		Bought office stationery.			

Correcting Errors After Posting Has Taken Place When an entry was journalized correctly but one of the amounts was posted incorrectly, correct the error by drawing a single line through the amount and recording the correct

Whether you are preparing accounting records manually or on computer, accuracy is of primary importance. Rapid and accurate ten-key skills are a must for the accountant or bookkeeper.

amount above. For example, an entry to record cash received for professional fees was correctly journalized as $400. However, it was posted as a debit to Cash for $400 and a credit to Professional Fees for $4,000. In the Professional Fees account, draw a line through $4,000 and insert $400 above. Change the running balance of the account and initial the corrections.

FYI

Use a ruler to draw a line through an error.

ACCOUNT **Professional Fees** ACCOUNT NO. **411**

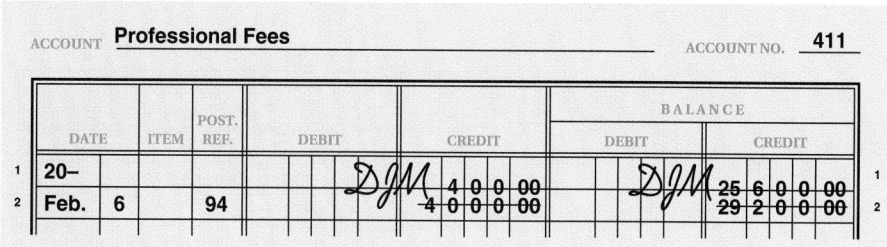

	DATE		ITEM	POST. REF.	DEBIT	CREDIT	BALANCE DEBIT	BALANCE CREDIT	
1	20–					DJM 400 00		DJM 25,600 00	1
2	Feb.	6		94		~~4,000 00~~		~~29,200 00~~	2

Correcting Entry Method

Objective 5

Correct entries using the correcting entry method.

You should use the correcting entry method when incorrectly journalized amounts have been posted. There are two correcting entry methods; they are

1. One-step method. Simply make one entry that undoes the error and provides the correct account.
2. Two-step method. The first step reverses the error made by the original entry. The second step includes the correct entry.

The correcting entry should *always* include an explanation. For example, on January 9, a $620 payment for advertising was incorrectly journalized and posted as a debit to Miscellaneous Expense for $620 and a credit to Cash for $620.

FYI

How you correct an error on a computer depends on whether the entry has been posted or not. Before posting, most software programs allow you to replace the incorrect account number or amount. If the entry has been posted, you may have to make a correcting entry to reverse the error, and then record the correct entry.

	DATE		DESCRIPTION	POST. REF.	DEBIT	CREDIT	
1	20–						1
2	Jan.	27	Advertising Expense		620 00		2
3			Miscellaneous Expense			620 00	3
4			To correct error of January 9				4
5			in which a payment for				5
6			Advertising Expense was				6
7			debited to Miscellaneous				7
8			Expense.				8

For example, if the original entry was recorded as a debit to Miscellaneous Expense and a credit to Cash, then reverse this entry by debiting Cash and crediting Miscellaneous Expense.

DATE		DESCRIPTION	POST. REF.	DEBIT	CREDIT
20–					
Jan.	27	Cash		620 00	
		Miscellaneous Expense			620 00
		To reverse out an incorrect			
		entry recorded January 9.			

DATE		DESCRIPTION	POST. REF.	DEBIT	CREDIT
20–					
Jan.	27	Advertising Expense		620 00	
		Cash			620 00
		To correct error of January 9			
		in which a payment for			
		Advertising Expense was			
		debited to Miscellaneous			
		Expense.			

After the correcting entry has been journalized, the accounts are posted as for any other entry. After posting, the account balances should be correct.

CHAPTER REVIEW

Review of Performance Objectives

1. Record a group of transactions pertaining to a service enterprise in a two-column general journal.

   Based on source documents, the transactions are analyzed to determine the accounts involved and whether the accounts are debited or credited. For each transaction, total debits must equal total credits. The journal is a book of original entry in which a day-by-day record of business transactions is maintained. The parts of a journal entry consist of the transaction date, the title of the account(s) debited, the title of the account(s) credited, the amounts recorded in the Debit and Credit columns, and an explanation.

2. Post entries from a two-column general journal to general ledger accounts.

   The ledger is a book that contains all the accounts, arranged according to the chart of accounts. Posting is the process of transferring information from the journal to the ledger accounts. The posting process consists of four steps:

   1. Write the date of the transaction in the account's Date column.
   2. Write the amount of the transaction in the Debit or Credit column, and enter the new balance in the Balance columns under Debit or Credit.
   3. Write the page number of the journal in the Post. Ref. column of the ledger account.
   4. Record the ledger account number in the Post. Ref. column of the journal.

3. Prepare a trial balance from the ledger accounts.

   The trial balance consists of a listing of account balances in two columns, one labeled Debit and one labeled Credit. The balances come from the ledger accounts.

4. Correct entries using the ruling method.

   The ruling method can be used if an error is discovered before or after an entry has been posted. Draw a line through the incorrect account title or amount, and write the correct account title or amount immediately above. Include your initials with the correction.

5. Correct entries using the correcting entry method.

   This method is used if an error is discovered after an incorrectly journalized entry has been posted. If the error consists of the wrong account(s), an entry is made to cancel out or reverse the incorrect account(s) and insert the correct account(s). Initial the correction.

Glossary

Account numbers The numbers assigned to accounts according to the chart of accounts. (76)

Cost principle The principle that a purchased asset should be recorded at its actual cost. (72)

Cross-reference The ledger account number in the Post. Ref. column of the journal and the journal page number in the Post. Ref. column of the ledger account. (78)

General ledger A loose-leaf book containing the activity (by accounts) of a business. (75)

Journal The book in which a person makes the original record of a business transaction; commonly referred to as a *book of original entry.* (68)

Journalizing The process of recording a business transaction in a journal. (68)

Ledger account A complete record of the transactions recorded in an individual account. (75)

Posting The process of transferring figures from the journal to the ledger accounts. (75)

Source documents Business papers, such as checks, invoices, receipts, letters, and memos, that furnish proof that a transaction has taken place. (68)

Two-column general journal A general journal in which there are two amount columns, one used for debit amounts and one used for credit amounts. (68)

QUESTIONS, EXERCISES, AND PROBLEMS

Discussion Questions

1. Why is the journal called a book of original entry?
2. How does the ledger differ from the journal?
3. What is the purpose of having a ledger account for each account?
4. List by account classification the sequence of the accounts in the general ledger.
5. Arrange the following steps in the posting process in proper order:
   a. Write the ledger account number in the Post. Ref. column of the journal.
   b. Write the amount of the transaction.
   c. Write the date of the transaction.
   d. Write the page number of the journal in the Post. Ref. column of the ledger account.
6. What does cross-referencing in the posting process mean?
7. Why is a source document important to the journalizing process?
8. In a chart of accounts listed by account number, what is the first number for each of the following accounts:
   a. Professional Fees
   b. Utilities Expense
   c. J. R. Watson, Capital
   d. Accounts Receivable
   e. Accounts Payable

Exercises

P.O. 1

Label parts of a journal entry.

Exercise 3-1 In the two-column journal below, the capital letters represent where parts of a journal entry appear. Write the numbers 1 through 8 on a piece of paper. After each number, associate or match the capital letter where these items should appear with the number of the item.

GENERAL JOURNAL PAGE 1

DATE		DESCRIPTION	POST. REF.	DEBIT	CREDIT
G					
H	I	J	O	M	
		K	P		N
		L			

1. Year
2. Month
3. Explanation

4. Title of account debited
5. Ledger account number of account credited
6. Amount of debit
7. Day of the month
8. Title of account credited

P.O. 1
Journalize transactions.

Exercise 3-2 Architectural Consulting Service completed the following transactions. Journalize the transactions in general journal form, including brief explanations.

Oct.	7	Received cash on account from Walter Tauscher, a customer, Inv. No. 312, $890.
	15	Paid on account to Mason Brothers, a creditor, $265, Ck. No. 2242.
	20	M. L. Nguyen, the owner, withdrew cash for personal use, $1,230, Ck. No. 2243.
	23	Bought store supplies for $87 and office supplies for $36 on account from Wilber Office Supply, Inv. No. 1040.
	29	M. L. Nguyen, the owner, invested $4,500 cash and $5,500 of his personal equipment.

P.O. 1
Journalize transactions.

Exercise 3-3 Dupree Tutoring Service completed the following transactions. Journalize the transactions in general journal form, including brief explanations.

Mar.	1	Bought equipment for $9,000 from Educational Systems, paying $3,000 in cash and placing the balance on account, Ck. No. 3230.
	10	Paid the wages for the first week of March, $1,836, Ck. No. 3231.
	15	Sold services for cash to Central School District, $1,100, Sales Inv. 121.
	26	Sold services on account to Mason School, $1,240, Sales Inv. 122.
	31	Paid on account to Educational Systems, $500, Ck. No. 3232.

P.O. 2
Post to a ledger account.

Exercise 3-4 The following May journal entries all involved cash.

Increases to Cash—Debits		Decreases to Cash—Credits	
5/1	10,000	5/3	900
5/9	1,700	5/8	700
5/16	5,400	5/12	3,200
5/23	700	5/25	4,600
5/30	4,300		

Post the amounts to the ledger account for Cash, Account No. 111. Assume that all transactions appeared on page 6 of the general journal.

P.O. 2
Determine steps in the posting process.

Exercise 3-5 Arrange the following steps in the posting process in proper order:

a. The amount of the balance of the ledger account is recorded in the Debit Balance or Credit Balance column.
b. The amount of the transaction is recorded in the Debit or Credit column of the ledger account.

c. The ledger account number is recorded in the Post. Ref. column of the journal.
d. The date of the transaction is recorded in the Date column of the ledger account.
e. The page number of the journal is recorded in the Post. Ref. column of the ledger account.

P.O. 3

Prepare a corrected trial balance.

Exercise 3-6 The bookkeeper for Rains Company has prepared the following trial balance.

Rains Company
Trial Balance
June 30, 20—

ACCOUNT NAME	DEBIT	CREDIT
Cash		2,500.00
Accounts Receivable	8,300.00	
Supplies	600.00	
Prepaid Insurance	650.00	
Equipment	15,300.00	
Accounts Payable		2,700.00
D. Rains, Capital		12,500.00
D. Rains, Drawing	4,890.00	
Professional Fees		17,540.00
Rent Expense	500.00	
Miscellaneous Expense	1,800.00	
	32,040.00	35,240.00

The bookkeeper has asked for your help. In examining the company's journal and ledger, you discover the following errors. Use this information to construct a corrected trial balance.

a. The debits to the Cash account total $8,000, and the credits total $3,300.
b. A $500 payment to a creditor was entered in the journal correctly but was not posted to the Accounts Payable account.
c. The first two numbers in the balance of the Accounts Receivable account were transposed in copying the balance from the ledger to the trial balance.
d. The $1,500 amount withdrawn by the owner for personal use was debited to Miscellaneous Expense by mistake—it was correctly credited to Cash.

P.O. 4,5

Determine the effect of errors.

Exercise 3-7 Determine the effect of the following errors on a company's total revenue, total expenses, and net income. Indicate the effect by writing O for "Overstated (too much)"; U for "Understated (too little)"; or NA for "Not Affected."

Transactions	Total Revenue	Total Expenses	Net Income
Example: A check for $425 was written to pay on account. The accountant debited Rent Expense for $425 and credited Cash for $425.	NA	O	U
a. $320 was received on account from customers. The accountant debited Cash for $320 and credited Professional Fees for $320.	320 "O"	NA	320 "O"
b. The owner withdrew $1,000 for personal use. The accountant debited Wages Expense for $1,000 and credited Cash for $1,000.	NA	1,000 "O"	1,000 "U"
c. A check was written for $1,250 to pay the rent. The accountant debited Rent Expense for $1,520 and credited Cash for $1,520. 1520 1250 270	NA	270 "O"	270 "U"
d. $1,500 was received on account from customers. The accountant debited Cash for $1,500 and credited the Capital account for $1,500.	NA	NA	NA
e. A check was written for $125 to pay the phone bill received and recorded earlier in the month. The accountant debited Phone Expense for $125 and credited Cash for $125.	NA	125 "O"	125 "U"

P.O. 4,5

Journalize correcting entries.

Exercise 3-8 Journalize correcting entries for each of the following errors and include a brief explanation.

a. A cash purchase of office equipment for $510 was journalized as a cash purchase of store equipment for $510. (Use the ruling method; assume the entry has not been posted.)
b. An entry for a $250 payment for office supplies was journalized as $520. (Use the ruling method; assume the entry has not been posted.)
c. A $620 payment for repairs was journalized and posted as a debit to Equipment instead of a debit to Repair Expense. (Use the correcting entry method to journalize the correction.)
d. A $750 bill for vehicle insurance was received and immediately paid. It was journalized and posted as $570. (Use the correcting entry method to journalize the correction.)

CONSIDER AND COMMUNICATE

Your bookkeeper friend is telling you how sometimes she accidentally debits an incorrect expense account. Your friend says she doesn't have time to make the corrections; besides, the boss will never know the difference. How would you explain to her the impact of these errors?

WHAT IF . . .

Your employee hands you a balanced trial balance. What if you then find out that one transaction was left out completely, another was recorded twice, and a third entry was journalized as $25 instead of $250? Your employee argues that the trial balance is in balance, so it must be correct. How would you explain this situation to your employee?

CRITICAL THINKING

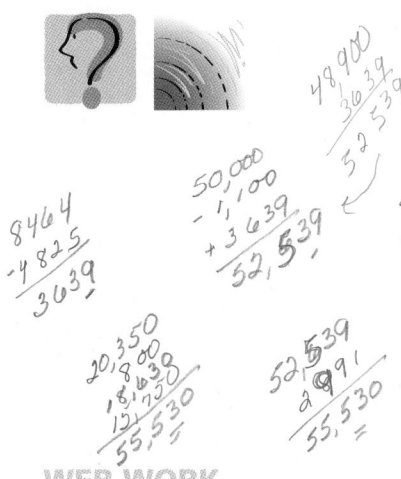

You work as an accounting clerk. You have received the following information supplied by a client from the client's bank, the client's tax returns, and a variety of other July documents. The client wants you to prepare an income statement, a statement of owner's equity, and a balance sheet for the month of July for Kristina L. Bialuski, Bialuski Company.

Income from Services	3,697	Rent Expense	1,500
Professional Fees	?	Wages Expense	2,850
Total Revenue	8,464	Utilities Expense	475
Beginning Capital	50,000	Drawing	1,100
Cash	20,350	Supplies	800
Truck	?	Equipment	18,630
Accounts Payable	?	Total Liabilities and Owner's Equity	55,530

WEB WORK

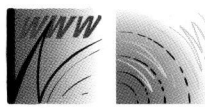

Using an Internet web browser, type in the search box the phrase *computerized accounting software* or *accounting software Peachtree.* Search for an article or find a home page that will provide you with information about computerized accounting. Narrow your search by adding accounting terms to the search box, for example, computerized accounting disadvantages or accounting practices manual. Discuss or write about your findings.

PROBLEM SET A

For additional help, see the demonstration problems at the beginning of each chapter in your Working Papers.

P.O. 1

Problem 3-1A The chart of accounts of the Brakke School is shown here, followed by the transactions that took place during October of this year:

Assets

111 Cash
113 Accounts Receivable
115 Prepaid Insurance
124 Equipment
127 Furniture

Liabilities

221 Accounts Payable

Owner's Equity

311 T. R. Brakke, Capital
312 T. R. Brakke, Drawing

Revenue

411 Tuition Income

Expenses

511 Salary Expense
512 Rent Expense
513 Gas and Oil Expense
514 Advertising Expense
515 Repair Expense
516 Telephone Expense
517 Utilities Expense
529 Miscellaneous Expense

Oct.	1	Bought liability insurance for one year, $1,540, Ck. No. 1527.
	3	Received a bill for advertising from the *Town Cryer,* $480.
	4	Paid the rent for the current month, $1,350, Ck. No. 1528.
	7	Received a bill for equipment repair from Fix-It Services, $186, Inv. No. 436.
	10	Received and deposited tuition from students, $4,603.
	11	Received and paid the telephone bill, $127, Ck. No. 1529.
	15	Bought desks and chairs from Bukola Furniture Company, $1,475, paying $775 in cash and placing the balance on account, Ck. No. 1530.
	18	Paid on account to the *Town Cryer,* a creditor, $480, Ck. No. 1531.
	21	T. R. Brakke withdrew $650 for personal use, Ck. No. 1532.
	24	Received a bill for gas and oil from Ott Oil Company, $358, Inv. 682.
	25	Received and deposited tuition from students $5,260.
	27	Paid the salary of the office assistant, $975, Ck. No. 1533.
	28	Bought a photocopier on account from Evergreen Office Machines, $1,300, Inv. No. 417.
	29	Received $600 tuition from a student who had charged the tuition on account last month.
	30	Received and paid the bill for utilities, $459, Ck. No. 1534.
	31	Paid for flower arrangements for front office, $48, Ck. No. 1535.
	31	T. R. Brakke invested his personal computer and printer, with a fair market value of $1,550, in the business.

Instructions

Record these transactions in the general journal, including a brief explanation for each entry. Number the journal pages 31, 32, and 33.

P.O. 2,3

Problem 3-2A The journal entries for August, Howell Car Care's second month of business, have been journalized in the general journal in your Working Papers. The balances of the accounts as of July 31 have been recorded in the general ledger in your working papers. Notice the word *Balance* in the Item column, the check mark in the Post. Ref. column, and that the amount is in the Balance column only.

Check Figure

Net Income, $10,503

Instructions

1. Write the owner's name, W. Howell, in the Capital and Drawing accounts.
2. Post the general journal entries to the general ledger accounts.
3. Prepare a trial balance as of August 31, 20—.
4. Prepare an income statement for the two months ended August 31, 20—.
5. Prepare a statement of owner's equity for the two months ended August 31, 20—.
6. Prepare a balance sheet as of August 31, 20—.

P.O. 1,2,3

Problem 3-3A Following is the chart of accounts of M. L. Haas, M.D.

Assets

111 Cash
113 Accounts Receivable
115 Supplies
117 Prepaid Insurance
124 Equipment

Liabilities

221 Accounts Payable

Owner's Equity

311 M. L. Haas, Capital
312 M. L. Haas, Drawing

Revenue

411 Professional Fees

Expenses

511 Salary Expense
512 Rent Expense
513 Laboratory Expense
514 Utilities Expense

Dr. Haas completed the following transactions during July:

July 1 Bought laboratory equipment on account from Stordeur Surgical Supply Company, $2,346, paying $1,500 in cash and placing the remainder on account, Ck. No. 1730.
3 Paid the office rent for the current month, $900, Ck. No. 1731.
5 Received cash on account from patients, $345.
6 Bought supplies on account from Turnbull Supply Company, $327, Inv. 3455.
7 Received and paid the bill for laboratory services, $874, Ck. No. 1732.
8 Bought insurance for one year, $1,135, Ck. No. 1733.
12 Performed medical services for patients on account, $2,368.
15 Performed medical services for patients for cash, $1,846.
16 Part of the equipment purchased on July 1 was found to be broken. Haas returned the damaged part and received a reduction in his bill, $168, Inv. 3162, Credit Memo No. 141.
18 Paid the salary of the part-time nurse, $985, Ck. No. 1734.
24 Received and paid the telephone bill for the month, $145, Ck. No. 1735.
28 Performed medical services for patients on account, $3,640.
29 Dr. Haas withdrew cash for his personal use, $1,800, Ck. No. 1736.

Check Figure
Trial balance total, $51,961

Instructions

1. Journalize the transactions for July in the general journal, beginning on page 21.
2. Write the name of the owner next to the Capital and Drawing accounts in the general ledger. The balances of the accounts as of June 30 have been recorded in the general ledger in your working papers. Notice the word *Balance* in the Item column, the check mark in the Post. Ref. column, and that the amount is in the Balance column only. This indicates a balance brought forward from a prior page or month.
3. Post the entries to the general ledger accounts.
4. Prepare a trial balance.

Instructions for General Ledger Software

1. Journalize the transactions in the general journal.
2. Post the entries to the general ledger.
3. Print a trial balance as of July 31.

P.O. 1,2,3

Problem 3-4A Vera's Landscaping Service has the following chart of accounts:

Assets

111 Cash
113 Accounts Receivable
115 Supplies
117 Prepaid Insurance
124 Equipment

Liabilities

221 Accounts Payable

Owner's Equity

311 V. Daily, Capital
312 V. Daily, Drawing

Revenue

411 Landscaping Income

Expenses

511 Salary Expense
512 Rent Expense
513 Gas and Oil Expense
514 Utilities Expense

The following transactions were completed by Vera's Landscaping Service:

Mar.	1	Daily deposited $20,000 in a bank account in the name of the business.
	4	Daily invested her personal gardening equipment, with a fair market value of $1,400, in the business.
	6	Bought a used trailer on account from Trailer Sales, $800, Inv. No. 314.
	7	Paid the rent for the current month, $485, Ck. No. 1000.
	9	Bought a used backhoe from Earth Equipment, $8,500, paying $4,000 in cash and placing the balance on account, Inv. No. 4166, Ck. No. 1001.
	10	Bought liability insurance for one year, $1,100, Ck. No. 1002.
	13	Sold landscaping services on account to Local Grocers, $1,225, Inv. 100.
	14	Bought supplies on account from Office Masters, $185, Inv. 5172.
	15	Sold landscaping services on account to C. Abrudan, $1,845, Inv. 101.
	17	Received and paid the bill from Grover Services for gas and oil for the equipment, $84, Ck. No. 1003.
	19	Sold landscaping services for cash to Chicz Company, $987, Inv. 102.
	22	Paid on account to Trailer Sales, a creditor, $600, Inv. 314, Ck. No. 1004.
	24	Received on account from Local Grocers, a customer, $500, Inv. 100.
	28	Sold landscaping services on account to Tsakuda Inc., $1,626, Inv. 103.
	29	Received and paid the telephone bill, $184, Ck. No. 1005.
	30	Paid the salary of the employee, $3,268, Ck. No. 1006.
	31	Daily withdrew cash for her personal use, $1,500, Ck. No. 1007.

Check Figure

Trial balance total, $31,968

Instructions

1. Journalize the transactions in the general journal, beginning on page 1. Write a brief explanation for each entry.
2. Write the name of the owner on the Capital and Drawing accounts.
3. Post the journal entries to the ledger accounts.
4. Prepare a trial balance dated March 31, 20—.

PROBLEM SET B

For additional help, see the demonstration problems at the beginning of each chapter in your Working Papers.

P.O. 1

Problem 3-1B The chart of accounts of the Bilson Language School is shown here, followed by the transactions that took place during December of this year:

Assets

111 Cash
113 Accounts Receivable
115 Prepaid Insurance
117 Supplies
124 Equipment
127 Furniture

Liabilities

221 Accounts Payable

Owner's Equity

311 T. L. Bilson, Capital
312 T. L. Bilson, Drawing

Revenue

411 Tuition Income

Expenses

511 Salary Expense
512 Rent Expense
513 Gas and Oil Expense
514 Advertising Expense
515 Repair Expense
516 Telephone Expense
517 Utilities Expense
529 Miscellaneous Expense

Dec. 1 Bought liability insurance for one year, $1,278, Ck. No. 1627.
11 Received a bill for advertising from the *City News,* $590, Statement No. 4267.
12 Paid the rent for the current month, $1,150, Ck. No. 1628.
13 Received a bill for equipment repair from Repair Services, $286, Inv. No. 547.
16 Received and deposited tuition from students, $3,970.
17 Received and paid the telephone bill, $216, Ck. No. 1629.
18 Bought desks and chairs from Siladke Furniture Company, $1,265, paying $600 in cash and placing the balance on account, Ck. No. 1630.
20 Paid on account to the *City News,* a creditor, $590, Statement No. 4233, Ck. No. 1631.
21 T. L. Bilson withdrew $750 for personal use, Ck. No. 1632.
26 Received a bill for gas and oil from DeMers Oil Company, $247, Inv. 591.
27 Received and deposited tuition from students, $4,370.
31 Paid the salary of the office assistant, $955, Ck. No. 1633.
31 Bought a fax machine on account from Central Office Machines, $899, Inv. 529.
31 Received $700 tuition from a student who had put the tuition on account last month.
31 Received and paid the bill for utilities, $348, Ck. No. 1634.
31 T. L. Bilson invested her personal computer and printer, with a fair market value of $1,425, in the business.
31 Bought supplies, $182, Ck. No. 1635.

Instructions

Record these transactions in the general journal, including a brief explanation for each entry. Number the journal pages 31, 32, and 33.

P.O. 2,3

Problem 3-2B The journal entries for May, Singh's Day Care's second month of business, have been journalized in the general journal in your working papers. The balances of the accounts as of April 30 have been recorded in the general ledger in your working papers. Notice the word *Balance* in the Item column, the check mark in the Post. Ref. column, and that the amount is in the Balance column only. This indicates a balance brought forward from a prior page or month.

Check Figure
Net Income, $5,538

Instructions

1. Write the owner's name, T. Singh, in the Capital and Drawing accounts.
2. Post the general journal entries to the general ledger accounts.
3. Prepare a trial balance as of May 31, 20—.
4. Prepare an income statement for the two months ended May 31, 20—.
5. Prepare a statement of owner's equity for the two months ended May 31, 20—.
6. Prepare a balance sheet as of May 31, 20—.

P.O. 1,2,3

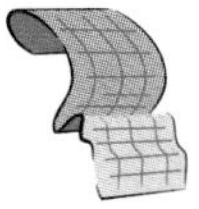

Problem 3-3B Following is the chart of accounts of D. L. Sargeant, M.D.

Assets
111 Cash
113 Accounts Receivable
115 Supplies
117 Prepaid Insurance
124 Equipment

Liabilities
221 Accounts Payable

Owner's Equity
311 D. L. Sargeant, Capital
312 D. L. Sargeant, Drawing

Revenue
411 Professional Fees

Expenses
511 Salary Expense
512 Rent Expense
513 Laboratory Expense
514 Utilities Expense

Dr. Sargeant completed the following transactions during July:

July 1 Bought laboratory equipment on account from Brady Surgical Supply Company, $3,235, paying $1,235 in cash and placing the remainder on account, Inv. No. 2071, Ck. No. 1930.

3 Paid the office rent for the current month, $950, Ck. No. 1931.

5 Received cash on account from patients, $2,456.

6 Bought supplies on account from Kuschak Supply Company, $304, Inv. 3455.

9 Received and paid the bill for laboratory services, $945, Ck. No. 1932.

10 Bought insurance for one year, $1,045, Ck. No. 1933.

12 Performed medical services for patients on account, $2,470.

14 Performed medical services for patients for cash, $2,738.

18 Part of the equipment purchased on July 1 was found to be broken. Sargeant returned the damaged part and received a reduction in her bill, $243, Inv. 2071, Credit Memo No. 218.

20 Paid the salary of the part-time nurse, $990, Ck. No. 1934.

22 Received and paid the telephone bill for the month, $185, Ck. No. 1935.

24 Performed medical services for patients on account, $3,820.

30 Dr. Sargeant withdrew cash for her personal use, $1,500, Ck. No. 1936.

Check Figure
Trial balance total, $37,893

Instructions

1. Journalize the transactions for July in the general journal, beginning on page 21.
2. Write the name of the owner next to the Capital and Drawing accounts in the general ledger. The balances of the accounts as of June 30 have been recorded in the general ledger in your working papers. Notice the word *Balance* in the Item column, the check mark in the Post. Ref. column, and that the amount is in the Balance column only. This indicates a balance brought forward from a prior page or month.
3. Post the entries to the general ledger accounts.
4. Prepare a trial balance.

Instructions for General Ledger Software

1. Journalize the transactions in the general journal.
2. Post the entries to the general ledger.
3. Print a trial balance as of July 31.

P.O. 1,2,3

Problem 3-4B Bill's Landscaping Service maintains the following chart of accounts.

Assets
111 Cash
113 Accounts Receivable
115 Supplies
117 Prepaid Insurance
124 Equipment

Liabilities
221 Accounts Payable

Owner's Equity
311 W. Drake, Capital
312 W. Drake, Drawing

Revenue
411 Landscaping Income

Expenses
511 Salary Expense
512 Rent Expense
513 Gas and Oil Expense
514 Utilities Expense

The following transactions were completed by Drake:

Apr.	1	Drake deposited $18,000 in a bank account in the name of the business.
	4	Drake invested his personal gardening equipment, with a fair market value of $1,500, in the business.
	6	Bought a used trailer on account from Roadside Sales, $900, Inv. No. 415.
	7	Paid the rent for the current month, $574, Ck. No. 100.
	9	Bought a used bulldozer from Trekoe Equipment, $9,500, paying $4,000 in cash and placing the balance on account, Inv. No. 3255, Ck. No. 101.
	10	Bought liability insurance for one year, $1,200, Ck. No. 102.
	13	Sold landscaping services on account to Morgan Homes, $2,116, Inv. 100.
	14	Bought supplies on account from Sanders Supply, $162, Inv. 4281.
	15	Sold landscaping services on account to Baskett Inc., $2,736, Inv. 101.
	17	Received and paid the bill from Le Services for gas and oil for the equipment, $84, Ck. No. 103.

Apr. 19 Sold landscaping services for cash to Marshall Company, $987, Inv. 102.
22 Paid on account to Roadside Sales, a creditor, $400, Inv. 415, Ck. No. 104.
24 Received on account from Morgan Homes, a customer, $500, Inv. 100.
28 Sold landscaping services on account to Hisayo Inc., $1,626, Inv. 103.
29 Received and paid the telephone bill, $145, Ck. No. 105.
30 Paid the salary of the employee, $2,268, Ck. No. 106.
30 Drake withdrew cash for his personal use, $1,400, Ck. No. 107.

Check Figure

Trial balance total, $33,127

Instructions

1. Journalize the transactions in the general journal that begins on page 1. Write a brief explanation for each entry.
2. Write the name of the owner on the Capital and Drawing accounts.
3. Post the journal entries to the general ledger accounts.
4. Prepare a trial balance dated April 30, 20—.

Continuous General Ledger Problem: Journalizing, Posting, and Trial Balance

J. Miracle, an expert art and furniture restorer, buys a studio where he has opened Like New, a sole proprietorship. His accountant has prepared the following chart of accounts. Some accounts may be unfamiliar to you at this time, but as you progress in your accounting education, these accounts will become necessary.

Chart of Accounts

Assets

111 Cash
113 Accounts Receivable
115 Supplies
117 Prepaid Insurance
142 Building
143 Accum. Dep., Building
144 Van
145 Accum. Dep., Van
146 Office Equipment
147 Accum. Dep., Office Equipment
148 Office Furniture
149 Accum. Dep., Office Furniture

Liabilities

211 Accounts Payable
212 Wages Payable
251 Mortgage Payable

Owner's Equity

312 J. Miracle, Capital
313 J. Miracle, Drawing
399 Income Summary

Revenue

411 Service Income

Expenses

511 Wages Expense
512 Utilities Expense
513 Advertising Expense
514 Repair Expense
519 Supplies Expense
520 Insurance Expense
521 Depr. Expense, Building
522 Depr. Expense, Van
523 Depr. Expense, Office Equip.
524 Depr. Expense, Office Furn.

Following are the transactions for May:

May 1 Miracle deposited $100,000 in a bank account in the name of the business, Dep. Slip No. 16262.

2 Miracle bought Like New for $125,400. The assets include a building, $90,000; van, $18,500; office equipment, $12,600; office furniture, $4,300. Paid $36,000 in cash (Ck. No. 1000) and placed the balance on a mortgage note. (Debit each asset separately and credit Cash and Mortgage Payable.)

4 Bought supplies on account from The Paint Pot, $2,290, Inv. 961.

5 Bought advertising on account from Adams Advertising, $841, Inv. 3162.

Note: The Continuous General Ledger Problem can be worked with Houghton Mifflin Windows General Ledger Package, Peachtree Release 5.01, QuickBooks 6.0, or other general ledger software packages.

May 7 Sold services on account to Adeline Harris, $1,256, Sales Inv. 2001.

9 Sold services for cash to customers, $4,167, Cash Receipt Nos. 1100–1106.

11 Bought insurance for the business from Drake Agency for one year, $1,153, Ck. No. 1001.

12 Bought office equipment on account from Office Ready, $698, Inv. 6136.

15 Paid wages of part-time assistant for the first half of the month, $850, Ck. No. 1002.

16 Received on account from J. Wilson, a customer, $540, Cash Receipt No. 1107.

17 Sold services for cash to customers, $5,173, Cash Receipt Nos. 1108–1116.

18 The owner withdrew cash for personal use, $1,100, Ck. No. 1003.

19 Received and paid the bill for repairs, $459, Ck. No. 1004.

21 Bought additional office furniture on account from Au Furniture, $723, Inv. 475.

22 Sold services on account to Jeff Isely, $1,536, Sales Inv. 2002.

23 Sold services on account to Mike Willen, $2,314, Sales Inv. 2003.

25 Received and paid for utility bill, $345, Ck. No. 1005.

27 Paid $300 on account to Office Ready, a creditor, $300, Ck. No. 1006, Inv. 6136.

31 Paid wages of part-time assistant for the second half of the month, $850, Ck. No. 1007.

Instructions

1. Open the general ledger software.
2. Create and save a new file as Likenew.
3. Print a copy of the chart of accounts for your convenience in planning journal entries.
4. Journalize the transactions in the general journal and post them to the general ledger.
5. Print the general journal.
6. Print the general ledger.
7. Print a trial balance.

Cumulative Self-Check: Chapters 1–3

PART I: MULTIPLE-CHOICE QUESTIONS

____ 1. Which of the following is not considered an account?

a. Cash
b. Prepaid Insurance
c. Equipment
d. Assets
e. Accounts Receivable

____ 2. In which of the following transactions would an expense be recorded?

a. Received a bill for utilities.
b. Paid on an account payable for the electric bill.
c. Received and paid a bill for repairs.
d. All of these should be recorded as an expense.
e. Only a and c should be recorded as an expense.

____ 3. The ending capital balance appears on which of the following statements?

a. Statement of owner's equity
b. Balance sheet
c. Income statement
d. Statement of owner's equity and balance sheet
e. Statement of owner's equity and income statement

____ 4. On a statement of owner's equity, if beginning capital is $41,000 and there are an additional investment of $6,000, a net loss of $8,000, and owner withdrawals of $15,000, the ending capital amount would be

a. $70,000.
b. $24,000.
c. $40,000.
d. $54,000.
e. none of these.

____ 5. If a $36 cash purchase of supplies is recorded as a $63 debit to Supplies and a $63 credit to Cash, the result will be that

a. the trial balance will be in balance.
b. the Supplies account will be overstated.
c. the Cash account will be understated.
d. Supplies will be overstated and Cash will be understated.
e. all of these will be true.

Note: Answers to the Cumulative Self-Check begin on page A-1.

____ 6. A person who wanted to know the balance of an account would look in

a. the ledger.
b. the chart of accounts.
c. the journal.
d. the source documents.
e. none of these.

PART II: PRACTICAL APPLICATION

Journalizing, Posting, Trial Balance, and Financial Statements

The accounts and their balances, as of December 1 of this year, for Stanfill Services are listed below:

111 Cash	$18,900	311 D. Stanfill, Capital	$49,590
112 Accounts Receivable	6,300	312 D. Stanfill, Drawing	11,200
113 Supplies	870	411 Service Income	39,600
114 Prepaid Insurance	1,230	511 Wages Expense	10,450
124 Equipment	31,200	512 Utilities Expense	2,760
221 Accounts Payable	6,340	513 Rent Expense	12,620

Check Figure
Net income, $13,158

Instructions

1. Journalize the following December transactions in general journal form on journal page 31.

Dec.	1	Stanfill deposited $10,000 in an account in the name of the business.
	4	Received and paid the bill for the rent for December, $900, Ck. No. 2331.
	11	Received $1,860 on account from customers, Cash Receipt Nos. 1430–1438.
	19	Sold services on account to M. Linares, $2,150, Sales Inv. No. 2591.
	22	Received and paid the bill for utilities, $197, Ck. No. 2332.
	23	Bought supplies on account from Staple Works, $248, Inv. No. 2606.
	31	Paid the wages for the month, $1,665, Ck. No. 2333.
	31	Stanfill withdrew $1,800 for personal use, Ck. No. 2334.

2. Label T accounts with the above account names.
3. Correctly place the plus and minus signs under all T accounts, and label the debit and credit sides of each T account.
4. Post the entries to the T accounts by date, and foot and balance the accounts.
5. Prepare a trial balance as of December 31.
6. Prepare an income statement for the year ended December 31.
7. Prepare a statement of owner's equity for the year ended December 31.
8. Prepare a balance sheet as of December 31.

4 Adjusting Entries and the Work Sheet

WINDOWS ON THE WORLD WIDE WEB

Do you Yahoo? With net revenues of $86,064,000 in the first quarter of 1999, Internet companies like Yahoo! attract a lot of investors. If you were writing adjusting entries for Yahoo!'s accounts, how would you handle the depreciation of the company's computer equipment? How would you make adjustments for accrued expenses of $43,572,000 for that same quarter? What would the income statement and balance sheet look like for Yahoo! in 1998? If you were thinking of investing in a service provider after reviewing Yahoo!'s annual report, would you want to put your money where your mouse is? Check out this URL to review Yahoo!'s annual report:
http://docs.yahoo.com/info/investor/ar98/yahoo98annualreport.pdf.
Or check out Yahoo!'s first quarter balance sheet for the period ending March 31, 1999: **http://docs.yahoo.com/docs/pr/1q99balance.html**.

Performance Objectives

After you have completed this chapter, you will be able to do the following:

1. Define a *fiscal period.*
2. List the classifications of the accounts that occupy each column of a ten-column work sheet.
3. Complete a work sheet for a service enterprise, involving adjustments for supplies used, expired insurance, depreciation, and accrued wages.
4. Prepare an income statement, a statement of owner's equity, and a balance sheet for a service business directly from the work sheet.
5. Journalize and post the adjusting entries.
6. Prepare an income statement and a balance sheet for a business with more than one revenue account and more than one accumulated depreciation account.

Remember!

Accounting steps:

Analyzing: Which accounts are involved?

Classifying: assets, liabilities, capital, revenue, and expenses

Recording: journalizing

Summarizing: financial statements

Interpreting: drawing conclusions

Relating to the *summarizing* step in the definition of accounting, here we introduce the work sheet and the financial statements. Now that you are familiar with the classifying and recording phases of accounting for a service business, let's look at the remaining steps in the accounting process.

FISCAL PERIOD

Objective 1

Define *fiscal period* and *fiscal year.*

A **fiscal period** is any period of time covering a complete accounting cycle. A **fiscal year** is a fiscal period consisting of twelve consecutive months. It does not have to coincide with the calendar year. If a business has seasonal peaks, it is a good idea to complete the accounting operations at the end of the most active season. At that time, management wants to know the results of the year and where the business stands financially. The fiscal year of a resort that operates during the summer may be from October 1 of one year to September 30 of the next. The government at some levels has a fiscal year from July 1 of one year to June 30 of the following year. Department stores often use a fiscal period from February 1 of one year to January 31 of the next. For income tax purposes, any period of twelve consecutive months may be selected. However, you have to be consistent and use the same fiscal period each year.

THE ACCOUNTING CYCLE

The **accounting cycle** represents the sequence of steps in the accounting process completed during the fiscal period. Figure 1 shows how we introduce these steps on a chapter-by-chapter basis. This outline brings you up to date on what we have accomplished so far and how each chapter fits into the steps in the accounting cycle.

FIGURE 1

Chapter 1	Analysis of Business Transactions Assets = Liabilities + Owner's Equity Analysis of Business Transactions Assets = Liabilities + Capital + Revenue − Expenses
Chapter 2	Analysis of Business Transactions Assets = Liabilities + Capital + Revenue − Expenses + | − − | + − | + − | + + | −
Chapter 3	Journalize and Post Business Transactions. Prepare a Trial Balance.
Chapter 4	Gather the Adjustment Data. Complete a Work Sheet. Prepare Financial Statements. Journalize and Post Adjusting Entries.
Chapter 5	Journalize and Post Closing Entries. Prepare a Post-Closing Trial Balance.

Remember!

The yellow color represents source documents, which are evidence of transactions.

THE WORK SHEET

FYI

The use of computerized accounting software can eliminate the preparation of the manual work sheet. It does not, however, eliminate the journalizing and posting of the adjusting entries.

The **work sheet** is a working paper used by accountants to record necessary adjustments and provide up-to-date account balances needed to prepare the financial statements. The work sheet is a tool that accountants use to help in preparing the financial statements. As a tool, the work sheet serves as a central place for bringing together the information needed to record the adjustments. With up-to-date account balances, the accountant can prepare the financial statements.

First, we present the work sheet form so that you can see the big picture. Next, we describe and show examples of adjustments. Finally, we show how the adjustments are entered on the work sheet and how the work sheet is completed.

For our purposes, we use a ten-column work sheet—so called because two amount columns are provided for each of the work sheet's five major sections. We will explain the function of each of these sections, again basing our discussion on the accounting activities of Cruz Auto Detail. But first we need to fill in the heading, which consists of three lines: (1) the name of the company, (2) the title of the working paper, and (3) the period of time covered.

Cruz Auto Detail
Work Sheet
For Month Ended June 30, 20—

	TRIAL BALANCE		ADJUSTMENTS		ADJUSTED TRIAL BALANCE		INCOME STATEMENT		BALANCE SHEET	
ACCOUNT NAME	DEBIT	CREDIT	DEBIT	CREDIT	DEBIT	CREDIT	DEBIT	CREDIT	DEBIT	CREDIT

Next, we want to point out the account classifications that are placed in each column. We start with the Trial Balance columns and then move across the work sheet, discussing each pair of columns separately.

The Columns of the Work Sheet

Objective 2

List the classifications of the accounts that occupy each column of a ten-column work sheet.

Trial Balance Columns When you use a work sheet, you do not have to prepare a trial balance on a separate sheet of paper. Instead, you enter the account balances from the general ledger in the first two amount columns of the work sheet. List the accounts that have balances in the Account Name column in the same order in which they appear in the chart of accounts. Assuming normal balances, the account classifications are listed in the Trial Balance Debit and Credit columns of the work sheet as shown at the top of the next page.

Remember!

You have already prepared a trial balance. Record the normal balances in the Trial Balance Debit or Credit column.

As we move along in this chapter, we will discuss the adjustments. The Adjusted Trial Balance columns contain the same account classifications as the Trial Balance columns. **The Adjusted Trial Balance columns are merely extensions of the Trial Balance columns, plus or minus any adjustment amounts.** If an adjustment is required, the amounts are carried from the Trial Balance columns through the Adjustments columns and into the Adjusted Trial Balance columns.

Account Name	Trial Balance		Adjustments		Adjusted Trial Balance		Income Statement		Balance Sheet	
	Debit	Credit	Debit	Credit	Debit	Credit	Debit	Credit	Debit	Credit
	Assets →				Assets					
		Liabilities →				Liabilities				
		Capital →				Capital				
	Drawing →				Drawing					
		Revenue →				Revenue				
	Expenses →				Expenses					

Income Statement Columns An income statement contains the revenues minus the expenses. Revenue accounts have credit balances, so they are recorded in the Income Statement Credit column. Expense accounts have debit balances, so they are recorded in the Income Statement Debit column.

Account Name	Trial Balance		Adjustments		Adjusted Trial Balance		Income Statement		Balance Sheet	
	Debit	Credit	Debit	Credit	Debit	Credit	Debit	Credit	Debit	Credit
	Assets →				Assets					
		Liabilities →				Liabilities				
		Capital →				Capital				
	Drawing →				Drawing					
		Revenue →				Revenue →		Revenue		
	Expenses →				Expenses →		Expenses			

Balance Sheet Columns As you recall, the balance sheet is a statement showing assets, liabilities, and owner's equity. Asset accounts have debit balances, so they are recorded in the Balance Sheet Debit column. Liability accounts have credit balances, so they are recorded in the Balance Sheet Credit column. The Capital account has a credit balance, so it is recorded in the Balance Sheet Credit column. Because the Drawing account is a deduction from Capital, it has a debit balance and is recorded in the Balance Sheet Debit column (the opposite column from that in which Capital is recorded).

Account Name	Trial Balance		Adjustments		Adjusted Trial Balance		Income Statement		Balance Sheet	
	Debit	Credit	Debit	Credit	Debit	Credit	Debit	Credit	Debit	Credit
	Assets →				Assets →				Assets	
		Liabilities →				Liabilities →				Liabilities
		Capital →				Capital →				Capital
	Drawing →				Drawing →				Drawing	
		Revenue →				Revenue →		Revenue		
	Expenses →				Expenses →		Expenses			

ADJUSTMENTS

Adjustments are a way of updating the ledger accounts. They may be considered *internal transactions.* They have not been recorded in the accounts up to this time because no outside party has been involved. Adjustments are determined after the trial balance has been prepared.

Objective 3

Complete a work sheet for a service enterprise, involving adjustments for supplies used, expired insurance, depreciation, and accrued wages.

Only a few accounts are adjusted. After you have acquired experience in accounting, these accounts will be easy to recognize. To describe the reasons for making adjustments, let's return to Cruz Auto Detail. First, we select the accounts that require adjustments. Next, we show the adjustments recorded in T accounts so you can see the effect on the accounts. **However, bear in mind that the adjustments are first recorded on the work sheet.**

Supplies

In the trial balance, the Supplies account has a balance of $800. When Cruz Auto Detail bought supplies, Cruz wrote the entry as a debit to Supplies and a credit to Accounts Payable. Thus she recorded the purchase of supplies as an increase in the Supplies account.

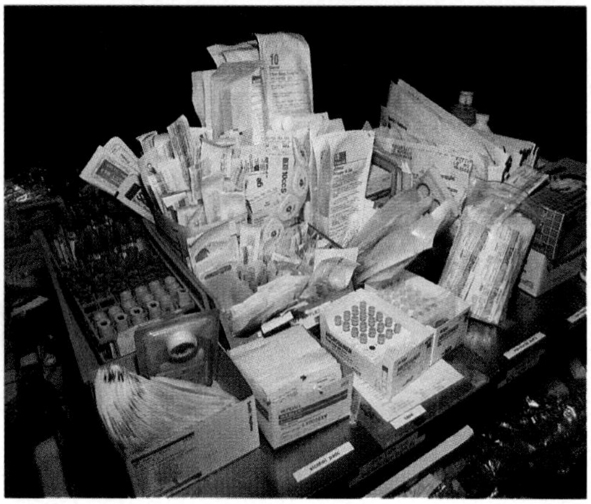

All businesses continually use up supplies in the process of doing business. Supplies that are unused, though, are considered an asset.

As long as supplies are unused, they are considered an asset. But we have not taken into consideration the fact that any business continually uses up supplies in the process of carrying on its activities. For Cruz Auto Detail, the items recorded under Supplies consist of buffer pads, cleaners, waxes, etc. Rather than going to the trouble of journalizing the supplies used each day, Cruz Auto Detail waits until the end of the month and then takes a physical count of the supplies left. **To find the amount of supplies used, subtract the amount left from the total supplies that were available.**

When Cruz counts the supplies on June 30, she finds that there is $260 worth of supplies left. The situation looks like this:

Balance of Supplies account $800	−	Amount of supplies left $260	=	Amount of supplies used and the adjusting entry amount $540

To record the amount of the supplies used, Cruz has to make an adjusting entry. The purpose of an **adjusting entry** is to bring the books up to date at the end of the accounting period. The journalizing of these adjustments is shown on page 125. Let's look at this in T account form. We need to take the amount of supplies used ($540) out of the Supplies account (credit Supplies) because we no longer have that much of the asset. Also, we need to put the amount of supplies used ($540) in the Supplies Expense account (debit Supplies Expense) because we have incurred this expense.

Remember!

For the adjustment of supplies, first find the amount used by subtracting the amount left from the balance of the Supplies account. In the adjusting entry, take the amount used out of Supplies and put it into Supplies Expense.

(a)

	Supplies +		−		**Supplies Expense** +		−
(Old)	Balance	800	Adjusting	540	Adjusting	540	
(New)	Balance	260					

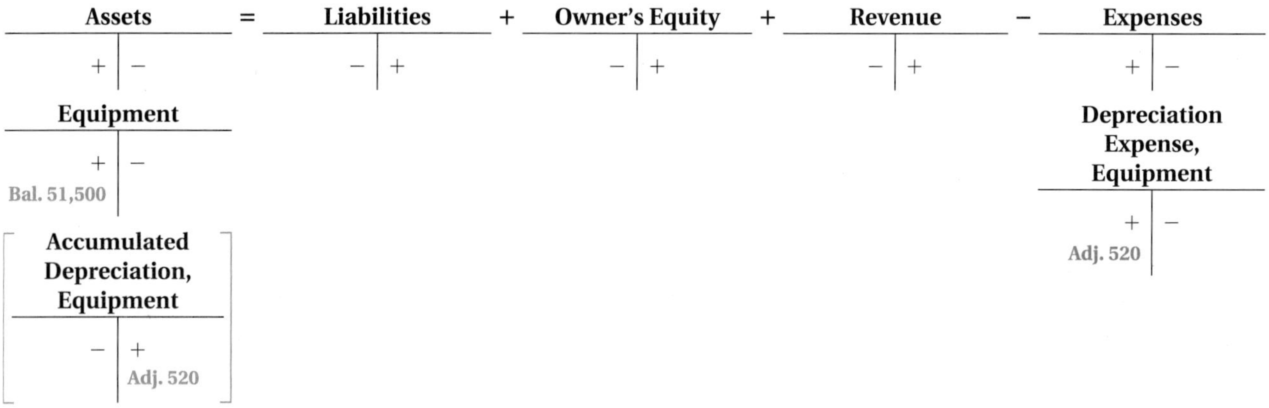
Assets = Liabilities + Owner's Equity + Revenue − Expenses
+ | −
− | +
− | +
− | +
+ | −
Equipment
+ | −
Bal. 51,500
Accumulated Depreciation, Equipment
− | +
Adj. 520
Depreciation Expense, Equipment
+ | −
Adj. 520

Remember!

The book value of an asset equals the cost of the asset minus the accumulated depreciation. Also, book value is not the same as market value.

Accumulated Depreciation, Equipment, as the title implies, is the total depreciation that the company has taken since the original purchase of the asset. Rather than crediting the Equipment account, Cruz Auto Detail keeps track of the total depreciation taken since it first acquired the asset in a separate account. The maximum depreciation it could take would be the cost of the equipment, $51,500, less trade-in value of $7,820. So, Accumulated Depreciation, Equipment, will increase at the rate of $520 per month, assuming that no additional equipment has been purchased. For example, at the end of the second month, Accumulated Depreciation, Equipment, will amount to $1,040 ($520 + $520), and the book value will be $50,460 ($51,500 − $1,040).

Wages Expense

The end of the fiscal period and the end of the employees' payroll period rarely fall on the same day. A diagram of the situation looks like this:

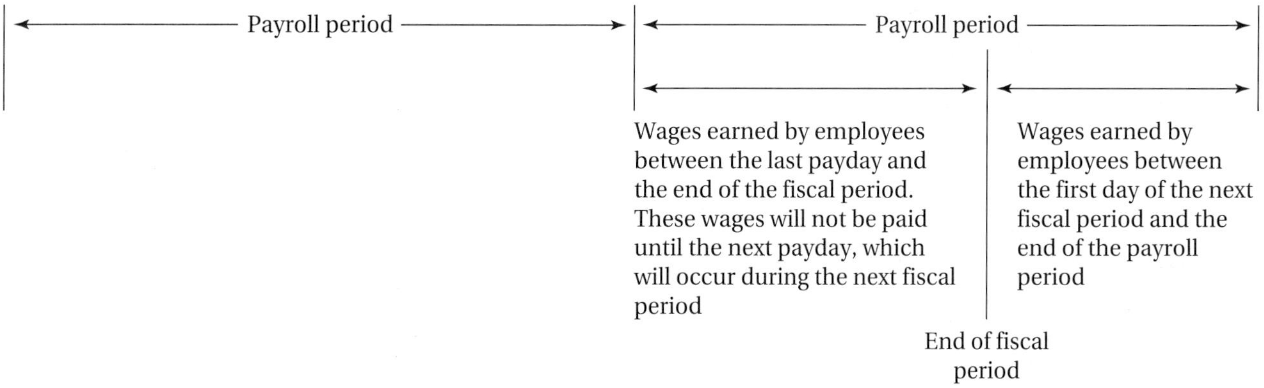
Payroll period
Payroll period
Wages earned by employees between the last payday and the end of the fiscal period. These wages will not be paid until the next payday, which will occur during the next fiscal period
Wages earned by employees between the first day of the next fiscal period and the end of the payroll period
End of fiscal period

Since the last day of the fiscal period falls in the middle of the payroll period, we have to split up the wages earned in that payroll period between the fiscal period just ending and the next fiscal period. We will use another company for this example.

Assume that this firm pays its employees a total of $400 per day and that payday falls on Friday throughout the year. The employees work a five-day week. When the employees pick up their paychecks on Friday, the amount of the checks includes their wages for that day and for the preceding four days. Suppose that the last day of the fiscal period falls on Wednesday, December 31. The diagram on the following page illustrates this situation.

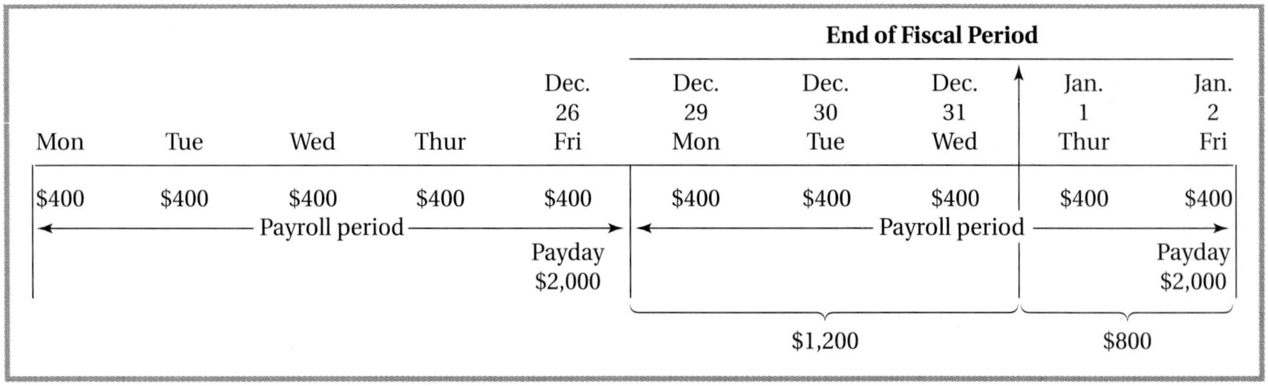
End of Fiscal Period
Dec. 26 Fri
Dec. 29 Mon
Dec. 30 Tue
Dec. 31 Wed
Jan. 1 Thur
Jan. 2 Fri
Mon
Tue
Wed
Thur
$400 $400 $400 $400 $400 $400 $400 $400 $400 $400
Payroll period
Payroll period
Payday $2,000
Payday $2,000
$1,200
$800

Remember!

If the end of the fiscal period (or end of the fiscal year) occurs during the middle of a payroll period, Wages Expense must be adjusted to bring it up to date. In the adjusting entry, add the amount employees have earned between the end of the last payroll period and the end of the fiscal period.

December

S	M	T	W	T	F	S
	1	2	3	4	(5)	6
7	8	9	10	11	(12)	13
14	15	16	17	18	(19)	20
21	22	23	24	25	(26)	27
28	29	30	31			

Paydays

To have the Wages Expense account show an accurate balance for the fiscal period, you need to add $1,200 for the cost of labor between the last payday, December 26, and the end of the year, December 31 ($400 for December 29; $400 for December 30; $400 for December 31). Because the $1,200 will not be paid at this time but is owed to the employees as of December 31, you also need to add $1,200 to Wages Payable, a liability account, because the company owes this amount to employees.

Wages Expense

+		−
(Old) Balance	104,000	
Adjusting	1,200	
(New) Balance	105,200	

Wages Payable

−	+	
	Adjusting	1,200

Returning to our illustration of Cruz Auto Detail, the last payday was June 24. Between June 24 and the end of the month, Cruz Auto Detail owes an additional $290 in wages to its employee. Accountants refer to this extra amount that has not been recorded at the end of the month as **accrued wages.** In accounting terms, **accrual** means recognition of an expense or a revenue that has been incurred (expense) or earned (revenue) but has not yet been recorded.

Remember!

In the adjusting entry for accrued wages, increase both the Wages Expense and the Wages Payable accounts.

(d) Wages Expense

+		−
(Old) Balance	1,400	
Adjusting	290	
(New) Balance	1,690	

Wages Payable

−	+	
	Adjusting	290

The Financial Picture
Before Adjustments
The Financial Picture
After Adjustments

Without adjustments, the financial statements would be out of focus. Adjustments fine tune the financial picture of the business.

You record the adjusting entry for accrued wages as a debit to Wages Expense and a credit to Wages Payable because both accounts need to be increased.

Placement of Accounts in the Work Sheet

We have to enter the adjustments on the work sheet, but before doing so, let's briefly discuss the Drawing and Accumulated Depreciation accounts, as well as net income, and their effect on the work sheet.

Capital and Drawing Account Balances The Drawing account is a contra account (contrary to Capital). In the statement of owner's equity, Drawing is deducted from Capital. To show one account as a deduction from another, the plus and minus signs are switched around. The T accounts look like this:

L.A. Cruz, Capital	
−	+
Debit	Credit Balance

L.A. Cruz, Drawing	
+	−
Debit Balance	Credit

The normal balance for the Capital account is recorded in the Credit columns of the Trial Balance, the Adjusted Trial Balance, and the Balance Sheet sections. The normal balance for the Drawing account is recorded in the Debit columns of the Trial Balance, the Adjusted Trial Balance, and the Balance Sheet sections.

Equipment and Accumulated Depreciation, Equipment, Account Balances The Accumulated Depreciation, Equipment, account is a contra account (contrary to Equipment). In the balance sheet, Accumulated Depreciation, Equipment, is deducted from Equipment. The T accounts look like this:

Equipment	
+	−
Debit Balance	Credit

Accumulated Depreciation, Equipment	
−	+
Debit	Credit Balance

The normal balance for the Equipment account is recorded in the Debit columns of the Trial Balance, the Adjusted Trial Balance, and the Balance Sheet sections. The normal balance for the Accumulated Depreciation, Equipment, account is recorded in the Credit columns of the Trial Balance, the Adjusted Trial Balance, and the Balance Sheet sections.

Net Income

Net income (or net loss) is the difference between revenue and expenses. It is used to balance the Income Statement columns; since revenue is normally larger than expenses, the balancing amount must be added to the expense side. Net income (or net loss) is also used to balance the Balance Sheet columns. As on the statement of owner's equity, you add net income to the owner's beginning Capital balance. Since the Capital balance is located in the Balance Sheet Credit column, net income must also be added to that side. The following diagram shows these relationships:

Account Name	Trial Balance		Adjustments		Adjusted Trial Balance		Income Statement		Balance Sheet	
	Debit	Credit	Debit	Credit	Debit	Credit	Debit	Credit	Debit	Credit
	A	Accum.			A	Accum.			A	Accum.
	+	Depr.			+	Depr.			+	Depr.
	Draw.	+			Draw.	+			Draw.	+
	+	L			+	L				L
	E	+			E	+				+
		Cap.				Cap.				Cap.
		+				+		R		
		R				R	E			
Net Income							NI			NI

Remember!

A net income amount is entered in the Income Statement Debit column and the Balance Sheet Credit column (same side as the increase side of Capital). A net loss is entered in the Income Statement Credit column and the Balance Sheet Debit column (same side as the decrease side of Capital).

On the other hand, if expenses are larger than revenue, the result is a net loss. You must add net loss to the revenue side to balance the Income Statement columns. Also, because a net loss is deducted from the owner's beginning Capital balance, you must include net loss in the debit side of the Balance Sheet columns, thereby balancing these columns. To show this, let's look at the Income Statement and Balance Sheet columns diagramed here.

	Income Statement		Balance Sheet	
	Debit	Credit	Debit	Credit
			A	Accum.
			+	Depr.
			Draw.	+
				L
				+
	E	R		Cap.
Net Loss		NL	NL	

Summary of Adjustments by T Accounts

To test your understanding, describe why the following adjustments are necessary. The answers are shown below the accounts.

(a)

Supplies				Supplies Expense			
	+	–			+	–	
Balance	800	Adjusting	540	Adjusting	540		

(b)

Prepaid Insurance				Insurance Expense			
	+	–			+	–	
Balance	360	Adjusting	30	Adjusting	30		

(c)

Depreciation Expense, Equipment				Accumulated Depreciation, Equipment			
	+	–			–	+	
Adjusting	520					Adjusting	520

(d)

Wages Expense				Wages Payable			
	+	–			–	+	
Balance	1,400						
Adjusting	290					Adjusting	290

Remember!

The amount of the adjusting entry for supplies used equals the balance of the Supplies account minus the amount of the supplies inventory (left over).

a. To record the cost of supplies used during June, $540.
b. To record the insurance expired during June, $30.
c. To record the depreciation for the month of June, $520.
d. To record accrued wages owed at the end of June, $290.

Mixed Accounts At this point, take special notice of the fact that **each adjusting entry contains an income statement account (revenue or expense) and a balance sheet account (asset, contra asset, or liability).** Accountants refer to these accounts as **mixed accounts**—accounts with balances that are partly income statement amounts and partly balance sheet amounts. The income statement and balance sheet accounts involved are separate accounts that have a part of their name in common, like Supplies Expense (an expense account) and Supplies (an asset account). For example, Supplies is recorded as $800 in the Trial Balance, but after adjustment, this amount is split up or apportioned as $540 in Supplies Expense in the Income Statement columns and $260 in Supplies in the Balance Sheet columns. Similarly, Prepaid Insurance is recorded as $360 in the Trial Balance columns but is apportioned as $30 in Insurance Expense in the Income Statement columns and $330 in Prepaid Insurance in the Balance Sheet columns. In other words, portions of these trial balance amounts are recorded in each section.

Remember!

Each of the accounts that is adjusted has a companion account. Supplies—companion account is Supplies Expense. Prepaid Insurance—companion account is Insurance Expense. Depreciation Expense—companion account is Accumulated Depreciation. Wages Expense—companion account is Wages Payable.

In the previous examples, we used T accounts to explain how to handle adjustments. T accounts help organize any type of accounting entry into debits and credits. But now it is time to record the adjustments on the work sheet. To help you remember which classifications of accounts appear in each column of the work sheet, we will label the columns with letters specifying each classification of accounts; for example, A for assets and L for liabilities as shown in Figure 2 on the following page.

Cruz Auto Detail
Work Sheet
For Month Ended June 30, 20—

	ACCOUNT NAME	TRIAL BALANCE DEBIT *A + Draw. + E*	TRIAL BALANCE CREDIT *Accum. Deprec. + L + C + R*	ADJUSTMENTS DEBIT	ADJUSTMENTS CREDIT
1	Cash	23,250.00			
2	Accounts Receivable	200.00			
3	Supplies	800.00			(a) 540.00
4	Prepaid Insurance	360.00			(b) 30.00
5	Equipment	51,500.00			
6	Accounts Payable		4,700.00		
7	L. A. Cruz, Capital		70,000.00		
8	L. A. Cruz, Drawing	3,000.00			
9	Income from Services		7,270.00		
10	Wages Expense	1,400.00		(d) 290.00	
11	Rent Expense	900.00			
12	Advertising Expense	400.00			
13	Utilities Expense	160.00			
14		81,970.00	81,970.00		
15	Supplies Expense			(a) 540.00	
16	Insurance Expense			(b) 30.00	
17	Depreciation Expense, Equipment			(c) 520.00	
18	Accumulated Depreciation, Equipment				(c) 520.00
19	Wages Payable				(d) 290.00
20				1,380.00	1,380.00

FIGURE 2

Steps in the Completion of the Work Sheet

Before we complete the work sheet, let's list the recommended steps to follow.

1. Complete the Trial Balance columns, total, and rule.
2. Complete the Adjustments columns, total, and rule.
3. Complete the Adjusted Trial Balance columns, total, and rule.
4. Record balances in the Income Statement and Balance Sheet columns and total each column.
5. Record net income or net loss in the Income Statement columns by subtracting the smaller side from the larger side and adding the difference to the smaller side, total, and rule.
6. Record net income or net loss in the Balance Sheet columns by subtracting the smaller side from the larger side and adding the difference to the smaller side (the amount should be the same as the difference between the Income Statement column totals—if not, there is an error), total, and rule.

Step 1: Trial Balance Columns Note that the trial balance in Figure 2 is the same trial balance for Cruz Auto Detail presented earlier. You will be able to follow the completion of the entire work sheet for Cruz Auto Detail in Figures 3 through 6 by turning the transparent pages, thus adding the next stage of its completion, and in Figure 7 on pages 122–123.

Remember!

After the first fiscal period, Accumulated Depreciation will have a balance, so it will be listed immediately below the asset being depreciated (which in this example is Equipment). Consequently, Accumulated Depreciation will not appear at the bottom of next month's work sheet.

Step 2: Adjustments Columns When we enter the adjustments, we identify them as **(a)**, **(b)**, **(c)**, and **(d)** to indicate the relationships between the debit and credit sides and the sequence of the individual adjusting entries (see Figure 4).

Note that Supplies Expense; Insurance Expense; Depreciation Expense, Equipment; Accumulated Depreciation, Equipment; and Wages Payable did not appear in the trial balance because there were no balances in the accounts at that time. We wrote them below the Trial Balance totals to complete the work sheet.

Here is a brief review of the adjustments:

a. To record the $540 cost of supplies used during June.
b. To record the $30 cost of insurance expired during June.
c. To record $520 depreciation for the month of June.
d. To record $290 of accrued wages owed at the end of June.

Now let's look at the work sheet shown in Figure 7 (pp. 122–123). To reinforce the idea of adjusting entries, see the brief explanation of each adjustment at the right of the work sheet. Again, the completed work sheet is shown on the transparent pages (Figures 3–6) between pages 120–121.

After the first fiscal period, Accumulated Depreciation will always have a balance until the related asset is sold or disposed of. Consequently, it will be listed in the Trial Balance columns immediately below the appropriate asset (Equipment, in this case).

Remember!

Supplies is adjusted for the amount used.

Insurance is adjusted by adding the amount expired to Insurance Expense while deducting the same amount from Prepaid Insurance.

Depreciation is added to both Depreciation Expense and Accumulated Depreciation.

Accrued wages are added to both Wages Expense and Wages Payable.

Regarding the work sheet, again, we emphasize that it is strictly a working paper or tool used to gather together all the up-to-date information needed to prepare the financial statements. **The adjustments are always recorded in the work sheet first.**

Step 3: Adjusted Trial Balance Columns Once the Adjustments columns are totaled and ruled, extend each Trial Balance amount, plus or minus any adjustment from the Adjustments columns, to the Adjusted Trial Balance columns as shown in Figure 5 or Figure 7.

Step 4: Income Statement and Balance Sheet Columns Extend the balances in the Adjusted Trial Balance columns to either the Income Statement or the Balance Sheet columns (see Figure 6).

Step 5: Net Income or Net Loss—Income Statement Columns Total each of the two Income Statement columns. Subtract the smaller side from the larger side, and write the difference under the smaller Income Statement column total, total and rule as shown in Figure 6.

DHL

Depreciation can occur from wear and tear of everyday use or assets can simply become obsolete.

Step 6: Net Income or Net Loss—Balance Sheet Columns Total each of the two Balance Sheet columns. Subtract the smaller side from the larger side, and write the difference under the smaller Balance Sheet column total (the amount should be the same as the difference between the Income Statement column totals—if not, there is an error), total and rule as shown in Figure 6.

If there is a net income, the credit side of the Income Statement columns will be larger than the debit side—more revenue than expenses. In this case, write Net Income in the Account Name column on the same line as the difference you calculated.

If there is a net loss, the debit side of the Income Statement columns will be larger than the credit side—more expenses than revenue. In this case,

FIGURE 7

Account Name	Trial Balance Debit A + Draw. + E	Trial Balance Credit Accum. Deprec. + L + C + R
Cash	23,250.00	
Accounts Receivable	200.00	
Supplies	800.00	
Prepaid Insurance	360.00	
Equipment	51,500.00	
Accounts Payable		4,700.00
L. A. Cruz, Capital		70,000.00
L. A. Cruz, Drawing	3,000.00	
Income from Services		7,270.00
Wages Expense	1,400.00	
Rent Expense	900.00	
Advertising Expense	400.00	
Utilities Expense	160.00	
	81,970.00	81,970.00
Supplies Expense	Step 1	
Insurance Expense		
Depreciation Expense, Equipment		
Accumulated Depreciation, Equipment		
Wages Payable		
(a) Supplies used, $540		
(b) Insurance expired, $30		
(c) Depreciation of equipment, $520		
(d) Accrued wages, $150		

write Net Loss in the Account Name column on the same line as the difference you calculated.

Work Sheet Requiring Two Pages

If a large number of accounts is involved, it may be necessary to continue the work sheet to a second page.

Remember!

When a work sheet requires two pages, the totals at the bottom of the first sheet do not have to be equal. Debits must equal credits by the end of the second page.

(First Page)

Account Name	Trial Balance		Adjustments	
Wages Expense	3,240 00		(c) 220 50	
Totals carried forward	98,312 00	91,146 10	962 50	126 50

Cruz Auto Detail
Work Sheet
For Month Ended June 30, 20—

Adjustments		Adjusted Trial Balance		Income Statement		Balance Sheet	
Debit	Credit	Debit A + Draw. + E	Credit Accum. Deprec. + L + C + R	Debit E	Credit R	Debit A + Draw.	Credit Accum. Deprec. + L + C
		23,250.00		*No adjustment, so carry over amount directly*			
		200.00					
	(a) 540.00	260.00		*Adjustment involved, subtract $540 (used) from $800*			
	(b) 30.00	330.00		*Adjustment involved, subtract $30 (expired) from $360*			
		51,500.00		*No adjustment, so carry over amount directly*			
			4,700.00				
			70,000.00				
		3,000.00					
			7,270.00				
(d) 290.00		1,690.00		*Adjustment involved, add $290 (accrued) to $1,400*			
		900.00		*No adjustment, so carry over amount directly*			
		400.00					
		160.00					
				This line is blank because of the trial balance total			
(a) 540.00		540.00		*Adjustment involved, carry $540 over to the same column*			
(b) 30.00		30.00		*Adjustment involved, carry $30 over to the same column*			
(c) 520.00		520.00		*Adjustment involved, carry $520 over to the same column*			
	(c) 520.00		520.00	*Adjustment involved, carry $520 over to the same column*			
	(d) 290.00		290.00	*Adjustment involved, carry $290 over to the same column*			
1,380.00	1,380.00	82,780.00	82,780.00				
Step 2		Step 3					

Note that the totals at the bottom of the first page are labeled “Totals carried forward” in the Account Name column. At the top of the second page, the totals are repeated and labeled “Totals brought forward” in the Account Name column. Continue listing account names and balances below the totals brought forward.

(Second Page)

Account Name	Trial Balance		Adjustments	
	Debit	Credit	Debit	Credit
Totals brought forward	98,312.00	91,146.10	962.50	126.50
Wages Payable				(c) 220.50

Finding Errors in the Income Statement and Balance Sheet Columns

As you have seen, the amount of the net income or net loss must be recorded in both an Income Statement column and a Balance Sheet column. Suppose that, after the net income is added to the Balance Sheet Credit column, the Balance Sheet columns are not equal. To find the error, follow this procedure:

1. Check to see that the amount of the net income or loss is recorded in the correct columns. For example, net income is placed in the Income Statement Debit column and the Balance Sheet Credit column.
2. Verify the addition of all the columns.
3. Look to see if the appropriate amounts have been recorded in the Income Statement and Balance Sheet columns. For example, asset amounts should be listed in the Balance Sheet Debit column, expense amounts should be listed in the Income Statement Debit column, and so forth.
4. Verify, by adding or subtracting across each line, that the amounts carried over from the Trial Balance columns through the Adjustments columns into the Adjusted Trial Balance columns are correct.
5. The correct amounts of the revenue and expense accounts are transferred to the income statement columns.
6. The correct amounts of assets, liabilities, and owner's equity accounts are transferred to the balance sheet columns.

Generally, one of these steps will expose the error.

Completion of the Financial Statements

Objective 4

Prepare an income statement, a statement of owner's equity, and a balance sheet for a service business directly from the work sheet.

As we stated, the purpose of the work sheet is to help the accountant prepare the financial statements. Since we have completed the work sheet for Cruz Auto Detail, we can now prepare the income statement, the statement of owner's equity, and the balance sheet by taking the figures directly from the work sheet. These statements are shown in Figure 8 on the facing page.

Note that you record Accumulated Depreciation, Equipment, in the asset section of the balance sheet as a direct deduction from Equipment. As we have said, accountants refer to this as a *contra asset account* because it is contrary to its companion account. The difference, $50,980, is called the book value or carrying value because it represents the cost of the asset after Accumulated Depreciation has been deducted.

When preparing the statement of owner's equity, always remember to check the beginning balance of Capital against the balance shown in the Capital account in the general ledger. An additional investment may have been made during the fiscal period, and you need to record any such additional investment in the statement of owner's equity.

JOURNALIZING ADJUSTING ENTRIES

Objective 5

Journalize and post the adjusting entries.

To change the balance of a ledger account, you need a journal entry as evidence of the change. So far, we have been listing adjustments only in the Adjustments columns of the work sheet. The work sheet is not a journal, so we must journalize the adjustments to update the ledger accounts. **Take the information for these entries directly from the Adjustments columns of the work sheet, debiting and crediting exactly the same accounts and amounts in the journal entries.**

FIGURE 8

Remember!

Money columns are not labeled Debit or Credit. Each column simply shows account balances. Amounts in these columns are either added or subtracted.

Cruz Auto Detail
Income Statement
For Month Ended June 30, 20—

Revenue:		
Income from Services		$7,270.00
Expenses:		
Wages Expense	$1,690.00	
Rent Expense	900.00	
Advertising Expense	400.00	
Utilities Expense	160.00	
Supplies Expense	540.00	
Insurance Expense	30.00	
Depreciation Expense, Equipment	520.00	
Total Expenses		4,240.00
Net Income		$3,030.00

Remember!

Ruling columns correctly is very important. Always draw a single rule below a column to be added or subtracted. Draw double rules below the totals.

Cruz Auto Detail
Statement of Owner's Equity
For Month Ended June 30, 20—

L. A. Cruz, Capital, June 1, 20—		$70,000.00
Net Income for June	$3,030.00	
Less Withdrawals for June	3,000.00	
Increase in Capital		30.00
L. A. Cruz, Capital, June 30, 20—		$70,030.00

Cruz Auto Detail
Balance Sheet
June 30, 20—

Assets		
Cash		$23,250.00
Accounts Receivable		200.00
Supplies		260.00
Prepaid Insurance		330.00
Equipment	$51,500.00	
Less Accumulated Depreciation	520.00	50,980.00
Total Assets		$75,020.00
Liabilities		
Accounts Payable	$4,700.00	
Wages Payable	290.00	
Total Liabilities		$4,990.00
Owner's Equity		
L. A. Cruz, Capital		70,030.00
Total Liabilities and Owner's Equity		$75,020.00

In the Description column of the general journal, write "Adjusting Entries" before you begin making these entries. This can eliminate the need to write an explanation for each entry. The adjusting entries for Cruz Auto Detail are shown in Figure 9.

FIGURE 9

GENERAL JOURNAL PAGE 4

	DATE		DESCRIPTION	POST. REF.	DEBIT	CREDIT	
1	20–		Adjusting Entries				1
2	June	30	Supplies Expense	515	540 00		2
3			Supplies	115		540 00	3
4							4
5		30	Insurance Expense	516	30 00		5
6			Prepaid Insurance	117		30 00	6
7							7
8		30	Dep. Expense, Equipment	517	520 00		8
9			Accum. Dep., Equipment	125		520 00	9
10							10
11		30	Wages Expense	511	290 00		11
12			Wages Payable	212		290 00	12

Remember!

Each adjusting entry consists of an income statement account and a balance sheet account.

When you post the adjusting entries to the ledger accounts, write the word "Adjusting" in the Item column of the ledger account. The adjusting entry for Supplies is posted as follows:

GENERAL LEDGER

ACCOUNT Supplies ACCOUNT NO. 115

	DATE		ITEM	POST. REF.	DEBIT	CREDIT	BALANCE DEBIT	BALANCE CREDIT	
1	20–								1
2	June	4		1	800 00		800 00		2
3		30	Adj.	4		540 00	260 00		3
4									4

ACCOUNT Supplies Expense ACCOUNT NO. 515

	DATE		ITEM	POST. REF.	DEBIT	CREDIT	BALANCE DEBIT	BALANCE CREDIT	
1	20–								1
2	June	30	Adj.	4	540 00		540 00		2
3									3
4									4

FYI

Many businesses produce monthly financial statements. Adjustments must be made every time a financial statement is done.

FIGURE 10

Karl Veterinary Clinic
Income Statement
For Year Ended December 31, 20—

Revenues:		
Professional Fees	$ 111,720.00	
Boarding Fees	22,080.00	
Total Revenues		$ 133,800.00
Expenses:		
Salaries Expense	$ 84,000.00	
Depreciation Expense, Building	6,480.00	
Depreciation Expense, Equipment	3,840.00	
Supplies Expense	3,720.00	
Insurance Expense	720.00	
Miscellaneous Expense	2,160.00	
Total Expenses		100,920.00
Net Income		$ 32,880.00

In the adjusted accounts, notice that the intent is to make sure that the expenses recorded match up or compare with the revenues for the same period of time. In other words, for the month of June, we record all the revenues for June and all the expenses for June. Thus the revenues and expenses for the same time period are matched. This is called the **matching principle**.

Objective 6

Prepare an income statement and a balance sheet for a business with more than one revenue account and more than one accumulated depreciation account.

Businesses with More than One Revenue Account and More than One Accumulated Depreciation Account

The only revenue account for Cruz Auto Detail is Income from Services. However, a business may have several distinct sources of revenue. For example, Karl Veterinary Clinic has two revenue accounts: Professional Fees and Boarding Fees. Figure 10 illustrates the placement of these accounts in the income statement.

In Figure 10, also note that the company has two assets subject to depreciation: Building and Equipment. In the financial statements, Depreciation Expense and Accumulated Depreciation must be listed for each asset.

MetLife

Prepaid insurance is an asset that expires as time goes on. You make adjustments using the Prepaid Insurance and Insurance Expense accounts. For the insurance company, however, prepaid insurance is a liability.

Land supposedly lasts forever, so land is not depreciated. Adjustments would have been made in the work sheet for depreciation of the equipment and the building. The balance sheet for Karl Veterinary Clinic is shown in Figure 11.

FIGURE 11

Karl Veterinary Clinic
Balance Sheet
December 31, 20—

Assets		
Cash		$ 6,240.00
Supplies		200.00
Land		4,400.00
Building	$117,700.00	
Less Accumulated Depreciation	36,400.00	81,300.00
Equipment	$ 42,600.00	
Less Accumulated Depreciation	29,200.00	13,400.00
Total Assets		$105,540.00
Liabilities		
Accounts Payable		$ 2,800.00
Owner's Equity		
Doris P. Karl, Capital		102,740.00
Total Liabilities and Owner's Equity		$105,540.00

CHAPTER REVIEW

Review of Performance Objectives

1. Define *fiscal period* and *fiscal year.*

   A fiscal period is any period of time covering a complete accounting cycle. A fiscal year consists of twelve consecutive months.

2. List the classifications of the accounts that occupy each column of a ten-column work sheet.

Trial Balance Debit	Assets + Drawing + Expenses
Trial Balance Credit	Accum. Deprec. + Liabilities + Capital + Revenue
Adjustments Debit	Expenses
Adjustments Credit	Assets + Liabilities
Adjusted Trial Balance Debit	Assets + Drawing + Expenses
Adjusted Trial Balance Credit	Accum. Deprec. + Liabilities + Capital + Revenue
Income Statement Debit	Expenses
Income Statement Credit	Revenue
Balance Sheet Debit	Assets + Drawing
Balance Sheet Credit	Accumulated Depreciation + Liabilities + Capital

3. Complete a work sheet for a service enterprise, involving adjustments for supplies used, expired insurance, depreciation, and accrued wages.

   Adjustment for supplies used: debit Supplies Expense and credit Supplies.
   Adjustment for expired insurance: debit Insurance Expense and credit Prepaid Insurance.
   Adjustment for depreciation: debit Depreciation Expense and credit Accumulated Depreciation.
   Adjustment for accrued wages: debit Wages Expense and credit Wages Payable.

4. Prepare an income statement, a statement of owner's equity, and a balance sheet for a service business directly from the work sheet.

   Prepare the income statement directly from the amounts listed in the Income Statement Debit and Credit columns. The net income should equal the net income previously determined on the work sheet. For the statement of owner's equity, use the amount of the beginning capital listed in the Balance Sheet Credit column after checking the general ledger for any additional investment(s), the amount of the net income from the Balance Sheet Credit column, and the amount of Drawing from the Balance Sheet Debit column. Prepare the balance sheet directly from the amounts listed in the Balance Sheet Debit and Credit columns (except Drawing and Capital).

5. Journalize and post the adjusting entries.

   Adjusting entries are taken directly from the Adjustments columns of the work sheet.

6. Prepare an income statement and a balance sheet for a business with more than one revenue account and more than one accumulated depreciation account.

   Businesses that have more than one source of revenue or more than one type of asset that is subject to depreciation must show a separate account for each on the income statement and the balance sheet.

Glossary

Accounting cycle The sequence of steps in the accounting process completed during the fiscal period. (109)

Accrual Recognition of an expense or a revenue that has been incurred or earned but has not yet been recorded. (116)

Accrued wages The amount of unpaid wages owed to employees for the time between the end of the last pay period and the end of the fiscal period. (116)

Adjusting entry An entry to help bring the books up to date at the end of the fiscal period. (112)

Adjustments Internal transactions that bring ledger accounts up to date, as a planned part of the accounting procedure. They are first recorded in the Adjustments columns of the work sheet. (112)

Book value or **carrying value** The cost of an asset minus the accumulated depreciation. (114)

Contra account An account that is contrary to, or a deduction from, another account; for example, Accumulated Depreciation is listed as a deduction from Equipment. (114)

Depreciation An expense based on the expectation that an asset will gradually decline in usefulness due to time, wear and tear, or obsolescence; the cost of the asset is therefore spread out over its estimated useful life. A part of depreciation expense is apportioned to each fiscal period. (113)

Fiscal period Any period of time covering a complete accounting cycle, generally consisting of twelve consecutive months. (109)

Fiscal year A fiscal period consisting of twelve consecutive months. (109)

Matching principle The principle that the revenue for one time period is matched up or compared with the related expenses for the same time period. (127)

Mixed accounts Certain accounts that appear in the trial balance with balances that are partly income statement amounts and partly balance sheet amounts—for example, Prepaid Insurance and Supplies. (119)

Straight-line depreciation A means of calculating depreciation in which the cost of an asset, less any trade-in value, is allocated evenly over the useful life of the asset. (113)

Work sheet A working paper used by accountants to record necessary adjustments and provide up-to-date account balances needed to prepare the financial statements. (110)

QUESTIONS, EXERCISES, AND PROBLEMS

Discussion Questions

1. What is the purpose of a work sheet?
2. What is the purpose of adjusting entries?
3. What is a mixed account? Give an example. What is a contra account? Give an example.
4. In which column of the work sheet—Income Statement (IS), Balance Sheet (BS)—would the adjusted balances of the following accounts appear?

Account	IS or BS?	Account	IS or BS?
a. Prepaid Insurance		e. Accumulated Depreciation, Equipment	
b. Supplies		f. T. Oglevan, Drawing	
c. Wages Payable		g. Insurance Expense	
d. Income from Services		h. Depreciation Expense, Equipment	

5. Why is it necessary to make an adjustment if wages for work performed for the pay period Monday through Friday are paid on Friday and the accounting period ends on a Wednesday?
6. Define depreciation as it relates to a truck you bought for your business.
7. What is the amount of the adjustment for supplies if the balance of supplies bought is $1,450 but the amount left when counted is $860?
8. Why is it necessary to journalize adjusting entries that you have prepared on the work sheet?

Exercises

P.O. 2

List account classifications in work sheet columns.

Exercise 4-1 List the following classifications of accounts in all the columns in which they appear in the work sheet, with the exception of the Adjustments columns. (Example: Assets.)

Assets	Capital
Accumulated Depreciation (with previous balance)	Drawing
Liabilities	Revenue
	Expenses

Write Net Income in the appropriate columns.

Account Name	Trial Balance		Adjustments		Adjusted Trial Balance		Income Statement		Balance Sheet	
	Debit	Credit	Debit	Credit	Debit	Credit	Debit	Credit	Debit	Credit
	Assets				Assets				Assets	
Net Income										

P.O. 2

Classify accounts and indicate normal balances and statement columns.

Exercise 4-2 Classify each of the accounts listed below as assets (A), liabilities (L), owner's equity (OE), revenue (R), or expenses (E). Indicate the normal debit or credit balance of each account. Indicate whether each account will appear in the Income Statement columns (IS) or the Balance Sheet columns (BS) of the work sheet. Item 0 is given as an example.

Account	Classification	Normal Balance	IS or BS Columns
0. Example: Wages Expense	E	Debit	IS
a. Prepaid Insurance			
b. Accounts Payable			
c. C. Kronenberg, Capital			
d. Accounts Receivable			
e. Accumulated Depreciation, Building			
f. C. Kronenberg, Drawing			
g. Rental Income			
h. Equipment			
i. Depreciation Expense, Equipment			
j. Supplies			

P.O. 3

Choose accounts that require adjustment.

Exercise 4-3 Place a check mark next to any account(s) requiring adjustment. Explain why those accounts must be adjusted.

✓	Account Name (in trial balance order)	Reason for Adjusting This Account
	a. Cash	
	b. Accounts Receivable	
	c. Supplies	
	d. Prepaid Insurance	
	e. Equipment	
	f. Accumulated Depreciation, Equipment	
	g. Accounts Payable	
	h. G. L. Johnson, Capital	
	i. G. L. Johnson, Drawing	
	j. Wages Expense	

P.O. 3

Prepare adjustments in the work sheet.

Exercise 4-4 Below is a partial work sheet for Megan's Place. Prepare the following adjustments in this work sheet:

a. Supplies inventory (left or unused), $135—calculate the expired or used-up supplies.
b. Expired or used-up insurance, $300.
c. Depreciation expense on equipment, $850—remember to credit the accumulated depreciation account for equipment, not Equipment.
d. Wages accrued or earned since the last payday, $124 (owed and to be paid on the next payday).

	ACCOUNT NAME	TRIAL BALANCE DEBIT	TRIAL BALANCE CREDIT	ADJUSTMENTS DEBIT	ADJUSTMENTS CREDIT
1	Cash	5,621.00			
2	Supplies	385.00			
3	Prepaid Insurance	900.00			
4	Equipment	4,680.00			
5	Accumulated Depreciation, Equipment		1,250.00		
6	Accounts Payable		2,649.00		
7	M. Megan, Capital		4,624.00		
8	M. Megan, Drawing	2,200.00			
9	Service Income		6,847.00		
10	Rent Expense	956.00			
11	Wages Expense	560.00			
12	Miscellaneous Expense	68.00			
13		15,370.00	15,370.00		
14					

P.O. 3

Prepare adjustments and adjusted trial balance.

Exercise 4-5 Complete the work sheet through the adjusted trial balance using the following adjustment information:

a. Supplies inventory (left or unused), $148—calculate the expired or used-up supplies.
b. Expired or used-up insurance, $450.
c. Depreciation expense on equipment, $970—remember to credit the accumulated depreciation account for equipment, not Equipment.
d. Wages accrued or earned since the last payday, $221 (owed and to be paid on the next payday).

		TRIAL BALANCE		ADJUSTMENTS		ADJUSTED TRIAL BALANCE	
	ACCOUNT NAME	DEBIT	CREDIT	DEBIT	CREDIT	DEBIT	CREDIT
1	Cash	4620 00					
2	Supplies	367 00					
3	Prepaid Insurance	1100 00					
4	Equipment	5678 00					
5	Accumulated Depreciation,						
6	Equipment		1456 00				
7	Accounts Payable		1975 00				
8	D. Lyon, Capital		6126 00				
9	D. Lyon, Drawing	1800 00					
10	Service Fees		5736 00				
11	Rent Expense	865 00					
12	Wages Expense	785 00					
13	Miscellaneous Expense	78 00					
14		15293 00	15293 00				
15							
16							
17							
18							
19							
20							
21							
22							
23							
24							
25							
26							
27							
28							

P.O. 3

Calculate the missing adjustments.

Exercise 4-6 Journalize the four adjusting entries from the partial work sheet on the following page for the month ended May 31. (*Hint:* Use what you know about extending numbers to the four statement columns.)

	Account Name	Income Statement Debit	Income Statement Credit	Balance Sheet Debit	Balance Sheet Credit	
1	Cash			4731 00		1
2	Supplies			266 00		2
3	Prepaid Insurance			841 00		3
4	Equipment			5832 00		4
5	Accumulated Depreciation, Equipment				1820 00	5
6	Accounts Payable				985 00	6
7	C. Peak, Capital				6810 00	7
8	C. Peak, Drawing			2150 00		8
9	Professional Fees		8673 00			9
10	Salary Expense	2787 00				10
11	Rent Expense	1200 00				11
12	Miscellaneous Expense	134 00				12
13						13
14	Supplies Expense	118 00				14
15	Insurance Expense	185 00				15
16	Depreciation Expense, Equipment	364 00				16
17	Salaries Payable				320 00	17
18		4788 00	8673 00	13820 00	9935 00	18
19	Net Income	3885 00			3885 00	19
20		8673 00	8673 00	13820 00	13820 00	20
21						21

P.O. 5
Journalize adjusting entries from the work sheet.

Exercise 4-7 Journalize the adjustments for the Jama Company as of August 31.

	Account Name	Trial Balance Debit	Trial Balance Credit	Adjustments Debit	Adjustments Credit
1	Cash	3971 00			
2	Supplies	462 00			(a) 201 00
3	Prepaid Insurance	4873 00			(b) 265 00
4	Equipment	5678 00			
5	Accumulated Depreciation, Equipment		645 00		(c) 206 00
6	Accounts Payable		843 00		
7	A. Jama, Capital		12551 00		
8	A. Jama, Drawing	2000 00			
9	Service Fees		4683 00		
10	Rent Expense	795 00			
11	Wages Expense	865 00		(d) 168 00	
12	Miscellaneous Expense	78 00			
13		18722 00	18722 00		
14	Supplies Expense			(a) 201 00	
15	Insurance Expense			(b) 265 00	
16	Depreciation Expense, Equipment			(c) 206 00	
17	Wages Payable				(d) 168 00
18				840 00	840 00
19					

P.O. 5
Journalize adjusting entries.

Exercise 4-8 Journalize the following adjusting entries that were included in the work sheet for the month ended December 31. Assume the financial statements have been prepared.

Dec.	31	Supplies inventory (left or unused), $196. The cost of supplies in the unadjusted trial balance was $534. The amount in the Adjustments column of the work sheet is $338 (verify).
	31	Salaries for two days are unpaid at December 31, $1,600 (verify). Salaries are $4,000 for a five-day week.
	31	Insurance was bought on September 1 for $1,800 for 12 months' coverage. Four months' coverage has expired, $600 (verify).
	31	Depreciation for the month on equipment, $50, based on an asset costing $4,500 with a trade-in value of $1,500 and an estimated life of 5 years (verify).

CONSIDER AND COMMUNICATE

Assume that you have completed the income statement, but the net income is not the same as you calculated on your work sheet. What should you check?

WHAT IF . . .

You find that your accounting clerk forgot to adjust for $300 in wages earned since the last payday. The next payday is in the next accounting period. Will this omission affect the ledger accounts, income statement, statement of owner's equity, and balance sheet? If so, how?

CRITICAL THINKING

Your supervisor has just handed you the partial work sheet (on the following page) for the month ended July 31 and asked you to journalize the adjusting entries. He apologizes for having spilled liquid on the first six columns of the work sheet.

WEB WORK

Select a major company in which you are interested. Using your web browser, key in the name of the company; for example jcpenney. Or, if you know the web address of the company, key it into the Location box; for example, gapinc.com. Once you are on the home page, search for phrases like *company information* or *about us.* Write a summary of the information you find about the company including the company's product, its mission or goals, sales information, and any other financial information you discover, including the web address where you found the information.

ACCOUNT NAME	INCOME STATEMENT DEBIT *E*	INCOME STATEMENT CREDIT *R*	BALANCE SHEET DEBIT *A + Draw.*	BALANCE SHEET CREDIT *Accum. Depr. + L + C*
Cash			3254 00	
Supplies			202 00	
Prepaid Insurance			550 00	
Equipment			4697 00	
Accumulated Depreciation, Equipment				1838 00
Accounts Payable				961 00
E. Walia, Capital				5115 00
E. Walia, Drawing			1200 00	
Service Income		4587 00		
Rent Expense	897 00			
Wages Expense	726 00			
Miscellaneous Expense	37 00			
Supplies Expense	256 00			
Insurance Expense	340 00			
Depreciation Expense, Equipment	600 00			
Wages Payable				258 00
	2856 00	4587 00	9903 00	8172 00
Net Income	1731 00			1731 00
	4587 00	4587 00	9903 00	9903 00

PROBLEM SET A

For additional help, see the demonstration problems at the beginning of each chapter in your Working Papers.

P.O. 3

Problem 4-1A The trial balance for the Reckis Insurance Agency as of August 31, after the firm has completed its first month of operations, follows:

Reckis Insurance Agency
Trial Balance
August 31, 20—

ACCOUNT NAME	DEBIT *A + Draw. + E*	CREDIT *Accum. Depr. + L + C + R*
Cash	3427 00	
Accounts Receivable	1319 00	
Prepaid Insurance	362 00	
Supplies	492 00	
Office Equipment	4939 00	
Accounts Payable		1071 00
M. Reckis, Capital		9020 00
M. Reckis, Drawing	900 00	
Commissions Earned		2520 00
Rent Expense	695 00	
Travel Expense	225 00	
Utilities Expense	198 00	
Miscellaneous Expense	54 00	
	12611 00	12611 00

Check Figure

Net Income, $161

Instructions

1. Record the amounts in the Trial Balance columns of the work sheet and record the owner's name in the Capital and Drawing accounts.
2. Complete the work sheet by making the following adjustments and lettering each adjustment:
   a. Expired or used-up insurance, $86.
   b. Supplies inventory (left or unused), $91—calculate the amount of supplies used up.
   c. Depreciation expense on office equipment, $700—remember to credit the accumulated depreciation account for office equipment, not Office Equipment.

P.O. 4,5

Problem 4-2A The completed work sheet for Wong Design for the month of March is in your Working Papers.

Check Figure

Total Assets, $15,480

Instructions

1. Prepare an income statement.
2. Prepare a statement of owner's equity. Assume that no additional investments were made in March.
3. Prepare a balance sheet.
4. Journalize the adjusting entries.

P.O. 3,5

Problem 4-3A The trial balance of The Fashion Center for the month ended September 30 is presented below.

The Fashion Center
Trial Balance
September 30, 20—

ACCOUNT NAME	DEBIT	CREDIT
Cash	2,378.00	
Supplies	864.00	
Prepaid Insurance	1,345.00	
Equipment	32,978.00	
Accumulated Depreciation, Equipment		16,235.00
Accounts Payable		2,751.00
C. Barkley, Capital		45,208.00
C. Barkley, Drawing	22,445.00	
Income from Services		43,791.00
Wages Expense	29,761.00	
Rent Expense	14,932.00	
Utilities Expense	1,573.00	
Telephone Expense	1,271.00	
Miscellaneous Expense	438.00	
	107,985.00	107,985.00

Data for the adjustments are as follows:

a. Supplies inventory (left or unused), $227—calculate the expired or used-up supplies.
b. Expired or used-up insurance, $320.

c. Depreciation expense on equipment, $2,800—remember to credit the accumulated depreciation account for equipment, not Equipment.
d. Wages accrued or earned since the last payday, $468 (owed and to be paid on the next payday).

Check Figure
Net Loss, $8,409

Instructions

1. Complete the work sheet.
2. Journalize the adjusting entries.

P.O. 3,4,5,6

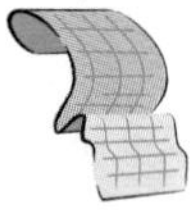

Problem 4-4A The trial balance for Wrye's Putt Putt Golf on June 30 is shown below.

Wrye's Putt Putt Golf
Trial Balance
June 30, 20—

ACCOUNT NAME	DEBIT	CREDIT
Cash	4,532.00	
Supplies	346.00	
Prepaid Insurance	1,284.00	
Equipment	23,687.00	
Accumulated Depreciation, Equipment		1,278.00
Repair Equipment	6,289.00	
Accumulated Depreciation, Repair Equipment		1,485.00
Accounts Payable		960.00
T. Wrye, Capital		23,010.00
T. Wrye, Drawing	1,565.00	
Golf Fees Income		12,387.00
Concessions Income		2,863.00
Wages Expense	2,163.00	
Rent Expense	1,350.00	
Utilities Expense	357.00	
Repair Expense	271.00	
Miscellaneous Expense	139.00	
	41,983.00	41,983.00

Data for month-end adjustments are as follows:

a. Supplies inventory (left or unused), $208 (calculate the expired or used-up supplies).
b. Expired or used-up insurance, $350.
c. Depreciation expense on Equipment, $800 (remember to credit the accumulated depreciation account for equipment, not Equipment).
d. Depreciation expense on Repair Equipment, $1,240 (remember to credit the accumulated depreciation account for repair equipment, not Repair Equipment).
e. Wages accrued or earned since the last payday, $385 (owed and to be paid on the next payday).

Check Figure
Net Income, $8,057

Instructions

1. Complete the work sheet for the month.

2. Prepare an income statement, a statement of owner's equity, and a balance sheet. Assume that no additional investments were made during June.
3. Journalize the adjusting entries.

Instructions for General Ledger Software

1. Journalize the adjusting entries in the general journal. (No work sheet is required.)
2. Post the adjusting entries.
3. Print an income statement, a statement of owner's equity, and a balance sheet. Assume that no additional investments were made during the month.

PROBLEM SET B

For additional help, see the demonstration problem at the beginning of each chapter in your Working Papers.

P.O. 3

Problem 4-1B The trial balance of the Marshall Insurance Agency as of September 30, after the firm has completed its first month of operations, follows:

Marshall Insurance Agency
Trial Balance
September 30, 20—

ACCOUNT NAME	DEBIT *A + Draw. + E*	CREDIT *Accum. Depr. + L + C + R*
Cash	3537 00	
Accounts Receivable	1228 00	
Prepaid Insurance	675 00	
Supplies	387 00	
Office Equipment	5246 00	
Accounts Payable		1267 00
N. Marshall, Capital		9628 00
N. Marshall, Drawing	1100 00	
Commissions Earned		2843 00
Rent Expense	785 00	
Travel Expense	488 00	
Utilities Expense	227 00	
Miscellaneous Expense	65 00	
	13738 00	13738 00

Check Figure
Net Income, $298

Instructions

1. Record the amounts in the Trial Balance columns of the work sheet and record the owner's name in the Capital and Drawing accounts.
2. Complete the work sheet by making the following adjustments and lettering each adjustment:
   a. Expired or used-up insurance, $100.
   b. Supplies inventory (left or unused), $107—calculate the amount of supplies used up.

c. Depreciation expense on office equipment, $600—remember to credit the accumulated depreciation account for office equipment, not Office Equipment.

P.O. 4,5

Problem 4-2B The completed work sheet for Clark Design for the month of March is in your Working Papers.

Check Figure
Total Assets, $20,458

Instructions

1. Prepare an income statement.
2. Prepare a statement of owner's equity. Assume no additional investments were made in March.
3. Prepare a balance sheet.
4. Journalize the adjusting entries.

P.O. 3,5

Problem 4-3B The trial balance of Quick Cleaners for the month ended September 30 is presented below.

Quick Cleaners
Trial Balance
September 30, 20—

ACCOUNT NAME	DEBIT	CREDIT
Cash	2,489.00	
Supplies	752.00	
Prepaid Insurance	1,236.00	
Equipment	22,752.00	
Accumulated Depreciation, Equipment		14,357.00
Accounts Payable		2,647.00
D. Stevenson, Capital		28,169.00
D. Stevenson, Drawing	20,359.00	
Income from Services		40,850.00
Wages Expense	24,983.00	
Rent Expense	10,673.00	
Utilities Expense	1,154.00	
Telephone Expense	1,244.00	
Miscellaneous Expense	381.00	
	86,023.00	86,023.00

Data for the adjustments are as follows:

a. Supplies inventory (left or unused), $345 (calculate the expired or used-up supplies).
b. Expired or used-up insurance, $895.
c. Depreciation expense on equipment, $3,200 (remember to credit the accumulated depreciation account for equipment, not Equipment).
d. Wages accrued or earned since the last payday, $595 (owed and to be paid on the next payday).

Check Figure
Net Loss, $2,682

Instructions

1. Complete the work sheet.
2. Journalize the adjusting entries.

P.O. 3,4,5,6

Problem 4-4B The trial balance for Scott's Game Town on July 31 is shown below.

Scott's Game Town
Trial Balance
July 31, 20—

ACCOUNT NAME	DEBIT	CREDIT
Cash	3,621.00	
Supplies	257.00	
Prepaid Insurance	1,295.00	
Equipment	28,642.00	
Accumulated Depreciation, Equipment		2,387.00
Repair Equipment	1,865.00	
Accumulated Depreciation, Repair Equipment		780.00
Accounts Payable		842.00
T. Scott, Capital		23,971.00
T. Scott, Drawing	1,000.00	
Golf Fees Income		8,954.00
Concessions Income		2,752.00
Wages Expense	1,268.00	
Rent Expense	980.00	
Utilities Expense	246.00	
Repair Expense	380.00	
Miscellaneous Expense	132.00	
	39,686.00	39,686.00

Data for month-end adjustments are as follows:

a. Supplies inventory (left or unused), $136 (calculate the expired or used-up supplies).
b. Expired or used-up insurance, $245.
c. Depreciation expense on equipment, $650 (remember to credit the accumulated depreciation account for equipment, not Equipment).
d. Depreciation expense on repair equipment, $450 (remember to credit the accumulated depreciation account for repair equipment, not Repair Equipment).
e. Wages accrued or earned since the last payday, $315 (owed and to be paid on the next payday).

Check Figure
Net Income, $6,919

Instructions

1. Complete the work sheet for the month.
2. Prepare an income statement, a statement of owner's equity, and a balance sheet. Assume that no additional investments were made during July.
3. Journalize the adjusting entries.

Instructions for General Ledger Software

1. Journalize the adjusting entries in the general journal. (No work sheet is required.)
2. Post the adjusting entries.
3. Print an income statement, a statement of owner's equity, and a balance sheet. Assume no additional investments were made during the month.

Continuous General Ledger Problem: Adjustments

Adjustment information for Like New is listed below.

Adjustment information:

a. Wages accrued or earned since the last payday, $42.50 (owed and to be paid on the next payday).
b. Depreciation expense on office furniture, $1,100—remember to credit the accumulated depreciation account for office furniture, not Office Furniture.
c. Depreciation expense on office equipment, $890—remember to credit the accumulated depreciation account for office equipment, not Office Equipment.
d. Depreciation expense on van, $1,100—remember to credit the accumulated depreciation account for van, not Van.
e. Depreciation expense on building, $3,500—remember to credit the accumulated depreciation account for building, not Building.
f. Expired or used-up insurance, $96.08.
g. Supplies inventory (left or unused), $1,336—calculate the amount of the expired or used-up supplies.

Instructions

1. Launch the accounting software and open the file you saved as Likenew.
2. Journalize and post the adjusting entries.
3. Print an income statement, statement of owner's equity, and balance sheet.
4. Print the general journal (if you can filter the entries, print only the adjusting entries).
5. Print the general ledger (if you can filter the entries, print only the accounts affected by the adjusting entries).
6. Save the file as Likenew2.

Note: The Continuous General Ledger Problem can be worked with Houghton Mifflin Windows General Ledger Package, Peachtree Release 5.01, QuickBooks 6.0, or other general ledger software packages.

APPENDIX

A Methods of Depreciation

Performance Objectives

After you have completed this appendix, you will be able to do the following:

1. Prepare a schedule of depreciation using the straight-line method.
2. Prepare a schedule of depreciation using the sum-of-the-years'-digits method.
3. Prepare a schedule of depreciation using the double-declining-balance method.
4. Prepare a schedule of depreciation for five-year property under the Modified Accelerated Cost Recovery System.

Three methods of depreciation will be illustrated using the example of a delivery truck. Assume that the truck was bought at the beginning of Year 1 and at a cost of $12,000. The truck is estimated to have a useful life of five years and a trade-in value of $3,000 at the end of the five-year period. The three methods to be described are straight-line, sum-of-the-years'-digits, and double-declining-balance.

STRAIGHT-LINE METHOD

Objective 1

Prepare a schedule of depreciation using the straight-line method.

We showed this method in Chapter 4, providing for an equal amount of depreciation each year.

$$\text{Yearly depreciation} = \frac{\text{Cost of asset} - \text{Trade-in value}}{\text{Years of life}} = \frac{\$12{,}000 - \$3{,}000}{5 \text{ years}}$$

$$= \frac{\$9{,}000}{5 \text{ years}} = \$1{,}800 \text{ per year}$$

Year	Depreciation for the Year	Accumulated Depreciation	Book Value (Cost Less Accumulated Depreciation)
1	$9,000 ÷ 5 years = $1,800	$1,800	$12,000 − $1,800 = $10,200
2	9,000 ÷ 5 years = 1,800	$1,800 + $1,800 = 3,600	12,000 − 3,600 = 8,400
3	9,000 ÷ 5 years = 1,800	3,600 + 1,800 = 5,400	12,000 − 5,400 = 6,600
4	9,000 ÷ 5 years = 1,800	5,400 + 1,800 = 7,200	12,000 − 7,200 = 4,800
5	9,000 ÷ 5 years = 1,800	7,200 + 1,800 = 9,000	12,000 − 9,000 = 3,000
	$9,000		

SUM-OF-THE-YEARS'-DIGITS METHOD

Objective 2

Prepare a schedule of depreciation using the sum-of-the-years'-digits method.

Add the number of years and use the sum as the denominator of the fractions. As numerators in the fractions, use the years in reverse order.

$$1 + 2 + 3 + 4 + 5 = 15$$

$$\frac{5}{15} + \frac{4}{15} + \frac{3}{15} + \frac{2}{15} + \frac{1}{15} = \frac{15}{15}$$

Year	Depreciation for the Year	Accumulated Depreciation	Book Value (Cost Less Accumulated Depreciation)
1	$9,000 × 5/15 = $3,000	$3,000	$12,000 − $3,000 = $9,000
2	9,000 × 4/15 = 2,400	$3,000 + $2,400 = 5,400	12,000 − 5,400 = 6,600
3	9,000 × 3/15 = 1,800	5,400 + 1,800 = 7,200	12,000 − 7,200 = 4,800
4	9,000 × 2/15 = 1,200	7,200 + 1,200 = 8,400	12,000 − 8,400 = 3,600
5	9,000 × 1/15 = 600	8,400 + 600 = 9,000	12,000 − 9,000 = 3,000
15	15/15 $9,000		

DOUBLE-DECLINING-BALANCE METHOD

Objective 3

Prepare a schedule of depreciation using the double-declining-balance method.

The term *double* refers to double the straight-line rate. With an estimated useful life of five years, the straight-line rate is ⅕, or .2. Twice, or double, the straight-line rate is ⅖ (⅕ × 2) or .4. **The trade-in value is not taken into account until the end of the schedule.** In calculating declining balance method depreciation, double the straight-line rate is multiplied by the book value without subtracting trade-in value. This differs from the straight-line and sum-of-the-years'-digits methods where the trade-in value is subtracted from the original cost to calculate periodic depreciation expense. Multiply *book value* at beginning of year by twice the straight-line rate. Notice that an asset cannot be depreciated below its trade-in value. In year 3, only the amount of depreciation expense—$1,320 or $4,320–3,000—necessary to reduce the asset to its trade-in value is allowed. No further depreciation expense is permitted in years 4 and 5.

Year	Depreciation for the Year	Accumulated Depreciation	Book Value (Cost Less Accumulated Depreciation)
1	$12,000 × .4 = $4,800	$4,800	$12,000 − $4,800 = $7,200
2	$7,200 × .4 = 2,880	$4,800 + $2,880 = 7,680	12,000 − 7,680 = 4,320
3	$4,320 − $3,000 = 1,320	7,680 + 1,320 = 9,000	12,000 − 9,000 = 3,000
4	0	9,000	12,000 − 9,000 = 3,000
5	0	9,000	12,000 − 9,000 = 3,000
	$9,000		

ASSETS PLACED IN SERVICE AFTER DECEMBER 31, 1986

Objective 4

Prepare a schedule of depreciation for five-year property under the Modified Accelerated Cost Recovery System.

As long as the method is used consistently, companies may choose any of the three methods for their own financial statements. However, for tax purposes, the Internal Revenue Service stipulates certain rates for specific classes of assets. The rates also vary depending on the time the assets were placed in service. We will show the most recent rates.

Most businesses use the Modified Accelerated Cost Recovery System (MACRS) as defined by the Internal Revenue Service for federal income tax purposes. The Accelerated Cost Recovery System (ACRS) first took effect in 1981 and was later modified for assets placed in service after December 31, 1986, by the Tax Reform Act of 1986. The term *recovery* is used because MACRS is a means of recovering or deducting the cost of an asset. According to MACRS, property is divided into nine classes, as follows:

3-year property—certain horses and tractor units for use over the road

5-year property—autos, trucks, computers, typewriters, and copiers

7-year property—office furniture and fixtures and any property that does not have a class life and that is not, by law, in any other class

10-year property—vessels, barges, tugs, and similar water transportation equipment

15-year property—wharves, roads, fences, and any municipal wastewater treatment plants

20-year property—certain farm buildings and municipal sewers

27.5-year residential rental property—rental houses and apartments

31.5-year real property—office buildings and warehouses

39-year property—nonresidential real property placed in service after May 13, 1993

Under MACRS, trade-in value is ignored.

Our light truck qualifies as five-year property. The approximate rates (rounded for the sake of this illustration) are: first year, 20 percent; second year, 32 percent; third year, 19 percent; fourth year, 15 percent; fifth year, 14 percent. Congress may change the lives of property and/or the rates at which property is taxed.

Year	Depreciation for the Year	Accumulated Depreciation	Book Value (Cost Less Accumulated Depreciation)
1	$12,000 × .20 = $2,400	$ 2,400	$12,000 − $ 2,400 = $9,600
2	12,000 × .32 = 3,840	$ 2,400 + $3,840 = 6,240	12,000 − 6,240 = 5,760
3	12,000 × .19 = 2,280	6,240 + 2,280 = 8,520	12,000 − 8,520 = 3,480
4	12,000 × .15 = 1,800	8,520 + 1,800 = 10,320	12,000 − 10,320 = 1,680
5	12,000 × .14 = 1,680	10,320 + 1,680 = 12,000	12,000 − 12,000 = 0

For federal income tax purposes, a company must use either the current MACRS for assets placed in service after December 31, 1986, or an alternative straight-line depreciation method, which differs slightly from the method presented in the text.

PROBLEMS

P.O. 1

Check Figure

Year 1 depreciation, $3,000

Problem A-1 A delivery van was bought for $15,000. The estimated life of the van is four years. The trade-in value at the end of four years is estimated to be $3,000. Prepare a depreciation schedule for the four-year period using the straight-line method.

P.O. 2

Check Figure

Year 2 depreciation, $3,600

Problem A-2 Using the information in Problem A-1, prepare a depreciation schedule using the sum-of-the-years'-digits method.

P.O. 4

Check Figure

Year 3 depreciation, $2,850

Problem A-3 Assume the van was purchased after January 1, 1991. Using the information in Problem A-1, prepare a schedule of depreciation under MACRS.

5 Closing Entries and the Post-Closing Trial Balance

WINDOWS ON THE WORLD WIDE WEB

Why would a company's accounting staff need to close or zero out the balance of revenues and expenses at the end of each year? Why not just keep a running total the entire time the firm is in business? How does this help the company prepare for a new accounting period? What advantage does annual reporting give investors? By the end of the 1990s, the clothing manufacturer, Tommy Hilfiger Corporation, reported net revenues of more than $800 million. What figure represents the year-end revenues for the present year? How would you record the financial data for this company if you were in charge of accounting for Tommy Hilfiger Corporation? What would be the difference between Tommy Hilfiger Corporation's trial balance and post-closing trial balance? Look up the financial highlights of Tommy Hilfiger Corporation at **http://www.tommypr.com/corporate/index5.htm**.

Performance Objectives

After you have completed this chapter, you will be able to do the following:

1. List the steps in the accounting cycle.
2. Journalize and post closing entries for a service enterprise.
3. Prepare a post-closing trial balance.
4. Define the following methods of accounting: accrual basis, cash-receipts-and-disbursements basis, modified cash basis.
5. Prepare interim statements.

Objective 1

List the steps in the accounting cycle.

Let's review the steps in the accounting cycle for an entire fiscal period. Remember that a fiscal period is generally twelve consecutive months, but can also consist of other time frames like three months or six months.

1. **Analyze source documents and record business transactions in a journal.**
2. **Post journal entries to the accounts in the ledger.**
3. **Prepare a trial balance.**

4. **Gather adjustment data and record the adjusting entries on a work sheet.**
5. **Complete the work sheet.**
6. **Prepare financial statements from the data on the work sheet.**
7. **Journalize and post the adjusting entries from the data on the work sheet.**
8. **Journalize and post the closing entries.**
9. **Prepare a post-closing trial balance.**

This chapter explains the procedure for completing the final steps: closing entries and the post-closing trial balance.

Adjusting entries, closing entries, and a post-closing trial balance are prepared at the end of a fiscal period. The number of months in a fiscal period varies. To introduce you to these final steps in the accounting cycle, we assume here that the fiscal period for Cruz Auto Detail is one month. We make this assumption so that we can thoroughly cover the material and give you a chance to practice its application. The entire accounting cycle is outlined in Figure 1.

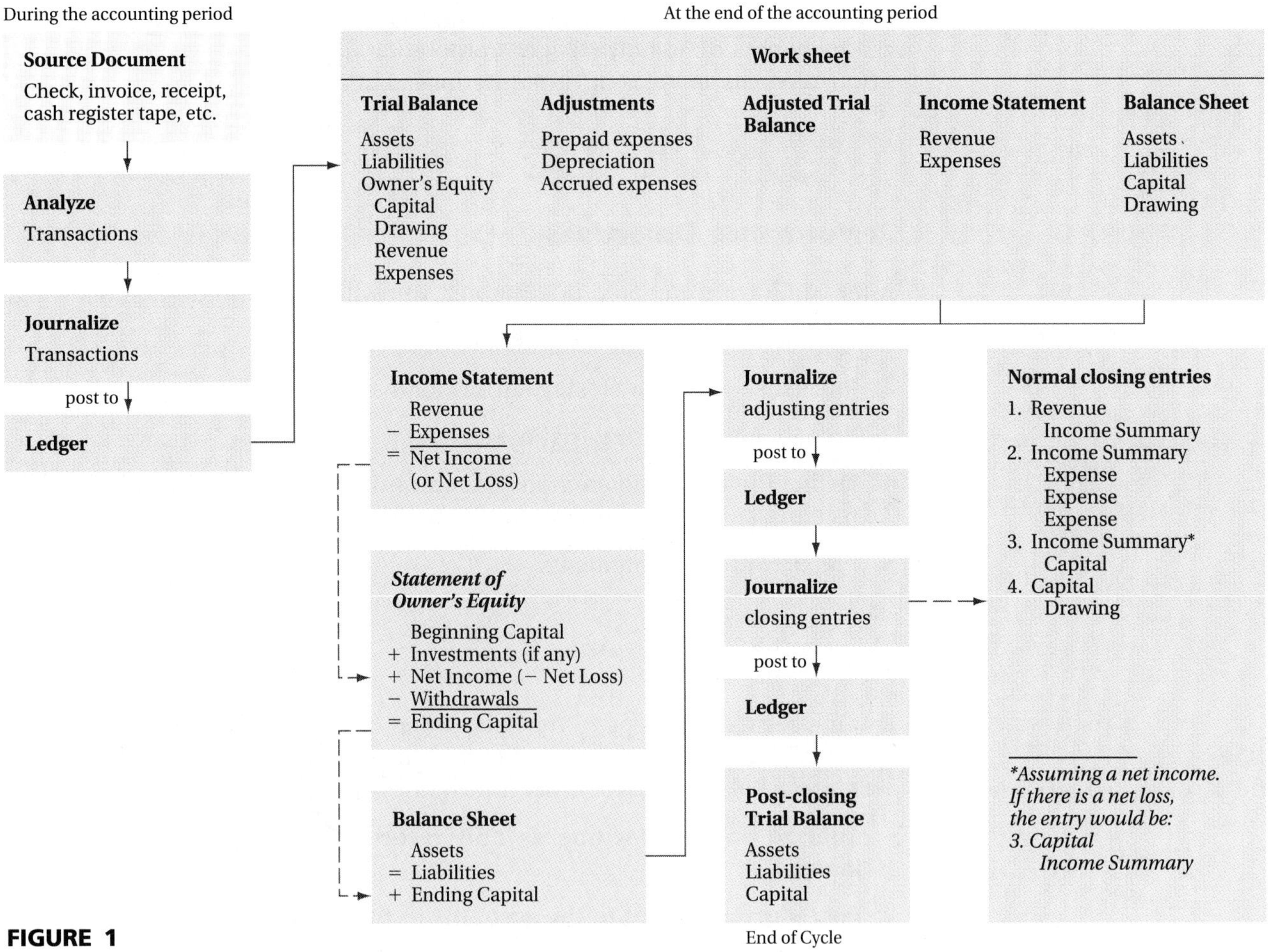
During the accounting period
At the end of the accounting period
Source Document
Check, invoice, receipt, cash register tape, etc.
Analyze
Transactions
Journalize
Transactions
post to
Ledger
Work sheet
Trial Balance
Assets
Liabilities
Owner's Equity
Capital
Drawing
Revenue
Expenses
Adjustments
Prepaid expenses
Depreciation
Accrued expenses
Adjusted Trial Balance
Income Statement
Revenue
Expenses
Balance Sheet
Assets
Liabilities
Capital
Drawing
Income Statement
Revenue
− Expenses
= Net Income
(or Net Loss)
Statement of Owner's Equity
Beginning Capital
+ Investments (if any)
+ Net Income (− Net Loss)
− Withdrawals
= Ending Capital
Balance Sheet
Assets
= Liabilities
+ Ending Capital
Journalize
adjusting entries
post to
Ledger
Journalize
closing entries
post to
Ledger
Post-closing Trial Balance
Assets
Liabilities
Capital
End of Cycle
Normal closing entries
1. Revenue
Income Summary
2. Income Summary
Expense
Expense
Expense
3. Income Summary*
Capital
4. Capital
Drawing
*Assuming a net income. If there is a net loss, the entry would be:
3. Capital
Income Summary

FIGURE 1

CLOSING ENTRIES

To help you understand the reason for the closing entries, let's repeat the fundamental accounting equation:

Assets = Liabilities + Owner's Equity + Revenue − Expenses

We know that the income statement, as stated in the third line of its heading, covers a period of time. The income statement consists of revenue minus expenses for this period of time only. So, when the next fiscal period begins, we should start with zero balances. We start all over again each period.

This year's revenue and expenses...
BEFORE CLOSING
AFTER CLOSING

Closing entries empty or zero out temporary owner's equity accounts and prepare the accounts for the new accounting period—emptying out folders for one year so they can be filled with the new year's revenue and expenses.

Purpose of Closing Entries

This brings us to the *purpose* of the **closing entries**, which is to close (or clear) the temporary-equity or nominal accounts (revenue, expense, and drawing accounts). We do this because their balances apply to only one fiscal period. Closing entries are made after the last adjusting entry. With the coming of the next fiscal period, we want to start from zero, recording revenue and expenses for the new fiscal period. The closing entries also update the owner's Capital account.

Accountants also refer to closing the accounts as clearing the accounts. For income tax purposes, this is certainly understandable. No one wants to pay income tax more than once on the same income, and the Internal Revenue Service doesn't allow you to count an expense more than once. So now we have this:

Assets = Liabilities + Owner's Equity (Capital) + ~~Revenue~~ (closed) − ~~Expenses~~ (closed)

Remember!

The matching principle is why we close revenue, expense, and drawing accounts.

The assets, the liabilities, and the owner's Capital account remain open. The balance sheet gives the present balances of these accounts. The accountant carries the asset, liability, and Capital account balances over to the next fiscal period.

Procedure for Closing

Objective 2

Journalize and post closing entries for a service enterprise.

The procedure for closing is simply to balance off the account; in other words, to make the balance *equal to zero.* This meets our objective, which is to start from zero in the next fiscal period. Let's illustrate this first with T accounts. Suppose an account to be closed has a debit balance of $960; then, to make the balance equal to zero, we *credit* the account for $960.

Debit		Credit	
Balance	960	Closing	960

At the end of a fiscal period, closing entries allow a business to start a new income statement period with a clean slate. Revenue and expense accounts are closed.

MEADOWLANDS
TOYOTA
$3500 REBATES
PLUS
GIANT DISCOUNTS
NOW

Now suppose an account to be closed has a credit balance of $1,200; then, to make the balance equal to zero, we *debit* the account for $1,200.

Debit		Credit	
Closing	1,200	Balance	1,200

Remember, every entry must have both a debit and a credit. So, to record the other half of the closing entry, we bring into existence the **Income Summary**. The Income Summary account does not have plus and minus signs, just debit and credit.

There are four steps in the closing procedure:

1. **Close the revenue accounts into Income Summary.**
2. **Close the expense accounts into Income Summary.**
3. **Close the Income Summary account into the Capital account, transferring the net income or loss to the Capital account.**
4. **Close the Drawing account into the Capital account.**

To illustrate, we return to Cruz Auto Detail. For the purpose of the illustration, assume that Cruz Auto Detail's fiscal period consists of one month. We have the following T account balances in the revenue and expense accounts after the adjustments have been posted.

FYI

Making closing entries using accounting software is frequently done instantaneously. The operator selects the instruction to close and the revenue, expense, and Drawing accounts are automatically closed. The net income (or loss) is sent to the Capital account. The bad news is that any errors made prior to closing are included. Always make a backup copy of your file prior to closing in case you have made a mistake.

Income from Services

	−	+	
		Balance	7,270

Utilities Expense

	+	−	
Balance	160		

Wages Expense

	+	−	
Balance	1,690		

Supplies Expense

	+	−	
Balance	540		

Rent Expense

	+	−	
Balance	900		

Insurance Expense

	+	−	
Balance	30		

Advertising Expense

	+	−	
Balance	400		

Depreciation Expense, Equipment

	+	−	
Balance	520		

Step 1 Close the revenue account or accounts into Income Summary. In order to make the balance of Income from Services equal to zero, we *balance it off,* or debit it, in the amount of $7,270. Because we need an offsetting credit, we credit Income Summary for the same amount. Notice that there are no signs in Income Summary, only Debit and Credit like the other accounts.

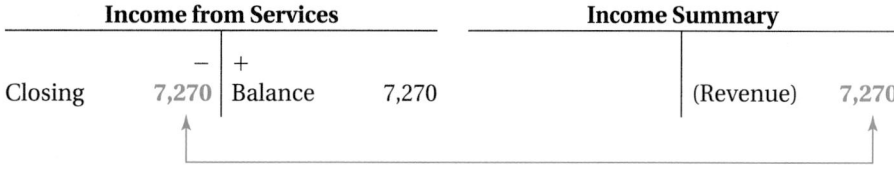

Income from Services

	−	+	
Closing	7,270	Balance	7,270

Income Summary

		(Revenue)	7,270

The balance of Income from Services is transferred to Income Summary.

Step 2 Close the expense accounts into Income Summary. To make the balances of the expense accounts equal to zero, we need to balance them off, or credit them. Again the T accounts are useful for formulating this journal entry.

Wages Expense

	+	−	
Balance	1,690	Closing	1,690

Rent Expense

	+	−	
Balance	900	Closing	900

Advertising Expense

	+	−	
Balance	400	Closing	400

Utilities Expense

	+	−	
Balance	160	Closing	160

Supplies Expense

	+	−	
Balance	540	Closing	540

Insurance Expense

	+	−	
Balance	30	Closing	30

Depreciation Expense, Equipment

	+	−	
Balance	520	Closing	520

Income Summary

(Expenses)	4,240	(Revenue)	7,270

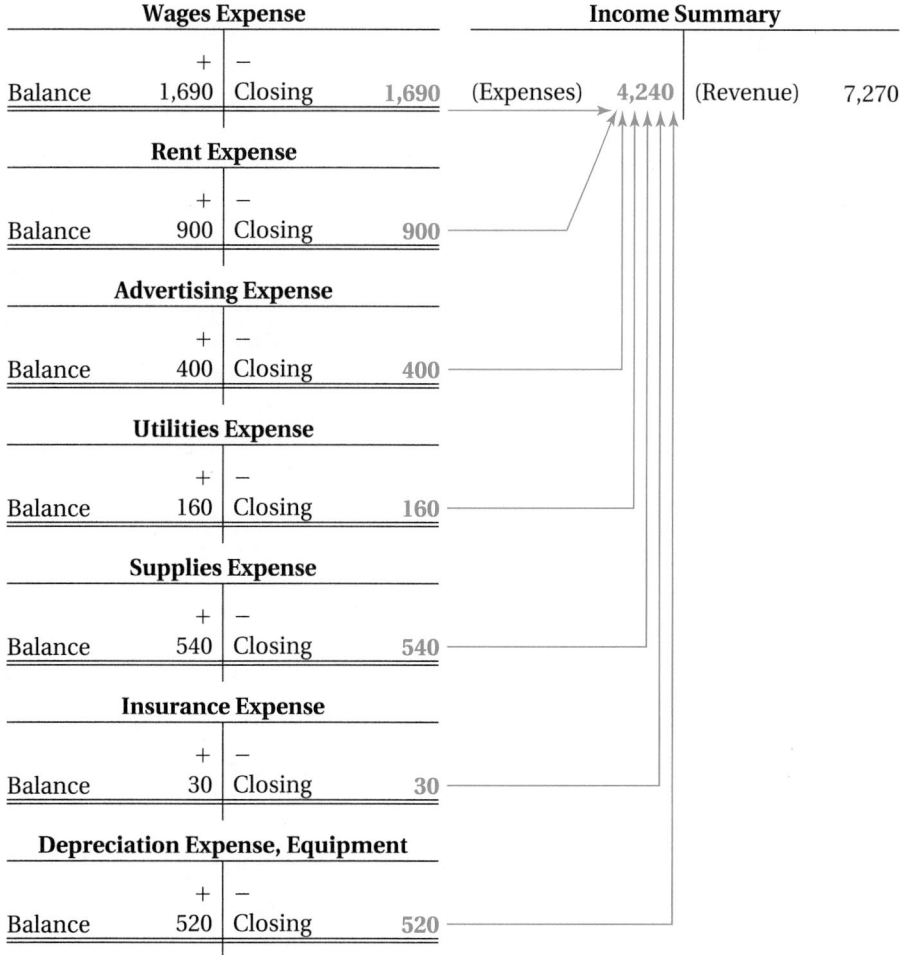

Step 3 Recall that we created Income Summary so that we could have a debit and a credit in each closing entry. Now that it has done its job, we close it out. We use the same procedure as before, in that we make the balance equal to zero, or balance off the account. We transfer, or close, the balance

of the Income Summary account into the Capital account, as shown in the T accounts and in Figure 2.

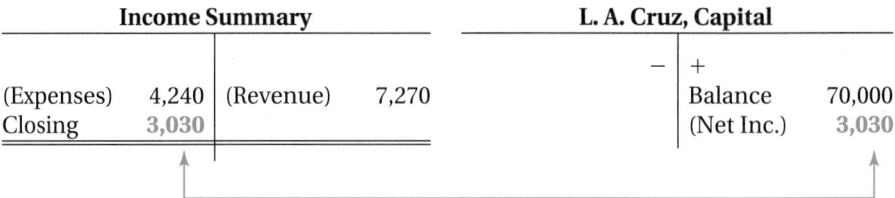

Income Summary			
(Expenses)	4,240	(Revenue)	7,270
Closing	3,030		

L. A. Cruz, Capital			
−		+	
		Balance	70,000
		(Net Inc.)	3,030

Income Summary is always closed into the Capital account by the amount of the net income (Revenue minus Expenses) or the net loss. Comparing net income or net loss on the work sheet with the closing entry for Income Summary can serve as a check point or verification for you.

FIGURE 2

GENERAL JOURNAL PAGE 4

	DATE	DESCRIPTION	POST. REF.	DEBIT	CREDIT
		Closing Entries			
Step 1	30	Income from Services		7,270.00	
		Income Summary			7,270.00
	30	Income Summary		4,240.00	
		Wages Expense			1,690.00
		Rent Expense			900.00
Step 2		Advertising Expense			400.00
		Utilities Expense			160.00
		Supplies Expense			540.00
		Insurance Expense			30.00
		Depreciation Expense,			
		Equipment			520.00
	30	Income Summary		3,030.00	
		L. A. Cruz, Capital			3,030.00

Net income is added (credited) to the Capital account because, as shown in the statement of owner's equity, net income is treated as an addition. Net loss, on the other hand, is subtracted from (debited) to the Capital account, because net loss is treated as a deduction in the statement of owner's equity. Here's how to close Income Summary for J. Doe Company (net loss of $200):

Income Summary			
(Expenses)	900	(Revenue)	700
		Closing	200

J. Doe, Capital			
	−	+	
(Net Loss)	200	Balance	30,000

The entry to close Income Summary into Doe's Capital account would look like the following.

GENERAL JOURNAL PAGE 3

DATE		DESCRIPTION	POST. REF.	DEBIT	CREDIT
		Closing Entries			
	31	J. Doe, Capital		200 00	
		Income Summary			200 00

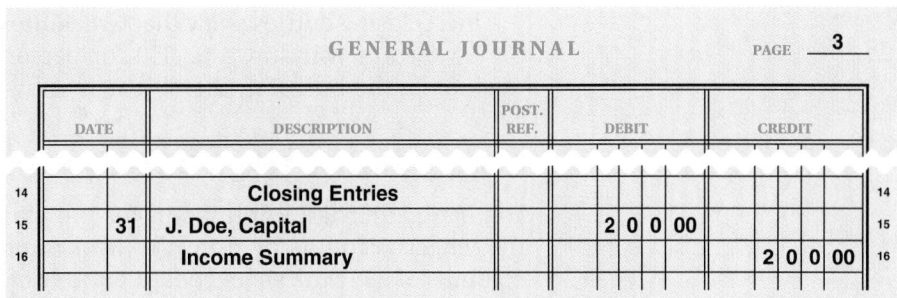

Step 4 Let's return to the example of Cruz Auto Detail. The Drawing account applies to only one fiscal period, and so it too must be closed. Drawing is not an expense because it did not help the business generate revenue. And because Drawing is not an expense, it cannot affect net income or net loss. It appears in the statement of owner's equity as a deduction from the Capital account, so it is closed directly into the Capital account. We balance off the Drawing account, or make the balance of it equal to zero. The balance of Drawing is transferred to the Capital account.

L. A. Cruz, Drawing

+	−
Balance 3,000	Closing 3,000

L. A. Cruz, Capital

−	+
3,000	Balance 70,000
	(Net Inc.) 3,030

The journal entries in the closing procedure are shown in Figure 3.

FIGURE 3

GENERAL JOURNAL PAGE 4

DATE		DESCRIPTION	POST. REF.	DEBIT	CREDIT
Step 1		**Closing Entries**			
	30	Income from Services		7,270 00	
		Income Summary			7,270 00
Step 2	30	Income Summary		4,240 00	
		Wages Expense			1,690 00
		Rent Expense			900 00
		Advertising Expense			400 00
		Utilities Expense			160 00
		Supplies Expense			540 00
		Insurance Expense			30 00
		Depreciation Expense,			
		Equipment			520 00
Step 3	30	Income Summary		3,030 00	
		L. A. Cruz, Capital			3,030 00
Step 4	30	L. A. Cruz, Capital		3,000 00	
		L. A. Cruz, Drawing			3,000 00

FYI

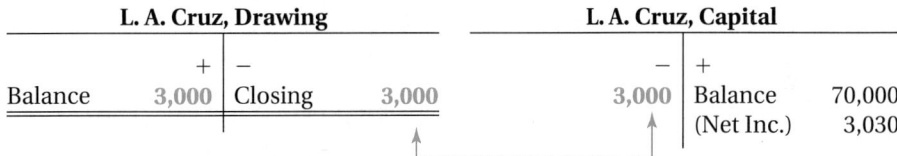

As a memory tool for the sequence of steps in the closing procedure, use the letters of the closing elements, **REID: R**evenue, **E**xpenses, **I**ncome Summary, **D**rawing.

These closing entries show that Cruz Auto Detail has net income of $3,030, the owner has withdrawn $3,000 for personal expenses, and $30 has been retained in the business, thereby increasing capital.

Closing Entries Taken Directly from the Work Sheet

You can gather the information for the closing entries either directly from the ledger accounts or from the work sheet. Since the Income Statement columns of the work sheet consist entirely of revenues and expenses, you can pick up the figures for three of the four closing entries from these columns. Figure 4 shows a partial work sheet for Cruz Auto Detail.

		TRIAL BALANCE		ADJUSTMENTS		INCOME STATEMENT	
	ACCOUNT NAME	DEBIT	CREDIT	DEBIT	CREDIT	DEBIT	CREDIT
1	Cash	23,250.00					
2	Accounts Receivable	200.00					
3	Supplies	800.00			(a) 540.00		
4	Prepaid Insurance	360.00			(b) 30.00		
5	Equipment	51,500.00					
6	Accounts Payable		4,700.00				
7	L. A. Cruz, Capital		70,000.00				
8	L. A. Cruz, Drawing	3,000.00					
9	Income from Services		7,270.00				7,270.00
10	Wages Expense	1,400.00		(d) 290.00		1,690.00	
11	Rent Expense	900.00				900.00	
12	Advertising Expense	400.00				400.00	
13	Utilities Expense	160.00				160.00	
14		81,970.00	81,970.00				
15	Supplies Expense			(a) 540.00		540.00	
16	Insurance Expense			(b) 30.00		30.00	
17	Depreciation Expense,						
18	Equipment			(c) 520.00		520.00	
19	Accumulated Dep.,						
20	Equipment				(c) 520.00		
21	Wages Payable				(d) 290.00		
22				1,380.00	1,380.00	4,240.00	7,270.00
23	Net Income					3,030.00	
24						7,270.00	7,270.00
25							
26							

FIGURE 4

You may plan the closing entries by balancing off all the figures that appear in the Income Statement columns. For example, in the Income Statement Credit column, there is a credit for $7,270 (Income from Services), so we debit that account for $7,270 and credit Income Summary for $7,270.

There are debits for $1,690, $900, $400, $160, $540, $30, and $520 (expense accounts). So now we *credit* these accounts for the same amounts, and we debit Income Summary for their total ($4,240).

Next, we close Income Summary into Capital, using the net income figure already shown on the work sheet in Figure 4.

We do, of course, have to get the last closing entry from the Balance Sheet columns to close Drawing.

Remember!

The temporary-equity accounts (revenue, expenses, Drawing, and Income Summary) are closed out because they apply to only one fiscal period.

Incidentally, accountants call the accounts that are to be closed (such as revenue, expenses, Income Summary, and Drawing) **nominal** or **temporary-equity accounts**. These accounts are *temporary* in that their balances apply to only one fiscal period. The *equity* aspect pertains because these accounts all come under the umbrella of owner's equity.

On the other hand, accountants call the accounts that remain open (such as assets, liabilities, and Capital) **real** or **permanent accounts**. These accounts have balances that will be carried over to the next fiscal period. They are *permanent* because as long as the company exists, there will be balances in these accounts.

Posting the Closing Entries

In the Item column of the ledger account, we write the word *Closing*. To show that the balance of an account is zero, we draw a line through both the Debit Balance and the Credit Balance columns.

After we have posted the closing entries, the Capital, Drawing, Income Summary, revenue, and expense accounts of Cruz Auto Detail appear as follows:

GENERAL LEDGER

ACCOUNT L. A. Cruz, Capital ACCOUNT NO. 311

DATE		ITEM	POST. REF.	DEBIT	CREDIT	BALANCE DEBIT	BALANCE CREDIT
20–							
June	1		1		70,000 00		70,000 00
	30		4		3,030 00		73,030 00
	30		4	3,000 00			70,030 00

ACCOUNT L. A. Cruz, Drawing ACCOUNT NO. 312

DATE		ITEM	POST. REF.	DEBIT	CREDIT	BALANCE DEBIT	BALANCE CREDIT
20–							
June	30		3	3,000 00		3,000 00	
	30	Closing	4		3,000 00	—	—

ACCOUNT Income Summary ACCOUNT NO. 313

DATE		ITEM	POST. REF.	DEBIT	CREDIT	BALANCE DEBIT	BALANCE CREDIT
20–							
June	30		4		7,270 00		7,270 00
	30		4	4,240 00			3,030 00
	30	Closing	4	3,030 00		—	—

ACCOUNT **Income from Services** ACCOUNT NO. **411**

DATE		ITEM	POST. REF.	DEBIT	CREDIT	BALANCE DEBIT	BALANCE CREDIT
20–							
June	7		1		3,520 00		3,520 00
	15		2		1,050 00		4,570 00
	30		3		2,700 00		7,270 00
	30	Closing	4	7,270 00		—	—

ACCOUNT **Wages Expense** ACCOUNT NO. **511**

DATE		ITEM	POST. REF.	DEBIT	CREDIT	BALANCE DEBIT	BALANCE CREDIT
20–							
June	24		2	1,400 00		1,400 00	
	30	Adj.	4	290 00		1,690 00	
	30	Closing	4		1,690 00	—	—

ACCOUNT **Rent Expense** ACCOUNT NO. **512**

DATE		ITEM	POST. REF.	DEBIT	CREDIT	BALANCE DEBIT	BALANCE CREDIT
20–							
June	8		1	900 00		900 00	
	30	Closing	4		900 00	—	—

ACCOUNT **Advertising Expense** ACCOUNT NO. **513**

DATE		ITEM	POST. REF.	DEBIT	CREDIT	BALANCE DEBIT	BALANCE CREDIT
20–							
June	14		2	400 00		400 00	
	30	Closing	4		400 00	—	—

ACCOUNT **Utilities Expense** ACCOUNT NO. **514**

DATE		ITEM	POST. REF.	DEBIT	CREDIT	BALANCE DEBIT	BALANCE CREDIT
20–							
June	18		2	160 00		160 00	
	30	Closing	4		160 00	—	—

Office supplies consist of a wide variety of items that are used up and reordered frequently in the course of doing business. W. B. Mason delivers all kinds of office supplies to keep businesses productive.

WHO BUT
W.B.MASON
FOR OFFICE FURNITURE, DESIGN & SUPPLIES
586-3434
W.B.M.

ACCOUNT **Supplies Expense** ACCOUNT NO. **515**

DATE		ITEM	POST. REF.	DEBIT	CREDIT	BALANCE DEBIT	BALANCE CREDIT
20–							
June	30	Adj.	4	540.00		540.00	
	30	Closing	4		540.00	—	—

ACCOUNT **Insurance Expense** ACCOUNT NO. **516**

DATE		ITEM	POST. REF.	DEBIT	CREDIT	BALANCE DEBIT	BALANCE CREDIT
20–							
June	30	Adj.	4	30.00		30.00	
	30	Closing	4		30.00	—	—

ACCOUNT **Depreciation Expense, Equipment** ACCOUNT NO. **517**

DATE		ITEM	POST. REF.	DEBIT	CREDIT	BALANCE DEBIT	BALANCE CREDIT
20–							
June	30	Adj.	4	520.00		520.00	
	30	Closing	4		520.00	—	—

THE POST-CLOSING TRIAL BALANCE

Objective 3

Prepare a post-closing trial balance.

After posting the closing entries and before going on to the next fiscal period, verify the balances of the accounts that remain open. To do so, prepare a **post-closing trial balance**, using the final balance figures from the ledger accounts. The purpose of the post-closing trial balance is to make sure that the debit balances equal the credit balances.

Note that the accounts listed in the post-closing trial balance (assets, liabilities, and Capital) are the *real* or *permanent accounts* (see Figure 5). The accountant carries forward the balances of the permanent accounts from one fiscal period to another.

FIGURE 5

Cruz Auto Detail
Post-Closing Trial Balance
June 30, 20—

ACCOUNT NAME	DEBIT	CREDIT
Cash	23,250.00	
Accounts Receivable	200.00	
Supplies	260.00	
Prepaid Insurance	330.00	
Equipment	51,500.00	
Accumulated Depreciation, Equipment		520.00
Accounts Payable		4,700.00
Wages Payable		290.00
L. A. Cruz, Capital		70,030.00
	75,540.00	75,540.00

Contrast this to the handling of *nominal* or *temporary-equity accounts* (revenue, expenses, Income Summary, and Drawing), which are closed at the end of each fiscal period.

If the total debits and total credits of the post-closing trial balance are not equal, here's a recommended procedure for tracking down the error.

1. Re-add the trial balance columns.
2. Check to see that the figures were correctly transferred from the ledger accounts to the post-closing trial balance.
3. Verify the posting of the adjusting entries and the recording of the new balances.
4. Make sure that the closing entries have been posted and that all revenue, expense, Income Summary, and Drawing accounts have zero balances.

THE ACCRUAL BASIS

Objective 4

Define the following methods of accounting: accrual basis, cash-receipts-and-disbursements basis, modified cash basis.

Up to this time, we have been using the accrual basis of accounting. **When we use the accrual basis, we record revenue when it is earned and expenses when they are incurred.** Revenues are inflows of assets, cash, or accounts receivable that result from selling goods or services. Expenses are outflows of used assets that result from selling goods or services. Revenues are recorded by the seller in the period that the buyer accepts delivery of the goods or services from the seller. Expenses are recorded by the seller in the same period in which the related revenue was recognized by the seller. This concept is called the *matching principle*. Cruz Auto Detail's transactions were recorded on the accrual basis. Let's recall two transactions.

Think different.

Companies using accrual basis accounting, like Apple Computer, Inc. would debit Accounts Payable and credit Cash for this advertising expense. Smaller or professional firms that use a modified cash basis would debit Advertising Expense and credit Cash.

Transaction (i) Received the bill for newspaper advertising, $400. The expense was recorded before it was paid in cash. The expense was matched up with the fiscal period in which it was incurred.

Advertising Expense			
(i)	400		

Accounts Payable			
		(i)	400

Transaction (j) Entered into a contract with Costello Taxi to perform detailing services on a credit basis. Billed Costello Taxi for services performed, $1,050.

Accounts Receivable			
(j)	1,050		

Income from Services			
		(j)	1,050

The revenue was recorded before it was received in cash. It was matched up with the fiscal period in which it was earned. Accountants feel strongly that the accrual basis gives the most realistic picture of the revenue and expense accounts and, hence, the net income. (Net income equals total revenue minus total expenses.)

CASH-RECEIPTS-AND-DISBURSEMENTS BASIS

When the **cash-receipts-and-disbursements basis** is used, all revenue is recorded only when it is received in cash, and all expenses are recorded only when they are paid in cash. *The cash-receipts-and-disbursements basis is not appropriate for most business firms.* This is true because most companies do have some equipment, and the Internal Revenue Service requires that equipment be depreciated over a period of years, resulting in an expense that does not involve cash.

The cash-receipts-and-disbursements basis is used mainly by individuals for their personal tax returns. Here, revenue in the form of salaries or wages, interest, and similar items is reported only when received in cash, and expenses to be included as personal deductions are reported only when paid in cash.

MODIFIED CASH BASIS

Professional enterprises and many small businesses, particularly service firms, use a **modified cash basis**. **Revenue is not recorded by the firm until it receives cash** from the customer. Here we are concerned with situations in which services are performed in one fiscal period, but the cash for these same services is not received until a later fiscal period. Under the modified cash basis, the revenue is recorded in the later period, when the cash is actually received.

Most expenses also are recorded only when they are paid in cash. An expense may be incurred in one fiscal period and paid in a later period.

Under the modified cash basis, the expense is recorded in the later period, when it is actually paid. For example, an employee's earnings for the month of December are paid on January 5. Under this basis, no entry is made for accrued salaries, but on January 5, an entry is made debiting Salary Expense and crediting Cash.

However, **under the modified cash basis, exceptions are made for expenditures on items having an economic life of more than one year and on some prepaid items.** Examples of such expenditures and prepaid items are equipment, supplies, and insurance. Costs of these items must be prorated or spread out over their useful lives, and so adjusting entries are made for depreciation of equipment, supplies used up, and expiration of insurance. As we stated, there is no need to make additional adjusting entries, such as an adjustment for accrued salaries or other accrued adjustments that we will introduce later. The Internal Revenue Service publications refer to the modified cash basis as a hybrid method because it combines some of the characteristics of both the accrual basis and the cash-receipts-and-disbursements basis of accounting.

Remember!

Under the modified cash system, exceptions are made for recording supplies expense, insurance expense, and depreciation expense.

Accrual Basis vs. Modified Cash Basis

As an illustration, we will show selected transactions of another business, so that you can see how these transactions are recorded using both the accrual basis and the modified cash basis. (Assume that the transactions recorded in T accounts on page 161 have first been journalized.) Abbreviated income statements are shown at the top of page 162.

	Accounting Basis	
Transaction	**Accrual**	**Modified Cash**
a. Billed customers for services rendered, $2,600.	Journalized (Revenue is recorded at this point.) Dr. Accounts Receivable Cr. Income from Services	Not journalized (Cash has not been received.)
b. Received bill for advertising from *Milton Daily World,* $220.	Journalized (Expense is recorded at this point.) Dr. Advertising Expense Cr. Accounts Payable	Not journalized (Cash has not been paid.)
c. Bought equipment on account from Stanton Company, $1,940.	Journalized Dr. Equipment Cr. Accounts Payable	Journalized (Cash will be paid later.) Dr. Equipment Cr. Accounts Payable
d. Received $2,000 from charge customers previously billed.	Journalized (Revenue was recorded previously.) Dr. Cash Cr. Accounts Receivable	Journalized (Cash has been received.) (Revenue is recorded at this point.) Dr. Cash Cr. Income from Services

	Accounting Basis	
Transaction	**Accrual**	**Modified Cash**
e. Paid $100 to *Milton Daily World* for advertising previously billed.	Journalized (Expense was recorded previously.) Dr. Accounts Payable Cr. Cash	Journalized (Cash has been paid.) (Expense is recorded at this point.) Dr. Advertising Expense Cr. Cash
f. Paid wages for the period, $1,400.	Journalized (Expense is recorded at this point.) Dr. Wages Expense Cr. Cash	Journalized (Cash has been paid.) (Expense is recorded at this point.) Dr. Wages Expense Cr. Cash
g. Recorded depreciation of equipment for the period, $380.	Journalized (Expense is recorded at this point.) Dr. Depreciation Expense Cr. Accumulated Depreciation	Journalized (Depreciation is an exception.) (Expense is recorded at this point.) Dr. Depreciation Expense Cr. Accumulated Depreciation

These journal entries are posted in the following T accounts.

Accrual Basis

Cash

	+		−
(d)	2,000	(e)	100
		(f)	1,400

Income from Services

	−		+
		(a)	2,600

Accounts Receivable

	+		−
(a)	2,600	(d)	2,000

Advertising Expense

	+		−
(b)	220		

Equipment

	+		−
(c)	1,940		

Wages Expense

	+		−
(f)	1,400		

Accumulated Depreciation

	−		+
		(g)	380

Depreciation Expense

	+		−
(g)	380		

Accounts Payable

	−		+
(e)	100	(b)	220
		(c)	1,940

Modified Cash Basis

Cash

	+		−
(d)	2,000	(e)	100
		(f)	1,400

Income from Services

	−		+
		(d)	2,000

Equipment

	+		−
(c)	1,940		

Advertising Expense

	+		−
(e)	100		

Accumulated Depreciation

	−		+
		(g)	380

Wages Expense

	+		−
(f)	1,400		

Accounts Payable

	−		+
		(c)	1,940

Depreciation Expense

	+		−
(g)	380		

Here's a comparison of the income statements under the accrual basis and the modified cash basis.

Accrual Basis

Income Statement		
Revenue:		
Income from Services		$2,600
Expenses:		
Advertising Expense	$ 220	
Wages Expense	1,400	
Depreciation Expense	380	
Total Expenses		2,000
Net Income		$ 600

Modified Cash Basis

Income Statement		
Revenue:		
Income from Services		$2,000
Expenses:		
Advertising Expense	$ 100	
Wages Expense	1,400	
Depreciation Expense	380	
Total Expenses		1,880
Net Income		$ 120

INTERIM STATEMENTS

Objective 5

Prepare interim statements.

As we said previously, a firm's fiscal year generally consists of twelve consecutive months. However, it is understandable that the owner of the business does not want to wait until the end of the twelve-month period to determine whether the company made a profit or a loss. Instead, most owners want financial statements at the end of each month. Financial statements prepared during the fiscal year, for periods of less than twelve months, are called **interim statements**. (They are given this name because they are prepared within the fiscal period.) For example, a business may prepare the income statement, the statement of owner's equity, and the balance sheet *monthly*. These statements provide up-to-date information about the results and status of operations. For example, a company might have the following interim statements:

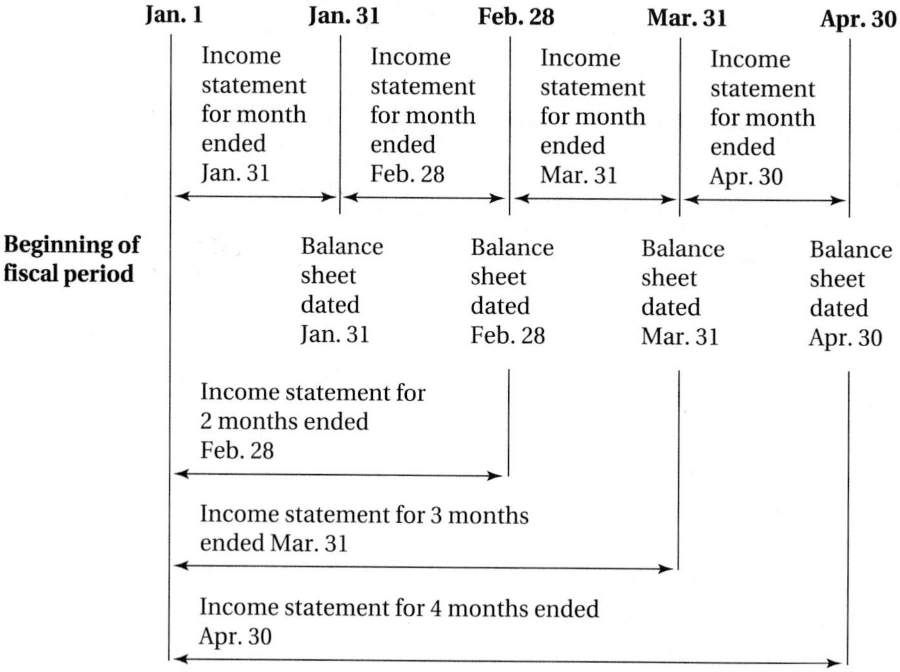
Jan. 1
Jan. 31
Feb. 28
Mar. 31
Apr. 30
Income statement for month ended Jan. 31
Income statement for month ended Feb. 28
Income statement for month ended Mar. 31
Income statement for month ended Apr. 30
Beginning of fiscal period
Balance sheet dated Jan. 31
Balance sheet dated Feb. 28
Balance sheet dated Mar. 31
Balance sheet dated Apr. 30
Income statement for 2 months ended Feb. 28
Income statement for 3 months ended Mar. 31
Income statement for 4 months ended Apr. 30

In this case, the accountant would prepare a work sheet at the end of each month. Next, based on these work sheets, he or she would prepare the financial statements. *However, the remaining steps—journalizing the adjusting and closing entries and preparing the post-closing trial balance—would be performed only at the end of the year.*

CHAPTER REVIEW

Review of Performance Objectives

1. List the steps in the accounting cycle.

    1. Analyze source documents and record business transactions in a journal.
    2. Post journal entries to the accounts in the ledger.
    3. Prepare a trial balance.
    4. Gather adjustment data and record the adjusting entries on a work sheet.
    5. Complete the work sheet.
    6. Prepare financial statements from the data on the work sheet.
    7. Journalize and post the adjusting entries from the data on the work sheet.
    8. Journalize and post the closing entries.
    9. Prepare a post-closing trial balance.

2. Journalize and post closing entries for a service enterprise.

    The four steps in the closing procedure are as follows:

    1. Close the revenue accounts into Income Summary.
    2. Close the expense accounts into Income Summary.
    3. Close the Income Summary account into the Capital account, transferring the net income or loss to the Capital account.
    4. Close the Drawing account into the Capital account.

3. Prepare a post-closing trial balance.

    A post-closing trial balance consists of the final balances of the accounts remaining open. It is the final proof that the debit balances equal the credit balances before the posting for the new fiscal period commences.

4. Define the following methods of accounting: accrual basis, cash-receipts-and-disbursements basis, modified cash basis.

    Under the *accrual basis* of accounting, revenue is recorded when earned, even if cash is received at a later date, and expenses are recorded when incurred, even if cash is to be paid at a later date. Under the *cash-receipts-and-disbursements basis,* revenue is recorded only when cash is received, and expenses are recorded only when paid in cash. This basis is used mainly by individuals for their income taxes.

    Under the *modified cash basis,* revenue is recorded only when cash is received, and most expenses are recorded only when paid in cash. However, exceptions are made for certain expenses, such as depreciation, supplies used, and insurance expired, allowing adjusting entries.

5. Prepare interim statements.

    Interim statements consist of year-to-date income statements, statements of owner's equity, and balance sheets as of various dates during the fiscal period.

Glossary

Accrual basis An accounting method under which revenue is recorded when it is earned, regardless of when it is received, and expenses are recorded when they are incurred, regardless of when they are paid. (158)

Cash-receipts-and-disbursements basis An accounting method under which all revenue is recorded only when it is received in cash, and all expenses are recorded only when they are paid in cash. (159)

Closing entries Entries made at the end of a fiscal period to close off the revenue, expense, and drawing accounts—that is, to make the balances of the temporary-equity accounts equal to zero. Closing is also called *clearing the accounts.* (149)

Income Summary An account brought into existence in order to have a debit and credit in each closing entry. The revenue and expense account balances are transferred to this account to allow calculations of net income or net loss. (150)

Interim statements Financial statements prepared during the fiscal year, covering a period of time less than twelve months. (162)

Modified cash basis An accounting method under which revenue is recorded only when it is received in cash. Most expenses are recorded only when they are paid in cash. However, exceptions are made for expenditures on items having a useful life of more than one year and for certain prepaid items. Expenditures for supplies and insurance premiums can be *prorated,* or spread out over the fiscal periods covered. Expenditures for long-lived items are recorded as assets and later depreciated as an expense over their useful lives. (159)

Nominal or **temporary-equity accounts** Accounts that apply to only one fiscal period and that are to be closed at the end of that fiscal period, such as revenue, expense, Income Summary, and Drawing accounts. This category may also be described as all accounts except assets, liabilities, and the Capital account. (155)

Post-closing trial balance The listing of the final balances of the real accounts at the end of the fiscal period. (157)

Real or **permanent accounts** The accounts that remain open (assets, liabilities, and the Capital account in owner's equity) and that have balances that will be carried over to the next fiscal period. (155)

QUESTIONS, EXERCISES, AND PROBLEMS

Discussion Questions

1. Number in order the following steps in the accounting cycle.
   a. Prepare a trial balance on the first two columns of the work sheet.
   b. Post journal entries to accounts in the ledger.
   c. Journalize and post adjusting entries.
   d. Analyze source documents and record transactions in the journal.
   e. Prepare financial statements.

f. Gather adjusting data and write adjusting entries on the work sheet.
g. Journalize and post closing entries.
h. Prepare a post-closing trial balance.
i. Complete the work sheet.

2. List the steps in the closing procedure.
3. What is the purpose of closing entries?
4. What are the two sources from which you can make closing entries?
5. What are real accounts? What are nominal accounts? Explain how they differ.
6. What is the purpose of the Income Summary, and how does it relate to the revenue and expense accounts?
7. What is the purpose of the post-closing trial balance? What is the difference between a trial balance and a post-closing trial balance?
8. Write the third closing entry to transfer the profit or loss to the P. Thompson, Capital, account for July 31, assuming the following:

   a. A profit of $3,847
   b. A loss of $1,278

Exercises

P.O. 2

Classify accounts and show where they are listed on the work sheet.

Exercise 5-1 Classify the accounts listed below as real (permanent) or nominal (temporary), and indicate with an x whether the account is closed. Also, indicate the financial statement in which each account will appear. The Building account is given as an example.

Account Title	Real	Nominal	Closed: Yes	Closed: No	Income Statement	Balance Sheet
0. Example: Building	X			X		X
a. Prepaid Insurance	X			X		X
b. Accounts Payable	X			X		X
c. Wages Payable	X			X		X
d. Services Income		X	X		X	
e. Rent Expense		X	X		X	
f. Supplies Expense		X	X		X	
g. Accum. Depr., Equip.	X			X		X

P.O. 2

Journalize closing entries from T account balances.

Exercise 5-2 Number the closing entries as steps 1 through 4. Journalize the closing entries on the following page.

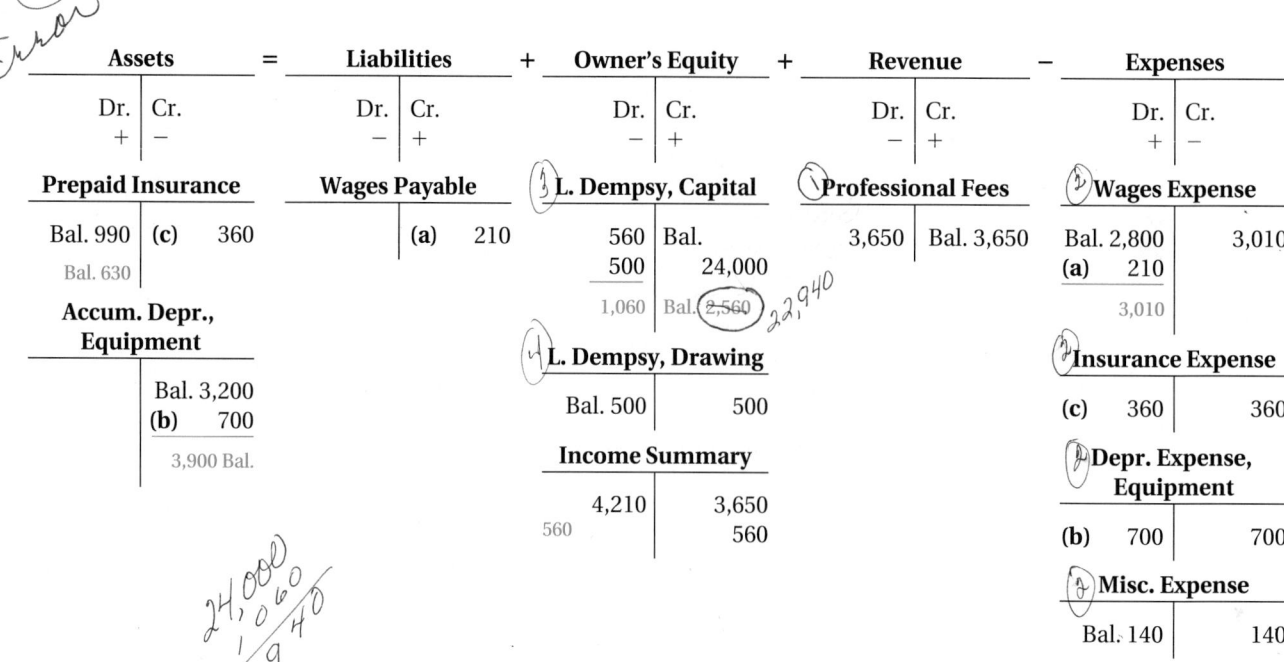

Assets		=	Liabilities		+	Owner's Equity		+	Revenue		−	Expenses	
Dr. +	Cr. −		Dr. −	Cr. +		Dr. −	Cr. +		Dr. −	Cr. +		Dr. +	Cr. −

Prepaid Insurance

Dr.	Cr.
Bal. 990	(c) 360
Bal. 630	

Accum. Depr., Equipment

Dr.	Cr.
	Bal. 3,200
	(b) 700
	3,900 Bal.

Wages Payable

Dr.	Cr.
	(a) 210

L. Dempsy, Capital

Dr.	Cr.
560	Bal.
500	24,000
1,060	Bal. 2,560

L. Dempsy, Drawing

Dr.	Cr.
Bal. 500	500

Income Summary

Dr.	Cr.
4,210	3,650
560	560

Professional Fees

Dr.	Cr.
3,650	Bal. 3,650

Wages Expense

Dr.	Cr.
Bal. 2,800	3,010
(a) 210	
3,010	

Insurance Expense

Dr.	Cr.
(c) 360	360

Depr. Expense, Equipment

Dr.	Cr.
(b) 700	700

Misc. Expense

Dr.	Cr.
Bal. 140	140

P.O. 2

Journalize closing entries from account balances.

Exercise 5-3 As of December 31, the end of the current year, the ledger of Diggs Company contained the following account balances after adjustment. All accounts have normal balances. Journalize the closing entries.

Cash	$ 8,540	W. O. Ryan, Drawing	$1,698
Equipment	11,486	Professional Fees	6,875
Accumulated Depreciation, Equipment	2,687	Wages Expense	1,468
Accounts Payable	1,574	Rent Expense	990
Wages Payable	658	Depreciation Expense, Equipment	1,243
W. O. Ryan, Capital	13,876	Miscellaneous Expense	245

P.O. 2

Journalize closing entries from work sheet columns—a profit.

Exercise 5-4 The Income Statement columns of the work sheet of R. Douglas Company for the fiscal year ended June 30 appear below. During the year, R. Douglas withdrew $4,100. Journalize the closing entries.

	ACCOUNT NAME	INCOME STATEMENT DEBIT	INCOME STATEMENT CREDIT
1	Service Income		68,970 00
2	Rental Income		26,760 00
3	Rent Expense	27,000 00	
4	Wages Expense	19,540 00	
5	Utilities Expense	3,650 00	
6	Miscellaneous Expense	1,590 00	
7		51,780 00	95,730 00
8	Net Income	43,950 00	
9		95,730 00	95,730 00

P.O. 2

Journalize closing entries from work sheet columns—a loss.

Exercise 5-5 The Income Statement columns of the work sheet of R. Mandel Company for the fiscal year ended December 31 appear below. During the year, R. Mandel withdrew $28,000. Journalize the closing entries.

		INCOME STATEMENT	
	ACCOUNT NAME	DEBIT	CREDIT
1	Service Income		32 7 4 0 00
2	Rental Income		12 0 0 0 00
3	Wages Expense	43 5 2 0 00	
4	Utilities Expense	4 6 3 0 00	
5	Miscellaneous Expense	15 2 0 0 00	
6		63 3 5 0 00	44 7 4 0 00
7	Net Loss		18 6 1 0 00
8		63 3 5 0 00	63 3 5 0 00

P.O. 2

Journalize closing entries three and four from account balances.

Exercise 5-6 After all revenue and expenses have been closed at the end of the fiscal period ended December 31, Income Summary has a debit of $35,450 and a credit of $31,430. On the same date, A. Morrison, Drawing, has a debit balance of $11,300, and A. Morrison, Capital, has a credit balance of $68,320.

a. Journalize the entries necessary to close the remaining temporary accounts.

b. What is the new balance of A. Morrison, Capital, after closing the remaining temporary accounts?

P.O. 5

Place accounts on financial statements.

Exercise 5-7 Indicate with an X whether each of the following would appear on the income statement, statement of owner's equity, or balance sheet. The first item is provided as an example.

Item	Income Statement	Statement of OE	Balance Sheet
0. Example: The total liabilities of the business at the end of the year.			X
a. The amount of the owner's Capital balance at the end of the year.			
b. The amount of depreciation expense on equipment during the year.			
c. The amount of the company's net income for the year.			
d. Supplies on hand at the end of the year.			
e. The book value of the equipment.			
f. Total insurance expired during the year.			
g. Total accounts receivable at the end of the year.			
h. Total withdrawals by the owner.			
i. The cost of supplies used during the year.			
j. The amount of the owner's Capital balance at the beginning of the year.			

P.O. 5

Prepare a statement of owner's equity from T accounts.

Exercise 5-8 Prepare a statement of owner's equity for VonBehren Veterinary Clinic for the year ended December 31. P. VonBehren's capital amount on January 1 was $140,000, and there was an additional investment of $8,000 on May 12 and withdrawals of $21,500 for the year. Net income for the year was $4,198.

CONSIDER AND COMMUNICATE

A friend of yours owns a small business and has completed part of an accounting class—through the chapter on adjustments. He is about to start a new fiscal period, and he sees no need for closing. Explain why the closing entries are so important to the accounting cycle and to his records.

CRITICAL THINKING

Your bookkeeper has submitted the following trial balance, marked "Post-Closing." Assume that the totals are correct.

a. Study the trial balance and prepare a response to what you have reviewed.
b. Journalize the closing entries. Prepare additional entries, if needed.
c. What is the net income or net loss for the period?
d. Was there an increase or a decrease in Capital?
e. What would be the ending amount of Capital?
f. What is the balance of the post-closing trial balance after posting the closing entries?

Post-Closing Trial Balance

ACCOUNT NAME	DEBIT *A + Draw. + E*	CREDIT *Accum. Deprec. + L + C + R*
Cash	2,327.00	
Accounts Receivable	919.00	
Prepaid Insurance	1,462.00	
Supplies	392.00	
Office Equipment	5,339.00	
Accounts Payable		
C. Horn, Capital		9,020.00
C. Horn, Drawing	1,000.00	
Commissions Earned		3,120.00
Rent Expense	795.00	
Advertising Expense	525.00	
Utilities Expense	298.00	
Miscellaneous Expense	154.00	
	13,211.00	13,211.00

A MATTER OF ETHICS

You are completing the accounting cycle for the company for which you work. You have made a post-closing trial balance, but it doesn't balance. You are tired, and besides, you don't think they pay you for this kind of headache.

You decide to increase the balance of an asset account to make the totals balance. Discuss this behavior and whether it is ethical or illegal.

WEB WORK

Using an Internet web browser, type the word *spreadsheets* in the search box. Search for an article or find a home page that provides information about computerized spreadsheets. Narrow your search by adding accounting terms to the search box, for example, *computerized* spreadsheet or *accounting tools.* Discuss or write about your findings.

PROBLEM SET A

For additional help, see the demonstration problems at the beginning of each chapter in your Working Papers.

P.O. 2

Problem 5-1A After the accountant posted the adjusting entries for M. Tigard, Designer, the general ledger contained the following account balances on May 31:

Comm Earn 3697
I. Sum 3697
I. Sum 1704
Rent Exp 790
Depr Exp 520
Util Exp 276
Misc. Exp 118
I Sum 1993
Capital 1993
Capital 1800
Draw 1800

	Account Name	Adjusted Trial Balance Debit (A + Draw. + E)	Adjusted Trial Balance Credit (Accum. Deprec. + L + C + R)
1	Cash	2,318.00	
2	Accounts Receivable	1,208.00	
3	Prepaid Insurance	987.00	
4	Supplies	381.00	
5	Office Equipment	5,790.00	
6	Accumulated Depreciation, Equipment		1,364.00
7	Accounts Payable		880.00
8	M. Tigard, Capital		8,247.00
9	M. Tigard, Drawing	1,800.00	
10	Commissions Earned		3,697.00
11	Rent Expense	790.00	
12	Depreciation Expense, Equipment	520.00	
13	Utilities Expense	276.00	
14	Miscellaneous Expense	118.00	
15		14,188.00	14,188.00

Check Figure
Net Income, $1,993

Instructions

a. Write the owner's name on the Capital and Drawing T accounts.
b. Record the account balances in the T accounts for owner's equity, revenue, and expenses.
c. Journalize the closing entries with the four steps in correct order. Number the closing entries 1–4.
d. Post the closing entries to the T accounts right after you journalize each one to see the effect of the closing entries. Number the closing entries 1–4.

P.O. 2

Problem 5-2A The partial work sheet for Kingman Consulting for the month of May is as follows:

	ACCOUNT NAME	INCOME STATEMENT		BALANCE SHEET	
		DEBIT E	CREDIT R	DEBIT A + Draw.	CREDIT Accum. Depr. + L + C
1	Cash			2248 00	
2	Supplies			220 00	
3	Prepaid Insurance			859 00	
4	Equipment			5731 00	
5	Accumulated Depreciation, Equipment				2379 00
6	Accounts Payable				841 00
7	K. Kingman, Capital				2415 00
8	K. Kingman, Drawing			1800 00	
9	Consulting Income		8546 00		
10	Rent Expense	800 00			
11	Wages Expense	1633 00			
12	Miscellaneous Expense	168 00			
13					
14	Supplies Expense	145 00			
15	Insurance Expense	264 00			
16	Depreciation Expense, Equipment	700 00			
17	Wages Payable				387 00
18		3710 00	8546 00	10858 00	6022 00
19	Net Income	4836 00			4836 00
20		8546 00	8546 00	10858 00	10858 00
21					

Check Figure

Debit to Income Summary, second entry, $3,710

Instructions

a. Write the owner's name on the Capital and Drawing T accounts.
b. Record the account balances in the T accounts for owner's equity, revenue, and expenses.
c. Journalize the closing entries with the four steps in correct order. Number the closing entries 1 through 4.
d. Post the closing entries to the T accounts right after you journalize each one to see the effect of the closing entries. Number the closing entries 1 through 4.

P.O. 1,2,3

Problem 5-3A The completed work sheet for Kathy's Tour Company as of December 31 is presented in your Working Papers, along with the general ledger as of December 31 before adjustments.

Check Figure

Post-closing trial balance total, $7,520

Instructions

1. Write the name of the owner in the Capital and Drawing accounts.
2. Write the balances from the unadjusted trial balance in the general ledger.
3. Journalize and post the adjusting entries.
4. Journalize and post the closing entries with the four steps in the correct order.
5. Prepare a post-closing trial balance.

P.O. 1,2,3

Problem 5-4A The account balances of Morrow Tutoring Service as of June 30, 20—, the end of the current fiscal year, are as follows:

	ACCOUNT NAME	TRIAL BALANCE DEBIT	TRIAL BALANCE CREDIT
1	Cash	5491 00	
2	Accounts Receivable	624 00	
3	Supplies	327 00	
4	Prepaid Insurance	1280 00	
5	Equipment	6497 00	
6	Accumulated Depreciation, Equipment		2672 00
7	Van	18674 00	
8	Accumulated Depreciation, Van		4368 00
9	Accounts Payable		1036 00
10	B. Morrow, Capital		4848 00
11	B. Morrow, Drawing	12000 00	
12	Fees Earned		53280 00
13	Salary Expense	18000 00	
14	Advertising Expense	1200 00	
15	Van Operating Expense	605 00	
16	Utilities Expense	1248 00	
17	Miscellaneous Expense	258 00	
18		66204 00	66204 00

Check Figure

Net income, $28,468

Instructions

1. Complete the work sheet:

   Data for the adjustments:

   a. Supplies inventory (left or unused), $180 (calculate the expired or used up supplies).
   b. Expired or used up insurance, $320.
   c. Depreciation expense on equipment, $890 (remember to credit the accumulated depreciation account for equipment, not Equipment).
   d. Depreciation expense on the van, $1,860 (remember to credit the accumulated depreciation account for the van, not Van).
   e. Salary accrued (earned) since the last payday, $284 (owed and to be paid on the next payday).
2. Prepare an income statement.
3. Prepare a statement of owner's equity; assume there was an additional investment of $2,000.
4. Prepare a balance sheet.
5. Journalize the adjusting entries.
6. Journalize the closing entries with the four steps in the proper sequence.

Instructions for General Ledger software

1. Print a trial balance.
2. Journalize the adjusting entries in the general journal and post to the general ledger. (No work sheet is required on the computer.)

3. Print an income statement, a statement of owner's equity, and a balance sheet.
4. Journalize the closing entries in the general journal.
5. Post the closing entries.
6. Print a post-closing trial balance.

PROBLEM SET B

For additional help, see the demonstration problems at the beginning of each chapter in your Working Papers.

P.O. 2

Problem 5-1B After the accountant posted the adjusting entries for K. Lu, Designer, the general ledger contained the following account balances on May 31:

	Account Name	Adjusted Trial Balance Debit (A + Draw. + E)	Adjusted Trial Balance Credit (Accum. Deprec. + L + C + R)
1	Cash	2,429.00	
2	Accounts Receivable	886.00	
3	Prepaid Insurance	1,460.00	
4	Supplies	570.00	
5	Office Equipment	4,672.00	
6	Accumulated Depreciation, Equipment		1,253.00
7	Accounts Payable		943.00
8	K. Lu, Capital		6,520.00
9	K. Lu, Drawing	1,650.00	
10	Commissions Earned		4,679.00
11	Rent Expense	895.00	
12	Depreciation Expense, Equipment	467.00	
13	Utilities Expense	264.00	
14	Miscellaneous Expense	102.00	
15		13,395.00	13,395.00

Check Figure
Net Income, $2,951

Instructions

a. Write the owner's name on the Capital and Drawing T accounts.
b. Record the account balances in the T accounts for owner's equity, revenue, and expenses.
c. Journalize the closing entries with the four steps in correct order. Number the closing entries 1 through 4.
d. Post the closing entries to the T accounts right after you journalize each one to see the effect of the closing entries. Number the closing entries 1 through 4.

P.O. 2

Problem 5-2B The partial work sheet for Colfeld Consulting for the month of June is as follows.

Account Name	Income Statement Debit (E)	Income Statement Credit (R)	Balance Sheet Debit (A + Draw.)	Balance Sheet Credit (Accum. Depr. + L + C)
Cash			6104 00	
Supplies			296 00	
Prepaid Insurance			1344 00	
Equipment			6751 00	
Accumulated Depreciation, Equipment				3393 00
Accounts Payable				1356 00
D. Colfeld, Capital				1367 00
D. Colfeld, Drawing			2400 00	
Consulting Income		15060 00		
Rent Expense	1100 00			
Wages Expense	1908 00			
Miscellaneous Expense	240 00			
Supplies Expense	136 00			
Insurance Expense	345 00			
Depreciation Expense, Equipment	900 00			
Wages Payable				348 00
	4629 00	15060 00	16895 00	6464 00
Net Income	10431 00			10431 00
	15060 00	15060 00	16895 00	16895 00

Check Figure

Debit to Income Summary, second entry, $4,629

Instructions

a. Write the owner's name on the Capital and Drawing T accounts.
b. Record the account balances in the T accounts for owner's equity, revenue, and expenses.
c. Journalize the closing entries with the four steps in correct order. Number the closing entries 1 through 4.
d. Post the closing entries to the T accounts right after you journalize each one to see the effect of the closing entries. Number closing entries 1–4.

P.O. 1,2,3

Problem 5-3B The completed work sheet for Dunn Insurance Agency as of December 31 is presented in your Working Papers, along with the general ledger as of December 31 before adjustments.

Check Figure

Post-closing trial balance total, $9,024

Instructions

1. Write the name of the owner in the Capital and Drawing accounts.
2. Write the balances from the unadjusted trial balance in the general ledger.
3. Journalize and post the adjusting entries.
4. Journalize and post the closing entries with the four steps in the correct order.
5. Prepare a post-closing trial balance.

P.O. 1,2,3

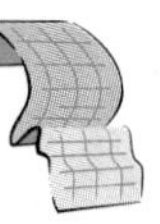

Problem 5-4B The account balances of Morton Company as of June 30, the end of the current fiscal year, are as follows.

	ACCOUNT NAME	TRIAL BALANCE DEBIT	TRIAL BALANCE CREDIT
1	Cash	4381 00	
2	Accounts Receivable	578 00	
3	Supplies	397 00	
4	Prepaid Insurance	1138 00	
5	Equipment	5713 00	
6	Accumulated Depreciation, Equipment		2487 00
7	Van	12678 00	
8	Accumulated Depreciation, Van		3318 00
9	Accounts Payable		997 00
10	S. Morton, Capital		5964 00
11	S. Morton, Drawing	18000 00	
12	Professional Fees		48317 00
13	Salary Expense	16000 00	
14	Advertising Expense	887 00	
15	Van Operating Expense	462 00	
16	Utilities Expense	685 00	
17	Miscellaneous Expense	164 00	
18		61083 00	61083 00

Check Figure

Net income, $27,127

Instructions

1. Complete the work sheet.

   Data for the adjustments:
   a. Supplies inventory (left or unused), $160 (calculate the expired or used up supplies).
   b. Expired or used up insurance, $482.
   c. Depreciation expense on equipment, $590 (remember to credit the accumulated depreciation account for equipment, not Equipment).
   d. Depreciation expense on the van, $1,032 (remember to credit the accumulated depreciation account for the van, not Van).
   e. Salary accrued (earned) since the last payday, $651 (owed and to be paid on the next payday).
2. Prepare an income statement.
3. Prepare a statement of owner's equity; assume there was an additional investment of $2,000.
4. Prepare a balance sheet.
5. Journalize the adjusting entries.
6. Journalize the closing entries with the four steps in the proper sequence.

Instructions for General Ledger software

1. Print a trial balance.
2. Journalize the adjusting entries in the general journal and post to the general ledger. (No work sheet is required on the computer.)
3. Print an income statement, a statement of owner's equity, and a balance sheet.
4. Journalize the closing entries in the general journal.
5. Post the closing entries.
6. Print a post-closing trial balance.

Continuous General Ledger Problem: Closing Entries

Check Figure

Post-Closing Trial Balance total $202,602.92

Instructions

1. Open the accounting software and open the file you saved as Likenew2.
2. Journalize and post the closing entries. Some software packages do not require that you journalize closing entries; you need only select a menu item to cause closing entries to happen. Check your software's menus and/or documentation.
3. Print the general journal (if you can filter the entries, print only the closing entries).
4. Print the general ledger (if you can filter the entries, print only the accounts affected by the closing entries).
5. Print a trial balance (a post-closing trial balance).
6. Save the file as Likenew3.

Note: The Continuous General Ledger Problem can be worked with Houghton Mifflin Windows General Ledger Package, Peachtree Release 5.01, QuickBooks 6.0, or other general ledger software packages.

Cumulative Self-Check: Chapters 4–5

PART I: MULTIPLE-CHOICE QUESTIONS

____ 1. The net income appears on all of the following statements except

a. the statement of owner's equity.
b. the balance sheet.
c. the income statement.
d. all of these.
e. none of these.

____ 2. Which of the following entries records the withdrawal of cash for personal use by Dolan, the owner of a business firm?

a. Debit Cash and credit Drawing.
b. Credit Cash and debit Salary Expense.
c. Debit Cash and credit Salary Expense.
d. Credit Cash and debit Drawing.
e. None of these.

____ 3. Which of the following errors, considered individually, would cause the trial balance totals to be unequal?

a. A payment of $62 for supplies was posted as a debit of $62 to Supplies and a credit of $26 to Cash.
b. A payment of $763 to a creditor was posted as a debit of $763 to Accounts Payable and a debit of $763 to Cash.
c. Cash received from customers on account was posted as a debit of $480 to Cash and a credit of $48 to Accounts Receivable.
d. All of these.
e. None of these.

____ 4. The balance in the Prepaid Insurance account before adjustment at the end of the year is $480. This represents six months' insurance paid on November 1. The adjusting entry required on December 31 is

a. debit Insurance Expense, $160; credit Prepaid Insurance, $160.
b. debit Prepaid Insurance, $80; credit Insurance Expense, $80.
c. debit Prepaid Insurance, $420; credit Insurance Expense, $420.
d. debit Insurance Expense, $420; credit Prepaid Insurance, $420.
e. none of these.

____ 5. If an accountant fails to make an adjusting entry to record expired insurance at the end of a fiscal period, the omission will cause

a. total expenses to be understated.
b. total revenue to be understated.
c. total assets to be understated.
d. all of these.
e. none of these.

Note: Answers to Cumulative Self-Check begin on page A-1.

___ 6. Faulkner Company bought equipment on January 2 of this year for $7,600. At the time of purchase, the equipment was estimated to have a useful life of eight years and a trade-in value of $400 at the end of eight years. Using the straight-line method, the amount of depreciation for the first year is

a. $1,000.
b. $900.
c. $800.
d. $950.
e. none of these.

___ 7. If expenses are greater than revenue, the Income Summary account will be closed by a debit to

a. Cash and a credit to Income Summary.
b. Income Summary and a credit to Cash.
c. Capital and a credit to Income Summary.
d. Income Summary and a credit to Capital.
e. none of these.

___ 8. In preparing closing entries, it is helpful to refer to which of the following columns of the work sheet first?

a. The Balance Sheet columns
b. The Adjusted Trial Balance columns
c. The Income Statement columns
d. Both the Adjusted Trial Balance and the Income Statement columns
e. None of these

PART II: PRACTICAL APPLICATION

On December 31, the ledger accounts of Hanley's Upholstery Shop have the following balances after all adjusting entries have been posted.

Cash	$1,200
Supplies	1,900
Equipment	5,400
Accumulated Depreciation, Equipment	1,100
Accounts Payable	300
T. L. Hanley, Capital	6,500
T. L. Hanley, Drawing	16,400
Income Summary	
Income from Services	$25,900
Wages Expense	1,500
Rent Expense	2,400
Utilities Expense	1,000
Depreciation Expense, Equipment	500
Supplies Expense	2,200
Miscellaneous Expense	900

Instructions

Journalize the four closing entries in the proper order.

PART III: MATCHING QUESTIONS

____ 1. Creditor	a. The book of original entry
____ 2. Business entity	b. One to whom money is owed
____ 3. Fundamental accounting equation	c. Accounts that are partly income statement and partly balance sheet accounts
____ 4. Income statement	d. Assets − Liabilities
____ 5. Owner's equity	e. A listing of the ending balances of all ledger accounts that proves the equality of total debits and total credits
____ 6. Accounts Receivable	f. The process of recording transactions in a journal
____ 7. Net loss	g. The left side of a T account
____ 8. Ledger	h. A business enterprise, separate and distinct from the person who owns its assets
____ 9. Credit	i. The process of transferring accounts and amounts from the journal to the ledger
____ 10. Compound entry	j. An account that is deducted from another account
____ 11. Trial balance	k. Amounts owed by charge customers
____ 12. Journalizing	l. Balance sheet accounts
____ 13. Posting	m. Assets = Liabilities + Owner's Equity
____ 14. Cross-reference	n. A bookkeeping device for referring from journal to ledger or ledger to journal
____ 15. Journal	o. The right side of a T account
____ 16. Work sheet	p. Allocation of the cost of a plant asset over its estimated life
____ 17. Book value	q. Financial statement that shows the net results of operations
____ 18. Depreciation	r. Accounts that belong to only one fiscal period and are closed out at the end of each fiscal period
____ 19. Accounting cycle	s. A transaction that has two or more debits and/or credits
____ 20. Fiscal year	t. Paper used to record adjustments and provide balances to prepare financial statements
____ 21. Contra account	u. Excess of total expenses over total revenues
____ 22. Mixed accounts	v. A period of 12 consecutive months
____ 23. Temporary-equity accounts	w. A book containing all the accounts of a business
____ 24. Real accounts	x. The cost of an asset minus its accumulated depreciation
____ 25. Debit	y. Steps in the accounting process, completed during the fiscal period

Accounting Cycle Review Problem A

This problem is designed to enable you to apply the knowledge you have acquired in the preceding chapters. In accounting, the ultimate test is being able to handle data in real-life situations. This problem will give you valuable experience.

Chart of Accounts

Assets

111 Cash
112 Accounts Receivable
113 Supplies
114 Prepaid Insurance
121 Land
122 Building
123 Accumulated Depreciation, Building
124 Pool/Slide Facility
125 Accumulated Depreciation, Pool/Slide Facility
126 Pool Furniture
127 Accumulated Depreciation, Pool Furniture

Liabilities

221 Accounts Payable
222 Wages Payable
223 Mortgage Payable

Owner's Equity

311 K. Taylor, Capital
312 K. Taylor, Drawing
313 Income Summary

Revenue

411 Income from Services
412 Concessions Income

Expenses

511 Pool Maintenance Expense
512 Wages Expense
513 Advertising Expense
514 Utilities Expense
515 Interest Expense
516 Supplies Expense
517 Insurance Expense
518 Depreciation Expense, Building
519 Depreciation Expense, Pool/Slide Facility
520 Depreciation Expense, Pool Furniture
522 Miscellaneous Expense

You are to record transactions in a two-column general journal. Assume that the fiscal period is one month. You will then be able to complete all the steps in the accounting cycle.

When you are analyzing the transactions, think them through by visualizing the T accounts or by writing them down on scratch paper. For unfamiliar types of transactions, specific instructions for recording them are included. However, reason them out for yourself as well. Check off each transaction as it is recorded.

July 1 Taylor deposited $156,000 in a bank account for the purpose of buying Fun World Waterslides. The business is a public recreation area offering three large waterslides (called "tubes"), one children's slide, an inner tube run, and a hot tub area.

2 Bought Fun World Waterslides in its entirety for a total price of $540,800. The assets include pool furniture, $2,500; the pool/slide facility (includes filter system, pools, pump, and slides), $147,800; building, $95,500; and land, $295,000. Paid $133,000 down and signed a mortgage note for the remainder. (Debit the assets, and credit Cash and Mortgage Payable.)

July 2 Received and paid the bill for a one-year premium for insurance, $10,036.

2 Bought 125 inner tubes from Wright's Tires for $3,125, paying $1,500 down, with the remainder due in twenty days. (Debit Supplies instead of an Equipment account because inner tubes generally last only a month or so.)

3 Signed a contract with a video game company to lease space for video games and to provide a food concession. The rental income agreed upon is 10 percent of the revenues generated from the machines and food, with the estimated monthly rental income paid in advance. Received cash payment for July, $380. (Debit Cash and credit Concessions Income.)

5 Received bills totaling $1,190 for the grand opening/Fourth of July party. The bill from Party Promotions for the promotional handouts, balloons, decorations, and prizes was $620, and the newspaper advertising bills from the *City Star* were $570. (These expenses should all be considered advertising expense.)

6 Signed a year contract for the pool maintenance with Crystal Clean Maintenance and paid the maintenance fee for July of $506.

6 Paid cash for employee picnic food and beverages, $103.24. (Debit Miscellaneous Expense.)

7 Received $14,056 in cash as income for the use of the facilities.

9 Bought parts for the filter system on account from Applewood Pool Supply, $956. (Debit Pool Maintenance Expense.)

14 Received $9,182 in cash as income for the use of the facilities.

15 Paid wages to employees for the period ending July 14, $10,080.

16 Paid $1,190 on account for promotional expenses recorded on July 5.

16 Taylor withdrew cash for personal use, $2,000.

17 Bought additional pool furniture from Leisure Products for $2,126; payment due in thirty days.

18 Paid cash to seamstress for alterations and repairs to the character costumes, $49.60. (Debit Miscellaneous Expense.)

21 Received $12,150 in cash as income for the use of the facilities.

21 Paid cash to Wright's Tires as partial payment on account, $812.50.

23 Received a $225 reduction of our account from Leisure Products for lawn chairs received in damaged condition.

25 Received and paid telephone bill, $176.

30 Paid wages for the period July 15 through 29 of $11,560.

31 Received $13,970 in cash as income for the use of the facilities.

31 Paid cash to Applewood Pool Supply to apply on account, $478.

31 Received and paid water bill, $2,029.

July 31 Paid cash as an installment payment on the mortgage, $4,788. Of this amount, $1,710 represents a reduction in the principal, and the remainder is interest. (Debit Mortgage Payable, debit Interest Expense, and credit Cash.)

31 Received and paid electric bill, $979.

31 Bought additional inner tubes from Wright's Tires for $536, paying $100 down, with the remainder due in thirty days.

31 Taylor withdrew cash for personal use, $2,500.

31 Sales for the video and food concessions amounted to $5,670, and 10 percent of $5,670 equals $567. Since you have already recorded $380 as concessions income, record the additional $187 revenue due from the concessionaire (cash was not received).

Check Figures

Trial balance total, $615,642.50
Net income, $15,122.16

Instructions

1. Journalize the transactions, starting on page 1 of the general journal.
2. Post the transactions to the ledger accounts.
3. Prepare a trial balance in the first two columns of the work sheet.
4. Complete the work sheet. Data for the adjustments are as follows:
   a. Insurance expired during the month, $836 (rounded off).
   b. Depreciation of building for the month, $350.
   c. Depreciation of pool/slide facility for the month, $570.
   d. Depreciation of pool furniture for the month, $50.
   e. Wages accrued at July 31, $589.
   f. Inner tubes on hand (supplies) at July 31, $1,960.
5. Prepare the income statement.
6. Prepare the statement of owner's equity.
7. Prepare the balance sheet.
8. Journalize adjusting entries.
9. Post adjusting entries to the ledger accounts.
10. Journalize closing entries.
11. Post closing entries to the ledger accounts.
12. Prepare a post-closing trial balance.

Accounting Cycle Review Problem B

This problem is designed to enable you to apply the knowledge you have acquired in the preceding chapters. In accounting, the ultimate test is being able to handle data in real-life situations. This problem will give you valuable experience.

Chart of Accounts

Assets

111 Cash
112 Accounts Receivable
114 Prepaid Insurance
121 Land
125 Pool Structure
126 Accumulated Depreciation, Pool Structure
127 Fan System
128 Accumulated Depreciation, Fan System
129 Sailboats
130 Accumulated Depreciation, Sailboats

Liabilities

221 Accounts Payable
222 Wages Payable
223 Mortgage Payable

Owner's Equity

311 J. Moore, Capital
312 J. Moore, Drawing
313 Income Summary

Revenue

411 Income from Services
412 Concessions Income

Expenses

511 Sailboat Rental Expense
512 Wages Expense
513 Advertising Expense
514 Utilities Expense
515 Interest Expense
516 Insurance Expense
517 Depreciation Expense, Pool Structure
518 Depreciation Expense, Fan System
519 Depreciation Expense, Sailboats
522 Miscellaneous Expense

You are to record transactions in a two-column general journal. Assume that the fiscal period is one month. You will then be able to complete all the steps in the accounting cycle.

When you are analyzing the transactions, think them through by visualizing the T accounts or by writing them down on scratch paper. For unfamiliar types of transactions, specific instructions for recording them are included. However, reason them out for yourself as well. Check off each transaction as it is recorded.

June 1 Moore deposited $83,200 in a bank account for the purpose of buying Lakeland Indoor Sailboats, a business offering the use of small sailboats to the public at a large indoor pool with a fan system that provides wind.

2 Bought Lakeland Indoor Sailboats in its entirety for a total price of $213,300. The assets include sailboats, $20,800; fan system, $8,500; pool structure, $144,000; land, $40,000. Paid $64,400 down, and signed a mortgage note for the remainder. (Debit each asset and credit Cash and the mortgage payable.)

3 Received and paid bill for newspaper advertising, $148.

June	3	Received and paid bill for a one-year premium for insurance, $1,036.
	3	Bought additional boats from A and M Manufacturing Co. for $6,520, paying $3,200 down, with the remainder due in thirty days.
	3	Signed a contract with a vending machine service to lease space for vending machines. The rental income agreed upon is 10 percent of the sales generated from the machines, with the estimated total rental income payable in advance. Received estimated cash payment for June, $180. (Debit Cash and credit Concessions Income.)
	3	Received bill from Quick Printing for promotional handouts, $368 (Advertising Expense).
	3	Signed a contract for leasing sailboats from Kelsey Boat Co. and paid rental fee for June, $632.
	5	Paid cash for miscellaneous expenses, $92.44.
	8	Received $2,632.50 in cash as income for the use of the boats.
	9	Bought an addition for the fan system on account from Stanwood Pool Supply, $836.
	15	Paid wages to employees for the period ending June 14, $4,200.
	16	Paid on account for promotional handouts already recorded on June 3.
	16	Moore withdrew cash for personal use, $1,052.
	16	Bought additional sails from Bergen Products, Inc., $854; payment due in thirty days. (Debit Sailboats.)
	16	Received $3,043 in cash as income for the use of the boats.
	19	Paid cash for miscellaneous expenses, $42.64.
	20	Paid cash to A and M Manufacturing Co. as part payment on account, $480.
	22	Received $5,082 in cash for the use of the boats (Income from Services).
	23	Received a reduction in the outstanding bill from A and M Manufacturing Co. for a boat received in a damaged condition, $452. (Debit Accounts Payable, credit Sailboats.)
	24	Received and paid telephone bill, $84.
	29	Paid wages for period June 15 through 28, $4,652.
	30	Paid cash to Stanwood Pool Supply to apply on account, $418.
	30	Received and paid electric bill, $42.
	30	Paid cash as an installment payment on the mortgage, $1,880. Of this amount, $680 represents a reduction in the principal, and the remainder is interest. (Debit Mortgage Payable, debit Interest Expense, and credit Cash.)
	30	Received and paid water bill, $432.
	30	Bought additional boats from Stanski and Son for $4,852, paying $452 down, with the remainder due in thirty days.

June	30	Moore withdrew cash for personal use, $1,156.
	30	Received $4,632 in cash as income for the use of the boats.
	30	Sales from vending machines for the month amounted to $2,320. Ten percent of $2,320 equals $232. Since you have already recorded $180 as concessions income, list the additional $52 revenue earned from the vending machine operator. (Cash was not received.)

Check Figures

Net income, $1,379.42; total of post-closing trial balance, $240,914.42

Instructions

1. Journalize the transactions, starting on page 1 of the general journal.
2. Post the transactions to the ledger accounts.
3. Prepare a trial balance in the first two columns of the work sheet.
4. Complete the work sheet. Data for the adjustments are as follows:
   a. Insurance expired during the month, $86 (rounded off).
   b. Depreciation of pool structure for the month, $600.
   c. Depreciation of fan system for the month, $163.
   d. Depreciation of sailboats for the month, $804.
   e. Wages accrued at June 30, $696.
5. Prepare the income statement.
6. Prepare the statement of owner's equity.
7. Prepare the balance sheet.
8. Journalize adjusting entries.
9. Post adjusting entries to the ledger accounts.
10. Journalize closing entries.
11. Post closing entries to the ledger accounts.
12. Prepare a post-closing trial balance.

6 Accounting for Professional Enterprises: The Combined Journal (Optional)

WINDOWS ON THE WORLD WIDE WEB

Accounting systems for professional companies such as architecture firms, law firms, and doctors' offices include documenting items such as fees for services rendered, utility bills, travel expenses, supplies, and insurance. When architect I. M. Pei designed the Rock and Roll Hall of Fame in Cleveland, Ohio, what kind of accounting records do you think his company kept? If you worked for an organization that owned both I.M. Pei's architectural firm and Pizza Hut, a service business, how would you enter the accounting information into a combined journal for both businesses? Any idea what I.M. Pei charged for his firm's design of the Museum? Can you get an idea from the average salary of an architect according to the American Institute of Architects? Learn more about the Rock and Roll Hall of Fame at **http://www.rockhall.com/visit/index.html**. Then read about salary information for architects: **http://stats.bls.gov/oco/ocos038.htm**.

Performance Objectives

After you have completed this chapter, you will be able to do the following:

1. Describe the accounting records for a professional enterprise.
2. Record transactions for both a professional and a service enterprise in a combined journal.
3. Post from the combined journal and determine the cash balance.
4. Prepare a work sheet for a professional enterprise.
5. Prepare financial statements for a professional enterprise.
6. Record adjusting and closing entries in a combined journal.

A professional enterprise offers a specialized service for a fee. The fee may be charged on a per hour basis, a per visit basis, or a per job or task basis. **Professional enterprises** include practices of medicine, dentistry, law, architecture, engineering, optometry, and so forth. Your knowledge of accounting procedures can be readily applied to professional enterprises. Professional enterprises generally use a modified cash basis.

EXAMPLE: RECORDS OF A DENTIST

Objective 1

Describe the accounting records for a professional enterprise.

To understand the modified cash system used by a professional enterprise, let's look at the records of Dr. S. A. Ogden, a dentist. The basic records used in his office are the appointment record and the patient's ledger record. Following is the chart of accounts for the office:

Chart of Accounts

Assets

111 Cash
112 X-ray Supplies
113 Dental Supplies
114 Office Supplies
115 Prepaid Insurance
121 Dental Equipment
122 Accumulated Depreciation, Dental Equipment
123 Office Furniture and Equipment
124 Accumulated Depreciation, Office Furniture and Equipment

Liabilities

211 Notes Payable

Owner's Equity

311 S. A. Ogden, Capital
312 S. A. Ogden, Drawing
313 Income Summary

Revenue

411 Professional Fees

Expenses

511 Dental Instruments Expense
512 Laundry and Cleaning Expense
513 Salary Expense
514 Laboratory Expense
515 Dental Supplies Expense
516 Rent Expense
517 Depreciation Expense, Dental Equipment
518 Depreciation Expense, Office Furniture and Equipment
519 X-ray Supplies Expense
521 Office Supplies Expense
522 Insurance Expense
523 Telephone Expense
524 Utilities Expense
525 Repairs and Maintenance Expense
526 Miscellaneous Expense

Appointment Record

The dentist's receptionist keeps a daily appointment record, showing the time of each appointment and the name of the patient, and gives a copy of the appointment record to the dentist the day before the scheduled appointments. Dr. Ogden's appointment record is shown in Figure 1.

Patient's Ledger Record

The receptionist also maintains a **patient's ledger record** card for each patient. One side of this card shows a daily record of the services performed, amount of any cost estimate given, plan of payment, and information regarding collections. This side of the card is shown in Figure 2 on page 188.

The other side of the card contains a diagram of the patient's teeth and a space for personal information about the patient.

FIGURE 1

APPOINTMENT RECORD

DATE 12/1/20—

HOUR	PATIENT	SERVICE RENDERED	FEES	RECEIPTS
8:00	Ella Berger			
15	John Lyons			
30				
45	Carlos Reyes			
9:00				
15				
30				
45	Donna Heller			
10:00	L. A. Corrick			
15				
30				
45	Ralph Warfield			
11:00	Peter Smithson			
15				
30				
45				
1:00	Donald C. Kraft			
15				
30	N. C. Byers			
45				
2:00	Mrs. N. D. West			
15				
30	John F. Piper			
45	Nolan F. Sanderson			
3:00				
15	Nancy Stacy			
30				
45	C. D. Harper			
4:00				
15	Ardis Holcomb			

After Dr. Ogden completes the work, he (or an assistant) describes the services performed and writes the amount of the fees in the debit column. The card is returned to the receptionist, who records the services rendered and the fees charged on the appointment record.

The patient's ledger record for L. A. Corrick is shown in Figure 2, on the next page. **As with Accounts Receivable, debits mean increases in the amounts owed by patients, and credits mean decreases in the amounts owed by patients.** The Balance column shows the amount owed by the patient at the time of the latest entry.

The services to be performed may require a number of appointments. Some patients may make partial payments each time they have an appointment. Others may pay the entire amount at—or after—the last appointment. Patients' bills are compiled directly from the patient's ledger record.

FIGURE 2

L. A. Corrick — 360-365-2619
2416 Bryan Ave., E — Account No. 46-4128
Chicago, IL 60644

DATE		SERVICE RENDERED	TIME	DEBIT	CREDIT	BALANCE
June	15	#31—M.O.D. (4)	10:00	105 00		105 00
July	4	Ck.			105 00	
	16	#27—D.O. (Amal.)	9:15	94 00		94 00
Aug.	5	Ck.			94 00	
Sept.	24	#25—P.J.C.	10:00	740 00		740 00
Oct.	6	Ck.			120 00	620 00
	18	#24—D. (Porc.)	9:00	80 00		700 00
Nov.	3	Ck.			120 00	580 00
	9	#18—full gold crown	10:00	550 00		1130 00
Dec.	1	B. W. X-rays (6)	10:00	96 00		1226 00
		Full upper denture		900 00		2126 00
	1	Ck.			200 00	1926 00

PLAN OF SERVICE	PLAN OF PAYMENT	COLLECTION EFFORTS
1–2 surf. } amalgam	30-day basis	
2–3 surf. } 1 full gold crown	or $100 per month	
1–1 surf. } 1 ceramic crown		
2 anterior porcelain		
ESTIMATE IF ANY		
$900 upper denture (6 appt.)	$150 per month	

The dentist or receptionist regularly reviews the patients' ledger records to determine which accounts are past due. Figure 3 shows the statement that was mailed to L. A. Corrick at the end of December.

Receipt of Payments from Patients

Depending on the size of the office, the person who receives payments may be the receptionist or the cashier in the accounting office. Whoever receives the payments issues a written receipt for all incoming cash, filled out in duplicate, sending the first copy to the patient and filing the second copy as evidence of the transaction. Receipts should be prenumbered so that they can be accounted for. The payment is recorded in the Receipts column of the appointment record.

When a patient sends in a payment, the receptionist records the amount on the appointment record and on the patient's ledger record in the credit column on the day the payment was received.

Remember!

The fees charged are not recorded in the Professional Fees account until they are received in cash.

The form in Figure 4 on page 190 is a typical appointment record for a day, showing services rendered, fees (recorded by the dentist on the patients' ledger records), and payments received (recorded by the receptionist). The receptionist deposits $1,349 in the bank. A journal entry would now be made debiting Cash and crediting Professional Fees for $1,349.

FIGURE 3

S. A. OGDEN, D.D.S.
1710 CARTER AVE., E
CHICAGO, IL 60642

STATEMENT

L. A. Corrick
2416 Bryan Ave., E
Chicago, IL 60644

December 31, 20—
Account No. 46-4128

DATE	PROFESSIONAL SERVICE	CHARGES	PAYMENTS	BALANCE
6/15	#31—MOD (4)	105 00		105 00
7/4	Ck.		105 00	——
7/16	#27—DO (Amal.)	94 00		94 00
8/5	Ck.		94 00	——
9/24	#25—PJC	740 00		740 00
10/6	Ck.		120 00	620 00
10/18	#24—D (Porc.)	80 00		700 00
11/3	Ck.		120 00	580 00
11/9	#18—full gold crown	550 00		1,130 00
12/1	B.W. X-rays (6)	96 00		1,226 00
	Full upper denture	900 00		2,126 00
12/1	Ck.		200 00	1,926 00

PAY LAST AMOUNT IN BALANCE COLUMN.

Summary of Procedures

1. Patients request appointments.
2. Receptionist records appointments on appointment record: date, time, and name of patient.
3. Receptionist furnishes dentist with appointment record for the day, plus the patients' ledger records.
4. Dentist performs services and records descriptions of the services performed on each patient's ledger card, listing the fees to be charged in the Debit column.
5. Receptionist accepts payments from patients both in the office and through the mail and records receipt of payments in the Receipts column of the appointment record. Any difference between the fee charged amount and the insurance company approved amount for the services rendered can be shown in the Debit column and a note made in the Service Rendered column. (For purposes of this text, cash receipts are recorded weekly.)
6. At the end of the day, receptionist deposits cash received in the bank.
7. Receptionist lists the description of services and the amount charged on the appointment record.
8. Receptionist records payments received on the patients' ledger cards in the Credit column. The source is the appointment record.
9. Receptionist compiles monthly statements directly from patient's ledger records.

FIGURE 4

APPOINTMENT RECORD

DATE 12/1/20—

HOUR	PATIENT	SERVICE RENDERED	FEES		RECEIPTS	
8:00	Ella Berger	Extraction	50	00		
15	John Lyons	Three amalgam fillings				
30		D.O. (3)	306	00	70	00
45	Carlos Reyes	Gold inlay filling	425	00		
9:00						
15						
30						
45	Donna Heller	Amalgam filling D.O.	92	00		
10:00	L. A. Corrick	B.W. X-rays (6)	96	00	200	00
15		Denture—full upper				
30		(6 appointments)	900	00		
45	Ralph Warfield	Prophylaxis	72	00	72	00
11:00	Peter Smithson	Endodontia treatment	220	00	50	00
15						
30						
45						
1:00	Donald C. Kraft	Amalgam filling M.O.D.	104	00	52	00
15						
30	N. C. Byers	Ceramco crown	585	00		
45						
2:00	Mrs. N. D. West	Extraction	50	00		
15						
30	John F. Piper	Amalgam filling 1 surf.	75	00		
45	Nolan F. Sanderson	Prophylaxis and full-				
3:00		mouth X-ray (14)	134	00		
15	Nancy Stacy	Fixed bridge 3 units				
30		(Gold) (5 appointments)	1,640	00	125	00
45	C. D. Harper	Prophylaxis & bitewing				
4:00		X-rays	92	00		
15	Ardis Holcomb	Periodontal treatment	284	00		
30						
45						
5:00						
15						
	Ronald T. McCaw				120	00
	Helen Bower				110	00
	Eugene Sampson				136	00
	Sidney Weeks				54	00
	C. D. Sanderson				186	00
	Roger Lindsay				74	00
	Gilbert Rae				100	00
			5,125	00	1,349	00

This procedure may vary, depending on the size of the office staff. Also, the monthly statement may consist of a duplicate copy of the patient's ledger card. If the size of the office staff is sufficiently large, the function of accepting and depositing money should be separated from the function of recording payments.

Here is a list of Dr. Ogden's transactions for December, the last month of the fiscal period. **To save time and space, cash receipts are recorded on a weekly basis.**

Dec. 1 Issued Ck. No. 416 for rent for December, $2,000.

1 Issued Ck. No. 417 for telephone bill for November, $71.

1 Issued Ck. No. 418 for electric bill for November, $112.

3 Issued Ck. No. 419 to First-Rate Printing for patient statement forms, $132.

5 Issued Ck. No. 420 to Milner Dental Supply for drills, $254.

5 Total cash received from patients during the week, $7,144.

8 Issued Ck. No. 421 to Garcia Office Supply for repair of copier, $92.

9 Issued Ck. No. 422 to S. A. Ogden for personal use, $750.

11 Issued Ck. No. 423 to Reliable Cleaning Service for janitorial service, $140.

We will first record these transactions in general journal form (Figure 5). However, since our objective is to introduce the combined journal, we will also record the same transactions in a combined journal.

FIGURE 5

GENERAL JOURNAL

DATE		DESCRIPTION	POST. REF.	DEBIT	CREDIT
20—					
Dec.	1	Rent Expense		2000 00	
		Cash			2000 00
		Rent for December,			
		Ck. No. 416.			
	1	Telephone Expense		71 00	
		Cash			71 00
		Telephone bill for November,			
		Ck. No. 417.			
	1	Utilities Expense		112 00	
		Cash			112 00
		Electric bill for November,			
		Ck. No. 418.			
	3	Office Supplies		132 00	
		Cash			132 00
		First-Rate Printing for			
		statement forms, Ck. No. 419.			

FIGURE 5 (continued)

	5	Dental Instruments Expense		254 00	
		Cash			254 00
		Milner Dental Supply for			
		drills, Ck. No. 420.			
	5	Cash		7,144 00	
		Professional Fees			7,144 00
		For period Dec. 1 through 5.			
	8	Repairs and Maint. Expense		92 00	
		Cash			92 00
		Garcia Office Supply, for			
		repair of copier, Ck. No. 421.			
	9	S. A. Ogden, Drawing		750 00	
		Cash			750 00
		For personal use, Ck. No. 422.			
	11	Laundry and Cleaning Expense		140 00	
		Cash			140 00
		Reliable Cleaning Service,			
		Ck. No. 423.			

THE COMBINED JOURNAL

Objective 2

Record transactions for both a professional and a service enterprise in a combined journal.

General Journal
OR
Combined Journal
NOT BOTH

The **combined journal** is designed to make the recording and posting of transactions more efficient. It is used widely by professional and service enterprises, where **it replaces the general journal.** No explanations are given in the combined journal. **Special columns** are set up to record accounts that are used frequently by a particular business. Most transactions can be recorded on one line.

Compare the first nine transactions in the combined journal in Figure 6 (pages 194 and 195) with the same transactions recorded in the general journal in Figure 5. In the first transaction (paid rent for the month, $2,000), the entry is a debit to Rent Expense and a credit to Cash. There is a Cash Credit column in the combined journal, so you list $2,000 in this column; that $2,000 will be posted as part of the column total. The Other Accounts columns are used to record any accounts for which there are no special columns. Since there is no Rent Expense Debit column, the $2,000 debit to Rent Expense must be recorded in the Other Accounts Debit column. Notice that the Other Accounts column does not tell you where to post the $2,000. Therefore, you need to write the title of the account to be posted in the Account Name column. This amount is posted separately.

In the December 5 entry to record professional fees received in cash, special columns are available to handle both the debit to Cash and the credit to Professional Fees. In cases where the special columns can handle both the entire debit and credit amounts, it is not necessary to use the Account Name

LAUNDRY
BAK'S
LAUNDRY
DRY CLEANING

Owners of dry cleaners and service stations as well as doctors and lawyers can buy premade combined journals targeted directly for their own professions. These combined journals are set up to help channel routine transactions into the journal.

column. To show that the Account Name column has not been overlooked, we draw a long line through it and put a dash in the Post. Ref. column. The individual amounts are posted as parts of the totals of the special columns. The rest of the month's transactions follow:

Dec. 12 Total cash received from patients during the week, $2,411.

16 Issued Ck. No. 424 to Davies Dental Supply for miscellaneous dental supplies, $432.

16 In payment of salaries, issued Ck. No. 425 to C. R. Jarvis, $970 and Ck. No. 426 to D. C. Smith, $970. (Use two lines.)

19 Bought new dental chair from Milner Dental Supply, $5,779. Issued Ck. No. 427 as a downpayment, $1,779. The balance is to be paid in ten monthly payments of $400 each (Notes Payable). (Use two lines.)

19 Total cash received from patients during the week, $1,120.

22 Issued Ck. No. 428 to S. A. Ogden for personal use, $810.

23 Issued Ck. No. 429 to Nollen Dental Laboratory for laboratory expense, $296.

23 Issued Ck. No. 430 to Milner Dental Supply as a contract payment (Notes Payable) on dental equipment purchased in October, $400.

27 Total cash received from patients during the week, $1,396.

29 Ogden wrote Ck. No. 431 payable to Briggs Automotive for repairing his car, $226 (to be recorded as Drawing).

31 Issued Ck. No. 432 to Milner Dental Supply for miscellaneous dental supplies, $219.

31 In payment of salaries, issued Ck. No. 433 to C. R. Jarvis, $970 and Ck. No. 434 to D. C. Smith, $970. (Use two lines.)

31 Issued Ck. No. 435 to S. A. Ogden for personal use, $1,190.

31 Issued Ck. No. 436 to Jersey Publishers Service for magazines for the office, $54.

31 Issued Ck. No. 437 to Clement Linen Supply for laundry services, $84.

31 Total cash received from patients this week up until last day of year, $1,976.

After you have added all columns at the end of the month, prove on scratch paper that the sum of the debit totals equals the sum of the credit totals.

Column	Debit totals	Credit totals
Cash	$14,047.00	$12,921.00
Other Accounts	8,840.00	4,000.00
Dental Supplies	651.00	
S. A. Ogden, Drawing	2,976.00	
Professional Fees		14,047.00
Laundry and Cleaning Expense	224.00	
Salary Expense	3,880.00	
Laboratory Expense	296.00	
Miscellaneous Expense	54.00	
	$30,968.00	$30,968.00

COMBINED JOURNAL

CASH		CK. NO.	DATE		ACCOUNT NAME	POST. REF.	OTHER ACCOUNTS	
DEBIT	CREDIT						DEBIT	CREDIT
			20—					
	2000 00	416	Dec.	1	Rent Expense	516	2000 00	
	71 00	417		1	Telephone Expense	523	71 00	
	112 00	418		1	Utilities Expense	524	112 00	
	132 00	419		3	Office Supplies	114	132 00	
	254 00	420		5	Dental Instruments Expense	511	254 00	
7144 00				5		–		
	92 00	421		8	Repairs and Maintenance Expense	525	92 00	
	750 00	422		9	S. A. Ogden	–		
	140 00	423		11	Reliable Cleaning Service	–		
2411 00				12		–		
	432 00	424		16	Davies Dental Supply	–		
	970 00	425		16	C. R. Jarvis	–		
	970 00	426		16	D. C. Smith	–		
				19	Dental Equipment	121	5779 00	
	1779 00	427		19	Notes Payable	211		4000 00
1120 00				19		–		
	810 00	428		22	S. A. Ogden	–		
	296 00	429		23	Nollen Dental Laboratory	–		
	400 00	430		23	Notes Payable	211	400 00	
1396 00				27		–		
	226 00	431		29	Briggs Automotive	–		
	219 00	432		31	Milner Dental Supply	–		
	970 00	433		31	C. R. Jarvis	–		
	970 00	434		31	D. C. Smith	–		
	1190 00	435		31	S. A. Ogden	–		
	54 00	436		31	Jersey Publishers Service	–		
	84 00	437		31	Clement Linen Supply	–		
1976 00				31		–		
14047 00	12921 00			31			8840 00	4000 00
(111)	(111)						(X)	(X)

END OF MONTH
Post the column totals to the Cash account in the general ledger at the end of the month. The account number in parentheses at the foot of each column indicates that posting has been completed.

DAILY
Post each amount in the Other Accounts columns to an account in the general ledger. The account number recorded in the Post. Ref. column indicates that posting has been completed. The (X) indicates that the column total is not to be posted.

FIGURE 6

PAGE 12

		DENTAL SUPPLIES	S. A. OGDEN, DRAWING	PROFESSIONAL FEES	LAUNDRY AND CLEANING EXPENSE	SALARY EXPENSE	LABORATORY EXPENSE	MISC. EXPENSE	
		DEBIT	DEBIT	CREDIT	DEBIT	DEBIT	DEBIT	DEBIT	
									1
									2
									3
									4
									5
									6
				7,144.00					7
									8
			750.00						9
					140.00				10
				2,411.00					11
		432.00							12
						970.00			13
						970.00			14
									15
									16
				1,120.00					17
			810.00						18
							296.00		19
									20
				1,396.00					21
			226.00						22
		219.00							23
						970.00			24
						970.00			25
			1,190.00						26
								54.00	27
					84.00				28
				1,976.00					29
		651.00	2,976.00	14,047.00	224.00	3,880.00	296.00	54.00	30
		(113)	(312)	(411)	(512)	(513)	(514)	(526)	31
									32
									33
									34

END OF MONTH
Post the column totals to their general ledger accounts. Account numbers in parentheses indicate that posting has been completed.

Posting from the Combined Journal

Objective 3

Post from the combined journal and determine the cash balance.

The person who keeps records posts items in the Other Accounts columns individually, usually daily, using the specific transaction date. **After posting the ledger account, the person records the ledger account number in the Post. Ref. column of the combined journal.** This procedure is similar to posting from a general journal.

Remember!

Special columns are posted as one total. Amounts in Other Accounts columns are posted individually.

Special columns, used only for debits or credits to specific accounts, are posted as totals at the end of the month. **After posting the ledger account, you record the ledger account number in the special column immediately below the total.** The account number is placed in parentheses. The total of the Cash Debit column in Figure 6 on pages 194–195 is an example. After the Cash account in the general ledger has been debited for $14,047.00, the account number of Cash (111) is placed in parentheses below the total of the Cash Debit column in the combined journal. Notice the X's in parentheses below the totals of the Other Accounts columns. These totals were not posted because the individual amounts recorded in the columns were posted separately to the accounts listed in the Account Name column. The separate amounts listed in the Other Accounts columns should not be posted twice.

The Cash, Dental Supplies, and Rent Expense accounts from Dr. Ogden's completed general ledger are shown in Figure 7 to illustrate the posting process.

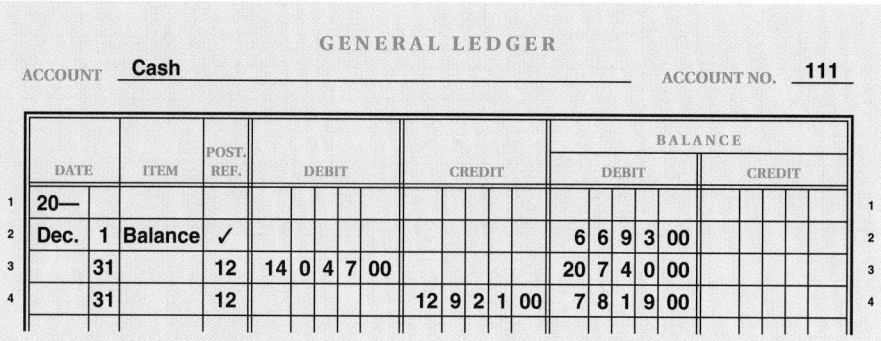

FIGURE 7

GENERAL LEDGER

ACCOUNT Cash ACCOUNT NO. 111

DATE		ITEM	POST. REF.	DEBIT	CREDIT	BALANCE DEBIT	BALANCE CREDIT
20—							
Dec.	1	Balance	✓			6 6 9 3 00	
	31		12	14 0 4 7 00		20 7 4 0 00	
	31		12		12 9 2 1 00	7 8 1 9 00	

ACCOUNT Dental Supplies ACCOUNT NO. 113

DATE		ITEM	POST. REF.	DEBIT	CREDIT	BALANCE DEBIT	BALANCE CREDIT
20—							
Dec.	1	Balance	✓			4 8 2 9 00	
	31		12	6 5 1 00		5 4 8 0 00	

ACCOUNT Rent Expense ACCOUNT NO. 516

DATE		ITEM	POST. REF.	DEBIT	CREDIT	BALANCE DEBIT	BALANCE CREDIT
20—							
Dec.	1	Balance	✓			16 0 0 0 00	
	1		12	2 0 0 0 00		18 0 0 0 00	

A combined journal allows businesses to set up special columns for frequently used accounts, such as Dental Supplies for this professional firm.

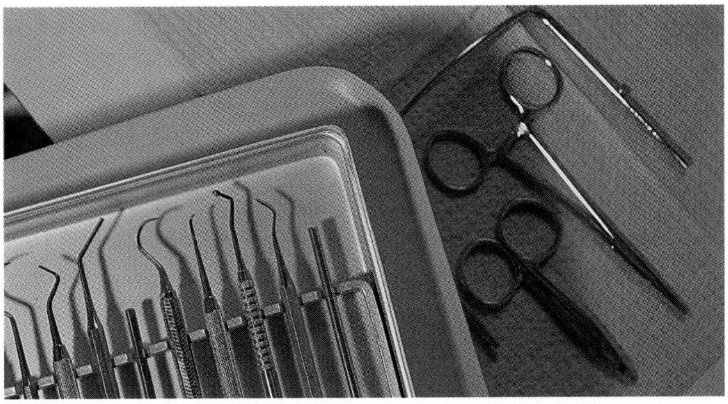

Determining Cash Balance

The cash balance may be determined at any time during the month by taking the beginning balance of cash, adding the total cash debits so far during the month, and subtracting the total cash credits so far during the month. For example, to determine the balance of cash on December 5:

COMBINED JOURNAL PAGE 12

	Cash Debit	Cash Credit	Ck. No.	Date		Account Name
1				20—		
2		2,000 00	416	Dec.	1	Rent Expense
3		71 00	417		1	Telephone Expense
4		112 00	418		1	Utilities Expense
5		132 00	419		3	Office Supplies
6		254 00	420		5	Dental Instruments Expense
7	7,144 00				5	———
8	7,144 00	2,569 00				

Beginning balance (Dec. 1)	$ 6,693
Add cash debits	7,144
Total	$13,837
Less cash credits	2,569
Ending balance (Dec. 5)	$11,268

Work Sheet for a Professional Enterprise

Objective 4

Prepare a work sheet for a professional enterprise.

Assume that Dr. Ogden's receptionist posted the journal entries to the ledger accounts and recorded the trial balance in the first two columns of the work sheet. Dr. Ogden uses the modified cash basis of accounting, recording revenue only when he has received it in cash and recording expenses only when he has paid for them in cash. However, when Dr. Ogden buys an item that is going to last a number of years, he records this item as an asset and writes it off or depreciates it by making an adjusting entry each year of its useful life. He also makes adjusting entries for expired insurance and for supplies used. Data for the adjustments are given below.

a. Additional depreciation on dental equipment, $8,400.
b. Additional depreciation on office furniture and equipment, $1,520.
c. Inventory of x-ray supplies, $618 (ending balance).
d. Inventory of dental supplies, $1,616 (ending balance).
e. Inventory of office supplies, $196 (ending balance).
f. Insurance expired, $1,836.

With these adjusting entries, the rest of the work sheet can be completed as shown in Figure 8. First the balances of the accounts that were adjusted are brought up to date in the Adjusted Trial Balance columns. Then these amounts are carried forward to the remaining columns.

FIGURE 8

	ACCOUNT NAME	TRIAL BALANCE DEBIT	TRIAL BALANCE CREDIT
1	Cash	7846 00	
2	X-ray Supplies	2762 00	
3	Dental Supplies	5480 00	
4	Office Supplies	1308 00	
5	Prepaid Insurance	2448 00	
6	Dental Equipment	115234 00	
7	Accumulated Depreciation, Dental Equipment		17200 00
8	Office Furniture and Equipment	7800 00	
9	Accum. Depr., Office Furniture and Equipment		4200 00
10	Notes Payable		7600 00
11	S. A. Ogden, Capital		71498 00
12	S. A. Ogden, Drawing	46280 00	
13	Professional Fees		161024 00
14	Dental Instruments Expense	1982 00	
15	Laundry and Cleaning Expense	3024 00	
16	Salary Expense	40800 00	
17	Laboratory Expense	5856 00	
18	Rent Expense	18000 00	
19	Telephone Expense	412 00	
20	Utilities Expense	778 00	
21	Repairs and Maintenance Expense	888 00	
22	Miscellaneous Expense	624 00	
23		261522 00	261522 00
24	Depreciation Expense, Dental Equipment		
25	Depreciation Expense, Office Furn. and Equipment		
26	X-ray Supplies Expense		
27	Dental Supplies Expense		
28	Office Supplies Expense		
29	Insurance Expense		
30			
31	Net Income		
32			
33			

Remember!

In adjusting for supplies, deduct the amount of the ending inventory from the amount recorded as Supplies.

Medical professionals have their uniforms or lab coats cleaned by outside services. Their work sheets are likely to include an account for Laundry and Cleaning Expense.

L&N
UNIFORM
SUPPLY CO.
Uniforms Coveralls Aprons Shop Towels Dust Control

S. A. Ogden, D.D.S.
Work Sheet
For Year Ended December 31, 20—

Adjustments		Adjusted Trial Balance		Income Statement		Balance Sheet	
Debit	Credit	Debit	Credit	Debit	Credit	Debit	Credit
		7,846.00				7,846.00	
	(c) 2,144.00	618.00				618.00	
	(d) 3,864.00	1,616.00				1,616.00	
	(e) 1,112.00	196.00				196.00	
	(f) 1,836.00	612.00				612.00	
		115,234.00				115,234.00	
	(a) 8,400.00		25,600.00				25,600.00
		7,800.00				7,800.00	
	(b) 1,520.00		5,720.00				5,720.00
			7,600.00				7,600.00
			71,498.00				71,498.00
		46,280.00				46,280.00	
			161,024.00		161,024.00		
		1,982.00		1,982.00			
		3,024.00		3,024.00			
		40,800.00		40,800.00			
		5,856.00		5,856.00			
		18,000.00		18,000.00			
		412.00		412.00			
		778.00		778.00			
		888.00		888.00			
		624.00		624.00			
(a) 8,400.00		8,400.00		8,400.00			
(b) 1,520.00		1,520.00		1,520.00			
(c) 2,144.00		2,144.00		2,144.00			
(d) 3,864.00		3,864.00		3,864.00			
(e) 1,112.00		1,112.00		1,112.00			
(f) 1,836.00		1,836.00		1,836.00			
18,876.00	18,876.00	271,442.00	271,442.00	91,240.00	161,024.00	180,202.00	110,418.00
				69,784.00			69,784.00
				161,024.00	161,024.00	180,202.00	180,202.00

Financial Statements

Objective 5

Prepare financial statements for a professional enterprise.

From the work sheet, Dr. Ogden's accountant prepares the financial statements shown in Figure 9. In this case, there was no additional investment made by S. A. Ogden during the year.

Adjusting and Closing Entries

Objective 6

Record adjusting and closing entries in a combined journal.

Dr. Ogden (or his receptionist) records the adjusting and closing entries entirely in the Other Accounts columns of the combined journal. These entries must be posted individually, so the special columns are never used for them.

FIGURE 9

S. A. Ogden, D.D.S.
Income Statement
For Year Ended December 31, 20—

Revenue:		
Professional Fees		$161,024.00
Expenses:		
Dental Instruments Expense	$ 1,982.00	
Laundry and Cleaning Expense	3,024.00	
Salary Expense	40,800.00	
Laboratory Expense	5,856.00	
Dental Supplies Expense	3,864.00	
Rent Expense	18,000.00	
Depreciation Expense, Dental Equipment	8,400.00	
Depreciation Expense, Office Furniture and Equipment	1,520.00	
X-ray Supplies Expense	2,144.00	
Office Supplies Expense	1,112.00	
Insurance Expense	1,836.00	
Telephone Expense	412.00	
Utilities Expense	778.00	
Repairs and Maintenance Expense	888.00	
Miscellaneous Expense	624.00	
Total Expenses		91,240.00
Net Income		$ 69,784.00

S. A. Ogden, D.D.S.
Statement of Owner's Equity
For Year Ended December 31, 20—

S. A. Ogden, Capital, January 1, 20—		$71,498.00
Net Income for Year	$69,784.00	
Less Withdrawals for Year	46,280.00	
Increase in Capital		23,504.00
S. A. Ogden, Capital, December 31, 20—		$95,002.00

Remember!

Whenever you are preparing a statement of owner's equity, always check the Capital account in the general ledger to see if any additional investment was recorded.

FIGURE 9 (continued)

S. A. Ogden, D.D.S.
Balance Sheet
December 31, 20—

Assets		
Cash		$ 7,846.00
X-ray Supplies		618.00
Dental Supplies		1,616.00
Office Supplies		196.00
Prepaid Insurance		612.00
Dental Equipment	$115,234.00	
Less Accumulated Depreciation	25,600.00	89,634.00
Office Furniture and Equipment	$ 7,800.00	
Less Accumulated Depreciation	5,720.00	2,080.00
Total Assets		$102,602.00
Liabilities		
Notes Payable		$ 7,600.00
Owner's Equity		
S. A. Ogden, Capital		95,002.00
Total Liabilities and Owner's Equity		$102,602.00

The adjusting and closing entries are shown in Figure 10 on pages 202–203, two pages of a shortened combined journal. These adjusting and closing entries are shown here on two pages to make the concept clear. In practice, the closing entries would be written right below the adjusting entries. Be careful not to split up any individual entry between two pages. The totals are included because it is customary to show totals of all columns of a combined journal. In the Account Name column, accounts to be credited do not have to be indented.

DESIGNING A COMBINED JOURNAL

Remember!

A combined journal can be used for either the accrual or the modified cash basis of accounting.

Since the combined journal is widely used in professional offices and service business firms, it is interesting to look over the varieties of combined journals available at stores selling office supplies. Some are bound journals; others are loose-leaf books. The number of columns varies from six to twenty, and they are available with or without column headings. Those that have printed column headings represent a "canned" type of combined journal. These journals are available for service stations, dry cleaners, doctors' offices, and many other types of businesses.

Combined journals with blank columns can be customized to meet the specific requirements of a given business. Prior to labeling the columns, first study the operations of the business and make up a chart of accounts. Next, identify those accounts that are likely to be used frequently to record typical transactions of the business. Naturally, if these accounts are used over and over, you need to set up special columns for them.

COMBINED JOURNAL

Cash Debit	Cash Credit	Ck. No.	Date		Account Name	Post. Ref.	Other Accounts Debit	Other Accounts Credit
			20—		Adjusting Entries			
			Dec.	31	Depr. Expense, Dental Equipment	517	8400 00	
					Accum. Depr., Dental Equipment	122		8400 00
				31	Depreciation Expense, Office			
					Furniture and Equipment	518	1520 00	
					Accumulated Depreciation, Office			
					Furniture and Equipment	124		1520 00
				31	X-ray Supplies Expense	519	2144 00	
					X-ray Supplies	112		2144 00
				31	Dental Supplies Expense	515	3864 00	
					Dental Supplies	113		3864 00
				31	Office Supplies Expense	521	1112 00	
					Office Supplies	114		1112 00
				31	Insurance Expense	522	1836 00	
					Prepaid Insurance	115		1836 00
				31			18876 00	18876 00
							(X)	(X)

FIGURE 10

CHAPTER REVIEW

Review of Learning Objectives

1. Describe the accounting records for a professional enterprise.

   The records for a professional enterprise generally consist of an appointment record, a recording of charges levied for services rendered, and patients' or clients' (customers') ledger cards. A combined journal is generally used to record transactions that are posted to a general ledger.

2. Record transactions for both a professional and a service enterprise in a combined journal.

   Special columns are set up to record transactions involving frequently used accounts. Transactions involving other accounts are recorded in the Other Accounts columns. A long line in the Account Name column and a dash in the Post. Ref. column indicate that all debits and credits for a transaction have been entered in special columns.

3. Post from the combined journal and determine the cash balance.

COMBINED JOURNAL

Cash Debit	Cash Credit	Ck. No.	Date		Account Name	Post. Ref.	Other Accounts Debit	Other Accounts Credit
			20—		Closing Entries			
			Dec.	31	Professional Fees	411	161,024.00	
					Income Summary	313		161,024.00
				31	Income Summary	313	91,240.00	
					Dental Instruments Expense	511		1,982.00
					Laundry and Cleaning Expense	512		3,024.00
					Salary Expense	513		40,800.00
					Laboratory Expense	514		5,856.00
					Dental Supplies Expense	515		3,864.00
					Rent Expense	516		18,000.00
					Depr. Expense, Dental Equipment	517		8,400.00
					Depr. Expense, Office Furniture			
					and Equipment	518		1,520.00
					X-ray Supplies Expense	519		2,144.00
					Office Supplies Expense	521		1,112.00
					Insurance Expense	522		1,836.00
					Telephone Expense	523		412.00
					Utilities Expense	524		778.00
					Repairs and Maintenance Expense	525		888.00
					Miscellaneous Expense	526		624.00
				31	Income Summary	313	69,784.00	
					S. A. Ogden, Capital	311		69,784.00
				31	S. A. Ogden, Capital	311	46,280.00	
					S. A. Ogden, Drawing	312		46,280.00
				31			368,328.00	368,328.00
							(X)	(X)

FIGURE 10 (continued)

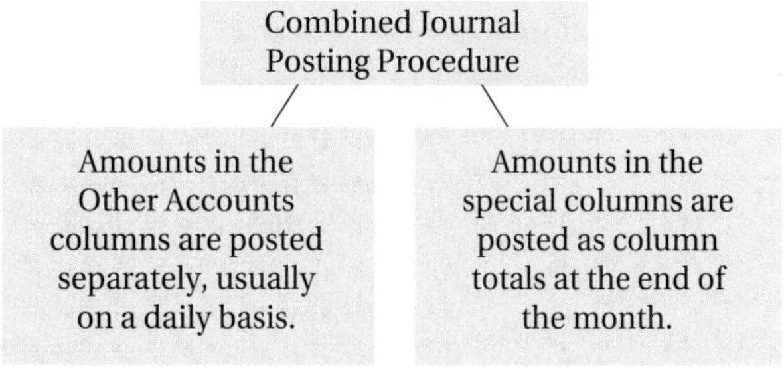
Combined Journal Posting Procedure
Amounts in the Other Accounts columns are posted separately, usually on a daily basis.
Amounts in the special columns are posted as column totals at the end of the month.

An account number in the Post. Ref. column indicates that the amount in the Other Accounts column has been posted; a dash in that column indicates that the amount is being posted as part of a column total. Below the totals of the Other Accounts columns, an X in parentheses indicates that the column total was not posted; accounts were posted individually. Below the totals of the special columns, the account numbers in parentheses indicate that each column has been posted.

4. Prepare a work sheet for a professional enterprise.

   The work sheet for a professional enterprise is the same as the work sheet presented in Chapter 4 for a service enterprise.

5. Prepare financial statements for a professional enterprise.

   The financial statements for professional enterprises are the same as the financial statements presented previously for service enterprises, except for some new account titles.

6. Record adjusting and closing entries in a combined journal.

   Adjusting and closing entries are recorded in the Account Name column and the Other Accounts Debit and Credit columns. The closing entries may be recorded immediately below the adjusting entries. However, if it is necessary to carry over any one entry to a second page, you should not split up the entry.

Glossary

Combined journal A journal format widely used by professional and service enterprises in place of a general journal; designed to make the recording and posting of transactions more efficient. (192)

Patient's ledger record A record of amounts charged to patients, amounts received from patients, estimates given, and the remaining amounts owed by patients, which are called debit balances. In the event that a patient overpaid, the remainder is called a credit balance, which indicates a liability exists to the patient. (186)

Professional enterprise A business that provides a highly specialized service for a fee. (185)

Special columns Columns in a journal that are used to record amounts that occur frequently. (192)

QUESTIONS, EXERCISES, AND PROBLEMS

Discussion Questions

1. Why do small businesses find the combined journal convenient to use?
2. Name four columns that should always appear in a combined journal.
3. What types of transactions are recorded in the Other Accounts Debit and Other Accounts Credit columns?
4. In the Post. Ref. column of a combined journal, what does a dash signify and what does a number indicate?
5. What is the meaning of X's and numbers in parentheses under the column totals of a combined journal?
6. When an amount is placed in the Other Accounts Debit or Other Accounts Credit column, why is it necessary to complete the Account Name column?
7. You have been asked to design a combined journal for Andrea's Hair Salon. Customers pay in cash only. The business buys supplies on account from creditors. Rent and utilities are paid monthly. Employees are paid wages weekly. The owner, Andrea Wilke, makes withdrawals weekly. The firm advertises frequently. List the special columns needed plus the four columns that always appear in a combined journal.
8. Describe the process of proving the combined journal at the end of the month.

Exercises

P.O. 1

Record receipt of cash under modified cash basis.

Exercise 6-1 On June 4, the appointment record for a chiropractor shows that the total of the fees column is $326 and the total of the receipts column is $197. At the end of the day, $197 is deposited in the bank. Record the journal entry for the deposit in the general journal. Assume that the modified cash basis is used.

P.O. 2

List the columns to record transactions.

Exercise 6-2 The Brandon Advertising Agency uses a combined journal with the following columns. Assume that the accrual basis of accounting is used.

Cash Debit	Accounts Receivable Debit
Cash Credit	Accounts Receivable Credit
Ck. No.	Accounts Payable Debit
Date	Accounts Payable Credit
Account Name	Commissions Income Credit
Post. Ref.	Salary Expense Debit
Other Accounts Debit	Utilities Expense Debit
Other Accounts Credit	

List the columns in which each of the following would be recorded.

a. Payment of rent for the month.
b. Charging a client a commission.
c. Payment of an electric bill.
d. Investment of equipment by the owner.

P.O. 2

Designate columns to record transactions.

Exercise 6-3 T. L. Lee, an attorney, uses a combined journal with the columns listed below. Indicate which columns would be used to enter the following transactions.

a. Cash Debit
b. Cash Credit
c. Other Accounts Debit
d. Other Accounts Credit
e. Accounts Receivable Debit
f. Accounts Receivable Credit
g. Fees Earned Credit
h. Office Supplies Debit
i. Salary Expense Debit
j. Travel Expense Debit

1. Issued a check for $249 for the purchase of a filing cabinet.
2. Sold services on account, $5,440.
3. Received and paid the electric bill, $98.
4. Received and paid the bill for airline ticket, $356.
5. Sold services for cash, $100.
6. Received and paid the bill for rent for the month, $1,000.
7. Received $4,200 on account from customers.
8. T. L. Lee withdrew $1,500 for personal use.
9. Issued a check for $50 payment of court fees on behalf of the client (client owes us).

P.O. 2

Designate columns to record transactions.

Exercise 6-4 The books of Binyon and Associates, Certified Public Accountants, are kept on a modified cash basis. The client record of Alice Benson is presented on the following page.

BINYON AND ASSOCIATES
CERTIFIED PUBLIC ACCOUNTANTS
242 SELVA AVENUE
MIAMI, FLORIDA 32906

CLIENT RECORD

Alice Benson
1429 Garfield Avenue
Miami, Florida 32909

DATE		SERVICE	CHG		REC		BAL	
20—								
May	6	Tax prep.	164	00			164	00
June	2				90	00	74	00

Record the June 2 transaction in a combined journal.

P.O. 2

Journalize a withdrawal.

Exercise 6-5 Assume that on June 14, Binyon and Associates issues business check number 311 for $950 to Miami National Bank for payment on N. Binyon's home mortgage. Explain how the transaction would be recorded in a combined journal.

P.O. 2

List the special columns to accommodate a situation.

Exercise 6-6 Baxter Dental Laboratory maintains charge accounts for nine dentists. The owner is R. A. Baxter. Frequent payments include supplies, salaries, delivery, and owner's withdrawals. List the special columns you would suggest for a combined journal.

P.O. 2

Describe the posting procedure.

Exercise 6-7 Kroyer Landscaping Services uses a combined journal that includes the following columns:

Cash Debit
Cash Credit
Other Accounts Debit
Other Accounts Credit
Fees Income
Truck Expense Debit
Supplies Expense Debit
Wages Expense Debit
Miscellaneous Expense Debit

Indicate the columns that are posted individually and those that are posted as a column total. Indicate the columns that are posted daily and those that are posted at the end of the month.

P.O. 3

Determine up-to-date cash balance.

Exercise 6-8 Determine the cash balance after November 8.

Cash	
Beginning Nov. 1 Bal. 642.50	

	CASH		CK.	DATE	
	DEBIT	CREDIT	NO.		
1				20—	
2	921 64			Nov.	1
3		75 42	121		3
4	389 00				5
5		416 20	122		8
6	840 00	219 00	123		9
7		84 59	124		11

CONSIDER AND COMMUNICATE

You do the bookkeeping for a veterinarian. She has no formal accounting system yet, but she does save all source documents.

1. Convince her of the benefits of a combined journal.
2. Design the format for a combined journal with debit or credit columns and headings to accommodate the entries for a veterinarian using the modified cash basis.

WHAT IF . . .

Your friend has been using a general journal for his sole proprietorship business. He needs a better journal solution because he does the accounting himself. Discuss how you think a combined journal could be the answer he is looking for.

A MATTER OF ETHICS

It is Friday at 5 P.M. It is your responsibility to count the money in the cash register, prepare the deposit slip for the bank, and lock up. You have counted the money, prepared the bank deposit, and cleared the cash register, when a customer comes in to buy something. You finish the sale for $9.50. The customer had the exact change. You are in a hurry and do not want to redo the deposit, so you put the $9.50 in your bag (the safe is locked and you don't have the combination). You intend to add it to Monday's deposit. Over the weekend you run out of gas and need the $9.50 for gas. Discuss the situation.

WEB WORK

Using an Internet web browser, type in the search box the phrase *professional business* or *service business accounting.* Search for an article or find a home page that provides information about accounting for small businesses. Summarize your findings in a 1–2 paragraph memorandum to the owner of a small business. Plan a short oral presentation for your class.

PROBLEM SET A

For additional help, see the demonstration problems at the beginning of each chapter in your Working Papers.

P.O. 2

Problem 6-1A M. L. Janes, M.D., uses the following chart of accounts:

Assets

111 Cash
112 Medical Supplies
113 X-ray Supplies
114 Office Supplies
121 Medical Equipment
122 Accumulated Depreciation, Medical Equipment
123 Office Furniture and Equipment
124 Accumulated Depreciation, Office Furniture and Equipment
125 Vehicle
126 Accumulated Depreciation, Vehicle

Liabilities

211 Notes Payable

Owner's Equity

311 M. L. Janes, Capital
312 M. L. Janes, Drawing
313 Income Summary

Revenue

411 Professional Fees

Expenses

511 Nurse Salary Expense
512 Office Salary Expense
513 Equipment Rental Expense
514 Rent Expense
515 Medical Supplies Expense
516 X-ray Supplies Expense
517 Laboratory Expense
518 Cleaning Expense
519 Office Supplies Expense
521 Depreciation Expense, Medical Equipment
522 Depreciation Expense, Office Furniture and Equipment
523 Depreciation Expense, Vehicle
524 Vehicle Expense
525 Insurance Expense
526 Telephone Expense
527 Utilities Expense
528 Miscellaneous Expense

Dr. Janes's records consist of an appointment record book, examination and charge reports, patients' ledger records, a combined journal, and a general ledger. The doctor fills out an examination and charge report each time a patient visits. The report contains a description or listing of the treatments and tests administered, and also the amounts of the charges. The charges are then recorded in the patient's ledger record. Monthly statements based on the patient's ledger record are mailed to the patient. Dr. Janes's books are kept on the modified cash basis. These transactions took place during April:

Apr. 1 Paid Krebs Realty for rent for the month, $1,680 (Ck. No. 636).
2 Paid salary to M. Lewis (part-time office person), $875 (Ck. No. 637).
4 Bought medical supplies for cash from Pike Medical Supply Co., $460 (Ck. No. 638).
6 Received cash from patients during week, $7,920.
9 Paid telephone bill to Acme Telephone Company, $97 (Ck. No. 639).
12 Paid Techno-Labs for laboratory expense, $465 (Ck. No. 640).
13 Total cash received from patients during week, $5,470.
15 Dr. M. L. Janes withdrew $850 for personal use (Ck. No. 641).
17 Bought x-ray supplies for cash from Tilly Supply Company, $214 (Ck. No. 642).
18 Paid Terry's Service Station for gas and oil for vehicle used in business, $87 (vehicle expense) (Ck. No. 643).

Apr. 20 Received cash from patients during week, $2,986.
23 Bought postage stamps for cash at post office, $10 (Miscellaneous Expense) (Ck. No. 644).
24 Paid $104 for laundry service to Crystal Laundry (Cleaning Expense) (Ck. No. 645).
27 Paid King News Service for magazines, $76.75 (Miscellaneous Expense) (Ck. No. 646).
30 Paid salary for the month to C. Doane (nurse), $2,010 (Ck. No. 647).
30 Paid Best Janitorial, $132 (Cleaning Expense) (Ck. No. 648).
30 Received cash from patients (April 21 through 30), $2,158.
30 Dr. M. L. Janes withdrew $1,820 for personal use (Ck. No. 649).

Check Figure
Total debits, $27,414.75

Instructions

1. Record these transactions on page 9 of the combined journal. Insert the name of the Drawing account.
2. Prove the equality of the debit and credit totals in the Account Name column below the totals.

P.O. 6

Problem 6-2A The completed work sheet for S. R. Lindell, Psychologist, is shown in Figure 11 on pages 210 and 211.

Check Figure
Total Other Accounts Debit column, $173,211.40

Instructions

Record the adjusting and closing entries in the combined journal. Remember to total the columns and insert an X in parentheses below each total.

P.O. 2,3

Problem 6-3A Dr. Terrence T. Cascone operates the Cascone Allergy Clinic. The transactions described below were completed during September of this year. His chart of accounts is as follows:

Assets

111 Cash
112 Accounts Receivable
113 Supplies
114 Prepaid Insurance
121 Equipment
122 Accumulated Depreciation, Equipment

Liabilities

221 Accounts Payable

Owner's Equity

311 T. T. Cascone, Capital
312 T. T. Cascone, Drawing
313 Income Summary

Revenue

411 Professional Fees

Expenses

511 Salary Expense
512 Rent Expense
513 Laboratory Expense
514 Utilities Expense
515 Depreciation Expense, Equipment
516 Miscellaneous Expense

Sept. 2 Bought medical equipment on account, $1,680, from Wing Medical Supplies. (Use two lines.)
2 Paid Jayco Realty for office rent for month, $1,050 (Ck. No. 516).
2 Received cash on account from patients, $829: D. R. Calvin, $152.50; Diane Stillman, $272; Jackson Niles, $317; Teresa Garrett, $87.50. (Dr. Cascone uses the accrual basis. Use four lines, recording individual amounts in both the Cash Debit column and the Accounts Receivable Credit column. List each patient's name in the Account Name column.)

FIGURE 11

Account Name	Trial Balance Debit	Trial Balance Credit
Cash	6,270.00	
Supplies	5,260.00	
Office Equipment	56,410.25	
Accumulated Depreciation, Office Equipment		16,984.16
S. R. Lindell, Capital		38,872.94
S. R. Lindell, Drawing	24,785.00	
Professional Fees		70,929.20
Salary Expense	16,324.60	
Advertising Expense	4,575.10	
Rent Expense	7,670.00	
Vehicle Expense	2,062.75	
Travel Expense	2,241.32	
Entertainment Expense	796.12	
Miscellaneous Expense	391.16	
	126,786.30	126,786.30
Depreciation Expense, Office Equipment		
Supplies Expense		
Net Income		

Sept. 3 Received cash for professional services rendered, $2,419.

5 Received and paid electric bill to Mid-State Power, $147.52 (Ck. No. 517).

8 Received and paid telephone bill to Western Telephone Company for month, $73 (Ck. No. 518).

9 Recorded fees charged to patients on account for professional services rendered $766.50: F. Radewan, $396.50; M. Parkhill, $370. (Use two lines.)

15 Paid salary of L. Macy (assistant), $757.50 (Ck. No. 519).

19 Received cash for professional services, $598.

23 Returned part of the equipment purchased on September 2 and received a reduction on the bill, $75.

28 Billed patients on account for professional services rendered, $1,133: C. C. Robbins, $575; Meredith Capwell, $316.50; Drew Hanson, $241.50.

30 Paid salary of C. Bates (part-time assistant), $820.75 (Ck. No. 520).

30 Paid salary of R. Cato (receptionist), $1,120 (Ck. No. 521).

30 Dr. Cascone withdrew $1,688.50 cash for personal use (Ck. No. 522).

Check Figure
Total debits, $13,157.77

Instructions

1. Record these transactions in the combined journal, page 37.
2. Prove the equality of the debit and credit totals in the Account Name column below the totals.

S. R. Lindell, Psychologist
Work Sheet
For Year Ended December 31, 20—

Adjustments Debit	Adjustments Credit	Adjusted Trial Balance Debit	Adjusted Trial Balance Credit	Income Statement Debit	Income Statement Credit	Balance Sheet Debit	Balance Sheet Credit
		6,270.00				6,270.00	
	(b) 585.20	4,674.80				4,674.80	
		56,410.25				56,410.25	
	(a) 5,982.80		22,966.96				22,966.96
			38,872.94				38,872.94
		24,785.00				24,785.00	
			70,929.20		70,929.20		
		16,324.60		16,324.60			
		4,575.10		4,575.10			
		7,670.00		7,670.00			
		2,062.75		2,062.75			
		2,241.32		2,241.32			
		796.12		796.12			
		391.16		391.16			
(a) 5,982.80		5,982.80		5,982.80			
(b) 585.20		585.20		585.20			
6,568.00	6,568.00	132,769.10	132,769.10	40,629.05	70,929.20	92,140.05	61,839.90
				30,300.15			30,300.15
				70,929.20	70,929.20	92,140.05	92,140.05

3. Fill in owner's equity accounts and post to the accounts in the general ledger.
4. Prepare a trial balance.

P.O. 2

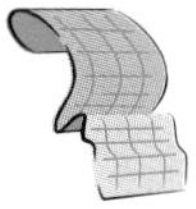

Problem 6-4A On September 1 of this year, T. W. Binford started a limousine service serving the local area. The following transactions related to Luxury Limousine Service were completed during September.

Sept.
- 1 Binford opened an account in the Golden State Bank in the name of the business and deposited $34,000.
- 2 Bought two used limousines from Laughlin Motors for $80,900, paying $20,900 down, with the balance payable in 30 days (Ck. No. 1).
- 3 Bought heavy-duty vacuum and car-cleaning equipment for $359 from Gehrig E. Schaums, paying cash (Ck. No. 2).
- 4 Paid Valley Service for gas and oil for limousines, $172 (Ck. No. 3).
- 5 Paid rent for subletting office space, $235 (Ck. No. 4).
- 7 Paid wages to L. Bain, $454 (Ck. No. 5).
- 7 Received revenue for the week, $1,214.
- 9 Paid for city business license, $86 (Ck. No. 6).
- 11 Bought desk and filing cabinet on account from Murray Office Supply, $279.
- 14 Paid for telephone answering service for the month, $136 (Ck. No. 7).

Sept. 14 Paid wages to L. Bain, $469 (Ck. No. 8).
14 Binford withdrew $750 for personal use (Ck. No. 9).
14 Received revenue for the week, $1,340.
17 Paid Laughlin Motors $3,000 as part payment on account (Ck. No. 10).
18 Paid $142 for advertising in the telephone directory (Ck. No. 11).
18 Paid Valley Service for gas and oil for limousines, $214 (Ck. No. 12).
20 Paid utilities for the month, $106 (Ck. No. 13).
21 Received revenue for the week $1,439.
23 Paid wages to L. Bain, $471 (Ck. No. 14).
30 Received revenue for the week, $1,010.
30 Paid Security Insurance Agency for vehicle insurance for six months, $757.
30 Paid wages to L. Bain, $444 (Ck. No. 15).
30 Binford withdrew $1,000 for personal use (Ck. No. 16).

Check Figure
Total debits, $128,977

Instructions

1. By reviewing the transactions for Luxury Limousine Service, develop a chart of accounts. The company will use the modified cash basis. All revenue is in the form of cash.
2. Label the appropriate columns in the combined journal. Next to the Date column, list a Ck. No. column and record checks beginning with number 1.
3. Record the transactions in the combined journal beginning with page 1.
4. Show proof of the equality of debit and credit totals in the Account Name column below the totals.

Instructions for General Ledger Software

1. Prepare a bank reconciliation as of July 31. Errors made by the company or the bank, as well as service charges, must be entered as debit or credit memos.
2. Print the bank reconciliation.
3. Record the necessary journal entries.
4. Print the journal entries.

PROBLEM SET B

For additional help, see the demonstration problems at the beginning of each chapter in your Working Papers.

P.O. 2

Problem 6-1B The following chart of accounts is used by C. Stevenson, M.D.:

Assets

111 Cash
112 Medical Supplies
113 X-ray Supplies
114 Office Supplies
121 Medical Equipment
122 Accumulated Depreciation, Medical Equipment
123 Office Furniture and Equipment
124 Accumulated Depreciation, Office Furniture and Equipment
125 Vehicle
126 Accumulated Depreciation, Vehicle

Liabilities

211 Notes Payable

Owner's Equity

311 C. Stevenson, Capital
312 C. Stevenson, Drawing
313 Income Summary

Revenue

411 Professional Fees

Expenses

511 Salary Expense
512 Rent Expense
513 Equipment Rental Expense
514 Medical Supplies Expense
515 X-ray Supplies Expense
516 Laboratory Expense
517 Cleaning Expense
518 Office Supplies Expense
519 Depreciation Expense, Medical Equipment
521 Depreciation Expense, Office Furniture and Equipment
522 Depreciation Expense, Vehicle
523 Vehicle Expense
524 Insurance Expense
525 Telephone Expense
526 Utilities Expense
527 Miscellaneous Expense

Dr. Stevenson's records consist of an appointment record book, examination and charge reports, patients' ledger records, a combined journal, and a general ledger. The doctor fills out an examination and charge report each time a patient visits. The reports contain a description or listing of the treatments and tests administered, along with the amounts of the charges. The charges are then recorded in the patient's ledger record. Monthly statements based on the patients' ledger records are mailed to patients. Dr. Stevenson's books are kept on the modified cash basis.

The following transactions took place during November:

Nov. 1 Bought medical supplies for cash from Mason Surgical Supply, $521.50 (Ck. No. 214).
1 Paid Kelsey Realty for rent for the month, $1,350 (Ck. No. 215).
4 Paid salary to C. Ortiz (part-time office person), $935 (Ck. No. 216).
6 Received cash from patients during the week, $8,412.
7 Bought an examination table from Shelly Surgical Supply, costing $1,680, paying $480 in cash and agreeing by contract to pay the balance in three monthly installments of $400 each (credit Notes Payable). (Issued Ck. No. 217.)
8 Paid Ruiz Laboratories for laboratory expense, $354 (Ck. No. 218).
9 Paid telephone bill to Region Telephone Company, $96 (Ck. No. 219).
13 Total cash received from patients during the week, $6,111.
16 Dr. C. Stevenson withdrew $1,000 for personal use (Ck. No. 220).
16 Bought x-ray supplies for cash from Saling's Supply Company, $198.50 (Ck. No. 221).
20 Total cash received from patients during the week, $2,595.
23 Bought postage stamps for cash at post office, $15 (Miscellaneous Expense) (Ck. No. 222).
26 Paid Sharkie's Service Station for gas and oil, $100.25 (Vehicle Expense) (Ck. No. 223).
28 Paid Strong and Company for janitorial service, $85 (Cleaning Expense) (Ck. No. 224).
30 Paid salary to L. Mackey (nurse), $2,305 (Ck. No. 225).
30 Dr. C. Stevenson withdrew $1,620 for personal use (Ck. No. 226).
30 Paid $102.10 to Economy Laundry for laundry service through November 30 (Cleaning Expense) (Ck. No. 227).

FIGURE 12

	ACCOUNT NAME	TRIAL BALANCE DEBIT	TRIAL BALANCE CREDIT
1	Cash	8,105.00	
2	Supplies	2,242.40	
3	Equipment	35,219.00	
4	Accumulated Depreciation, Equipment		7,490.00
5	T. R. Berman, Capital		27,945.40
6	T. R. Berman, Drawing	14,880.00	
7	Professional Fees		65,952.00
8	Salary Expense	31,315.00	
9	Advertising Expense	1,060.80	
10	Rent Expense	1,830.00	
11	Vehicle Expense	1,975.00	
12	Travel Expense	3,124.60	
13	Entertainment Expense	935.00	
14	Miscellaneous Expense	700.60	
15		101,387.40	101,387.40
16	Depreciation Expense, Equipment		
17	Supplies Expense		
18			
19	Net Income		
20			
21			

Check Figure
Total debits, $27,480.35

Instructions

1. Record these transactions in the combined journal, page 26. Insert the name in the Drawing account.
2. Prove the equality of the debits and credits in the Account Name column below the totals.

P.O. 6

Problem 6-2B The completed work sheet for Berman Development Company is shown in Figure 12 above.

Check Figure
Total Other Accounts Debit column, $150,045.40

Instructions

Record the adjusting and closing entries in the combined journal. Remember to total the columns and insert an X in parentheses below each total.

P.O. 2,3

Problem 6-3B Teresa K. Muller, D.C., operates the Muller Chiropractic Clinic. The transactions described on pages 215–216 were completed during September of this year. Her chart of accounts is as follows:

Assets

111 Cash
112 Accounts Receivable
113 Supplies
114 Prepaid Insurance
121 Equipment
122 Accumulated Depreciation, Equipment

Liabilities

221 Accounts Payable

Owner's Equity

311 T. K. Muller, Capital
312 T. K. Muller, Drawing
313 Income Summary

Berman Development Company
Work Sheet
For Month Ended December 31, 20—

Adjustments Debit	Adjustments Credit	Adjusted Trial Balance Debit	Adjusted Trial Balance Credit	Income Statement Debit	Income Statement Credit	Balance Sheet Debit	Balance Sheet Credit
		8,105.00				8,105.00	
	(b) 2,040.40	202.00				202.00	
		35,219.00				35,219.00	
	(a) 1,221.00		8,711.00				8,711.00
			27,945.40				27,945.40
		14,880.00				14,880.00	
			65,952.00		65,952.00		
		31,315.00		31,315.00			
		1,060.80		1,060.80			
		1,830.00		1,830.00			
		1,975.00		1,975.00			
		3,124.60		3,124.60			
		935.00		935.00			
		700.60		700.60			
(a) 1,221.00		1,221.00		1,221.00			
(b) 2,040.40		2,040.40		2,040.40			
3,261.40	3,261.40	102,608.40	102,608.40	44,202.40	65,952.00	58,406.00	36,656.40
				21,749.60			21,749.60
				65,952.00	65,952.00	58,406.00	58,406.00

Revenue

411 Professional Fees

Expenses

511 Salary Expense
512 Rent Expense
513 Laboratory Expense
514 Utilities Expense
515 Depreciation Expense, Equipment
516 Miscellaneous Expense

Sept. 1 Bought x-ray equipment on account from Radiological Associates, $1,680. (Use two lines.)
2 Paid N. Barnes for office rent for the month, $925 (Ck. No. 423).
2 Received cash on account from patients, $816: Ralph Whitehall, $285; Eileen Butterick, $321; Anthony Clark, $210. (Dr. Gilman uses the accrual basis. Use three lines, recording individual amounts in both the Cash Debit column and the Accounts Receivable Credit column. List each patient's name in the Account Name column.)
4 Received cash for professional services rendered, $1,890.50.
6 Received and paid electric bill to Universal Electric, $135.50 (Ck. No. 424).
7 Received and paid telephone bill for month to Southern Telephone Company, $42 (Ck. No. 425).

KVCC Arcadia Commons Campus Library

Sept. 9 Recorded fees charged to patients on account for professional services rendered, $891.50: T. R. Swenson, $420; Hubert Cooke, $471.50. (Use two lines.)

15 Paid salary of A. Olivera (assistant), $1,120 (Ck. No. 426).

19 Received cash for professional services, $585.

22 Returned part of equipment purchased on September 1 and received a reduction on the bill, $175.

27 Billed patients on account for professional services rendered, $690: N. R. Cranston, $160; J. R. Perez, $285; S. N. Appleton, $245.

30 Paid salary of D. Curry (part-time assistant), $522.50 (Ck. No. 427).

30 Paid salary of V. Green (receptionist), $1,040 for the month (Ck. No. 428).

30 Dr. Muller withdrew $1,520 cash for personal use (Ck. No. 429).

Check Figure
Total debits, $12,033

Instructions

1. Record these transactions in the combined journal, page 43.
2. Prove the equality of the debit and credit totals in the Account Name column below the money column totals.
3. Fill in owner's equity accounts and post to the accounts in the general ledger.
4. Prepare a trial balance.

P.O. 2

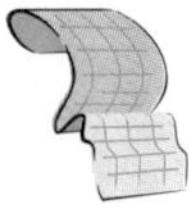

Problem 6-4B On July 1 of this year, K. A. Boehm started a landscaping business. The following transactions relating to Boehm's Landscaping were completed during July.

July 1 Boehm opened an account at the Carter National Bank in the name of the business and deposited $15,000.

1 Paid rent for office and warehouse space for the month, $525 (Ck. No. 1).

2 Bought a used truck from Nielsen Motors for $18,200, paying $4,000 as a downpayment, with the balance on account due in 30 days (Ck. No. 2).

3 Bought landscaping equipment from Greene Equipment for $3,500, paying $1,500 as a downpayment, with the balance due in 30 days (Ck. No. 3).

3 Paid Zippie's Fast Serve for gas and oil for the truck, $149 (Ck. No. 4).

4 Received and paid bill for advertising from the *City Lights Review*, $158 (Ck. No. 5).

4 Bought fertilizers on account from Date's Lawn and Garden Store, $1,060.

4 Bought beauty bark from O&P Distributing Company on account, $300.

6 Received revenue for the week, $1,492.

7 Paid wages to part-time employee, $292 (Ck. No. 6).

7 Paid for telephone answering service for the week, $144 (Ck. No. 7).

10 Paid Zippie's Fast Serve for gas and oil for the truck, $135 (Ck. No. 8).

13 Received revenue for the week, $1,601.

17 Boehm withdrew $1,020 for personal use (Ck. No. 9).

20 Received revenue for the week, $1,288.

July 21 Paid wages to part-time employee, $312 (Ck. No. 10).
27 Paid $67 for city business license (Ck. No. 11).
27 Paid utilities for the month, $126 (Ck. No. 12).
30 Paid Nielsen Motors $2,000 to apply on account (Ck. No. 13).
30 Paid Zippie's Fast Serve for gas and oil for the truck, $45, plus $95 for a tune-up (Ck. No. 14).
31 Received revenue for the week, $1,625.
31 Paid wages to part-time employee, $321 (Ck. No. 15).
31 Boehm withdrew $850 for personal use (Ck. No. 16).

Check Figure
Total debits, $50,305

Instructions

1. By reviewing the transactions for Boehm's Landscaping, formulate a chart of accounts. Boehm will use the modified cash basis of accounting.
2. Label the appropriate columns in the combined journal. Next to the Date column, list a Ck. No. column and record checks beginning with number 1.
3. Record the transactions in the combined journal beginning with page 1.
4. Show proof of the equality of debit and credit totals in the Account Name column below the totals.

Instructions for General Ledger Software

1. Prepare a bank reconciliation as of July 31. Errors made by the company or the bank, as well as service charges, must be entered as debit or credit memos.
2. Print the bank reconciliation.
3. Record the necessary journal entries.
4. Print the journal entries.

7 Bank Accounts and Cash Funds

WINDOWS ON THE WORLD WIDE WEB

Want to be as rich as Chicago Cub Sammy Sosa? After finishing college you may only earn a fraction of his income. Want some tips on growing your dough? Learn how to build wealth, manage credit-card debt, and decide how to spend your money. Are you better off buying a $174,000 house, a $100,000 condo, or renting an apartment for $550 per month? How do you reconcile your bank statements? Would you reconcile your bank account any differently if you were Sammy Sosa? Check out AOL's money management web site for helpful tips you can use to better handle finances at **http://www.aol.com/timesavers/money.html**. And to find out what Sammy Sosa and the other Chicago Cubs made this year, see **http://cbs.sports.com/u/baseball/mlb/teams/CHC/salaries.htm**.

Performance Objectives

After you have completed this chapter, you will be able to do the following:

1. Describe the procedure for depositing checks.
2. Reconcile a bank statement.
3. Record the required journal entries directly from the bank reconciliation.
4. Record journal entries to establish and reimburse a Petty Cash Fund.
5. Complete petty cash vouchers and petty cash payments records.
6. Record the journal entries to establish a Change Fund.
7. Record journal entries for transactions involving Cash Short and Over.

A very important aspect of any system of financial accounting, either for an individual or for a business enterprise, is the accurate and efficient management of cash. For a business of any size, all cash received during a work day should be deposited at the end of the day, and all disbursements—with the exception of payments from Petty Cash—should be made by check. When we talk about cash, we mean currency, coins, checks, money orders, traveler's checks, and bank drafts or bank cashier's checks. Personal checks are accepted conditionally—that is, based on the condition that they are valid. In other words, we consider checks to be good until they are otherwise proven not to be good.

In this chapter, besides discussing bank accounts, we are going to talk about **cash funds**—petty cash funds and change funds—which are separately held reserves of cash set aside for specific purposes.

Internal control of cash is a critical activity in a business. Divide the cash activities among several people to deter mishandling.

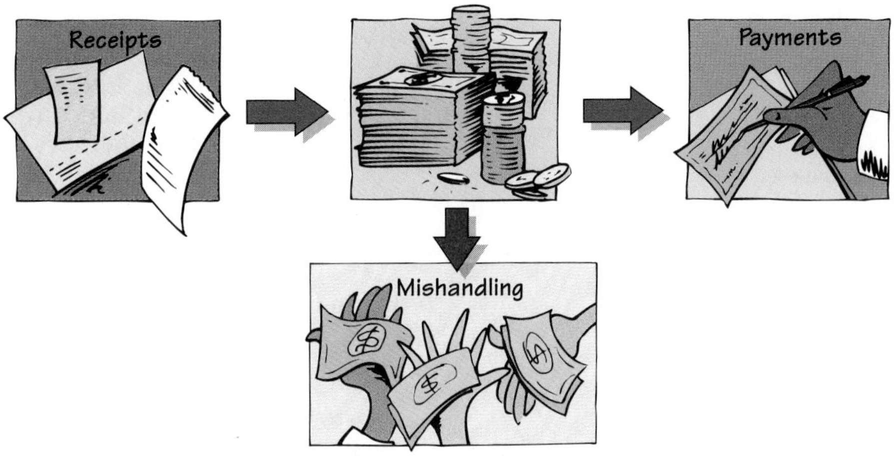
Receipts
Payments
Mishandling

USING A CHECKING ACCOUNT

Although you may be familiar with the process of opening a checking account, making deposits, and writing checks, let's review these and other procedures associated with opening and maintaining a business checking account. We will discuss signature cards, deposit slips, automated teller machines, night deposits, and endorsements.

Signature Card

When Roberta C. Bryan founded Bryan Floral, a full-service florist, she opened a checking account in the name of the business. When she made her first deposit, she filled out a **signature card** for the bank's files. Bryan gave her assistant, Maria R. Figueroa, the right to sign checks too, so the assistant also signed the card. The signature card gives the bank a copy of the official signatures of any persons authorized to sign checks. The bank can use it to verify the signatures on any checks of Bryan Floral presented for payment. This card helps the bank detect forgeries. Figure 1 shows a typical signature card.

FYI

As a means of preventing employee theft, many companies require more than one signature on their checks.

FIGURE 1

Title **Bryan Floral**

Account Number 5008-3007

In consideration of the acceptance by BARNETT NATIONAL BANK of my/our account of the type indicated below, I/we agree to be bound by such rules and regulations and/or such schedules of interest, fees and charges applicable to such account as may now or hereafter be adopted by and in effect at said Bank, and also by the provisions printed hereon. It is understood that the acceptance by said Bank of my/our account is subject to the receipt by said Bank of satisfactory credit information.

(1) Sign Here *Roberta C. Bryan*

(2) Sign Here *Maria R. Figueroa*

Address **1424 Garber Avenue**

City **San Diego** State **California** Zip **92109**

☑ CHECKING ☐ MULTIPLE MATURITY ☐ CASH MANAGER

☐ SAVINGS ☐ GUARANTEED INTEREST (Multiple Maturity) ☐ SAFE DEPOSIT ☐ OTHER ____________

IF THIS IS A JOINT ACCOUNT, BOTH OWNERS MUST SIGN ABOVE

Each of the signers guarantees the genuineness of the signature of the other. Each signer also agrees with the other and the Bank that deposits now or hereafter made to this account may be withdrawn in whole or part by either or survivor, and that each may endorse for deposit to this account any instrument payable to the order of either or both. Provisions respecting this agreement shall be modified only upon receipt by the Bank of written notice, signed by both.

Deposit Slips

Objective 1

Describe the procedure for depositing checks.

The bank provides printed **deposit slips** or deposit tickets on which customers record the amount of coins and currency they are depositing and list each individual check being deposited. A typical deposit slip is shown in Figure 2.

FIGURE 2

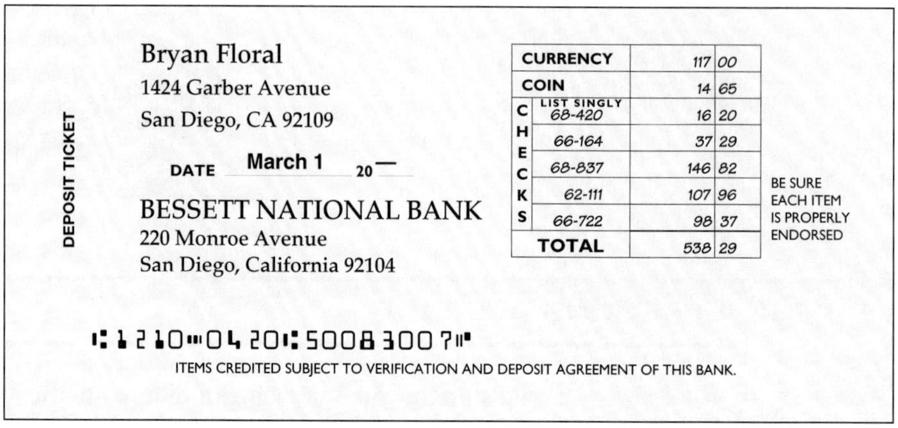

DEPOSIT TICKET

Bryan Floral
1424 Garber Avenue
San Diego, CA 92109

DATE March 1 20—

BESSETT NATIONAL BANK
220 Monroe Avenue
San Diego, California 92104

CURRENCY		117	00
COIN		14	65
CHECKS (LIST SINGLY)	68-420	16	20
	66-164	37	29
	68-837	146	82
	62-111	107	96
	66-722	98	37
TOTAL		538	29

BE SURE EACH ITEM IS PROPERLY ENDORSED

⑆1210⑈04 20⑆ 5008 300 7⑈

ITEMS CREDITED SUBJECT TO VERIFICATION AND DEPOSIT AGREEMENT OF THIS BANK.

Each check should be listed according to its American Bankers Association (ABA) transit number. The **ABA number** is the small fraction located in the upper right corner of a check. The numerator (top of the fraction) indicates the city or state in which the bank is located and the specific bank on which the check is drawn. The denominator (bottom of the fraction) indicates the Federal Reserve District in which the check is cleared and the routing number used by the Federal Reserve Bank. For example,

$$\frac{68\text{-}420}{1210}$$

FYI

The 12 in the denominator represents the Twelfth Federal Reserve District, and the 10 represents the routing number used by the Federal Reserve Bank.

The 68 identifies the city or state, and the 420 indicates the specific bank within that area (see Figures 3 and 5).

For a business account, the depositor fills out the deposit slip in duplicate, giving the original to the bank teller and keeping the copy. (This procedure may vary from bank to bank.)

When the bank receives the deposited checks, it prints the amount of each check on the lower right side of the check in a very distinctive script called **MICR**, which stands for *magnetic ink character recognition.* The routing number (as well as the depositor's number) used by the Federal Reserve Bank was printed on the lower left side of the blank check before it was sent to the account holder. The reason banks use this MICR script is that the electronic equipment used to process the checks is able to rapidly read the script identifying the bank on which the check is drawn and the amount of the check.

Automated Teller Machines

Deposits, withdrawals, and transfers can be made at all hours at banks with **ATMs** (automated teller machines). Each depositor uses a plastic card that contains a code number. The amount to be deposited, withdrawn, or transferred is keyed in by the depositor. To make a deposit, the customer inserts an envelope containing cash and/or checks and a copy of the deposit slip into the ATM. To make a withdrawal, the customer requests an amount, the ATM dispenses it, and the customer removes the cash. In addition to deposits and withdrawals, a customer may transfer amounts from one account to another (for example, from savings to checking).

Night Deposits

Most banks also provide night depositories so that firms and individuals can make deposits after regular banking hours. Depositories are secured chutes into which a firm's representative can drop a bag of cash and checks, knowing that the day's receipts will be safe until the bank opens in the morning.

Endorsements

The bank may not accept for deposit a check made out to a firm until someone from the firm has endorsed the check. The endorsement may be made by signature or by stamp. The endorsement should appear on the back of the left end of a check, as it does in Figure 3. The **endorsement** (1) transfers title to the money and (2) authorizes the payment of the check. In other words, if the check is not good, NSF (not sufficient funds), then the bank, in order to protect itself, will deduct the amount of the check from the depositor's account.

FIGURE 3

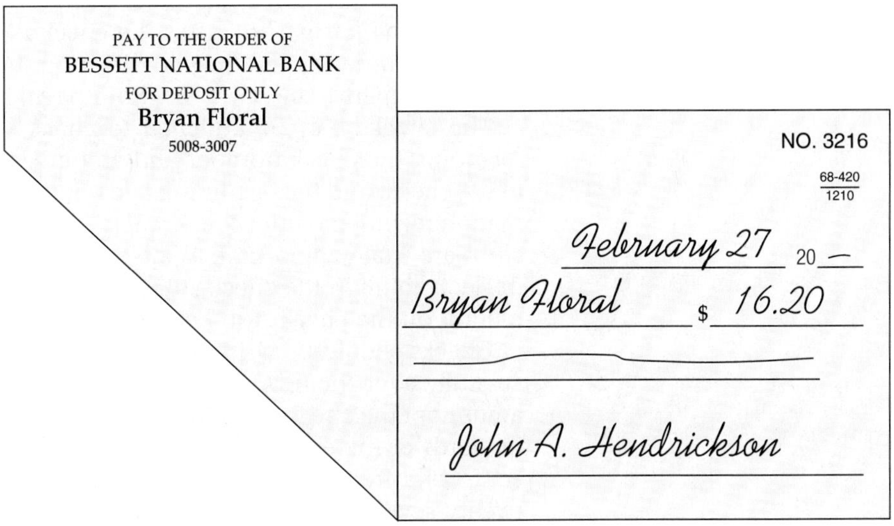
PAY TO THE ORDER OF
BESSETT NATIONAL BANK
FOR DEPOSIT ONLY
Bryan Floral
5008-3007
NO. 3216
68-420
1210
February 27
20 —
Bryan Floral
$ 16.20
John A. Hendrickson

Restrictive Endorsement All checks made payable to Bryan Floral are endorsed by stamping on the back of the checks "Pay to the Order of Bessett National Bank, For Deposit Only, Bryan Floral." This is called a **restrictive endorsement** because it restricts or limits any further transfer of the check. This endorsement also forces the deposit of the check, because the endorsement is not valid for any other purpose.

Blank Endorsement When the party to whom a check is made payable (the payee) endorses the check by signing only her or his name on the back of the check, this is known as a **blank endorsement** (Figure 4). With a blank endorsement, there are no restrictions attached.

FIGURE 4

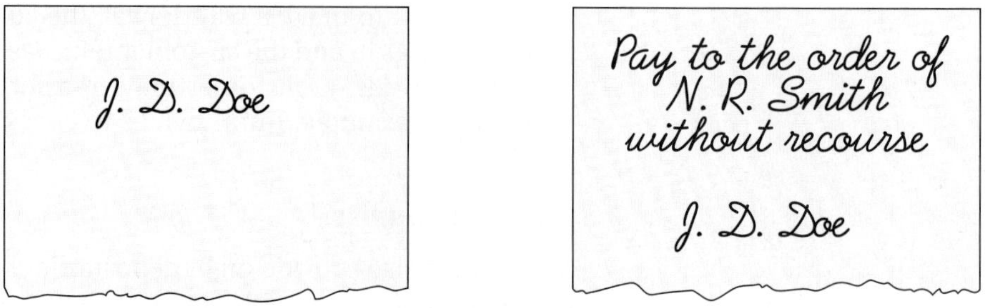
J. D. Doe
Pay to the order of
N. R. Smith
without recourse
J. D. Doe

Blank Endorsement   Qualified Endorsement

Qualified Endorsement A third type of endorsement is a **qualified endorsement** (see Figure 4), which generally includes the phrase "Pay to the order of," followed by the name of the person to whom the check is being transferred, and then followed by the phrase "without recourse." Such an endorsement frees the endorser from future liability in case the drawer of the check does not have sufficient funds to cover the check.

WRITING CHECKS

People generally use a check to withdraw money from a bank checking account. The party who writes the check is called the **drawer**. A check represents an order by the drawer, directing the bank to pay a designated person or company. The party to whom payment is to be made is the **payee**.

The checks may be attached to check stubs. Each stub has spaces for recording the check number and amount, the date and payee, the purpose of the check, and the beginning and ending balances of cash. *Note:* The information recorded on the check stub is the basis for the journal entry, so check stubs are vitally important. A person in a hurry or under pressure sometimes neglects to fill in the check stubs. Therefore, it is best to record all the information on the check stub *before making out the check.*

Checks should be written carefully so that no dishonest person can successfully alter them. Write the payee's name on the first long line. Write the amount of the check in figures close to the dollar sign, then write the amount in words at the extreme left of the line provided for this information. Write cents as a fraction of 100. For example, write $727.50 as "seven hundred twenty-seven 50/100," or $89.00 as "eighty-nine and NO/100." From a legal standpoint, if there is a discrepancy between the amount in figures and the written amount, the written amount prevails. However, as a general practice, the bank gets in touch with the drawer and asks what the correct amount should be.

Computerized firms print their checks electronically. Some firms use a **check writer**, which is a machine that imprints the amount in figures and words on the check itself. Using this machine neatly prevents anyone from altering the amount of the check.

Finally, the drawer's signature on the face of the check should match that on the signature card on file at the drawer's bank.

Figure 5 is a check, with the accompanying stub, drawn on the account of Bryan Floral.

A description of the script appears in Figure 6.

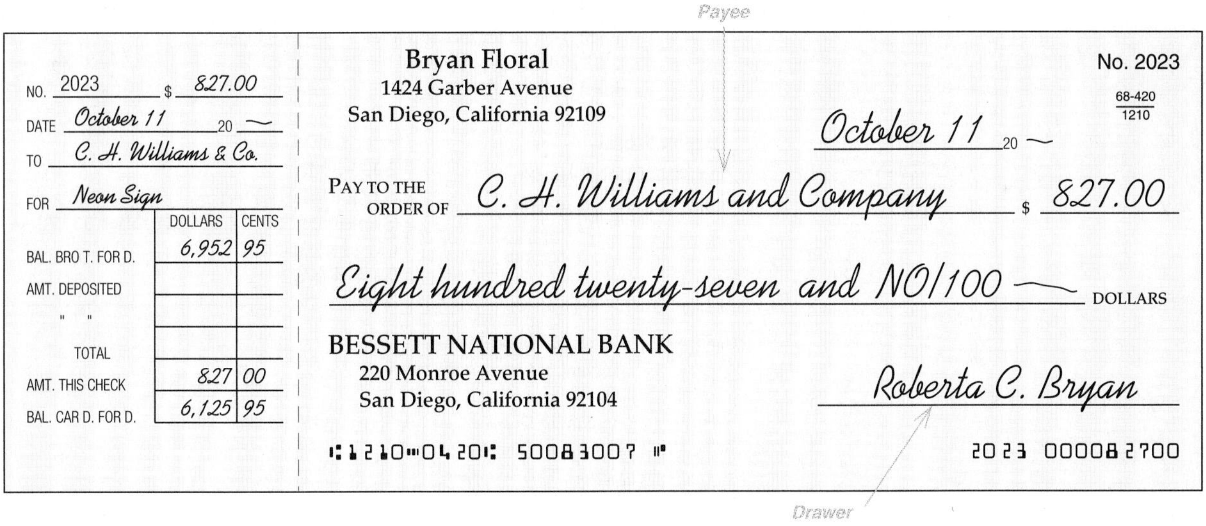
Payee
NO. 2023 $ 827.00
DATE October 11 20 —
TO C. H. Williams & Co.
FOR Neon Sign
DOLLARS CENTS
BAL. BRO T. FOR D. 6,952 95
AMT. DEPOSITED
TOTAL
AMT. THIS CHECK 827 00
BAL. CAR D. FOR D. 6,125 95
Bryan Floral
1424 Garber Avenue
San Diego, California 92109
No. 2023
68-420
1210
October 11 20 —
PAY TO THE ORDER OF C. H. Williams and Company $ 827.00
Eight hundred twenty-seven and NO/100 — DOLLARS
BESSETT NATIONAL BANK
220 Monroe Avenue
San Diego, California 92104
Roberta C. Bryan
Drawer

FIGURE 5

FIGURE 6

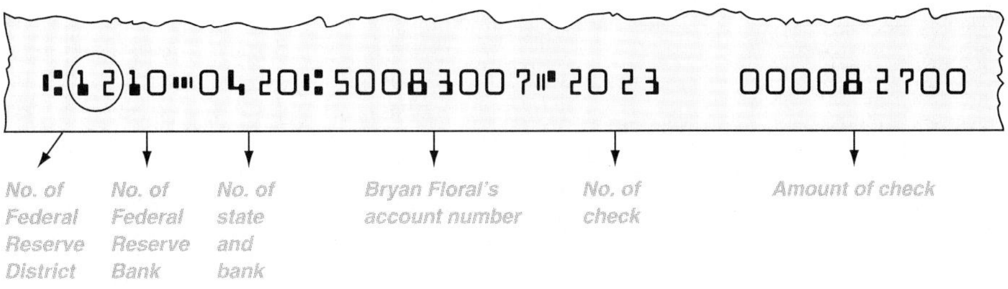
No. of Federal Reserve District
No. of Federal Reserve Bank
No. of state and bank
Bryan Floral's account number
No. of check
Amount of check

BANK STATEMENTS

Once a month the bank sends each of its customers a **bank statement**. This statement provides the following information about customers' cash accounts:

- The balance at the beginning of the month
- Additions in the form of deposits and credit memos
- Deductions in the form of checks and debit memos
- The final balance at the end of the month

A bank statement for Bryan Floral is shown in Figure 7 on page 224. The following legend of symbols is listed on the bottom of the statement:

- **CM (credit memo)** Increases in or credits to the account, such as notes or accounts left with the bank for collection.
- **DM (debit memo)** Decreases in or debits to the account, such as NSF checks, ATM withdrawals, and service charges. Service charges are based on the number of items processed and the average account balance. Special charges may also be levied against the account for collections and other services performed, including check printing.
- **PBP (pay by phone)** Transactions made by telephone using the number keypad instead of writing checks.

BESSETT NATIONAL BANK
220 Monroe Avenue
San Diego, California 92104

STATEMENT OF ACCOUNT

Bryan Floral
1424 Garber Avenue
San Diego, CA 92109

ACCOUNT NUMBER
5008-3007
STATEMENT DATE
September 30, 20 — - October 31, 20 —
TAX ID NUMBER
83-424 9732

SUMMARY

Balance Last Statement	$7,089.13
Amount of Checks and Debits	$25,154.91
Number of Checks	66
Amount of Deposits and Credits	$27,031.78
Number of Deposits	23
Balance This Statement	$8,966.00

CHECKS/OTHER DEBITS

CHECKS

CHECK NUMBER	DATE POSTED	AMOUNT	CHECK NUMBER	DATE POSTED	AMOUNT
1952	10-01	50.00	1988	10-17	61.22
1953	10-01	200.00	1989	10-17	463.29
1954	10-01	400.00	1990	10-18	520.00
1955	10-02	46.00	1991	10-19	14.57
1956	10-02	174.23	1992	10-19	23.98
1957	10-02	671.74	1993	10-19	115.16
1958	10-03	846.20	1994	10-20	117.37
1984	10-14	664.56	2018	10-30	126.70
1985	10-15	719.00	2019	10-30	943.64
1986	10-16	61.68	2020	10-31	843.17
1987	10-16	591.84	2021	10-31	21.92

OTHER DEBITS

DESCRIPTION	DATE POSTED	AMOUNT
DM NSF check from D. M. Scott	10-15	125.00
DM Automated Teller Trans. 062142 customer N3162241 at terminal 30962—cash	10-16	20.00
DM Service charge	10-31	5.50

DEPOSITS/OTHER CREDITS

DEPOSITS

DATE POSTED	AMOUNT	DATE POSTED	AMOUNT
10-01	921.00	10-17	873.19
10-02	1,476.22	10-18	946.78
10-03	463.62	10-21	329.49
10-04	789.44	10-22	1,116.27
10-07	1,063.14	10-23	734.13
10-08	1,211.96	10-26	227.69
10-14	992.27	10-28	439.45
10-15	759.41	10-29	611.12
10-16	641.33	10-30	764.35

OTHER CREDITS

DESCRIPTION	DATE POSTED	AMOUNT
CM Note collected, principal $600, interest $6	10-29	606.00

PLEASE EXAMINE THIS STATEMENT CAREFULLY. REPORT ANY POSSIBLE ERRORS IN 10 DAYS.

CODE SYMBOLS

CM Credit Memo	OD Overdraft
DM Debit Memo	EC Error Correction
PBP Pay by Phone	

FIGURE 7

- **OD (overdraft)** The withdrawal of more than the cash balance in the account, resulting in a negative balance.
- **EC (error correction)** Corrections of errors made by the bank, such as mistakes in transferring figures.

The bank statement is a valuable aid to efficiency and accuracy because it provides a double record of the Cash account. If a business entity deposits all cash receipts in the bank and makes all payments by check, then the bank is keeping an independent record of the firm's cash. You might think that the two balances—the firm's and the bank's—should be equal, but this is unlikely. Some transactions may have been recorded in the firm's account before being entered in the bank's records. In addition, there are unavoidable delays (by either the firm or the bank) in recording transactions. Ordinarily, there is a delay of one or more days between the date on which a check is written and the date when it is presented to the bank for payment. Also, banks may not record deposits until the following business day. During this time lag, deposits made or checks written are recorded in the firm's checkbook, but they are not yet listed on the bank statement.

Remember!

Debit memos represent deductions from and credit memos represent additions to a bank account.

The bank mails statements to its depositors each month. The **canceled checks** (checks that have been paid or cleared by the bank) are listed on the bank statement. They are called *canceled checks* because they are canceled by a stamp or perforation, indicating that they have been paid. Debit or credit memos are generally mailed with the statement.

Recording Deposits or Withdrawals

Each business entity keeps its accounts from its *own* point of view. As far as the bank is concerned, each customer's deposits are liabilities, in that the bank owes the customer the amount of the deposits. Using T accounts, it looks like this:

Liabilities

−	+
Debits	Credits

Deposits Payable

	−	+	
	Debits	Credits	
Debit memos	Checks written	Deposits	Credit memos
	Service charges	Notes	
	NSF checks	collected	
	ATM withdrawls		

When the bank receives a cash deposit from a customer, the bank credits Deposits Payable, because it owes more to its customer. When the bank cashes a check (pays out) for a customer, the bank debits Deposits Payable, because it owes less to its customer.

The customer, on the other hand, uses the account titled Cash, or Cash in Bank, or simply the name of the bank. Deposits are recorded as debits, and withdrawals are recorded as credits in the account. On a bank reconciliation, the balance of the account is listed as the **ledger balance of cash** before reconciliation with the bank statement.

Need for Reconciling Bank Balance and Ledger Balance

Objective 2

Reconcile a bank statement.

FYI

When a bank agrees to accept payments on behalf of a customer, the fee the bank charges does not necessarily mean that the bank will follow up on collection of a payment or notify the customer that the payment is late.

Bank Bal — unknowns

My Bal — unknowns

Since the bank statement balance and the ledger balance of cash are not equal, a firm prepares a **bank reconciliation** to uncover the reasons for the difference between the two balances and to correct any errors that may have been made by either the bank or the firm. This makes it possible to arrive at the same balance in each account, which is called the *adjusted balance,* or *true balance,* of the Cash account.

There are a variety of reasons for differences between the bank statement balance and the customer's cash balance. Here are some of the more common ones:

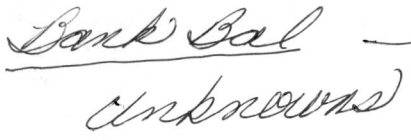

- **Deposit in transit** A deposit made after the bank statement was issued. The depositor has naturally already added the amount to the Cash account in his or her books, but the deposit has not been recorded by the bank (this is also called a *late deposit*).
- **Outstanding checks** Checks that have been written by the company but not yet received for payment by the time the bank sends out its statement. The company employee, when writing checks, deducted the amounts from the Cash account in the company's books, which explains the difference.
- **Collections** When the bank acts as a collection point for its customers by accepting payments on their behalf, it adds the proceeds to the customer's bank account and sends a credit memorandum to notify the customer of the transaction or includes it on the next bank statement.
- **Interest income** Some checking accounts are interest bearing or earning. The depositor will not learn how much interest the bank has credited to the bank account until the bank statement is received.
- **NSF (not sufficient funds) check** When a bank customer deposits a check, it is recorded as cash on the customer's books. Occasionally, however, a check is not paid (bounces). When the bank notifies the customer of this, the customer must make a deduction from the Cash account. Simultaneously, the depositor records an increase in accounts receivable because the client's debt to the depositor remains unpaid. An NSF check may also be called a *dishonored check.*
- **Service charge** A bank charge for services rendered: for handling checks, for collecting money, for receiving payment of notes turned over to it by the customer for collection, for check printing, and for other such services. The bank immediately deducts the fee from the balance of the bank account and notifies the depositor with a debit memorandum.
- **Errors** In spite of internal controls and systems designed to double-check to prevent errors, sometimes either the customer or the bank makes a mistake. Often these errors do not become evident until the bank reconciliation is performed.

Steps in Reconciling the Bank Statement

Follow these steps to reconcile a bank statement:

1. **Canceled checks**
   a. Compare the amount of each canceled check with the bank statement and note any differences. The amount of the machine-readable characters should appear at the lower right-hand corner of the check, which should match the amount written on the check and the bank statements.

b. In the checkbook beside the check number, list the date of the bank statement. In some cases, a bank may not pay a check until one or two months after it was written. If a question arises as to whether or not you have paid a particular bill, you can look at the checkbook. Then you can refer directly to the bank statement to pick up the accompanying canceled check as proof of payment.

2. **Deposits**
   a. Compare the deposits in transit (not recorded by the bank at the time of the statement) listed on last month's bank reconciliation with the deposits shown on the bank statement. All of last month's deposits in transit should be listed on this month's bank statement. If they are not, notify the bank immediately.
   b. Compare the remaining deposits listed on this month's bank statement with deposits written in the company's accounting records. Consider any deposits not shown on the bank statement as deposits in transit.

3. **Outstanding checks**
   a. Arrange the canceled checks in order by check number.
   b. Look over the list of outstanding checks left over from last month's bank reconciliation, and note the checks that have now been returned or cleared.
   c. For each canceled check, compare the amount recorded in MICR numbers at the lower right-hand corner of the check with the amount recorded in the checkbook. Next, compare the canceled checks with the numerical listing in the statement. Use a check mark (✓) to indicate that the check has been paid and that the amount is correct. Any payments that have not been marked off, including the outstanding checks from last month's bank reconciliation, are the present outstanding checks.
   d. Review the endorsements on the backs of the checks to verify that money has been sent to the correct payee.

4. **Bank memoranda** Trace the credit memos and debit memos to the journal. If the memos have not been recorded, make separate entries for them.

A large firm should require that the reconciliation be prepared by an employee who is not involved in recording business transactions or in handling cash receipts and disbursements.

ITT
CHASE
1431
1349
1384
312
332

Besides their core activities of providing financial transactions, many banks are actively committed to community service by supporting various causes, such as Chase Manhattan Bank's sponsorship of the Chase Corporate Challenge.

Examples of Bank Reconciliations

Let's go through the reconciliation process for two firms, L. A. Chapton Company and Bryan Floral.

L. A. Chapton Company The bank statement of L. A. Chapton Company indicates a balance of $2,119 as of March 31. The balance of the Cash account in Chapton's ledger as of that date is $1,552. Chapton's accountant has taken the following steps:

1. Verified that canceled checks were recorded correctly on the bank statement.
2. Noted that the deposit made on March 31 was not recorded on the bank statement, $762.
3. Noted outstanding checks: no. 921, $626; no. 985, $69; no. 986, $438.
4. Noted credit memo: note collected by the bank from S. Ellers, $200, not recorded in the journal.
5. Noted debit memo: collection charge and service charge not recorded in the journal, $4.

The note received from S. Ellers is called a promissory note. A **promissory note** is a written promise to pay a definite amount at a definite future time. Let's assume that L. A. Chapton Company received the sixty-day non-interest-bearing note from S. Ellers for services performed. In recording the transaction, Chapton's accountant debited Notes Receivable and credited Income from Services. (The account Notes Receivable is similar to Accounts Receivable. However, Accounts Receivable is reserved for customer charge accounts, with payments usually due in thirty days.) Next, L. A. Chapton Company turned the note over to its bank for collection.

The bank will use a credit memo form to notify L. A. Chapton Company that the note has been collected and that the company's bank account has been increased by the amount of the note. Based on the credit memo, Chapton's accountant will make a journal entry debiting Cash and crediting Notes Receivable.

Think of the bank reconciliation in terms of the following:

1. Bring the bank statement balance up to date by recording the events that we knew about but the bank did not know about when it prepared the statement (deposits in transit and outstanding checks as shown in our checkbook, for example).
2. Bring the balance of the Cash account up to date by recording the events that the bank knew about but we did not know about until we received the statement (debit memos and credit memos as shown on the bank statement, for example).

The bank reconciliation may be prepared on a separate sheet of paper or on the back of the bank statement. Figure 8 shows L. A. Chapton's bank reconciliation. The items in the reconciliation that require journal entries are shown in color, and the entries are shown below.

Objective 3

Record the required journal entries directly from the bank reconciliation.

Note that the journal entries are based on the items used to adjust the ledger balance of Cash. These items represent the transactions that the bank has knowledge of but the firm does not. According to the bank reconciliation, the true balance of Cash is $1,748, which is the balance we wish to show on the firm's books. We can't change the balance of an account unless we first make a journal entry and then post the entry to the accounts involved. **Consequently, we have to make journal entries for items in the Ledger Balance**

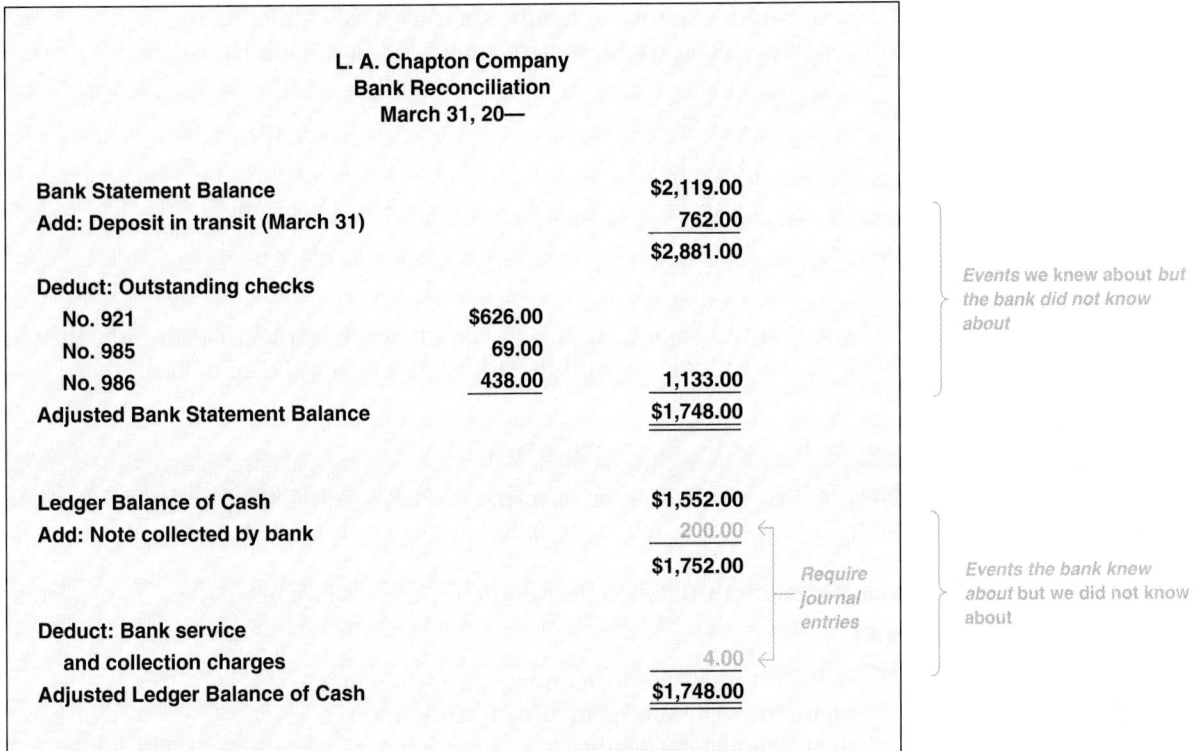

L. A. Chapton Company Bank Reconciliation March 31, 20—			
Bank Statement Balance		$2,119.00	
Add: Deposit in transit (March 31)		762.00	
		$2,881.00	
Deduct: Outstanding checks			Events we knew about but the bank did not know about
No. 921	$626.00		
No. 985	69.00		
No. 986	438.00	1,133.00	
Adjusted Bank Statement Balance		$1,748.00	
Ledger Balance of Cash		$1,552.00	
Add: Note collected by bank		200.00	Require journal entries
		$1,752.00	Events the bank knew about but we did not know about
Deduct: Bank service and collection charges		4.00	Require journal entries
Adjusted Ledger Balance of Cash		$1,748.00	

FIGURE 8

of Cash section of the bank reconciliation. In the Ledger Balance of Cash section, the additions are debited to the Cash account, and the deductions are credited to the Cash account. L. A. Chapton Company records the entries in its general journal:

GENERAL JOURNAL PAGE ____

DATE		DESCRIPTION	POST. REF.	DEBIT	CREDIT
20—					
Mar.	31	Cash		200 00	
		Notes Receivable			200 00
		Non-interest-bearing note			
		signed by S. Ellers was			
		collected by the bank.			
	31	Miscellaneous Expense		4 00	
		Cash			4 00
		Service charge and collection			
		charge levied by bank.			

Here bank service and collection charges are recorded in Miscellaneous Expense because the amounts are relatively small. Some accountants may use a separate expense account, such as Bank Charge Expense. After the entries have been posted, the T account for Cash looks like this:

Cash			
Balance	1,552	Mar. 31	4
Mar. 31	200		
	1,752		
Bal. 1,748			

Note that the balance in the T account is now equal to both the adjusted bank statement balance and the adjusted ledger balance of cash.

Remember!

When placing each item on the bank reconciliation, ask yourself if it has been recorded only by the bank or only by the depositor. If an item has been recorded by both the bank and the depositor, there is nothing to do. If an item has been recorded only by the bank, then record it in a similar manner in the Ledger Balance of Cash section. If an item has been recorded only by the depositor, then record it in a similar manner in the Bank Statement Balance section.

Form of Bank Reconciliation

Now that you have seen an example of a bank reconciliation, let's look at the standard form of a bank reconciliation for an imaginary company.

Bank Statement Balance (last figure on the statement)		$4,000
Add		
Deposits in transit (deposits made after the bank statement was issued and already added to the ledger balance of Cash)	$300	
Bank errors (that understate balance)	20	320
		$4,320
Deduct		
Outstanding checks (they have already been deducted from the Cash account)	$960	
Bank errors (that overstate balance)	40	1,000
Adjusted Bank Statement Balance (the true balance of Cash)		$3,320
Ledger Balance of Cash (the latest balance of the Cash account if it has been posted up to date; otherwise take the beginning balance of Cash, plus cash receipts and minus cash payments)		$2,850
Add		
Credit memos (additions by the bank not recorded in the Cash account, such as collections of notes)	$500	
Book errors (that understate balance)	40	540
		$3,390
Deduct		
Debit memos (deductions by the bank not recorded in the Cash account, such as service charges or collection charges and NSF checks)	$ 20	
Book errors (that overstate balance)	50	70
Adjusted Ledger Balance of Cash (the true balance of Cash)		$3,320

Bryan Floral The bank statement of Bryan Floral shows a final balance of $8,966 as of October 31 (see Figure 9). The present balance of the Cash account in the ledger, after Bryan's accountant has posted from the journal, is $8,030.50. The accountant took the following steps:

1. Verified that canceled checks were recorded correctly on the bank statement.
2. Discovered that a deposit of $1,003 made on October 31 was not recorded on the bank statement.
3. Noted outstanding checks: no. 1916, $461; no. 2022, $119; no. 2023, $827; no. 2024, $67.
4. Noted that a credit memo for a note collected by the bank from Lee and Brock, $600 principal plus $6 interest, was not recorded in the journal.
5. Found that check no. 2001 for $523, payable to Davis, Inc., on account, was recorded in the journal as $532. (The correct amount is $523.)
6. Noted that a debit memo for a collection charge and service charge of $5.50 was not recorded in the journal.
7. Noted that a debit memo for an NSF check for $125 from D. M. Scott was not recorded.
8. Noted that a $20 personal withdrawal by Roberta C. Bryan, the owner, using an ATM, was not recorded.

Look at Figure 9 to see how each step relates to the bank reconciliation.

The accountant makes journal entries for the items indicated in Figure 9 to change the balance of the Cash account from its present balance of

FIGURE 9

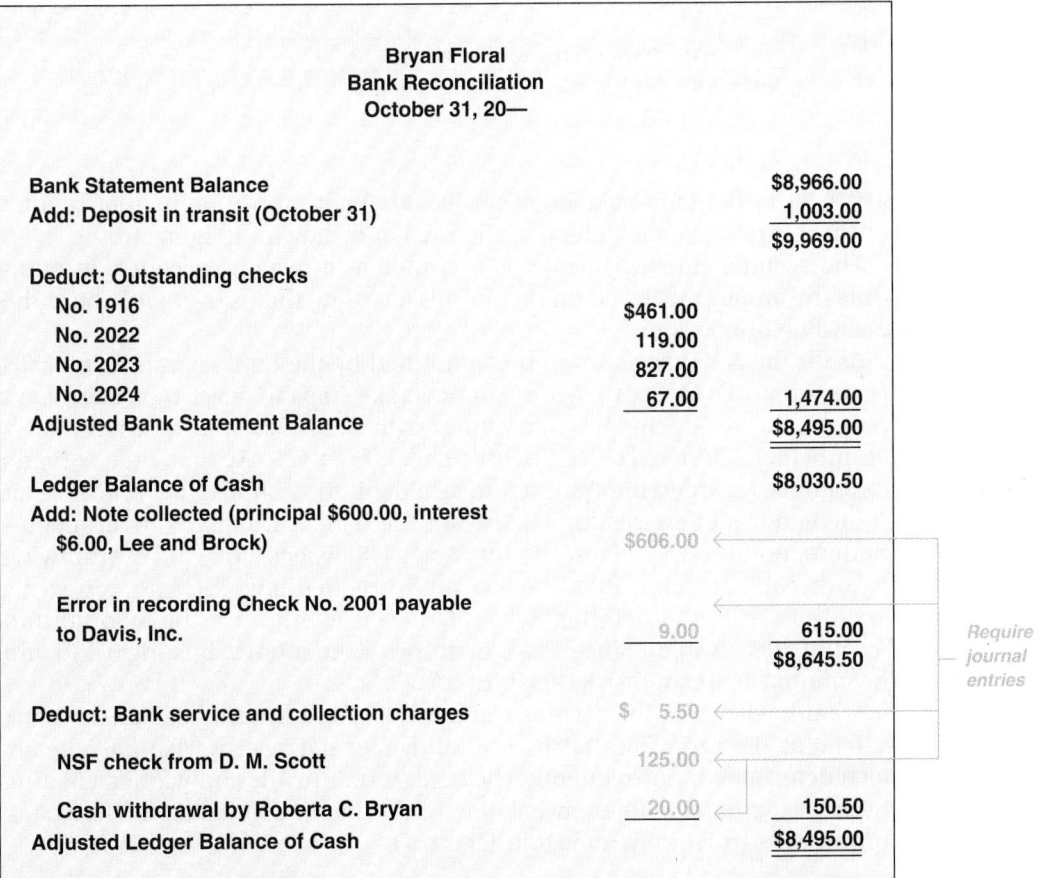

Bryan Floral
Bank Reconciliation
October 31, 20—

Bank Statement Balance		$8,966.00	
Add: Deposit in transit (October 31)		1,003.00	
		$9,969.00	
Deduct: Outstanding checks			
No. 1916	$461.00		
No. 2022	119.00		
No. 2023	827.00		
No. 2024	67.00	1,474.00	
Adjusted Bank Statement Balance		$8,495.00	
Ledger Balance of Cash		$8,030.50	
Add: Note collected (principal $600.00, interest $6.00, Lee and Brock)	$606.00		Require journal entries
Error in recording Check No. 2001 payable to Davis, Inc.	9.00	615.00	
		$8,645.50	
Deduct: Bank service and collection charges	$ 5.50		
NSF check from D. M. Scott	125.00		
Cash withdrawal by Roberta C. Bryan	20.00	150.50	
Adjusted Ledger Balance of Cash		$8,495.00	

FIGURE 10

GENERAL JOURNAL PAGE ______

DATE		DESCRIPTION	POST. REF.	DEBIT	CREDIT
20—					
Oct.	31	Cash		606 00	
		Notes Receivable			600 00
		Interest Income			6 00
		Bank collected note signed			
		by Lee and Brock.			
	31	Cash		9 00	
		Accounts Payable			9 00
		Error in recording check no.			
		2001 payable to Davis, Inc.			
	31	Miscellaneous Expense		5 50	
		Cash			5 50
		Bank service charge and			
		collection charge.			
	31	Accounts Receivable		125 00	
		Cash			125 00
		NSF check received from			
		D. M. Scott			
	31	R. C. Bryan, Drawing		20 00	
		Cash			20 00
		Withdrawal for personal use.			

$8,030.50 to the true balance of $8,495.00. Again, those items that require journal entries are highlighted in Figure 9 and shown in Figure 10.

The account Interest Income is classified as a revenue account. It represents the amount received on the promissory note that is over and above the face value of the note.

As for the NSF check, upon being notified by the bank, Bryan Floral calls its customer (D. M. Scott). Scott can now take steps to cover the check. Let's back up and review Bryan's transaction with D. M. Scott. In return for service provided, Bryan received Scott's check for $125. At that time, Bryan's accountant recorded the transaction as a debit to Cash for $125 and a credit to Income from Services for $125. Then the bank, through its debit memorandum, notifies Bryan Floral about Scott's NSF check. To avoid overdrawing its own bank account, Bryan makes an entry crediting Cash (to correct its record of Cash) and debiting Accounts Receivable (to put the amount into Accounts Receivable). Since D. M. Scott owes the money, it is logical to add the amount to Accounts Receivable.

Remember!

When you are reconciling a bank statement, always double-check for any outstanding checks or deposits from previous statements that have been carried forward. Also double-check for any bank service charges.

A bank reconciliation form is ordinarily printed on the back of the bank statement. The adjusted balance of the ledger balance of cash has already been determined. Consequently, the bank form provides only for calculating the adjusted bank statement balance of the bank reconciliation. The bank form for Bryan Floral is shown in Figure 11.

THIS FORM IS PROVIDED TO HELP YOU BALANCE YOUR BANK STATEMENT

CHECKS OUTSTANDING—NOT CHARGED TO ACCOUNT

NO. 1916	$ 461	00
2022	119	00
2023	827	00
2024	67	00
TOTAL	$ 1,474	00

BEFORE YOU START—

PLEASE BE SURE YOU HAVE ENTERED IN YOUR CHECKBOOK ALL AUTOMATIC TRANSACTIONS SHOWN ON THE FRONT OF YOUR STATEMENT.

YOU SHOULD HAVE ADDED IF ANY OCCURRED:

1. Loan advances.
2. Credit memos.
3. Other automatic deposits.

YOU SHOULD HAVE SUBTRACTED IF ANY OCCURRED:

1. Automatic loan payments.
2. Automatic savings transfers.
3. Service charges.
4. Debit memos.
5. Other automatic deductions and payments.

BANK BALANCE SHOWN ON THIS STATEMENT	$ 8,966.00
ADD	
DEPOSITS NOT SHOWN ON THIS STATEMENT *(IF ANY)*	$ 1,003.00
TOTAL	$ 9,969.00
SUBTRACT—	
► CHECKS OUTSTANDING	$ 1,474.00
BALANCE	$ 8,495.00

SHOULD AGREE WITH YOUR CHECKBOOK BALANCE AFTER DEDUCTING SERVICE CHARGE (IF ANY) SHOWN ON THIS STATEMENT.

Please examine immediately and report if incorrect. If no reply is received within 15 days the account will be considered correct.

FIGURE 11

THE PETTY CASH FUND

Day after day, business firms are confronted with transactions requiring small immediate payments, such as paying for delivery charges, a birthday card, or a new toner cartridge. If the firm had to go through the usual procedure of making all payments by check, the time consumed would be frustrating and the whole process would be unduly expensive. For many firms, the cost of writing each check is more than $10; this includes the cost of an employee's time for writing and reconciling the check. Suppose you buy 5 stamps from an employee for $1.65, and you want to reimburse her for that money. To write a check would not be practical. It only makes sense to pay in cash, using the **Petty Cash Fund**. *Petty* means "small," so the firm sets a maximum amount that can be paid immediately out of petty cash. Payments that exceed this maximum must be processed by regular check through the journal.

Establishing the Petty Cash Fund

Objective 4

Record journal entries to establish and reimburse Petty Cash Fund.

Petty Cash

After the firm has set the maximum amount of a payment from petty cash, next step is to estimate how much cash will be needed during a given period of time, such as a month. It is also important to consider the element of security when keeping cash in the office. If the risk is great, the amount kept in the fund should be small. Bryan Floral decides to establish a Petty Cash Fund of $50 and put it under the control of the assistant. Accordingly, Bryan's accountant writes a check, cashes it at the bank, and records this transaction in the journal as follows:

Establish

Replenish

GENERAL JOURNAL PAGE ____

	DATE		DESCRIPTION	POST. REF.	DEBIT	CREDIT	
1	20—						1
2	Sept.	1	Petty Cash Fund		50 00		2
3			Cash			50 00	3
4			Established a Petty Cash				4
5			Fund.				5

T accounts for the entry look like this:

Petty Cash Fund	
+	−
50	

Cash	
+	−
	50

Because the Petty Cash Fund is an asset account, it is listed on the balance sheet immediately below Cash.

Once the fund has been created, it is not debited again unless the original amount is not large enough to handle the necessary transactions. In that case, the accountant has to increase the Petty Cash Fund—perhaps from $50 to $75. **But, barring such a change in the size of the fund, Petty Cash Fund is debited only once.**

Remember!

The Petty Cash Fund account is debited only once, and this happens when the fund is first established.

The check is written to the assistant, say, "John Doe, Petty Cash Fund." He or she converts it into convenient **denominations**, which are varieties of coins and currency, such as quarters and dimes and $1 and $5 bills. Then the assistant puts the money in a locked drawer and will not pay anything larger than $5 (or whatever is the agreed-upon amount) out of petty cash.

Payments from the Petty Cash Fund

Objective 5

Complete petty cash vouchers and petty cash payments records.

The assistant now takes the responsibility for the Petty Cash Fund. He or she is designated as the only person who can make payments from it. In case of his or her illness, some other employee should be named as stand-in. A **petty cash voucher** must be used to account for every payment from the fund. The voucher constitutes a receipt signed by the person who authorized the payment and by the person who received payment as well as the purpose of the petty cash payment. Thus, even for small payments of $5 or less, there would have to be collusion between the payee and the assistant for any theft to occur. Figure 12 is a petty cash voucher.

FIGURE 12

PETTY CASH VOUCHER

No. 1 Date September 2, 20—

Paid to Mark Delivery Service $ 2.00

For Delivery

Account Delivery Expense

Approved by M. Figueroa *Payment received by* D. Stanton

Petty Cash Payments Record

Rockwell's
ee Delivery
714-669-9310

A petty cash fund is an effective and efficient way to deal with small cash payments that need to be made immediately. These caterers, delivering food for an office party, can be paid on the spot, saving their own company the expense of billing and the recipient the expense of writing a check.

Some firms prefer to have a written record on one sheet of paper, so they keep a **petty cash payments record**. In a petty cash payments record, petty cash vouchers and the accounts that are to be charged are listed as well as the purpose of the expenditure. Special columns for frequent types of expenditures are included in the Distribution of Payments section. The petty cash payments record is not a journal.

Bryan Floral made the following payments from its Petty Cash Fund during September:

Sept.	2	Paid $2 to Mark Delivery Service, voucher no. 1.
	3	Bought pencils and pens, $3.09, voucher no. 2.
	5	Paid local newspaper for advertising, $5, voucher no. 3.
	7	Paid postage on incoming packages, $2.90, voucher no. 4.
	10	Roberta C. Bryan, the owner, withdrew $5 for personal use, voucher no. 5.
	14	Reimbursed employee for stamps, $1.65, voucher no. 6.
	21	Bought stick-on tabs, $4.10, voucher no. 7.
	22	Paid $3 to Mark Delivery Service, voucher no. 8.
	26	Paid for mailing packages, $3.80, voucher no. 9.
	27	Paid $3.50 to Fast Way Delivery, voucher no. 10.
	29	Bought memo pads, $4.40, voucher no. 11.
	29	Paid for making duplicate keys, $2.60, voucher no. 12.
	30	Paid $3.20 to Mark Delivery Service, voucher no. 13.
	30	Paid for trash removal, $5, voucher no. 14.

Figure 13 on pages 236–237 shows how these payments are recorded.

Petty Cash Payments Record
Month of September 20—

DATE		VOU. NO.	EXPLANATION		PAYMENTS	OFFICE SUPPLIES
Sept.	1		Established fund, check no. 90, $50			
	2	1	Mark Delivery Service		2 00	
	3	2	Pencils and pens		3 09	3 09
	5	3	Local newspaper		5 00	
	7	4	Postage on incoming mail		2 90	
	10	5	Roberta C. Bryan		5 00	
	14	6	Reimburse employee for stamps		1 65	
	21	7	Stick-on tabs		4 10	4 10
	22	8	Mark Delivery Service		3 00	
	26	9	Postage for mailings		3 80	
	27	10	Fast Way Delivery		3 50	
	29	11	Memo pads		4 40	4 40
	29	12	Making duplicate keys		2 60	
	30	13	Mark Delivery Service		3 20	
	30	14	Trash removal		5 00	
	30		Totals		49 24	11 59
			Balance in Fund	$ .76		
			Reimbursed check no. 136	49.24		
			Total	$50.00		

FIGURE 13

Reimbursement of the Petty Cash Fund

To bring the fund back up to the original amount when it is nearly exhausted (for instance, at the end of the month), the accountant reimburses the fund for expenditures made. Consequently, the Petty Cash Fund may be considered a revolving fund. If the amount initially put in the Petty Cash Fund is $50 and at the end of the month only $.76 is left, the accountant puts $49.24 in the fund as a reimbursement, thereby bringing the fund back up to $50 to start the new month.

Remember!

The petty cash payments record or calculator tapes are not journals; they are simply used as a basis for compiling information for the journal entry. Remember, to change an account, we have to make a journal entry.

Bear in mind that the petty cash payments record is only a supplementary record for gathering information. A less formal way of compiling the information concerning petty cash payments might consist of collecting one month's petty cash vouchers, then sorting them by accounts, such as Office Supplies, Delivery Expense, and the like. Then run a calculator tape for each account. At the end of the month, the accountant makes a summarizing entry to officially journalize the transactions that have taken place. The journal and T accounts of Bryan Floral are shown at the bottom of page 237.

Note that, in the summarizing entry, the accountant debits the accounts on whose behalf the payments were made and credits the Cash account. She or he leaves the Petty Cash Fund account alone. Then the assistant cashes a check for $49.24 and puts the cash in a locked place, thereby restoring the amount in the Petty Cash Fund to the original $50.

PAGE 1

DISTRIBUTION OF PAYMENTS		OTHER ACCOUNTS	
DELIVERY EXPENSE	MISCELLANEOUS EXPENSE	ACCOUNT	AMOUNT
2.00			
		Advertising Expense	5.00
2.90			
		R. C. Bryan, Drawing	5.00
	1.65		
3.00			
3.80			
3.50			
	2.60		
3.20			
	5.00		
18.40	9.25		10.00

GENERAL JOURNAL PAGE ____

DATE		DESCRIPTION	POST. REF.	DEBIT	CREDIT
20—					
Sept.	30	Office Supplies		11.59	
		Delivery Expense		18.40	
		Miscellaneous Expense		9.25	
		Advertising Expense		5.00	
		R. C. Bryan, Drawing		5.00	
		Cash			49.24
		Reimbursed the Petty Cash			
		Fund, Ck. No. 136.			

Cash	
+	−
	49.24

R. C. Bryan, Drawing	
+	−
5.00	

Miscellaneous Expense	
+	−
9.25	

Office Supplies	
+	−
11.59	

Delivery Expense	
+	−
18.40	

Advertising Expense	
+	−
5.00	

THE CHANGE FUND

Anyone who has ever tried to pay for a small item with a $20 bill knows that any firm that carries out numerous cash transactions needs a **Change Fund**.

Establishing the Change Fund

Objective 6

Record the journal entries to establish a Change Fund.

Before setting up a Change Fund, you have to decide two things: (1) how much money needs to be in the fund, and (2) what denominations of bills and coins are needed. Like the Petty Cash Fund, **the Change Fund is debited only once: when it is established.** It is left at the initial figure unless the person in charge decides to make it larger. The Change Fund account, like the Petty Cash Fund account, is an asset. It is recorded in the balance sheet immediately below Cash. If the Petty Cash Fund account is larger than the Change Fund account, it precedes the Change Fund.

The owner of Bryan Floral, Roberta C. Bryan, decides to establish a change fund; she decides this at the same time she sets up the company's petty cash fund. The entries for the two transactions look like this:

GENERAL JOURNAL PAGE ____

DATE		DESCRIPTION	POST. REF.	DEBIT	CREDIT
20—					
Sept.	1	Petty Cash Fund		50 00	
		Cash			50 00
		Established a petty cash fund.			
	1	Change Fund		120 00	
		Cash			120 00
		Established a change fund.			

The T accounts for establishing the fund are as follows:

Change Fund	
+	−
120	

Cash	
+	−
	120

Bryan cashes a check for $120 and gets the money in several denominations. She is now prepared to make change for any normal business transactions.

Depositing Cash

At the end of each business day, Bryan deposits the cash taken in during the day, but she holds back the amount of the Change Fund, being sure that it is in convenient denominations. Let's say that on September 1, Bryan Floral had $425 on hand at the end of the day.

$425	Total cash count
− 120	Change fund
$305	New cash deposit

The T accounts look like this:

Cash		Floral Sales Income	
+	−	−	+
305			305

The day's receipts are journalized as follows:

GENERAL JOURNAL PAGE ____

DATE		DESCRIPTION	POST. REF.	DEBIT	CREDIT
20—					
Sept.	1	Cash		305 00	
		Floral Sales Income			305 00
		To record revenue earned			
		during the day.			

The amount of the cash deposit is the total cash count less the amount of the Change Fund. This should be equal to the income earned.

On September 9, the cash count is $537. So Bryan deposits $417 ($537 – $120). Bryan's accountant makes the following entry to record the day's receipts:

GENERAL JOURNAL PAGE ____

DATE		DESCRIPTION	POST. REF.	DEBIT	CREDIT
20—					
Sept.	9	Cash		417 00	
		Floral Sales Income			417 00
		To record revenue earned			
		during the day.			

Some businesses label the Cash account *Cash in Bank* and label the Change Fund *Cash on Hand.*

CASH SHORT AND OVER

Objective 7

Record journal entries for transactions involving Cash Short and Over.

There is an inherent danger in making change: Human beings make mistakes, especially when there are many customers to be waited on or when the business is temporarily short-handed. Because mistakes do happen, accounting records must be set up to cope with the situation. One reason that a business uses a cash register is to detect mistakes in handling cash. **If, after removing the Change Fund, the day's receipts are less than the register reading, then a cash shortage exists. Conversely, when the day's receipts are greater than the register reading, a cash overage exists.** Both shortages and overages are recorded in the same account, which is called Cash Short and Over. Shortages are considered an expense of operating a business, and therefore shortages are recorded on the debit side of the account. Overages are treated as another form of revenue, and therefore overages are recorded on the credit side of the account.

FYI

The Cash Short and Over account may also be used to handle shortages and overages in the Petty Cash Fund.

Let's say that on September 14, Bryan Floral is faced with the following situation:

Cash Register Tape	Cash Count	Amount of the Change Fund
$490	$607	$120

After deducting the $120 in the Change Fund, Bryan will deposit $487 ($607 − $120). Note that this amount is $3 less than the amount indicated by the cash register ($490 − $487); therefore, a $3 cash shortage exists. The following T accounts show how Bryan entered this transaction into the books:

FYI

Like the Income Summary account, which has no normal balance, the Cash Short and Over account has no signs.

Cash		Floral Sales Income		Cash Short and Over	
+	−	−	+		
487			490	3	

Short & Over New account Cash Short & Over Placement

The next day, September 15, the pendulum happens to swing in the other direction:

Cash Register Tape	Cash Count	Amount of the Change Fund
$559	$680	$120

The amount to be deposited is $560 ($680 − $120). This figure is $1 greater than the $559 in floral sales income indicated by the cash register tape. Thus, there is a $1 cash overage ($560 − $559). The analysis of this transaction is shown in the following T accounts:

Cash		Floral Sales Income		Cash Short and Over	
+	−	−	+		
560			559		1

A scanner can speed counting and costing of goods, whether for the customer at the check-out counter or taking inventory of goods still on the shelves. The scanner, however, is only as accurate as the amount for each item entered in the computer.

Bryan Floral's revenue for September 14 and 15 is recorded in the general journal as follows:

GENERAL JOURNAL PAGE ____

DATE		DESCRIPTION	POST. REF.	DEBIT	CREDIT
20—					
Sept.	14	Cash		487 00	
		Cash Short and Over		3 00	
		Floral Sales Income			490 00
		To record revenue earned			
		for the day involving a			
		cash shortage of $3.			
	15	Cash		560 00	
		Floral Sales Income			559 00
		Cash Short and Over			1 00
		To record revenue earned			
		during the day involving a			
		cash overage of $1.			

As far as errors are concerned, one would think that shortages would be offset by overages. However, customers receiving change are more likely to report shortages than overages. **Consequently, the firm usually experiences a greater number of shortages.** A firm may set a tolerance level for the cashiers. If the shortages consistently exceed the level of tolerance, either fraud is being committed or somebody is making entirely too many careless mistakes.

Now let's summarize our discussion of the Cash Short and Over account by drawing the following conclusions from the illustration:

1. At the close of the business day, the firm deposits the difference between the amount in the cash drawer and the amount in the Change Fund.
2. The firm records the amount shown on the cash register tape as its floral sales income.
3. If the amount of the cash deposit disagrees with the record of receipts, Cash Short and Over makes up the difference. In the first situation just described, there was a shortage of $3, and so there was a debit to Cash Short and Over. In the second situation, there was an overage of $1, and so there was a credit to Cash Short and Over. It is apparent that, as a result of these transactions, the account looks like this:

Cash Short and Over

Shortage	3	Overage	1

Throughout any fiscal period, the accountant must continually record shortages and overages in the Cash Short and Over account. Let's say that Bryan's final balance is $21 on the debit side. Bryan winds up with a net shortage of $21.

At the end of the fiscal period, **if the account has a debit balance or net shortage, the accountant classifies it as an expense and credits Cash Short and Over and debits Miscellaneous Expense, so that the amount is put in the income statement under Miscellaneous Expense.** The T account would look like this:

Cash Short and Over

Short	3	Over	1
	4		1
	3		2
	7		2
	5		1
	2		2
	3		1
	4		10
Bal. 21	31		

Conversely, **if the account has a credit balance or net overage, the accountant classifies it as a revenue account and debits Cash Short and Over and credits Miscellaneous Income, so that the amount is put in the income statement under Miscellaneous Income.** This is an exception to the policy of recording accounts under their exact account title in financial statements. Rather than attaching plus and minus signs to the Cash Short and Over account immediately, we wait until we find out its final balance, then make a journal entry to send the balance to the correct account classification.

CHAPTER REVIEW

Review of Performance Objectives

1. Describe the procedure for depositing checks.

   The procedure for depositing checks consists of first endorsing each check and then completing a deposit slip. On the deposit slip, record the date, the amount of currency to be deposited, the amount and ABA number of each check, and the total amount to be deposited. The checks to be deposited should accompany the deposit slip.

2. Reconcile a bank statement.

   The standard form for a bank reconciliation is as follows:

   Bank Statement Balance

   Add

   Deposits in transit
   Bank errors that understate bank statement balance

   Deduct

   Outstanding checks
   Bank errors that overstate bank statement balance

   Adjusted Bank Statement Balance

Ledger Balance of Cash

Add

Notes collected
Interest income earned
Checkbook errors that understate the ledger balance of cash
Bank credit memos

Deduct

Bank service charges
Checkbook errors that overstate the ledger balance of cash
NSF checks
Bank debit memos

Adjusted Ledger Balance of Cash

3. Record the required journal entries directly from the bank reconciliation.

   Journal entries for the Ledger Balance of Cash section are required. The entry for notes and interest collected is a debit to Cash and credits to Notes Receivable and Interest Income. The entry for a bank service charge is a debit to Miscellaneous Expense and a credit to Cash. The entry for an NSF check is a debit to Accounts Receivable and a credit to Cash.

4. Record journal entries to establish and reimburse Petty Cash Fund.

   The entry to establish a Petty Cash Fund is a debit to Petty Cash Fund and a credit to Cash. The entry to reimburse the Petty Cash Fund consists of debits to the items for which payments from the Petty Cash Fund were made and one credit to Cash for the total payments.

5. Complete petty cash vouchers and petty cash payments records.

   A petty cash voucher is made out for each payment from the Petty Cash Fund. In the petty cash payments record, each voucher is listed and a notation is made concerning the accounts involved; also, an explanation of why the money was paid out is recorded. The petty cash payments record is used as a source of information for making the journal entry to reimburse the Petty Cash Fund.

6. Record the journal entries to establish a Change Fund.

   The entry to establish the Change Fund is a debit to Change Fund and a credit to Cash.

7. Record journal entries for transactions involving Cash Short and Over.

   The Cash Short and Over account provides a way to keep a record of errors in making change. A debit balance in Cash Short and Over denotes a shortage, which is listed as Miscellaneous Expense; the entry is a debit to Miscellaneous Expense and a credit to Cash Short and Over. A credit balance in Cash Short and Over denotes an overage, which becomes Miscellaneous Income; the entry is a debit to Cash Short and Over and a credit to Miscellaneous Income.

Glossary

ABA number The number assigned by the American Bankers Association to a given bank. The first part of the numerator denotes the city or state in which the bank is located; the second part denotes the bank on which the check is drawn. The denominator indicates the Federal Reserve District in which the check is cleared and the routing number used by the Federal Reserve Bank. (220)

ATM (automated teller machine) A machine that enables depositors to make deposits, withdrawals, and transfers using a coded plastic card. (220)

Bank reconciliation A process by which an accountant determines whether and why there is a difference between the balance shown on the bank statement and the balance of the Cash account in the firm's general ledger. The object is to determine the adjusted (or true) balance of the Cash account. (226)

Bank statement A periodic statement that a bank sends to the drawer/depositor of a checking account listing deposits received and checks paid by the bank, debit and credit memos, and beginning and ending balances. (223)

Blank endorsement An endorsement in which the holder (payee) of a check simply signs her or his name on the back of the check. There are no restrictions attached. (221)

Canceled checks Checks issued by the depositor that have been paid (cleared) by the bank and listed on the bank statement. They are called canceled checks because they are canceled by a stamp or perforation, indicating that they have been paid. (225)

Cash funds Separately held reserves of cash set aside for specific purposes. (218)

Change Fund A cash fund used by a firm to make change for customers who pay cash for goods or services. (238)

Check writer A machine that imprints the amount of a check in figures and words on the check itself. (222)

Collections Payments collected by the bank and added to the customer's bank account in the form of a credit memorandum. (226)

Denominations Varieties of coins and currency, such as quarters, dimes, and nickels and $1 and $5 bills and so on. (234)

Deposit in transit A deposit not recorded on the bank statement because the deposit was made between the time of the bank's closing date for compiling items for its statement and the time the statement is received by the depositor; also known as a *late deposit.* (226)

Deposit slips Printed forms provided by a bank on which customers can list all items being deposited; also known as *deposit tickets.* (220)

Drawer The party who writes the check. (222)

Endorsement The process by which the payee transfers ownership of the check to a bank or another party. A check must be endorsed when deposited in a bank, because the bank must have legal title to it in order to collect payment from the drawer of the check (the person or firm who wrote the check). In case the check cannot be collected, the endorser guarantees all subsequent holders (*exception:* an endorsement "without recourse"). (221)

Ledger balance of cash The balance of the Cash account in the general ledger before it is reconciled with the bank statement. (225)

MICR Magnetic ink character recognition; the characters the bank uses to print the number of the depositor's account and the bank's number at the bottom of checks and deposit slips. The bank also prints the amount of the check in MICR when the check is deposited. A number written in these characters can be read by electronic equipment used by banks in clearing checks. (220)

NSF (not sufficient funds) checks Checks drawn against an account in which there are *not sufficient funds* and returned by the payee's bank to the drawer's bank because of nonpayment; also known as *dishonored checks.* (226)

Outstanding checks Checks that have been written by the drawer and deducted on his or her records but have not reached the bank for payment and are not deducted from the bank balance by the time the bank issues its statement. (226)

Payee The person to whom a check is payable. (222)

Petty Cash Fund A cash fund used to make small immediate cash payments. (234)

Petty cash payments record A record indicating the amount of each petty cash voucher, the accounts to which it should be charged, and the purpose of the expenditure. (235)

Petty cash voucher A form stating who requested cash from the Petty Cash Fund, signed by (1) the person in charge of the fund and (2) the person who received the cash, and indicating the purpose of the petty cash payment. (235)

Promissory note A written promise to pay a definite sum at a definite future time. (228)

Qualified endorsement An endorsement in which the holder (payee) of a check avoids future liability, in case the drawer of the check does not have sufficient funds to cover the check, by adding the words "Pay to the order of" and "without recourse" to the endorsement on the back of the check. (222)

Restrictive endorsement An endorsement, such as "Pay to the order of (name of bank), for deposit only," that restricts or limits any further negotiation of a check. It forces the check's deposit, because the endorsement is not valid for any other purpose. (221)

Service charge The fee the bank charges for handling checks, collections, and other items. It is in the form of a debit memorandum. (226)

Signature card The form a depositor signs to give the bank a copy of the official signatures of any persons authorized to sign checks. The bank can use it to verify the depositors' signatures on checks. (219)

QUESTIONS, EXERCISES, AND PROBLEMS

Discussion Questions

1. What is the purpose of a signature card?
2. What are the purposes served by endorsing checks?
3. Why is there generally a difference between the balance in the Cash account on the company's books and the balance on the bank statement?
4. On the bank statement reconciliation, what is the similarity between outstanding checks and NSF checks?
5. Indicate whether the following items in a bank reconciliation should be (1) added to the Cash account balance, (2) deducted from the Cash account balance, (3) added to the bank statement balance, or (4) deducted from the bank statement balance.
   a. NSF check
   b. Deposit in transit
   c. Outstanding check
   d. Bank error charging the firm's account with another company's check
   e. Bank service charge

6. Why is it unnecessary to make general journal entries for the bank statement side of the bank reconciliation?
7. a. Explain the purpose served by a Petty Cash Fund.
   b. Describe the entries to establish and reimburse the fund.
8. a. What does a debit balance in Cash Short and Over represent?
   b. Where does a debit balance in Cash Short and Over appear in the financial statements?
   c. What does a credit balance in Cash Short and Over represent?
   d. Where does a credit balance in Cash Short and Over appear in the financial statements?

Exercises

P.O. 2

Determine missing amounts on a bank reconciliation.

Exercise 7-1 Fill in the missing amounts for the following bank reconciliation:

Bank Reconciliation
March 31, 20—

Bank Statement Balance		$3,754.00
Add: Deposit in transit		(a)
		$4,021.00
Deduct: Outstanding checks		
No. 210	$210.00	
No. 224	(b)	
No. 227	320.00	851.00
Adjusted Bank Statement Balance		(c)
Ledger Balance of Cash		$2,840.00
Add: Note collected by bank		427.00
		(d)
Deduct: Bank service charge	(e)	
NSF check from customer	85.00	97.00
Adjusted Ledger Balance of Cash		(f)

P.O. 3

Journalize entries from a bank reconciliation.

Exercise 7-2 The Ledger Balance of Cash section of the bank reconciliation for Jeon Company for July 31 is shown below.

Ledger Balance of Cash		$6,357.00
Add: Note collected (principal, $700.00, interest $41, signed by L. Hyde)	$741.00	
Error in recording Ck. No. 2225 payable to Fenton Company (recorded check for $18 too much)	18.00	759.00
		$7,116.00
Deduct: NSF check from J. Kelton	$ 85.00	
Bank service and collection charges	21.00	106.00
		$7,010.00

Journalize the entries required to bring the general ledger up to date as of July 31 of this year.

P.O. 2
Determine amount of outstanding checks.

Exercise 7-3 When the bank statement is received on December 3, it shows a balance of $3,000 as of November 30, before reconciliation. After reconciliation, the adjusted balance is $2,500. If there was one deposit in transit amounting to $500, what was the total of the outstanding checks, assuming that there were no other adjustments to be made to the bank statement?

P.O. 2
Place items on a bank reconciliation.

Exercise 7-4 Write a check mark in the column that indicates the location of each item that would be found on a bank reconciliation. The checks are written correctly.

Item	Add to Bank Statement Balance	Subtract from Bank Statement Balance	Add to Ledger Balance of Cash	Subtract from Ledger Balance of Cash
a. A check-printing charge				
b. An outstanding check				
c. A deposit for $187 listed incorrectly on the bank statement as $178				
d. A collection charge the bank made for a note it collected for its depositor				
e. A check written for $40.73 and recorded incorrectly in the checkbook as $40.37				
f. A deposit in transit				
g. An NSF check received from a customer				
h. A check written for $72.39 and recorded incorrectly in the checkbook as $720.39				

P.O. 2
Determine the adjusted ledger balance of cash.

Exercise 7-5 The Mysung Company's Cash account shows a balance of $752.00 as of August 31 of this year. The balance on the bank statement on that date is $1,250.50. Checks for $263.70, $437.05, and $327.00 are outstanding. The bank statement shows a check issued by another depositor for $237.25 (in other words, the bank made an error and charged Mysung Company for a check written by another company). The bank statement also shows an NSF check for $280.00 received from one of Mysung's customers. Service charges for the month were $12.00. What is the adjusted ledger balance of cash as of August 31?

P.O. 4
Journalize entries pertaining to a Petty Cash Fund.

Exercise 7-6 Make entries in general journal form to record the following:

a. Established a Petty Cash Fund, $150. Issued Ck. No. 857.
b. Reimbursed the Petty Cash Fund for expenditures of $102: Store Supplies, $28; Office Supplies, $36; Miscellaneous Expense, $38. Issued Ck. No. 889.
c. Increased the amount of the fund by an additional $25. Issued Ck. No. 891.

d. Reimbursed the Petty Cash Fund for expenditures of $91.84: Store Supplies, $45.92; Delivery Expense, $36.00; Miscellaneous Expense, $9.92. Issued Ck. No. 936.

P.O. 6,7

Journalize entry for the receipt of cash.

Exercise 7-7 At the end of the day, the cash register tape lists $827.27 as total income from services. Cash on hand consists of $15.27 in coins, $694.00 in currency, $80 in traveler's checks, and $236.00 in customers' checks. The amount of the Change Fund is $200. In general journal form, record the entry to record the day's cash revenue.

P.O. 6,7

Describe entries related to the Change Fund and Cash Short and Over.

Exercise 7-8

a. Describe the entries that have been posted to the following accounts after the Change Fund was established.

Change Fund

Debit	Credit
200	

Sales

Debit	Credit
	Jan. 3 1,521
	Jan. 4 1,420
	Jan. 6 1,663

Cash

Debit	Credit
Jan. 3 1,523	
Jan. 4 1,419	
Jan. 6 1,660	

Cash Short and Over

Debit		Credit	
Jan. 4	1	Jan. 3	2
Jan. 6	3		

b. How will the balance of Cash Short and Over be reported on the income statement?

CONSIDER AND COMMUNICATE

Your friend owns a small clothing alterations business. To make change for a customer, your friend must take money out of her own wallet. How would you explain the separate entity concept, along with how a Change Fund account might help the situation?

CRITICAL THINKING

William Croxton, a college student, plans to provide résumé and thesis typing services to graduate students at the university near his home. He must determine how much money to deposit initially in his business account to pay for the start-up costs of the new business. After start-up costs, he must be left with a balance of $5,000 in his business account. He plans to buy a computer and printer and a copier for $3,500, and he will make a down payment of $1,500. The fax machine and telephone system he needs are available for $360 cash. He will buy paper for the copier, printer, and fax machine for $325 on account.

1. How much should William's investment be on May 1 if he plans to meet his goal of having $5,000 in his business account after the anticipated transactions?
2. Prepare a balance sheet for William's business as of May 15, 20—.

Transaction	Cash	Equipment	Supplies	Accounts Payable	W. Croxton, Capital
a. Make beginning investment (unknown at this time)					
Balance					
b. Buy computer/printer/copier for $3,500, paying $1,500 down, and placing the rest on account.					
Balance					
c. Bought fax/telephone for $360 cash.					
Balance					
d. Bought paper supplies for $325 on account.					
Balance					

A MATTER OF ETHICS

You work as a cashier in a service business. Some days you are short of cash at the end of the day, and some days you have more cash than the cash register tape says was earned. You are embarrassed when your cash is short and don't want the owner to know, so you take money from your wallet and make up the difference. On days when you are over, you keep the difference to help pay back what you paid to cover your shortages. Comment on this practice.

WEB WORK

Using an Internet web browser, type the phrase *small business accounting* or *sba.gov* for the home page of the Small Business Administration in the search box. Search for information about embezzlement or internal control systems. Discuss your findings in a five-minute presentation to your class, or summarize them in a one-page memorandum.

PROBLEM SET A

For additional help, see the demonstration problem at the beginning of each chapter in your Working Papers.

P.O. 2,3

Problem 7-1A Carver Men's Shop deposits all receipts in the bank each evening and makes all payments by check. On September 30 its Cash in Bank account has a balance of $2,041.60. The bank statement of September 30 shows a balance of $2,268.43. The following information pertains to reconciling the bank statement:

a. The reconciliation for August, the previous month, showed three checks outstanding on August 31: no. 1516 for $75; no. 1519 for $65.40, and no. 1520 for $120. Checks no. 1516 and 1520 were returned with the September bank statement; however, check no. 1519 was not returned.

b. Checks no. 1599 for $87.50, no. 1616 for $18.61, no. 1617 for $52.87, and no. 1618 for $40.79 were written during September and have not been returned by the bank.
c. A deposit of $442.34 was placed in the night depository on September 30 and did not appear on the bank statement.
d. The canceled checks were compared with the entries in the checkbook, and it was observed that check no. 1587, for $89, payable to C. T. Carver, the owner, for personal use, was written correctly but was recorded in the checkbook as $108.
e. There is a bank debit memo for service charges, $13.
f. There is a bank credit memo for collection of a note signed by J. L. Yung, $398, including $380 principal and $18 interest.

Check Figure
Adjusted ledger balance of cash, $2,445.60

Instructions

1. Prepare a bank reconciliation as of September 30, assuming that the debit and credit memos have not been recorded.
2. Record the necessary entries in general journal form, page 12.

P.O. 4,5

Problem 7-2A On July 1, Driskol and Company established a Petty Cash Fund. The following petty cash transactions took place during the month:

July 1 Cashed check no. 1956 for $125 to establish a Petty Cash Fund, and put the $125 in a locked drawer in the office.
3 Bought postage stamps, $13.60, voucher no. 1 (Miscellaneous Expense).
4 Issued voucher no. 2 for taxi fare, $18 (Miscellaneous Expense).
6 Issued voucher no. 3 for delivery charges on outgoing parts, $3.80.
9 N. Driskol withdrew $18 for personal use, voucher no. 4.
13 Paid $6.80 for postage, voucher no. 5 (Miscellaneous Expense).
19 Bought pens for office, $12.15, voucher no. 6.
23 Paid $2.18 for a box of staples, voucher no. 7.
28 Paid $22 for window cleaning service, voucher no. 8 (Miscellaneous Expense).
29 Paid $12.18 for pencils for office, voucher no. 9.
31 Issued for cash check no. 1974 for $108.71 to reimburse Petty Cash Fund.

Check Figure
Office Supplies, $26.51

Instructions

1. Journalize the entry establishing the Petty Cash Fund in the general journal, page 3.
2. Record the disbursements of petty cash in the petty cash payments record, page 1.
3. Journalize the summarizing entry to reimburse the Petty Cash Fund.

P.O. 6,7

Problem 7-3A M. Cho, owner of Cho's Crafts, makes bank deposits in the night depository at the close of each business day. The following information for the last three days of June is available.

	June		
	28	29	30
Cash register tape	$756.18	$835.60	$ 912.50
Cash count	854.97	934.40	1,014.70

Check Figure

Cash Short and Over, June 30, $2.20 over

Instructions

In general journal form, record the cash deposit for each day, assuming that there is a $100 Change Fund.

P.O. 2,3

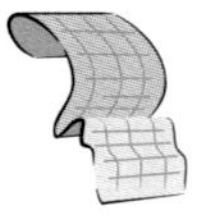

Problem 7-4A On August 31, Kravsnik Company receives its bank statement. The company deposits its receipts in the bank and makes all payments by check. The debit memo for $149 is for an NSF check written by N. Carlton. Check no. 1924 for $336, payable to Garner Company (a creditor), was incorrectly recorded in the checkbook and journal as $200.

The balance of the Cash account as of August 31 is $1,509. Outstanding checks as of August 31 are: no. 1928, $119; no. 1929, $243. The accountant notes that the deposit of August 31 for $261 did not appear on the bank statement.

Check Figure

Adjusted ledger balance of cash, $1,212

Instructions

1. Prepare a bank reconciliation as of August 31, assuming that the debit memos have not been recorded.
2. Record the necessary journal entries.
3. Complete the bank form to determine the adjusted balance of cash.

PEABODY NATIONAL BANK

Kravsnik Company
416 Seneca Avenue
Kansas City, Missouri 64102

ACCOUNT NO.
152-6 55-217

STATEMENT DATE
August 1–31, 20—

SUMMARY

Balance Last Statement	$1,360.00
Amount of Checks and Debits	$2,698.00
Number of Checks	11
Amount of Deposits and Credits	$2,651.00
Number of Deposits	7
Balance This Statement	$1,313.00

CHECKS/ OTHER DEBITS

CHECKS

CHECK NUMBER	DATE POSTED	AMOUNT	CHECK NUMBER	DATE POSTED	AMOUNT
1917	8-04	172.00	1923	8-09	621.00
1918	8-04	76.00	1924	8-17	336.00
1919	8-05	146.00	1925	8-17	14.00
1920	8-07	206.00	1926	8-23	533.00
1921	8-07	139.00	1927	8-28	94.00
1922	8-08	200.00			

OTHER DEBITS

DESCRIPTION	DATE POSTED	AMOUNT
DM NSF check	8-31	149.00
DM Service charge	8-31	12.00

DEPOSITS/ OTHER CREDITS

DEPOSITS

DATE POSTED	AMOUNT	DATE POSTED	AMOUNT
8-02	326.00	8-18	419.00
8-05	412.00	8-24	398.00
8-09	437.00	8-28	291.00
8-14	368.00		

PLEASE EXAMINE THIS STATEMENT CAREFULLY. REPORT ANY POSSIBLE ERRORS IN 10 DAYS.

CODE SYMBOLS

CM Credit Memo **DM** Debit Memo **OD** Overdraft **EC** Error Correction

Instructions for General Ledger Software

1. Prepare a bank reconciliation as of August 31. Errors made by the company or the bank, as well as service charges, must be entered as debit or credit memos.
2. Print the bank reconciliation.
3. Record the necessary journal entries.
4. Print the journal entries.

PROBLEM SET B

For additional help, see the demonstration problem at the beginning of each chapter in your Working Papers.

P.O. 2,3

Problem 7-1B The Malamura Company deposits all receipts in the bank and makes all payments by check. On November 30 its Cash account has a balance of $2,289.00. The bank statement on November 30 shows a balance of $2,894.00. You are given the following information with which to reconcile the bank statement:

a. A deposit of $320.00 was placed in the night depository on November 30 and did not appear on the bank statement.
b. The reconciliation for October, the previous month, showed three checks outstanding on October 31: no. 1727 for $81.30, no. 1730 for $127.40, and no. 1732 for $62.40. Checks no. 1727 and 1730 were returned with the November bank statement; however, check no. 1732 was not returned.
c. Check no. 1742 for $98.50, no. 1743 for $46.27, no. 1744 for $37.92, and no. 1745 for $200.91 were written during November but were not returned by the bank.
d. You compare the canceled checks with the entries in the checkbook and find that check no. 1737 for $58, payable to C. R. Malamura, the owner, for her personal use, was written correctly. However, the check was recorded in the checkbook as $85.
e. Included in the bank statement was a bank debit memo for service charges, $12.
f. A bank credit memo was also enclosed for the collection of a note signed by L. B. Norman, $464, including $436 principal and $28 interest.

Check Figure
Adjusted ledger balance of cash, $2,768.00

Instructions

1. Prepare a bank reconciliation as of November 30, assuming that the debit and credit memos have not been recorded.
2. Record the necessary entries in general journal form, page 4.

P.O. 4,5

Problem 7-2B On March 1 of this year, the Stenn Company established a Petty Cash Fund, and the following petty cash transactions took place during the month:

Mar.	1	Cashed check no. 1314 for $110 to establish a Petty Cash Fund, and put the $110 in a locked drawer in the office.
	4	Issued voucher no. 1 for taxi fare, $14 (Miscellaneous Expense).
	7	Issued voucher no. 2 for memo pads, $4.10.

Mar. 9 Paid $17.50 for an advertisement in a college basketball program, voucher no. 3.
16 Bought postage stamps, $16, voucher no. 4 (Miscellaneous Expense).
20 Paid $18.50 to have snow removed from office front sidewalk, voucher no. 5 (Miscellaneous Expense).
25 Issued voucher no. 6 for delivery charge, $3.45.
28 R. C. Do, the owner, withdrew $19 for personal use, voucher no. 7.
29 Paid $3.50 for postage, voucher no. 8 (Miscellaneous Expense).
30 Paid $8.40 for delivery charge, voucher no. 9.
31 Issued for cash check no. 1372 for $104.45 to reimburse Petty Cash Fund.

Check Figure
Office Supplies, $4.10

Instructions

1. Journalize the entry establishing the Petty Cash Fund in the general journal, page 3.
2. Record the disbursements of petty cash in the petty cash payments record.
3. Journalize the summarizing entry to reimburse the Petty Cash Fund.

P.O. 6

Problem 7-3B Melissa Smith, owner of Melissa's Beauty Salon, makes bank deposits in the night depository at the close of each business day. The following information for the first three days of April is available.

	April		
	1	2	3
Cash register tape	$358.20	$418.52	$424.79
Cash count	457.28	520.55	523.59

Check Figure
Cash Short and Over, April 3, $1.20 short

Instructions

In general journal form, record the cash deposit for each day, assuming that there is a $100 Change Fund.

P.O. 2,3

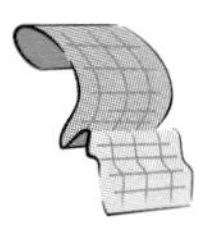

Problem 7-4B On August 2, Eastside Hotel receives its bank statement. The company deposits its receipts in the bank and makes all payments by check. The debit memo for $137 is for an NSF check written by T. N. Klein. Check no. 1617 for $63.80, payable to Wrye Company (a creditor), was incorrectly recorded in the checkbook and journal as $36.80.

The balance of the Cash account as of July 31 is $2,167.40. Outstanding checks as of July 31 are: no. 1631, $21.64; no. 1632, $91.23; no. 1633, $154.29. The accountant notes that the July 31 deposit of $268 did not appear on the bank statement.

Check Figure
Adjusted ledger balance of cash, $1,990.30

Instructions

1. Prepare a bank reconciliation as of July 31, assuming that the debit memos have not been recorded.
2. Record the necessary journal entries.

3. Complete the bank form to determine the adjusted balance of cash.

STANTON NATIONAL BANK

Eastside Hotel
410 W. Lang Street
Rockford, Illinois 61104

ACCOUNT NO.
761-145-792
STATEMENT DATE
July 1–31, 20—

SUMMARY

Balance Last Statement	$2,168.50
Amount of Checks and Debits	$2,707.21
Number of Checks	14
Amount of Deposits and Credits	$2,528.17
Number of Deposits	7
Balance This Statement	$1,989.46

CHECKS/OTHER DEBITS

CHECKS

CHECK NUMBER	DATE POSTED	AMOUNT	CHECK NUMBER	DATE POSTED	AMOUNT
1617	7-03	63.80	1624	7-08	120.00
1618	7-03	167.00	1625	7-09	429.60
1619	7-03	124.20	1626	7-12	37.40
1620	7-05	137.20	1627	7-14	38.49
1621	7-06	236.25	1628	7-22	182.71
1622	7-06	159.89	1629	7-25	96.87
1623	7-08	244.50	1630	7-26	19.20

OTHER DEBITS

DESCRIPTION	DATE POSTED	AMOUNT
DM NSF check	7-22	137.00
DM Service charge	7-31	13.10

DEPOSITS/OTHER CREDITS

DEPOSITS

DATE POSTED	AMOUNT	DATE POSTED	AMOUNT
7-03	491.50	7-15	291.76
7-06	415.72	7-18	142.90
7-09	439.16	7-28	368.93
7-11	378.20		

PLEASE EXAMINE THIS STATEMENT CAREFULLY. REPORT ANY POSSIBLE ERRORS IN 10 DAYS.

CODE SYMBOLS

CM Credit Memo **DM** Debit Memo **OD** Overdraft **EC** Error Correction

Instructions for General Ledger Software

1. Prepare a bank reconciliation as of July 31. Errors made by the company or the bank, as well as service charges, must be entered as debit or credit memos.
2. Print the bank reconciliation.
3. Record the necessary journal entries.
4. Print the journal entries.

APPENDIX

B Bad Debts

Performance Objectives

After you have completed this appendix, you will be able to do the following:

1. Prepare the adjusting entry for bad debts using the allowance method, based on a percentage of credit sales.
2. Prepare the entry to write off an account as uncollectible when the allowance method is used.
3. Prepare the entry to write off an account as uncollectible when the specific charge-off method is used.

As you know, not all credit customers pay their bills. In this appendix, we turn our attention to the accounts receivable that will not be collected. There are two basic methods of providing for writing or charging off credit customers' accounts that are considered uncollectible. They are the allowance method and the specific charge-off method.

ALLOWANCE METHOD

The allowance method provides for bad debt losses in advance, by estimating them. Though there are a number of ways to estimate the amount of future losses from open accounts, we will base our estimate on a percentage of credit sales.

For example, based on its experience with bad debt losses, the Mosier Company estimates that 1 percent of its revenue from services on account for the year will be uncollectible. Obviously, Mosier does not know which credit customers will not pay their bills. If the company were certain that a particular customer would not pay his or her bill, then it wouldn't perform services without requiring cash in advance.

Adjusting Entry and Writing Off an Account

Objective 1
Prepare the adjusting entry for bad debts using the allowance method, based on a percentage of credit sales.

Mosier's total income from services on account for last year was $300,000. One percent of $300,000 is $3,000. On its work sheet, Mosier makes an adjusting entry. We show this in T account form.

Bad Debts Expense

+	−
Dec. 31 Adjusting 3,000	

Allowance for Doubtful Accounts

−	+
	Dec. 31 Adjusting 3,000

Allowance for Doubtful Accounts is treated as a deduction from Accounts Receivable. Consequently, Allowance for Doubtful Accounts is a contra account. The adjusting entry is similar to the entry for depreciation in that there is a debit to an expense account and a credit to a contra account. In T account form, the adjustment for depreciation looks like this:

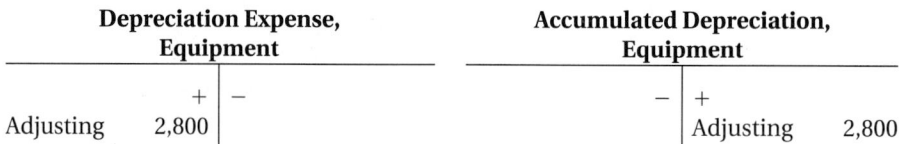

Depreciation Expense, Equipment

+	−
Adjusting 2,800	

Accumulated Depreciation, Equipment

−	+
	Adjusting 2,800

Assume that Mosier Company's balance of Accounts Receivable is $90,000 and its balance of Equipment is $75,000. Let's show the accounts and the adjusting entries in T account form.

Assets = **Liabilities** + **Owner's Equity** + **Revenue** − **Expenses**

Assets (+ / −)	Liabilities (− / +)	Owner's Equity (− / +)	Revenue (− / +)	Expenses (+ / −)

Assets

Accounts Receivable

+	−
Bal. 90,000	

Allowance for Doubtful Accounts

−	+
	Bal. 170
	Adj. 3,000
	Bal. 3,170

Equipment

+	−
Bal. 75,000	

Accumulated Depreciation, Equipment

−	+
	Bal. 7,000
	Adj. 2,800
	Bal. 9,800

Revenue

Income from Services

−	+
	Bal. 300,000

Expenses

Bad Debts Expense

+	−
Adj. 3,000	

Depreciation Expense, Equipment

+	−
Adj. 2,800	

The Depreciation Expense, Equipment, account comes into existence as an adjusting entry at the end of the year. It is closed immediately after being brought into existence. The same thing happens to Bad Debts Expense; it comes into existence as an adjusting entry, and then it is immediately closed during the closing process.

FYI

Companies generally have a credit balance left in the Allowance account.

As certain charge customers' accounts are determined to be uncollectible and are written off, the losses are taken out of Allowance for Doubtful Accounts. Think of the Allowance for Doubtful Accounts as a reservoir. By means of the adjusting entry, the account is filled up at the end of the year and then is gradually drained off (reduced) during the next year by write-offs of charge customer accounts. The $170 balance in Allowance for Doubtful Accounts at the end of the year indicates that less accounts receivable were actually written off as uncollectible during the year than previously estimated. As a result, Bad Debts Expense in the period was overstated and therefore net income understated.

Objective 2

Prepare the entry to write off an account as uncollectible when the allowance method is used.

Let's go on to the next year. On January 2, the Mosier Company finally gives up on its attempts to collect $720 from its credit customer A. N. Brady, which is included in Accounts Receivable. The Mosier Company now writes off the account in the amount of $720, shown below in T account form.

Accounts Receivable

+		−	
Bal.	90,000	Jan. 2 (write-off)	720
Bal.	89,280		

Allowance for Doubtful Accounts

−		+	
Jan. 2 (write-off)	720	Bal.	3,170
		Bal.	2,450

As you can see, the write-off has reduced both the balance of Accounts Receivable and the balance of Allowance for Doubtful Accounts but has not changed the net realizable value of accounts receivable. The general journal entry is shown below.

PAGE ____

	DATE		DESCRIPTION	POST. REF.	DEBIT	CREDIT	
1	20—						1
2	Jan.	2	Allowance for Doubtful Accounts		720 00		2
3			Accounts Receivable			720 00	3
4			Wrote off the account of				4
5			A. N. Brady as uncollectible.				5
6							6

An Advantage and a Disadvantage of the Allowance Method

The allowance method is consistent with the accrual basis of accounting in that it matches revenues of one year with expenses of the same year. The bad-debt loss potential is provided in the same year in which the revenue is earned. The conformity with the matching principle places the allowance method in compliance with generally accepted accounting principles as recognized by the FASB. However, the allowance method cannot be used for federal income tax purposes. This means that if a business uses the allowance method, the net income shown on the company's income statement will differ from the net income shown on its federal income tax return.

SPECIFIC CHARGE-OFF METHOD

Objective 3

Prepare the entry to write off an account as uncollectible when the specific charge-off method is used.

Under the specific charge-off method, when a credit customer's account is determined to be uncollectible, the account is simply written off. The terms *write-off* and *charge-off* mean the same thing. No allowance account is used with the specific charge-off method because no estimate of uncollectible accounts receivable is calculated. As an illustration, Walton Company uses the specific charge-off method. On May 5, Walton Company writes off the account of L. C. Garber, $220. For the purpose of this example, we will use a separate Accounts Receivable account for L. C. Garber. T accounts pertaining to Garber's account look like this:

Accounts Receivable			
	+	−	
Balance	220	May 5 (write-off)	220

Bad Debts Expense			
	+	−	
May 5 (write-off)	220		

The general journal entry is shown below.

PAGE ____

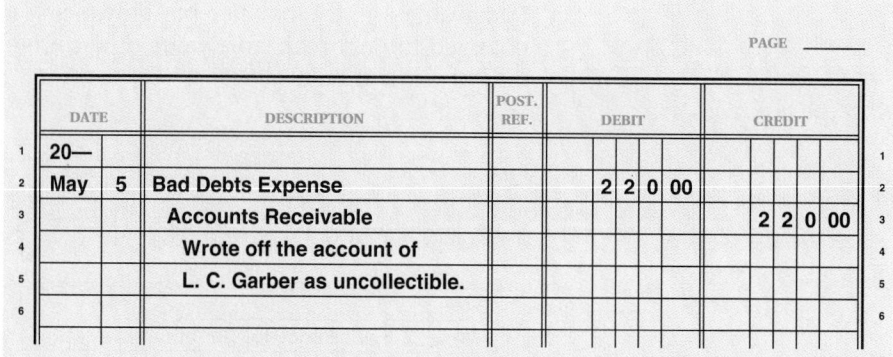

	DATE		DESCRIPTION	POST. REF.	DEBIT	CREDIT	
1	20—						1
2	May	5	Bad Debts Expense		220 00		2
3			Accounts Receivable			220 00	3
4			Wrote off the account of				4
5			L. C. Garber as uncollectible.				5
6							6

Under this method, entries will be made directly into the Bad Debts Expense account during the year. No adjusting entry is needed, and Allowance for Doubtful Accounts is not used.

Advantage of the Specific Charge-off Method

The main advantage is that the method may be used for federal income tax purposes. It is not necessary to make an adjusting entry. Also, one less account (Allowance for Doubtful Accounts) is required.

Disadvantage of the Specific Charge-off Method

This method is not consistent with the accrual basis of accounting (recognizing revenue when it is earned and expenses when they are incurred). The method does not match up the revenue of one year with the expense of the same year. This lack of conformity with the matching principle places the specific charge-off method in violation of generally accepted accounting principles. For example, the sale of services on account to L. C. Garber could have been made four years ago. Since the account receivable will never be collected, the revenue for that year was too high (overstated). Consequently, net income is also overstated during that year. Now, four years later, $220 is written off as an expense. So net income for this year is too low (understated) because of the added expense.

PROBLEMS

P.O. 1,2

Check Figure

Adjusting entry amount, $3,620

Problem B-1 Ramos Company's total sales on account for the year amounted to $362,000. The company, which uses the allowance method, estimated bad debts at 1 percent of its charge sales. Journalize the following selected entries:

2000		
Dec.	31	The adjusting entry.
2001		
Mar.	2	Write-off of the account of B. L. Hulse as uncollectible, $264.
June	6	Write-off of the account of A. P. Tolland as uncollectible, $341.

P.O. 1,2

Check Figure

Adjusting entry amount, $1,431.53

Problem B-2 Harron's Landscape Service's total revenue on account for 2000 amounted to $286,305. The company, which uses the allowance method, estimates bad debts at ½ percent of total revenue on account. Journalize the following selected entries:

2000		
Dec.	12	Performed services on account for D. A. Wagner, $114.
	31	The adjusting entry.
	31	The closing entry.
2001		
Feb.	18	Wrote off the account of D. A. Wagner as uncollectible, $114.

P.O. 3

Check Figure

Name of debit account, Bad Debts Expense

Problem B-3 Jump City uses the specific charge-off method for recording bad debts. Journalize the following selected entries:

2000		
Apr.	10	Write-off of the account of J. C. Sonja as uncollectible, $195.
July	27	Write-off of the account of B. R. West as uncollectible, $142.

8 Employee Earnings and Deductions

WINDOWS ON THE WORLD WIDE WEB

When you graduate from college, where will you work? What will you earn? Will you be paid by the hour, by commission, or with a salary? If you land a job at a large corporation like Microsoft, you can expect to receive benefits such as employer-paid coverage for medical, dental, and vision care for you and your family members. In addition, you will be entitled to life insurance, a 401K plan, and even free soft drinks, as well as discounts on Microsoft products at the company store.

If your job were in Microsoft's accounting department, you would need to keep records on payroll taxes paid and employee income tax withholding. You'd want to make sure paychecks were processed on time and were accurate. For more information on Microsoft benefits and job opportunities, go to **http://www.microsoft.com/jobs/**.

Performance Objectives

After you have completed this chapter, you will be able to do the following:

1. Calculate total earnings based on an hourly, piece-rate, or commission basis.
2. Determine deductions from tables of employees' income tax withholding.
3. Complete a payroll register.
4. Journalize the payroll entry from a payroll register.
5. Maintain employees' individual earnings records.

Up to now, we've been recording employees' earnings as a debit to Salaries or Wages Expense and a credit to Cash, but we've really been talking only about **gross pay**: the total amount of an employee's pay before deductions. We haven't mentioned the various deductions that we all know are taken out of our gross pay before we get to the **net pay**, or take-home pay. In this chapter, we talk about types of deductions and how to enter them in the payroll records, and about journal entries to record the payroll and pay the employees.

OBJECTIVES OF PAYROLL RECORDS AND ACCOUNTING

There are two primary reasons to maintain accurate payroll records. First, we must collect the data necessary to compute the compensation for each employee for each payroll period.

Second, we must provide the information needed to complete the various government reports—federal and state—required of all employers. All business enterprises, both large and small, are required by law to withhold certain amounts from employees' pay for taxes, to make payments to government agencies by specific deadlines, and to submit reports on official forms. Because governments impose penalties if the requirements are not met, employers are vitally concerned with payroll accounting. Anyone going into accounting or involved with the management of any business should be thoroughly acquainted with payroll accounting.

The employer is required to keep records of the following information:

1. **Personal data on employee** Name, address, Social Security number, date of birth
2. **Data on wage payments** Dates and amounts of payments, and payroll periods
3. **Amount of taxable wages paid** Dates and amount earned year to date for the calendar year involved
4. **Amount of tax withheld from each employee's earnings by pay period**

EMPLOYER/EMPLOYEE RELATIONSHIPS

FYI

Examples of independent contractors include a self-employed appliance repair person, plumber, or CPA.

Payroll accounting is concerned with employees and their compensation, withholdings, records, reports, and taxes. There is a distinction between an employee and an independent contractor. An **employee** is one who is under the direction and control of the employer, such as a secretary, bookkeeper, salesclerk, vice president, controller, and so on. An **independent contractor** is engaged for a definite job or service and may choose her or his own means of doing the work. Payments made to independent contractors are in the form of fees or charges. Independent contractors submit bills or invoices for the work they do. The payment is not subject to any withholding or payroll taxes by the person or firm paying that invoice.

HOW EMPLOYEES GET PAID

Employees may be paid a salary or wages, depending on the type of work and the period of time covered. Money paid to a person for managerial or administrative services is usually called a salary, and the time period covered is generally a month or a year. Money paid for either skilled or unskilled labor is usually called wages, and the time period covered is hours or weeks. Wages may also be paid on a piecework basis. A company may supplement an employee's salary or wage by commissions, bonuses, cost-of-living adjustments, and profit-sharing plans. As a rule, employees are paid by check, in cash, or by a direct deposit to their bank account. However, their compensation may take the form of merchandise, lodging, meals, or other property as well. When the compensation is in these forms, you have to determine the fair value of the property or service given in payment for an employee's labor.

Calculating Total Earnings

Objective 1

Calculate total earnings based on an hourly, piece-rate, or commission basis.

When compensation is based on the amount of time worked, the accountant has to have a record of the number of hours worked by each employee. When there are only a few employees, this can be accomplished by means of a time book. When there are many employees, time clocks or other electronic time-keeping systems are used.

FIGURE 1

TIME CARD

Name: Asino, Matte E.

Week ending: Oct. 7, 20—

Day	In	Out	In	Out	Hours Worked	
					Regular	Overtime
M	757	1200	1220	432	8	
T	756	1206	1236	437	8	
W	757	1202	1231	431	8	
T	800	1211	1240	632	8	2
F	800	1203	1233	533	8	1
S	759	1102				3
S						

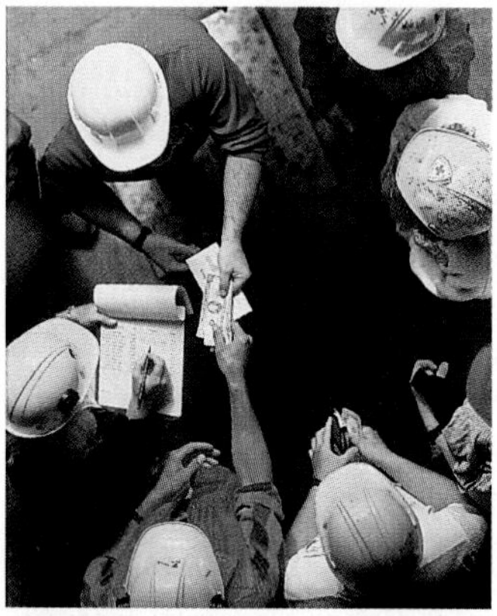

Although wages are more often paid by check or direct deposit, some industries or companies still pay employees in cash. From an internal control point of view, however, it is better to have a permanent record, which a check or direct deposit slip provides.

Employees may be paid weekly, biweekly, semimonthly, or monthly. Biweekly is every two weeks. Semimonthly is twice a month.

Wages

Consider Matte E. Asino, who works for Greg Company. His regular rate of pay is $22.84 per hour. The company pays time-and-a-half for hours worked in excess of 40 per week. In addition, it pays him double time for any work he does on Sundays and holidays. Asino has a ½-hour lunch break during an 8½-hour day. He is not paid for the lunch break nor is he paid for minutes before 8 AM or after 4:30 PM unless hours of overtime were authorized in advance. His time card for the week is shown in Figure 1.

Asino's gross wages can be computed by one of two methods. The first method works like this:

40 hours at straight time	40 × $22.84 per hour =	$ 913.60
2 hours overtime on Thursday	2 × $34.26 per hour =	$ 68.52
1 hour overtime on Friday	1 × $34.26 per hour =	$ 34.26
3 hours overtime on Saturday	3 × $34.26 per hour =	$ 102.78
Total gross wages	46	$1,119.16

The second method of calculating gross wages is often used when it is necessary to identify or track overtime premium.

46 hours at straight time: 46 × $22.84 per hour =	$1,050.64
Overtime premium:	
6 hours × $11.42 per hour premium =	68.52
Total gross wages	$1,119.16

FYI

Minimum wages are set by Congress or state legislature—whichever is higher. Originally, the minimum wage was $.25 per hour.

Salaries

Employees who are paid a regular salary may also be entitled to extra pay for overtime. It is necessary to figure out their regular hourly rate of pay before you can determine their overtime rate. Consider R. Helvi, who gets a salary of \$2,250 per month. She is entitled to overtime pay for all hours worked in excess of 40 during a week at the rate of 1½ times her regular hourly rate. This past week she worked 44 hours, so we calculate her overtime pay as follows:

\$2,250 per month × 12 months = \$27,000 per year
\$27,000 per year ÷ 52 weeks = \$519.23 per week
\$519.23 per week ÷ 40 hours = \$12.98 per regular hour

Earnings for 44 hours:		
40 hours at straight time	40 × \$12.98 =	\$519.20
4 hours overtime	4 × \$19.47 =	\$ 77.88
Total gross earnings		\$597.08

Piece Rate

Workers under the piece-rate system are paid at the rate of so much per unit of production. For example, Bob Faulk, a pear picker, gets paid \$9 for picking a bin of pears. If he picks 6 bins during the day, his total earnings are 6 × \$9 = \$54.

Commissions

Some salespersons are paid on a purely commission basis. However, a more common arrangement is a salary plus a commission or bonus. Assume that Lena Breski receives an annual salary of \$18,000. Her employer agrees to pay her a 5 percent commission on all sales during the year in excess of \$100,000. Her sales for the year total \$240,000. Her commission is \$7,000 (\$140,000 × .05). Therefore, her total earnings are \$25,000 (\$18,000 + \$7,000).

Workers paid by the piece-rate system are paid according to how much they produce. The number of heads of lettuce picked or shirts sewn determines the worker's total compensation.

VACUUM COOLED
VACUUM COOLED
LETTUCE

DEDUCTIONS FROM TOTAL EARNINGS

Anyone who has ever earned a paycheck has encountered some of the many types of deductions. Total earnings minus deductions equal net pay. The most usual deductions are for

1. Federal income tax withholding
2. State income tax withholding
3. FICA tax (Social Security and Medicare), employee's share
4. Purchase of U.S. savings bonds
5. Union dues
6. Medical and life insurance premiums
7. Contributions to a charitable organization
8. Repayment of personal loans from the company credit union
9. Savings through the company credit union

Employees' Federal Income Tax Withholding

FYI

Federal tax rates change frequently, but the procedure stays the same. We will use the tax table given in this chapter for all computations.

Employers are required not only to withhold employees' taxes and then pay them to the Internal Revenue Service, but also to keep records of the names and addresses of persons employed, their **taxable earnings** (the earnings subject to tax) and withholdings, and the amounts and dates of payment. The employer has to submit reports to the Internal Revenue Service quarterly (Form 941) and to the employee annually (W-2 form). With few exceptions, this requirement applies to employers of one or more persons.

The amount of federal income tax withheld from an employee's earnings depends on the amount of her or his total earnings, marital status, and the number of withholding allowances claimed. A **withholding allowance** is an amount of an individual's earnings that is exempt from income taxes (nontaxable). An employee is entitled to one personal allowance for the taxpayer, one for his or her spouse, and one for each dependent. An **exemption** is an amount of an employee's annual earnings not subject to income tax. Each employee has to fill out an **Employee's Withholding Allowance Certificate (Form W-4)**, shown in Figure 2.

The employer retains this form as authorization to withhold money for the employee's federal income tax.

Circular E, Employer's Tax Guide

Objective 2

Determine deductions using tables of employees' income tax withholding.

Circular E contains withholding tables for federal income, Social Security, and Medicare taxes, along with the rules for depositing these taxes. It is regularly updated to reflect changes in tax laws and withholding rates. It also describes filing requirements for official employer reports. Circular E is provided free of charge by the Internal Revenue Service. Accountants responsible for preparation of payroll registers and forms should be familiar with the contents of Circular E.

FYI

Circular E is sometimes referred to as the payroll bible.

The **wage-bracket tax tables** cover monthly, semimonthly, biweekly, weekly, and daily payroll periods. The tables are also subdivided on the basis of marital status. First locate the wage bracket in the first two columns of the table. Next, find the column for the number of allowances claimed and read down this column until you get to the appropriate wage-bracket line. A portion of the weekly federal income tax withholding table for married persons is reproduced in Figure 3 on page 266.

Form **W-4**
Department of the Treasury
Internal Revenue Service

Employee's Withholding Allowance Certificate

▶ **For Privacy Act and Paperwork Reduction Act Notice, see page 2.**

OMB No. 1545-0010

20XX

1 Type or print your first name and middle initial Matte E.	Last name Asino	2 Your social security number 5 4 3 2 4 1 6 8 0
Home address (number and street or rural route) 6242 Baxter Drive	3 ☐ Single ☒ Married ☐ Married, but withhold at higher Single rate. **Note:** *If married, but legally separated, or spouse is a nonresident alien, check the Single box.*	
City or town, state, and ZIP code Bangor, Maine 04412	4 If your last name differs from that on your social security card, check here. **You** must call 1-800-772-1213 for a new card . . . ▶ ☐	

5 Total number of allowances you are claiming (from line H above or from the worksheets on page 2 if they apply) . | 5 | 2

6 Additional amount, if any, you want withheld from each paycheck . . . . | 6 | $

7 I claim exemption from withholding for 1999, and I certify that I meet **BOTH** of the following conditions for exemption:
- Last year I had a right to a refund of **ALL** Federal income tax withheld because I had **NO** tax liability **AND**
- This year I expect a refund of **ALL** Federal income tax withheld because I expect to have **NO** tax liability.

If you meet both conditions, write "EXEMPT" here . . . . ▶ | 7 |

Under penalties of perjury, I certify that I am entitled to the number of withholding allowances claimed on this certificate, or I am entitled to claim exempt status.

Employee's signature
(Form is not valid
unless you sign it) ▶ *Matte E. Asino* **Date** ▶ *February 1, 20–*

8 Employer's name and address (Employer: Complete 8 and 10 only if sending to the IRS)	9 Office code (optional)	10 Employer identification number

FIGURE 2

Assume that Matte E. Asino, who claims two allowances, has gross wages of $1,119.16 for the week. As $1,119.16 falls in the $1,110–$1,120 bracket, you can see from the table that $148 should be withheld.

Note the headings of the bracket columns: "At least" and "But less than." A strict interpretation of the $1,110–$1,120 bracket really means $1,110–$1,119.99. Therefore, if Asino's salary were $1,120, it would fall into the $1,120–$1,130 bracket.

Employees' State Income Tax Withholding

Many states that levy state income taxes also furnish employers with withholding tables. Other states use a fixed percentage of the federal income tax withholding as the amount to be withheld for state taxes. In our illustration, we assume that the amount of each employee's state income tax deduction is 20 percent of that employee's federal income tax deduction.

Employees' FICA Tax Withholding (Social Security and Medicare)

The Federal Insurance Contributions Act provides for retirement pensions after a worker reaches age 62, disability benefits for any worker who becomes disabled (and for her or his dependents), and a health insurance program after age 65 (Medicare). Both the employee and the employer have to pay **FICA taxes**, which are commonly referred to as **Social Security taxes** and **Medicare taxes**. The employer withholds FICA taxes from employees' wages and pays them to the U.S. Treasury Department.

FICA tax rates apply to the gross earnings of an employee during the **calendar year** (January 1 through December 31). After an employee has paid

MARRIED Persons—WEEKLY Payroll Period

If the wages are–		And the number of withholding allowances claimed is—										
At least	But less than	0	1	2	3	4	5	6	7	8	9	10
		The amount of income tax to be withheld is—										
$740	$750	93	85	78	70	62	54	46	39	31	23	15
750	760	95	87	79	71	63	56	48	40	32	25	17
760	770	96	88	81	73	65	57	49	42	34	26	18
770	780	98	90	82	74	66	59	51	43	35	28	20
780	790	99	91	84	76	68	60	52	45	37	29	21
790	800	101	93	85	77	69	62	54	46	38	31	23
800	810	102	94	87	79	71	63	55	48	40	32	24
810	820	104	96	88	80	72	65	57	49	41	34	26
820	830	105	97	90	82	74	66	58	51	43	35	27
830	840	107	99	91	83	75	68	60	52	44	37	29
840	850	108	100	93	85	77	69	61	54	46	38	30
850	860	110	102	94	86	78	71	63	55	47	40	32
860	870	111	103	96	88	80	72	64	57	49	41	33
870	880	113	105	97	89	81	74	66	58	50	43	35
880	890	114	106	99	91	83	75	67	60	52	44	36
890	900	116	108	100	92	84	77	69	61	53	46	38
900	910	118	109	102	94	86	78	70	63	55	47	39
910	920	121	111	103	95	87	80	72	64	56	49	41
920	930	124	112	105	97	89	81	73	66	58	50	42
930	940	126	114	106	98	90	83	75	67	59	52	44
940	950	129	115	108	100	92	84	76	69	61	53	45
950	960	132	117	109	101	93	86	78	70	62	55	47
960	970	135	120	111	103	95	87	79	72	64	56	48
970	980	138	123	112	104	96	89	81	73	65	58	50
980	990	140	126	114	106	98	90	82	75	67	59	51
990	1,000	143	129	115	107	99	92	84	76	68	61	53
1,000	1,010	146	131	117	109	101	93	85	78	70	62	54
1,010	1,020	149	134	120	110	102	95	87	79	71	64	56
1,020	1,030	152	137	122	112	104	96	88	81	73	65	57
1,030	1,040	154	140	125	113	105	98	90	82	74	67	59
1,040	1,050	157	143	128	115	107	99	91	84	76	68	60
1,050	1,060	160	145	131	116	108	101	93	85	77	70	62
1,060	1,070	163	148	134	119	110	102	94	87	79	71	63
1,070	1,080	166	151	136	122	111	104	96	88	80	73	65
1,080	1,090	168	154	139	125	113	105	97	90	82	74	66
1,090	1,100	171	157	142	128	114	107	99	91	83	76	68
1,100	1,110	174	159	145	130	116	108	100	93	85	77	69
1,110	1,120	177	162	148	133	119	110	102	94	86	79	71
1,120	1,130	180	165	150	136	121	111	103	96	88	80	72
1,130	1,140	182	168	153	139	124	113	105	97	89	82	74
1,140	1,150	185	171	156	142	127	114	106	99	91	83	75
1,150	1,160	188	173	159	144	130	116	108	100	92	85	77
1,160	1,170	191	176	162	147	133	118	109	102	94	86	78
1,170	1,180	194	179	164	150	135	121	111	103	95	88	80
1,180	1,190	196	182	167	153	138	124	112	105	97	89	81
1,190	1,200	199	185	170	156	141	126	114	106	98	91	83
1,200	1,210	202	187	173	158	144	129	115	108	100	92	84
1,210	1,220	205	190	176	161	147	132	117	109	101	94	86
1,220	1,230	208	193	178	164	149	135	120	111	103	95	87
1,230	1,240	210	196	181	167	152	138	123	112	104	97	89
1,240	1,250	213	199	184	170	155	140	126	114	106	98	90
1,250	1,260	216	201	187	172	158	143	129	115	107	100	92
1,260	1,270	219	204	190	175	161	146	131	117	109	101	93
1,270	1,280	222	207	192	178	163						
1,280	1,290	224	210	195	181	166						
1,290	1,300	227	213	198	184	169						
1,300	1,310	230	215	201	186	172						
1,310	1,320	233	218	204	189	175						
1,320	1,330	236	221	206	192	177						
1,330	1,340	238	224	209	195	180						
1,340	1,350	241	227	212	198	183						
1,350	1,360	244	229	215	200	186						
1,360	1,370	247	232	218	203	189						
1,370	1,380	250	235	220	206	191						
1,380	1,390	252	238	223	209	194						
$1,390 and over		Use Table 1(b) for a **MARRIED person**										

1 (b) MARRIED person—

If the amount of wages (after subtracting withholding allowances) is:		The amount of income tax to withhold is:	
Not over $124		$0	
Over—	**But not over—**		**of excess over—**
$124	—$899 . .	15%	—$124
$899	—$1,855 . .	$116.25 plus 28%	—$899
$1,855	—$3,084 . .	$383.93 plus 31%	—$1,855
$3,084	—$5,439 . .	$764.92 plus 36%	—$3,084
$5,439	. . . .	$1,612.72 plus 39.6%	—$5,439

FIGURE 3

FYI

At one time, Social Security and Medicare were not separated for tax computation, and at a later date there was a $125,000 limit on Medicare taxable earnings. Now all earnings are taxable for Medicare.

Social Security tax on the maximum taxable earnings, the employer stops deducting Social Security tax until the next calendar year begins. Congress has frequently changed the schedule of rates and taxable incomes.

In this text, we assume a Social Security rate of 6.2 percent of the first $68,400 for each employee and a Medicare rate of 1.45 percent of all earnings for each employee. Both tax rates apply to earnings during the calendar year. (Tables for Social Security and Medicare tax withholdings are available in the Internal Revenue Service Circular E, Employer's Tax Guide, also called Publication 15.)

Let's return to Matte E. Asino, who had gross wages of $1,119.16 for the week ending October 7. Suppose that his total accumulated gross wages earned this year prior to this payroll period are $32,890. Asino's total gross wages including this payroll period were $34,009.16 ($32,890 + $1,119.16). Since the Social Security tax applies to the first $68,400 and the Medicare tax applies to all earnings, Asino's earnings are subject to both taxes. For Asino's Social Security tax, multiply $1,119.16 by 6.2 percent ($1,119.16 × .062 = $69.39). For Asino's Medicare tax, multiply $1,119.16 by .0145 = $16.23.

Here's another example. Assume that Sharlet Wilson had cumulative earnings of $70,400 at the beginning of the pay period. During this pay period, she earned $4,000. Since her cumulative earnings are greater than $68,400, she is exempt from the Social Security tax. However, because the Medicare tax applies to all earnings, she is not exempt from the Medicare tax. Her Medicare tax is $58 ($4,000 × .0145).

PAYROLL REGISTER

Objective 3

Complete a payroll register.

The payroll register is a multicolumn form prepared for each payroll period listing the earnings, deductions, and net pay for each employee. In Figure 4 (shown on the next page) we see a payroll register that shows the data for each employee on a separate line. This would be suitable for a firm, like Greg Company, that has a small number of employees.

First, we'll show the entire payroll register, then we'll break it down and explain it column by column. The number at the foot of each column refers to the related text description.

The payroll period shown in Figure 4 covers October 1 through October 7. The first part consists of employees' names, hours worked, beginning cumulative earnings, and taxable earnings.

(1) **Total Hours**—Taken from employees' time cards.

(2) **Beginning Cumulative Earnings**—The amount each employee has earned between January 1 and September 30 (the last day of the previous payroll period). It is taken from each employee's individual earnings record. (See Figure 7, pages 274–275.)

(3) **Regular Earnings**—Earnings for hours worked up to and including 40. In other words, the first 40 hours multiplied by each employee's regular hourly rate.

(4) **Overtime Earnings**—Hours in excess of 40 (relative to a 40-hour week) worked by each employee, multiplied by that employee's overtime rate.

(5) **Total Earnings**—Regular earnings plus overtime earnings.

(6) **Ending Cumulative Earnings**—Beginning Cumulative Earnings plus Total Earnings.

	NAME	TOTAL HOURS	BEGINNING CUMULATIVE EARNINGS	EARNINGS: REGULAR	EARNINGS: OVERTIME	EARNINGS: TOTAL	ENDING CUMULATIVE EARNINGS	UNEMPLOYMENT
1	Asino, Matte E.	46	32 890 00	913 60	205 56	1 119 16	34 009 16	
2	Boritsky, Olga	45	6 192 00	619 20	116 10	735 30	6 927 30	735 30
3	Dray, Greg G.	49	6 846 00	684 60	231 05	915 65	7 761 65	154 00
4	Foulkes, Bob L.	40	38 637 00	1 073 25	0 00	1 073 25	39 710 25	
5	Groyer, Milli K.	40	68 000 00	1 888 89	0 00	1 888 89	69 888 89	
6	Kramer, Ada A.	40	68 100 00	1 891 67	0 00	1 891 67	69 991 67	
7	Minkowitz, John L.	55	36 840 00	1 023 33	575 63	1 598 96	38 438 96	
8	Orleons, Janet C.	40	45 783 00	1 271 75	0 00	1 271 75	47 054 75	
9	Pinkovich, Mark S.	44	46 970 00	1 304 72	195 71	1 500 43	48 470 43	
10	Romero, Sheila J.	45	54 978 00	1 527 17	286 34	1 813 51	56 791 51	
11	Tivoli, Jake T.	40	42 078 00	1 168 83	0 00	1 168 83	43 246 83	
12	Wilson, Sharlet D.	52	68 600 00	1 905 56	857 50	2 763 06	71 363 06	
13			515 914 00	15 272 57	2 467 89	17 740 46	533 654 46	889 30
14		(1)	(2)	(3)	(4)	(5)	(6)	(7A)
15								

15,272.57 + 2,467.89 = 17,740.46

515,914.00 + 17,740.46 = 533,654.46

FIGURE 4

(7) **Taxable Earnings**—The amount of earnings subject to taxation, **not the tax itself.** We'll use these columns later to figure the amount of each tax. In other words, **Taxable Earnings is the base on which to figure the tax. Taxable Earnings multiplied by the tax rate equals the amount of the tax.**

(7A) **Unemployment Taxable Earnings—**In our illustration, we are using a maximum of $7,000 for unemployment tax liability on the employer for each employee. This column represents the previously untaxed portion remaining of the $7,000 for the individual employees. **Unemployment tax is paid only by the employer in most states. An unemployment tax may be paid both to the state and to the federal government.** Actually, states may use different maximum earnings and different rates than does the federal government. However, many states use $7,000, which at the time of this writing is the amount used by the federal government. There are three possibilities for Unemployment Taxable Earnings, as follows:

a. **Employee's cumulative earnings including this pay period have not reached $7,000.** When an employee's cumulative earnings so far during the calendar year (since January 1) are less than $7,000, we record the total earnings for the payroll period in the Unemployment Taxable Earnings column. For example, Olga Boritsky's cumulative earnings before this week were $6,192. Olga's cumulative earnings after this week are $6,927.30 ($6,192 + $735.30). Because Olga's cumulative earnings are still less than $7,000, the entire $735.30 in wages earned during this pay period is listed in the Unemployment Taxable Earnings column.

PAYROLL REGISTER FOR WEEK ENDED October 7, 20—

(7) TAXABLE EARNINGS		(8) DEDUCTIONS						
SOCIAL SECURITY	MEDICARE	FEDERAL INCOME TAX	STATE INCOME TAX	SOCIAL SECURITY TAX	MEDICARE TAX	MEDICAL INSURANCE	OTHER	
1119 16	1119 16	177 00	35 40	69 39	16 23	11 19	—	
735 30	735 30	90 00	18 00	45 59	10 66	11 03	UW	12 00
915 65	915 65	103 00	20 60	56 77	13 28	13 73	UW	15 00
1073 25	1073 25	122 00	24 40	66 54	15 56	16 10	—	
400 00	1888 89	394 44	78 89	24 80	27 39	28 33	—	
300 00	1891 67	395 30	79 06	18 60	27 43	28 38	UW	10 00
1598 96	1598 96	312 24	62 45	99 14	23 18	23 98	UW	12 00
1271 75	1271 75	222 00	44 40	78 85	18 44	19 08	UW	20 00
1500 43	1500 43	284 65	56 93	93 03	21 76	22 51	—	
1813 51	1813 51	372 31	74 46	112 44	26 30	27 20	AR	50 00
1168 83	1168 83	176 00	35 20	72 47	16 95	17 53	UW	25 00
—	2763 06	665 43	133 09	—	40 06	41 44	UW	30 00
11896 84	17740 46	3314 37	662 88	737 62	257 24	260 50		174 00
(7B)	(7C)	(8A)	(8B)	(8C)	(8D)	(8E)		(8F)

3,314.37 + 662.88 + 737.62 + 257.24 + 260.50 + 174.00 = 5,406.61

PAGE 68

	(9) PAYMENTS		(10) EXPENSE ACCOUNT DEBITED		
TOTAL	NET AMOUNT	CK. NO.	SALES WAGES EXPENSE	OFFICE WAGES EXPENSE	
309 21	809 95	931	1119 16		1
187 28	548 02	932	735 30		2
222 38	693 27	933	915 65		3
244 60	828 65	934		1073 25	4
553 85	1335 04	935	1888 89		5
558 77	1332 90	936		1891 67	6
532 99	1065 97	937	1598 96		7
402 77	868 98	938		1271 75	8
478 88	1021 55	939	1500 43		9
662 71	1150 80	940	1813 51		10
343 15	825 68	941	1168 83		11
910 02	1853 04	942	2763 06		12
5406 61	12333 85		13503 79	4236 67	13
(8G)	(9A)	(9B)	(10A)	(10B)	14
					15

5,406.61 + 12,333.85 = 17,740.46

13,503.79 + 4,236.67 = 17,740.46

FYI

Social Security and Medicare taxes are recorded separately in the payroll register because there is no limit on Medicare as there is on Social Security.

Remember!

Unemployment taxable earnings are used for calculating the amount of the unemployment tax, which is paid by the employer only.

b. **Employee's cumulative earnings were less than $7,000 before this week and are more than $7,000 after this week.** Look at the line for Greg Dray and notice that his cumulative earnings before this week were $6,846. Dray's new cumulative earnings (ending) are $7,761.65 ($6,846 + $915.65), putting him over the $7,000 maximum. Therefore, to bring Dray up to the $7,000 limit, $154 ($7,000 − $6,846) of his earnings for the week are taxable. After this week, none of Dray's earnings for the remainder of this calendar year will be taxable for unemployment.

c. **Employee's cumulative earnings before this week were more than $7,000.** After an employee's earnings top $7,000 during the calendar year, record a dash in the Unemployment Taxable Earnings column to indicate that the column has not been forgotten or overlooked. For example, Matte Asino's total earnings before the payroll period ended October 7 (beginning) were $32,890 (as shown in his individual earnings record in Figure 7). Since he had previously earned more than $7,000 this year, we record a dash in the Unemployment Taxable Earnings column.

Remember!

Taxable earnings is the base on which to figure the tax, not the tax itself.

(7B) **Social Security Taxable Earnings**—The first $68,400 for each employee. We assume a Social Security tax rate of 6.2 percent of the first $68,400 paid to each employee during the calendar year.

a. **Employee's cumulative earnings including this pay period have not reached $68,400.** When an employee's cumulative earnings so far during the year are less than $68,400, we record the total earnings for the payroll period in the Social Security Taxable Earnings column. For example, Olga Boritsky's cumulative earnings so far this year amount to $6,192. Because Olga's total earnings are less than $68,400, the entire $735.30 of wages earned during this pay period is listed in the Social Security Taxable Earnings column. Note that this is true of all the employees except Sharlet Wilson.

b. **Employee's cumulative earnings before the week were more than $68,400.** After an employee's earnings top $68,400 during the calendar year, record a dash to indicate that the column has not been forgotten or overlooked. (Use the same procedure as for the Unemployment Taxable Earnings column.) For example, Sharlet Wilson's cumulative earnings before the payroll period ended October 7 were $68,600. Since she had previously earned more than $68,400, we record a dash in the Social Security Taxable Earnings column.

(7C) **Medicare Taxable Earnings**—All earnings for this period. We have assumed a Medicare tax rate of 1.45 percent on all earnings that are paid to each employee during the calendar year. Therefore, all earnings for this period are taxable and are recorded in the Medicare Taxable Earnings column.

(8) **Deductions**—Amounts taken away (withheld) from total earnings.

(8A) **Federal Income Tax Deductions**—The amount of the federal income tax deduction for each employee can be located directly on the wage bracket tables.

(8B) **State Income Tax Deductions**—States that impose income taxes also provide wage-bracket tables. The state tax deduction for each employee can be located directly in the appropriate table. As stated previously, we are assuming a rate of 20 percent of the federal income tax.

(8C) **Social Security Tax Deductions**—For each employee's Social Security tax deduction, we first go to the Social Security Taxable Earnings column and note the amount subject to tax. Next, we multiply the Social Security taxable earnings by 6.2 percent. For example, Boritsky's

The United Way is a huge charitable organization that collects and compiles contributions from companies and individuals and allocates funds to various agencies under its umbrella. United Way agencies reach out to all ages as well as providing funding for research on many health issues.

Remember!

Taxable earnings multiplied by the tax rate equals the tax.

taxable earnings are $735.30, and her Social Security tax deduction is $45.59 ($735.30 × .062).

(8D) **Medicare Tax Deductions**—For each employee's Medicare tax deduction, we go to the Medicare Taxable Earnings column and note the amount subject to tax. Next, we multiply the Medicare taxable earnings by 1.45 percent. For example, Boritsky's taxable earnings are $735.30, and her Medicare tax deduction is $10.66 ($735.30 × .0145).

(8E) **Medical Insurance Deductions**—Premiums paid by the employee through payroll withholding. The amount of the premium for each employee depends on the number of dependents claimed. For example, Boritsky's premium is $11.03 per week.

(8F) **Other Deductions**—Employees' voluntary withholdings. In our illustration, UW represents the United Way, and AR stands for Accounts Receivable (employee pays charge account to the company). For example, Sheila Romero paid $50 on her charge account.

(8G) **Total Deductions**—The combined total of each employee's deductions for taxes, insurance, and other. For example, Boritsky's total deduction is $187.28 ($90.00 + $18.00 + $45.59 + $10.66 + $11.03 + $12.00).

(9) **Payments**—The amount of each employee's payroll check (take-home pay).

(9A) **Net Amount**—Each employee's Total Earnings minus Total Deductions. For example, Boritsky's net amount is $548.02 ($735.30 − $187.28).

(9B) **Ck. No.**—The number of each employee's payroll check.

(10) **Expense Account Debited**—Columns used for distributing each amount into the appropriate wages expense account. Greg Company uses Sales Wages Expense and Office Wages Expense. The sum of these two columns equals the total earnings.

(10A) **Sales Wages Expense**—Amounts earned by employees involved in sales activities.

(10B) **Office Wages Expense**—Amounts earned by employees involved in office activities.

THE PAYROLL ENTRY

Objective 4

Journalize the payroll entry from a payroll register.

Because the payroll register summarizes the payroll data for the period, it is used as the basis for recording the payroll in the ledger accounts. Since the payroll register does not have the status of a journal, a journal entry is necessary. Figure 5 shows the entry in general journal form.

FIGURE 5

GENERAL JOURNAL PAGE 31

DATE		DESCRIPTION	POST. REF.	DEBIT	CREDIT
20–					
Oct.	7	Sales Wages Expense		13,503.79	
		Office Wages Expense		4,236.67	
		Employees' Federal Income			
		Tax Payable			3,314.37
		FICA Tax Payable			994.86
		Employees' State Income Tax			
		Payable			662.88
		Employees' Medical Insurance			
		Payable			260.50
		Employees' United Way			
		Payable			124.00
		Accounts Receivable			50.00
		Wages Payable			12,333.85
		Payroll register, page 68,			
		for week ended October 7.			

Remember!

The totals from the payroll register are the amounts used in the payroll entry.

Note that the accountant records the total cost to the company for services of employees as debits to the Wages Expense accounts.

Also note that the total Social Security tax deductions ($737.62) and the total Medicare tax deductions ($257.24) are combined to become FICA Tax Payable of $994.86 ($737.62 + $257.24). The two tax deductions are combined into the one liability account because they are paid together at the same time. Social Security and Medicare taxes are recorded separately in the payroll register because they must be listed separately on each employee's W-2 form (Wage and Tax Statement).

To pay the employees from the company's regular checking account, the accountant now makes the following journal entry:

Remember!

The amount shown as Wages Payable is the employees' take-home pay.

DATE		DESCRIPTION	POST. REF.	DEBIT	CREDIT
	8	Wages Payable		12,333.85	
		Cash—M. Asino			809.95
		Cash—O. Boritsky			548.02
		Cash—G. Dray			693.27
		Cash—B. Foulkes			828.65
		Cash—M. Groyer			1,335.04
		Cash—A. Kramer			1,332.90
		Cash—J. Minkowitz			1,065.97
		Cash—J. Orleons			868.98
		Cash—M. Pinkovich			1,021.55
		Cash—S. Romero			1,150.80
		Cash—J. Tivoli			825.68
		Cash—S. Wilson			1,853.04

Special Payroll Bank Account—An Alternative

FYI

A company with a small number of employees would probably use its regular bank account to issue a check to each employee.

A firm with a large number of employees would probably open a special **payroll bank account** with its bank. One check drawn on the regular bank account is made payable to the special payroll account for the amount of the total net pay for a payroll period. All payroll checks for the period are then written on the special payroll account. To record this, the accountant makes the following journal entry. In this book, assume the entry to debit Cash—Payroll Bank Account and to credit Cash has already been made.

FYI

With the use of the special payroll bank account, if employees delay cashing their paychecks, then the checks do not have to be listed on the bank reconciliation of the firm's regular bank account. Balances of Employees' Medical Insurance Payable, Employees' United Way Payable, and other employee deductions are paid out of the firm's regular bank account.

GENERAL JOURNAL PAGE 1

DATE		DESCRIPTION	POST. REF.	DEBIT	CREDIT
	8	Wages Payable		12,333.85	
		Cash—Payroll Bank Account			12,333.85
		Paid wages for week			
		ended October 7.			

Paycheck

All the data needed to make out a payroll check are available in the payroll register. Matte E. Asino's paycheck is shown in Figure 6.

FIGURE 6

EMPLOYEE	TOTAL HOURS	O.T. HOURS	REG. PAY	O.T. PREM. PAY	GROSS PAY	FED INC. TAX	STATE INC. TAX	SOCIAL SECURITY TAX	MEDICARE TAX	MEDICAL INSURANCE	OTHER	TOTAL DED.	NET PAY
Matte E. Asino	46	6	913.60	205.56	1119.16	177.00	35.40	69.39	16.23	11.19	—	309.21	809.95

CENTRAL NATIONAL BANK 98-461/252

Payroll Account

Greg Company
610 First Avenue
Bangor, Maine 04412

October 8 20 — No. 931

PAY TO THE ORDER OF Matte E. Asino $ 809.95

Eight hundred nine and 95/100 DOLLARS

Ella D. Greg

⑆252⑈0461⑆

EMPLOYEE'S INDIVIDUAL EARNINGS RECORD

NAME Matte E. Asino
ADDRESS 6242 Baxter Drive
Bangor, Maine 04412
MALE X
FEMALE
MARRIED X
SINGLE
PHONE NO. 663-2556
DATE OF BIRTH 9/19/72
EMPLOYEE NO. 5
SOC. SEC. NO. 543-24-1680
PAY RATE $22.84
EQUIVALENT HOURLY RATE $22.84
DATE TERMINATED
CLASSIFICATION FOR WORKERS' COMPENSATION INSURANCE Sales floor

			HOURS WORKED		EARNINGS					
	PERIOD ENDED	DATE PAID	REG	O.T.	REGULAR	OVERTIME	TOTAL	ENDING CUMULATIVE EARNINGS	FEDERAL INCOME TAX	STATE INCOME TAX
40	9/3	9/4	40	8	913 60	274 08	1187 68	28721 70	167 00	33 40
41	9/10	9/11	40	2	913 60	68 52	982 12	29909 38	114 00	22 80
42	9/17	9/18	40	2	913 60	68 52	982 12	30891 50	114 00	22 80
43	9/24	9/25	40	5	913 60	171 30	1084 90	31873 62	139 00	27 80
44	9/30	10/1	40	4	913 60	137 04	1050 64	32958 52	131 00	26 20
45	10/7	10/8	40	6	913 60	205 56	1119 16	34009 16	177 00	35 40

FIGURE 7

Employees' Individual Earnings Records

Objective 5

Maintain employees' individual earnings records.

To comply with government regulations, a firm has to keep current data on each employee's accumulated earnings, deductions, and net pay. The information contained in the payroll register is recorded each payday in each **employee's individual earnings record**. Figure 7 shows a portion of the earnings record for Matte E. Asino.

CHAPTER REVIEW

Review of Performance Objectives

1. Calculate total earnings based on an hourly, piece-rate, or commission basis.

   Earnings calculated on an *hourly basis* equal the hourly rate multiplied by the number of hours worked. Earnings calculated on a *piece-rate basis* equal the total number of products produced multiplied by the rate per unit of product. Earnings calculated on a *commission basis* equal the total number of units sold or the price of units sold multiplied by the commission rate.

2. Determine deductions using tables of employees' income tax withholding.

   Using the appropriate income tax withholding table in IRS Circular E, first determine marital status and payroll period and then locate the wage bracket containing the amount of earnings. Next, on the same horizontal line, select the vertical column containing the number of allowances claimed.

3. Complete a payroll register.

   List the employees' names, hours worked, and beginning cumulative earnings. Add the total earnings to the beginning cumulative earnings to get ending cumulative earnings. The Unemployment Taxable Earnings column is used for the first $7,000 of each employee's earnings for FUTA and SUTA. The Social Security Taxable Earnings column is used for an assumed first $68,400. The Medicare Taxable Earnings column is used for all earnings. Under the Deductions columns, list the

DATE EMPLOYED 2/1/—

NO. OF EXEMPTIONS 2

PER HOUR X PER DAY

PER WEEK PER MONTH

DEDUCTIONS						PAID	
SOCIAL SECURITY TAX	MEDICARE TAX	MEDICAL INSURANCE	OTHER CODE	OTHER AMOUNT	TOTAL	NET AMOUNT	CK. NO.
73.64	17.22	11.19	UW	5.00	307.45	880.23	877
60.89	14.24	11.19	UW	—	223.12	759.00	889
60.89	14.24	11.19	UW	5.00	228.12	754.00	901
67.26	15.73	11.19	UW	—	260.98	823.92	913
65.14	15.23	11.19	UW	5.00	253.76	796.88	925
69.39	16.23	11.19	UW	—	309.21	809.95	931

income taxes withheld, the Social Security taxes withheld, the Medicare taxes withheld, and other deductions. The Social Security tax deduction equals the Social Security taxable earnings multiplied by an assumed rate of 6.2 percent. The Medicare tax deduction equals the Medicare taxable earnings multiplied by an assumed rate of 1.45 percent. Net amount equals total (gross) earnings minus total deductions. The Expense Account Debited columns are used to distribute salary and wages expense to the appropriate accounts.

4. Journalize the payroll entry from a payroll register.

Totals are taken directly from the payroll register. For the following entry, assume that one check is made payable to a special payroll bank account. The entry to transfer the cash to the payroll bank account is not shown here.

GENERAL JOURNAL PAGE 31

DATE		DESCRIPTION	POST. REF.	DEBIT	CREDIT
20–					
Oct.	7	Sales Wages Expense		13,503.79	
		Office Wages Expense		4,236.67	
		Employees' Federal Income			
		Tax Payable			3,314.37
		FICA Tax Payable			994.86
		Employees' State Income Tax			
		Payable			662.88
		Employees' Medical Insurance			
		Payable			260.50
		Employees' United Way			
		Payable			124.00
		Accounts Receivable			50.00
		Wages Payable			12,333.85
		Payroll register, page 68,			
		for week ended October 7.			

The following entry is used to pay the employees:

18		8	Wages Payable		12 3 3 3 85	
19			Cash			12 3 3 3 85
20			Paid wages for week			
21			ended October 7.			
22						
23						
24						

5. Maintain employees' individual earnings records.

   In the employees' individual earnings records, list the personal data for each employee. Based on the information contained in the payroll register, record the earnings and deductions for each payroll period.

Glossary

Calendar year A twelve-month period beginning on January 1 and ending on December 31 of the same year. (265)

Employee One who works for compensation under the direction and control of the employer. (261)

Employee's individual earnings record A supplementary record for each employee showing personal payroll data and yearly cumulative earnings, deductions, and net pay. (274)

Employee's Withholding Allowance Certificate (Form W-4) A form that specifies the number of allowances claimed by each employee and gives the employer the authority to withhold money for an employee's federal income taxes and FICA taxes. (264)

Exemption An amount of an employee's annual earnings not subject to income tax for the taxpayer, taxpayer's spouse, and dependents (usually children). (264)

FICA taxes Social Security taxes plus Medicare taxes, paid by both employee and employer under the provisions of the Federal Insurance Contributions Act. The proceeds are used to pay old-age and disability pensions and to fund the Medicare program. (265)

Gross pay The total amount of an employee's pay before any deductions. (260)

Independent contractor Someone who is engaged for a definite job or service, and who may choose her or his own means of doing the work. This person is not an employee of the firm for which the service is provided. (261)

Medicare taxes Federal government taxes levied on employees and employers; proceeds are used for medical insurance for eligible people age 65 or over. (265)

Net pay Gross pay minus deductions. Also called *take-home pay.* (260)

Payroll bank account A special checking account used to pay a company's employees. (273)

Payroll register A multicolumn form prepared for each payroll period listing the earnings, deductions, and net pay for each employee. (267)

Social Security taxes Federal government taxes levied on employees and employers; proceeds are used for old-age pensions and disability benefits. (265)

Taxable earnings The amount of an employee's earnings subject to a tax. (264)

Wage-bracket tax tables A chart providing the amounts to be deducted for income taxes based on amount of earnings, marital status, and number of allowances claimed. (264)

Withholding allowance An amount of an employee's annual earnings not subject to income tax. (264)

QUESTIONS, EXERCISES, AND PROBLEMS

Discussion Questions

1. What is the purpose of the employee's individual earnings record, and how is it related to the payroll register?
2. What is the purpose of the payroll register?
3. What information is included in an employee's individual earnings record?
4. Explain how gross earnings differ from net earnings for a payroll period.
5. Describe how a special payroll bank account is useful in paying the wages and salaries of employees.
6. List three required deductions and four voluntary deductions from an employee's total earnings.
7. What is the difference between an employee and an independent contractor? List three examples of an independent contractor.
8. What information is included in a wage-bracket withholding table? Are there overlapping amounts of gross earnings in the table?

Exercises

P.O. 1
Calculate gross pay.

Exercise 8-1 Determine the gross pay for each employee listed below.

a. Gary Dillon is paid time-and-a-half for all hours over forty. He worked forty-five hours during the week. His regular pay rate is $10.40 per hour.
b. Mai Do worked fifty-two hours during the week. She is entitled to time-and-a-half for all hours in excess of forty per week. Her regular pay rate is $12.30 per hour.
c. Latisha Morgan is paid a commission of 9 percent of her sales, which amounted to $10,474.
d. May Belski's yearly salary is $40,400. During the week, Belski worked forty-two hours, and she is entitled to time-and-a-half for all hours over forty.

P.O. 1,2

Determine gross pay and withholding.

Exercise 8-2 Lester Ramirez works for Pell Company, which pays its employees time-and-a-half for all hours worked in excess of forty per week. Ramirez's pay rate is $15.50 per hour. His wages are subject to federal income tax, a Social Security tax deduction at the rate of 6.2 percent, and a Medicare tax deduction at the rate of 1.45 percent. He is married and claims three allowances. Ramirez has a half-hour lunch break during an eight-and-one-half-hour day. He is paid for hours between 8 and 4:30 and overtime for increments greater that 30 minutes on a given day. Ramirez's beginning cumulative earnings are $36,722.

Complete the following using Ramirez's time card shown below:

a. 40 hours at straight time × $15.50 per hour — $620
b. 10 hours overtime × $23.25 per hour — 232.50
c. Total gross pay — $852.50
d. Federal income tax withholding (from tax tables in Figure 3, page 266) — $86
e. Social Security tax withholding at 6.2 percent — 52.86
f. Medicare tax withholding at 1.45 percent — 12.36
g. Total withholding — 151.22
h. Net pay — $701.28

TIME CARD

Name: Ramirez, Lester

Week ending: March 11, 20—

Day	In	Out	In	Out	Hours Worked: Regular	Hours Worked: Overtime
M	756	1209	1239	432	8	
T	752	1205	1235	504	8	½
W	759	1220	1240	503	8	½
T	800	1208	1238	434	8	
F	756	1209	1239	633	8	2
S	800	1201	1240	340		7
S						

FIGURE 8

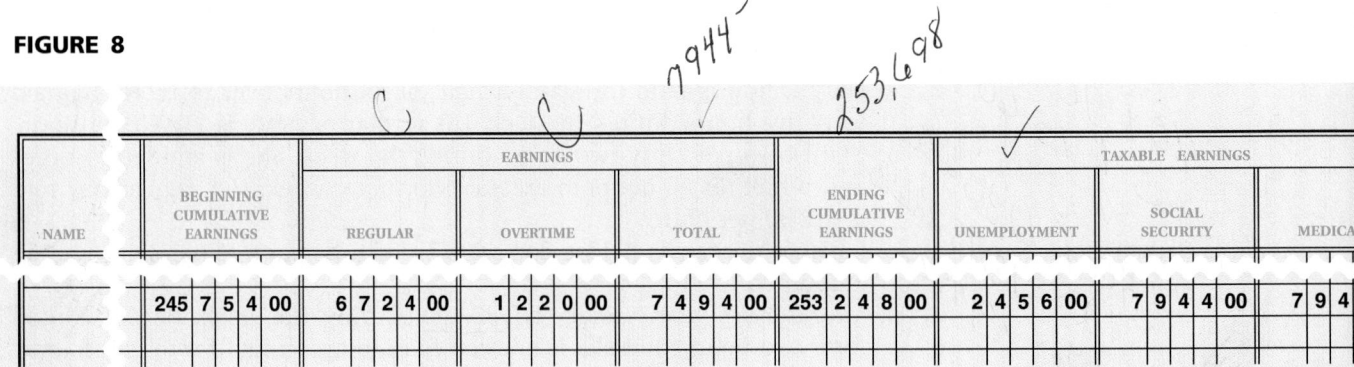

Name	Beginning Cumulative Earnings	Earnings: Regular	Earnings: Overtime	Earnings: Total	Ending Cumulative Earnings	Taxable Earnings: Unemployment	Taxable Earnings: Social Security	Taxable Earnings: Medica[re]
	245754 00	6724 00	1220 00	7494 00	253248 00	2456 00	7944 00	794

P.O. 2,3
Determine net pay.

Exercise 8-3 Using the income tax withholding table in Figure 3, page 266, for each employee of Tri-State Company, determine the net pay for the week ended January 21. Assume a Social Security tax of 6.2 percent and a Medicare tax of 1.45 percent. All employees have cumulative earnings of less than $68,400. Assume all employees are married.

Employee	Allowances	Total Earnings	Social Security Tax Withheld	Medicare Tax Withheld	Federal Income Tax Withheld	Union Dues Withheld	Medical Insurance Withheld	Net Pay
a. Alster, C. A.	1	$ 880	$	$	$	$ 25	$ 30	$
b. Drake, R. N.	2	820				25	26	
c. Finn, T. C.	3	1,010				—	30	
d. Handy, L. O.	0	1,075				25	30	
e. Nguyen, M. E.	2	930				25	30	
Totals		$4,715	$	$	$	$100	$146	$

P.O. 3
Locate errors in a payroll register.

Exercise 8-4 For the week ended September 7, the totals of the payroll register for Brennan, Inc., are presented in Figure 8. The regular and overtime earnings are correct. List six errors that exist. All earnings are subject to Social Security and Medicare taxes.

P.O. 3
Determine taxable earnings.

Exercise 8-5 For tax purposes, assume that the maximum taxable earnings are $68,400 for Social Security and $7,000 for the unemployment tax, and that all earnings are taxable for Medicare. For the payroll register for the month of November in Figure 9 (page 280), determine the taxable earnings for each employee.

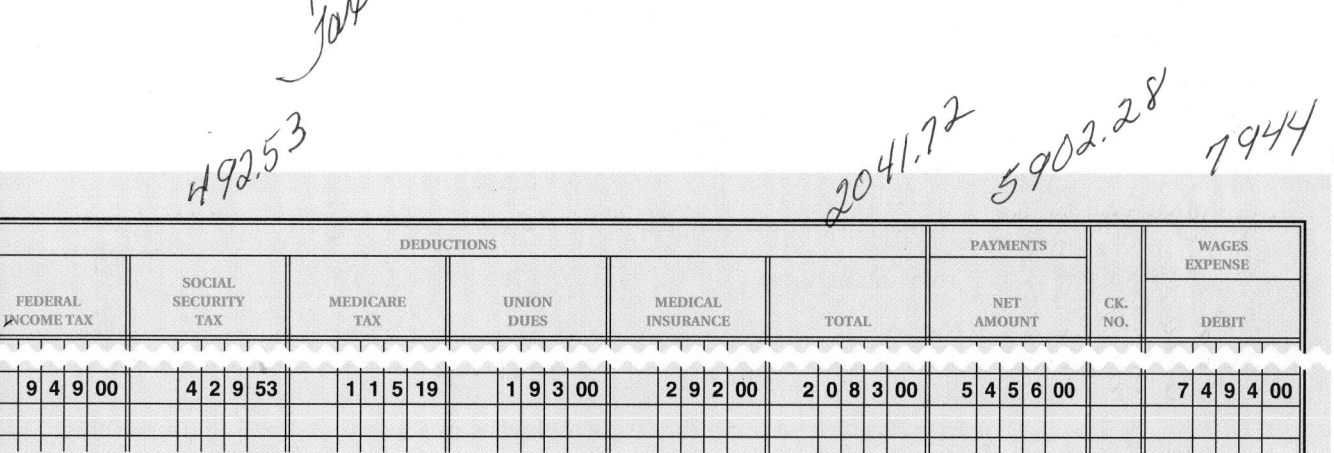

DEDUCTIONS						PAYMENTS		WAGES EXPENSE
FEDERAL INCOME TAX	SOCIAL SECURITY TAX	MEDICARE TAX	UNION DUES	MEDICAL INSURANCE	TOTAL	NET AMOUNT	CK. NO.	DEBIT
949 00	429 53	115 19	193 00	292 00	2,083 00	5,456 00		7,494 00

Employee	Beginning Cumulative Earnings	Total Earnings	Ending Cumulative Earnings	Taxable Earnings: Unemployment	Taxable Earnings: Social Security	Taxable Earnings: Medicare
Alston, J.	63 173 00	4 767 00	67 940 00			
Ely, B.	33 219 00	3 830 00	37 049 00			
Glenn, C.	30 550 00	2 730 00	33 280 00			
Johns, A.	3 751 00	1 463 00	5 214 00			
Newkirk, J.	5 436 00	1 284 00	6 720 00			

FIGURE 9

P.O. 3,4

Determine FICA withholdings and journalize payroll entry.

Exercise 8-6 On January 21, the column totals of the payroll register for Kraal Company showed that its sales employees had earned $14,280, its driver employees had earned $9,340, and its office employees had earned $7,484. Social Security taxes were withheld at an assumed rate of 6.2 percent, and Medicare taxes were withheld at an assumed rate of 1.45 percent. Other deductions consisted of federal income tax, $3,732; medical insurance, $1,561; union dues, $486. Determine the amount of Social Security and Medicare taxes withheld, and record the general journal entry for the payroll, crediting Salaries Payable for the net pay. All earnings were taxable.

P.O. 1,2

Determine missing amounts.

Exercise 8-7 Lien Labs has two employees. The information shown below was taken from their individual earnings records for the month of September. Determine the missing amounts, assuming that the Social Security tax is 6.2 percent and the Medicare tax is 1.45 percent. All earnings are subject to Social Security and Medicare taxes. Round amounts to nearest dollar.

	Bandor	Ringness	Total
Regular earnings	$1,600	$?	$?
Overtime earnings	?	105	?
Total earnings	$1,740	$?	$?
Federal income tax withheld	$ 330	$?	$?
State income tax withheld	?	85	?
Social Security tax withheld	108	92	?
Medicare tax withheld	25	22	?
Medical insurance withheld	104	98	?
Total deductions	$ 679	$ 476	$?
Net pay	$?	$1,009	$?

P.O. 4

Journalize the payroll entry.

Exercise 8-8 Assume that the employees in Exercise 8-7 are paid from the company's regular bank account (check numbers 931 and 932). Record the payroll entry in general journal form, dated September 30.

CONSIDER AND COMMUNICATE

Nguyen Company pays its employees weekly by issuing checks on its regular bank account. The owner thinks it would be too much trouble to have a second checking account. Respond to the owner's concern.

WHAT IF . . .

You have just completed the payroll register for this week's payroll. You have crossfooted the register—that is, you have added the columns vertically and horizontally. There is just one problem: The total of the Net Amount column does not equal the total of the Gross Amount column minus the total of the Total Deductions column. How could this happen? What would you do to obtain correctly crossfooted totals?

A MATTER OF ETHICS

An employee who is married and has two children submits a W-4 form to his employer indicating that he is single and claims zero deductions. Is this action ethical, unethical, or illegal? Explain your reasoning.

WEB WORK

Using an Internet web browser, type in the search box the phrase *payroll accounting* for the home pages of firms that specialize in payroll services. Search for information about payroll services. Discuss your findings in a small group. Write a one-page recommendation to the owner of a business.

PROBLEM SET A

For additional help, see the demonstration problem at the beginning of each chapter in your Working Papers.

P.O. 1,2

Problem 8-1A Vadim Barsk, an employee of Myer Company, worked forty-six hours during the week of February 9 through 15. His rate of pay is $15.50 per hour, and he gets time-and-a-half for work in excess of forty hours per week. He is married and claims one allowance on his W-4 form. His wages are subject to the following deductions:

a. Federal income tax (use the table in Figure 3, page 266).
b. Social Security tax at 6.2 percent.
c. Medicare tax at 1.45 percent.
d. Union dues, $10.00.
e. Medical insurance, $12.00.

Check Figure
Net pay, $592.40

Instructions

Compute his regular pay, overtime pay, gross pay, and net pay.

P.O. 1,3,4

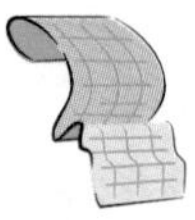

Problem 8-2A Rutger Homes has the following payroll information for the week ended February 21:

Name	Earnings at End of Previous Week	Daily Time S	M	T	W	T	F	S	Pay Rate	Federal Income Tax
Ager, A. C.	1,920.00	8	8	8	8	8			10.65	30.00
Bell, D. R.	2,030.00			8	8	8	8	8	10.50	37.00
Cole, H. A.	2,064.00	8	8	8			8	8	10.95	39.00
Field, P. N.	628.00				8	8			20.00	15.00
Gray, L. B.	2,597.00	8	8	8			8	8	10.90	47.00
Harris, G. W.	2,075.00	8	8		8	8	8	8	10.00	27.00

Taxable earnings for Social Security are based on the first $68,400. Taxable earnings for Medicare are based on all earnings. Taxable earnings for federal and state unemployment are based on the first $7,000. Employees are paid time-and-a-half for work in excess of forty hours per week.

Check Figure
Net Amount, $2,169.16

Instructions

1. Complete the payroll register, page 37. The Social Security tax rate is 6.2 percent, and the Medicare tax rate is 1.45 percent.
2. Prepare a general journal entry to record the payroll. The firm's general ledger contains a Wages Expense account and a Wages Payable account.
3. Assuming that the firm transfers funds from its regular bank account to its special payroll bank account, and that that entry has been made, prepare a general journal entry to record the payment of wages. Begin payroll checks with no. 206.

P.O. 1,2,3,4

Problem 8-3A The Toler Company pays its employees time-and-a-half for hours worked in excess of forty per week. The information available from time cards and employees' individual earnings records for the pay period ended October 14 is shown in the chart at the top of page 283.

Taxable earnings for Social Security are based on the first $68,400. Taxable earnings for Medicare are based on all earnings. Taxable earnings for federal and state unemployment are based on the first $7,000.

Name	Earnings at End of Previous Week	Daily Time M	T	W	T	F	S	Pay Rate	Income Tax Allowances
Baxter, J. C.	42,827.00	8	8	8	8	8	0	19.30	2
Choy, A. K.	43,539.00	8	8	8	8	10	8	19.60	1
Dray, W. L.	43,225.00	8	8	10	8	8	0	19.50	1
Gary, S. P.	49,831.00	8	8	8	8	8	0	20.00	3
Nye, M. B.	44,985.00	8	8	8	8	8	4	19.40	3
Otis, N. B.	41,131.00	8	8	8	8	8	0	19.00	1
Rega, J. B.	6,529.00	8	8	8	8	8	4	18.50	1
Sange, P. W.	43,013.00	8	8	8	8	8	4	19.25	2

Check Figure
Net Amount, $5,559.28

Instructions

1. Complete the payroll register, page 72, using the wage-bracket income tax withholding table in Figure 3 (page 266). The Social Security tax rate is 6.2 percent, and the Medicare tax rate is 1.45 percent. Assume that all employees are married.
2. Prepare a general journal entry to record the payroll. The firm's general ledger contains a Wages Expense account and a Wages Payable account.
3. Assuming that the firm has transferred funds from its regular bank account to its special payroll bank account, and that this entry has been made, prepare a general journal entry to record the payment of wages. In the payroll register, begin payroll checks with number 942.

P.O. 3,4

Problem 8-4A The information for the Saranga Company, shown in the chart at the top of page 284, is available from Saranga's time cards and the employees' individual earnings records for the pay period ended December 22.

Taxable earnings for Social Security are based on the first $68,400. Taxable earnings for Medicare are based on all earnings. Taxable earnings for federal and state unemployment are based on the first $7,000.

Check Figure
Net Amount, $6,953.41

Instructions

1. Complete the payroll register, page 56, using a Social Security tax rate of 6.2 percent and a Medicare tax rate of 1.45 percent. (The total of Social Security tax deduction and Medicare tax deduction for D. C. Lang is $62.63. Check this figure.) Concerning Other Deductions, AR refers to Accounts Receivable and UW refers to United Way. Begin payroll checks in the payroll register with number 971.
2. Prepare the general journal entry to record the payroll.

Name	Hours Worked	Earnings at End of Previous Week	Total Earnings	Class.	Federal Income Tax	Other Deduct.	
Coy, C. E.	44	32,950	750	Sales	79.00	UW	16.50
Dara, V. A.	40	37,410	850	Sales	102.00	AR	80.00
Farr, J. P.	40	36,860	838	Sales	99.00	UW	16.50
Gant, N. D.	44	32,490	735	Office	85.00	UW	15.00
Jong, J. W.	48	36,980	840	Office	108.00	UW	16.00
Lang, D. C.	40	67,750	1,540	Office	295.00	UW	12.00
Mory, R. G.	40	36,860	836	Sales	91.00	AR	54.00
Nge, P. M.	40	36,750	830	Sales	107.00	UW	16.00
Orr, T. B.	44	33,480	760	Sales	96.00	UW	16.50
Tye, K. C.	42	47,000	1,070	Sales	136.00	UW	18.00

3. Prepare the general journal entry to pay the payroll. Assume that funds for this payroll have been transferred to Cash—Payroll Bank Account and that this entry has been made.

PROBLEM SET B

For additional help, see the demonstration problem at the beginning of each chapter in your Working Papers.

P.O. 1,2

Problem 8-1B Inez Parr, an employee of Kellen Company, worked forty-four hours during the week of October 11 through 17. Her rate of pay is $17.50 per hour, and she receives time-and-a-half for all work in excess of forty hours per week. Parr is married and claims two allowances on her W-4 form. Her wages are subject to the following deductions:

a. Federal income tax (use the table in Figure 3, page 266).
b. Social Security tax at 6.2 percent.
c. Medicare tax at 1.45 percent.
d. Union dues, $15.25.
e. Medical insurance, $34.75.

Check Figure
Net pay, $606.42

Instructions

Compute her regular pay, overtime pay, gross pay, and net pay.

P.O. 1,3,4

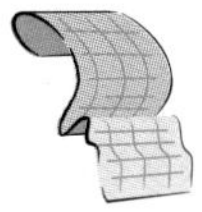

Problem 8-2B Hagen Company has the following payroll information for the pay period ended May 14:

Name	Earnings at End of Previous Week	Daily Time M	T	W	T	F	S	Pay Rate	Federal Income Tax
Gilam, N. C.	7,455.00	8	8	8	8	8	0	8.80	27.00
Hardt, A. L.	6,513.00	8	8	8	8	8	0	8.50	33.00
Loren, D. R.	6,843.00	0	8	8	8	8	8	8.60	25.00
Ngo, N. A.	9,536.00	8	8	8	0	8	8	9.80	41.00
Sorley, B. M.	6,632.00	8	8	8	8	8	8	8.90	36.00
Unger, P. R.	7,467.00	0	8	8	8	8	8	9.20	21.00

Taxable earnings for Social Security are based on the first $68,400. Taxable earnings for Medicare are based on all earnings. Taxable earnings for federal and state unemployment are based on the first $7,000. Employees are paid time-and-a-half for work in excess of forty hours per week.

Check Figure

Net Amount, $1,903.01

Instructions

1. Complete the payroll register, page 34. The Social Security tax rate is 6.2 percent, and the Medicare tax rate is 1.45 percent.
2. Prepare a general journal entry to record the payroll.
3. Assuming that the firm has transferred funds from its regular bank account to its special payroll bank account, and that this entry has been made, prepare a journal entry to record the payment of wages. Begin payroll checks with No. 744.

P.O. 1,2,3,4

Problem 8-3B The Sorelle Company pays its employees time-and-a-half for hours worked in excess of forty per week. The information in the chart at the top of page 286 is available from time cards and employees' individual earnings records for the pay period ended September 21.

Taxable earnings for Social Security are based on the first $68,400. Taxable earnings for Medicare are based on all earnings. Taxable earnings for federal and state unemployment are based on the first $7,000.

Check Figure

Net Amount, $5,740.49

Instructions

1. Complete the payroll register, page 72, using the wage-bracket income tax withholding table in Figure 3 (page 266). The Social Security tax rate is 6.2 percent, and the Medicare tax rate is 1.45 percent. Assume that all employees are married.

Name	Earnings at End of Previous Week	Daily Time M	T	W	T	F	S	Pay Rate	Income Tax Allowances
Brit, A. C.	6,565.00	8	8	8	10	8	0	17.50	1
Dorn, B. N.	35,338.00	8	8	8	8	8	0	23.25	2
Gorst, A. J.	33,250.00	8	10	8	8	8	0	22.00	2
Ingle, D. G.	36,224.00	8	8	8	8	8	4	24.00	3
Jeon, H. O.	34,655.00	8	8	8	8	8	0	23.00	0
Lemer, J. E.	28,827.00	8	8	9	8	8	0	18.50	2
Orse, D. W.	6,843.00	8	8	8	9	9	4	18.70	1
Worfe, W. L.	26,386.00	8	8	10	8	8	0	18.30	1

2. Prepare a general journal entry to record the payroll. The firm's general ledger contains a Wages Expense account and a Wages Payable account.
3. Assuming that the firm has transferred funds from its regular bank account to its special payroll bank account, and that this entry has been made, prepare a general journal entry to record the payment of wages. In the payroll register, begin payroll checks with Ck. No. 863.

PO 3,4

Problem 8-4B For the Saranga Company, the information in the chart on the following page is available from the time books and employees' individual earnings records for the pay period ended December 29.

Taxable earnings for Social Security are based on the first $68,400. Taxable earnings for Medicare are based on all earnings. Taxable earnings for federal and state unemployment are based on the first $7,000.

Check Figure
Net Amount, $7,183.23

Instructions

1. Complete the payroll register, page 56, using a Social Security tax rate of 6.2 percent and a Medicare tax rate of 1.45 percent. (The total of Social Security tax deduction and Medicare tax deduction for D. C. Lang is $22.33. Check this figure.) Concerning Other Deductions, AR refers to Accounts Receivable, and UW refers to United Way. Begin payroll checks in the payroll register with check no. 914.
2. Prepare the general journal entry to record the payroll.
3. Prepare the general journal entry to pay the payroll. Assume that funds for this payroll have been transferred to Cash—Payroll Bank Account and that this entry has been made.

Name	Hours Worked	Earnings at End of Previous Week	Total Earnings	Class.	Federal Income Tax	Other Deduct.	
Coy, C. E.	44	33,700	750.00	Sales	79.00	AR	75.00
Dara, V. A.	42	38,260	910.00	Sales	111.00	UW	16.50
Farr, J. P.	40	37,698	838.00	Sales	99.00	UW	16.50
Gant, N. D.	44	33,225	735.00	Office	85.00		
Jong, J. W.	48	37,820	840.00	Office	108.00	UW	16.00
Lang, D. C.	40	69,290	1,540.00	Office	295.00	UW	12.00
Mory, R. G.	43	37,696	926.00	Sales	105.00	UW	16.00
Nge, P. M.	40	37,580	830.00	Sales	107.00		
Orr, T. B.	44	34,240	760.00	Sales	96.00	AR	16.50
Tye, K. C.	42	48,070	1,070.00	Sales	136.00	UW	18.00

9 Employer Taxes, Payments, and Reports

WINDOWS ON THE WORLD WIDE WEB

What are your social security taxes paying for? Where does this money go? What taxes does your employer have to pay? How are your social security benefits and Medicare taxes calculated? Who figures your state and federal unemployment taxes and workers' compensation insurance amounts? How can you be sure your employers have paid FICA taxes correctly? The Social Security Administration web site allows you to request your social security statement of earnings and benefits. This report estimates your future social security benefits and tells you how to qualify for those benefits. By requesting your statement, you can check an estimate of your retirement and disability benefits and obtain complete earnings and social security tax history. Beginning in 1999 on an annual basis, this statement is mailed automatically to people older than 25 years old who pay social security but do not currently receive social security benefits. Check out other social security issues and get a free copy of your statement of earnings and benefits at **http://www.ssa.gov/**.

Performance Objectives

After you have completed this chapter, you will be able to do the following:

1. Calculate the amount of payroll tax expense and journalize the related entry.
2. Journalize the entry for the deposit of employees' federal income taxes withheld and FICA taxes (both employees' withheld and employer's matching share) and prepare the deposit coupon.
3. Journalize the entries for the payment of employer's state and federal unemployment taxes.
4. Journalize the entry for the deposit of employees' state income taxes withheld.
5. Complete Employer's Quarterly Federal Tax Return, Form 941.
6. Prepare W-2 and W-3 forms and Form 940.
7. Calculate the premium for workers' compensation insurance, and prepare the entry for payment in advance.
8. Determine the amount of the end-of-the-year adjustments for (a) workers' compensation insurance and (b) accrued salaries and wages, and record the adjustments.

We have talked about computing and recording such payroll data as gross pay, employees' income tax withheld, employees' FICA tax withheld, and various deductions requested by employees. Now we will pay these withholding liabilities and the taxes levied on the employer based on the total payroll.

EMPLOYER IDENTIFICATION NUMBER

Everyone who works must have a Social Security number, a vital part of federal income tax returns. An employer's counterpart to the Social Security number is the **employer identification number** assigned by the Internal Revenue Service. Employers of one or more persons are required to have such a number, and it must be listed on all reports and payments of employees' federal income tax withholding and FICA taxes.

EMPLOYER'S PAYROLL TAXES

An employer's payroll taxes are based on the gross wages paid to employees. Payroll taxes—like property taxes—are an expense of doing business. Greg Company records these taxes in the **Payroll Tax Expense** account and debits the account for the company's portion of FICA taxes and for state and federal unemployment taxes. In T account form, Payroll Tax Expense for Greg Company would look like the following example.

Payroll Tax Expense

+	–
FICA tax (employer's matching portion) State unemployment tax Federal unemployment tax	Closed at the end of the year along with all other expense accounts

As you can see, **FICA tax (employer's share), state unemployment tax, and federal unemployment tax are included under the umbrella of Payroll Tax Expense.** In most states, the unemployment taxes are levied on the employer only.

Employer's Matching Portion of FICA Tax (Social Security Plus Medicare)

FICA tax is imposed equally on both employer and employee. After the firm's accountant deducts the employee's share from gross wages and records it in the payroll entry under FICA Tax Payable, he or she then determines the

HEAL
MEDICARE
Keep It Strong,
Pass It Along!
PROTECT MEDICARE!

The skyrocketing costs of Medicare have caused Congress to try to make sweeping reforms. The issues are far-reaching, however, because Medicare affects such a large percentage of the population—who fear their benefits may be reduced.

employer's share by multiplying the employer's tax rates (assumed to be 6.2 percent for Social Security and 1.45 percent for Medicare) by the taxable earnings (assumed to be $68,400 for Social Security and all earnings for Medicare). The same tax rates apply to both the employer and the employees.

The accountant gets the Social Security and Medicare taxable earnings amounts from the payroll register. In Figure 1 we present the Taxable Earnings columns taken from the payroll register for the week ended October 7.

Before we look at the journal entry to record the employer's share of FICA tax, let's look at the entry in T account form.

Payroll Tax Expense

+	−
994.84	

FICA Tax Payable

−	+		
	Balance	994.86	(employees' share of FICA tax as posted from the payroll entry)
		994.84	(employers' share of FICA tax)

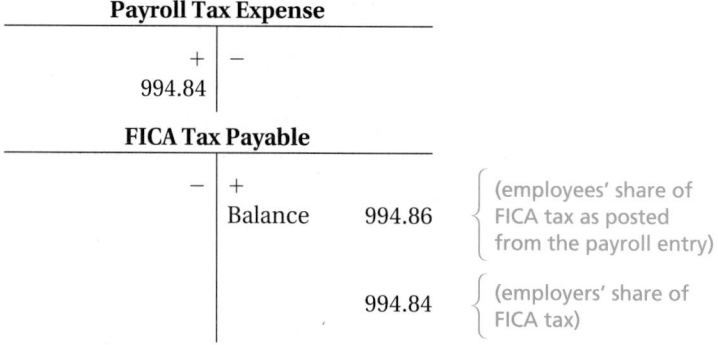

Note particularly that the FICA Tax Payable account is often used for both the tax liability of the employer and the amounts withheld from the employees. This is logical because both FICA taxes are paid at the same time

Amount of employees' earnings for the period that has not, as yet, been taxed as part of the $7,000 maximum liability (Unemployment column)

Amount of employees' earnings that are less than $68,400 per employee for the year (Social Security column)

Amount of all employees' earnings (Medicare column)

	NAME	TOTAL HOURS	TOTAL	ENDING CUMULATIVE EARNINGS	(7) TAXABLE EARNINGS: UNEMPLOYMENT	SOCIAL SECURITY	MEDICARE
1	Asino, Matte E.	46	1,119.16	34,009.16	—	1,119.16	1,119.16
2	Boritsky, Olga	45	735.30	6,927.30	735.30	735.30	735.30
3	Dray, Greg G.	49	915.65	7,761.65	154.00	915.65	915.65
4	Foulkes, Bob L.	40	1,073.25	39,710.25	—	1,073.25	1,073.25
5	Groyer, Milli K.	40	1,888.89	69,888.89	—	400.00	1,888.89
6	Kramer, Ada A.	40	1,891.67	69,991.67	—	300.00	1,891.67
7	Minkowitz, John L.	55	1,598.96	38,438.96	—	1,598.96	1,598.96
8	Orleons, Janet C.	40	1,271.75	47,054.75	—	1,271.75	1,271.75
9	Pinkovich, Mark S.	44	1,500.43	48,470.43	—	1,500.43	1,500.43
10	Romero, Sheila J.	45	1,813.51	56,791.51	—	1,813.51	1,813.51
11	Tivoli, Jake T.	40	1,168.83	43,246.83	—	1,168.83	1,168.83
12	Wilson, Charles D.	52	2,763.06	71,363.06	—	—	2,763.06
13			17,740.46	533,654.46	889.30	11,896.84	17,740.46

FIGURE 1

Employer's state unemployment tax $889.30 × .054 = $48.02

Employer's Social Security tax $11,896.84 × .062 = $737.60

Employer's Medicare tax $17,740.46 × .0145 = $257.24

Employer's federal unemployment tax $899.30 × .008 = $7.19

Combined Employer's FICA tax ($737.60 + $257.24) = $994.84

and to the same place. There may be a slight difference between the employer's and the employees' share of FICA taxes because of the rounding process. For the employees' share, the accountant uses the total of the employees' Social Security and Medicare tax deductions. For the employer's share, the accountant multiplies the total taxable earnings (Social Security and Medicare) by the tax rates.

Employer's State Unemployment Tax

The state unemployment tax (SUTA) is levied only on the employer in most states, the proceeds to be used to pay subsistence benefits to unemployed workers. The rate of the state unemployment tax varies considerably among the states. Assume that Greg Company is subject to a rate of 5.4 percent of the first $7,000 of each employee's earnings (the same base amount as for the federal unemployment tax). As shown in the portion of the payroll register illustrated in Figure 1, $889.30 of earnings are subject to the state unemployment tax. Accordingly, by T accounts, the state unemployment tax based on taxable earnings is as follows.

Payroll Tax Expense		State Unemployment Tax Payable	
+	–	–	+
(889.30 × .054) 48.02			(889.30 × .054) 48.02

Employer's Federal Unemployment Tax

The federal unemployment tax (FUTA) **is paid only by the employer.** Congress may from time to time change the rate. Let's assume a rate of .8 percent (.008) of the first $7,000 earned by each employee during the calendar year. For the weekly payroll period for Greg Company, the tax liability is $7.11 ($889.30 of unemployment taxable earnings, taken from the payroll register, multiplied by .008, the tax rate). The T account is as follows:

Payroll Tax Expense		Federal Unemployment Tax Payable	
+	–	–	+
(889.30 × .008) 7.11			(889.30 × .008) 7.11

Objective 1

Calculate the amount of payroll tax expense and journalize the related entry.

To make things clearer, figures for the three employer's payroll taxes have been presented separately. Now let's combine all of this information into one entry, which follows the regular payroll entry. Greg Company pays its employees weekly, so it also makes its Payroll Tax Expense entry weekly.

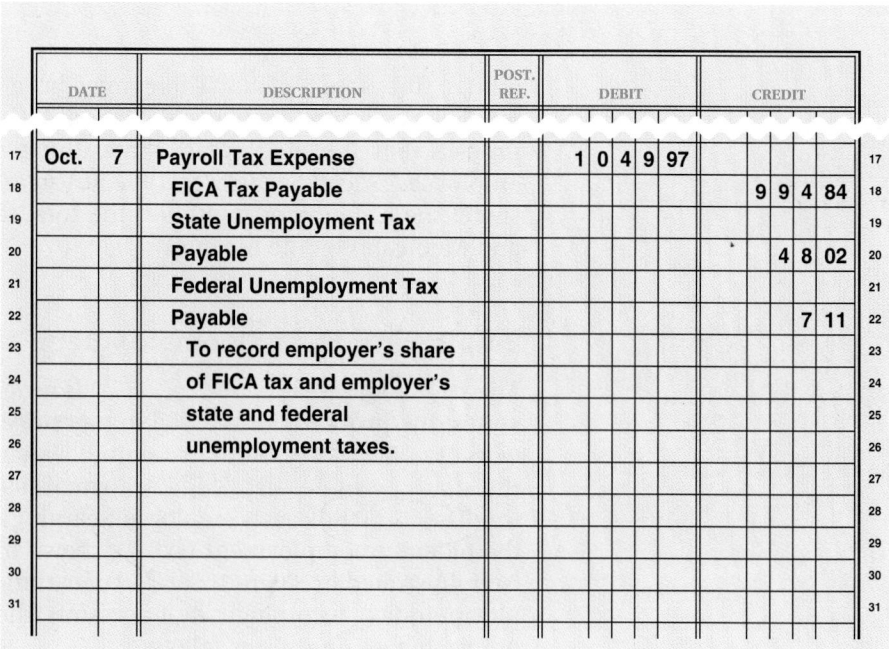

	DATE		DESCRIPTION	POST. REF.	DEBIT	CREDIT	
17	Oct.	7	Payroll Tax Expense		1 0 4 9 97		17
18			FICA Tax Payable			9 9 4 84	18
19			State Unemployment Tax				19
20			Payable			4 8 02	20
21			Federal Unemployment Tax				21
22			Payable			7 11	22
23			To record employer's share				23
24			of FICA tax and employer's				24
25			state and federal				25
26			unemployment taxes.				26
27							27
28							28
29							29
30							30
31							31

JOURNAL ENTRIES FOR RECORDING PAYROLL

At this point, let's restate in general journal form the entries that have already been recorded. We'll do this so that you can see the sequence of the payroll entries. First, the entry to record the payroll is journalized.

DATE		DESCRIPTION	POST. REF.	DEBIT	CREDIT
20–					
Oct.	7	Sales Wages Expense		13503 79	
		Office Wages Expense		4236 67	
		Employees' Federal Income			
		Tax Payable			3314 37
		FICA Tax Payable			994 86
		Employees' State Income Tax			
		Payable			662 88
		Employees' Medical Insurance			
		Payable			260 50
		Employees' United Way			
		Payable			124 00
		Accounts Receivable			50 00
		Wages Payable			12333 85
		Payroll register, page 68,			
		for week ended October 7.			

Next, the entry to record the employer's payroll taxes is journalized.

Remember!

The sequence of steps for recording the payroll entries is: (1) record the payroll for the present period in the payroll register; (2) based on the payroll register, record the payroll entry in the journal; (3) based on the Taxable Earnings columns of the payroll register, record Payroll Tax Expense in the journal; (4) make a journal entry to pay the employees.

DATE		DESCRIPTION	POST. REF.	DEBIT	CREDIT
	7	Payroll Tax Expense		1049 97	
		FICA Tax Payable			994 84
		State Unemployment Tax			
		Payable			48 02
		Federal Unemployment Tax			
		Payable			7 11
		To record employer's share			
		of FICA tax and employer's			
		state and federal			
		unemployment taxes.			

Finally, the entry to pay the employees is journalized. Greg Company issues one check payable to a payroll bank account. To pay its employees, it will draw separate payroll checks on this payroll account. (The entry to transfer cash to the payroll bank account is not shown here.)

DATE		DESCRIPTION	POST. REF.	DEBIT	CREDIT
	8	Wages Payable		12 3 3 3 85	
		Cash—Payroll Bank Account			12 3 3 3 85
		Paid salaries for week			
		ended October 7.			

As stated previously, in the first payroll entry, small employers will credit Cash directly instead of Wages Payable. These employers issue separate checks out of their regular bank accounts for each employee.

Next, we describe the entries for paying withholdings for employees' federal income tax and FICA tax and the employer's matching share of FICA tax. We also show the entries for paying the federal and state unemployment taxes and the withholdings for employees' state income tax.

PAYMENTS OF FICA TAX AND EMPLOYEES' FEDERAL INCOME TAX WITHHOLDING

Objective 2

Journalize the entry for the deposit of employees' federal income taxes withheld and FICA taxes (both employees' withheld and employer's matching share) and prepare the deposit coupon.

FYI

There are penalties applied for late deposits of federal taxes.

After paying employees, the employer must make payments in the form of federal tax deposits. A deposit includes the combined total of three items: (1) employees' federal income taxes withheld, (2) employees' FICA taxes withheld, and (3) employer's share of FICA taxes. Employers make these deposits on a pay-as-you-go basis.

Deposits are made to authorized commercial banks or Federal Reserve banks. The deposits are forwarded to the U.S. Treasury. The timing of these deposits depends on the amounts owed. The calendar year is broken into days, semiweekly periods, months, and **quarters** (3 consecutive months).

Employers submit a return, Form 941, every quarter. The due dates for filing this return are as follows:

Quarter	Ending Date of Quarter	Due Date for Form 941
January–February–March	March 31	April 30
April–May–June	June 30	July 31
July–August–September	September 30	October 31
October–November–December	December 31	January 31

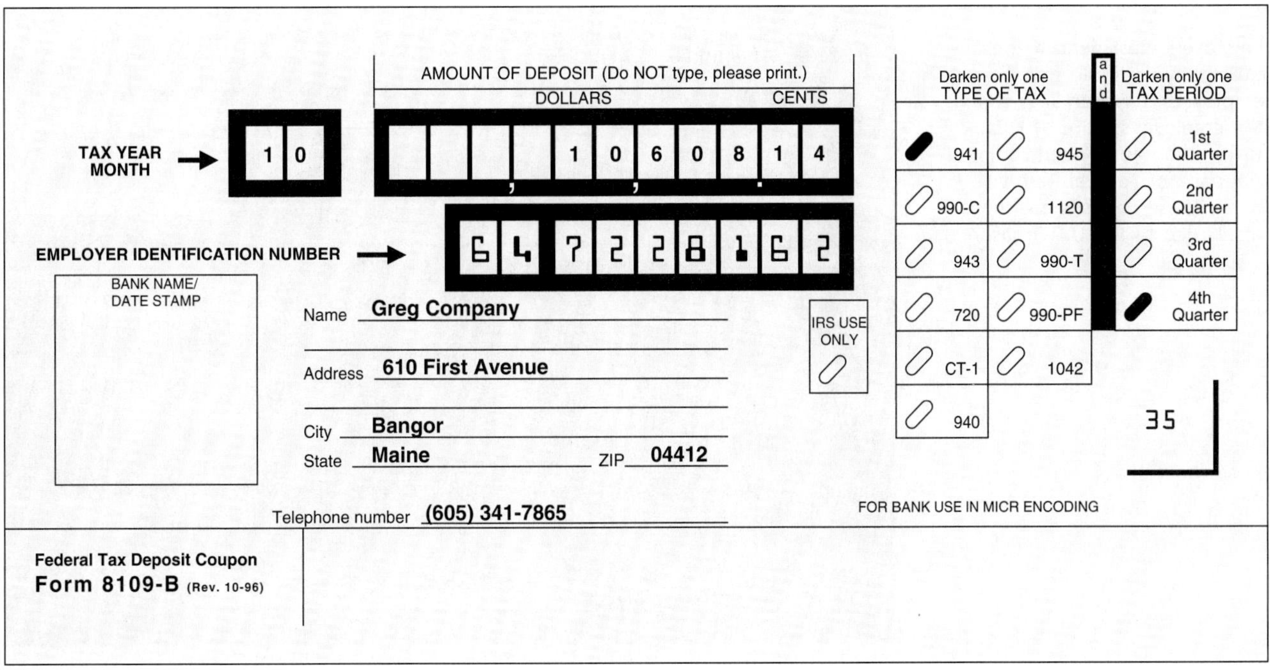
AMOUNT OF DEPOSIT (Do NOT type, please print.)
DOLLARS CENTS

TAX YEAR MONTH → 1 0

1 0 6 0 8 1 4

EMPLOYER IDENTIFICATION NUMBER → 6 4 7 2 2 8 1 6 2

BANK NAME/ DATE STAMP

Name Greg Company

Address 610 First Avenue

City Bangor

State Maine ZIP 04412

Telephone number (605) 341-7865

IRS USE ONLY

Darken only one TYPE OF TAX: 941 (darkened), 945, 990-C, 1120, 943, 990-T, 720, 990-PF, CT-1, 1042, 940

and

Darken only one TAX PERIOD: 1st Quarter, 2nd Quarter, 3rd Quarter, 4th Quarter (darkened)

35

FOR BANK USE IN MICR ENCODING

Federal Tax Deposit Coupon
Form 8109-B (Rev. 10-96)

FIGURE 2

Federal Tax Deposit Coupon

Let's go back to Greg Company, where taxes were previously paid up to date. From the payroll of October 7, the following federal taxes are owed:

Employees' federal income taxes withheld	$3,314.37
Employees' FICA taxes withheld	994.86
Employer's share of FICA taxes	994.84
Total federal undeposited taxes	$5,304.07

We continue on for the next payroll period, ended October 14:

	Oct. 7	Oct. 14	Total
Employees' federal income taxes withheld	$3,314.37	$3,314.37	$ 6,628.74
Employees' FICA taxes withheld	994.86	994.86	1,989.72
Employer's share of FICA taxes	994.84	994.84	1,989.68
Total federal undeposited taxes	$5,304.07	$5,304.07	$10,608.14

Greg Company, which deposits monthly, receives a federal tax deposit card (printed with the company's name and tax number) from the Internal Revenue Service (Figure 2).

The accountant records the amount of the deposit, the employer identification number, the type of tax, the tax period, and the name and address of the company. The entry in general journal form to record the deposit of two weeks' taxes looks like the following.

FYI

We will show a Form 941 later in this chapter.

FYI

Employers must deposit the taxes they withhold from employees' paychecks, as well as the employer's share of FICA taxes, in an authorized commercial bank or Federal Reserve bank on designated schedules based on the amount of the deductions and contributions. These deposits are then forwarded to the U.S. Treasury.

FYI

Because of rounding differences, the employee and employer amounts of FICA taxes may differ slightly. Line 9 of the 941 Form accommodates this difference.

Employers must deposit the taxes they withhold from employees' paychecks, as well as the employer's share of FICA taxes, in an authorized commercial bank or Federal Reserve bank. These deposits are then forwarded to the U.S. Treasury.

DATE		DESCRIPTION	POST. REF.	DEBIT	CREDIT
20–					
Nov.	15	Employees' Federal Income Tax			
		Payable		6,628.74	
		FICA Tax Payable		3,979.40	
		Cash			10,608.14
		Issued check for federal tax			
		deposit, Bangor Bank.			

PAYMENTS OF STATE UNEMPLOYMENT INSURANCE

Objective 3

Journalize the entries for the payment of employer's state and federal unemployment taxes.

As we stated before, states differ with regard to both the rate and the taxable base for unemployment insurance. In our example, we assume that the state tax is 5.4 percent of the first \$7,000 paid to each employee during the calendar year. **The state tax is usually paid quarterly and is due by the end of the month following the end of the quarter (the same as the due dates for Form 941).** Here's the entry in general journal form made by Greg Company for the first quarter (covering the months of January, February, and March). We assume that \$60,436 was taxable for the quarter. The amount of the tax is \$3,263.54 (\$60,436 × .054).

	DATE		DESCRIPTION	POST. REF.	DEBIT	CREDIT	
1	20–						1
2	Apr.	30	State Unemployment Tax				2
3			Payable		3 2 6 3 54		3
4			Cash			3 2 6 3 54	4
5			Issued check for payment of				5
6			state unemployment tax.				6
7							7

The T accounts are as follows:

Cash				State Unemployment Tax Payable			
	+	−			−	+	
		Apr. 30	3,263.54	Apr. 30	3,263.54	Mar. 31	
						Balance	3,263.54

The balance in State Unemployment Tax Payable is the result of weekly entries recording the state unemployment portion of payroll tax expense.

PAYMENTS OF FEDERAL UNEMPLOYMENT TAX

The FUTA tax is calculated quarterly, during the month following the end of each calendar quarter and is used to administer the funds. **If the accumulated tax liability is greater than $100, the tax is deposited in a commercial bank or Federal Reserve bank, accompanied by a preprinted federal tax deposit card** like that used to deposit employees' federal income tax withholding and FICA taxes. The due date for this deposit is the last day of the month following the end of the quarter, the same as the due dates for the Employer's Quarterly Federal Tax Return and for state unemployment taxes.

Here is the entry in general journal form made by Greg Company for the first quarter. In our example, since the FUTA and state unemployment taxable earnings are the same (the first $7,000 for each employee), we assume that $60,436 was taxable for the quarter. The amount of the tax is $483.49 ($60,436 × .008).

	DATE		DESCRIPTION	POST. REF.	DEBIT	CREDIT	
1	20–						1
2	Apr.	30	Federal Unemployment Tax				2
3			Payable		4 8 3 49		3
4			Cash			4 8 3 49	4
5			Issued check for deposit of				5
6			federal unemployment tax.				6
7							7

The T accounts are as follows:

Cash				Federal Unemployment Tax Payable			
+		–		–		+	
		Apr. 30	483.49	Apr. 30	483.49	Mar. 31 Balance	483.49

The balance in Federal Unemployment Tax Payable is the result of weekly entries recording the federal unemployment portion of payroll tax expense.

DEPOSITS OF EMPLOYEES' STATE INCOME TAX WITHHOLDING

Objective 4

Journalize the entry for the deposit of employees' state income taxes withheld.

Assume that the withholdings for employees' state income taxes are deposited on a quarterly basis, payable at the same time as state unemployment tax. Also, as of March 31, the credit balance of Employees' State Income Tax Payable is $1,526.08. The entry in general journal form to record the payment for the first quarter looks like this:

	DATE		DESCRIPTION	POST. REF.	DEBIT	CREDIT	
1	20–						1
2	Apr.	30	Employees' State Income Tax				2
3			Payable		1 5 2 6 08		3
4			Cash			1 5 2 6 08	4
5			Issued check for state				5
6			income tax deposit.				6
7							7

The T accounts are as follows:

Cash				Employees' State Income Tax Payable			
+		–		–		+	
		Apr. 30	1,526.08	Apr. 30	1,526.08	Mar. 31 Balance	1,526.08

EMPLOYER'S QUARTERLY FEDERAL TAX RETURN (FORM 941)

Objective 5

Complete Employer's Quarterly Federal Tax Return, Form 941.

The purpose of **Form 941** is to report the tax liability for withholdings of employees' federal income tax and FICA taxes, and also the employer's share of FICA taxes. Total tax deposits are also listed. As the title implies, the time period is three months. Remember that the due dates for the calendar year are: first quarter, April 30; second quarter, July 31; third quarter, October 31; fourth quarter, January 31.

A completed Form 941 for Greg Company is shown in Figure 3. Note that there are three main sections, which may be completed in the order

Form **941** (Rev. January 1999)
Department of the Treasury
Internal Revenue Service

Employer's Quarterly Federal Tax Return

▶ **See separate instructions for information on completing this return.**

Please type or print.

Enter state code for state in which deposits were made ONLY if different from state in address to the right ▶ (see page 2 of instructions).

Name (as distinguished from trade name)	Date quarter ended: December 31, 20—	OMB No. 1545-0029
Trade name, if any: Greg Company	Employer identification number: 64-7228162	T / FF / FD / FP / I / T
Address (number and street): 610 First Avenue	City, state, and ZIP code: Bangor, Maine 04412	

If address is different from prior return, check here ▶ ☐ (IRS Use)

If you do not have to file returns in the future, check here ▶ ☐ and enter date final wages paid ▶

If you are a seasonal employer, see **Seasonal employers** on page 1 of the instructions and check here ▶ ☐

Line	Description		Amount
1	Number of employees in the pay period that includes March 12th ▶	12	
2	Total wages and tips, plus other compensation	2	216,252 00
3	Total income tax withheld from wages, tips, and sick pay	3	39,768 00
4	Adjustment of withheld income tax for preceding quarters of calendar year	4	——
5	Adjusted total of income tax withheld (line 3 as adjusted by line 4—see instructions)	5	39,768 00
6	Taxable social security wages — 6a 130,080 00 × 12.4% (.124) =	6b	16,129 92
	Taxable social security tips — 6c × 12.4% (.124) =	6d	——
7	Taxable Medicare wages and tips — 7a 216,252 00 × 2.9% (.029) =	7b	6,271 31
8	Total social security and Medicare taxes (add lines 6b, 6d, and 7b). Check here if wages are not subject to social security and/or Medicare tax ▶ ☐	8	22,401 23
9	Adjustment of social security and Medicare taxes (see instructions for required explanation) Sick Pay $ ____ ± Fractions of Cents $ ____ ± Other $ ____ =	9	——
10	Adjusted total of social security and Medicare taxes (line 8 as adjusted by line 9—see instructions)	10	22,401 23
11	**Total taxes** (add lines 5 and 10)	11	62,169 23
12	Advance earned income credit (EIC) payments made to employees	12	——
13	Net taxes (subtract line 12 from line 11). **If $1,000 or more, this must equal line 17, column (d) below (or line D of Schedule B (Form 941))**	13	62,169 23
14	Total deposits for quarter, including overpayment applied from a prior quarter	14	62,169 23
15	**Balance due** (subtract line 14 from line 13). See instructions	15	—0—

16 **Overpayment.** If line 14 is more than line 13, enter excess here ▶ $ ____
and check if to be: ☐ Applied to next return OR ☐ Refunded.

- **All filers:** If line 13 is less than $1,000, you need not complete line 17 or Schedule B (Form 941).
- **Semiweekly schedule depositors:** Complete Schedule B (Form 941) and check here ▶ ☐
- **Monthly schedule depositors:** Complete line 17, columns (a) through (d), and check here ▶ ☑

17 Monthly Summary of Federal Tax Liability. Do not complete if you were a semiweekly schedule depositor.

(a) First month liability	(b) Second month liability	(c) Third month liability	(d) Total liability for quarter
18,236.45	20,956.56	22,976.22	62,169.23

Sign Here Under penalties of perjury, I declare that I have examined this return, including accompanying schedules and statements, and to the best of my knowledge and belief, it is true, correct, and complete.

Signature ▶ *Ellen D. Greg* Print Your Name and Title ▶ Ellen D. Greg, Owner Date ▶ *Jan. 31, 20—*

For Privacy Act and Paperwork Reduction Act Notice, see back of form. Cat. No. 17001Z Form **941** (Rev. 1-99)

FIGURE 3

presented below. (The Internal Revenue Service has frequently changed the arrangement and questions on Form 941.)

Heading

Once an employer has secured an identification number and has filed her or his first return, the Internal Revenue Service sends forms directly to the employer. These forms have the employer's name, address, and identification number filled in.

Monthly Summary of Federal Tax Liability

For each month, list the combined total of employees' federal income and FICA taxes withheld and employer's share of FICA.

Questions Listed on Form 941 (Figure 3)

Read each question line by line.

1. Total number of employees.
2. Total wages and tips, plus other compensation, subject to federal tax withholding.
3. Total federal income tax withheld—shown as credits in the Employees' Federal Income Tax Payable account.
4. Adjustment of withheld income tax for preceding quarters of calendar year.
5. Adjusted total of income tax withheld—the total of income tax withheld after any adjustment for withheld income tax for preceding quarters.
6. Taxable Social Security wages paid—total of the Social Security Taxable Earnings listed in the payroll register for the three-month quarter; 12.4 percent equals the employees' 6.2 percent plus the employer's 6.2 percent.
   Taxable Social Security tips—refers to customer tips reported by employees; the employer withholds 6.2 percent.
7. Taxable Medicare wages and tips—total of the Medicare Taxable Earnings listed in the payroll register for the three-month quarter; 2.9 percent equals the employees' 1.45 percent plus the employer's 1.45 percent.
8. Total Social Security and Medicare taxes—shown as credits in the FICA Tax Payable account.
9. Adjustment of Social Security and Medicare taxes—used to record corrections in Social Security taxes reported on earlier returns and for rounding differences.
10. Adjusted total of Social Security and Medicare taxes.
11. Total taxes—the total of various taxes withheld from employees' pay and the taxes imposed on the employer.
12. Advance earned income credit (EIC) payments—payments made in advance to qualified employees for earned income credit. For qualifying low-income taxpayers, the earned income credit is a deduction from income tax owed.
13. Net taxes—the total federal tax liability for the quarter (this is the same amount as the total of the Monthly Summary of Federal Tax Liability section).
14. Total deposits for quarter—total of the debits to the Employees' Federal Income Tax Payable and the FICA Tax Payable accounts for the three-month quarter.

15. Balance due.
16. Overpayment.

The amount of wages subject to tax may differ in blocks 1, 3, 5, 17, and 20. Qualified employee contributions to retirement plans, such as 401k and 403b plans, reduce the amount of wages subject to federal income tax but not social security tax or Medicare tax. Whether employee retirement contributions reduce taxable state and local wages depends upon the appropriate state and local laws.

Wage Withholding Statements for Employees (Forms W-2)

Objective 6

Prepare W-2 and W-3 forms and Form 940.

After the end of a year (December 31) and by the following January 31, the employer must furnish for each employee a Wage and Tax Statement, known as **Form W-2**. This form contains information about the employee's earnings and tax deductions for the year. The source of the information used to complete Form W-2 is the employee's individual earnings record. The amounts used to complete Matte E. Asino's W-2 form (in Figure 4) represent the amounts taken from his earnings record at the end of the calendar year, December 31.

FIGURE 4

a Control number 22222	Void ☐	**For Official Use Only ▶** **OMB No. 1545-0008**

b Employer identification number 64-7228162	**1** Wages, tips, other compensation 46,330	**2** Federal income tax withheld 8,573
c Employer's name, address, and ZIP code Greg Company 610 First Avenue Bangor, Maine 04412	**3** Social security wages 46,330	**4** Social security tax withheld 2,872.46
	5 Medicare wages and tips 46,330	**6** Medicare tax withheld 671.79
	7 Social security tips 0	**8** Allocated tips 0
d Employee's social security number 543-24-1680	**9** Advance EIC payment 0	**10** Dependent care benefits 0
e Employee's name (first, middle initial, last) Matte E. Asino 6242 Baxter Drive Bangor, Maine 04412	**11** Nonqualified plans 0	**12** Benefits included in box 1 0
	13 See instrs. for box 13	**14** Other
f Employee's address and ZIP code	**15** Statutory employee ☐ Deceased ☐ Pension plan ☐ Legal rep. ☐ Hshld. emp. ☐ Subtotal ☐ Deferred compensation ☐	

16 State	Employer's state I.D. No.	**17** State wages, tips, etc.	**18** State income tax	**19** Locality name	**20** Local wages, tips, etc.	**21** Local income tax
ME	464-729	46,330	1,735	0	0	0

Department of the Treasury—Internal Revenue Service

Form **W-2** **Wage and Tax Statement** **2000**

For Privacy Act and Paperwork Reduction Act Notice, see separate instructions.

Copy A For Social Security Administration–Send this entire page with Form W-3 to the Social Security Administration; photocopies are **Not** acceptable.

Cat. No. 10134D

Block 9 shows the total paid to the employee as advance earned income credit (EIC) payments. Block 13 is used for miscellaneous items, such as sick pay that is not included in income because the employee contributed to the sick pay plan. This box is also used for employer-provided group term life insurance in excess of $50,000. Box 14 may include the value of noncash fringe benefits, such as providing a vehicle for the employee. In box 15, statutory employees are life insurance and traveling salespersons, and legal representatives include attorneys and parents.

The accountant will prepare at least four copies of the W-2 form for each employee.

FYI

A copy is also sent (if applicable) to the state and/or local tax department, and a copy is given to the employee to attach to the state/local tax return.

Copy A—Employer sends to the Social Security Administration.
Copy B—Employer gives to employee to be attached to the employee's individual federal income tax return.
Copy C—Employer gives to employee to be kept for his or her personal records.
Copy D—Employer keeps this copy as a record of payments made.

If state and local income taxes are withheld, the employer prepares additional copies to be sent to the appropriate tax agency.

Employer's Annual Federal Income Tax Reports (Form W-3)

Accompanying copy A of the employees' W-2 forms, Greg Company sends **Form W-3**, Transmittal of Wage and Tax Statements, to the Social Security Administration. This form is due on February 28, following the end of the calendar year.

For all employees, Form W-3 shows the total wages and tips, total federal income tax withheld, total Social Security and Medicare taxable wages, total Social Security and Medicare tax withheld, and other information. These amounts must be the same as the grand totals of the W-2 forms and the four quarterly 941 forms for the year. Greg Company's completed Form W-3 is presented in Figure 5.

Some boxes deserve an explanation. Box d, establishment number, may be used for a company that has separate establishments, with each establishment filing W-2 and W-3 forms separately. Box 9 is used for recording the amount of advance earned income credits shown on W-2 forms for qualified employees. Box h is used by a company that had more than one employer identification number (EIN) during the year.

To sum up thus far: The employer must submit the following at the end of the calendar year: Employer's Quarterly Federal Tax Return, Form 941, for the fourth quarter by January 31; Wage and Tax Statements, Form W-2, for all employees by January 31; Transmittal of Wage and Tax Statements, Form W-3, by February 28.

REPORTS AND PAYMENTS OF FEDERAL UNEMPLOYMENT TAX

Remember!

If the accumulated FUTA tax liability at the end of a quarter is greater than $100, a deposit must be made.

As we stated previously, generally all employers are subject to the Federal Unemployment Tax Act. These employers must submit an Employer's Annual Federal Unemployment Tax Return, Form 940, not later than January 31 following the close of the calendar year. This deadline may be extended until February 10 if the employer has made deposits paying the FUTA tax liability

DO NOT STAPLE

a Control number	33333	**For Official Use Only ▶** **OMB No. 1545-0008**

b **Kind of Payer** ▶ 941 [X] Military [ ] 943 [ ] CT-1 [ ] Hshld. emp. [ ] Medicare govt. emp. [ ]	1 Wages, tips, other compensation **865,008**	2 Federal income tax withheld **103,801**
	3 Social security wages **778,836**	4 Social security tax withheld **52,557.90**
c Total number of Forms W-2 **12** / d Establishment number ———	5 Medicare wages and tips **865,008**	6 Medicare tax withheld **12,542.62**
e Employer identification number **64-7228162**	7 Social security tips **0**	8 Allocated tips **0**
f Employer's name **Greg Company** **610 First Avenue** **Bangor, Maine 04412**	9 Advance EIC payments **0**	10 Dependent care benefits **0**
	11 Nonqualified plans **0**	12 Deferred compensation **0**
g Employer's address and ZIP code	13	14
h Other EIN used this year **0**	15 Income tax withheld by third-party payer **0**	
i Employer's state I.D. no. **464-729**		

Contact person	Telephone number	Fax number	E-mail address
Ellen D. Greg	**(605) 341-7865**	**(605) 341-1463**	**GregCo@not.com**

Under penalties of perjury, I declare that I have examined this return and accompanying documents, and, to the best of my knowledge and belief, they are true, correct, and complete.

Signature ▶ *Ellen D. Greg* Title ▶ *Owner* Date ▶ *2/27/20–*

Form **W-3 Transmittal of Wage and Tax Statements 2000** Department of the Treasury Internal Revenue Service

Send this entire page with the entire Copy A page of Forms W-2 to the Social Security Administration. Photocopies are NOT acceptable.
Do not send any remittance (cash, checks, money orders, etc.) with FORMS W-2 and W-3.

FIGURE 5

in full. **Form 940** shows total wages paid to employees, total wages subject to federal unemployment tax, and other information.

Using Greg Company as our example, federal unemployment taxable earnings by quarter are as follows:

Federal Unemployment Tax	1st Quarter	2nd Quarter	3rd Quarter	4th Quarter	Cumulative Total
Taxable earnings	$60,436	$9,536	$10,427	$3,601	$84,000
Tax rate	× .008	× .008	× .008	× .008	× .008
Tax liability	$483.49	$76.29	$ 83.42	$28.80*	$672.00

* Rounding

We now repeat the journal entry for the first quarter, in which $483.49 was deposited on April 30.

	DATE		DESCRIPTION	POST. REF.	DEBIT	CREDIT	
1	20–						1
2	Apr.	30	Federal Unemployment Tax				2
3			Payable		483.49		3
4			Cash			483.49	4
5			Issued check for deposit of				5
6			federal unemployment tax.				6
7							7

During the second quarter, many employees' total earnings passed the $7,000 limit of taxable earnings, and the firm's tax liability was reduced accordingly. Because Greg's total accumulated liability ($76.29) was less than $100, a deposit covering that quarter was not made. However, because of an expansion of the company, three new employees were hired during the middle of the quarter.

For the third quarter, the tax liability amounted to $83.42. The total cumulative tax liability was now $159.71 ($76.29 second quarter plus $83.42 third quarter). Consequently, $159.71 was deposited on October 31.

By the end of the fourth quarter, each of the twelve employees' earnings passed the $7,000 mark. The total liability for the quarter is $28.80. This amount will be paid by January 31, accompanied by the completed Employer's Annual Federal Unemployment Tax Return, Form 940.

The T account for Federal Unemployment Tax Payable follows. The credits to the account were part of the entries to record the federal unemployment tax portion of Payroll Tax Expense for each payroll period.

Federal Unemployment Tax Payable

	–	+	
Apr. 30 deposit	483.49	1st quarter (liability)	483.49
Oct. 31 deposit	159.71	2nd quarter (liability)	76.29
		3rd quarter (liability)	83.42
Jan. 31 deposit	28.80	4th quarter (liability)	28.80

Employer's Annual Federal Unemployment (FUTA) Tax Return (Form 940)

Figure 6 shows a completed Form 940-EZ for Greg Company. This form has three sections. (Bear in mind that this form changes from time to time.)

Part I Line 1 Record total wages paid.

Line 2 Record certain exempt wages—this includes such items as agricultural labor, family employment, and the value of meals and lodging.

Form **940-EZ**
Department of the Treasury
Internal Revenue Service (99)

Employer's Annual Federal Unemployment (FUTA) Tax Return

▶ See separate **Instructions for Form 940-EZ** for information on completing this form.

OMB No. 1545-1110

2000

T	
FF	
FD	
FP	
I	
T	

Name (as distinguished from trade name)

Calendar year
20—

Trade name, if any
Greg Company

Address and ZIP code
610 First Avenue
Bangor, Maine 04412

Employer identification number
64 : 7228162

*Answer the questions under **Who May Use Form 940-EZ** on page 2. If you cannot use Form 940-EZ, you must use Form 940.*

A Enter the amount of contributions paid to your state unemployment fund. (See separate instructions.) . . . ▶ $ ....

B (1) Enter the name of the state where you have to pay contributions . . . . ▶ ....
(2) Enter your state reporting number as shown on your state unemployment tax return ▶

If you will not have to file returns in the future, check here (see **Who Must File** in separate instructions), **and complete and sign the return.** ▶ ☐

If this is an Amended Return, check here . . . . ▶ ☐

Part I Taxable Wages and FUTA Tax

Line	Description			Line	Amount
1	Total payments (including payments shown on lines 2 and 3) during the calendar year for services of employees			1	865,008 00
2	Exempt payments. (Explain all exempt payments, attaching additional sheets if necessary.) ▶	2	———		
3	Payments of more than $7,000 for services. Enter only amounts over the first $7,000 paid to each employee. Do not include any exempt payments from line 2. The $7,000 amount is the Federal wage base. Your state wage base may be different. **Do not use your state wage limitation**	3	781,008 00		
4	Total exempt payments (add lines 2 and 3)			4	781,008 00
5	**Total taxable wages** (subtract line 4 from line 1) . . . . ▶			5	84,000 00
6	**FUTA tax.** Multiply the wages on line 5 by .008 and enter here. **(If the result is over $100, also complete Part II.)**			6	672 00
7	Total FUTA tax deposited for the year, including any overpayment applied from a prior year			7	672 00
8	**Balance due** (subtract line 7 from line 6). Pay to the "United States Treasury" . . . . ▶ If you owe more than $100, see **Depositing FUTA tax** in separate instructions.			8	———
9	**Overpayment** (subtract line 6 from line 7). Check if it is to be: ☐ **Applied to next return** or ☐ **Refunded** ▶			9	———

Part II Record of Quarterly Federal Unemployment Tax Liability (Do not include state liability.) **Complete only if line 6 is over $100.**

Quarter	First (Jan. 1 – Mar. 31)	Second (Apr. 1 – June 30)	Third (July 1 – Sept. 30)	Fourth (Oct. 1 – Dec. 31)	Total for year
Liability for quarter	483.49	76.29	83.42	28.80	672.00

Under penalties of perjury, I declare that I have examined this return, including accompanying schedules and statements, and, to the best of my knowledge and belief, it is true, correct, and complete, and that no part of any payment made to a state unemployment fund claimed as a credit was, or is to be, deducted from the payments to employees.

Signature ▶ *Ellen D. Greg* **Title (Owner, etc.)** ▶ *Owner* **Date** ▶ *1/31/20–*

For Privacy Act and Paperwork Reduction Act Notice, see separate instructions. Cat. No. 10983G Form **940-EZ** (2000)

DETACH HERE

FIGURE 6

Line 3 Record exempt wages paid—wages paid to each employee over and above $7,000 for the calendar year.
Line 4 Total exempt payments.
Line 5 Total taxable wages.
Line 6 Computation of tax due.
Line 7 Total FUTA tax deposited.
Line 8 Balance due.
Line 9 Overpayment.

Part II Record of Quarterly Federal Unemployment Tax Liability.

WORKERS' COMPENSATION INSURANCE

Objective 7

Calculate the premium for workers' compensation insurance, and prepare the entry for payment in advance.

Most states require employers to provide **workers' compensation insurance** or industrial accident insurance for employees killed or injured on the job, either through plans administered by the state or through private insurance companies authorized by the state. The employer usually has to pay all the premiums. The premium rate varies with the amount of risk the job entails and the company's claims history. For example, handling molten steel ingots is much more dangerous than typing reports. Thus, it is very important that employees be identified properly in terms of the insurance premium classifications. The rates as percentages of the payroll may be .15 percent for office work, .5 percent for sales work, and 3.5 percent for industrial labor in heavy manufacturing. These same rates may be expressed as $.15 per $100 of the salaries or wages for office work, $.50 per $100 for sales work, and $3.50 per $100 for industrial labor.

Remember!

Workers' compensation for the year is first estimated based on the anticipated year's payroll; debit Prepaid Insurance, Workers' Compensation, and credit Cash. At the end of the year, when the actual payroll is known, the exact insurance premium is calculated; debit Workers' Compensation Insurance Expense and credit Prepaid Insurance, Workers' Compensation, for the amount paid at the beginning of the year.

If the amount of the estimated payroll is less than the actual payroll, debit Workers' Compensation Insurance Expense and credit Workers' Compensation Insurance Payable for the difference between the actual premium and the estimated premium.

Generally, the employer pays a premium in advance, based on the estimated payroll for the year. After the year ends, the employer knows the exact amount of the payroll and can calculate the exact premium. At that time, depending on the difference between the estimated and the exact premium, the employer either pays an additional premium or gets a credit for overpayment.

At Greg Company, there are two work classifications: office work and sales work. At the beginning of the year, the firm's accountant computed the estimated annual premium as follows:

Classification	Predicted Payroll	Rate (Percent)	Estimated Premium
Office work	$187,000	.15	$187,000 × .0015 = $ 280.50
Sales work	663,000	.50	663,000 × .0050 = 3,315.00
			Total estimated premium $3,595.50

As shown by T accounts, the accountant made the following entry.

Prepaid Insurance, Workers' Compensation

+	−
Jan. 10 3,595.50	

Cash

+	−
	Jan. 10 3,595.50

Pay estimated

Then, at the end of the calendar year, the accountant calculated the exact premium:

Classification	Exact Payroll	Rate (Percent)	Exact Premium
Office work	$192,000	.15	$192,000 × .0015 = $ 288.00
Sales work	673,000	.50	673,000 × .0050 = 3,365.00
			Total exact premium $3,653.00

End of year Figure Exact

Workers' compensation premiums are based upon the level of risk involved. A rating is given to the employer for each type of job.

Therefore, the amount of the unpaid premium is

$3,653.00	Total exact premium
$3,595.50	Less total estimated premium paid
$ 58.00	Additional premium owed

Objective 8a

Determine the amount of the end-of-the-year adjustment for workers' compensation insurance, and record the adjustment.

Now the accountant makes an adjusting entry, similar to the adjusting entry for expired insurance; this entry appears on the work sheet. The accountant then makes an additional adjusting entry for the extra premium owed. By T accounts, the entries are as follows:

Prepaid Insurance, Workers' Compensation

+		−	
Jan. 10 Bal.	3,595.00	Dec. 31 Adj.	3,595.00

Workers' Compensation Insurance Payable

−		+	
		Dec. 31 Adj.	58.00

Workers' Compensation Insurance Expense

+		−	
Dec. 31 Adj.	3,595.00		
Dec. 31 Adj.	58.00		

FYI

Workers' compensation premiums are based upon the level of risk involved. A rating is given to the employer for each type of job.

Greg Company will pay $58.00, the amount of unpaid premium, in January, together with the estimated premium for the next year.

ADJUSTING FOR ACCRUED SALARIES AND WAGES

Objective 8b

Determine the amount of the end-of-the-year adjustment for accrued salaries and wages, and record the adjustment.

Assume that $1,000 of salaries accrue for the time between the last payday and the end of the year. An adjusting entry is necessary.

	DATE		DESCRIPTION	POST. REF.	DEBIT	CREDIT	
1	20–		Adjusting Entry				1
2	Dec.	31	Salary Expense		1 0 0 0 00		2
3			Salaries Payable			1 0 0 0 00	3
4							4

Salaries Payable is considered a liability account, as are employees' withholding taxes and deductions payable. Federal income tax and FICA tax levied on employees do not become legal obligations until the employees are paid. Therefore, for the purpose of recording the adjusting entry, the entire liability of the gross salaries and wages is included under Salaries Payable or Wages Payable. In other words, in the adjusting entry, such accounts as Employees' Income Tax Payable, FICA Tax Payable (employees' share), and Employees' Union Dues Payable are not used.

Adjusting Entry for Accrual of Payroll Taxes

As you have seen, the following taxes come under the umbrella of the Payroll Tax Expense account: the employer's share of the FICA tax, the state unemployment tax, and the federal unemployment tax. The employer becomes liable for these taxes only when the employees are actually paid, rather than at the time the liability to the employees is incurred. From the standpoint of legal liability, there should be no adjusting entry for Payroll Tax Expense.

TAX CALENDAR

Now let's put it all together. To keep up with the task of paying and reporting the various taxes, the accountant compiles a chronological list of the due dates. We are including only the payroll taxes here, but sales taxes and property taxes should also be listed. When you think about the penalties for nonpayment of taxes by the due dates, this chronological list seems to be well worth the effort.

Jan.	10	Pay estimated annual premium for workers' compensation insurance. (This is an approximate date, as it varies among the states.)
	15	Make federal tax deposit for employees' income tax withholding, employees' FICA taxes withheld, and employer's FICA taxes for wages paid during the month of December.
	31	Complete Employer's Quarterly Federal Tax Return, Form 941, for the fourth quarter.
	31	Issue copies B and C of Wage and Tax Statement, Form W-2, to employees.
	31	Pay state unemployment tax liability for the previous quarter, and submit state return, employer's tax report.
	31	Pay any remaining federal unemployment tax liability for the previous year, and submit Form 940, Employer's Annual Federal Unemployment Tax Return.
	31	Make state deposit for employees' state income tax withholding and submit any required state payroll reports. (Timing and required reports may differ from state to state.)
Feb.	15	Make federal tax deposit for employees' income tax withholding, employees' FICA tax withholding, and employer's FICA tax for wages paid during the month of January.
	28	Complete Transmittal of Wage and Tax Statements, Form W-3, and attach copy A of W-2 forms for employees.
Mar.	15	Make federal tax deposit for employees' income tax withholding, employees' FICA tax withholding, and employer's FICA tax for wages paid during the month of February.

Compiling a chronological list of tax due dates helps accountants keep up with paying and reporting the various taxes.

Apr. 15 Make federal tax deposit for employees' income tax witholding, employees' FICA tax withholding, and employer's FICA tax for wages paid during the month of March.

30 Pay state unemployment tax liability for the previous quarter and submit state return, employer's tax report.

30 Complete Employer's Quarterly Federal Tax Return, Form 941, for the first quarter.

30 Make federal tax deposit for federal unemployment tax liability if it exceeds $100.

30 Make state deposit for employees' state income tax withholding.

CHAPTER REVIEW

Review of Performance Objectives

1. Calculate the amount of payroll tax expense and journalize the related entry.

Payroll tax expense consists of the employer's matching portion of FICA taxes, plus the state unemployment tax, plus the federal unemployment tax. The *FICA tax* consists of Social Security and Medicare taxes. *Social Security tax* equals total Social Security taxable earnings multiplied by .062 (6.2 percent assumed rate) on the taxable earnings. For this text, the maximum taxable is $68,400. Total *Medicare tax* equals Medicare taxable earnings multiplied by .0145 (1.45 percent assumed rate). There is no maximum limit for Medicare—all earnings are taxable. *State unemployment tax* equals unemployment taxable earnings multiplied by .054 (5.4 percent assumed rate). *Federal unemployment tax* equals unemployment taxable earnings multiplied by .008 (.8 percent assumed rate). The related journal entry is as follows:

DATE		DESCRIPTION	POST. REF.	DEBIT	CREDIT
Oct.	7	Payroll Tax Expense		1,049.97	
		FICA Tax Payable			994.84
		State Unemployment Tax			
		Payable			48.02
		Federal Unemployment Tax			
		Payable			7.11
		To record employer's share			
		of FICA tax and employer's			
		state and federal			
		unemployment taxes.			

2. Journalize the entry for the deposit of employees' federal income taxes withheld and FICA taxes (both employees' withheld and employer's matching share) and prepare the deposit coupon.

DATE		DESCRIPTION	POST. REF.	DEBIT	CREDIT
20–					
Nov.	15	Employees' Federal Income Tax			
		Payable		6628 74	
		FICA Tax Payable		3979 40	
		Cash			10608 14
		Issued check for federal tax			
		deposit, Bangor Bank.			

3. Journalize the entries for the payment of employer's state and federal unemployment taxes.

State unemployment tax is paid on a quarterly basis. Payment is due by the end of the next month following the end of the calendar quarter.

DATE		DESCRIPTION	POST. REF.	DEBIT	CREDIT
20–					
Apr.	30	State Unemployment Tax			
		Payable		3263 54	
		Cash			3263 54
		Issued check for payment of			
		state unemployment tax.			

If the amount of the accumulated federal unemployment tax liability exceeds $100 at the end of any quarter, the tax is due by the end of the next month following the end of the quarter. If the federal unemployment tax payable is less than $100 at the end of the year, it is due by January 31 of the next year.

DATE		DESCRIPTION	POST. REF.	DEBIT	CREDIT
20–					
Apr.	30	Federal Unemployment Tax			
		Payable		483 49	
		Cash			483 49
		Issued check for deposit of			
		federal unemployment tax.			

4. Journalize the entry for the deposit of employees' state income taxes withheld.

   Employees' state income taxes withheld are paid on a quarterly basis or as required by your state. Payment may be due by the end of the next month following the end of the calendar quarter.

DATE		DESCRIPTION	POST. REF.	DEBIT	CREDIT
20–					
Apr.	30	Employees' State Income Tax			
		Payable		1526 08	
		Cash			1526 08
		Issued check for state			
		income tax deposit.			

5. Complete Employer's Quarterly Federal Tax Return, Form 941.

   Form 941 is illustrated on page 299.

6. Prepare W-2 and W-3 forms and Form 940.

   W-2 form (Wage and Tax Statement) is illustrated on page 301. W-3 form (Transmittal of Wage and Tax Statements) is illustrated on page 303. Form 940 is illustrated on page 305.

7. Calculate the premium for workers' compensation insurance, and prepare the entry for payment in advance.

   Rates vary depending on the degree of physical risk involved in different occupations. The amount of the premium equals the predicted annual payroll multiplied by the premium rate. The entry is a debit to Prepaid Insurance, Workers' Compensation, and a credit to Cash.

8. Determine the amount of the end-of-the-year adjustments for (a) workers' compensation insurance and (b) accrued salaries and wages, and record the adjustments.

When the total annual payroll is known, the exact cost of workers' compensation insurance can be determined by multiplying the total payroll by the premium rate. Two adjusting entries are required. The first adjusting entry records the expired insurance as a debit to Workers' Compensation Insurance Expense and a credit to Prepaid Insurance, Workers' Compensation. The second adjusting entry records the difference between the estimated and the actual premiums. If the actual premium is greater than the premium that was paid in advance, the entry is a debit to Workers' Compensation Insurance Expense and a credit to Workers' Compensation Insurance Payable. The adjustment for accrued salaries and wages accounts for the additional amount of salaries or wages paid in the next payroll that are incurred in the current fiscal period—a debit to Wages (or Salaries) Expense. The credit to Salaries (or Wages) Payable accounts for the additional amount of liability incurred in the current period that will be paid with the next payroll that occurs in the following fiscal period.

Glossary

Employer identification number The number assigned each employer by the Internal Revenue Service for use in the submission of reports and payments for FICA taxes and federal income tax withheld. (289)

Federal unemployment tax (FUTA) A tax levied only on the employer, equal to .8 percent of the first $7,000 of total earnings paid to each employee during the calendar year. This tax is used to administer the funds. (292)

Form 940 An annual report filed by employers showing total wages paid to employees, total wages subject to federal unemployment tax, total federal unemployment tax, and other information. Also called the *Employer's Annual Federal Unemployment Tax Return.* (303)

Form 941 A quarterly report showing the tax liability for withholdings of employees' federal income tax and FICA tax and the employer's share of FICA tax. Total tax deposits made in the quarter are also listed on this Employer's Quarterly Federal Tax Return. (298)

Form W-2 A form containing information about employee earnings and tax deductions for the year. Also called *Wage and Tax Statement.* (301)

Form W-3 An annual report sent to the Social Security Administration listing the total wages and tips, total federal income tax withheld, total Social Security and Medicare taxable wages, total Social Security and Medicare tax withheld, and other information for all employees of a firm. Also called the *Transmittal of Wage and Tax Statements.* (302)

Payroll Tax Expense A general expense account used for recording the employer's matching portion of the FICA tax, the federal unemployment tax, and the state unemployment tax. (289)

Quarters Three consecutive months, also referred to as *calendar quarters.* (294)

State unemployment tax (SUTA) A tax levied only on the employer in most states. Rates differ among the various states; however, they are generally 5.4 percent or higher of the first $7,000 of total earnings paid to each employee during the calendar year. The proceeds are used to pay subsistence benefits to unemployed workers. (291)

Workers' compensation insurance This insurance, primarily paid for by the employer, provides benefits for employees injured or killed on the job. The rates vary according to the degree of risk inherent in the job. The plans may be sponsored by states or by private firms. The employer pays the premium in advance at the beginning of the year, based on the estimated payroll. The rates are adjusted after the exact payroll is known. (306)

QUESTIONS, EXERCISES, AND PROBLEMS

Discussion Questions

1. What payroll taxes are included under the Payroll Tax Expense account?
2. List the correct sequence of the steps for recording payroll entries, and identify the specific source of information for each entry.
3. Explain the deposit requirement for federal unemployment tax.
4. What is the purpose of Form 941? How often is it prepared, and what are the due dates?
5. How many copies are made of a Form W-2, and who uses the copies of the W-2 form?
6. What is the purpose of Form 940? How often is it prepared, and what is the due date?
7. Generally, what is the time schedule for payment of workers' compensation insurance premiums?
8. Explain the advantage of establishing a tax calendar.

Exercises

P.O. 1

Journalize the entry for payroll tax expense.

Exercise 9-1 West Company's partial payroll register for the week ended January 7 is shown below.

NAME	BEGINNING CUMULATIVE EARNINGS	TOTAL EARNINGS	ENDING CUMULATIVE EARNINGS	TAXABLE EARNINGS: UNEMPLOYMENT	TAXABLE EARNINGS: SOCIAL SECURITY	TAXABLE EARNINGS: MEDICARE
Bonner, R. S.	—	895 00	895 00	895 00	895 00	895 00
Falk, M. C.	—	567 00	567 00	567 00	567 00	567 00
Hagen, W. O.	—	483 00	483 00	483 00	483 00	483 00
Lien, Loan	—	679 00	679 00	679 00	679 00	679 00
Parker, S. J.	—	578 00	578 00	578 00	578 00	578 00
Tinker, E. B.	—	446 00	446 00	446 00	446 00	446 00
		3648 00	3648 00	3648 00	3648 00	3648 00

Assume that the payroll is subject to a Social Security tax of 6.2 percent of the first $68,400 and a Medicare tax of 1.45 percent on all earnings. Also assume that the federal unemployment tax is .8 percent of the first $7,000, and the state unemployment tax is 5.4 percent of the first $7,000. Give the entry in general journal form to record the payroll tax expense.

P.O. 1

Journalize the entry for payroll tax expense.

Exercise 9-2 On January 14, at the end of the second week of the year, the totals of Kwan Company's payroll register showed that its store employees' wages amounted to $30,432 and its warehouse wages amounted to $12,360. Withholdings consisted of federal income taxes, $4,152; Social Security taxes at the rate of 6.2 percent of the first $68,400; Medicare taxes at the rate of 1.45 percent on all earnings; union dues, $811.

a. Calculate the amount of Social Security and Medicare taxes to be withheld, and write the general journal entry to record the payroll.
b. Write the general journal entry to record the employer's payroll taxes, assuming that the federal unemployment tax is .8 percent of the first $7,000 and the state unemployment tax is 5.4 percent of the same base, and that no employee has surpassed the $7,000 limit.

P.O. 1

Journalize the payroll entries.

Exercise 9-3 File Systems had the following payroll data for wages for the week ended February 5:

TOTAL EARNINGS	ENDING CUMULATIVE EARNINGS	TAXABLE EARNINGS: UNEMPLOYMENT	TAXABLE EARNINGS: SOCIAL SECURITY	TAXABLE EARNINGS: MEDICARE	DEDUCTIONS: FEDERAL INCOME TAX	DEDUCTIONS: STATE INCOME TAX	DEDUCTIONS: SOCIAL SECURITY TAX	DEDUCTIONS: MEDICARE TAX
6750 00	72830 00	6750 00	6750 00	6750 00	822 00	155 00	418 50	97 88

a. Write the general journal entry to record the payroll.
b. Write the general journal entry to record the employer's payroll taxes. Assume rates of .8 percent for federal unemployment tax and 5.4 percent for state unemployment tax based on the first $7,000 for each employee and that no employee has earned more than $7,000.

P.O. 1

Journalize the entry for payroll tax expense.

Exercise 9-4 The following information on earnings and deductions for the pay period ended December 14 is from Lamba Company's payroll records:

Name	Gross Pay	Beginning Cumulative Earnings
Bremer, A. F.	$ 310	$ 6,620
Dugger, L. D.	760	38,100
Spulak, C. R.	1,080	62,800
Recknagle, L. W.	290	38,700
Carlisle, M. E.	590	62,400
Stevenson, D. H.	950	6,810

For each employee, the Social Security tax is 6.2 percent of the first $68,400, and the Medicare tax is 1.45 percent on all earnings. The federal unemployment tax is .8 percent of the first $7,000 of earnings of each employee. The state unemployment tax is 5.4 percent of the same base. Determine the total taxable earnings for unemployment, Social Security, and Medicare. Prepare a general journal entry to record the employer's payroll taxes.

P.O. 2

Journalize entries for payment of federal payroll taxes.

Exercise 9-5 Selected columns of Lau Company's payroll register for the month of January are as follows. The employees' FICA taxes are matched by the employer.

Payment Date	Employees' Federal Income Tax	Employees' Social Security Tax	Employees' Medicare Tax
Jan. 7	1,092.00	485.00	114.25
14	1,124.00	510.14	120.31
21	1,205.00	562.62	126.24
28	1,431.00	581.27	141.26

Lau Company deposits taxes monthly. Record the entry for payment of FICA and federal income taxes for employees and employer in general journal form.

P.O. 2,3

Journalize entries for payment of payroll taxes.

Exercise 9-6 On September 30, Krabb Company's selected account balances are as follows:

Employees' Federal Income Tax Payable	$ 2,169
FICA Tax Payable (employer and employee)	2,319
State Unemployment Tax Payable	1,308
Federal Unemployment Tax Payable	201
Salaries Payable	1,906
Salary Expense	32,738
Payroll Tax Expense	2,126

In general journal form, prepare the entries to record the following:

Oct. 15 Payment of liabilities for FICA and federal income tax.
31 Payment of liability for state unemployment tax.
31 Payment of liability for federal unemployment tax.

P.O. 2,3

Journalize entries for payment of payroll taxes.

Exercise 9-7 On September 30, Michilak Company's selected payroll accounts are as follows.

FICA Tax Payable			
−	+		
	Sept. 30	2,213.86	
	Sept. 30	2,213.86	

State Unemployment Tax Payable		
−	+	
	Sept. 30	1,217.83

Federal Unemployment Tax Payable		
−	+	
	Sept. 30	201.14

Employees' Federal Income Tax Payable		
−	+	
	Sept. 30	3,312.74

Prepare general journal entries to record the following:

Oct. 15 Payment of federal tax deposit of FICA and federal income tax.
31 Payment of state unemployment tax.
31 Payment of federal unemployment tax.

P.O. 7,8

Journalize entries for workers' compensation insurance.

Exercise 9-8 Mayeno Company received a premium notice on January 2 for workers' compensation insurance stating the rates for the new year. Estimated employees' earnings for the year are as follows:

Classification	Estimated Wages and Salaries	Rate Per Hundred	Estimated Premium
Office clerical	$ 91,000	.11	$ 100.10
Warehouse work	28,000	.92	257.60
Manufacturing	$265,000	1.20	3,180.00
			$3,537.70

At the end of the year, the exact figures for the payroll are as follows:

Classification	Estimated Wages and Salaries	Rate Per Hundred	Exact Premium
Office clerical	$ 92,000	.11	$ 101.20
Warehouse work	27,000	.92	248.40
Manufacturing	$268,000	1.20	3,216.00
			$3,565.60

a. Record the entry in general journal form for payment of the estimated premium.
b. Record the adjusting entries on December 31 for the insurance expired and for the additional premium.

WHAT IF . . .

The payroll clerk is working on the payroll register, specifically the Taxable Earnings columns for federal and state unemployment taxes and FICA taxes. The problem is that several employees' gross earnings are about to exceed the limits for unemployment and FICA taxes. For each employee whose cumulative earnings were near the limit, the payroll clerk multiplied the tax rate by the amount by which the employee's earnings exceeded the tax ceiling (not the amount between the beginning cumulative earnings and the tax limit). Comment on this procedure.

CRITICAL THINKING

It is December 15, and you are the payroll clerk for Listel Company. The owner has come to you for help; two employees have asked for a 4 percent pay raise, and the owner wants to know how much more such a raise will cost her next year. Present gross salaries are as follows:

Employee A		
$40,000/year	Married, with 2 allowances	Paid weekly
Employee B		
$42,000/year	Married, with 1 allowance	Paid weekly

Assume the following tax rates and limits:

Social Security, 6.2 percent with a limit of $68,400
Medicare, 1.45 percent with no limit (all earnings taxable)
SUTA, 5.4 percent with a limit of $7,000
FUTA, .8 percent with a limit of $7,000

What will be the cost to the employer of giving Employee A and Employee B the pay raise?

A MATTER OF ETHICS

An employer prepares the payroll and correctly computes the necessary withholding taxes. The employer pays accumulated employment taxes on the fifteenth of the next month. Payday is the last day of the month. However, between the end of one month and the fifteenth day of the next month, the balance in the employer's business bank account has been getting smaller and smaller. The employer has used the funds withheld from employees to pay some of the business's bills. He anticipates that enough of the customers who owe him money will pay their outstanding debts. If this assumption is true, the checking account will have enough in it to pay the federal deposit on the fifteenth of the month. Is the employer acting ethically, because he intends to have enough money in the account for the deposit?

WEB WORK

Using an Internet web browser, type *employment laws* in the search box and search for information about laws of hiring and firing in your state. Discuss or write your findings.

PROBLEM SET A

For additional help, see the demonstration problem at the beginning of each chapter in your Working Papers.

P.O. 1

Problem 9-1A Mezistrano Labs had the following payroll for the week ended February 28:

Salaries	
Technicians' salaries	$6,842.00
Office salaries	2,064.00
Total	$8,906.00

Deductions	
Federal income tax withheld	$ 684.00
Social Security tax withheld	552.17
Medicare tax withheld	129.14
Union dues withheld	180.00
Medical insurance	460.00
Total	$2,005.31

Assumed tax rates are as follows:

a. FICA: Social Security, 6.2 percent (.062) on the first $68,400 for each employee, and Medicare, 1.45 percent (.0145) on all earnings for each employee.

b. State unemployment tax, 5.4 percent (.054) on the first $7,000 for each employee.

c. Federal unemployment tax, .8 percent (.008) on the first $7,000 for each employee.

Check Figure
Payroll Tax Expense, $1,067.20

Instructions

Record the following entries in general journal form:

1. The payroll entry as of February 28.
2. The entry to record the employer's payroll taxes as of February 28, assuming that the total payroll is subject to the FICA tax (combined Social Security and Medicare) and that $6,224.00 is subject to unemployment taxes.
3. The payment of the employees on March 2 (assume that the company has transferred cash to Cash—Payroll Bank Account for this payroll).

P.O. 1

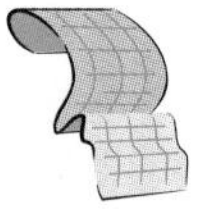

Problem 9-2A Temp Services has the following payroll information for the week ended December 7.

			Deductions	
Name	Beginning Cumulative Earnings	Total Earnings	Federal Income Tax	State Income Tax
Barker, T. C.	6,820.00	480.00	46.00	5.52
Ellis, M. R.	6,840.00	470.00	45.00	5.40
Fisk, B. L.	36,320.00	740.00	85.00	10.20
Janus, V. O.	26,200.00	540.00	55.00	6.60
Lenski, A. D.	68,523.00	1,389.00	238.00	28.56
Mais, E. G.	28,426.00	605.00	64.00	7.68

Assumed tax rates are as follows:

a. FICA: Social Security, 6.2 percent (.062) on the first $68,400 for each employee, and Medicare, 1.45 percent (.0145) on all earnings for each employee.
b. State unemployment tax, 5.4 percent (.054) on the first $7,000 for each employee.
c. Federal unemployment tax, .8 percent (.008) on the first $7,000 for each employee.

Check Figure
Payroll Tax Expense, $258.10

Instructions

1. Complete the payroll register, page 72.
2. Prepare a general journal entry to record the payroll as of December 7.
3. Prepare a general journal entry to record the payroll taxes as of December 7.
4. Journalize the entry to pay the payroll on December 9. (Assume that the company has transferred cash to the Cash—Payroll Bank Account for this payroll.)

P.O. 5

Problem 9-3A For the third quarter of the year, Jiang Company, 6227 Circle Avenue, Chicago, Illinois 60652, received Form 941 from the Internal Revenue Service. The identification number of Jiang Company is 76-4213171. Its payroll for the quarter ended September 30 is as follows.

	NAME	TOTAL EARNINGS	TAXABLE EARNINGS: UNEMPLOYMENT	TAXABLE EARNINGS: SOCIAL SECURITY	TAXABLE EARNINGS: MEDICARE	DEDUCTIONS: FEDERAL INCOME TAX	DEDUCTIONS: SOCIAL SECURITY TAX	DEDUCTIONS: MEDICARE TAX
1	Bailey, D. D.	6,579.00	421.00	6,579.00	6,579.00	646.00	407.90	95.40
2	Carter, L. E.	8,428.00	—	8,428.00	8,428.00	752.00	522.54	122.21
3	Dravski, P. A.	4,712.00	5,144.00	4,712.00	4,712.00	568.00	292.14	68.32
4	Gregor, V. O.	3,627.00	3,627.00	3,627.00	3,627.00	395.00	224.87	52.59
5	Temple, T. C.	7,830.00	—	7,830.00	7,830.00	702.00	485.46	113.54
6	Vorisky, O. T.	5,060.00	—	5,060.00	5,060.00	632.00	313.72	73.37
7		36,236.00	9,192.00	36,236.00	36,236.00	3,695.00	2,246.63	525.42

The company has had six employees throughout the year. Assume that the Social Security tax is 6.2 percent of the first $68,400, and that the Medicare tax is 1.45 percent of all earnings. The employer matches the employees' FICA (Social Security and Medicare) taxes. There are no taxable tips, adjustments, backup withholding, or earned income credits. Jiang Company has submitted the following federal tax deposits and written the accompanying checks:

	On August 15 for the July Payroll	On September 15 for the August Payroll	On October 15 for the September Payroll
Employees' income tax withheld	$1,280.00	$1,392.00	$1,023.00
Employees' Social Security and Medicare tax withheld	851.10	875.92	1,045.03
Employer's Social Security and Medicare tax contributed	851.10	875.92	1,045.03
	$2,982.20	$3,143.84	$3,113.06

Check Figure

Total taxes, $9,239.10

Instructions

Complete Form 941 dated October 31 for the owner, Byung Jiang.

P.O. 1,2,3

Problem 9-4A The Lautman Company has the following balances in its general ledger as of June 1 of this year:

a. FICA Tax Payable (liability for May), $1,806.42.
b. Employees' Federal Income Tax Payable (liability for May), $998.00.
c. Federal Unemployment Tax Payable (liability for April and May), $180.36.
d. State Unemployment Tax Payable (liability for April and May), $1,306.84.
e. Employees' Medical Insurance Payable (liability for April and May), $1,282.00.

The company completed the following transactions involving the payroll during June and July:

June 13 Issued check for $2,804.42, payable to Security Bank, for the monthly deposit of May FICA taxes and employees' federal income tax withheld.

30 Recorded the payroll entry in the general journal from the payroll register for June. The payroll register has the following column totals:

Sales salaries	$10,130.00	
Office salaries	4,068.00	
Total earnings		$14,198.00
Employees' federal income tax deductions	$ 1,422.00	
Employees' Social Security tax deductions	880.28	
Employees' Medicare tax deductions	205.87	
Employees' medical insurance deductions	710.00	
Total deductions		3,218.15
Net pay		$10,979.85

30 Recorded payroll taxes. Employer matches the employees' FICA taxes. State unemployment tax is 5.4 percent, and federal unemployment tax is .8 percent. At this time, all employees' earnings are taxable for FICA and unemployment taxes.

30 Issued check for $10,979.85 from Cash—Payroll Bank Account to pay salaries for the month.

July 14 Issued check for $1,992, payable to Careso Insurance Company, in payment of employees' medical insurance for April, May, and June.

14 Issued check for $3,594.30, payable to Security Bank, for the monthly deposit of June FICA taxes and employees' federal income tax withheld.

31 Issued check for $2,073.53, payable to the State Tax Commission, for state unemployment tax for April, May, and June. The check was accompanied by the quarterly tax return.

31 Issued check for $293.94, payable to Security Bank, for the deposit of federal unemployment tax for the months of April, May, and June.

Check Figure

Payroll Tax Expense, $1,966.42

Instructions

Record the transactions in the general journal, page 77.

Instructions for General Ledger Software

1. Record the transactions in the general journal.
2. Print the journal entries.

PROBLEM SET B

For additional help, see the demonstration problem at the beginning of each chapter in your Working Papers.

P.O. 1

Problem 9-1B Kovach Company had the following payroll for the week ended March 21:

Salaries		**Deductions**	
Sales salaries	$7,420.00	Federal income tax withheld	$ 790.00
Office salaries	1,791.00	Social Security tax withheld	571.08
Total	$9,211.00	Medicare tax withheld	133.56
		State income tax withheld	186.00
		U.S. savings bonds	200.00
		Total	$1,880.64

Assumed tax rates are as follows:

a. FICA: Social Security, 6.2 percent (.062) on the first $68,400 for each employee, and Medicare, 1.45 percent (.0145) on all earnings for each employee.
b. State unemployment tax, 5.4 percent (.054) on the first $7,000 for each employee.
c. Federal unemployment tax, .8 percent (.008) on the first $7,000 for each employee.

Check Figure
Payroll Tax Expense, $999.76

Instructions

Record the following entries in general journal form:

1. The payroll entry as of March 21.
2. The entry to record the employer's payroll taxes as of March 21, assuming that the total payroll is subject to the FICA tax (combined Social Security and Medicare) and that $4,760 is subject to unemployment taxes.
3. The payment of the employees on March 23. (Assume that the company has transferred cash to Cash—Payroll Bank Account for this payroll.)

P.O. 1

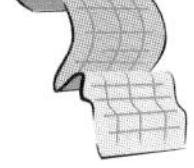

Problem 9-2B Kuo Agency has the following information for the week ended December 14:

	NAME	BEGINNING CUMULATIVE EARNINGS	TOTAL EARNINGS	DEDUCTIONS: FEDERAL INCOME TAX	DEDUCTIONS: STATE INCOME TAX
1	Born, R. E.	10,650.00	460.00	43.00	5.00
2	Gorzel, T. S.	38,820.00	970.00	123.00	27.00
3	Junko, E. G.	67,804.00	1,095.00	157.00	42.00
4	Long, P. D.	6,750.00	385.00	31.00	15.00
5	Phillips, S. D.	31,670.00	694.00	78.00	18.00
6	Quinn, D. L.	48,961.00	1,040.00	143.00	35.00
7					

Assumed tax rates are as follows:

a. FICA: Social Security, 6.2 percent (.062) on the first $68,400 for each employee, and Medicare, 1.45 percent (.0145) on all earnings for each employee.
b. State unemployment tax, 5.4 percent (.054) on the first $7,000 for each employee.
c. Federal unemployment tax, .8 percent (.008) on the first $7,000 for each employee.

Check Figure
Payroll Tax Expense, $339.83

Instructions

1. Complete the payroll register, page 72.
2. Prepare a general journal entry to record the payroll as of December 14. The company's general ledger contains a Salary Expense account and a Salaries Payable account.
3. Prepare a general journal entry to record the payroll taxes as of December 14.
4. Journalize the entry to pay the payroll on December 16. (Assume that the company has transferred cash to the Cash—Payroll bank account for this payroll.) Payroll checks begin with Ck. No. 923 in the payroll register.

P.O. 5

Problem 9-3B For the third quarter of the year, Freeman Construction, of 7144 Stone Boulevard, San Francisco, California 94421, received Form 941 from the District Office of the Internal Revenue Service. The identification number for Freeman Construction is 77-6271161. Its payroll for the quarter ended September 30 is as follows:

			TAXABLE EARNINGS			DEDUCTIONS		
	NAME	TOTAL EARNINGS	UNEMPLOYMENT	SOCIAL SECURITY	MEDICARE	FEDERAL INCOME TAX	SOCIAL SECURITY TAX	MEDICARE TAX
1	Brinnon, D. L.	3387 00	652 00	3387 00	3387 00	310 00	209 99	49 11
2	Finn, J. A.	6753 00	—	6753 00	6753 00	704 00	418 69	97 92
3	Harrell, N. E.	7780 00	—	7780 00	7780 00	820 00	482 36	112 81
4	Kelly, T. L.	6243 00	—	6243 00	6243 00	660 00	387 07	90 52
5	Morton, S. M.	4215 00	785 00	4215 00	4215 00	384 00	261 33	61 12
6	Rieck, A. J.	10264 00	—	10264 00	10264 00	1224 00	636 37	148 83
7		38642 00	1437 00	38642 00	38642 00	4102 00	2395 81	560 31

The company has had six employees throughout the year. Assume that the Social Security tax is 6.2 percent of the first $68,400 and that the Medicare tax is 1.45 percent of all earnings. The employer matches the employees' FICA (Social Security and Medicare) taxes. There are no taxable tips, adjustments, backup withholding, or earned income credits. Freeman Construction has submitted the following federal tax deposits and written the accompanying checks:

On August 15 for the July Payroll		On September 15 for the August Payroll		On October 15 for the September Payroll	
Employees' income tax withheld	$1,452.00	Employees' income tax withheld	$1,378.00	Employees' income tax withheld	$1,272.00
Employees' Social Security and Medicare tax withheld	984.80	Employees' Social Security and Medicare tax withheld	1,138.40	Employees' Social Security and Medicare tax withheld	832.92
Employer's Social Security and Medicare tax contributed	984.80	Employer's Social Security and Medicare tax contributed	1,138.40	Employer's Social Security and Medicare tax contributed	832.92
	$3,421.60		$3,654.80		$2,937.84

Check Figure
Total taxes, $10,014.24

Instructions

Complete Form 941 dated October 29 for the owner, Tony Freeman. *Note:* The .01 difference is recorded on line 9, Fraction of Cents.

P.O. 1,2,3

Problem 9-4B The Deupree Company has the following balances in its general ledger as of March 1 of this year:

a. FICA Tax Payable (liability for February), $1,405.20.
b. Employees' Federal Income Tax Payable (liability for February), $815.00.
c. State Unemployment Tax Payable (liability for January and February), $975.40.
d. Federal Unemployment Tax Payable (liability for January and February), $140.60.
e. Employees' Medical Insurance Payable (liability for January and February), $940.00.

The company completed the following transactions involving the payroll during March and April:

Mar. 12 Issued check for $2,220.20 payable to Coastal Bank, for monthly deposit of February FICA taxes and employees' federal income tax withheld.

31 Recorded the payroll entry in the general journal from the payroll register for March. The payroll register had the following column totals:

Sales salaries	$7,426.00	
Office salaries	1,837.00	
Total earnings		$9,263.00
Employees' federal income tax deductions	$ 752.00	
Employees' Social Security tax deductions	574.31	
Employees' Medicare tax deductions	134.31	
Employees' medical insurance deductions	490.00	
Total deductions		1,950.62
Net pay		$7,312.38

Mar. 31 Recorded payroll taxes. Employer matches the employees' FICA taxes. State unemployment tax is 5.4 percent. Federal unemployment tax is .8 percent. At this time, all employees' earnings are taxable for FICA and unemployment taxes.

31 Issued check for $7,312.38 from Cash—Payroll Bank Account to pay the salaries for the month.

Apr. 3 Issued check for $1,430, payable to Angel Insurance Company, for employees' medical insurance for January, February, and March.

14 Issued check for $2,169.24, payable to Coastal Bank, for monthly deposit of March FICA taxes and employees' federal income tax withheld.

30 Issued check for $1,475.60, payable to State Department of Revenue, for state unemployment tax for January, February, and March. The check was accompanied by the quarterly tax return.

30 Issued check, payable to Coastal Bank, for deposit of federal unemployment tax for January, February, and March, $214.70.

Check Figure

Payroll Tax Expense, $1,282.92

Instructions

Record the transactions in the general journal, page 77.

Instructions for General Ledger Software

1. Record the transactions in the general journal.
2. Print the journal entries.

Cumulative Self-Check: Chapters 7–9

PART I: COMPLETION

1. Checks issued by the depositor that have been paid or have cleared the bank are called ______________ checks.
2. A deposit that is not recorded on the bank statement because it was made after the bank's closing date for preparation of bank statements is called a(n) ______________.
3. The process by which the payee transfers ownership of the check to a bank or other party is called a(n) ______________.
4. The person to whom a check is payable is called the ______________.
5. A cash fund used to make small immediate cash payments is called a(n) ______________.

PART II: APPLICATION

1. Cora Thomas's salary is $1,775 per month. If she works more than 40 hours in one week, she is entitled to overtime pay at the rate of 1½ times her regular hourly rate. During the current week, she worked 45 hours. Calculate her gross pay.
2. On June 30, the column totals of Midway Cleaning's payroll register showed that its cleaning employees had earned $9,000 and its office employees had earned $3,000. Social Security taxes were withheld at 6.2 percent, and Medicare taxes were withheld at 1.45 percent. All earnings are taxable. Other deductions consisted of federal income tax, $1,500; U.S. savings bonds, $500; and medical insurance, $962. Determine the amount of Social Security and Medicare taxes that should be withheld. Record the general journal entry to record the payroll, crediting Salaries Payable for the net pay.
3. Rensel Company's payroll for the week ended December 31 is as follows:

Gross earnings of employees	$155,000
Social Security taxable earnings	143,000
Medicare taxable earnings	155,000
Federal unemployment taxable earnings	22,000
State unemployment taxable earnings	22,000

Note: Answers to the Cumulative Self-Check begin on page A-1.

Assume that the payroll is subject to Social Security tax of 6.2 percent (.062), Medicare tax of 1.45 percent (.0145), federal unemployment tax of .8 percent (.008), and state unemployment tax of 5.4 percent (.054). Write the entry in general journal form to record the employer's payroll tax expense.

PART III: TRUE/FALSE

T F 1. There is no limit on the amount of taxable earnings for Medicare.

T F 2. When journalizing the entry to reimburse the Petty Cash Fund, include a credit to Petty Cash Fund.

T F 3. When journalizing the entry to account for a customer's NSF check, debit Accounts Payable.

T F 4. An employee's net pay is the result of subtracting his or her deductions from gross pay.

T F 5. The gross pay for an employee who works 45 hours, earns \$8.50 per hour, and receives time and a half for hours worked past 40 hours is \$402.75.

10 The Sales Journal

WINDOWS ON THE WORLD WIDE WEB

If you bought a four-door Ford Explorer, Eddie Bauer edition, for around $35,000, Ford bookkeepers would record the transaction in a sales journal. If you changed your mind the next day and returned the Explorer to buy a Dodge Durango for $31,000 instead, Ford's records would need to show a sales return. Sales tax would have to be accounted for in the return as well. Your return of the Explorer affects numbers on Ford's income statement. And the dealership will have to make a journal entry to reduce sales totals for the month. Compare the price of new sport utility vehicles with financial statements for Ford Motor Company. For new car Blue Book values, visit Kelley Blue Book at **http://www.kbb.com/**. See Ford's annual reports at **http://www.ford.com/default.asp?pageid=37F**.

Performance Objectives

After you have completed this chapter, you will be able to do the following:

1. Describe the specific accounts used by a merchandising firm.
2. Record transactions in sales journals.
3. Post from sales journals to an accounts receivable ledger and a general ledger.
4. Prepare a schedule of accounts receivable.
5. Journalize sales returns and allowances, including credit memorandums and returns involving sales tax, and post to the ledger account.
6. Locate errors.
7. Post directly from sales invoices to an accounts receivable ledger and journalize and post a summarizing entry in the general journal.

By now you have had enough experience to complete the full accounting cycle for service and professional enterprises. To increase your accounting knowledge, let's introduce accounting systems for merchandising enterprises. This chapter describes specific accounts of merchandising firms; a merchandising firm can be anything from a dress shop to a supermarket. The sales journal and the accounts receivable ledger are also presented. We will use Jackson Electric Supply as a continuing example of a merchandising business.

SPECIAL JOURNALS

Any accounting system must be as efficient as possible. As a matter of fact, accounting is a means by which to measure efficiency in a business. Consequently, you should take shortcuts wherever possible without sacrificing internal control.

Special journals are books of original entry in which specialized types of repetitive transactions are recorded. Using a two-column general journal for recording transactions that take place over and over, day after day, is extremely time-consuming, because each individual debit and credit entry must be posted separately. Special journals save time by making it easier to handle specialized repetitive transactions and to divide up work.

The four most commonly used special journals are the sales journal (S) for sales of merchandise on account only, the purchases journal (P) for purchases of merchandise on account only (Ch. 11), the cash receipts journal (CR) for cash received (Ch. 12), and the cash payments journal (CP) for cash paid out (Ch. 12). If any or even all of these four journals are used, the general journal must still be used to record any *non*specialized transactions—in other words, any transactions that the special journals cannot handle. When a business uses more than one journal, it is necessary to use a letter in addition to the page number of the journal when posting to the ledger. **The letter designation for the general journal is J.**

SPECIFIC ACCOUNTS FOR MERCHANDISING FIRMS

Objective 1

Describe the specific accounts used by a merchandising firm.

A service or professional enterprise depends on the sale of its services for its revenue. Thus, a service or professional enterprise uses such accounts as Income from Services or Professional Fees. A merchandising business, on the other hand, depends on the sale of goods or merchandise for its revenue, recording the amount as credits to the Sales account.

Merchandise inventory consists of a stock of goods that a company buys and intends to resell, in the same physical condition, at a profit. Merchandise should be differentiated from other assets, such as equipment and supplies, that are acquired for use in the business and are not for resale.

Because the merchandising firm has to record transactions involving the purchase, handling, and sale of its merchandise, it uses accounts and procedures that we have not yet discussed. Let's look at the fundamental accounting equation with the new T accounts that are introduced in this and subsequent chapters.

The **Sales account** is a revenue account used for recording sales of merchandise.

The **Purchases account** is used strictly to record the cost of merchandise bought for resale. The plus and minus signs are the same as the signs for Merchandise Inventory. Purchases is placed under the heading of Expenses only because the accountant closes it along with the expense accounts at the end of the fiscal period.

The **Sales Returns and Allowances account** is used to record the physical return of merchandise by customers or a reduction in a bill because merchandise was damaged. It is treated as a deduction from Sales.

The **Purchases Returns and Allowances account** is used to record the company's returns of merchandise it has purchased from suppliers or reductions in bills because of damaged merchandise. It is treated as a deduction from Purchases.

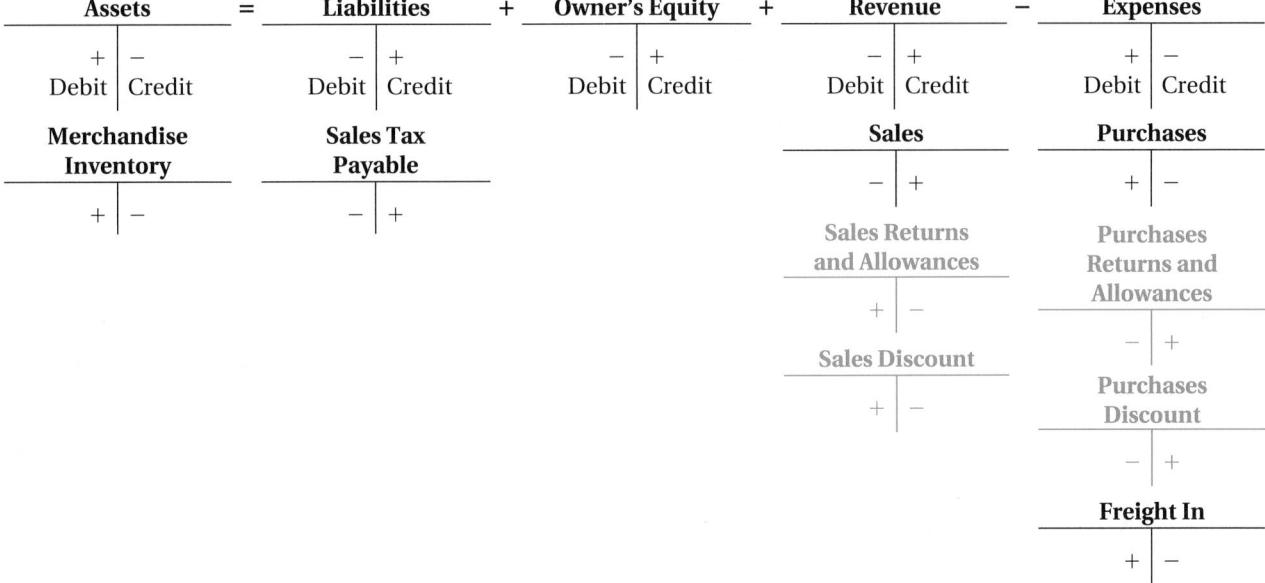

Assets		Liabilities		Owner's Equity		Revenue		Expenses
+ Debit | − Credit	=	− Debit | + Credit	+	− Debit | + Credit	+	− Debit | + Credit	−	+ Debit | − Credit
Merchandise Inventory + | −		**Sales Tax Payable** − | +				**Sales** − | +		**Purchases** + | −
						Sales Returns and Allowances + | −		**Purchases Returns and Allowances** − | +
						Sales Discount + | −		**Purchases Discount** − | +
								Freight In + | −

The **Sales Discount account** and **Purchases Discount account** are used to record cash discounts granted for prompt payments, in accordance with the credit terms.

The **Freight In account** is used to record the transportation charges on incoming merchandise intended for resale. Debits to this account increase the cost of purchases.

The T accounts for returns and allowances and for discounts are shown in green to emphasize that we are treating them as deductions from the related accounts placed above them. We list these accounts as deductions because they appear as deductions in the financial statements. Their relationship is similar to that between the Drawing account and the Capital account; remember that we deduct Drawing from Capital in the statement of owner's equity.

The type of transaction most frequently encountered in a merchandising business is the sale of merchandise. Some businesses sell on a cash-and-carry basis only; others sell only on credit. Many firms offer both arrangements. The same general types of entries pertain to retail and wholesale enterprises.

Sam Goody's
musicland
GOODY
GOT IT
SPECIAL VALUE
COMPACT DISCS

Merchandising firms such as Sam Goody's must differentiate merchandise—or goods bought to be resold at a profit—from other assets like equipment and supplies (goods used in the business but not resold).

RECORDING SALES ON ACCOUNT

Sales are recorded only in response to a customer order. The routines for processing orders and recording sales vary with the type and size of the business. However, a sale of merchandise on credit, such as a sale for $200, would be entered in a sales journal. Here's what this sale would look like in T accounts as a debit to Accounts Receivable and a credit to Sales.

Accounts Receivable		Sales	
+	−	−	+
200			200

In a retail business, a salesperson usually prepares a sales ticket in either duplicate or triplicate for a sale on account. One copy goes to the customer and another to the accounting department, where it serves as the basis for an entry in the sales journal. A third copy may be used as a record of sales—to compute sales commissions or control inventory, for example.

In a wholesale business, the company usually receives a written order from a customer or from a salesperson who obtained the order from the customer. The credit department approves the order, then sends it to the billing department, where the sales invoice is prepared.

Invoices are prepared in multiple copies. Figure 1 shows one possible distribution of sales invoice copies to various parties.

Our model business, Jackson Electric Supply, is a wholesaler. One of its invoices is shown in Figure 2.

We introduce the sales journal by looking at three transactions on the books of Jackson Electric Supply:

Aug. 1 Sold merchandise on account to L. A. Long Company, invoice no. 320, $424.00.

FIGURE 1

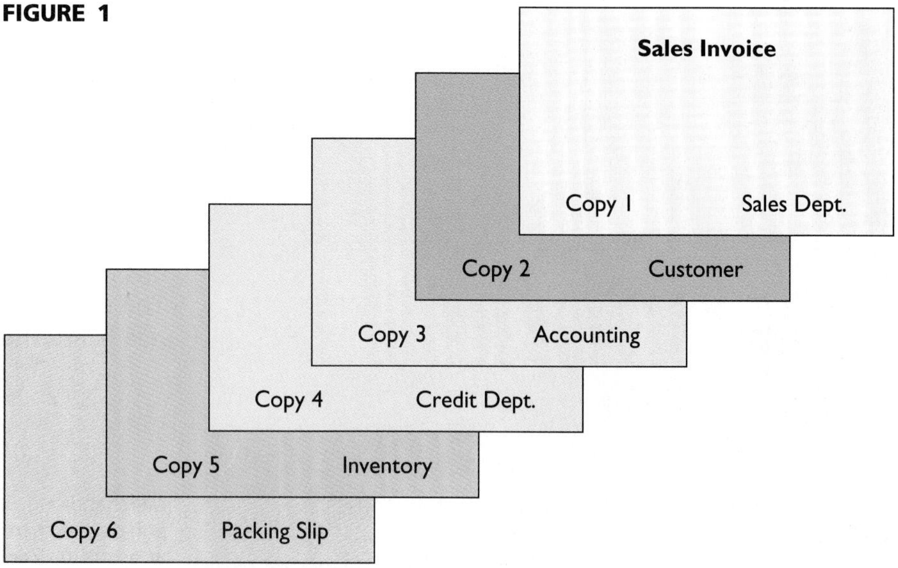
Sales Invoice
Copy I
Sales Dept.
Copy 2
Customer
Copy 3
Accounting
Copy 4
Credit Dept.
Copy 5
Inventory
Copy 6
Packing Slip

FIGURE 2

Jackson Electric Supply
625 N.E. Manor Avenue
Portland, Oregon 97201

INVOICE

SOLD TO L. A. Long Company
620 S.W. Kennedy Street
Portland, OR 97110

DATE: August 1, 20–
INVOICE NO.: 320
ORDER NO.: 5384
SHIPPED BY: Their truck
TERMS: 2/10, n/30

QUANTITY	DESCRIPTION	UNIT PRICE		TOTAL	
1000	Ivory duplex outlet cover		32	320	00
50	Ceiling junction box		96	48	00
40	Junction box (stud mount)	1	40	56	00
	TOTAL			424	00

Aug. 3 Sold merchandise on account to Marin, Inc., invoice no. 321, $116.
6 Sold merchandise on account to Arreloa Construction, invoice no. 322, $394.

We can use T accounts to visualize these transactions:

Accounts Receivable

+	−
424.00	
116.00	
394.00	

Sales

−	+
	424.00
	116.00
	394.00

If the transactions were recorded in a general journal, they would appear as they do in Figure 3 on the following page.

Next, the journal entries would be posted to the accounts in the general ledger (see Figure 3). As the last step in the posting process, the ledger account numbers would be recorded in the Post. Ref. column of the journal. (In each of the following ledger accounts, assume that there are no beginning balances.)

Obviously, there is a great deal of repetition in both journalizing and posting. The credit sales require three separate journal entries, three debit postings to Accounts Receivable, and three credit postings to Sales. We have presented all of this to show the advantages of the sales journal, which eliminates all this repetition.

FIGURE 3

GENERAL JOURNAL PAGE 23

	DATE		DESCRIPTION	POST. REF.	DEBIT	CREDIT	
1	20–						1
2	Aug.	1	Accounts Receivable	113	424 00		2
3			Sales	411		424 00	3
4			Invoice no. 320, L. A. Long				4
5			Company.				5
6							6
7		3	Accounts Receivable	113	116 00		7
8			Sales	411		116 00	8
9			Invoice no. 321, Marin, Inc.				9
10							10
11		6	Accounts Receivable	113	394 00		11
12			Sales	411		394 00	12
13			Invoice no. 322, Arreloa				13
14			Construction.				14
15							15
16							16
17							17

GENERAL LEDGER

ACCOUNT Accounts Receivable ACCOUNT NO. 113

	DATE		ITEM	POST. REF.	DEBIT	CREDIT	BALANCE DEBIT	BALANCE CREDIT	
1	20–								1
2	Aug.	1		23	424 00		424 00		2
3		3		23	116 00		540 00		3
4		6		23	394 00		934 00		4
5									5
6									6
7									7

ACCOUNT Sales ACCOUNT NO. 411

	DATE		ITEM	POST. REF.	DEBIT	CREDIT	BALANCE DEBIT	BALANCE CREDIT	
1	20–								1
2	Aug.	1		23		424 00		424 00	2
3		3		23		116 00		540 00	3
4		6		23		394 00		934 00	4
5									5
6									6
7									7

THE SALES JOURNAL

Objective 2

Record transactions in sales journals.

The **sales journal** records sales of merchandise *on account only.* This specialized type of transaction calls for debits to Accounts Receivable and credits to Sales. Let's see how to record the three transactions for Jackson Electric Supply in the sales journal *instead of* in the general journal.

Remember!

The sales journal is a book of original entry. Do not duplicate the transaction in the general journal.

SALES JOURNAL PAGE 38

	DATE		INV. NO.	CUSTOMER'S NAME	POST. REF.	ACCOUNTS RECEIVABLE DR. SALES CR.	
1	20–						1
2	Aug.	1	320	L. A. Long Company		424 00	2
3		3	321	Marin, Inc.		116 00	3
4		6	322	Arreloa Construction		394 00	4
5							5

Because *one* money column is headed Accounts Receivable Dr./Sales Cr., each transaction requires only a single line. Repetition is avoided, and all entries for sales of merchandise on account are found in one place. Listing the invoice number makes it easier to check the details of a particular sale at a later date.

Posting from the Sales Journal

Objective 3

Post from sales journals to an accounts receivable ledger and a general ledger.

Using the sales journal also saves time and space in posting to the ledger accounts. The transactions involving the sales of merchandise on account for the entire month of August are shown in Figure 4 on page 336.

Because every entry is a debit to Accounts Receivable and a credit to Sales, you can make a single posting to these accounts for the amount of the total as of the last day of the month. This entry is called a **summarizing entry** because it summarizes one month's transactions. In the Post. Ref. columns of the ledger accounts, the letter S designates the sales journal.

DISCOVER GOLD
Pepsi $1.79

A grocery store may have several sales accounts—one for groceries, one for produce, and one for meats, as well as one for sales tax.

FIGURE 4

SALES JOURNAL — PAGE 38

	DATE		INV. NO.	CUSTOMER'S NAME	POST. REF.	ACCOUNTS RECEIVABLE DR. SALES CR.	
1	20–						1
2	Aug.	1	320	L. A. Long Company		424 00	2
3		3	321	Marin, Inc.		116 00	3
4		6	322	Arreloa Construction		394 00	4
5		9	323	Markam Service Company		961 00	5
6		11	324	Colmer Company		772 24	6
7		16	325	Howard and Sons, Inc.		441 00	7
8		20	326	Hazen Electric		710 00	8
9		23	327	Baker Company		384 00	9
10		24	328	Colmer Company		293 22	10
11		28	329	Howard and Sons, Inc.		487 00	11
12		30	330	Baker Company		614 00	12
13		31	331	L. A. Long Company		375 50	13
14		31	332	F. A. Barnes, Inc.		861 00	14
15		31				6,832 96	15
16						(113)(411)	16
17							17

GENERAL LEDGER

ACCOUNT Accounts Receivable — ACCOUNT NO. 113

	DATE		ITEM	POST. REF.	DEBIT	CREDIT	BALANCE DEBIT	BALANCE CREDIT	
1	20–								1
2	Aug.	31		S38	6,832 96		6,832 96		2
3									3
4									4
5									5

ACCOUNT Sales — ACCOUNT NO. 411

	DATE		ITEM	POST. REF.	DEBIT	CREDIT	BALANCE DEBIT	BALANCE CREDIT	
1	20–								1
2	Aug.	31		S38		6,832 96		6,832 96	2
3									3
4									4
5									5

After posting the total of the Sales Journal to the Accounts Receivable account in the general ledger, write the account number of Accounts Receivable at the left below the total of the Sales Journal. Repeat the process of posting for the total of the Sales Journal to the general ledger, placing the account number of Sales at the right below the total of the sales journal. **Don't record these account numbers until you have completed the postings.**

If you should find an error, do not erase it. The same procedure for error correction that you learned earlier applies to special journals. If you catch the error in the journal entry before it is posted to the ledger, draw a single line through the error with a ruler, write in the correct information, and add your initials. If an amount is entered in the ledger incorrectly (although the journal entry is correct), follow the same procedure. However, if an entry included the wrong accounts, you must prepare a new journal entry to correct the first entry.

Remember!

The purpose of posting reference numbers is to tell where in the ledger an amount was posted or the journal from which it came.

Sales Journal Provision for Sales Tax

Most states and some cities levy a **sales tax** on retail sales of goods and services. The retailer collects the sales tax from customers and later pays it to the tax authorities.

When goods or services are sold on credit, the sales tax is charged to the customer and recorded at the time of the sale. The sales journal must be designed to handle this type of transaction. For example, if a retail store sells an item for $100 and the sales tax is 4 percent, the transaction would be recorded in T accounts like this:

Accounts Receivable		Sales		Sales Tax Payable	
+	−	−	+	−	+
104			100		4

Incidentally, when the sales tax is paid to the state, the accountant debits Sales Tax Payable and credits Cash.

Because we want to illustrate a sales journal for a retail merchandising firm operating in a state that has a sales tax, we will talk about the transactions of Freel Toy Center, another company. Its sales journal follows.

SALES JOURNAL PAGE 96

DATE		INV. NO.	CUSTOMER'S NAME	POST. REF.	ACCOUNTS RECEIVABLE DEBIT	SALES TAX PAYABLE CREDIT	SALES CREDIT
20–							
Apr.	1	9382	D. E. Bates		16 64	64	16 00
	1	9383	Center Child Care		22 88	88	22 00
	1	9384	Randy Kelley		52 00	2 00	50 00
	2	9385	R. M. Kale		12 48	48	12 00
	30	10121	L. O. Link		124 80	4 80	120 00
	30				2518 80	96 80	2422 00
					(113)	(214)	(411)

Remember!

With a sales journal that has more than one column, use the column totals to prove that the total debits equal the total credits. Do this before posting to the general ledger accounts.

The total of each column is posted to the ledger accounts at the end of the month. After posting the figures, the accountant records the account numbers in parentheses immediately below the totals. Note that Freel Toy Center's charge customers owe the total amount of the sales plus the sales tax, $2,518.80 ($2,422 + $96.80 = $2,518.80).

GENERAL LEDGER

ACCOUNT **Accounts Receivable** ACCOUNT NO. **113**

DATE		ITEM	POST. REF.	DEBIT	CREDIT	BALANCE DEBIT	BALANCE CREDIT
20–							
Apr.	30		S96	2 5 1 8 80		2 5 1 8 80	

ACCOUNT **Sales Tax Payable** ACCOUNT NO. **214**

DATE		ITEM	POST. REF.	DEBIT	CREDIT	BALANCE DEBIT	BALANCE CREDIT
20–							
Apr.	30		S96		9 6 80		9 6 80

ACCOUNT **Sales** ACCOUNT NO. **411**

DATE		ITEM	POST. REF.	DEBIT	CREDIT	BALANCE DEBIT	BALANCE CREDIT
20–							
Apr.	30		S96		2 4 2 2 00		2 4 2 2 00

THE ACCOUNTS RECEIVABLE LEDGER

Accounts Receivable represents the total amount owed to a business by its charge customers. The information in this account is incomplete, however. The business can't tell at a glance *how much each* individual charge customer owes. To correct this shortcoming, businesses keep a separate account for each charge customer.

When a business has very few charge customers, it is possible to have a separate Accounts Receivable account in the general ledger for each charge customer. However, when there are many charge customers, which is usually the case, this arrangement is too cumbersome. Listing each charge customer's account makes the trial balance very long and there is a greater likelihood of errors.

It is more practical to have a separate book containing a list of all the charge customers with their respective balances. This is called the **accounts receivable ledger**. In the accounts receivable ledger, the individual charge customer accounts are listed in either alphabetical or numerical order. If the company's accounting system is not computerized, accountants prefer a loose-leaf binder, so that they can insert accounts for new customers and remove closed accounts.

The Accounts Receivable account in the general ledger should still be maintained. When all the postings are up to date, the balance of this account should equal the total of all the charge customers' individual balances. The Accounts Receivable account in the general ledger is called a **controlling account**. The accounts receivable *ledger,* containing the accounts of all the charge customers, is really a special ledger, called a **subsidiary ledger**. Figure 5 diagrams the interrelationship of these ledgers.

FIGURE 5

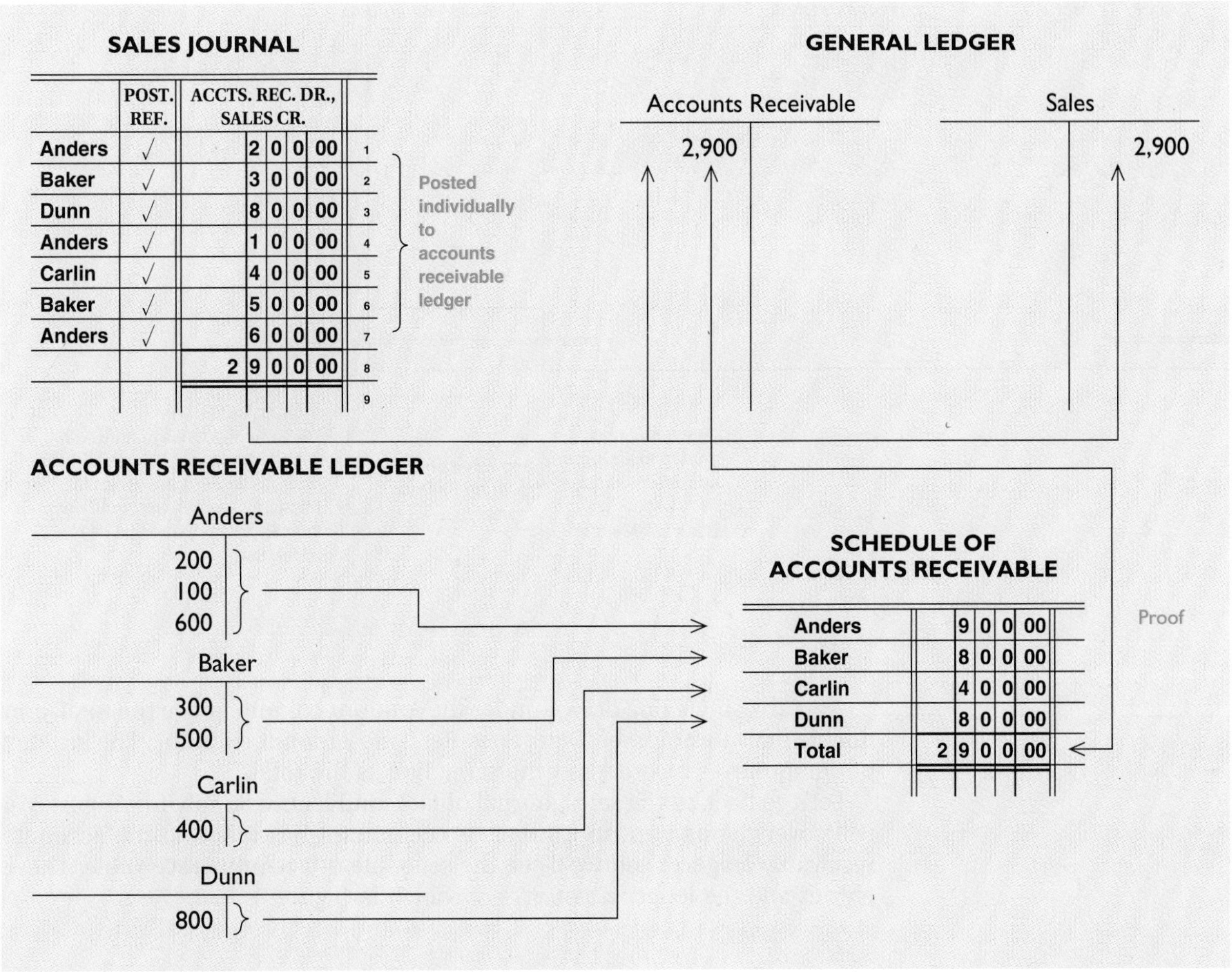
SALES JOURNAL
POST. REF.
ACCTS. REC. DR., SALES CR.
Anders √ 200 00 1
Baker √ 300 00 2
Dunn √ 800 00 3
Anders √ 100 00 4
Carlin √ 400 00 5
Baker √ 500 00 6
Anders √ 600 00 7
2,900 00 8
9
Posted individually to accounts receivable ledger
GENERAL LEDGER
Accounts Receivable
2,900
Sales
2,900
ACCOUNTS RECEIVABLE LEDGER
Anders
200
100
600
Baker
300
500
Carlin
400
Dunn
800
SCHEDULE OF ACCOUNTS RECEIVABLE
Anders 900 00
Baker 800 00
Carlin 400 00
Dunn 800 00
Total 2,900 00
Proof

■ ■ ■

Remember!

The balance of the Accounts Receivable controlling account at the end of the month must equal the total of the balances of the charge customer accounts in the accounts receivable ledger.

The accountant posts the individual amounts to the accounts receivable ledger every day, so that this ledger will have up-to-date information. At the end of the month, the accountant posts the total of the sales journal of $2,900 (in Figure 5) to the general ledger accounts as a debit to the Accounts Receivable controlling account and a credit to the Sales account. The schedule of accounts receivable is merely a listing of charge customers' individual balances.

In the simplified illustration in Figure 5, it just so happens that, since no payments were received from charge customers, the total of the sales journal equals the balance of Accounts Receivable. However, if $1,200 had been received from charge customers, both the balance of the Accounts Receivable controlling account and the total of the schedule of accounts receivable would be $1,700 ($2,900 − $1,200). The total of the sales journal would still be $2,900.

After you post an amount from the sales journal to a charge customer's account in the accounts receivable ledger, put a check mark (✓) in the Post. Ref. column of the sales journal. Figure 6 shows the posting procedure for a single-column sales journal.

FIGURE 6

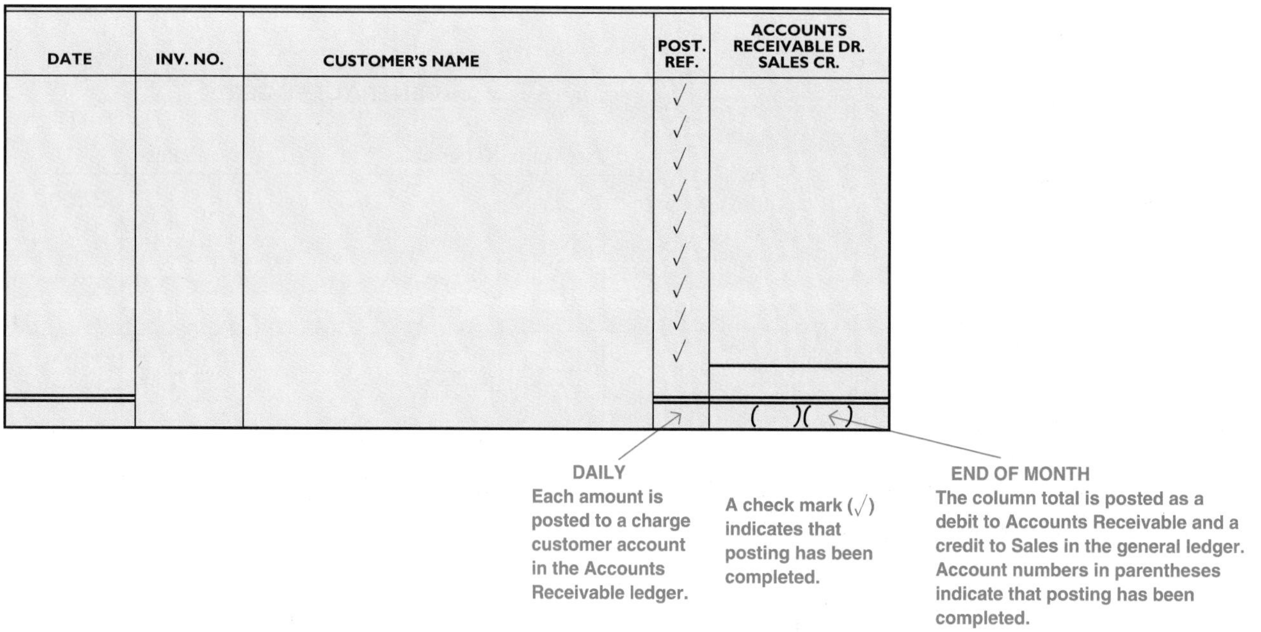

DATE	INV. NO.	CUSTOMER'S NAME	POST. REF.	ACCOUNTS RECEIVABLE DR. SALES CR.
			✓	
			✓	
			✓	
			✓	
			✓	
			✓	
			✓	
			✓	
			✓	
			↗	( )(↵)

DAILY
Each amount is posted to a charge customer account in the Accounts Receivable ledger.

A check mark (√) indicates that posting has been completed.

END OF MONTH
The column total is posted as a debit to Accounts Receivable and a credit to Sales in the general ledger. Account numbers in parentheses indicate that posting has been completed.

Note the single line drawn under the Amount column above the total, and double lines through the Date, Post. Ref., and Amount columns. The last day of the month is recorded on the same line as the total.

Let's go back to the sales journal of Jackson Electric Supply for August. We will cover the daily postings that its accountant has made to the accounts receivable ledger. Then we'll see the schedule of accounts receivable. These entries and the ledger accounts are shown in Figure 7.

FIGURE 7

Remember!

The check marks in the Post. Ref. column indicate that the amounts have been posted to the individual charge customer accounts in the accounts receivable ledger.

SALES JOURNAL PAGE 38

DATE		INV. NO.	CUSTOMER'S NAME	POST. REF.	ACCOUNTS RECEIVABLE DR. SALES CR.
20–					
Aug.	1	320	L. A. Long Company	✓	424.00
	3	321	Marin, Inc.	✓	116.00
	6	322	Arreloa Construction	✓	394.00
	9	323	Markam Service Company	✓	961.00
	11	324	Colmer Company	✓	772.24
	16	325	Howard and Sons, Inc.	✓	441.00
	20	326	Hazen Electric	✓	710.00
	23	327	Baker Company	✓	384.00
	24	328	Colmer Company	✓	293.22
	28	329	Howard and Sons, Inc.	✓	487.00
	30	330	Baker Company	✓	614.00
	31	331	L. A. Long Company	✓	375.50
	31	332	F. A. Barnes, Inc.	✓	861.00
	31				6,832.96
					(113)(411)

Remember!

The normal balance in the accounts receivable ledger is a debit, because the customer accounts represent assets.

ACCOUNTS RECEIVABLE LEDGER

NAME Arreloa Construction
ADDRESS 1016 Broad Street, S.W.
Seattle, WA 98102

DATE		ITEM	POST. REF.	DEBIT	CREDIT	BALANCE
20–						
Aug.	6		S38	394.00		394.00

NAME Baker Company
ADDRESS 271 N. Kinman Street
Bishop, WA 98792

DATE		ITEM	POST. REF.	DEBIT	CREDIT	BALANCE
20–						
Aug.	23		S38	384.00		384.00
	30		S38	614.00		998.00

FIGURE 7 (continued)

NAME F. A. Barnes, Inc.
ADDRESS 424 Fifteenth Street
Bridger, OR 97816

DATE		ITEM	POST. REF.	DEBIT	CREDIT	BALANCE
20–						
Aug.	31		S38	861.00		861.00

NAME Colmer Company
ADDRESS 2168 Tenth Street
Southridge, WA 98206

DATE		ITEM	POST. REF.	DEBIT	CREDIT	BALANCE
20–						
Aug.	11		S38	772.24		772.24
	24		S38	293.22		1,065.46

NAME Hazen Electric
ADDRESS 1620 Salazar Road
Brighton, OR 97414

DATE		ITEM	POST. REF.	DEBIT	CREDIT	BALANCE
20–						
Aug.	20		S38	710.00		710.00

NAME Howard and Sons, Inc.
ADDRESS 4142 Lucientes Avenue
Pender, OR 97512

DATE		ITEM	POST. REF.	DEBIT	CREDIT	BALANCE
20–						
Aug.	16		S38	441.00		441.00
	28		S38	487.00		928.00

FIGURE 7 (continued)

NAME **L. A. Long Company**
ADDRESS **620 S.W. Kennedy Street**
Portland, OR 97110

DATE		ITEM	POST. REF.	DEBIT	CREDIT	BALANCE
20–						
Aug.	1		S38	424.00		424.00
	31		S38	375.50		799.50

NAME **Marin, Inc.**
ADDRESS **1457 Megler Avenue**
Gabriola, OR 97316

DATE		ITEM	POST. REF.	DEBIT	CREDIT	BALANCE
20–						
Aug.	3		S38	116.00		116.00

NAME **Markam Service Company**
ADDRESS **2720 N.W. 43rd Ave.**
Portland, OR 97210

DATE		ITEM	POST. REF.	DEBIT	CREDIT	BALANCE
20–						
Aug.	9		S38	961.00		961.00

Objective 4

Prepare a schedule of accounts receivable.

Next, the accountant prepares a schedule of accounts receivable, listing each charge customer's balance. For this example, we assume that these were the only transactions involving charge customers.

Jackson Electric Supply
Schedule of Accounts Receivable
August 31, 20—

Arreloa Construction	394.00
Baker Company	998.00
F. A. Barnes, Inc.	861.00
Colmer Company	1,065.46
Hazen Electric	710.00
Howard and Sons, Inc.	928.00
L. A. Long Company	799.50
Marin, Inc.	116.00
Markam Service Company	961.00
Total Accounts Receivable	6,832.96

Again assume that there were no previous balances in the customers' accounts. The Accounts Receivable controlling account in the general ledger will have the same balance, $6,832.96, as the schedule of accounts receivable.

GENERAL LEDGER

ACCOUNT **Accounts Receivable** ACCOUNT NO. **113**

DATE		ITEM	POST. REF.	DEBIT	CREDIT	BALANCE DEBIT	BALANCE CREDIT
20–							
Aug.	31		S38	6,832.96		6,832.96	

SALES RETURNS AND ALLOWANCES

Objective 5

Journalize sales returns and allowances, including credit memorandums and returns involving sales tax, and post to the ledger accounts.

The Sales Returns and Allowances account handles two types of transactions having to do with merchandise that has previously been sold. A *return* is a physical return of the goods. An *allowance* is a reduction from the original price because the goods were defective or damaged. It may not be economically worthwhile to have customers return the goods; each situation is a special case. To avoid writing a separate letter each time to inform customers of their account adjustments, businesses use a special form called a **credit memorandum**. A credit memorandum (Figure 8) is a written statement indicating a seller's willingness to reduce the amount of a buyer's debt.

FIGURE 8

Jackson Electric Supply
625 N.E. Manor Avenue
Portland, Oregon 97201

CREDIT MEMORANDUM **No. 69**

CREDIT TO: Baker Company
271 N. Kinman Street
Bishop, WA 98792

DATE: September 2, 20–

WE CREDIT YOUR ACCOUNT AS FOLLOWS:

QUANTITY	DESCRIPTION	TOTAL
1	Entrance panel circuit breaker, 100 amp 120v-12 circuits	54.00

FYI

A company must manage its return policy carefully. Customers often take advantage of return privileges, creating significant handling costs for the merchant.

The Sales Returns and Allowances account is a deduction from Sales. Using an account separate from Sales provides a better record of the total returns and allowances. Accountants deduct Sales Returns and Allowances from Sales on the income statement.

Using T accounts, here's an example of a return. The original sale is shown first, followed by the issuance of a credit memorandum.

Transaction (a) On August 30, Jackson Electric Supply sold merchandise on account to Baker Company, $614, and recorded the sale in the sales journal.

Transaction (b) On September 2, Baker Company returned $54 worth of the merchandise. Jackson Electric Supply issued credit memorandum no. 69 (see Figure 8).

Assets		=	**Liabilities**		+	**Owner's Equity**		+	**Revenue**		−	**Expenses**	
+	−		−	+		−	+		−	+		+	−
Debit	Credit		Debit	Credit		Debit	Credit		Debit	Credit		Debit	Credit

Accounts Receivable

+	−
(a) 614	(b) 54

Sales

−	+
	(a) 614

Sales Returns and Allowances

+	−
(b) 54	

Remember!

Since Sales Returns and Allowances is a deduction from Sales, the plus and minus signs are reversed.

Jackson Electric Supply's accountant debits Sales Returns and Allowances because Jackson Electric Supply has more returns and allowances than it had before. The accountant credits Accounts Receivable because the charge customer, Baker Company, owes less than before.

You use the word *credit* in "credit memorandum" because the seller has to credit Accounts Receivable. Suppose that Jackson Electric Supply issues two credit memoranda during September and makes the following entries in the general journal:

GENERAL JOURNAL PAGE 27

	Date		Description	Post. Ref.	Debit	Credit	
1	20–						1
2	Sept.	2	Sales Returns and Allowances		54 00		2
3			Accounts Receivable,				3
4			Baker Company			54 00	4
5			Issued credit memo no. 69.				5
6							6
7		2	Sales Returns and Allowances		127 00		7
8			Accounts Receivable,				8
9			Markam Service Company			127 00	9
10			Issued credit memo no. 70.				10

Remember!

When a credit memo is issued, it means we have given the customer permission to return the goods or to receive an allowance.

The general journal entry serves as the posting source for crediting the Accounts Receivable controlling account in the general ledger. It also serves as the posting source for updating the accounts receivable ledger and therefore includes the name of the charge customer. If the balance of the Accounts Receivable controlling account is to equal the total of the individual balances in the accounts receivable ledger, you must post the amount to *both* the Accounts Receivable account in the general ledger *and* the account of Baker Company in the accounts receivable ledger. To take care of this dual posting, draw a slanted line in the Post. Ref. column. When the amount has been posted as a credit to the general ledger account, write the account number of Accounts Receivable in the left part of the Post. Ref. column. After the amount has been posted as a credit to the account of Baker Company, draw a check mark in the right portion of the Post. Ref. column. Sales Returns and Allowances is posted in the usual manner. Here are the entries after posting is complete:

GENERAL JOURNAL PAGE 27

	DATE		DESCRIPTION	POST. REF.	DEBIT	CREDIT	
1	20–						1
2	Sept.	2	Sales Returns and Allowances	412	54 00		2
3			Accounts Receivable,				3
4			Baker Company	113/✓		54 00	4
5			Issued credit memo no. 69.				5
6							6
7		2	Sales Returns and Allowances	412	127 00		7
8			Accounts Receivable,				8
9			Markam Service Company	113/✓		127 00	9
10			Issued credit memo no. 70.				10

GENERAL LEDGER

ACCOUNT Accounts Receivable ACCOUNT NO. 113

	DATE		ITEM	POST. REF.	DEBIT	CREDIT	BALANCE DEBIT	BALANCE CREDIT	
1	20–								1
2	Aug.	31		S38	6,832 96		6,832 96		2
3	Sept.	2		J27		54 00	6,778 96		3
4		2		J27		127 00	6,651 96		4
5									5

ACCOUNT Sales Returns and Allowances ACCOUNT NO. 412

	DATE		ITEM	POST. REF.	DEBIT	CREDIT	BALANCE DEBIT	BALANCE CREDIT	
1	20–								1
2	Sept.	2		J27	54 00		54 00		2
3		2		J27	127 00		181 00		3

ACCOUNTS RECEIVABLE LEDGER

NAME Baker Company
ADDRESS 271 N. Kinman Steet
Bishop, WA 98792

DATE		ITEM	POST. REF.	DEBIT	CREDIT	BALANCE
20–						
Aug.	23		S38	384 00		384 00
	30		S38	614 00		998 00
Sept.	2		J27		54 00	944 00

NAME Markam Service Company
ADDRESS 2720 N.W. 43rd Ave.
Portland, OR 97210

DATE		ITEM	POST. REF.	DEBIT	CREDIT	BALANCE
20–						
Aug.	9		S38	961 00		961 00
Sept.	2		J27		127 00	834 00

NO REFUNDS
EXCHANGES OR CREDIT ONLY

When a customer returns merchandise bought on account, the business issues a credit memorandum, which is a written statement that the seller is willing to reduce the buyer's debt. The entry is entered in the general journal if the sale was on account.

Sales Return Involving a Sales Tax

If a customer who returns merchandise to a retail store was originally charged a sales tax, the sales tax must be returned to the customer. Refer back to the sales journal of Freel Toy Center on page 337, which included sales taxes. On April 3, assume that D. E. Bates returns the merchandise bought on April 1 for $16 plus $.64 sales tax. Following is the general journal entry required for this type of return:

GENERAL JOURNAL PAGE 12

	DATE		DESCRIPTION	POST. REF.	DEBIT	CREDIT	
1	20–						1
2	Apr.	3	Sales Returns and Allowances		16 00		2
3			Sales Tax Payable		64		3
4			Accounts Receivable, D. E. Bates			16 64	4
5			Issued credit memo no. 371.				5
6							6
7							7

Procedure for Locating Errors

Objective 6

Locate errors.

Suppose you are facing a situation where the total of the schedule of accounts receivable does not equal the balance of the Accounts Receivable controlling account. To locate possible errors, do everything in reverse. Here is a suggested order:

1. Re-add the schedule of accounts receivable.
2. Check the balances transferred from the customer accounts in the accounts receivable ledger to the schedule of accounts receivable.
3. Verify the balances of the customer accounts in the accounts receivable ledger.
4. Verify the postings from the sales and general journals to the Accounts Receivable controlling account.
5. Re-add the sales journal.
6. Check the postings from the sales and general journals to the customer accounts in the accounts receivable ledger.

POSTING DIRECTLY FROM SALES INVOICES (AN ALTERNATIVE TO USING A SALES JOURNAL)

Objective 7

Post directly from sales invoices to an accounts receivable ledger and journalize and post a summarizing entry in the general journal.

Companies that have a large volume of sales on account sometimes use duplicate copies of their sales invoices as a sales journal. The accountant posts daily to the charge customer accounts in the accounts receivable ledger, working directly from the copies of the sales invoices or sales slips. He or she writes the invoice number rather than the journal page in the Post. Ref. column of the customer's account. A file is maintained for the copies of the sales invoices. Then, at the end of the month, the accountant brings the Accounts Receivable controlling account up to date by totaling all the sales invoices for the month and then making a general journal entry debiting Accounts Receivable and crediting Sales.

Let's use a different firm to show how this procedure works. Gordon Sports Equipment Company posts directly from its sales invoices; the total of its sales invoices for December is $37,426. Its accountant journalizes and posts the entry as follows:

Remember!

Posting directly from sales invoices is an alternative to the special sales journal; don't do both.

GENERAL JOURNAL PAGE 36

DATE		DESCRIPTION	POST. REF.	DEBIT	CREDIT
20–					
Dec.	31	Accounts Receivable	113	37 4 2 6 00	
		Sales	411		37 4 2 6 00
		Summarizing entry for the total			
		of the sales invoices for the			
		month.			

GENERAL LEDGER

ACCOUNT Accounts Receivable ACCOUNT NO. 113

DATE		ITEM	POST. REF.	DEBIT	CREDIT	BALANCE DEBIT	BALANCE CREDIT
20–							
Dec.	31		J36	37,426.00		37,426.00	

ACCOUNT Sales ACCOUNT NO. 411

DATE		ITEM	POST. REF.	DEBIT	CREDIT	BALANCE DEBIT	BALANCE CREDIT
20–							
Dec.	31		J36		37,426.00		37,426.00

This journal entry is a *summarizing entry* because it summarizes the credit sales for one month. Because the accountant posts the entry to the accounts in the general ledger, there is no need for a sales journal; the one summarizing entry in the general journal records the total sales for the month.

One invoice and the corresponding entry in the accounts receivable ledger might look like Figure 9 and the accompanying ledger account on the following page. The $855 is posted to the general ledger as a part of the total in the monthly summarizing entry.

FIGURE 9

Gordon Sports Equipment Company
1620 Santa Rosa Avenue
San Francisco, California 94133

INVOICE

SOLD TO Norton Sporting Goods
225 N.W. Satsop Ave.
Portland, OR 97201

DATE: Dec. 4, 20–
INVOICE NO.: 6075
ORDER NO.: 359
SHIPPED BY: Express Collect
TERMS: 2/10, n/30

QUANTITY	DESCRIPTION	UNIT PRICE	TOTAL
10	Fentris cartop bicycle carrier No. 561N	85.50	855.00

Remember!

The process of posting directly from sales invoices is a shortcut, but it does not eliminate the need to keep the accounts of individual charge customers current. Otherwise, you could not bill customers accurately, let alone collect from them.

ACCOUNTS RECEIVABLE LEDGER

NAME Norton Sporting Goods
ADDRESS 225 N.W. Satsop Ave.
Portland, OR 97201

DATE		ITEM	POST. REF.	DEBIT	CREDIT	BALANCE
20–						
Dec.	4		6075	855 00		855 00

CHAPTER REVIEW

Review of Performance Objectives

1. Describe the specific accounts used by a merchandising firm.

   The Merchandise Inventory account is an asset account representing the cost of goods bought for resale. The Sales Tax Payable account is a liability account representing amounts owed to each appropriate entity. The Sales account is a revenue account representing the total sales of merchandise. The Sales Returns and Allowances account is a deduction from the Sales account, representing amounts allowed for returns of merchandise and damaged goods. The Sales Discount account is a deduction from the Sales account, representing amounts deducted for prompt payments. The Purchases account is a cost (expense) account representing the costs of goods bought for resale. The Purchases Returns and Allowances account is a deduction from the Purchases account, representing amounts granted by suppliers for the return of merchandise or damaged goods. The Purchases Discount account is a deduction from the Purchases account, representing amounts suppliers allow for prompt payments. The Freight In account is a cost representing the transportation charges on incoming merchandise.

2. Record transactions in sales journals.

   The sales journal is used to record sales of merchandise on account only. An entry can be recorded on one line. The date, invoice number, and customer's name are listed, along with the amount of the invoice in the Accounts Receivable Dr./Sales Cr. column. In states where there is a sales tax an additional column exists called Sales Tax Payable Cr. In this multicolumn sales journal the sales plus the sales tax represents the amount owed by the customer.

3. Post from sales journals to an accounts receivable ledger and a general ledger.

   The entries are posted daily to the accounts receivable ledger. At the end of the month, the total is posted to the general ledger as a debit to the Accounts Receivable controlling account and a credit to the Sales account.

4. Prepare a schedule of accounts receivable.

   The schedule of accounts receivable consists of a listing of the individual account balances of the charge customers taken from the accounts receivable ledger.

5. Journalize sales returns and allowances, including credit memorandums and returns involving sales tax, and post to the ledger accounts.

When a customer returns merchandise, or when his or her bill is reduced owing to an allowance for defective or damaged merchandise, the Sales Returns and Allowances account is debited and the Accounts Receivable account is credited. The entry is recorded in the general journal and posted to both the general ledger and the accounts receivable ledger.

6. Locate errors.

   If, at the end of the month, the balance of the Accounts Receivable controlling account does not equal the total of the schedule of accounts receivable, accountants must retrace their steps to locate the errors.

7. Post directly from sales invoices to an accounts receivable ledger and journalize and post a summarizing entry in the general journal.

   Another shortcut is using sales invoices or sales slips as a sales journal, thereby doing away with the sales journal. Post to the charge customer accounts in the accounts receivable ledger directly from the sales invoices. At the end of the month, add all the sales invoices and make a summarizing entry in the general journal for the amount of the total. This entry is a debit to Accounts Receivable and a credit to Sales.

Glossary

Accounts receivable ledger A subsidiary ledger that lists the individual accounts of charge customers in either alphabetical or numerical order, with their respective balances. (339)

Controlling account An account in the general ledger that summarizes the balances of a subsidiary ledger. (339)

Credit memorandum A written statement indicating a seller's willingness to reduce the amount of a buyer's debt. The seller records the amount of the credit memorandum in the Sales Returns and Allowances account. (344)

Freight In account The account used to record transportation charges on incoming merchandise intended for resale. (331)

Merchandise inventory A stock of goods (an asset account) that a company buys and intends to resell, in the same physical condition, at a profit. (330)

Purchases account An account for recording the cost of merchandise acquired for resale. (330)

Purchases Discount account An account that records cash discounts granted by suppliers in return for prompt payment; it is treated as a deduction from Purchases. (331)

Purchases Returns and Allowances account An account that records a company's return of merchandise it has purchased or a reduction in the bill because of damaged merchandise; it is treated as a deduction from Purchases. (331)

Sales account A revenue account for recording the sale of merchandise. (330)

Sales Discount account An account that records a deduction from the original price, granted by the seller to the buyer for the prompt payment of an invoice. (331)

Sales journal A special journal for recording the sale of merchandise on account only. (335)

Sales Returns and Allowances account The account a seller uses to record the physical return of merchandise by customers or a reduction in a bill because merchandise was damaged. Sales Returns and Allowances is treated as a deduction from Sales. This account is usually evidenced by a credit memorandum issued by the seller. (330)

Sales tax A tax levied by a state or city government on the retail sale of goods and services. The tax is paid by the consumer but collected by the retailer. (337)

Special journals Books of original entry in which specialized types of repetitive transactions are recorded. (330)

Subsidiary ledger A group of accounts representing individual subdivisions of a controlling account. (339)

Summarizing entry An entry made to post the column totals of a special journal to the appropriate accounts in the general ledger. It is also used when individual sales invoices are posted directly to the accounts receivable ledger. (335)

QUESTIONS, EXERCISES, AND PROBLEMS

Discussion Questions

1. What information typically appears on a sales invoice?
2. Describe the posting procedure for totaling and ruling the sales journal.
3. What is the purpose of a schedule of accounts receivable?
4. Describe the procedure for posting from the sales journal to the accounts receivable ledger.
5. What is the difference between a sales return and a sales allowance?
6. Why is it worthwhile to set up an account for sales returns and allowances, when one could just debit the Sales account for any transaction involving a return or an allowance?
7. Why is an accounts receivable ledger necessary for a business with a large number of charge customers?
8. Describe the method of posting directly from sales invoices.

Exercises

P.O. 3

Post to general and accounts receivable ledgers.

Exercise 10-1 Describe how this sales journal would be posted to the ledgers:

SALES JOURNAL PAGE 94

DATE		INV. NO.	CUSTOMER'S NAME	POST. REF.	ACCOUNTS RECEIVABLE DR. SALES CR.
20–					
Oct.	3	414	Henderson Company		543 24
	4	415	R. T. Holcomb		1426 90
	7	416	Gray Company		1547 00
	11	417	Mercer Mobil		3212 16
	16	418	J. L. Anthony		2030 00
	22	419	C. A. Goldman		1844 05
	31	420	F. A. Baumann		2891 00
	31				13494 35

P.O. 5

Record sales return.

Exercise 10-2 Using the following source document (credit memo issued by Heald Electronics), record the transaction in general journal form on the books of Heald Electronics.

Heald Electronics
4160 Broad Street
Chicago, Illinois 60627

CREDIT MEMORANDUM No. **121**

DATE: **November 6, 20—**

CREDIT TO:

The Merchandise Mart
2241 Sullivan Street
Chicago, Illinois 60632

Your account has been credited for:

1 Benton 27" color TV (1xf27) **$623.00**

P.O. 5

Entries involving sales returns and allowances.

Exercise 10-3 Record the following transactions in a general journal for Denley Company:

Oct. 10 Mayer Company returned $520 of merchandise (wrong color) previously purchased on account. Issued credit memo no. 104. Mayer's original purchase was for $2,930.

17 Dolen Company returned $260 of defective merchandise previously purchased on account. Issued credit memo no. 105. Dolen's original purchase was for $720.

23 Denley Company issued credit memo no. 106 to Kily Company for $230 as an allowance for damaged merchandise. Kily's original purchase was for $3,530.

P.O. 5

Post to general and accounts receivable ledgers.

Exercise 10-4 Post the following entry to the general ledger and subsidiary ledger:

GENERAL JOURNAL PAGE 52

DATE		DESCRIPTION	POST. REF.	DEBIT	CREDIT
20–					
June	16	Sales Returns and Allowances		241 27	
		Accounts Receivable, R. D. Moen			241 27
		Issued credit memo no. 131.			

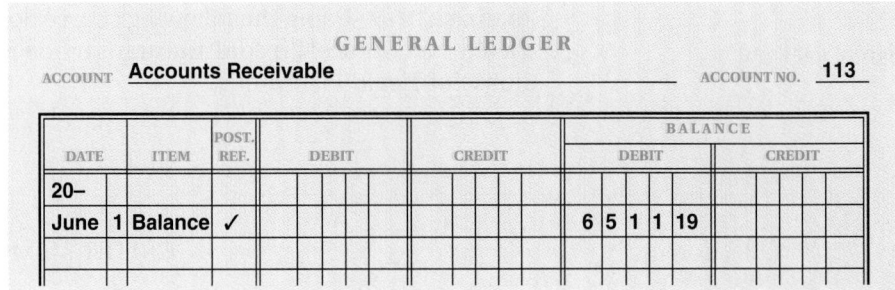

GENERAL LEDGER

ACCOUNT Accounts Receivable ACCOUNT NO. 113

DATE		ITEM	POST. REF.	DEBIT	CREDIT	BALANCE DEBIT	BALANCE CREDIT
20–							
June	1	Balance	✓			6,511.19	

ACCOUNT Sales Returns and Allowances ACCOUNT NO. 412

DATE		ITEM	POST. REF.	DEBIT	CREDIT	BALANCE DEBIT	BALANCE CREDIT
20–							
June	1	Balance	✓			314.60	

ACCOUNTS RECEIVABLE LEDGER

NAME R. D. Moen
ADDRESS 416 Fifth Avenue
Dallas, Texas 75204

DATE		ITEM	POST. REF.	DEBIT	CREDIT	BALANCE
20–						
May	31		S26	312.60		312.60

P.O. 3,5

Describe transactions involving a sale, a return, and a payment.

Exercise 10-5 Describe the transactions recorded in the following T accounts:

Cash

Debit	Credit
(c) 541	

Sales Tax Payable

Debit	Credit
(b) 8.20	(a) 49.20

Sales Returns and Allowances

Debit	Credit
(b) 100	

Accounts Receivable

Debit	Credit
(a) 649.20	(b) 108.20
	(c) 541

Sales

Debit	Credit
	(a) 600

P.O. 5

Entries involving a sale, a return, and a receipt of cash.

Exercise 10-6 Record the following transactions in general journal form:

a. Sold merchandise on account to C. C. Hall, $360 plus $18.00 sales tax (invoice no. D446).

b. Hall returned $90 of the merchandise. Issued credit memo no. 114 for $94.50 ($90 for the amount of the sale plus $4.50 for the amount of the sales tax).
c. Received $283.50 from C. C. Hall in full payment of account.

P.O. 6

Corrections involving a sales journal and an accounts receivable ledger.

Exercise 10-7 An accountant made the following errors in journalizing sales of merchandise on account in a single-column sales journal and in posting to the general ledger and the accounts receivable ledger. The errors were discovered at the end of the month before the closing entries were journalized and posted. Describe how to correct the errors.

a. The sales journal was footed correctly as $31,180, but it was posted as a debit and credit for $31,810.
b. A sale correctly recorded at $84 to N. P. Hale was posted to his account as $8.40.
c. A sale correctly recorded at $26 to N. A. Ales was posted to her account as $62.

P.O. 7

Summarizing entries for direct posting of sales and sales returns.

Exercise 10-8 A business uses copies of its sales invoices to record sales of merchandise on account and copies of its credit memorandums to record sales returns and allowances. During November the company issued 427 invoices for $148,941.20 and 16 credit memorandums for $9,427.18. Present the summarizing entries, dated November 30, in general journal form to record the sales and sales returns and allowances.

CONSIDER AND COMMUNICATE

After you finished the month's posting, the total of the schedule of accounts receivable matched the balance of the Accounts Receivable (controlling) account in the general ledger. You therefore mailed the statements to customers. You have received a phone call from Customer A, who is irritated and claims he was overcharged $43.97. Customer B calls to ask why her statement does not include her purchase of a blender for $43.97. She says she lost her original sales slip and needs a copy of the itemized bill so that she can return the item. Assume that the customers are correct. Explain how this could happen.

CRITICAL THINKING

TO: Accounting Clerk SUBJECT: Errors in trial balance
FROM: Senior Accountant DATE: April 1, 20—

Following is a trial balance prepared just before you were hired. There are two accounts missing, and the amount for Sales is off. Here are a few facts to consider. Our business is in a state that collects sales tax. I ran some totals, and we collected $1,400 in sales tax. Customers returned $800 in goods, which would reduce the above sales tax by $70. Our books need to reflect these events. The former accounting clerk said she did record everything—somewhere. Please determine the missing accounts and correct the accounts that are off.

Newkirk Retail Outlet
Trial Balance
March 31, 20—

ACCOUNT NAME	DEBIT	CREDIT
Cash	8,940.00	
Accounts Receivable	480.00	
Supplies	175.00	
Store Equipment	9,460.00	
Accounts Payable		958.00
D. Newkirk, Capital		11,959.00
D. Newkirk, Drawing	4,480.00	
Sales		18,000.00
Rent Expense	2,400.00	
Wages Expense	4,864.00	
Miscellaneous Expense	118.00	
	30,917.00	30,917.00

1. Think about where these amounts might have been put, think about what accounts are missing, and use T accounts to solve the problems.
2. Prepare a corrected trial balance.

A MATTER OF ETHICS

Ms. Hopper, an employee, accidentally dropped a pallet of boxes containing televisions off the forklift she was driving in the warehouse. No one saw what happened. She couldn't see (or hear) any damage to the televisions, so she reloaded the boxes and did not tell her supervisor. Is Ms. Hopper behaving in an ethical manner when she withholds this information? Assume that the sets were damaged and were delivered to customers. How would this damage affect the income statement?

WEB WORK

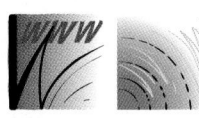

Using an Internet web browser, type *accounting* in the search box and search for information about a major company that interests you. Specifically look for sales information on the income statement. Discuss your findings in a small group. Write a one-page summary of your findings.

PROBLEM SET A

For additional help, see the demonstration problem at the beginning of each chapter in your Working Papers.

P.O. 2,3,4,5

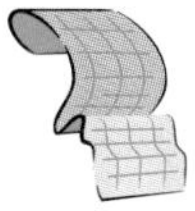

Problem 10-1A Landon's Beauty Supplies had the following sales of merchandise on account and sales returns and allowances during November:

Nov. 5 Sold merchandise on account to The Hair Stop, invoice no. 71, $153.70.

9 Sold merchandise on account to Shear Touch, invoice no. 72, $218.87.

11 Sold merchandise on account to The Coiffure Center, invoice no. 73, $338.46.

15 Sold merchandise on account to Lia's Hair Design, invoice no. 74, $370.50.

16 Issued credit memo no. 14, $85.18, to Shear Touch for merchandise returned.

21 Sold merchandise on account to The Hair Stop, invoice no. 75, $495.72.

22 Issued credit memo no. 15, $37.15, to The Coiffure Center for merchandise returned.

26 Sold merchandise on account to Lia's Hair Design, invoice no. 76, $318.42.

28 Sold merchandise on account to Shear Touch, invoice no. 77, $296.38.

29 Sold merchandise on account to The Hair Stop, invoice no. 78, $107.64.

30 Issued credit memo no. 16 to Lia's Hair Design for damage done to merchandise during shipping, $18.92.

Check Figure

Sales account balance, $8,615.89 credit

Instructions

1. Record these sales of merchandise on account in the sales journal (page 34). Record the sales returns and allowances in the general journal (page 59).
2. Immediately after recording each transaction, post to the accounts receivable ledger.
3. Post the amounts from the general journal daily. Post the sales journal amounts as a total at the end of the month: 113, Accounts Receivable; 411, Sales; 412, Sales Returns and Allowances.
4. Prepare a schedule of accounts receivable. Compare the balance of the Accounts Receivable controlling account with the total of the schedule of accounts receivable.

P.O. 2,3,4,5

Problem 10-2A Bradey Company sells electrical supplies on a wholesale basis. The following transactions took place during April of this year:

Apr. 1 Sold merchandise on account to Mayhew Company, invoice no. 761, $573.21.

5 Sold merchandise on account to L. R. Friedel Company, invoice no. 762, $301.46.

6 Issued credit memo no. 50 to Mayhew Company for merchandise returned, $51.50.

10 Sold merchandise on account to Danson Hardware, invoice no. 763, $551.41.

14 Sold merchandise on account to Benson Company, invoice no. 764, $838.33.

17 Sold merchandise on account to Porter Company, invoice no. 765, $511.27.

21 Issued credit memo no. 51 to Benson Company for merchandise returned, $81.36.

Apr. 24 Sold merchandise on account to Overall Company, invoice no. 766, $627.89.
26 Sold merchandise on account to Danson Hardware, invoice no. 767, $736.32.
30 Issued credit memo no. 52 to Danson Hardware for damage to merchandise, $101.40.

Check Figure

Accounts Receivable account balance, $5,075.05 debit

Instructions

1. Record these sales of merchandise on account in the sales journal (page 39). Record the sales returns and allowances in the general journal (page 74).
2. Immediately after recording each transaction, post to the accounts receivable ledger.
3. Post the amounts from the general journal daily. Post the sales journal amounts as a total at the end of the month: 113, Accounts Receivable; 411, Sales; 412, Sales Returns and Allowances.
4. Prepare a schedule of accounts receivable. Compare the balance of the Accounts Receivable controlling account with the total of the schedule of accounts receivable.

Instructions for General Ledger Software

1. Record these transactions in either the sales journal or the general journal and post.
2. Print the entries from the general journal.
3. Print the entries from the sales journal.
4. Print a schedule of accounts receivable and compare its total with the Accounts Receivable account.

P.O. 2,3,4,5

Problem 10-3A Mandel Florists sells flowers on a retail basis. Most of the sales are for cash; however, a few steady customers have charge accounts. Mandel's sales staff fills out a sales slip for each sale. The state government levies a 5 percent retail sales tax, which is collected by the retailer. The following represent Mandel Florists' charge sales for March:

Mar. 4 Sold potted plant on account to C. Milo, sales slip no. 242, $48, plus sales tax of $2.40, total $50.40.
6 Sold floral arrangement on account to R. Droy, sales slip no. 243, $46, plus sales tax of $2.30, total $48.30.
12 Sold corsage on account to B. Carr, sales slip no. 244, $16, plus sales tax of $.80, total $16.80.
16 Sold wreath on account to American Club, sales slip no. 245, $65, plus sales tax of $3.25, total $68.25.
18 Sold floral arrangements on account to Troy Funeral Home, sales slip no. 246, $214, plus sales tax of $10.70, total $224.70.
21 Troy Funeral Home returned a flower spray. Delivery of the spray occurred after the funeral was over. Mandel allowed full credit on the sale of $98 and the sales tax of $4.90 Credit memo no. 27.
23 Sold flower arrangements on account to Piedmont Savings and Loan Association for its anniversary, sales slip no. 247, $120 plus sales tax of $6, total $126.
24 Allowed Piedmont Savings and Loan Association credit, $28, plus $1.40 tax, because of withered blossoms in floral arrangements, credit memo no. 28.

Check Figure

Schedule of Accounts Receivable total, $540.37

Instructions

1. Record these transactions in either the sales journal (page 23) or the general journal (page 57).
2. Immediately after recording each transaction, post to the accounts receivable ledger.
3. Post the amounts from the general journal daily. Post the sales journal amounts as a total at the end of the month: 113, Accounts Receivable; 411, Sales; 214, Sales Tax Payable; 412, Sales Returns and Allowances.
4. Prepare a schedule of accounts receivable and compare its total with the Accounts Receivable account.

P.O. 4,7

Problem 10-4A Rory Sporting Goods uses duplicate copies of its charge sales invoices as a sales journal and posts to the accounts receivable ledger directly from the sales invoices. At the end of the month, the accountant totals the invoices and makes an entry in the general journal summarizing the charge sales for the month. The charge sales invoices for December are as follows:

Dec.	3	R. A. Finch Company, invoice no. 5214, $580.
	9	C. T. Baker, invoice no. 5237, $792.
	11	Soro Athletic Supply, invoice no. 5245, $326.
	13	Jason Company, invoice no. 5261, $1,137.
	17	Matthews, Inc., invoice no. 5277, $732.
	19	Travalina Company, invoice no. 5291, $564.
	23	Richard and Company, invoice no. 5309, $1,015.
	30	Soro Athletic Supply, invoice no. 5322, $1,238.

Check Figure

Schedule of Accounts Receivable total, $7,163.00

Instructions

1. Post to the accounts receivable ledger directly from the sales invoices, listing the invoice number in the Post. Ref. column.
2. Record the summarizing entry in the general journal (page 33) for the total amount of the sales invoices.
3. Post the general journal entry to the appropriate accounts in the general ledger: 113, Accounts Receivable; 411, Sales.
4. Prepare a schedule of accounts receivable and compare its total with the Accounts Receivable account.

PROBLEM SET B

For additional help, see the demonstration problem at the beginning of each chapter in your Working Papers.

P.O. 2,3,4,5

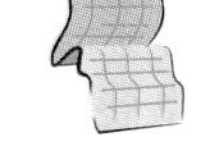

Problem 10-1B Darnold Beauty Supplies had the following sales of merchandise on account and sales returns and allowances during June.

Nov.	2	Sold merchandise on account to The Hair Stop, invoice no. 91, $267.52.
	8	Sold merchandise on account to Shear Touch, invoice no. 92, $236.40.
	10	Sold merchandise on account to The Coiffure Center, invoice no. 93, $317.31.

Nov. 15 Sold merchandise on account to Lia's Hair Design, invoice no. 94, $215.80.

16 Issued credit memo no. 12, $65.70, to Shear Touch, for merchandise returned.

21 Sold merchandise on account to The Hair Stop, invoice no. 95, $235.64.

23 Issued credit memo no. 13, $120.40, to The Coiffure Center, for merchandise returned.

26 Sold merchandise on account to Lia's Hair Design, invoice no. 96, $135.36.

28 Sold merchandise on account to Shear Touch, invoice no. 97, $247.21.

29 Sold merchandise on account to The Hair Stop, invoice no. 98, $57.48.

30 Issued credit memo no. 14, $36.72, to Lia's Hair Design for merchandise damaged in transit.

Check Figure

Sales account balance, $8,028.92 credit

Instructions

1. Record these sales of merchandise on account in the sales journal (page 34). Record the sales returns and allowances in the general journal (page 59).
2. Immediately after recording each transaction, post to the accounts receivable ledger. Fill in the names of companies where necessary.
3. Post the amounts from the general journal daily. Post the sales journal amount as a total at the end of the month: 113, Accounts Receivable; 411, Sales; 412, Sales Returns and Allowances.
4. Prepare a schedule of accounts receivable. Compare the balance of the Accounts Receivable controlling account with the total of the schedule of accounts receivable.

P.O. 2,3,4,5

Problem 10-2B Mandelli Company sells food supplies on a wholesale basis. The following transactions took place during November of this year:

Apr. 3 Sold merchandise on account to Mayhew Company, invoice no. 822, $530.19.

7 Sold merchandise on account to L. R. Friedel Company, invoice no. 823, $418.40.

8 Sold merchandise on account to Danson Hardware, invoice no. 824, $281.16.

13 Issued credit memo no. 61 to L. R. Friedel Company for merchandise returned, $49.95.

15 Sold merchandise on account to Benson Company, invoice no. 825, $723.88.

21 Sold merchandise on account to Porter Company, invoice no. 826, $792.53.

24 Issued credit memo no. 62 to Benson Company for merchandise returned, $87.41.

26 Sold merchandise on account to Overall Company, invoice no. 827, $576.34.

28 Issued credit memo no. 63 to Danson Hardware for damage to merchandise, $44.84.

30 Sold merchandise on account to Danson Hardware, invoice no. 828, $831.92.

Check Figure
Accounts Receivable account balance, $5,141.64 debit

Instructions

1. Record these sales of merchandise on account in the sales journal (page 39). Record the sales returns and allowances in the general journal (page 74).
2. Immediately after recording each transaction, post to the accounts receivable ledger.
3. Post the amounts from the general journal daily. Post the sales journal amount as a total at the end of the month: 113, Accounts Receivable; 411, Sales; 412, Sales Returns and Allowances.
4. Prepare a schedule of accounts receivable. Compare the balance of the Accounts Receivable controlling account with the total of the schedule of accounts receivable.

Instructions for General Ledger Software

1. Record these transactions in either the sales journal or the general journal and post.
2. Print the entries from the general journal.
3. Print the entries from the sales journal.
4. Print a schedule of accounts receivable and compare its total with the balance of Accounts Receivable.

P.O. 2,3,4,5

Problem 10-3B Scarvaglierri Florists sells flowers on a retail basis. Most of the sales are for cash; however, a few steady customers have charge accounts. Scarvaglierri's sales staff fills out a sales slip for each sale. The state government levies a 5 percent retail sales tax, which is collected by the retailer. Scarvaglierri Florists' charge sales for January are as follows:

Mar. 4 Sold floral arrangement on account to C. Milo, sales slip no. 236, $44, plus sales tax of $2.20, total $46.20.

7 Sold potted plant on account to R. Droy, sales slip no. 237, $19, plus sales tax of $.95, total $19.95.

12 Sold wreath on account to American Club, sales slip no. 238, $72, plus sales tax of $3.60, total $75.60.

17 Sold flower spray on account to Troy Funeral Home, sales slip no. 239, $190, plus sales tax of $9.50, total $199.50.

20 Troy Funeral Home returned the flower spray. Delivery of the spray occurred after the funeral was over. Scarvaglierri allowed full credit on the sale of $190 and the sales tax of $9.50, credit memo no. 27.

21 Sold flower arrangements on account to Piedmont Savings and Loan Association for it's anniversary, sales slip no. 240, $180, plus sales tax of $9, total $189.

22 Allowed Piedmont Savings and Loan Association credit, $25 plus $1.25 tax, because of withered blossoms in floral arrangements, credit memo no. 28.

27 Sold corsage on account to B. Carr, sales slip no. 241, $12, plus sales tax of $.60, total $12.60.

Check Figure
Schedule of Accounts Receivable total, $455.32

Instructions

1. Record these transactions in either the sales journal (page 23) or the general journal (page 57).
2. Immediately after recording each transaction, post to the accounts receivable ledger.

3. Post the amounts from the general journal daily. Post the sales journal amount as a total at the end of the month: 113, Accounts Receivable; 411, Sales; 214, Sales Tax Payable; 412, Sales Returns and Allowances.
4. Prepare a schedule of accounts receivable and compare its total with the balance of Accounts Receivable.

P.O. 4,7

Problem 10-4B Cullen Sporting Goods uses duplicate copies of its charge sales invoices as a sales journal and posts to the accounts receivable ledger directly from the sales invoices. The invoices are totaled at the end of the month, and an entry is made in the general journal to summarize the charge sales for the month. The charge sales invoices for December are as follows:

Dec.	4	R. A. Finch Company, invoice no. 5216, $562.
	9	C. T. Baker, invoice no. 5240, $658.
	11	Soro Athletic Supply, invoice no. 5242, $452.
	18	Jason Company, invoice no. 5267, $370.
	24	Matthew's, Inc., invoice no. 5287, $502.
	27	Travalina Company, invoice no. 5294, $567.
	28	Richard and Company, invoice no. 5311, $345.
	31	Soro Athletic Supply, invoice no. 5317, $205.

Check Figure

Schedule of Accounts Receivable total, $4,440.00

Instructions

1. Post to the accounts receivable ledger directly from the sales invoices, listing the invoice number in the Post. Ref. column.
2. Record the summarizing entry in the general journal (page 33) for the total amount of the sales invoices.
3. Post the general journal entry to the appropriate accounts in the general ledger: 113, Accounts Receivable; 411, Sales.
4. Prepare a schedule of accounts receivable and compare its total with the balance of Accounts Receivable.

Continuous General Ledger Problem: Sales Journal

The Like New sole proprietorship began as a service business, selling its services as an art and furniture restorer. It is owned by J. Miracle. The books were adjusted and closed on May 31, 2000. Following is the trial balance for Like New on May 31, 2000, after closing.

Place to START

Like New

General Ledger Trial Balance

As of May 31, 2000

Account	Account Description	Debit Amt	Credit Amt
111	Cash	68,823.00	
113	Accounts Receivable	4,566.00	
115	Supplies	1,336.00	
117	Prepaid Insurance	1,056.92	
142	Building	90,000.00	
143	Accum. Depreciation, Building		3,500.00
144	Van	18,500.00	
145	Accum. Depreciation, Van		1,100.00
146	Office Equipment	13,298.00	
147	Accum. Depr., Office Equipment		890.00
148	Office Furniture	5,023.00	
149	Accum. Depr., Office Furniture		1,100.00
211	Accounts Payable		4,252.00
212	Wages Payable		42.50
251	Mortgage Payable		89,400.00
312	J. Miracle, Capital		102,318.42
	Total:	**202,602.92**	**202,602.92**

Like New has decided to sell restored artwork and furniture in addition to its restoration services. Miracle has decided to add a sales journal to the records along with the general journal. The sales journal will receive entries for sales of merchandise on account only.

As the accountant for Like New, you will journalize and post the following June transactions. Journalize all sales of merchandise on account in the sales journal. The remainder of the journal entries will be journalized in the general journal.

If this is the first time you have worked for Like New, you will need to do a company setup on the general ledger accounting package you are using. This would include company information, customer names and balances, the chart of accounts, and beginning general ledger balances. Notice that the expense

Note: The Continuous General Ledger Problem can be worked with Houghton Mifflin Windows General Ledger Package, Peachtree Release 5.01, QuickBooks 6.0, or other general ledger software packages.

accounts are in the 600 category to leave 500-level accounts for the purchase of merchandise in the next chapter. Following are the transactions for June:

June	1	Miracle invested his personal facsimile machine, $269 (Office Equipment).
	2	Bought supplies on account from the Paint Pot, $374, Inv. 980.
	4	Sold two rocking chairs on account to Gail Murdock, $1,142, Sales Inv. 2004.
	5	Sold four frames on account to Image Place, $392, Sales Inv. 2005.
	6	Paid $500 on account to the Paint Pot, Ck. No. 1008.
	7	Paid $300 on account to Au Furniture, Ck. No. 1009.
	8	Paid the remaining $398 on account to Office Ready, Ck. No. 1010.
	10	Sold one desk on account to Baker Inn, $897, Sales Inv. 2006.
	11	Paid $1,140 interest (debit Interest Expense) and $261 on the principal of the mortgage (debit Mortgage Payable), $1,401, Ck. No. 1011.
	12	Sold a clock on account to Adeline Harris, $947, Sales Inv. 2007.
	13	Issued a credit memorandum to Image Place for one frame, $54, CM No. 1 (debit Sales Returns and Allowances and credit Accounts Receivable/Image Place).
	14	Sold two tapestries on account to Baker Inn, $1,281, Sales Inv. 2008.
	15	Paid wages of part-time assistant for the first half of the month, $850, Ck. No. 1012 (debit Wages Expense $807.50, debit Wages Payable $42.50).
	16	Sold services for cash to customers, $6,476, Cash Receipt Nos. 1117–1124.
	19	The owner withdrew cash for personal use, $1,644, Ck. No. 1013.
	22	Received cash on account from Adeline Harris, $1,256, Cash Receipt No. 1125.
	23	Received cash on account from Jeff Isely, $500, Cash Receipt No. 1126.
	24	Sold a coat tree on account to Baker Inn, $128, Sales Inv. 2009.
	25	Issued a credit memorandum to Baker Inn for one tapestry, $480, CM No. 2 (debit Sales Returns and Allowances and credit Accounts Receivable/Baker Inn).
	26	Received cash of account from Mike Willen, $1,000, Cash Receipt No. 1127.
	28	Paid $841 on account to Adams Advertising, Ck. No. 1014.
	30	Paid wages of part-time assistant for the second half of the month, $850, Ck. No. 1015.

Instructions

1. Launch the general ledger software.
2. Create a new file called likenews (*s* for sales journal). Enter the company name, chart of accounts (change the expenses to begin with a 6, e.g., 611 for Wages Expense), customer names and balances, vendor names and balances, and beginning general ledger balances.
3. Print a copy of the chart of accounts for your convenience in planning journal entries.
4. Journalize and post the transactions in either the general journal or the sales journal.
5. Print a trial balance ($212,706.42).
6. Print a schedule of accounts receivable ($6,603). Compare this number with the balance of Accounts Receivable in the trial balance in Direction 5. Are they the same? They should be.

11 The Purchases Journal

WINDOWS ON THE WORLD WIDE WEB

When you buy your next pair of Nike running shoes, ask yourself how far those shoes traveled before you laced them on your feet. Nike has more than 500 contract factories in 45 countries around the world. Your shoes may have been produced in Tae Kwang Vina, a Nike factory in Vietnam. Or maybe your feet are encased in shoe leather that a worker in China, Thailand, or Indonesia last touched. Nike's accounting department must account for the cost of moving those shoes or "goods" from the manufacturing plant to your favorite NikeTown retail location. The cost of travel, whether by air, ship, truck, or train, is known as "Freight In." This freight cost is passed on to you, the consumer. Do you want to learn more about Nike's global financial arm? Go to Nike's annual report menu at **http://www.nikebiz.com/invest/main_ar.shtml**.

Performance Objectives

After you have completed this chapter, you will be able to do the following:

1. Journalize transactions in a three-column purchases journal.
2. Post from a three-column purchases journal to an accounts payable ledger and a general ledger.
3. Journalize transactions involving purchases returns and allowances in a general journal.
4. Prepare a schedule of accounts payable.
5. Journalize transactions in a multicolumn purchases journal.
6. Post from a multicolumn purchases journal to an accounts payable ledger and a general ledger.
7. Post directly from purchase invoices to an accounts payable ledger and journalize and post a summarizing entry in the general journal.

We have been talking about the procedures, accounts, and special journals used to record the *sale* of merchandise. Now let's talk about those same elements as they apply to *buying* merchandise. We will be dealing with the Purchases account and with Purchases Returns and Allowances. In this chapter, you'll see that Accounts Payable, like Accounts Receivable, is a controlling account.

PURCHASING PROCEDURES

When you think of the great variety of types and sizes of merchandising firms, it should come as no surprise to learn that there is also considerable variety in the procedures used to buy goods for resale. Some purchases may be for cash; however, in most cases, purchases are on a credit basis. In a small retail store, the owner may do the buying. In large retail and wholesale concerns, department heads or division managers do the buying, after which the Purchasing Department goes into action: It places purchase orders, follows up the orders, and sees that deliveries are made to the right departments. The Purchasing Department also acts as a source of information on current prices, price trends, quality of goods, prospective suppliers, and reliability of suppliers.

The Purchasing Department normally requires that any requests to buy merchandise be in writing, in the form of a **purchase requisition**. After the purchase requisition is approved, the Purchasing Department sends a purchase order to the supplier. A **purchase order** is the company's written offer to buy certain goods. The accountant does not make any entry at this point because the supplier has not yet indicated acceptance of the order. A purchase order has at least four copies. The original goes to the supplier; copies go to the Purchasing Department (as proof of what was ordered), the department that issued the requisition (telling it that the goods it wanted have been ordered), and the Accounting Department, and a blind copy (with quantities omitted) goes to Receiving.

To continue with the accounts of Jackson Electric Supply, the Cable Department submits a purchase requisition to the Purchasing Department, as shown in Figure 1.

FIGURE 1

Jackson Electric Supply
625 N. E. Manor Avenue
Portland, Oregon 97201

No. C-726

PURCHASE REQUISITION

DEPARTMENT Cable DATE OF REQUEST July 2, 20—
ADVISE ON DELIVERY C. Carson DATE REQUIRED Aug. 5, 20—

QUANTITY	DESCRIPTION
10	Jacketed copper cable, 6 ga., 65 amp. (100' roll)

APPROVED BY *R. L. Schmidt* REQUESTED BY *J. C. Garcia*

FOR PURCHASING DEPT. USE ONLY

PURCHASE ORDER NO. 7918
DATE July 5, 20—

ISSUED TO: Draper, Inc.
1614 Olivera St.
San Francisco, CA 94129

FIGURE 2

Jackson Electric Supply
625 N. E. Manor Avenue
Portland, Oregon 97201

PURCHASE ORDER

TO: Draper, Inc.
1614 Olivera St.
San Francisco, CA 94129

DATE: July 5, 20—
ORDER NO.: 7918
SHIPPED BY:
TERMS: 2/10, n/30

QUANTITY	DESCRIPTION	UNIT PRICE	TOTAL
10	Jacketed copper cable, 6 ga., 65 amp. (100' roll)	39	390 00
	Total		390 00

R. L. Schmidt

The Purchasing Department completes the rest of the purchase requisition and then sends out the purchase order shown in Figure 2.

The seller then sends an **invoice** to the buyer. The invoice is a business form prepared by the seller that lists the items shipped, their cost, the terms, and mode of shipping. This invoice should arrive before the goods (or at least *with* the goods). From the seller's point of view, this is a sales invoice. If the sale is on credit, the seller's accountant makes an entry debiting Accounts Receivable and crediting Sales. To the buyer, this is a purchase invoice. Customarily, when the merchandise is received, the buyer's accountant makes an entry debiting Purchases and crediting Accounts Payable. Jackson Electric Supply receives the invoice shown in Figure 3 on page 368 from Draper, Inc.

Below are T accounts used in buying and selling goods.

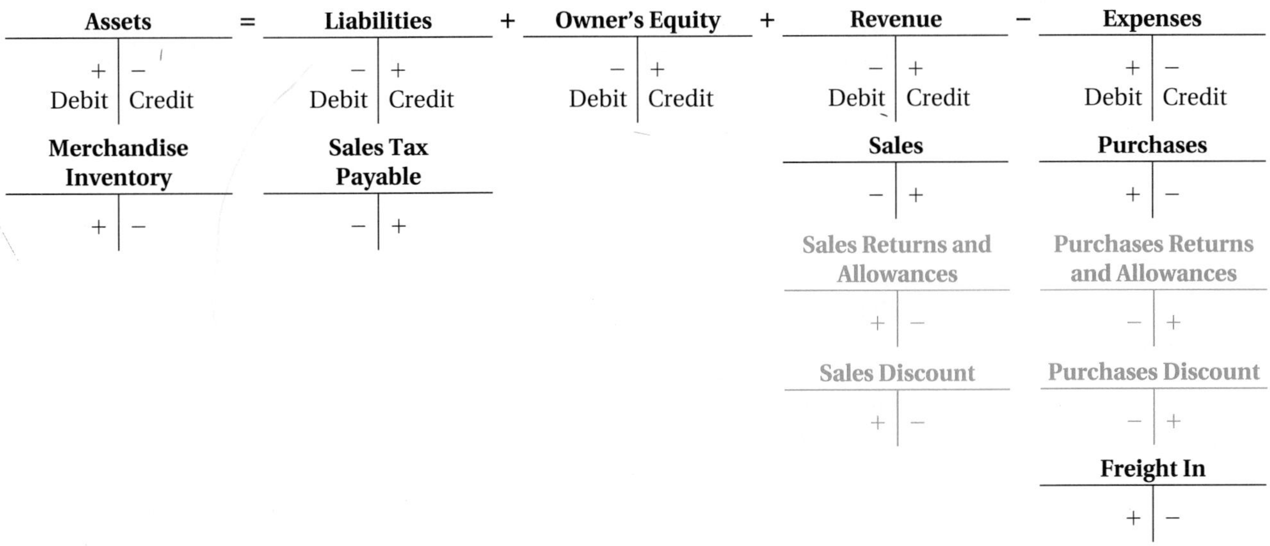

Assets = Liabilities + Owner's Equity + Revenue − Expenses
Assets: + − Debit Credit
Liabilities: − + Debit Credit
Owner's Equity: − + Debit Credit
Revenue: − + Debit Credit
Expenses: + − Debit Credit
Merchandise Inventory: + −
Sales Tax Payable: − +
Sales: − +
Purchases: + −
Sales Returns and Allowances: + −
Purchases Returns and Allowances: − +
Sales Discount: + −
Purchases Discount: − +
Freight In: + −

FIGURE 3

Draper, Inc.
1614 Olivera Street
San Francisco, CA 94129

No. 2706

INVOICE

SOLD TO Jackson Electric Supply
625 N. E. Manor Avenue
Portland, Oregon 97201

DATE: July 31, 20—
ORDER NO.: 7918
SHIPPED BY: Pacific Freight Line
TERMS: 2/10, n/30

YOUR ORDER NO.	SALESPERSON	TERMS
7918	C. L.	2/10, n/30
DATE SHIPPED	SHIPPED BY	FOB
July 31, 20—	Pacific Freight Line	San Francisco

QUANTITY	DESCRIPTION	UNIT PRICE	TOTAL
10	Jacketed copper cable, 6 ga., 65 amp. (100' roll)	39	390 00
	Freight		30 00
	Total		420 00

FOB-Free on Board
1) Destination
2) Shipping Point
* Supplier loads Free!

Bear in mind that the Purchases account is used exclusively for merchandise intended for resale. *If the firm buys anything else, the accountant records the amount under the appropriate asset or expense account.* At the end of the fiscal period, the balance in the Purchases account represents the total cost of merchandise bought during the period. Remember that Purchases is classified as an expense only for the sake of convenience. The classification is permissible because Purchases is closed along with the expense accounts at the end of the fiscal period.

Purchases Returns and Allowances is a deduction from Purchases. A separate account is set up to keep track of the amount of returns and reductions in bills because of damaged merchandise. On the income statement, we treat Purchases Returns and Allowances and Purchases Discount as deductions from Purchases; therefore, for consistency, they are presented below Purchases in the fundamental accounting equation just shown.

Freight Charges on Incoming Merchandise

FYI

Some accountants call the Freight In account *Transportation In*.

FOB Dest Seller pays
Fob Shipping Point Purchaser pays

Companies use the Freight In account to keep a record of all separately charged delivery costs on incoming merchandise.

Freight costs are expressed as FOB (free on board) destination or shipping point. **(Destination is the buyer's location; shipping point is the seller's location.)** In both cases, the supplier loads the goods free on board the carrier. Beyond that point, there must be an understanding as to who is responsible for paying the freight charges. **If the seller assumes the entire cost of transportation, without any reimbursement from the buyer, the terms are FOB destination**. In this case, title or ownership changes hands when the

FRISIA

To record the transportation costs of merchandise purchased for resale such as automobiles, accountants use an expense account called Freight In (also called Transportation In).

buyer receives the goods. **If the buyer is responsible for paying the freight cost, the shipping terms are called** **FOB shipping point**. In this case, title or ownership changes hands when goods are transferred to a common carrier (freight company).

Briefly, when goods are shipped FOB destination, the freight charges are not stated, and the seller simply pays the amount of the freight. Suppose Jackson Electric Supply (remember, it's in Portland) buys merchandise from a supplier in Chicago with shipping terms of FOB Portland listed on the invoice. The total of the invoice is $1,740, and there is no separate listing of freight charges. In other words, the seller has included the transportation costs in the price. NOTE

On the other hand, when goods are shipped FOB shipping point, with the buyer responsible for paying the freight charges, transportation costs may be handled in two ways:

1. The buyer may pay the freight charges directly to the transportation company. For example, an automobile dealer in Houston buys cars FOB Detroit. In this case, the automobile dealer makes one check payable to the manufacturer and another check payable to the carrier for the freight charges. (FOB Detroit is the same as FOB shipping point.)
2. The transportation costs may be listed separately on the invoice. For example, suppose a person orders a refrigerator from a mail order company. The mail order company has prepaid (paid in advance) the freight charges as a favor or convenience for the buyer. However, the freight charges are listed on the bill or invoice, and the buyer is responsible for reimbursing the mail order company for the freight charges. Similarly, when a business buys merchandise, the amount of the freight charges may be prepaid by the seller and listed separately on the invoice.

FYI

The cost of the goods sold by a company is usually its largest deduction in determining its gross profit.

FYI

Unless the title to the goods is expressly reserved by the seller, whoever pays the freight charges customarily has title to the goods.

Look again at the invoice of Draper, Inc. Note that the freight cost is listed separately, and so the terms are FOB shipping point (San Francisco). Draper paid the transportation cost, but Jackson must reimburse Draper for this cost.

Let's proceed with three other transactions for Jackson Electric Supply. We first record the transactions in a general journal. Then, as a means of reemphasizing the advantages of special journals as opposed to a general journal, we record the same transactions in a special journal. In practice, the transactions would be recorded in only one journal, not both.

During the first week in August, the following transactions took place:

Remember!

The transactions of August 2 and 3 are FOB shipping point, in which the seller pays the freight cost and adds it to the bill. The buyer pays the entire bill, including the freight cost.

Aug. 2 Bought merchandise on account from Draper, Inc., $390, its invoice no. 2706, dated July 31; terms 2/10, n/30; FOB San Francisco; freight prepaid and added to the invoice, $30 (total $420).

3 Bought merchandise on account from Reilly and Peters, $708, its invoice no. 982, dated August 2; terms net 30 days; FOB Cleveland; freight prepaid and added to the invoice, $52 (total $760).

5 Bought merchandise on account from Adkins Manufacturing Company, $692, its invoice no. 10611, dated August 3; terms 2/10, n/30; FOB Los Angeles.

Notice that the transactions with Draper, Inc., and Reilly and Peters are both FOB shipping point with the freight charges listed separately. Consequently, the buyer (Jackson) must reimburse the sellers for the transportation costs by paying the total of the invoices. However, in the transaction with Adkins Manufacturing, which is FOB shipping point without freight charges listed, the buyer (Jackson) must pay the freight costs separately, perhaps when the goods are delivered.

For now, we are concerned with journalizing the three purchases. Let's visualize these transactions using T accounts.

Purchases			Freight In			Accounts Payable	
+	−		+	−		−	+
Aug. 2 390			Aug. 2 30				Aug. 2 420
3 708			3 52				3 760
5 692							5 692

If these transactions are journalized in a general journal, they look like Figure 4. The general journal entries are then posted to the general ledger.

FIGURE 4

GENERAL JOURNAL PAGE 22

DATE		DESCRIPTION	POST. REF.	DEBIT	CREDIT
20–					
Aug.	2	Purchases	511	390 00	
		Freight In	514	30 00	
		Accounts Payable	221		420 00
		Draper, Inc., its invoice			
		no. 2706, dated July 31,			
		terms 2/10, n/30.			
	3	Purchases	511	708 00	
		Freight In	514	52 00	
		Accounts Payable	221		760 00
		Reilly and Peters, its			
		invoice no. 982, dated			
		August 2, terms net 30 days.			
	5	Purchases	511	692 00	
		Accounts Payable	221		692 00
		Adkins Manufacturing Co.,			
		its invoice no. 10611, dated			
		August 3, terms 2/10, n/30.			

GENERAL LEDGER

ACCOUNT Accounts Payable ACCOUNT NO. 221

DATE		ITEM	POST. REF.	DEBIT	CREDIT	BALANCE DEBIT	BALANCE CREDIT
20–							
Aug.	1	Balance	✓				356 00
	2		J22		420 00		776 00
	3		J22		760 00		1,536 00
	5		J22		692 00		2,228 00

FIGURE 4 (continued)

ACCOUNT **Purchases** ACCOUNT NO. **511**

DATE		ITEM	POST. REF.	DEBIT	CREDIT	BALANCE DEBIT	BALANCE CREDIT
20–							
Aug.	1	Balance	✓			20,612.00	
	2		J22	390.00		21,002.00	
	3		J22	708.00		21,710.00	
	5		J22	692.00		22,402.00	

ACCOUNT **Freight In** ACCOUNT NO. **514**

DATE		ITEM	POST. REF.	DEBIT	CREDIT	BALANCE DEBIT	BALANCE CREDIT
20–							
Aug.	1	Balance	✓			1,502.00	
	2		J22	30.00		1,532.00	
	3		J22	52.00		1,584.00	

Let's take a minute to explain the terms in the transactions. The notation "net 30 days" or "n/30" means that the bill is due within 30 days after the date of the invoice. The notation "2/10, n/30" refers to the **purchases discount** or cash discount. It means that the seller offers a 2 percent discount if the bill is paid within 10 days after the date of the invoice. Otherwise, the gross amount must be paid within 30 days after the invoice date.

PURCHASES JOURNAL (THREE-COLUMN)

Objective 1

Journalize transactions in a three-column purchases journal.

The repetition illustrated in our example can be avoided if the accountant uses a **purchases journal** instead of the general journal. This purchases journal is used to record the purchase of merchandise *on account only.* Some businesses prefer multicolumn purchases journals, which include all purchases on accounts. We look at this journal later in the chapter.

PURCHASES JOURNAL PAGE **29**

DATE		SUPPLIER'S NAME	INVOICE NO.	INVOICE DATE	TERMS	POST. REF.	ACCOUNTS PAYABLE CREDIT	FREIGHT IN DEBIT	PURCHASES DEBIT
20–									
Aug.	2	Draper, Inc.	2706	7/31	2/10, n/30		420.00	30.00	390.00
	3	Reilly and Peters	982	8/2	n/30		760.00	52.00	708.00
	5	Adkins Manufacturing Co.	10611	8/3	2/10, n/30		692.00		692.00

Posting from the Purchases Journal to the General Ledger

Objective 2

Post from a three-column purchases journal to an accounts payable ledger and a general ledger.

Figure 5 shows the journal entries for all transactions involving the purchase of merchandise on account for August and the related ledger accounts for the same time period. In the Post. Ref. column of the ledger accounts, P designates the purchases journal. After posting the column totals for the month to the ledger accounts, the accountant goes back to the purchases journal and records the account numbers in parentheses directly below the total.

FIGURE 5

PURCHASES JOURNAL — PAGE 29

	DATE		SUPPLIER'S NAME	INVOICE NO.	INVOICE DATE	TERMS	POST. REF.	ACCOUNTS PAYABLE CREDIT	FREIGHT IN DEBIT	PURCHASES DEBIT	
1	20–										1
2	Aug.	2	Draper, Inc.	2706	7/31	2/10, n/30		420.00	30.00	390.00	2
3		3	Reilly and Peters	982	8/2	n/30		760.00	52.00	708.00	3
4		5	Adkins Manufacturing Co.	10611	8/3	2/10, n/30		692.00		692.00	4
5		9	Sullivan Products Co.	B643	8/6	1/10, n/30		165.00	10.00	155.00	5
6		18	T. R. Wetzel	46812	8/17	n/60		228.00		228.00	6
7		25	Donaldson and Farr	1024	8/23	2/10, n/30		376.00	14.00	362.00	7
8		26	Draper, Inc.	2801	8/25	2/10, n/30		406.00	22.00	384.00	8
9		31						3,047.00	128.00	2,919.00	9
10								(221)	(514)	(511)	10
11											11
12											12

Remember!

Transactions involving the buying of supplies or other assets should not be journalized in the three-column purchases journal, because this purchases journal may be used only for purchases of merchandise for resale.

GENERAL LEDGER

ACCOUNT Accounts Payable — ACCOUNT NO. 221

	DATE		ITEM	POST. REF.	DEBIT	CREDIT	BALANCE DEBIT	BALANCE CREDIT	
1	20–								1
2	Aug.	1	Balance	✓				356.00	2
3		31		P29		3,047.00		3,403.00	3
4									4

ACCOUNT Purchases — ACCOUNT NO. 511

	DATE		ITEM	POST. REF.	DEBIT	CREDIT	BALANCE DEBIT	BALANCE CREDIT	
1	20–								1
2	Aug.	1	Balance	✓			20,612.00		2
3		31		P29	2,919.00		23,531.00		3
4									4

ENVELOPES

If a company were to purchase office supplies on account from a store like this, the company would not use a purchases journal unless it intended to then resell the supplies. Instead, the company would record the transaction in an accounts payable ledger.

FIGURE 5 (continued)

ACCOUNT Freight In ACCOUNT NO. 514

	DATE		ITEM	POST. REF.	DEBIT	CREDIT	BALANCE DEBIT	BALANCE CREDIT	
1	20–								1
2	Aug.	1	Balance	✓			1,502.00		2
3		31		P29	128.00		1,630.00		3
4									4

THE ACCOUNTS PAYABLE LEDGER

You know that the Accounts Receivable account in the general ledger is a controlling account, and that the accounts receivable ledger consists of an individual account for each charge customer. You also know that the accountant posts to the accounts receivable ledger every day.

Accounts Payable is a parallel case; it, too, is a controlling account in the general ledger. **The accounts payable ledger is a subsidiary ledger, and it consists of individual accounts for all the creditors.** Again, posting to the accounts payable ledger is usually done daily. After posting to the individual creditors' accounts, the accountant puts a check mark (✓) in the Post. Ref. column of the purchases journal. After the accountant has finished all the posting to the controlling account at the end of the period, the total of the schedule of accounts payable should equal the balance of the Accounts Payable (controlling) account. The three-column form is used for the accounts payable ledger.

Remember!

Creditors are companies or individuals to whom we owe money.

Remember!

Increases in Accounts Payable are recorded in the Credit column. Decreases in Accounts Payable are recorded in the Debit column.

Now let's look at the purchases journal (Figure 6) and the postings to the ledger (Figure 7) on page 374. Note that in the accounts payable ledger—as in the accounts receivable ledger—the accounts of the individual creditors are listed in either alphabetical or numerical order. Firms that handle all of their bookkeeping and accounting on computer may assign an account number to each individual account.

PURCHASES JOURNAL PAGE 29

DATE		SUPPLIER'S NAME	INVOICE NO.	INVOICE DATE	TERMS	POST. REF.	ACCOUNTS PAYABLE CREDIT	FREIGHT IN DEBIT	PURCHASES DEBIT
20–									
Aug.	2	Draper, Inc.	2706	7/31	2/10, n/30	✓	420 00	30 00	390 00
	3	Reilly and Peters	982	8/2	n/30	✓	760 00	52 00	708 00
	5	Adkins Manufacturing Co.	10611	8/3	2/10, n/30	✓	692 00		692 00
	9	Sullivan Products Co.	B643	8/6	1/10, n/30	✓	165 00	10 00	155 00
	18	T. R. Wetzel	46812	8/17	n/60	✓	228 00		228 00
	25	Donaldson and Farr	1024	8/23	2/10, n/30	✓	376 00	14 00	362 00
	26	Draper, Inc.	2801	8/25	2/10, n/30	✓	406 00	22 00	384 00
	31						3047 00	128 00	2919 00
							(221)	(514)	(511)

FIGURE 6

FIGURE 7

ACCOUNTS PAYABLE LEDGER

NAME Adkins Manufacturing Company
ADDRESS 254 Calle Mancha
Los Angeles, CA 90025

DATE		ITEM	POST. REF.	DEBIT	CREDIT	BALANCE
20–						
Aug.	5		P29		692 00	692 00

NAME Draper, Inc.
ADDRESS 1614 Olivera Street
San Francisco, CA 94129

DATE		ITEM	POST. REF.	DEBIT	CREDIT	BALANCE
20–						
Aug.	2		P29		420 00	420 00
	26		P29		406 00	826 00

NAME Donaldson and Farr
ADDRESS 2426 Reilly Way, N.E.
Seattle, WA 98102

DATE		ITEM	POST. REF.	DEBIT	CREDIT	BALANCE
20–						
Aug.	25		P29		376 00	376 00

FIGURE 7 (continued)

NAME Reilly and Peters
ADDRESS 2154 Springer St.
Boston, MA 02107

DATE		ITEM	POST. REF.	DEBIT	CREDIT	BALANCE
20–						
July	27		P28		180 00	180 00
Aug.	3		P29		760 00	940 00

NAME Sullivan Products Company
ADDRESS 142 Grant Road
Cleveland, OH 44102

DATE		ITEM	POST. REF.	DEBIT	CREDIT	BALANCE
20–						
Aug.	9		P29		165 00	165 00

NAME T. R. Wetzel
ADDRESS 1620 Minard St.
San Jose, CA 95101

DATE		ITEM	POST. REF.	DEBIT	CREDIT	BALANCE
20–						
July	29		P28		176 00	176 00
Aug.	18		P29		228 00	404 00

PURCHASES RETURNS AND ALLOWANCES

Objective 3

Journalize transactions involving purchases returns and allowances in a general journal.

As its title implies, the Purchases Returns and Allowances account handles either a return of merchandise previously purchased or an allowance made for merchandise that arrived in damaged condition. In both cases, there is a reduction in the amount owed to the supplier. The buyer sends a letter or printed form to the supplier, who acknowledges the reduction by sending a credit memorandum. The buyer should wait for notice that the deduction has been agreed to before making an entry.

The Purchases Returns and Allowances account is considered a deduction from Purchases. Using a separate account provides a better record for management of quality control of the total returns and allowances. Purchases Returns and Allowances is deducted from the Purchases account on the income statement. (We'll talk about this point later.) For now, let's look at an example consisting of two entries on the books of Jackson Electric Supply.

Transaction (a) On August 5, bought merchandise on account from Adkins Manufacturing Company, $692, its invoice no. 10611 of August 3; terms 2/10, n/30; FOB Los Angeles. Recorded this as a debit to Purchases and a credit to Accounts Payable. On August 6 returned merchandise costing $70. Made no entry.

Transaction (b) On August 8, received credit memorandum no. 629 from Adkins Manufacturing Company for $70. Recorded this as a debit to Accounts Payable and a credit to Purchases Returns and Allowances.

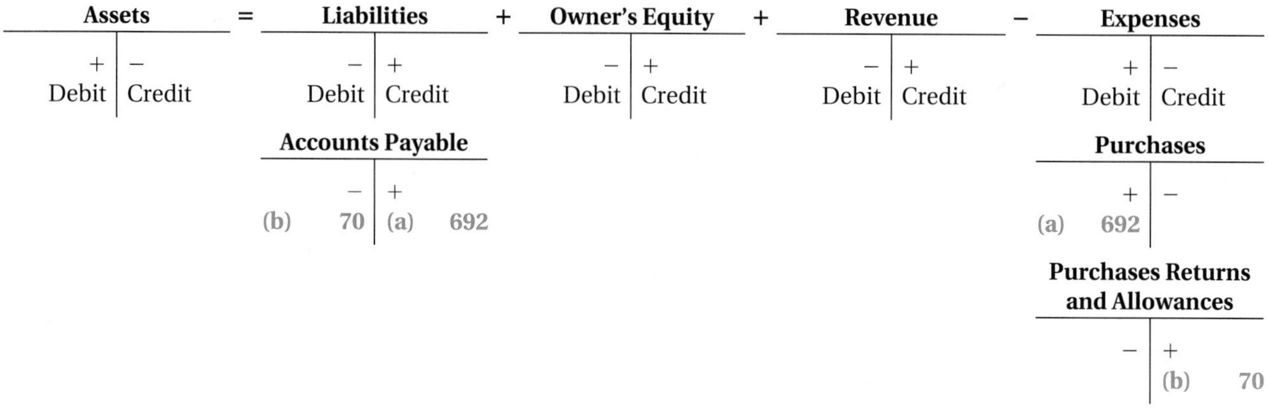

Assets = Liabilities + Owner's Equity + Revenue − Expenses
+ − Debit Credit
− + Debit Credit
− + Debit Credit
− + Debit Credit
+ − Debit Credit
Accounts Payable
− +
(b) 70 (a) 692
Purchases
+ −
(a) 692
Purchases Returns and Allowances
− +
(b) 70

Purchases Returns and Allowances is credited because Jackson Electric Supply's returns and allowances have increased. Accounts Payable is debited because Jackson Electric Supply owes less than before.

On August 12, suppose that Jackson Electric Supply also received credit memo no. 482 from Sullivan Products Company for $36 as an allowance for damaged merchandise. The entries in the general journal for journalizing the two credit memos are as follows:

GENERAL JOURNAL PAGE 27

DATE		DESCRIPTION	POST. REF.	DEBIT	CREDIT
20–					
Aug.	8	Accounts Payable, Adkins			
		Manufacturing Company		70 00	
		Purchases Returns and			
		Allowances			70 00
		Credit memo no. 629 for			
		return of merchandise.			
	12	Accounts Payable, Sullivan			
		Products Company		36 00	
		Purchases Returns and			
		Allowances			36 00
		Credit memo no. 482 as an			
		allowance for damaged			
		merchandise.			

Remember!

A credit memo received by the buyer means a reduction in the amount the buyer owes.

In these entries, Accounts Payable is followed by the name of the individual creditor's account. **The accountant must post the amount to both the Accounts Payable control account and the individual creditor's account in the accounts payable ledger.** The journal entries are shown here as they appear when the posting is completed. The account numbers in the Post. Ref. column indicate postings to the accounts in the general ledger, and the check marks indicate postings to the accounts in the accounts payable ledger.

Remember!

From the viewpoint of the buyer, a credit memo is journalized as a debit to Accounts Payable and a credit to Purchases Returns and Allowances. From the viewpoint of the seller, a credit memo is journalized as a debit to Sales Returns and Allowances and a credit to Accounts Receivable.

GENERAL JOURNAL PAGE 27

DATE		DESCRIPTION	POST. REF.	DEBIT	CREDIT
20–					
Aug.	8	Accounts Payable, Adkins			
		Manufacturing Company	221/✓	70 00	
		Purchases Returns and			
		Allowances	512		70 00
		Credit memo no. 629 for			
		return of merchandise.			
	12	Accounts Payable, Sullivan			
		Products Company	221/✓	36 00	
		Purchases Returns and			
		Allowances	512		36 00
		Credit memo no. 482 as an			
		allowance for damaged			
		merchandise.			

Many computer stores charge a 15 percent restocking fee to anyone who returns a computer. This helps reduce handling costs. The purchases returns and allowances account is used to record this fee.

GENERAL LEDGER

ACCOUNT Accounts Payable ACCOUNT NO. 221

DATE		ITEM	POST. REF.	DEBIT	CREDIT	BALANCE DEBIT	BALANCE CREDIT
20–							
Aug.	1	Balance	✓				356 00
	8		J27	70 00			286 00
	12		J27	36 00			250 00

ACCOUNT Purchases Returns and Allowances ACCOUNT NO. 512

DATE		ITEM	POST. REF.	DEBIT	CREDIT	BALANCE DEBIT	BALANCE CREDIT
20–							
Aug.	1	Balance	✓		70 00		640 00
	8		J27		36 00		710 00
	12		J27				746 00

ACCOUNTS PAYABLE LEDGER

NAME Adkins Manufacturing Company
ADDRESS 254 Calle Mancha
Los Angeles, CA 90025

DATE		ITEM	POST. REF.	DEBIT	CREDIT	BALANCE
20–						
Aug.	5		P29		692.00	692.00
	8		J27	70.00		622.00

NAME Sullivan Products Company
ADDRESS 2154 Springer St.
Boston, MA 02107

DATE		ITEM	POST. REF.	DEBIT	CREDIT	BALANCE
20–						
Aug.	9		P29		165.00	165.00
	12		J27	36.00		129.00

Schedule of Accounts Payable

Objective 4

Prepare a schedule of accounts payable.

Assuming that no other transactions involved Accounts Payable, the schedule of accounts payable would appear as follows. Note that the balances of the creditors' accounts, with the exception of the accounts for Adkins Manufacturing Company and Sullivan Products Company, are taken from the accounts payable ledger shown in Figure 7 on pages 374–375.

Jackson Electric Supply
Schedule of Accounts Payable
August 31, 20—

Adkins Manufacturing Company		$ 622.00
Draper, Inc.		826.00
Donaldson and Farr		376.00
Reilly and Peters		940.00
Sullivan Products Company		129.00
T. R. Wetzel		404.00
Total Accounts Payable		$3,297.00

The Accounts Payable controlling account in the general ledger is now posted up to date.

GENERAL LEDGER

ACCOUNT **Accounts Payable** ACCOUNT NO. **221**

DATE		ITEM	POST. REF.	DEBIT	CREDIT	BALANCE DEBIT	BALANCE CREDIT
20–							
Aug.	1	Balance	✓				356 00
	8		J27	70 00			286 00
	12		J27	36 00			250 00
	31		P29		3,047 00		3,297 00

SUBSIDIARY LEDGERS

The place of subsidiary ledgers in the accounting cycle is shown in Figure 8. The figure also shows how the schedules of accounts receivable and accounts payable fit into the accounting cycle.

FIGURE 8

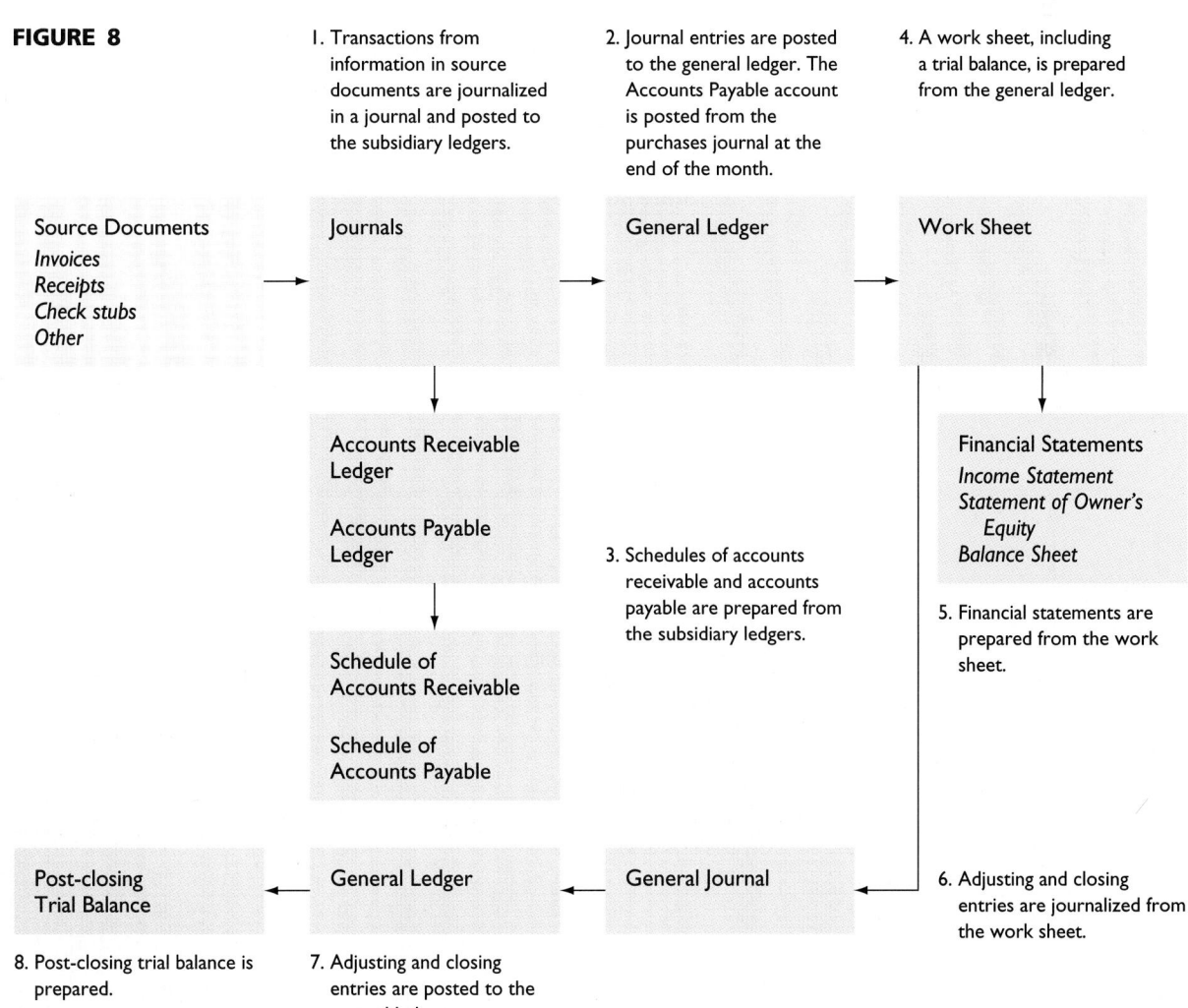

1. Transactions from information in source documents are journalized in a journal and posted to the subsidiary ledgers.
2. Journal entries are posted to the general ledger. The Accounts Payable account is posted from the purchases journal at the end of the month.
4. A work sheet, including a trial balance, is prepared from the general ledger.

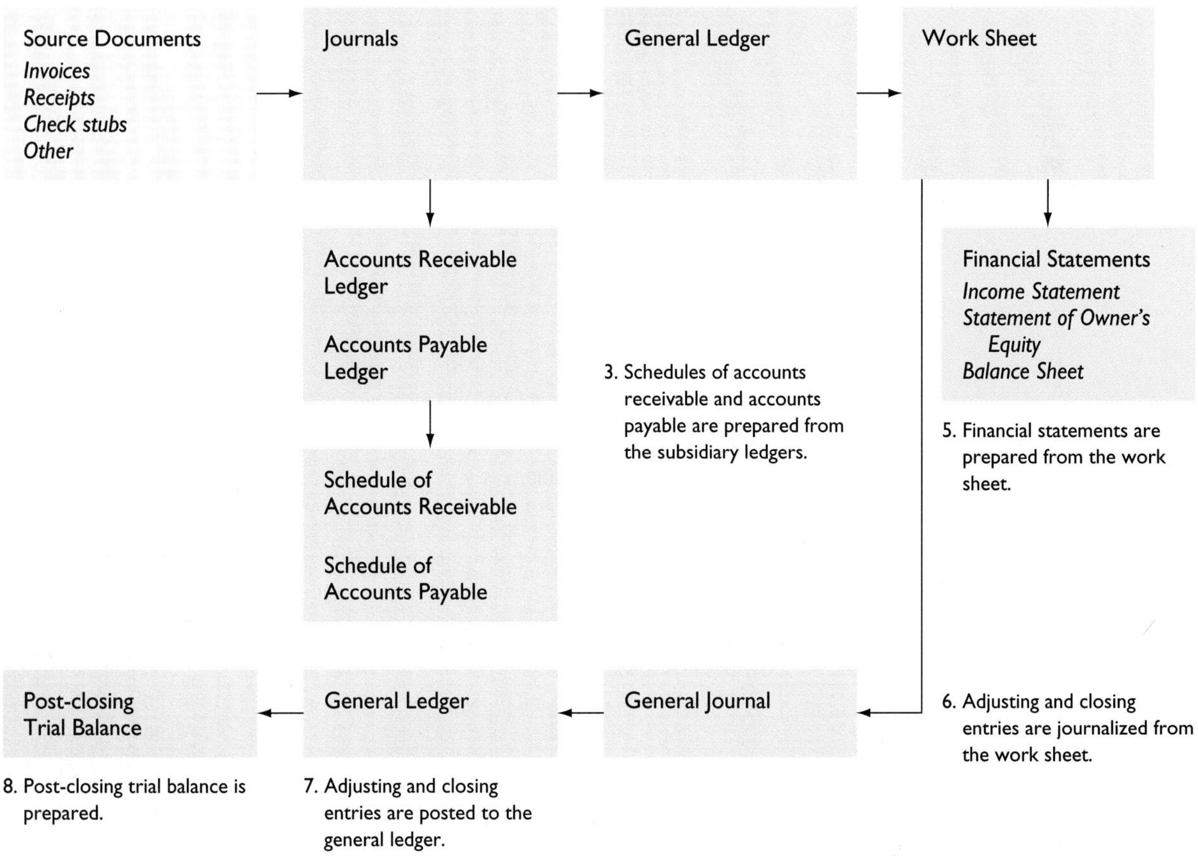
Source Documents
Invoices
Receipts
Check stubs
Other
Journals
General Ledger
Work Sheet
Accounts Receivable Ledger
Accounts Payable Ledger
Schedule of Accounts Receivable
Schedule of Accounts Payable
3. Schedules of accounts receivable and accounts payable are prepared from the subsidiary ledgers.
Financial Statements
Income Statement
Statement of Owner's Equity
Balance Sheet
5. Financial statements are prepared from the work sheet.
Post-closing Trial Balance
General Ledger
General Journal
6. Adjusting and closing entries are journalized from the work sheet.
8. Post-closing trial balance is prepared.
7. Adjusting and closing entries are posted to the general ledger.

MULTICOLUMN PURCHASES JOURNAL (INVOICE REGISTER)

Objective 5

Journalize transactions in a multicolumn purchases journal.

Instead of the three-column purchases journal, some businesses prefer to use a multicolumn purchases journal or invoice register, which handles not only freight charges and purchases of merchandise but anything bought on account. Items other than merchandise usually consist of supplies and equipment acquired for use in the firm. The advantage of a multicolumn purchases journal is that all types of purchases on account are journalized in one journal.

As an illustration, let's use another company, Cortez's Gift Shop. Here are three transactions that occurred during the first week in May:

May 2 Bought merchandise on account from Chase Specialty Company, \$610, its invoice no. L311, dated May 1; terms 2/10, n/30; FOB shipping point, freight prepaid and added to the invoice \$36 (total \$646).

Purchases		Freight In		Accounts Payable	
+	−	+	−	−	+
610		36			646

May 4 Bought packaging material on account from Benton Paper Products, its invoice no. 962D, dated May 4; terms n/30, \$98.

Store Supplies		Accounts Payable	
+	−	−	+
98			98

FIGURE 9

PURCHASES JOURNAL

DATE		SUPPLIER'S NAME	INVOICE NO.	INVOICE DATE	TERMS	POST. REF.	ACCOUNTS PAYABLE CREDIT	PURCHASES DEBIT	FREIGHT IN DEBIT
20–									
May	2	Chase Specialty Company	L311	5/1	2/10, n/30	✓	646 00	610 00	36 00
	4	Benton Paper Products	962D	5/4	n/30	✓	98 00		
	5	Lee Cabinet Shop	4273	5/5	n/30	✓	629 00		
	9	C. B. Boles Company	C-349	5/7	1/10, n/30	✓	416 00	404 00	12 00
	16	Gable and Son	124-9	5/15	2/10, n/30	✓	392 00	392 00	
	24	Moore Office Machines	N92	5/23	n/30	✓	515 71		
	27	Curtis, Inc.	517R	5/26	1/15, n/60	✓	304 00	304 00	
	30	Coe Office Supplies	5119	5/30	n/30	✓	42 36		
	31	Brice Corporation	D274	5/29	2/10, n/30	✓	277 20	264 20	13 00
	31						3,320 27	1,974 20	61 00
							(221)	(511)	(514)

Remember!

To save time in posting, special columns are set up for frequently used accounts.

May 5 Bought a display case on account from Lee Cabinet Shop, its invoice no. 4273, dated May 5; terms n/30, $629.

Store Equipment	
+	−
629	

Accounts Payable	
−	+
	629

These transactions, as well as others during the month, are now journalized in the multicolumn purchases journal shown in Figure 9.

For each transaction journalized in the multicolumn purchases journal, the amount to be credited is entered in the Accounts Payable Credit column. The next three columns are used to journalize the particular accounts most frequently affected. These are called special columns because each column has its own special account name. The final set of columns, under the heading Other Accounts Debit, is used to journalize the purchase of items that are not provided for in the special debit columns.

Posting from the Multicolumn Purchases Journal

Objective 6

Post from a multicolumn purchases journal to an accounts payable ledger and a general ledger.

Posting to the creditors' accounts in the accounts payable ledger from a multicolumn purchases journal is similar to posting from a three-column purchases journal. Posting is done daily, and the check marks (✓) in the Post. Ref. column indicate that the amounts have been posted separately.

The amounts listed in the Other Accounts Debit column are posted separately—usually on a daily basis. The posting process is the same as for posting from a general journal. The account numbers recorded in the Post. Ref. column indicate that the amounts have been posted.

At the end of the month, first prove that the sum of the debit totals equals the total of the Accounts Payable Credit column by making sure that debits equal credits horizontally for each entry and vertically as totals. This process is referred to as **crossfooting** the journal.

PAGE 62

STORE SUPPLIES DEBIT	OTHER ACCOUNTS DEBIT ACCOUNT	POST. REF.	AMOUNT	
				1
				2
98 00				3
	Store Equipment	125	629 00	4
				5
				6
	Office Equipment	127	515 71	7
				8
42 36				9
				10
140 36			1144 71	11
(114)			(X)	12
				13

	Debit Totals		Credit Total
Purchases	$1,974.20	Accounts Payable	$3,320.27
Freight In	61.00		
Store Supplies	140.36		
Other Accounts	1,144.71		
	$3,320.27		

Next, the accountant posts the special columns as totals. After posting the total amount, he or she records the ledger account number in parentheses below the total in the appropriate column. The (X) placed below the total of the Other Accounts Debit column means "this amount was not posted"—because the figures have already been posted separately.

POSTING DIRECTLY FROM PURCHASE INVOICES (AN ALTERNATIVE TO USING A PURCHASES JOURNAL)

Objective 7

Post directly from purchase invoices to an accounts payable ledger and journalize and post a summarizing entry in the general journal.

Posting from purchase invoices is a shortcut, like posting from sales invoices. Daily, the accountant posts to the individual creditors' accounts, working directly from the purchase invoices. The suppliers' invoice numbers rather than journal page numbers are recorded in the Post. Ref. column. The Accounts Payable controlling account in the general ledger is brought up to date at the end of the month by making a summarizing entry in the general journal. The accountant debits Purchases and Freight In, and also the appropriate asset account for any goods and services the company bought on account, and credits Accounts Payable.

Since posting directly from purchase invoices is a variation of the accounting system, we will use a different example: Don's RV Service. This firm sorts its invoices for the month and finds that the totals are as follows: purchases of merchandise, $9,164; freight charges on merchandise, $291; store supplies, $168; office supplies, $126; and store equipment, $520. The accountant then makes a summarizing entry in the general journal as follows:

GENERAL JOURNAL PAGE 37

	DATE		DESCRIPTION	POST. REF.	DEBIT	CREDIT	
1	20–						1
2	Oct.	31	Purchases	511	9 1 6 4 00		2
3			Freight In	514	2 9 1 00		3
4			Store Supplies	114	1 6 8 00		4
5			Office Supplies	115	1 2 6 00		5
6			Store Equipment	125	5 2 0 00		6
7			Accounts Payable	221		10 2 6 9 00	7
8			Summarizing entry for total				8
9			purchase of goods on				9
10			account.				10

The accountant posts the above entry to the general ledger accounts.

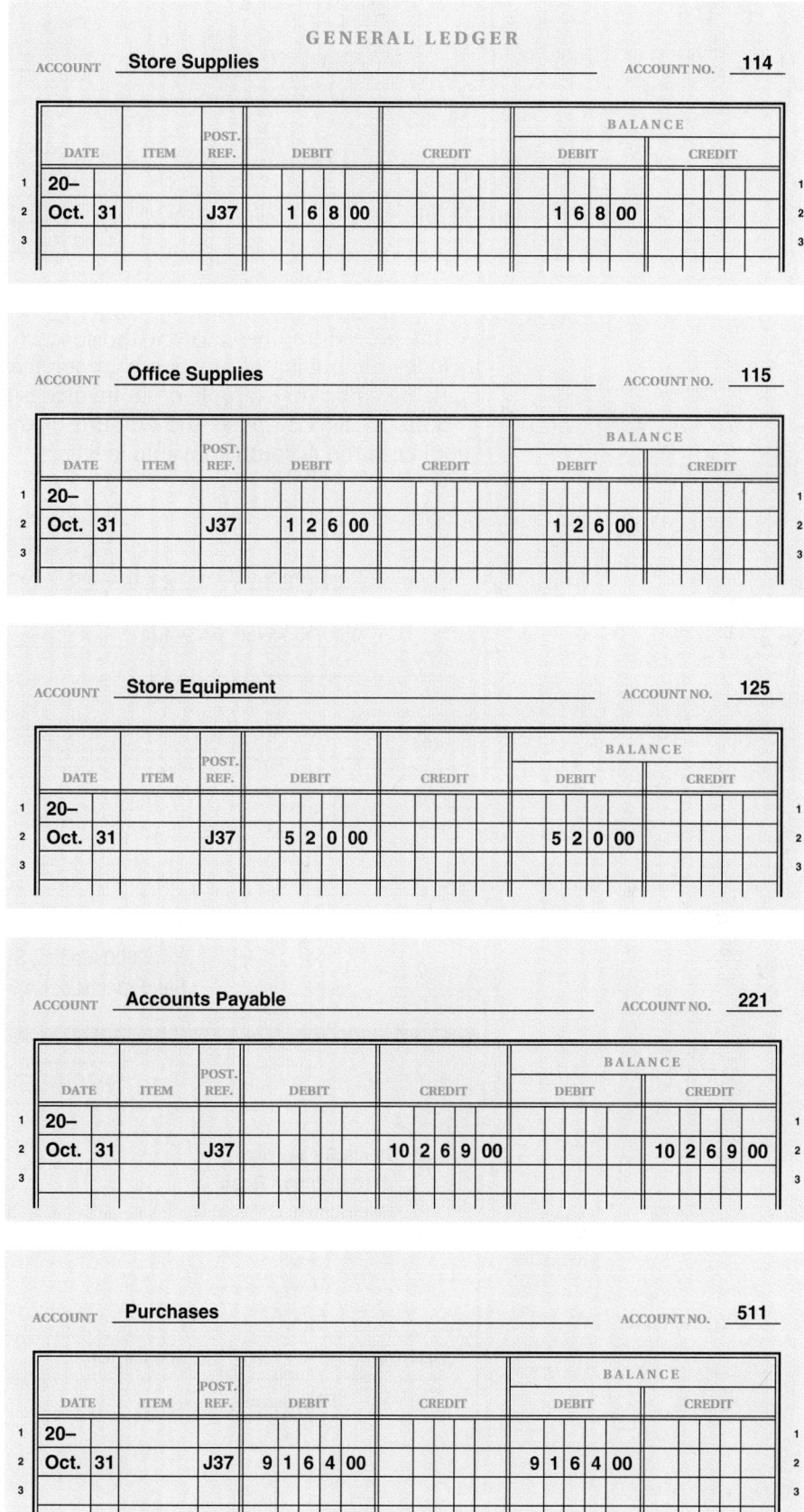

GENERAL LEDGER

ACCOUNT Store Supplies ACCOUNT NO. 114

DATE		ITEM	POST. REF.	DEBIT	CREDIT	BALANCE DEBIT	BALANCE CREDIT
20–							
Oct.	31		J37	168 00		168 00	

ACCOUNT Office Supplies ACCOUNT NO. 115

DATE		ITEM	POST. REF.	DEBIT	CREDIT	BALANCE DEBIT	BALANCE CREDIT
20–							
Oct.	31		J37	126 00		126 00	

ACCOUNT Store Equipment ACCOUNT NO. 125

DATE		ITEM	POST. REF.	DEBIT	CREDIT	BALANCE DEBIT	BALANCE CREDIT
20–							
Oct.	31		J37	520 00		520 00	

ACCOUNT Accounts Payable ACCOUNT NO. 221

DATE		ITEM	POST. REF.	DEBIT	CREDIT	BALANCE DEBIT	BALANCE CREDIT
20–							
Oct.	31		J37		10269 00		10269 00

ACCOUNT Purchases ACCOUNT NO. 511

DATE		ITEM	POST. REF.	DEBIT	CREDIT	BALANCE DEBIT	BALANCE CREDIT
20–							
Oct.	31		J37	9164 00		9164 00	

ACCOUNT **Freight In** ACCOUNT NO. **514**

	DATE		ITEM	POST. REF.	DEBIT	CREDIT	BALANCE DEBIT	BALANCE CREDIT	
1	20–								1
2	Oct.	31		J37	291.00		291.00		2
3									3

This procedure does away with the need for a purchases journal, and it includes the buying of any goods or services on account in the same summarizing entry. An example of an invoice is shown in Figure 10.

Don's RV Service posts the amount of the invoice to the account of the supplier in the accounts payable ledger:

ACCOUNTS PAYABLE LEDGER

NAME **Bingham Mobile Home Sales and Service**
ADDRESS **9600 Madera St.**
San Francisco, CA 94132

DATE		ITEM	POST. REF.	DEBIT	CREDIT	BALANCE
20–						
Oct.	7		13168		176.00	176.00

FIGURE 10

Bingham Mobile Home Sales and Service
9600 Madera St.
San Francisco, CA 94132

INVOICE

SOLD TO Don's RV Service
2716 Brighton Road
Burlingame, CA 94011

Rec'd October 7, 20–

DATE: Oct. 4, 20—
NO.: 13168
ORDER NO.: 1635
SHIPPED BY: Pacific Express Co.
TERMS: 1/10, n/30
FOB Burlingame

QUANTITY	DESCRIPTION	UNIT PRICE	TOTAL
20	TV antennas	8.80	176.00
	Total		176.00

Don's RV Service also includes the $176 figure in the summarizing entry recorded in the general journal, debiting Purchases and crediting Accounts Payable. Note that the supplier's invoice number is recorded in the Post. Ref. column in the Bingham Mobile Home Sales and Service account in the Accounts Payable ledger.

TRANSPORTATION CHARGES ON THE BUYING OF GOODS AND SERVICES OTHER THAN MERCHANDISE

Remember!

Freight In is used only to record the incoming transportation charges on merchandise intended for resale.

Any freight charges incurred when buying any other assets, such as supplies or equipment, should be debited to the respective asset accounts. Let's return to Jackson Electric Supply and assume that this company bought display cases on account from Coster Cabinet Shop, at a cost of $2,700 plus freight charges of $90. The seller of the display cases prepaid the transportation costs for Jackson Electric Supply and then added the $90 to the invoice price of the cases. Let's visualize this with T accounts.

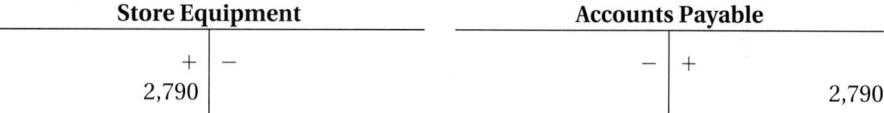

Store Equipment		Accounts Payable	
+	−	−	+
2,790			2,790

If Jackson Electric Supply had paid the freight charges separately, the entry for the payment would be a debit to Store Equipment for $90 and a credit to Cash for $90.

INTERNAL CONTROL

You know that the efficient management of cash is critical to a firm. All payments should be made either by check or from the petty cash fund, and all cash received should be deposited in the bank at the end of the day. The handling of cash in this manner is an example of **internal control**. Internal control embraces plans and procedures for the control of operations as a part of the accounting system. This is necessary when the owner or management must delegate authority. The owner has to take measures to (1) protect assets against fraud and waste, (2) provide for accurate accounting data, (3) promote an efficient operation, and (4) encourage adherence to management policies.

Internal Control of Purchases

Purchases is one of the areas in which internal control is essential. Efficiency and security require most companies to work out careful procedures for buying and paying for goods. This is understandable, as large sums of money are usually involved. The control aspect generally involves the following measures:

1. Purchases are made only after proper authorization is given. Purchase requisitions and purchase orders are all prenumbered, so that each form can be accounted for.

2. The receiving department carefully checks all goods upon receipt for count, damages, and description. Later, the report of the receiving department is verified against the purchase order and the purchase invoice.
3. The person who authorizes the payment is neither the person doing the ordering nor the person actually writing the check. Payment is authorized only after verifying the purchase invoice data with the receiving report and purchase order.
4. The person who actually writes the check has not been involved in any of the foregoing purchasing procedures.

CHAPTER REVIEW

Review of Performance Objectives

1. Journalize transactions in a three-column purchases journal.

   The three-column purchases journal handles the purchase of merchandise on account and freight charges that are prepaid by the seller and included in the invoice total. A transaction is journalized on one line including the date, supplier's name, invoice number, invoice date, terms, Accounts Payable Credit, Freight In Debit, and Purchases Debit.

2. Post from a three-column purchases journal to an accounts payable ledger and a general ledger.

   Amounts in the Accounts Payable Credit column are posted daily to the accounts payable ledger. At the end of the month, the totals are posted to the general ledger as a debit to Purchases, a debit to Freight In, and a credit to Accounts Payable.

3. Journalize transactions involving purchases returns and allowances in a general journal.

   When a credit memo is received for the return of merchandise or as an allowance for damaged merchandise, the buyer credits Purchases Returns and Allowances. If the merchandise was bought on account, the buyer debits Accounts Payable. The transaction is journalized in the general journal.

4. Prepare a schedule of accounts payable.

   A schedule of accounts payable, listing the balance of each individual creditor's account, is prepared from the accounts payable ledger.

5. Journalize transactions in a multicolumn purchases journal.

   A multicolumn purchases journal handles transactions involving the buying of anything on account, as well as freight charges prepaid by suppliers on behalf of the buyer. Most transactions can be journalized on one line. There are special columns for the most frequently used accounts and an Other Accounts Debit column for all other purchases on account.

6. Post from a multicolumn purchases journal to an accounts payable ledger and a general ledger.

   Amounts in the Accounts Payable Credit column are posted daily to the accounts payable ledger. Amounts in the Other Accounts Debit column are posted daily to the general ledger. At the end of the month, the totals of the special columns are posted to the general ledger.

7. Post directly from purchase invoices to an accounts payable ledger and journalize and post a summarizing entry in the general journal.

As a further shortcut, the firm may post to the accounts of the individual creditors in the accounts payable ledger directly from invoices of purchases of merchandise bought on credit. At the end of the month, the accountant makes a summarizing entry in the general journal, debiting Purchases, Freight In, and assets that were acquired and crediting Accounts Payable for the total of the invoices.

Glossary

Accounts payable ledger A subsidiary ledger that lists the individual accounts of creditors in either alphabetical or numerical order. (373)

Crossfooting Horizontal and vertical addition of column totals to prove that the total debits equal the total credits vertically and horizontally. (381)

FOB destination Shipping terms under which the seller pays the freight charges and includes them in the selling price. Title or ownership changes hands when the buyer receives the goods. (368)

FOB shipping point Shipping terms under which the buyer pays the freight charges between the point of shipment and the destination. Payment may be made directly to the carrier upon receiving the goods or to the supplier, if the supplier prepaid the freight charges on behalf of the buyer. Title or ownership changes hands when goods are transferred to the freight company. (369)

Internal control Plans and procedures built into the accounting system with the following objectives: (1) to protect assets against fraud and waste; (2) to provide accurate accounting data; (3) to promote an efficient operation; and (4) to encourage adherence to management policies. (385)

Invoice A business form prepared by the seller that lists the items shipped, their cost, the terms of the sale, and the mode of shipment. It may also state the freight charges. The buyer considers it a purchase invoice; the seller considers it a sales invoice. (367)

Purchase order A written order from the buyer of goods to the supplier, listing the items wanted and the terms of the transaction. (366)

Purchase requisition A form used to request that the Purchasing Department buy something. This form is intended for internal use within a company. (366)

Purchases discount A cash discount allowed for prompt payment of an invoice; for example, 2 percent if the bill is paid within 10 days. (371)

Purchases journal A special journal used to record the buying of goods on account. It may be used to record the purchase of merchandise only. It may also be a multicolumn journal, or invoice register, used to record the buying of anything on account. (371)

QUESTIONS, EXERCISES, AND PROBLEMS

Discussion Questions

1. How can a computer be considered merchandise by one company and office equipment by another?
2. Explain the purpose of the purchase requisition, the purchase order, and the purchase invoice. Which form is used as the basis for a journal entry?

3. What special account columns in a purchases journal would you recommend in situations in which a company frequently buys merchandise and the seller pays the freight charges as a convenience to the buyer and lists the amounts in the purchase invoices?
4. Why is it good practice to post daily to the accounts payable ledger?
5. Explain the meaning and importance of the shipping terms *FOB destination* and *FOB shipping point.* Who has title to the goods once they have been shipped?
6. Describe the four procedures that most companies follow to maintain internal control of purchases.
7. Explain the procedure of posting directly from purchase invoices.
8. Explain the process of proving the totals of a multicolumn purchases journal. What is this process called?

Exercises

P.O. 1

Record journal entries relating to purchases FOB shipping point and FOB destination.

Exercise 11-1 Journalize the following transactions in general journal form:

a. Bought merchandise on account from Berg Company, invoice no. 711N, $941; net 30 days; FOB shipping point.
b. Paid West Express for shipping charges on Berg Company purchase, $64.
c. Bought merchandise on account from Anders, Inc., invoice no. D312, $1,342; net 30 days; freight prepaid and added to invoice, $112 (total $1,454).
d. Paid Berg Company account in full, invoice no. 711N.
e. Paid Anders, Inc., account in full, invoice no. D312.

P.O. 3

Describe entries involving a purchase and return.

Exercise 11-2 Describe the transactions in the T accounts.

Cash

		(c)	750

Purchases

(a)	760		

Accounts Payable

(b)	50	(a)	800
(c)	750		

Purchases Returns and Allowances

		(b)	50

Freight In

(a)	40		

P.O. 3

Record journal entries for a purchase and return.

Exercise 11-3 Journalize the following transactions in general journal form:

a. Bought merchandise on account from Westro, Inc., invoice no. C229; net 30 days; FOB destination, $1,010.
b. Received credit memo no. 117 from Westro, Inc., for merchandise returned, $102.
c. Issued a check to Westro, Inc., in full payment of account.

P.O. 3

Post to accounts payable ledger and general ledger.

Exercise 11-4 Post the following entry to the general ledger and the subsidiary ledger:

GENERAL JOURNAL PAGE 92

	DATE		DESCRIPTION	POST. REF.	DEBIT	CREDIT	
1	20–						1
2	July	14	Accounts Payable, Bullock and				2
3			Hendricks		192 30		3
4			Purchases Returns and				4
5			Allowances			192 30	5
6			Credit memo no. 942 for				6
7			return of merchandise.				7
8							8

GENERAL LEDGER

ACCOUNT Accounts Payable ACCOUNT NO. 221

	DATE		ITEM	POST. REF.	DEBIT	CREDIT	BALANCE DEBIT	BALANCE CREDIT	
1	20–								1
2	July	1	Balance	✓				2,761 24	2
3									3

ACCOUNT Purchases Returns and Allowances ACCOUNT NO. 512

	DATE		ITEM	POST. REF.	DEBIT	CREDIT	BALANCE DEBIT	BALANCE CREDIT	
1	20–								1
2	July	1	Balance	✓				230 16	2
3									3

ACCOUNTS PAYABLE LEDGER

NAME Bullock and Hendricks

ADDRESS 542 Roselle Blvd.

Richmond, CA 94879

DATE		ITEM	POST. REF.	DEBIT	CREDIT	BALANCE
20–						
June	13		P73		218 00	218 00

P.O. 7

Record and post purchases directly from invoices.

Exercise 11-5 A business firm posts directly from its purchase invoices. After the invoices for the month have been sorted, the totals are as follows: purchases of merchandise, $9,583; freight charges on merchandise, $162; store supplies, $187; office supplies, $115; store equipment, $1,347. Journalize the summarizing entry in the general journal.

P.O. 3

Record journal entries for purchase and return of assets.

Exercise 11-6 Journalize the following transactions in general journal form:

a. Moi Company buys five different cash registers for use by cashiers on account from Reo Business Machines, invoice 142N, $10,416; net 30 days; FOB shipping point.
b. Paid Fastgo Freight Lines $204 for shipping charges on Reo Business Machines purchase.
c. One of the cash registers purchased for $2,010 is defective and is returned to the supplier. Reo Business Machines paid the freight charges. Moi Company received a credit memorandum from Reo Business Machines.
d. Paid Reo Business Machines in full, invoice no. 142N.

P.O. 2

Determine how errors will be exposed.

Exercise 11-7 The following errors were made in recording transactions in the purchases journal or in posting from it. How will each error come to the attention of the accountant?

a. An invoice of $470 for merchandise from Bellow Company was incorrectly recorded as having been received from Behlo Company.
b. A credit of $720 to the Holst Company account in the accounts payable ledger (controlling account) was posted as $270.
c. The Accounts Payable column of the purchases journal was overstated by $100.

P.O. 3

Correct journal entries.

Exercise 11-8 Journalize entries in general journal form to correct each error described below. Assume that the incorrect entries had been posted, and that the corrections are recorded in the same fiscal period in which the error occurred.

a. A $317 cash purchase of merchandise from L. B. Cho Company was journalized as a purchase on account.
b. The $1,810 cost of defective office equipment returned to the supplier was journalized as a credit to Purchases Returns and Allowances.
c. Transportation cost of $62 incurred on store equipment bought for use in the business was debited to Freight In.
d. Store supplies bought on account costing $91 were journalized as Purchases.

CONSIDER AND COMMUNICATE

You are the bookkeeper at a small merchandising firm. You are comparing the income statements from the last three years. You notice that the Purchases Returns and Allowances account (as a percentage of net sales) has been increasing at an alarming rate. If you were a manager, who would you speak to in the organization to help you understand why?

WHAT IF . . .

You have asked your client, a florist, to prepare a list of her accounts receivable by customer name, so that you may compare the balance with the balance of the control account in the general ledger.

She sent you the following list: Wholesome Florists, $750; Floral Supply, $505; Pretty Petals, $840.

You recognize the names as those of her suppliers, not her customers. You ask her again for the accounts receivable list, and she sends the same list, adding that those are the people who need to *receive* a payment from her. When you list a few of her customers' names, she tells you that these are the accounts payable because those are people who need to *pay* her.

Is she confused? If so, explain how she is confused about accounts receivable and accounts payable. Also suggest ways to avoid communication problems in the future.

A MATTER OF ETHICS

You work in a retail store selling computers. One of the employees asks you to write up the sales invoice for the sale of a computer to him at cost without the owner's approval. This employee knows that the owner sometimes sells computers to the employees at a discount and insists that it will not be any money out of the owner's pocket if you do this. Can you do this for the employee? If the owner would approve the sale only at a smaller discount, are you behaving ethically if you write up the sale at cost?

WEB WORK

Using an Internet web browser, type *inventory* in the search box and search for information about a major company that interests you. Specifically look for the percentage of Cost of Goods Sold that Purchases and Merchandise Inventory represent. Discuss your findings or write about them in a memo to the CFO (chief financial officer).

PROBLEM SET A

For additional help, see the demonstration problem at the beginning of each chapter in your Working Papers.

P.O. 1,2,4

Problem 11-1A Melor Appliance uses a three-column purchases journal. The company is located in Oakland, California. On January 1 of this year, the balances of the ledger accounts are Accounts Payable, $756.87; Purchases, zero; Freight In, zero. In addition to a general ledger, Melor Appliance also uses an accounts payable ledger. Transactions for January related to the buying of merchandise are as follows:

Jan. 2 Bought eighty 12-inch, 3-speed Brisk Oscillating Fans from Sueto Company, $995.50, invoice no. 268J, dated January 2; terms net 60 days; FOB Oakland.

4 Bought ten Cool Humidifiers from Meeker Company, $1,840, invoice no. 39426, dated January 2; terms 2/10, n/30; FOB Denver, freight prepaid and added to the invoice, $70 (total $1,910).

7 Bought ten Airy Window Fans from Tolan Company, $310, invoice no. 452A, dated January 6; terms 1/10, n/30; FOB Oakland.

Jan. 10 Bought twenty-four 2-speed Ceiling Fans, Model 2760, from Akel Company, $3,527, invoice no. 7742, dated January 7; terms 2/10, n/30; FOB Napa, freight prepaid and added to the invoice, $102 (total $3,629).

14 Bought four Sharpie Electric Hedge Trimmers from Grass Products, $182, invoice no. 2542, dated January 13; terms net 30 days; FOB Oakland.

22 Bought forty Pesty Electric Bug Killers from Sueto Company, $2,570, invoice no. 392J, dated January 22; terms net 60 days; FOB Oakland.

28 Bought ten Breezy Electric Blowers from Grass Products, $736, invoice no. 2691, dated January 27; terms net 30 days; FOB Oakland.

30 Bought ten Apex Powered Attic Ventilators from Poe Manufacturing, $356, invoice no. 664C, dated January 27; terms 2/10, n/30; FOB Seattle, freight prepaid and added to the invoice, $51 (total $407).

Check Figure

Accounts Payable account balance, $11,496.37

Instructions

1. Open the following accounts in the accounts payable ledger and record the January 1 balances, if any, as given: Akel Company; Grass Products; Meeker Company, $185.20; Poe Manufacturing Company, $250.07; Sueto Company; Tolan Company, $321.60. For the accounts having balances, write "Balance" in the Item column and place a check mark in the Post. Ref. column.
2. Record the balance of $756.87 in the Accounts Payable controlling account as of January 1. Write "Balance" in the Item column and place a check mark in the Post. Ref. column.
3. Journalize the transactions in the three-column purchases journal beginning on page 81.
4. Post to the accounts payable ledger daily.
5. Post to the general ledger at the end of the month.
6. Prepare a schedule of accounts payable, and compare the balance of the Accounts Payable controlling account with the total of the schedule of accounts payable.

P.O. 3,4,5

Problem 11-2A Rascal Boutique is located in New York City. The company had the following purchases of merchandise and other assets and related returns and allowances during May of this year.

May 4 Bought merchandise on account from Velour, Inc., $818.41, invoice no. 24812, dated May 2; terms 2/10, n/30; FOB New York.

6 Bought merchandise on account from Festival, Inc., $557.27, invoice no. L123, dated May 4; terms net 30 days; FOB Fort Lee, freight prepaid and added to the invoice, $41 (total $598.27).

9 Bought store supplies on account from Roja Company, $214.86, invoice no. B1164, dated May 8; terms net 30 days; FOB New York.

11 Bought office supplies on account from Jet Office Supply, $196.41, invoice no. 2465, dated May 10; terms net 30 days; FOB New Rochelle, freight prepaid and added to the invoice, $11 (total $207.41). (Record Office Supplies for $207.41.)

14 Received credit memo from Pelon Company for merchandise returned, $45, credit memo no. 772.

May 16 Bought merchandise on account from Velour, Inc., $1,484.27, invoice no. 26453, dated May 16; terms 2/10, n/30; FOB New York.
21 Bought merchandise on account from Kim Company, $913.46, invoice no. H2695, dated May 19; terms net 30 days; FOB Newark, freight prepaid and added to the invoice, $51 (total $964.46).
26 Bought merchandise on account from Delo Company, $813.43, invoice no. 52478, dated May 24; terms 2/10, n/30; FOB New York.
29 Received a credit memo from Festival, Inc., for merchandise returned, $91, credit memo no. 344.
30 Bought merchandise on account from Pelon Company, $1,342.86, invoice no. B8042, dated May 28; terms 2/10, n/30; FOB Newark, freight prepaid and added to the invoice, $118 (total $1,460.86).
31 Bought merchandise on account from Delo Company, $274.27, invoice no. 61994, dated May 30; terms 2/10, n/30; FOB New York.
31 Bought merchandise on account from Festival, Inc., $505.36, invoice no. L285, dated May 29; terms net 30 days; FOB Fort Lee, freight prepaid and added to the invoice, $35 (total $540.36).

Check Figure

Accounts Payable account balance, $11,378.68

Instructions

1. Open the following accounts in the general ledger and enter the balances as of May 1.

114 Store Supplies	$ 396.41	511 Purchases	$7,683.19
115 Office Supplies	192.85	512 Purchases Returns and Allowances	296.41
221 Accounts Payable	4,138.08	514 Freight In	591.52

For the accounts having balances, write "Balance" in the Item column and place a check mark in the Post. Ref. column.
2. Open the following accounts in the accounts payable ledger and record the May 1 balances, if any, as given: Delo Company, $1,246.87; Festival, Inc.; Jet Office Supply; Kim Company; Pelon Company, $1,432.92; Roja Company; Velour, Inc., $1,458.29. For the accounts having balances, write "Balance" in the Item column and place a check mark in the Post. Ref. column.
3. Journalize the transactions either in the general journal, starting on page 27, or on page 6 of the multicolumn purchases journal as appropriate.
4. Post the entries to the creditors' accounts in the accounts payable ledger immediately after you make each journal entry.
5. Post the entries in the general journal and the Other Accounts Debit column of the purchases journal immediately after you make each journal entry.
6. In the space below the purchases journal, show proof that the sum of the debit totals equals the total of the Accounts Payable Credit column.
7. Post the totals of the special columns of the purchases journal at the end of the month.
8. Prepare a schedule of accounts payable, and compare the balance of the Accounts Payable controlling account with the total of the schedule of accounts payable.

P.O. 7

no **Problem 11-3A** The Dole Products Company of Dallas, Texas, records sales of merchandise daily by posting directly from its sales invoices to the accounts receivable ledger. At the end of the month, a summarizing entry is made in the general journal. The purchase of goods on account is recorded in a similar manner. Each day's posting is done directly from the invoices to the accounts payable ledger, and a summarizing entry is made in the general journal at the end of the month. Sales of merchandise and purchases of goods on account during May of this year were as follows.

Sales of Merchandise on Account

May	4	Lemon and Fay, no. 3522, $536.41.
	7	C. L. Favor, Inc., no. 3523, $1,232.30.
	11	P. R. Kevo and Company, no. 3524, $687.91.
	15	Mako Company, no. 3525, $392.74.
	22	C. D. Swick, no. 3526, $232.81.
	24	Lester Jaco, no. 3527, $494.88.
	25	Shelley Tai, no. 3528, $767.45.
	28	Milo Corporation, no. 3529, $844.97.
	30	Howard and Company, no. 3530, $936.54.
	31	C. L. Favor, Inc., no. 3531, $1,127.22.

Purchases of Merchandise, Supplies, and Equipment on Account

May	3	Russel Company, merchandise, $231.46; FOB Dallas.
	9	Galer Manufacturing Company, merchandise, $645.54; FOB Dallas.
	11	Quick Supply Company, office supplies, $118.49; FOB Dallas.
	19	Goodrow Company, merchandise, $3,427; FOB Houston, freight prepaid and added to the invoice, $86 (total $3,513).
	21	Turow Company, store supplies, $210.40; FOB Dallas.
	27	Wilson Specialty Products, merchandise, $2,467.10; FOB Dallas.
	31	Spring Distributing Company, store equipment, $1,010; FOB Dallas.

Check Figure
Total Sales, $7,253.23

Instructions

1. Journalize the summarizing entry for sales of merchandise on account in the general journal, page 27.
2. Journalize the summarizing entry for the purchase of goods on account in the general journal.

P.O. 1,2,3,4

Problem 11-4A The following transactions relate to the Stellar Company of Atlanta during April of this year. Terms of sale are 2/10, n/30.

Apr.	2	Sold merchandise on account to Stroud and Company, invoice no. 1126, $836.
	4	Bought merchandise on account from Plagge Manufacturing Company, invoice no. 16521, $657; terms 1/10, n/30; dated April 2; FOB Atlanta.
	9	Sold merchandise on account to Plover and Lee, invoice no. 1127, $1,265.
	12	Bought merchandise on account from Vick Company, invoice no. L8552, $2,143; terms 2/10, n/30; dated April 11; FOB Rome, freight prepaid and added to the invoice, $51 (total $2,194).
	15	Received credit memo no. 79 for merchandise returned to Keller Company, for $127.
	17	Sold merchandise on account to C. N. Horn, Inc., invoice no. 1128, $1,002.
	19	Issued credit memo no. 34 to Plover and Lee for merchandise returned, $89.

Apr. 26 Bought merchandise on account from M. R. Penn, Inc., invoice no. 7447, $1,686; terms 2/10, n/30; dated April 23; FOB Macon, freight prepaid and added to the invoice, $41 (total $1,727).
29 Bought office supplies on account from Taylor Stationery Company, invoice no. S336, dated April 29, $187; terms net 30 days.
29 Sold merchandise on account to Spencer Company, invoice no. 1129, $2,643.
30 Issued credit memo no. 35 to Spencer Company for merchandise returned, $171.

Check Figure

Accounts Payable account balance, $5,205.00

Instructions

1. Open the following accounts in the accounts receivable ledger and record the balances, if any, as of April 1: C. N. Horn, Inc.; Plover and Lee, $516; Spencer Company, $884; Stroud and Company. For the accounts having balances, write "Balance" in the Item column and place a check mark in the Post. Ref. column. Total the amounts and record the balance in the controlling account in the general ledger. (Verify: $1,400.)
2. Open the following accounts in the accounts payable ledger and record the balances, if any, as of April 1: Keller Company, $371; M. R. Penn, Inc., $196; Plagge Manufacturing Company; Taylor Stationery Company; Vick Company. For the accounts having balances, write "Balance" in the Item column and place a check mark in the Post. Ref. column. Total the amounts and record the balance in the controlling account in the general ledger. (Verify: $567.)
3. Journalize the transactions in the sales, purchases, or general journal, as appropriate (sales journal, page 24; purchases journal, page 18; general journal, page 68).
4. Post the entries to the accounts receivable ledger daily.
5. Post the entries to the accounts payable ledger daily.
6. Post the entries in the general journal immediately after you make each journal entry.
7. Post the totals from the special journals at the end of the month.
8. Prepare a schedule of accounts receivable.
9. Prepare a schedule of accounts payable.
10. Compare the totals of the schedules with the balances of the controlling accounts.

Instructions for General Ledger Software

1. Journalize the transactions in the sales, purchases, or general journal.
   a. For efficiency, analyze the transactions, indicate into which journal each transaction goes, and key the entries in three batches—the sales journal, the purchases journal, and the general journal.
   b. If the program uses a single-column purchases journal, add the amount of the freight to the amount of purchases.
2. Print the journals.
3. Post the amounts from the sales, purchases, and general journals to the subsidiary ledgers and to the general ledger.
4. Print the general ledger.
5. Print a schedule of accounts receivable and compare the total with the balance of the Accounts Receivable control account.
6. Print a schedule of accounts payable and compare the total with the balance of the Accounts Payable control account.

PROBLEM SET B

For additional help, see the demonstration problem at the beginning of each chapter in your Working Papers.

P.O. 1,2,4

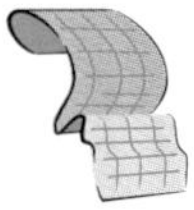

Problem 11-1B The Urban Bicycle Shop uses a three-column purchases journal. The company is located in Oak Park, Illinois. On January 1 of this year, the balances of the ledger accounts are Accounts Payable, $542.14; Purchases, zero; Freight In, zero. In addition to a general ledger, the company also uses an accounts payable ledger. Transactions for January related to the purchase of merchandise are as follows:

Jan. 4 Bought sixty 10-speed bicycles from Nagara Company, $5,986, invoice no. 26145, dated January 3; terms net 60 days; FOB Oak Park.

7 Bought tires from Biggs' Tire Company, $931, invoice no. 9763, dated January 5; terms 2/10, n/30; FOB Oak Park.

8 Bought bicycle lights and reflectors from Gannon Products, $341, invoice no. 17317, dated January 6; terms net 30 days; FOB Oak Park.

11 Bought hand brakes from Best, Inc., $361, invoice no. 291GE, dated January 9; terms 1/10, n/30; FOB Chicago, freight prepaid and added to the invoice, $21 (total $382).

19 Bought handle grips from Gannon Products, $184.60, invoice no. 17520, dated January 17; terms net 30 days; FOB Oak Park.

24 Bought thirty 5-speed bicycles from Nagara Company, $1,518, invoice no. 26942, dated January 23; terms net 60 days; FOB Oak Park.

29 Bought knapsacks from Minsky Manufacturing Company, $315.10, invoice no. 762AC, dated January 26; terms 2/10, n/30; FOB Oak Park.

31 Bought locks from Laker Security, $310.41, invoice no. 27712, dated January 26; terms 2/10, n/30; FOB Chicago, freight prepaid and added to the invoice, $12 (total $322.41).

Check Figure

Accounts Payable account balance, $10,522.25

Instructions

1. Open the following creditor accounts in the accounts payable ledger and record the January 1 balances, if any, as given: Best, Inc.; Biggs' Tire Company, $211; Gannon Products; Laker Security, $181.04; Minsky Manufacturing Company, $150.10; Nagara Company. For the accounts having balances, write "Balance" in the Item column and place a check mark in the Post. Ref. column.
2. Record the balance of $542.14 in the Accounts Payable controlling account as of January 1. Write "Balance" in the Item column and place a check mark in the Post. Ref. column.
3. Journalize the transactions in the three-column purchases journal beginning with page 81.
4. Post to the accounts payable ledger daily.
5. Post to the general ledger at the end of the month.
6. Prepare a schedule of accounts payable, and compare the balance of the Accounts Payable controlling account with the total of the schedule of accounts payable.

P.O. 3,4,5

Problem 11-2B World Camera is located in Portland. The company bought the following merchandise and supplies and had the following returns and allowances during April of this year.

Apr. 3 Bought merchandise on account from Draeger Imports, $855, invoice no. C4581, dated April 1; terms 2/10, n/30; FOB Chicago, freight prepaid and added to the invoice, $30 (total $885).

4 Bought merchandise on account from Ness Company, $805, invoice no. 561AM, dated April 2; terms 1/10, n/30; FOB Portland.

7 Bought merchandise on account from Ross Photo Supply, $592, invoice no. 65872, dated April 5; terms net 30 days; FOB Portland.

11 Bought office supplies on account from Mackey, Inc., $290, invoice no. 5639, dated April 11; terms net 30 days; FOB Portland.

13 Received a credit memo from Ness Company for merchandise returned, $36, credit memo no. 617.

16 Bought merchandise on account from Askey Company, $805, invoice no. 41832, dated April 15; terms 1/10, n/30; FOB Phoenix, freight prepaid and added to the invoice, $38 (total $843).

22 Bought equipment on account from Robo Company, $992, invoice no. L21654, dated April 19; terms net 30 days; FOB Portland.

27 Bought merchandise on account from Ness Company, $765, invoice no. 598AM, dated April 25; terms 1/10, n/30; FOB Portland.

28 Received a credit memo from Ross Photo Supply for merchandise returned, $82, credit memo no. 922.

29 Bought merchandise on account from Draeger Imports, $1,428, invoice no. C4721, dated April 27; terms 2/10, n/30; FOB Chicago, freight prepaid and added to the invoice, $102 (total $1,530).

30 Bought store supplies on account from N. D. Rice, Inc., $86, invoice no. 61875, dated April 29; terms net 30 days; FOB Portland.

30 Bought merchandise on account from Askey Company, $570, invoice no. 42003, dated April 27; terms 1/10, n/30; FOB Phoenix, freight prepaid and added to the invoice, $41 (total $611).

Check Figure

Accounts Payable account balance, $9,866.00

Instructions

1. Open the following accounts in the general ledger and enter the balances as of April 1.

114 Store Supplies	$ 352.00	511 Purchases	$8,467.91
115 Office Supplies	180.00	512 Purchases Returns and Allowances	310.05
124 Equipment	10,420.00		
221 Accounts Payable	2,585.00	514 Freight In	506.50

For the accounts having balances, write "Balance" in the Item column and place a check mark in the Post. Ref. column.

2. Open the following accounts in the accounts payable ledger and enter the April 1 balances, if any, as given: Askey Company, $1,220.10; Draeger Imports, $850.30; Mackey, Inc.; Ness Company; N. D. Rice, Inc.; Robo Company; Ross Photo Supply, $514.60. For the accounts having balances, write "Balance" in the Item column and place a check mark in the Post. Ref. column.
3. Journalize the transactions in either the general journal, starting on page 27, or the multicolumn purchases journal, on page 6, as appropriate.
4. Post the entries to the creditors' accounts in the accounts payable ledger immediately after you make each journal entry.

5. Post the entries in the Other Accounts Debit column of the purchases journal and in the general journal immediately after you make each of those journal entries.
6. In the space below the purchases journal, show proof that the sum of the debit totals equals the total of the Accounts Payable Credit column.
7. Post the totals of the special columns of the purchases journal at the end of the month.
8. Prepare a schedule of accounts payable, and compare the balance of the Accounts Payable controlling account with the total of the schedule of accounts payable.

P.O. 7

Problem 11-3B Hatch Products, Houston, records sales of merchandise daily by posting directly from its sales invoices to the accounts receivable ledger. At the end of the month, it makes a summarizing entry in the general journal. It records purchases of goods on account the same way, posting directly from the invoices to the accounts payable ledger daily and making a summarizing entry in the general journal at the end of the month. Sales of merchandise and purchases of goods on account during September of this year were as follows.

Sales of Merchandise on Account

Sept. 4 Stacy Corp., no. 2818, $1,348.41.
7 I. D. Kent, no. 2819, $939.29.
11 M. R. Braskey Company, no. 2820, $1,050.11.
15 The Place, no. 2821, $686.57.
21 Frank R. Baldwin, no. 2822, $899.51.
23 C. R. Kelly, no. 2823, $527.32.
25 Dave P. Hill, no. 2824, $716.82.
26 Brisko C. Johns, no. 2825, $421.20.
28 R. A. Casey, no. 2826, $227.94.
29 Harry C. Wells, no. 2827, $332.92.
30 C. P. Cole, no. 2828, $118.99.

Purchases of Merchandise, Supplies, and Equipment on Account

Sept. 3 Peel Corporation, merchandise, $3,740.50; FOB Houston.
7 Landry Company, merchandise, $2,518.42; FOB San Francisco, freight prepaid and added to the invoice, $116 (total $2,634.42).
9 Sutton Manufacturing Company, merchandise, $1,298.18; FOB Houston.
17 Hess, Inc., store supplies, $427; FOB Houston.
22 Peel Corporation, merchandise, $814.20; FOB Houston.
26 Castor Specialty Products, merchandise, $3,471.14; FOB Boston, freight prepaid and added to the invoice, $152 (total $3,623.14).
30 Jenson Office Furnishings, office equipment, $918.30; FOB Houston.
30 D. C. Cane, Inc., merchandise, $1,210.50; FOB Houston.

Check Figure

Total Sales, $7,269.08

Instructions

1. Journalize the summarizing entry for the sales of merchandise on account in the general journal, page 27.
2. Journalize the summarizing entry for the purchase of goods on account in the general journal.

P.O. 1,2,3,4

Problem 11-4B The following transactions relate to Crest Products during April of this year. Terms of sale are 2/10, n/30. The company is located in Los Angeles.

Apr. 1 Sold merchandise on account to Hagen Hardware, invoice no. 5522, $672.00.

4 Bought merchandise on account from Sely Manufacturing Company, invoice no. C1142, $438; terms 1/10, n/30; dated April 2; FOB San Diego, freight prepaid and added to the invoice, $32 (total $470).

9 Sold merchandise on account to Becker Stores, invoice no. 5523, $1,118.

11 Bought merchandise on account from Barns Products, invoice no. 8990, $1,732.65; terms 2/10, n/30; dated April 11; FOB San Francisco, freight prepaid and added to the invoice, $72 (total $1,804.65).

16 Sold merchandise on account to B. R. Akers, invoice no. 5524, $845.32.

19 Issued credit memo no. 32 to Becker Stores for merchandise returned, $86.

24 Bought merchandise on account from Ashland Manufacturing Company, invoice no. P1981, $1,450.70; terms 2/10, n/30; dated April 22; FOB Santa Rosa, freight prepaid and added to the invoice, $87 (total $1,537.70).

27 Bought office supplies on account from Castle's, invoice no. E621A, dated April 25, $97.41; net 30 days.

28 Sold merchandise on account to Graham Specialty Company, invoice no. 5525, $3,960.00.

29 Issued credit memo no. 33 to B. R. Akers for allowance on damaged merchandise, $91.

30 Received credit memo no. 356 for merchandise returned to Boswell, Inc., for $155.86.

Check Figure

Accounts Payable account balance, $4,198.22

Instructions

1. Open the following accounts in the accounts receivable ledger and record the balances as of April 1: B. R. Akers; Becker Stores, $481.10; Graham Specialty Company, $327.50; Hagen Hardware, $836.00. For the accounts having balances, write "Balance" in the Item column and place a check mark in the Post. Ref. column. Total the amounts and record the balance in the controlling account in the general ledger. (Verify: $1,644.60.)
2. Open the following accounts in the accounts payable ledger and record the balances as of April 1: Ashland Manufacturing Company; Barns Products, $186.40; Boswell, Inc., $257.92; Castle's; Sely Manufacturing Company. For the accounts having balances, write "Balance" in the Item column and place a check mark in the Post Ref. column. Total the amounts and record the balance in the controlling account in the general ledger. (Verify: $444.32.)
3. Journalize the transactions in the sales, purchases, or general journal, as appropriate (sales journal, page 24; purchases journal, page 18; general journal, page 68).
4. Post the entries to the accounts receivable ledger daily.
5. Post the entries to the accounts payable ledger daily.
6. Post the entries in the general journal immediately after you make each journal entry.

7. Post the totals from the special journals at month end.
8. Prepare a schedule of accounts receivable.
9. Prepare a schedule of accounts payable.
10. Compare the totals of the schedules with the balances of the controlling accounts.

Instructions for General Ledger Software

1. Record the transactions in the sales, purchases, or general journal.
   a. For efficiency, analyze the transactions, indicate into which journal each transaction goes, and key the entries in three batches—the sales journal, the purchases journal, and the general journal.
   b. If the program uses a single-column purchases journal, add the amount of the freight to the amount of purchases.
2. Print the journals.
3. Post the amounts from the sales, purchases, and general journals.
4. Print the general ledger.
5. Print a schedule of accounts receivable and compare the total with the balance of the Accounts Receivable control account.
6. Print a schedule of accounts payable and compare the total with the balance of the Accounts Payable control account.

Continuous General Ledger Problem: Purchases Journal

Last month, Like New began to sell restored artwork and furniture in addition to selling its restoration services. Miracle also added a sales journal to the records last month to receive entries for sales of merchandise on account only. This month, Miracle has added a purchases journal to the records to receive entries for purchases of merchandise (for resale) on account only. As the accountant for Like New, you are to journalize and post the following July transactions. All sales on account are 2/10, n/30.

July 1 Sold merchandise on account to Baker Inn, Sales Inv. 2010, $688.

2 Paid $1,140 interest (debit Interest Expense) and $261 on the principal of the mortgage (debit Mortgage Payable), $1,401, Ck. No. 1016.

3 Bought merchandise on account from Frame Co., Inv. no. 1000, $436; terms 2/10, n/30; dated July 3; freight prepaid and added to the invoice, $24 (total $460).

8 Sold merchandise on account to Adeline Harris, Sales Inv. 2011, $327.

10 Bought merchandise on account from Unique Furniture, Inv. no. 3455, $1,261; terms 2/10, n/30; dated July 10; freight prepaid and added to the invoice, $64 (total $1,325).

15 Sold merchandise on account to Gail Murdock, Sales Inv. 2012, $844.60.

16 Paid wages of part-time assistant for the first half of the month, $850, Ck. No. 1017.

20 Issued credit memo no. 3 to Adeline Harris for merchandise returned, $86, Sales Inv. 2011.

23 Bought merchandise on account from Au Furniture, Inv. no. 494, $1,522.50; terms 2/10, n/30; dated July 23; freight prepaid and added to the invoice, $83 (total $1,605.50).

27 Bought supplies on account from The Paint Pot, Inv. no. 998, dated July 26, $46.36; net 30 days.

28 Paid the utility bill for two months, $247, Ck. No. 1018.

29 Sold merchandise on account to Mike Wallen, Sales Inv. 2013, $2,459.

30 Issued credit memo no. 4 to Gail Murdock as an allowance on damaged merchandise, $94, Sales Inv. 2012.

31 Received credit memo no. 17 for merchandise returned to Au Furniture, Inv. no. 494, $144.42.

31 Paid wages of part-time assistant for the second half of the month, $850, Ck. No. 1019.

Note: The Continuous General Ledger Problem can be worked with Houghton Mifflin Windows General Ledger Package, Peachtree Release 5.01, QuickBooks 6.0, or other general ledger software packages.

Instructions

1. Launch the general ledger software.
2. Open the likenew (June) file and rename it for July.
3. Add the following new accounts:

   511 Purchases 512 Purchases Returns and Allowances
   614 Utilities Expense

4. Add the following vendor names and their current balances:

   The Paint Pot $2,164 Au Furniture $423

5. Journalize and post the transactions in either the general journal or one of the two special journals—Sales Journal or Purchases Journal.
6. Print a trial balance ($220,176.88).
7. Print a schedule of accounts receivable ($10,741.60). Compare the total with the Accounts Receivable account in the trial balance. They should be the same. If not, there is an error; reverse the process until you find the error.
8. Print a schedule of accounts payable ($5,855.44). Compare the total with the Accounts Payable account in the trial balance. They should be the same. If not, there is an error; reverse the process until you find the error.

12 The Cash Receipts Journal and the Cash Payments Journal

WINDOWS ON THE WORLD WIDE WEB

The next time you write out a check at your favorite hair salon or barbershop, think about the salon's cash receipts journal and how your sale might be recorded. If you pay by credit card, the salon must pay a bank credit-card expense to cover processing fees for your charge. The Redken highlighter or hair dye used on your hair may have been purchased by the salon at a discount. L'Oréal may give hair salons a trade discount on its Redken brand of hair-care products. Yet if you want to stock up on Redken styling products you will have to pay full price unless you take out a bank loan and open your own shop. So how well is L'Oréal doing financially, despite giving trade discounts? See L'Oréal's web site to find out at **http://www.loreal.com/us/group/index.asp**.

Performance Objectives

After you have completed this chapter, you will be able to do the following:

1. Journalize transactions for a retail merchandising business in a cash receipts journal.
2. Post from a cash receipts journal to a general ledger and an accounts receivable ledger.
3. Determine cash discounts according to credit terms, and record cash receipts from charge customers who are entitled to deduct the cash discount.
4. Journalize transactions in a cash payments journal for a service enterprise.
5. Post from a cash payments journal to a general ledger and an accounts payable ledger.
6. Journalize transactions involving cash discounts in a cash payments journal for a merchandising enterprise.
7. Journalize transactions in a check register.
8. Journalize transactions involving trade discounts.

We have seen that using a sales journal and a purchases journal enables an accountant to carry out the journalizing and posting processes much more efficiently. These special journals make it possible to post column totals rather than individual figures. They also make the division of labor more efficient because the journalizing functions can be delegated to different persons. The *cash receipts journal* and the *cash payments journal* further extend these advantages.

THE CASH RECEIPTS JOURNAL

Objective 1

Journalize transactions for a retail merchandising business in a cash receipts journal.

The **cash receipts journal** contains all transactions in which cash is received, or increases. When a cash receipts journal is used, all transactions in which cash is debited *must* be recorded in it. It may be used for a service as well as a merchandising business. Let's list some typical transactions of a retail merchandising business that result in an increase in cash. To get a better picture of the transactions, let's first record them in T accounts.

May 3 Sold merchandise for cash, $100, plus $8 sales tax.

Cash		Sales		Sales Tax Payable	
+	−	−	+	−	+
108			100		8

A customer using a bank charge card is actually borrowing the money (the total of the sale plus the sales tax) from the issuing bank. The merchandiser is still responsible for remitting the sales tax to the state revenue department.

May 4 Sold merchandise, $100, plus $8 sales tax, and the customer used a bank charge card. The bank issuing the card bills the customer directly each month. The business, on the other hand, deposits the bank credit card receipts every day. The bank *deducts a discount* and credits the firm's account with cash. We will assume that the discount is 4 percent. The firm therefore records the amount of the discount under Credit Card Expense: $108.00 × .04 = $4.32 credit card expense; $100.00 + $8.00 − $4.32 = $103.68.

Cash		Credit Card Expense		Sales Tax Payable		Sales	
+	−	+	−	−	+	−	+
103.68		4.32			8.00		100.00

May 5 Collected cash on account from L. R. Reed, a charge customer, $216.

Cash		Accounts Receivable	
+	−	+	−
216			216

May 7 The owner, G. H. Hall, invested cash in the business, $4,000.

Cash		G. H. Hall, Capital	
+	−	−	+
4,000			4,000

May 8 Sold equipment for cash at cost, $150.

Cash		Equipment	
+	−	+	−
150			150

The same transactions are shown in general journal form as follows:

GENERAL JOURNAL PAGE ______

DATE		DESCRIPTION	POST. REF.	DEBIT	CREDIT
20–					
May	3	Cash		108 00	
		Sales			100 00
		Sales Tax Payable			8 00
		Sold merchandise for cash.			
	4	Cash		103 68	
		Credit Card Expense		4 32	
		Sales			100 00
		Sales Tax Payable			8 00
		Sold merchandise involving			
		a bank charge card.			
	5	Cash		216 00	
		Accounts Receiv., L. R. Reed			216 00
		Collected cash on account.			
	7	Cash		4000 00	
		G. H. Hall, Capital			4000 00
		Owner invested cash.			
	8	Cash		150 00	
		Equipment			150 00
		Sold equipment at cost.			

UPS regularly uses an electronic tablet to record a customer's signature. This provides an instantaneous record to verify delivery. No paper is generated, and the signature can be read by customer service representatives who may have to respond to customer queries.

42507

Now let's analyze these five transactions: The first three would occur frequently; the last two would occur less frequently. When designing a cash receipts journal, it is logical to include a Cash Debit column because all the transactions involve an increase in cash. If a business regularly collects cash from charge customers, there should be an Accounts Receivable Credit column. If a firm often sells merchandise for cash and collects a sales tax, there should be a Sales Credit column and a Sales Tax Payable Credit column. If the business honors bank charge cards and wants to record the amount of the discount at the time of each transaction, there should be a Credit Card Expense Debit column for the amount deducted by the bank.

However, the credit to G. H. Hall, Capital, and the credit to Equipment occur very seldom, so it would not be practical to set up special columns for these credits. They can be handled adequately by an Other Accounts Credit column, which can be used for credits to all accounts that have no special column.

CASH RECEIPTS JOURNAL PAGE 41

	DATE		ACCOUNT CREDITED	POST. REF.	OTHER ACCOUNTS CREDIT	ACCOUNTS RECEIVABLE CREDIT	SALES CREDIT	SALES TAX PAYABLE CREDIT	CREDIT CARD EXPENSE DEBIT	CASH DEBIT	
1	20–										1
2	May	3	___				100 00	8 00		108 00	2
3		4	___				100 00	8 00	4 32	103 68	3
4		5	L. R. Reed			216 00				216 00	4
5		7	G. H. Hall,								5
6			Capital		4000 00					4000 00	6
7		8	Equipment		150 00					150 00	7
8											8

FIGURE 1

Now let's record these transactions in a cash receipts journal (see Figure 1). First, we repeat the transactions:

May 3 Sold merchandise for cash, $100, plus $8 sales tax.
4 Sold merchandise, $100, plus $8 sales tax, and the customer used a bank charge card. Discount charged by the bank is 4 percent of the total of sales plus sales tax.
5 Collected cash on account from L. R. Reed, a charge customer, $216.
7 The owner, G. H. Hall, invested cash in the business, $4,000.
8 Sold equipment for cash at cost, $150.

Remember!

The amount of credit card expense is based on the total of sales *plus* sales tax payable.

Remember!

Special journals include a sales journal, a purchases journal, a cash receipts journal, and a cash payments journal. They are used to save time by posting totals of the special columns rather than individual amounts to the general ledger.

As an alternative, many firms postpone recording the amount of bank credit card expense until they actually receive notification from their bank on their bank statement. For example, total credit card sales for a restaurant for a time period amount to $1,600 plus 6 percent sales tax. The entry is as follows:

Cash	
+	−
1,696	

Sales	
−	+
	1,600

Sales Tax Payable	
−	+
	96

The restaurant's next bank statement includes a debit memorandum for credit card charges of $67.84, using an assumed 4 percent discount rate ($1,696.00 × .04). The firm handles this in a similar manner to a check service charge:

Credit Card Expense	
+	−
67.84	

Cash	
+	−
	67.84

Posting from the Cash Receipts Journal

Here are some other transactions made during the month that involve increases in cash. (Remember that these transactions are for a retail business.)

May 11 Borrowed $300 from the bank, receiving cash and giving the bank a promissory note.
16 Sold merchandise for cash, $200, plus $16 sales tax.
21 Sold merchandise, $50, plus $4 sales tax; customer used a bank charge card. Credit card expense charge is 4 percent of sales plus sales tax.
26 Collected cash from B. Sanchez, a charge customer, on account, $62.40.
28 Sold merchandise for cash, $40, plus $3.20 sales tax.
31 Sold merchandise, $150, plus $12 sales tax; customer used a bank charge card. Credit card expense charge is 4 percent of sales plus sales tax.
31 Collected cash from T. Nguyen, a charge customer, on account, $26.

In the transaction of May 11, in which $300 was borrowed from the bank, the bank was given a **promissory note** (a written promise to pay a specified amount at a specified time) as evidence of the debt. The account **Notes Payable**, instead of Accounts Payable, is used to represent the amount owed on the promissory note. The Accounts Payable account is reserved for charge accounts with creditors, which are normally paid on a thirty-day basis.

Objective 2

Post from a cash receipts journal to a general ledger and an accounts receivable ledger.

Let's assume that all the month's transactions involving debits to Cash have now been recorded in the cash receipts journal. The cash receipts journal (see Figure 2 on the following page) and the T accounts following it illustrate the postings to the general ledger and the accounts receivable ledger.

Individual amounts in the Accounts Receivable Credit column of the cash receipts journal are usually posted daily to the accounts receivable ledger. Individual amounts in the Other Accounts Credit column are usually posted daily.

At the end of the month, we can post the special column totals in the cash receipts journal to the general ledger accounts. These columns include Accounts Receivable Credit, Sales Credit, Sales Tax Payable Credit, Credit Card Expense Debit, and Cash Debit.

FYI

The dash is a placeholder indicating that nothing has been left out or forgotten.

In the Post. Ref. column, the check marks (✓) indicate that the amounts in the Accounts Receivable Credit column have been posted to the individual charge customers' accounts as credits. The account numbers show that the amounts in the Other Accounts Credit column have been posted separately to the accounts described in the Account Credited column. An (X) goes under the total of the Other Accounts Credit column; it means "do not post—the figures have already been posted separately." This column is totaled to make it easier to prove that the debits equal the credits.

Note the ruling. A single rule is placed above the column totals, and double rules extend through all but the Account Credited column. Also, on the last line, the last day of the month is recorded in the Date column.

Let's say it's the end of the month. Total the columns first. Then begin **crossfooting** the journal by proving that the sum of the debit totals equals the sum of the credit totals. This process must be done before you post the totals to the general ledger accounts.

CASH RECEIPTS JOURNAL PAGE 41

DATE		ACCOUNT CREDITED	POST. REF.	OTHER ACCOUNTS CREDIT	ACCOUNTS RECEIVABLE CREDIT	SALES CREDIT	SALES TAX PAYABLE CREDIT	CREDIT CARD EXPENSE DEBIT	CASH DEBIT
20–									
May	3	———	—			100 00	8 00		108 00
	4	———	—			100 00	8 00	4 32	103 68
	5	L. R. Reed	✓		216 00				216 00
	7	G. H. Hall,							
		Capital	311	4000 00					4000 00
	8	Equipment	124	150 00					150 00
	11	Notes							
		Payable	211	300 00					300 00
	16	———	—			200 00	16 00		216 00
	21	———	—			50 00	4 00	2 16	51 84
	26	B. Sanchez	✓		62 40				62 40
	28	———	—			40 00	3 20		43 20
	31	———	—			150 00	12 00	6 48	155 52
	31	T. Nguyen	✓		26 00				26 00
	31			4450 00	304 40	640 00	51 20	12 96	5432 64
				(X)	(113)	(411)	(213)	(515)	(111)

Accounts Receivable Ledger

T. Nguyen

+	−	
	May 31	26.00

L. R. Reed

+	−	
	May 5	216.00

B. Sanchez

+	−	
	May 26	62.40

General Ledger

Cash 111

+		−
May 31	5,432.64	

Accounts Receivable 113

+	−	
	May 31	304.40

Equipment 124

+	−	
	May 8	150.00

Notes Payable 211

−	+	
	May 11	300.00

Sales Tax Payable 213

−	+	
	May 31	51.20

G. H. Hall, Capital 311

−	+	
	May 7	4,000.00

Sales 411

−	+	
	May 31	640.00

Credit Card Expense 515

+		−
May 31	12.96	

FIGURE 2

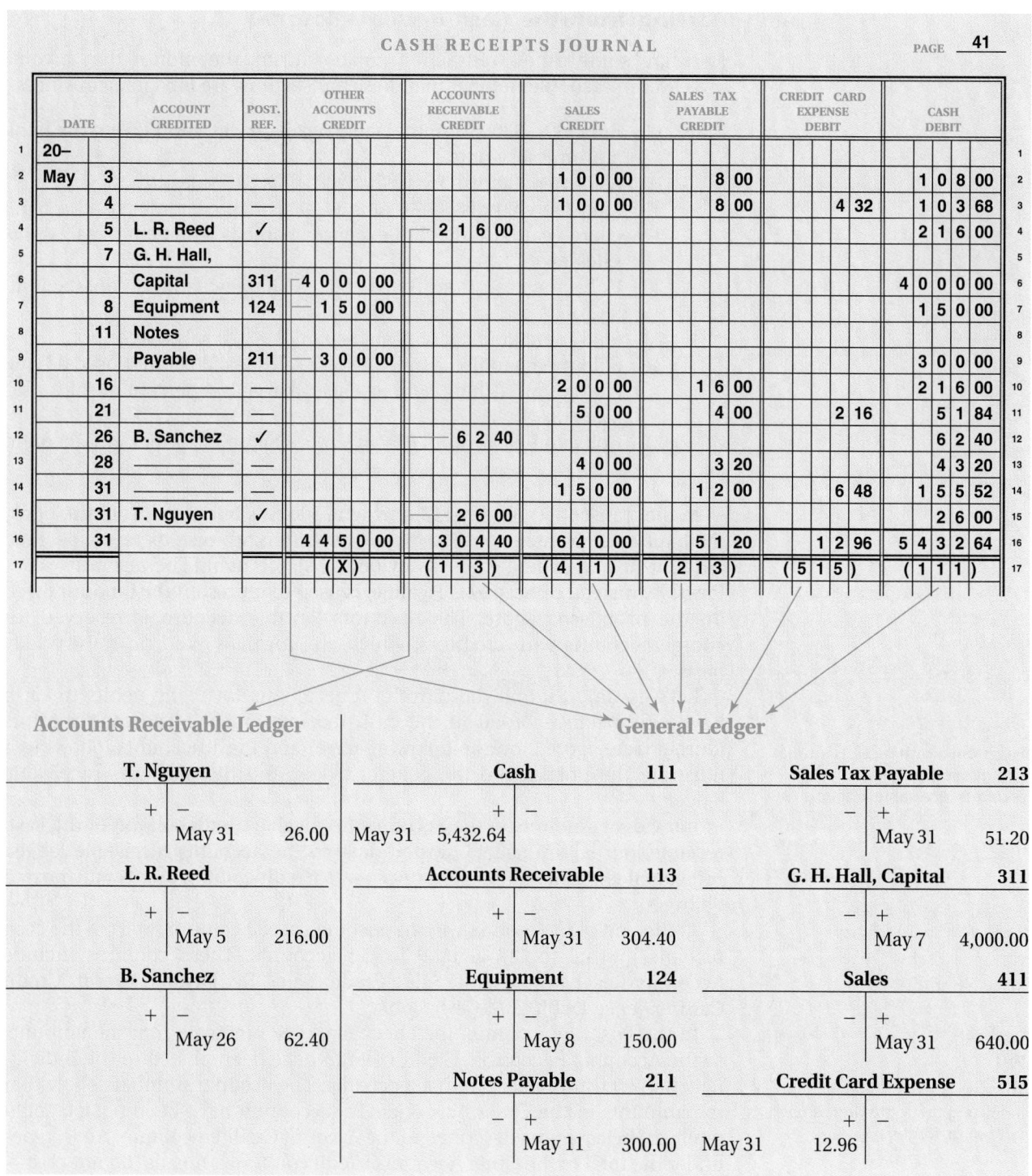

Debit Totals		**Credit Totals**	
Cash	$5,432.64	Other Accounts	$4,450.00
Credit Card Expense	12.96	Accounts Receivable	304.40
		Sales	640.00
		Sales Tax Payable	51.20
	$5,445.60		$5,445.60

Post the special column totals to the general ledger, using the letters CR as the posting reference. Next, write the general ledger account number in parentheses below the total in the appropriate column.

Advantages of a Cash Receipts Journal

1. Transactions generally can be recorded on one line.
2. All transactions involving debits to Cash are recorded in one place.
3. It eliminates much repetition in posting when there are numerous transactions involving Cash debits. The Cash Debit side can be posted as one total.
4. Special columns can be used for specialized transactions and posted as one total.

CREDIT TERMS

Objective 3

Determine cash discounts according to credit terms, and record cash receipts from charge customers who are entitled to deduct the cash discount.

The seller always stipulates credit terms: How much credit can a customer be allowed? And, how much time should the customer be given to pay the full amount? The **credit period** is the time the seller allows the buyer before full payment has to be made. Retailers generally allow twenty-five to thirty days.

Wholesalers and manufacturers often specify a **cash discount** in their credit terms. A cash discount is an amount that a customer can deduct if a bill is paid within a specified time. The discount is based on the *total amount of the invoice after any returns and allowances and freight charges billed on the invoice have been deducted.* Naturally, this discount acts as an incentive for charge customers to pay their bills promptly.

Let's say that a wholesaler offers customers credit terms of 2/10, n/30. These terms mean that the customer gets a 2 percent discount if the bill is paid within ten days after the invoice date. The discount period begins the day after the invoice date. If the bill is not paid within the ten days, the entire amount is due within thirty days after the invoice date. Other cash discounts that may be used are the following:

The cash receipts journal and the cash payments journal are used by both service and merchandising businesses to record all transactions in which cash comes into or goes out of the business.

- **1/15, n/60** The seller offers a 1 percent discount if the bill is paid within fifteen days after the invoice date, and the whole bill must be paid within sixty days after the invoice date.
- **2/10, EOM, n/60** The seller offers a 2 percent discount if the bill is paid within ten days after the end of the month, and the whole bill must be paid within sixty days after the last day of the month.

Patients are expected to pay for services when they are rendered.

A wholesaler or manufacturer that offers a cash discount adopts a single cash discount as a credit policy and makes this available to all its customers. The seller considers cash discounts as sales discounts; the buyer, on the other hand, considers cash discounts as purchases discounts. In this section we are concerned with the sales discount. *The Sales Discount account, like Sales Returns and Allowances, is a deduction from Sales.*

To illustrate, we return to Jackson Electric Supply. We record the following transactions in T accounts.

Transaction (a) August 1: Sold merchandise on account to L. A. Long Company, invoice no. 320; terms 2/10, n/30; $424.

Transaction (b) August 10: Received check from L. A. Long Company for $415.52 in payment of invoice no. 320, less cash discount ($424.00 × .02 = $8.48; $424.00 − $8.48 = $415.52).

Assets		=	Liabilities		+	Owner's Equity		+	Revenue		−	Expenses	
+ Debit	− Credit		− Debit	+ Credit		− Debit	+ Credit		− Debit	+ Credit		+ Debit	− Credit

Cash

+	−
(b) 415.52	

Accounts Receivable

+	−
(a) 424.00	(b) 424.00

Sales

−	+
	(a) 424.00

Sales Discount

+	−
(b) 8.48	

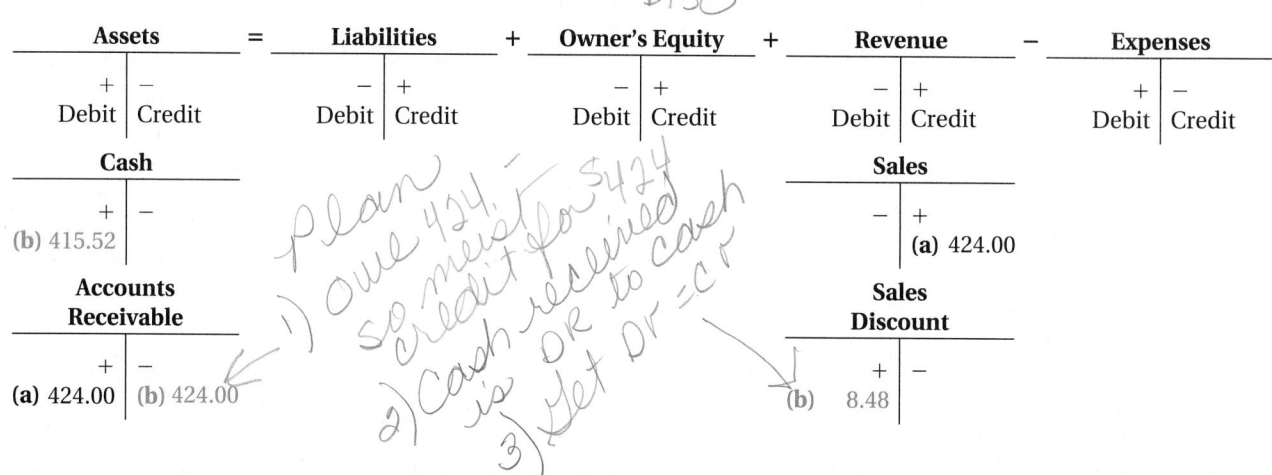

Since Jackson Electric Supply offers this cash discount to all its customers, and since charge customers often pay their bills within the discount period, Jackson Electric Supply sets up a Sales Discount Debit column in the cash receipts journal. Note that Jackson Electric Supply is a wholesaler. Therefore, a column for Sales Tax Payable is not used, since few states levy a tax on sales at the wholesale level.

CASH RECEIPTS JOURNAL PAGE 18

	Date		Account Credited	Post. Ref.	Other Accounts Credit	Accounts Receivable Credit	Sales Credit	Sales Discount Debit	Cash Debit	
1	20–									1
2	Aug.	10	L. A. Long Company			424 00		8 48	415 52	2
3										3

Several other transactions of Jackson Electric Supply during August involve increases in cash. Remember that the standard credit terms for all charge customers are 2/10, n/30.

Aug. 15 Cash sales for first half of the month, $1,460.

16 Received check from Arreloa Construction for $386.12 in payment of invoice no. 322, less cash discount ($394.00 − $7.88 = $386.12).

17 Received payment on a promissory note given by Nancy Turner, $300 principal, plus $3 interest. (The amount of the interest is recorded in Interest Income.)

Aug.	21	Received a check from Colmer Company for $756.80 in payment of invoice no. 324, less cash discount ($772.24 − $15.44 = $756.80).
	23	Sold equipment for cash at cost, $126.
	26	N. C. Jackson, the owner, invested an additional $4,000 cash in the business.
	26	Received a check from Howard and Sons, Inc., for $432.18 in payment of invoice no. 325 less the cash discount ($441.00 − $8.82 = $432.18).
	30	Received a check from Hazen Electric for $695.80 in payment of invoice no. 326, less cash discount ($710.00 − $14.20 = $695.80).
	31	Cash sales for second half of the month, $1,620.
	31	Received a check from Marin, Inc., in payment of invoice no. 321, for $116. (This is longer than the ten-day period, so Marin missed the cash discount.)

Jackson Electric Supply records these transactions in its cash receipts journal (Figure 3).

The company's accountant then proves the equality of debits and credits:

Remember!

When journalizing a cash receipt involving a sales discount, be sure to credit Accounts Receivable for the total amount of the sales transaction.

Debit Totals		**Credit Totals**	
Cash	$10,311.42	Other Accounts	$ 4,429.00
Sales Discount	54.82	Accounts Receivable	2,857.24
		Sales	3,080.00
	$10,366.24		$10,366.24

FIGURE 3

CASH RECEIPTS JOURNAL PAGE 18

DATE		ACCOUNT CREDITED	POST. REF.	OTHER ACCOUNTS CREDIT	ACCOUNTS RECEIVABLE CREDIT	SALES CREDIT	SALES DISCOUNT DEBIT	CASH DEBIT
20–								
Aug.	10	L. A. Long Company	✓		424 00		8 48	415 52
	15	———	—			1460 00		1460 00
	16	Arreloa Construction	✓		394 00		7 88	386 12
	17	Notes Receivable	112	300 00				
		Interest Income	422	3 00				303 00
	21	Colmer Company	✓		772 24		15 44	756 80
	23	Equipment	124	126 00				126 00
	26	N. C. Jackson, Capital	311	4000 00				4000 00
	26	Howard and Sons, Inc.	✓		441 00		8 82	432 18
	30	Hazen Electric	✓		710 00		14 20	695 80
	31	———	—			1620 00		1620 00
	31	Marin, Inc.	✓		116 00			116 00
	31			4429 00	2857 24	3080 00	54 82	10311 42
				(X)	(113)	(411)	(413)	(111)

SALES RETURNS AND ALLOWANCES AND SALES DISCOUNTS ON AN INCOME STATEMENT

In the fundamental accounting equation, to be consistent with the income statement, we placed Sales Returns and Allowances and Sales Discounts under Sales with the plus and minus signs reversed. Both accounts are contra revenue accounts, so we subtract their totals from Sales on the income statement. Here is the Revenue from Sales section of the annual income statement of Jackson Electric Supply.

Jackson Electric Supply
Income Statement
For Year Ended December 31, 20—

Revenue from Sales:			
Sales		$235,180.00	
Less: Sales Returns and Allowances	$ 840.00		
Sales Discounts	1,880.00	2,720.00	
Net Sales			$232,460.00

THE CASH PAYMENTS JOURNAL: SERVICE ENTERPRISE

The **cash payments journal**, as the name implies, is a special journal used to record all transactions in which cash goes out, or decreases. When the cash payments journal is used, all transactions in which cash is credited *must* be recorded in it. This journal may be used for either a service or a merchandising business.

To get acquainted with the cash payments journal, let's list some typical transactions of a service firm (such as a dry cleaner or a bowling alley) or a professional enterprise (such as a lawyer's office) that result in a decrease in cash. To illustrate, we record the following transactions in T accounts:

May 2 Paid L. N. Brown Company, a creditor, on account, Ck. No. 63, $1,220.

Accounts Payable		Cash	
−	+	+	−
1,220			1,220

May 4 Paid cash for supplies, Ck. No. 64, $190.

Supplies		Cash	
+	−	+	−
190			190

May 5 Paid wages for two weeks, Ck. No. 65, $1,216 (previously recorded in the payroll entry).

Wages Payable	
−	+
1,216	

Cash	
+	−
	1,216

May 6 Paid rent for the month, Ck. No. 66, $950.

Rent Expense	
+	−
950	

Cash	
+	−
	950

The same transactions are now shown in general journal form.

GENERAL JOURNAL PAGE ______

DATE		DESCRIPTION	POST. REF.	DEBIT	CREDIT
20–					
May	2	Accounts Payable,			
		L. N. Brown Co.		1220 00	
		Cash			1220 00
		Paid on account, Ck. No. 63.			
	4	Supplies		190 00	
		Cash			190 00
		Paid cash for supplies,			
		Ck. No. 64.			
	5	Wages Payable		1216 00	
		Cash			1216 00
		Paid wages for two weeks,			
		Ck. No. 65.			
	6	Rent Expense		950 00	
		Cash			950 00
		Paid rent for month,			
		Ck. No. 66.			

Let's analyze these four transactions. The first one would occur frequently, as payments to creditors are made several times a month. Of the last three transactions, the debit to Wages Payable might occur twice a month, the debit to Rent Expense once a month, and the debit to Supplies only occasionally.

It is logical to include a Cash Credit column in a cash payments journal because all transactions recorded in this journal involve a decrease in cash. Since payments to creditors are made often, there should also be an

Accounts Payable Debit column. You can set up any other column that is used often enough to warrant it. Otherwise, an Other Accounts Debit column takes care of all the other transactions.

Objective 4

Journalize transactions in a cash payments journal for a service enterprise.

Now let's record these same transactions in a cash payments journal and include a column titled Ck. No. If you think a moment, you will see that this is consistent with good management of cash. All expenditures except Petty Cash expenditures should be paid for by check. Let's repeat the transactions.

May 2 Paid L. N. Brown Company, a creditor, on account, Ck. No. 63, $1,220.
4 Paid cash for supplies, Ck. No. 64, $190.
5 Paid wages for two weeks, Ck. No. 65, $1,216 (previously recorded in the payroll entry).
6 Paid rent for the month, Ck. No. 66, $950.

CASH PAYMENTS JOURNAL PAGE 62

	DATE		CK. NO.	ACCOUNT DEBITED	POST. REF.	OTHER ACCOUNTS DEBIT	ACCOUNTS PAYABLE DEBIT	CASH CREDIT	
1	20–								1
2	May	2	63	L. N. Brown Co.			1,220.00	1,220.00	2
3		4	64	Supplies		190.00		190.00	3
4		5	65	Wages Payable		1,216.00		1,216.00	4
5		6	66	Rent Expense		950.00		950.00	5
6									6

Other transactions involving decreases in cash during May are as follows:

May 7 Paid a one-year premium for fire insurance, Ck. No. 67, $360.
9 Paid Morris, Inc., a creditor, on account, Ck. No. 68, $418.
11 Issued Ck. No. 69 in payment of delivery expense, $62.
14 Paid Russet and Son, a creditor, on account, Ck. No. 70, $110.
16 Issued Ck. No. 71 to the Logan State Bank for a Note Payable, $660, $600 on the principal and $60 interest.
19 Voided Ck. No. 72.
19 Bought equipment from Snyder Company for $200. Issued Ck. No. 73.
20 Paid wages for two weeks, Ck. No. 74, $1,340 (previously recorded in the payroll entry).
22 Issued Ck. No. 75 to Scheel Advertising Agency for advertising, $94 (not previously recorded).
26 Paid telephone bill, Ck. No. 76, $26.
31 Issued check for freight bill on equipment purchased on May 19, Ck. No. 77, $28.
31 Paid Lynn and Trask, a creditor, on account, Ck. No. 78, $160.

You should list all checks in consecutive order, even those checks that must be voided. In this way, *every* check is accounted for, which is necessary for internal control.

These transactions are recorded in the cash payments journal illustrated in Figure 4. Notice that an (X) is placed under the Other Accounts column. That means "do not post—the individual figures have already been posted."

FIGURE 4

CASH PAYMENTS JOURNAL PAGE 62

DATE		CK. NO.	ACCOUNT DEBITED	POST. REF.	OTHER ACCOUNTS DEBIT	ACCOUNTS PAYABLE DEBIT	CASH CREDIT
20–							
May	2	63	L. N. Brown Co.	✓		1220 00	1220 00
	4	64	Supplies	113	190 00		190 00
	5	65	Wages Payable	214	1216 00		1216 00
	6	66	Rent Expense	512	950 00		950 00
	7	67	Prepaid Insurance	114	360 00		360 00
	9	68	Morris, Inc.	✓		418 00	418 00
	11	69	Delivery Expense	513	62 00		62 00
	14	70	Russet and Son	✓		110 00	110 00
	16	71	Notes Payable	211	600 00		
			Interest Expense	518	60 00		660 00
	19	72	Void	—			
	19	73	Equipment	121	200 00		200 00
	20	74	Wages Payable	214	1340 00		1340 00
	22	75	Advertising				
			Expense	515	94 00		94 00
	26	76	Telephone				
			Expense	516	26 00		26 00
	31	77	Equipment	121	28 00		28 00
	31	78	Lynn and Trask	✓		160 00	160 00
	31				5126 00	1908 00	7034 00
					(X)	(221)	(111)

At the end of the month, after totaling the columns, check the accuracy of the footings by proving that the sum of the debit totals equals the sum of the credit totals. Since you have posted the individual amounts in the Other Accounts Debit column to the general ledger, the only posting that remains is the credit to the Cash account for $7,034 and the debit to the Accounts Payable (controlling) account for $1,908.

Debit Totals		**Credit Totals**	
Other Accounts	$5,126.00	Cash	$7,034.00
Accounts Payable	1,908.00		
	$7,034.00		$7,034.00

Objective 5

Post from a cash payments journal to a general ledger and an accounts payable ledger.

The posting process for the cash payments journal is similar to the posting process for the cash receipts journal. Individual amounts in the Accounts Payable Debit column are usually posted daily to the subsidiary ledger. After posting, put a check mark (✓) in the Post. Ref. column. Individual amounts in the Other Accounts Debit column are usually posted daily to the general ledger. Post these figures individually, then place the account number in the Post. Ref. column. Totals of the Cash Credit column and the Accounts Payable Debit column are posted to the general ledger accounts at the end of the month. Write the appropriate general ledger account number in parentheses below the column totals. Print an (X) below the total of the Other Accounts Debit column to indicate that the total amount is not posted. The posting letter designation for the cash payments journal is CP.

Remember!

The (X) below the total of the Other Accounts Debit column means "do not post total."

The advantages of the cash payments journal are similar to the advantages of the cash receipts journal:

1. Transactions generally can be recorded on one line.
2. All the transactions involving credits to Cash are recorded in one place.
3. For numerous transactions involving Cash credits, the Cash Credit side can be posted as one total.
4. Special columns can be used for specialized transactions and posted as one total.

THE CASH PAYMENTS JOURNAL: MERCHANDISING ENTERPRISE

Objective 6

Journalize transactions involving cash discounts in a cash payments journal for a merchandising enterprise.

There is one slight difference between the cash payments journal for a merchandising enterprise and that for a service enterprise. This difference has to do with the cash discounts available to a merchandising business. Recall that a cash discount is the amount that the buyer may deduct from the bill; this acts as an incentive to get the buyer to pay the bill promptly. The buyer considers the cash discount to be a purchases discount, because it relates to the buyer's purchase of merchandise. The Purchases Discount account, like Purchases Returns and Allowances, is treated as a deduction from Purchases on the buyer's income statement.

Let's return to Jackson Electric Supply and assume that the following transactions take place. To demonstrate the debits and credits, we show some typical transactions in the form of T accounts.

Transaction (a) August 2: Bought merchandise on account from Draper, Inc., $420, its invoice no. 2706, dated July 31; terms 2/10, n/30; FOB San Francisco, freight prepaid and added to the invoice, $30 (total invoice $450).

Remember!

The cash discount does not apply to freight charges billed separately on an invoice.

Transaction (b) August 8: Issued Ck. No. 76 to Draper, Inc., in payment of invoice no. 2706 less the cash discount of $8.40, $441.60 ($450.00 − $8.40), which is recorded in the cash payments journal. Notice that the discount applies only to the amount billed for the merchandise (2 percent of $420). Here are the transactions shown in T accounts:

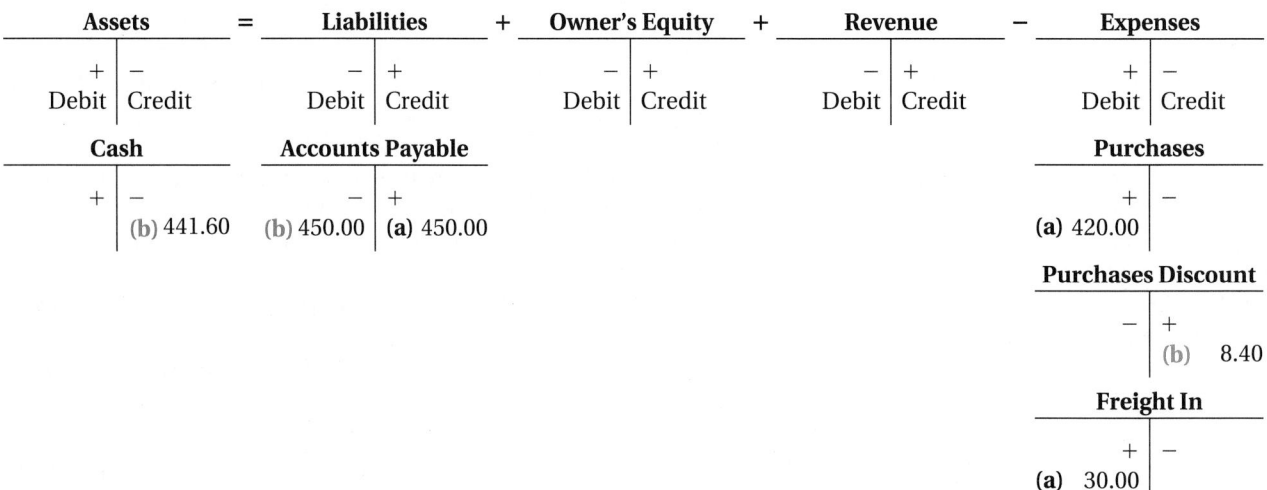

Assets		=	Liabilities		+	Owner's Equity		+	Revenue		−	Expenses	
+	−		−	+		−	+		−	+		+	−
Debit	Credit		Debit	Credit		Debit	Credit		Debit	Credit		Debit	Credit

Cash

+	−
	(b) 441.60

Accounts Payable

−	+
(b) 450.00	(a) 450.00

Purchases

+	−
(a) 420.00	

Purchases Discount

−	+
	(b) 8.40

Freight In

+	−
(a) 30.00	

Any well-managed business takes advantage of a purchases discount whenever possible. So, if a discount is generally available to the business, it is worthwhile to set up a special Purchases Discount Credit column in the cash payments journal. Transaction **(b),** August 8, looks like this in the cash payments journal:

CASH PAYMENTS JOURNAL — PAGE 26

DATE		CK. NO.	ACCOUNT DEBITED	POST. REF.	OTHER ACCOUNTS DEBIT	ACCOUNTS PAYABLE DEBIT	PURCHASES DISCOUNT CREDIT	CASH CREDIT
20–								
Aug.	8	76	Draper, Inc.			450 00	8 40	441 60

Here are some other transactions of Jackson Electric Supply involving decreases in cash during August. Note that credit terms vary among the different creditors. Detailed information on the purchase invoices paid below is available in the purchases journal on page 372.

Aug. 10 Paid wages for two-week period, Ck. No. 77, $1,680 (previously recorded in the payroll entry).

11 Issued Ck. No. 78 to Adkins Manufacturing Company, in payment of invoice no. 10611 ($692), less return ($70); less cash discount, 2/10, n/30; $609.56 ($692 − $70 = $622; $622.00 × .02 = $12.44; $622.00 − $12.44 = $609.56).

12 Bought supplies for cash; issued Ck. No. 79 payable to Dillon Office Supplies, $70.

15 Issued Ck. No. 80 to Sullivan Products Company in payment of its invoice no. B643 ($165) less return ($36); less cash discount, 1/10, n/30; $127.81 [$165 − $36 = $129; freight charges totaled $10.00 ($129 − $10 = $119); $119.00 × .01 = $1.19; $129.00 − $1.19 = $127.81].

16 Bought merchandise for cash, Ck. No. 81, payable to James and Son, $200.

19 Received bill and issued Ck. No. 82 to Mullin Express for freight charges on merchandise purchased earlier from Adkins Manufacturing Company, $60.

23 Voided Ck. No. 83.

23 Issued Ck. No. 84 to Amco Fire Insurance Company for insurance premium for one year, $420.

25 Paid wages for two-week period, Ck. No. 85, $1,750 (previously recorded in the payroll entry).

27 Paid G. O. Fromer for merchandise he returned on a cash sale, Ck. No. 86, $51.

31 Issued Ck. No. 87 to Reilly and Peters in partial payment of invoice no. 982, net 30 days, $180.

Remember!

After posting to the accounts payable subsidiary ledger from the cash payments journal, record a check mark in the Post. Ref. column in the cash payments journal.

The transaction of August 19 (Mullin Express) increases the Freight In account because the transportation charges are for merchandise purchased.

CASH PAYMENTS JOURNAL PAGE 26

DATE		CK. NO.	ACCOUNT DEBITED	POST. REF.	OTHER ACCOUNTS DEBIT	ACCOUNTS PAYABLE DEBIT	PURCHASES DISCOUNT CREDIT	CASH CREDIT
20–								
Aug.	8	76	Draper, Inc.	✓		450.00	8.40	441.60
	10	77	Wages Payable	214	1,680.00			1,680.00
	11	78	Adkins Manufacturing Company	✓		622.00	12.44	609.56
	12	79	Supplies	115	70.00			70.00
	15	80	Sullivan Products Company	✓		129.00	1.19	127.81
	16	81	Purchases	551	200.00			200.00
	19	82	Freight In	514	60.00			60.00
	23	83	Void	—				
	23	84	Prepaid Insurance	114	420.00			420.00
	25	85	Wages Payable	214	1,750.00			1,750.00
	27	86	Sales Returns and Allowances	412	51.00			51.00
	31	87	Reilly and Peters	✓		180.00		180.00
	31				4,231.00	1,381.00	22.03	5,589.97
					(X)	(221)	(513)	(111)

FIGURE 5

Now let's record these transactions in the cash payments journal (Figure 5). Jackson Electric Supply's accountant then proves the equality of debits and credits:

Debit Totals		**Credit Totals**	
Other Accounts	$4,231.00	Cash	$5,589.97
Accounts Payable	1,381.00	Purchases Discount	22.03
	$5,612.00		$5,612.00

CHECK REGISTER

Objective 7

Journalize transactions in a check register.

Instead of using a cash payments journal as a book of original entry, you can use a check register. The **check register** is merely a large checkbook with perforations that make it easy to tear out the checks. The page opposite the checks has columns labeled for special accounts, such as Bank Credit (in place of Cash), Accounts Payable Debit, and so on. The checks are prenumbered, and each check issued is recorded on the columnar sheet. This is common practice for a small business in which the owner writes the checks personally. Transactions are posted directly from the check register.

Suppose Jackson Electric Supply had used a check register instead of the cash payments journal. Its August transactions would appear as they do in Figure 6.

what Differences

CHECK REGISTER PAGE ______

DATE		CK. NO.	PAYEE	ACCOUNT DEBITED	POST. REF.	OTHER ACCOUNTS DEBIT	ACCOUNTS PAYABLE DEBIT	PURCHASES DISCOUNT CREDIT	CITY BANK CREDIT
20–									
Aug.	8	76	Draper, Inc.	Draper, Inc.	✓		450 00	8 40	441 60
	10	77	Payroll	Wages Payable	214	1680 00			1680 00
	11	78	Adkins	Adkins					
			Manufacturing Co.	Manufacturing	✓		622 00	12 44	609 56
	12	79	Dillon Office						
			Supplies	Supplies	115	70 00			70 00
	15	80	Sullivan	Sullivan					
			Products Co.	Products Co.	✓		129 00	1 19	127 81
	16	81	James and Son	Purchases	511	200 00			200 00
	19	82	Mullin Express	Freight In	514	60 00			60 00
	23	83	Void	————	—				
	23	84	Amco Fire	Prepaid					
			Insurance Co.	Insurance	114	420 00			420 00
	25	85	Payroll	Wages Payable	214	1750 00			1750 00
	27	86	G. O. Fromer	Sales Ret. and					
				Allowances	412	51 00			51 00
	31	87	Reilly and Peters	Reilly and Peters	✓		180 00		180 00
	31					4231 00	1381 00	22 03	5589 97
						(X)	(221)	(513)	(111)

FIGURE 6

Remember!

In the Post. Ref. column, a check mark indicates that the amount has been posted to the creditor's account in the accounts payable ledger; below the total of the Other Accounts Debit column, an (X) indicates that the total is not to be posted.

You can see that the difference between the cash payments journal and the check register is minor. The Bank Credit column substitutes for the Cash Credit column. The check register lists the payee of the check.

Two additional columns, Deposits and Bank Balance, can be added to give the current balance of the City Bank or Cash account. The posting process for each book of original entry is the same.

In a small business, the owner or manager usually signs all the checks. However, if the owner delegates the authority to sign checks to some other person, that person should *not* have access to the accounting records. Why? This helps prevent fraud, because a dishonest employee could conceal a cash disbursement in the accounting records. In other words, for a medium- to large-size business, a manager should keep a separate book, which in this case is the cash payments journal. One person writes the checks; another person records the checks in the cash payments journal; and a third person does the bank reconciliation. In this way, each person acts as a control on the others. There would have to be cooperation among the three people for embezzlement to take place. This precaution is consistent with a good system of internal control, because more than one person is involved in the process of recording cash payments. This system also provides protection against errors. One person can double-check the other person's work.

Comparison of Transactions for Two Companies' Purchases and Sales

Remember!

To the seller, a cash discount is a sales discount and is recorded in the cash receipts journal as a debit. To the purchaser, a cash discount is a purchases discount and is recorded in the cash payments journal as a credit.

Purchaser's Books—Able Company	Seller's Books—Baker Company
Bought merchandise from Baker Company, $500; terms 2/10, n/30.	Sold merchandise to Able Company, $500; terms 2/10, n/30.
Dr. Purchases, $500 Cr. Accounts Payable, $500	Dr. Accounts Receivable, $500 Cr. Sales, $500
Received credit memo from Baker Company for return of merchandise, $100.	Issued credit memo to Able Company for return of merchandise, $100.
Dr. Accounts Payable, $100 Cr. Purchases Returns and Allowances, $100	Dr. Sales Returns and Allowances, $100 Cr. Accounts Receivable, $100
Paid Baker Company within the discount period, $392 ($500 − $100 = $400; $400 × .02 = $8; $400 − $8 = $392).	Received cash from Able Company within the discount period, $392.
Dr. Accounts Payable, $400 Cr. Cash, $392 Cr. Purchases Discount, $8	Dr. Cash, $392 Dr. Sales Discount, $8 Cr. Accounts Receivable, $400

TRADE DISCOUNTS

Objective 8

Journalize transactions involving trade discounts.

Manufacturers and wholesalers of many lines of products publish annual catalogs listing their products at retail prices. These organizations offer their customers substantial reductions (often as much as 40 percent) from the list or catalog prices. The reductions from the list prices are called **trade discounts**. Trade discounts are not journalized. Remember, firms grant cash discounts for prompt payment of invoices. Trade discounts are *not related* to cash payments. Manufacturers and wholesalers use trade discounts to avoid the high cost of reprinting catalogs when selling prices change. To change prices, the manufacturer or wholesaler simply issues a sheet showing a new list of trade discounts to be applied to the catalog prices. Trade discounts can also be used to differentiate between classes of customers. For example, a manufacturer may use one schedule of trade discounts for wholesalers and another schedule for retailers.

Firms may quote trade discounts as a single percentage. *Example:* A distributor of furnaces grants a single discount of 40 percent off the listed catalog price of $8,000. In this case, the selling price is calculated as follows:

List or catalog price	$8,000
Less trade discount of 40% ($8,000 × .4)	3,200
Selling price	$4,800

Neither the seller nor the buyer records trade discounts in the accounts; they enter only the selling price. Using T accounts, the furnace distributor records the sale like this:

Accounts Receivable		Sales	
+	−	−	+
4,800			4,800

The buyer records the purchase as follows:

Purchases		Accounts Payable	
+	−	−	+
4,800			4,800

Firms may also quote trade discounts as a chain, or series, of percentages. For example, a distributor of automobile parts grants discounts of 30 percent, 10 percent, and 10 percent off the listed catalog price of $900. In this case, the selling price is calculated as follows:

List or catalog price	$900.00
Less first trade discount of 30% ($900 × .3)	270.00
Remainder after first discount	$630.00
Less second trade discount of 10% ($630 × .1)	63.00
Remainder after second discount	$567.00
Less third discount of 10% ($567 × .1)	56.70
Selling price	$510.30

Using T accounts, the automobile parts distributor records the sale as follows:

Accounts Receivable		Sales	
+	−	−	+
510.30			510.30

The buyer records the purchase as follows:

Purchases		Accounts Payable	
+	−	−	+
510.30			510.30

In the situation involving a chain of discounts, the additional discounts are granted for large-volume transactions, either in dollar amount or in size of shipment, such as carload lots.

Cash discounts could also apply in situations involving trade discounts. *Example:* Suppose that the credit terms of the preceding sale include a cash discount of 2/10, n/30, and that the buyer pays the invoice within ten days. The seller applies the cash discount to the selling price. The seller records the transaction as shown on the following page.

Cash		Sales Discount		Accounts Receivable	
+	−	+	−	+	−
500.09		10.21			510.30

The buyer records the transaction as follows:

Cash		Purchases Discount		Accounts Payable	
+	−	−	+	−	+
	500.09		10.21	510.30	

COMPARISON OF THE FIVE TYPES OF JOURNALS

We have now looked at four special journals and the general journal. It is very important for a business to select and use the journals that provide the most efficient accounting system possible. Figure 7 summarizes the applications of the journals we have discussed and correct procedures for using them.

FIGURE 7

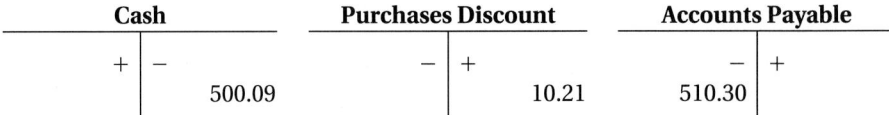

		Types of Transactions		
Sale of merchandise on account	Purchase of merchandise on account	Receipt of cash	Payment of cash	All other
		Evidenced by Source Documents		
Sales invoice	Purchase invoice	Credit card receipts Cash Checks	Check stub	Miscellaneous
		Types of Journals		
Sales journal	Purchases journal	Cash receipts journal	Cash payments journal	General journal
		Posting to Ledger Accounts		
Individual amounts posted daily to the accounts receivable ledger and the total posted monthly to the general ledger.	*Individual amounts posted daily to the accounts payable ledger and the totals of the special columns posted monthly to the general ledger.*	*Individual amounts in the Accounts Receivable Credit column posted daily to the accounts receivable ledger.* *Individual amounts in the Other Accounts columns posted daily to the general ledger.* *Totals of special columns posted monthly.*	*Individual amounts in the Accounts Payable Debit column posted daily to the accounts payable ledger.* *Individual amounts in the Other Accounts columns posted daily to the general ledger.* *Totals of special columns posted monthly.*	*Entries posted daily to the subsidiary ledgers and the general ledger.*

Recommended Order of Posting to the Subsidiary Ledgers and the General Ledger

To avoid errors and negative balances in accounts, post from the special journals in this order:

1. Sales journal
2. Purchases journal
3. Cash receipts journal
4. Cash payments journal

Posting of general journal entries depends on the dates of the specific transactions.

CHAPTER REVIEW

Review of Performance Objectives

1. Journalize transactions for a retail merchandising business in a cash receipts journal.

   A transaction for a retail merchandising business can be recorded on one line in a cash receipts journal. The cash receipts journal usually contains the following columns: Date, Account Credited, Post. Ref., Other Accounts Credit, Accounts Receivable Credit, Sales Credit, Sales Tax Payable Credit, Credit Card Expense Debit, and Cash Debit.

2. Post from a cash receipts journal to a general ledger and an accounts receivable ledger.

   The accountant posts daily from the Accounts Receivable Credit column to the individual charge customers' accounts in the accounts receivable ledger. After posting, the accountant puts a check mark (✓) in the Post. Ref. column. The accountant also posts the amounts in the Other Accounts Credit column daily and records the account numbers in the Post. Ref. column. The special columns are posted as totals at the end of the month. The accountant then writes the account numbers in parentheses under the totals. An (X) below the total of the Other Accounts Credit column shows that amounts are posted individually and the total is not posted.

3. Determine cash discounts according to credit terms, and record cash receipts from charge customers who are entitled to deduct the cash discount.

   The same cash discount is available to all the supplier's customers. The amount of the discount is determined by multiplying the invoice total (excluding freight charges and any returns and allowances) by the cash discount rate (usually 1 or 2 percent). The amount of the discount is recorded as a debit to Sales Discount.

4. Journalize transactions in a cash payments journal for a service enterprise.

   A cash payment by a service enterprise can be handled on one line in a cash payments journal. The cash payments journal usually contains the following columns: Date, Ck. No., Account Debited, Post. Ref., Other Accounts Debit, Accounts Payable Debit, and Cash Credit.

5. Post from a cash payments journal to a general ledger and an accounts payable ledger.

The accountant posts daily from the Accounts Payable Debit column to the individual suppliers' accounts in the accounts payable ledger. After posting, the accountant puts a check mark (✓) in the Post. Ref. column. The accountant also posts the amounts in the Other Accounts Debit column daily and records the account numbers in the Post. Ref. column. The special columns are posted as totals at the end of the month. The accountant then writes the account numbers in parentheses under the totals. An (X) below the total of the Other Accounts Debit column shows that amounts are posted individually and the total is not posted.

6. Journalize transactions involving cash discounts in a cash payments journal for a merchandising enterprise.

   A cash payment by a merchandising enterprise that includes a purchase discount can be recorded on one line in a cash payments journal. The cash payments journal usually contains the following columns: Date, Ck. No., Account Debited, Post. Ref., Other Accounts Debit, Accounts Payable Debit, Purchases Discount Credit, and Cash Credit.

7. Journalize transactions in a check register.

   Transactions can be recorded on one line in a check register. The check register is similar to the cash payments journal. However, the check register has an additional column entitled Payee, and instead of a Cash Credit column there is often a column with the name of the bank (City Bank Credit, for example).

8. Journalize transactions involving trade discounts.

   In transactions involving trade discounts, the trade discounts are deducted from the list prices to arrive at the selling prices. Both sellers and buyers record the transactions at the selling prices.

Glossary

Bank charge card A bank credit card, like the credit cards used by millions of private citizens. The cardholder pays what she or he owes directly to the issuing bank. The business firm deposits the credit card receipts; the amount of the deposit equals the total of the receipts, less a discount deducted by the bank. (404)

Cash discount The amount a customer can deduct for paying a bill within a specified period of time; used to encourage prompt payment. Not all sellers offer cash discounts. (409)

Cash payments journal A special journal used to record all transactions involving cash payments or decreases. (412)

Cash receipts journal A special journal used to record all transactions involving cash receipts or increases. (404)

Check register A journal in which checks are listed as they are written. A check register replaces a cash payments journal. (418)

Credit period The time the seller allows the buyer before full payment on a charge sale has to be made. (409)

Notes Payable The account containing the balance of promissory notes. (407)

Promissory note A written promise to pay a specified amount at a specified time. (407)

Trade discount A substantial discount from the list or catalog prices of goods, granted by the seller; not recorded by the buyer or the seller. (420)

QUESTIONS, EXERCISES, AND PROBLEMS

Discussion Questions

1. What are the normal balances of (a) Purchases? (b) Sales Discount? (c) Purchases Returns and Allowances? (d) Sales? (e) Purchases Discount? (f) Sales Returns and Allowances?
2. What does an (X) below the total of a special journal's Other Accounts column signify?
3. Explain the following credit terms: (a) n/30; (b) 2/10, n/60; (c) 1/15, EOM, n/30.
4. In a cash receipts journal, both the Accounts Receivable Credit column and the Cash Debit column were mistakenly understated by $100. How will this error be discovered?
5. If a cash payments journal is supposed to save writing, why are there so many entries in the Other Accounts Debit column?
6. Describe the posting procedure for a cash payments journal with an Other Accounts Debit column and several special columns, including an Accounts Payable Debit column.
7. An electronics business purchased speakers for resale. The total of the invoice is $3,600, and it is subject to trade discounts of 15 percent, 10 percent, and 5 percent. Compute the amount the dealer will pay for the speakers.
8. What is the difference between a cash discount and a trade discount?

Exercises

P.O. 1

Describe a recorded transaction involving sale of merchandise with sales tax, paid by credit card.

Exercise 12-1 Describe the transaction recorded.

Cash (Dr.)	Cash (Cr.)	Sales Tax Payable (Dr.)	Sales Tax Payable (Cr.)	Sales (Dr.)	Sales (Cr.)	Credit Card Expense (Dr.)	Credit Card Expense (Cr.)
424.20			21.00		420.00	16.80	

P.O. 1,3

Label column headings.

Exercise 12-2 Label the blanks in the column heads as either debit or credit.

CASH RECEIPTS JOURNAL PAGE ____

	DATE	ACCOUNT CREDITED	POST. REF.	OTHER ACCOUNTS ____	ACCOUNTS RECEIVABLE ____	SALES ____	SALES DISCOUNT ____	CASH ____	
1									1

P.O. 6

Describe posted transactions.

Exercise 12-3 Describe the transactions recorded in the following T accounts.

Cash	
	(c) 1,479.80

Accounts Payable	
(b) 170	(a) 1,680
(c) 1,510	

Purchases	
(a) 1,680	

Purchases Returns and Allowances	
	(b) 170

Purchases Discount	
	(c) 30.20

P.O. 6

Calculate amounts paid for merchandise purchases involving returns and cash discounts.

Exercise 12-4 For the following purchases of merchandise, determine the amount of cash to be paid:

Purchase	Invoice Date	Credit Terms	FOB	Amount of Purchase	Freight Charges	Total Invoice Amount	Returns and Allowances	Date Paid
a.	June 1	2/10, n/30	Destination	$460	—	$ 460	—	June 30
b.	June 12	1/10, n/30	Destination	700	—	700	$100	June 21
c.	June 14	2/10, n/30	Shipping point	860	$60	920	—	June 20
d.	June 21	n/30	Shipping point	930	70	1,000	130	July 12
e.	June 24	1/10, n/30	Shipping point	660	50	710	90	July 3

P.O. 1,6

Designate the appropriate journal.

Exercise 12-5 Indicate the journal in which each of the following transactions should be recorded. Assume a three-column purchases journal.

	Journal				
Transaction	S	P	CR	CP	J
a. Paid a creditor on account.					
b. Bought merchandise on account.					
c. Sold merchandise for cash.					
d. Adjusted for insurance expired.					
e. Received payment on account from a charge customer.					
f. Received a credit memo for merchandise returned.					
g. Bought equipment on credit.					
h. Sold merchandise on account.					
i. Recorded a customer's NSF check.					
j. Invested personal noncash assets in the business.					
k. Withdrew cash for personal use.					

P.O. 3

Journalize transactions involving sales and purchases of merchandise with returns and cash discounts.

Exercise 12-6 Journalize the following transactions in general journal form:

May 4 Sold merchandise on account to Secor, Inc.; 2/10, n/30; $690.
10 Purchased merchandise on account from the Manly Company; 1/10, n/60; FOB shipping point; $940.
11 Paid freight bill on merchandise purchased from the Manly Company, $37, to Golden Freight Lines.
13 Received full payment from Secor, Inc.
14 Received a credit memo from the Manly Company for defective merchandise returned, $104.
19 Paid the Manly Company in full within the discount period.
28 Bought merchandise on account from Beal Company, $910; 2/10, n/30; freight prepaid and added to the invoice, $37 (total, $947).

P.O. 3

Journalize transactions involving sale and purchase of merchandise, a return, and a cash discount.

Exercise 12-7 Journalize the following transactions in general journal form, first on the books of the seller (Rye Company) and then on the books of the buyer (Low Company).

Rye Company

a. Sold merchandise on account to Low Company; 2/10, n/30; $1,500.
b. Issued a credit memo to Low Company for damaged merchandise, $100.
c. Low Company paid the account in full within the discount period.

Low Company

a. Purchased merchandise on account from Rye Company; 2/10, n/30; $1,500.
b. Received a credit memo from Rye Company for damaged merchandise, $100.
c. Paid the Rye Company account in full within the discount period.

P.O. 8

Make correcting entries involving freight charges, returns, and trade discounts.

Exercise 12-8 Journalize general journal entries to correct the errors described below. Assume that the incorrect entries were posted in the same period in which the errors occurred.

a. A freight cost of $55 incurred on equipment purchased for use in the business was debited to Freight In.
b. The issuance of a credit memo to Sorino Company for $96 for merchandise returned was recorded as a debit to Purchases Returns and Allowances and a credit to Accounts Receivable, Sorino Company.
c. A cash purchase of $118 of store supplies for the business was recorded as office supplies.
d. A cash sale of $72 to M. A. Max was recorded as a sale on account.
e. A purchase of merchandise from Arms Company in the amount of $1,000 with a 30 percent trade discount was recorded as a debit to Purchases and a credit to Accounts Payable of $1,000 each.

CONSIDER AND COMMUNICATE

You are the manager of the Accounts Receivable Department for a merchandising business. Your billing clerk sent a bill for $2 to a customer who had charged $100 in goods with terms 2/10, n/30. The customer has called and indicated his displeasure; he can't understand an error like this, since he paid on time. Explain to your billing clerk why Accounts Receivable is credited for $100 and not $98. How was permission given to send less than the full amount?

CRITICAL THINKING

You work for Dawson Plumbing Supply. You are responsible for training a new accounting clerk. He has the following questions for you to answer about this invoice:

Dawson Plumbing Supply
1400 Jackson Avenue
Chicago, Illinois 60612

No. 320

INVOICE

SOLD TO C. P. Lind Company
5210 Gilman Avenue
San Diego, CA 92102

DATE: August 1, 20–
ORDER NO.: 5384
SHIPPED BY: Fast Freight
TERMS: 2/10, n/30
SALESPERSON: H. M.

QUANTITY	DESCRIPTION	UNIT PRICE	TOTAL
6	Olin single-control tub shower faucet #44B652	51 50	309 00
6	Olin dual-control washerless lavatory faucet #59B641	22 20	133 20
12	Olin massage shower head, antique brass #37B411	11 56	138 72
	Subtotal		580 92
	Freight		63 80
	Total		644 72

1. Who is the buyer?
2. Who is paying the freight?
3. What is the customer's order number?
4. What percentage of the goods bought is the cost of the freight?
5. What are the credit terms and what do they mean?
6. How much will the buyer actually have to pay if it sends the money in ten days?
7. What is the dollar amount of the discount?
8. Who receives the discount?
9. What is the due date for payment to get the discount?
10. Why would a seller give a buyer a discount?

A MATTER OF ETHICS

When the new accountant started work, the owner took him out to lunch each Friday to discuss problems, progress, and suggestions to improve the business. One Friday, the owner couldn't go to lunch with the accountant. The accountant took the money for his lunch from petty cash and charged it to the owner's drawing account. He reasoned that the owner always took him to lunch on Friday, and he didn't have money for lunch. This happened several Fridays during the year. Was this a fair assumption for the accountant to make? Was it ethical?

WEB WORK

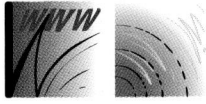

Using an Internet web browser, type the phrase for the home page of a company selling accounting software in the search box. Search for information about different brands of general ledger software. Compare the packages for features, modules, cost, the size of the company the software is designed to serve, the level of accounting knowledge needed by the user, and technical assistance. Discuss or write your findings in a memo to your supervisor.

PROBLEM SET A

For additional help, see the demonstration problem at the beginning of each chapter in your Working Papers.

P.O. 1,2

Problem 12-1A Freddy and Company, a retail carpet store, sells on the bases of (1) cash, (2) charge accounts, and (3) bank credit cards. The following transactions involved cash receipts for the firm during May of this year. The bank charges 4 percent on the total of the credit card sales plus sales tax. (For all sales involving credit cards, record credit card expense at the time of the sale.)

May	8	Total cash sales for the week, $1,380, plus $69 sales tax.
	8	Total sales for the week paid for by bank credit cards, $1,600, plus $80 sales tax.
	11	D. C. Colter, the owner, invested an additional $4,000.
	11	Collected cash from N. D. Poyor, a charge customer, $82.50.
	12	Sold store equipment at cost for cash, $270.
	15	Total cash sales for the week, $1,880, plus $94 sales tax.
	15	Total sales for the week paid for by bank credit cards, $950, plus $47.50 sales tax.
	19	Borrowed $2,500 from the bank; receiving the same in cash and giving the bank a promissory note.
	21	Collected cash from R. Brace, a charge customer, $86.
	22	Total cash sales for the week, $2,105, plus $105.25 sales tax.
	22	Total sales for the week paid for by bank credit cards, $1,375, plus $68.75 sales tax.
	24	Received cash as refund for the return of merchandise purchased, $152.60.
	26	Collected cash from C. Fely, a charge customer, $158.
	31	Total cash sales for the remainder of the month, $2,486, plus $124.30 sales tax.
	31	Total sales for the remainder of the month paid for by bank credit cards, $1,050, plus $52.50 sales tax.
	31	Collected cash from R. D. Thor, a charge customer, $157.60.

Check Figure

Total Sales Credit, $12,826

Instructions

1. Open the following accounts in the accounts receivable ledger and record the May 1 balances as given: R. Brace, $86; C. Fely, $188; S. R. Page, $114.72; N. D. Poyor, $82.50; R. D. Thor, $157.60; F. N. Wicks, $72.45. Place a check mark in the Post. Ref. column.
2. Record a balance of $701.27 in the Accounts Receivable controlling account as of May 1.
3. Journalize the transactions in the cash receipts journal beginning with page 62.
4. Post daily to the accounts receivable ledger.
5. Total and rule the cash receipts journal.
6. Prove the equality of debit and credit totals.
7. Post to the Accounts Receivable account in the general ledger.
8. Prepare a schedule of accounts receivable. Compare the total with the balance of the Accounts Receivable account.

P.O. 1,3

Problem 12-2A Pearson Company sells candy wholesale to vending machine operators. Terms of sales on account are 2/10, n/30, FOB shipping point. The following transactions involving cash receipts and sales of merchandise took place in May of this year:

May	1	Received $1,058.40 cash from L. Rich in payment of April 22 invoice of $1,080, less cash discount.
	4	Received $1,026 cash in payment of $950 note receivable and interest of $76.
	7	Received $882 cash from K. L. Shane in payment of April 29 invoice of $900, less cash discount.
	8	Sold merchandise on account to D. Pane, invoice no. 272, $572.
	16	Cash sales for first half of May, $4,741.
	17	Received cash from D. Pane in payment of invoice no. 272, less cash discount.
	20	Received $342 cash from L. N. Shay in payment of April 16 invoice, no discount.
	21	Sold merchandise on account to R. O. Wexel, invoice no. 285, $820.
	24	Received $371 cash refund for return of defective equipment that was originally bought for cash.
	27	Sold merchandise on account to R. Jones, invoice no. 292, $536.
	31	Cash sales for second half of May, $4,241.

Check Figure

Total sales on account, $1,928

Instructions

1. Journalize the transactions for May in the cash receipts journal and the sales journal.
2. Total and rule the journals.
3. Prove the equality of debit and credit totals.

P.O. 7

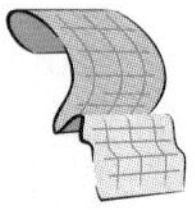

Problem 12-3A The Book Worm uses a check register to keep track of expenditures. The following transactions occurred during February of this year:

Feb.	3	Issued check no. 4312, $725.20, to Kent Company for the amount of its invoice no. 681 recorded previously for $740, less 2 percent cash discount.
	4	Paid freight bill to King Express Company, $58, for books purchased; issued check no. 4313.
	6	Paid rent for the month, $750; check no. 4314, to Mayer Company.

Feb. 11 Received and paid bill for advertising in the *Eastside News*, $155; check no. 4315.
11 Paid Conley Book Company $841.50, check no. 4316, for its invoice no. A331 recorded previously for $850 less 1 percent cash discount.
17 Paid wages recorded previously for first half of February, $550; check no. 4317.
21 R. D. Macky, the owner, withdrew $800 for personal use; check no. 4318.
26 Made payment on bank loan, $940; check no. 4319, consisting of $870 on the principal and $70 interest, Coast National Bank.
27 Paid Gary Publishing Company $1,200, check no. 4320, for its invoice no. 7768 recorded previously (no discount).
28 Voided check no. 4321.
28 Paid wages expense recorded previously for second half of February, $550; check no. 4322.

Check Figure
Total First Nat'l Bank Credit, $6,569.70

Instructions

1. Journalize the transactions in the check register.
2. Total and rule the check register.
3. Prove the equality of the debit and credit totals.

P.O. 1,2,3,5,6

Problem 12-4A The following transactions were completed by Hayden Auto Supply during January, which is the first month of this fiscal year. Terms of sale are 2/10, n/30.

Jan. 2 Paid rent for the month, $650; check no. 6981.
2 J. Helena, the owner, invested an additional $2,500 in the business.
4 Bought merchandise on account from Vicks and Company, $2,930; its invoice no. A691, dated January 2; terms 2/10, n/30.
4 Received check from Van Appliance for $1,176 in payment of $1,200 invoice less discount.
4 Sold merchandise on account to L. Parks, $950, invoice no. 6483.
6 Received check from Peters, Inc., for $735 in payment of $750 invoice less discount.
7 Issued check no. 6982, $686, to Franklin Company in payment of its invoice no. C1272 for $700 less discount.
7 Bought supplies on account from Dobson Office Supply, $108; its invoice no. 1906B; terms net 30 days.
7 Sold merchandise on account to Engle Company, $990, invoice no. 6484.
9 Issued credit memo no. 43 to L. Parks, $40, for merchandise returned.
11 Cash sales for January 1 to January 10, $4,943.
11 Paid Vicks and Company $2,871.40; check no. 6983, in payment of $2,930 invoice less discount.
14 Sold merchandise on account to Van Appliance, $2,140, invoice no. 6485.
18 Bought merchandise on account from Cross Products, $4,120; its invoice no. 7281D, dated January 16; FOB shipping point, freight prepaid and added to the invoice $150 (total invoice, $4,270); terms 2/10, n/60.
21 Issued check no. 6984, $370, to *The Shopper* for advertising not recorded previously (Miscellaneous Expense).
21 Cash sales for January 11 to January 20, $3,640.

Jan. 23 Received and paid invoice from Fast Freight; check no. 6985, $96, for freight charges on merchandise purchased on January 4.
23 Received credit memo no. 163, $315, from Cross Products for merchandise returned.
29 Sold merchandise on account to Byron Supply, $1,710, invoice no. 6486.
31 Cash sales, January 21 to January 31, $4,786.
31 Issued check no. 6986 for $56 payable to M. Dore for miscellaneous expenses.
31 Recorded payroll entry from the payroll register; total salaries, $6,200; employees' federal income tax withheld, $904; FICA tax withheld, $465.
31 Recorded the payroll taxes: FICA, $465; state unemployment tax, $334.80; federal unemployment tax, $49.60.
31 Issued check no. 6987, $4,831, for salaries for the month.
31 J. Helena, the owner, withdrew $900 for personal use, check no. 6988.

Check Figure

Trial balance totals, $63,328

Instructions

1. Journalize the transactions for January, using a sales journal, page 73; a purchases journal, page 56; a cash receipts journal, page 38; a cash payments journal, page 45; a general journal, page 100. The chart of accounts is as follows:

111 Cash
113 Accounts Receivable
114 Merchandise Inventory
115 Supplies
116 Prepaid Insurance
121 Equipment

215 Salaries Payable
216 Employees' Federal Income Tax Payable
217 FICA Tax Payable
218 State Unemployment Tax Payable
219 Federal Unemployment Tax Payable
221 Accounts Payable

311 J. Helena, Capital
312 J. Helena, Drawing

411 Sales
412 Sales Returns and Allowances
413 Sales Discount

511 Purchases
512 Purchases Returns and Allowances
513 Purchases Discount
514 Freight In

621 Salary Expense
622 Payroll Tax Expense
627 Rent Expense
631 Miscellaneous Expense

2. Post daily all entries involving customer accounts to the accounts receivable ledger.
3. Post daily all entries involving creditor accounts to the accounts payable ledger.
4. Post daily those entries involving the Other Accounts columns and the general journal to the general ledger. Write the owner's name in the Capital and Drawing accounts.
5. Add the columns of the special journals, and prove the equality of debit and credit totals on scratch paper.

6. Post the appropriate totals of the special journals to the general ledger.
7. Prepare a trial balance.
8. Prepare a schedule of accounts receivable and a schedule of accounts payable. Do the totals equal the balances of the related controlling accounts?

Instructions for General Ledger Software

1. Journalize the transactions in the sales journal, purchases journal, cash receipts journal, cash payments journal, and general journal.
   a. For efficiency, analyze the transactions, indicate what journal each transaction goes into, and key the entries in five groups or batches, one for each journal.
   b. Because the program uses a single-column purchases journal, add the amount of the freight to the amount of purchases.
2. Print the journals.
3. Post the amounts from the sales, purchases, cash receipts, cash payments, and general journals.
4. Print a trial balance.
5. Print a schedule of accounts receivable and compare the total with the balance of the Accounts Receivable controlling account.
6. Print a schedule of accounts payable and compare the total with the balance of the Accounts Payable controlling account.

PROBLEM SET B

For additional help, see the demonstration problem at the beginning of each chapter in your Working Papers.

P.O. 1,2

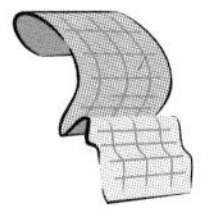

Problem 12-1B Low-Cost Furniture, a home furnishings store, sells on the bases of (1) cash, (2) charge accounts, and (3) bank credit cards. The following transactions involve cash receipts for the firm for November of this year. The bank charges 4 percent of the total credit card sales plus tax. (For all sales involving credit cards, record credit card expense at the time of the sale.)

Nov. 7 Total cash sales for the week, $1,900, plus $95 sales tax.
7 Total sales from bank credit cards for the week, $2,300, plus $115 sales tax.
11 M. R. Vaa, the owner, invested an additional $4,500.
12 Collected cash from T. R. Allard, a charge customer, $162.40.
12 Sold office equipment for cash, $425.
14 Total cash sales for the week, $2,734.60, plus $136.73 sales tax.
14 Total sales from bank credit cards for the week, $1,980, plus $99 sales tax.
18 Borrowed $5,000 from the bank, signing a promissory note.
19 Collected cash from N. P. Troy, a charge customer, $192.40.
21 Total cash sales for the week, $3,840, plus $192 sales tax.
21 Total sales from bank credit cards for the week, $2,260, plus $113 sales tax.
22 Low-Cost Furniture received cash as a refund for the return of merchandise it purchased, $271.

Nov. 24 Collected cash from C. E. Barry, a charge customer, $255.46.
30 Total cash sales for the remainder of the month, $4,531.50, plus $226.58 sales tax.
30 Total sales from bank credit cards for the remainder of the month, $397.10, plus $19.86 sales tax.
30 Collected cash from O. Harris, a charge customer, $182.17.

Check Figure

Total Sales Credit, $19,943.20

Instructions

1. Open the following accounts in the accounts receivable ledger and record the November 1 balances as given: T. R. Allard, $162.40; C. E. Barry, $255.46; L. R. Cao, $106.46; L. P. Drew, $179.52; O. Harris, $182,17; N. P. Troy, $192.40. Place a check mark in the Post. Ref. column.
2. Record a balance of $1,078.41 in the Accounts Receivable controlling account as of November 1.
3. Journalize the transactions in the cash receipts journal beginning with page 16.
4. Post daily to the accounts receivable ledger.
5. Total and rule the cash receipts journal.
6. Prove the equality of debit and credit totals.
7. Post to the Accounts Receivable account in the general ledger.
8. Prepare a schedule of accounts receivable. Compare the total with the balance of the Accounts Receivable account.

P.O. 1,3

Problem 12-2B The C. R. Mitchel Company sells candy wholesale, primarily to vending machine operators. Terms of sales on account are 2/10, n/30, FOB shipping point. The following transactions involving cash receipts and sales of merchandise took place in May of this year:

May 2 Received $823.20 cash from N. Rockney in payment of April 23 invoice of $840 less cash discount.
5 Received $594 cash in payment of $550 note receivable and interest of $44.
8 Sold merchandise on account to G. Sellers, invoice no. 862, $511.
9 Received $627.20 in cash from D. Marks in payment of April 30 invoice of $640, less cash discount.
15 Cash sales for first half of May, $3,857.
16 Received cash from G. Sellers in payment of invoice no. 862, less discount.
19 Received $353 in cash from R. O. Hays in payment of April 14 invoice, no discount.
22 Sold merchandise on account to N. T. Jakes, invoice no. 887, $684.
25 Received $218 cash refund for return of defective equipment bought in April for cash.
28 Sold merchandise on account to M. E. Mars, invoice no. 910, $818.
31 Cash sales for the second half of May, $3,449.

Check Figure

Total sales on account, $2,013

Instructions

1. Journalize the transactions for May in the cash receipts journal and the sales journal.
2. Total and rule the journals.
3. Prove the equality of debit and credit totals.

P.O. 7

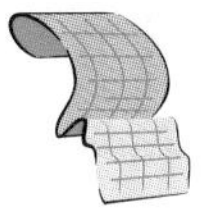

Problem 12-3B Newkirk Company uses a check register to keep track of expenditures. The following transactions occurred during February of this year:

Feb. 1 Issued check no. 4311 to Benson Company for its invoice no. 3113 recorded previously; $870 less cash discount of $17.40, $852.60.
2 Paid freight bill to The Express Company, $64, for merchandise purchased, issuing check no. 4312.
4 Paid rent for month of February, $550; check no. 4313 to Drexel Realty.
9 Received and paid bill for advertising in *Neighborhood News;* check no. 4314, $236.
10 Paid Delaney Company $1,202.85, check no. 4315, for its invoice no. D642 recorded previously in the amount of $1,215 less 1 percent cash discount.
15 Paid wages for first half of month, $1,562; check no. 4316 (payroll entry was previously recorded).
19 R. Newkirk, the owner, withdrew $700 for personal use; check no. 4317.
25 Made payment on bank loan, $648; check no. 4318, consisting of $600 on principal and $48 interest, Second National Bank.
27 Issued to Lacy Publishing Company check no. 4319, $528, for its invoice no. 6317 recorded previously (no discount).
28 Voided check no. 4320.
28 Paid wages recorded previously for second half of month; $1,562, check no. 4321.

Check Figure

Total First Nat'l Bank Credit, $7,905.45

Instructions

1. Journalize the transactions in the check register.
2. Total and rule the check register.
3. Prove the equality of the debit and credit totals.

P.O. 1,2,3,6

Problem 12-4B The following transactions were completed by Top Restaurant Equipment during January, the first month of this fiscal year. Terms of sale are 2/10, n/30.

Jan. 2 Paid rent for the month, $675; check no. 6981.
2 E. Yu, the owner, invested an additional $2,500 in the business.
4 Bought merchandise on account from Vicks and Company, $2,430; its invoice no. A694, terms 2/10, n/30; dated January 2.
4 Received check from Van Appliance for $1,176 in payment of invoice for $1,200 less discount.
4 Sold merchandise on account to L. Parks, $860, invoice no. 6483.
6 Received check from Peters, Inc., for $735 in payment of $750 invoice less discount.
7 Issued check no. 6982, $686, to Franklin Company in payment of its invoice no. C127 for $700, less discount.
7 Bought supplies on account from Dobson Office Supply, $104.50, its invoice no. 1906B; terms net 30 days.
7 Sold merchandise on account to Engle Company, $910, invoice no. 6484.
9 Issued credit memo no. 43 to L. Parks, $45, for merchandise returned.

Jan. 11 Cash sales for January 1 to January 10, $4,120.18.
11 Paid Vicks and Company $2,381.40; check no. 6983, in payment of its $2,430 invoice, less discount.
14 Sold merchandise on account to Van Appliance, $1,830, invoice no. 6485.
18 Bought merchandise on account from Cross Products, $3,250; its invoice no. 7281, dated January 16; terms 2/10, n/60; FOB shipping point, freight prepaid and added to invoice, $110 (total invoice, $3,360).
21 Issued check no. 6984, $270, for advertising to Barclay Agency not recorded previously (Miscellaneous Expense).
21 Cash sales for January 11 through January 20, $3,911.
23 Received and paid invoice from Fast Freight; check no. 6985, $102, for freight charges on merchandise purchased January 4.
23 Received credit memo no. 163, $82, from Cross Products for merchandise returned.
29 Sold merchandise on account to Byron Supply, $1,720, invoice no. 6486.
31 Cash sales for January 21 through January 31, $4,104.
31 Issued check no. 6986, $55, to M. Dore for miscellaneous expenses not recorded previously.
31 Recorded payroll entry from the payroll register: total salaries, $6,050; employees' federal income tax withheld, $918; FICA tax withheld, $462.83.
31 Recorded the payroll taxes: FICA, $462.83; state unemployment tax, $326.70; federal unemployment tax, $48.40.
31 Issued check no. 6987, $4,669.17, for salaries for the month.
31 E. Yu, the owner, withdrew $800 for personal use, check no. 6988.

Check Figure
Trial balance totals, $60,701.04

Instructions

1. Journalize the transactions for January, using a sales journal, page 73; a purchases journal, page 74; a cash receipts journal, page 56; a cash payments journal, page 63; a general journal, page 119. The chart of accounts is as follows:

111 Cash
113 Accounts Receivable
114 Merchandise Inventory
115 Supplies
116 Prepaid Insurance
121 Equipment

215 Salaries Payable
216 Employees' Federal Income Tax Payable
217 FICA Tax Payable
218 State Unemployment Tax Payable
219 Federal Unemployment Tax Payable
221 Accounts Payable

311 E. Yu, Capital
312 E. Yu, Drawing

411 Sales
412 Sales Returns and Allowances
413 Sales Discount

511 Purchases
512 Purchases Returns and Allowances
513 Purchases Discount
514 Freight In

621 Salary Expense
622 Payroll Tax Expense
627 Rent Expense
631 Miscellaneous Expense

2. Post daily all entries involving customer accounts to the accounts receivable ledger.
3. Post daily all entries involving creditor accounts to the accounts payable ledger.
4. Post daily those entries involving the Other Accounts columns and the general journal to the general ledger. Write the owner's name in the Capital and Drawing accounts.
5. Add the columns of the special journals, and prove the equality of debit and credit totals on scratch paper.
6. Post the appropriate totals of the special journals to the general ledger.
7. Prepare a trial balance.
8. Prepare a schedule of accounts receivable and a schedule of accounts payable. Do the totals equal the balances of the related controlling accounts?

Instructions for General Ledger Software

1. Journalize the transactions in the sales journal, purchases journal, cash receipts journal, cash payments journal, and general journal.
   a. For efficiency, analyze the transactions, indicate what journal each transaction goes into, and key the entries in five groups or batches, one for each journal.
   b. Because the program uses a single-column purchases journal, add the amount of the freight to the amount of purchases.
2. Print the journals.
3. Post the amounts from the sales, purchases, cash receipts, cash payments, and general journals.
4. Print a trial balance.
5. Print a schedule of accounts receivable and compare the total with the balance of the Accounts Receivable controlling account.
6. Print a schedule of accounts payable and compare the total with the balance of the Accounts Payable controlling account.

Continuous General Ledger Problem: Cash Receipts and Cash Payments Journals

During June and July, Like New added a sales journal and a purchases journal to the records to reduce writing and to save time. This month, August, Miracle has added a cash receipts journal (for all entries that increase cash) and a cash payments journal (for all entries that decrease cash). As the accountant for Like New, you are to journalize and post the following August transactions. All sales on account are 2/10, n/30.

Aug. 1 J. Miracle, the owner, invested a photocopy machine in the business, $350 (Office Equipment).

2 Paid the $1,140 interest (debit Interest Expense) and $261 on the principal of the mortgage (debit Mortgage Payable), $1,401, Ck. No. 1020.

3 Bought merchandise on account from Frame Co., Inv. no. 1054, $1,130; terms 2/10, n/30; dated August 3; freight prepaid and added to the invoice, $118 (total $1,248).

4 Received a check for $3,697.54 from Mike Wallen on account, $3,773 less 2% discount.

7 Received a check for $500 from Baker Inn on account, Sales Inv. 2011, no discount.

8 Issued a check for $1,605.50 to Au Furniture in payment of its invoice no. 494 for $1,605.50, Ck. No. 1021. Too late for discount.

9 Bought supplies on account from Office Ready, $43, invoice no. 416; terms net 30 days.

10 Sold merchandise on account to Baker Inn, Sales Inv. 2015, $1,788.

11 Cash sales for August 1 through August 10, $1,790.82 (Service Income) and $2,004.40 (Merchandise Income).

12 Paid Unique Furniture $1,325 in payment of its invoice no. 3455 for $1,325, Ck. No. 1022. Too late for the discount.

14 Bought merchandise on account from Au Furniture, Inv. no. 3474, $4,905; terms 2/10, n/30; dated August 14; freight prepaid and added to the invoice, $187 (total $5,092).

15 Sold merchandise on account to Mike Wallen, Sales Inv. 2016, $1,294.

16 Paid wages of part-time assistant for the first half of the month, $850, Ck. No. 1023.

18 Bought merchandise on account from Au Furniture, Inv. no. 502, $4,908; terms 2/10, n/30; dated July 23.

19 Issued a check for $876 for advertising to Castle Ads, Ck. No. 1024 (Advertising Expense).

19 Paid the utility bill, $125, Ck. No. 1025.

Note: The Continuous General Ledger Problem can be worked with Houghton Mifflin Windows General Ledger Package, Peachtree Release 5.01, QuickBooks 6.0, or other general ledger software packages.

Aug. 20 Cash sales for August 11 through August 20, $2,100 (Service Income) and $2,060 (Merchandise Income).

21 Received credit memo no. 24 for merchandise returned to Au Furniture, Inv. no. 502, $108.

24 Sold merchandise on account to Gail Murdock, Sales Inv. 2017, $1,916.

25 Received and paid invoice 2760 from WayFast Freight, Ck. No. 1026, $186, for freight purchased on August 18.

26 Issued Ck. No. 1027 to M. Pierce for $86 for flowers (Miscellaneous Expense).

27 J. Miracle, owner, withdrew $435 for personal use, Ck. No. 1028.

31 Cash sales for August 21 through August 31, $1,309 (Service Income) and $2,309 (Merchandise Income).

31 Paid wages of part-time assistant for the second half of the month, $850, Ck. No. 1029.

Instructions

1. Launch the general ledger software.
2. Open the likenew (July) file and rename it for August.
3. Add the following new accounts:

416 Sales Discount	614 Miscellaneous Expense
514 Freight In	615 Advertising Expense

4. Add the following vendor: Office Ready.
5. Journalize and post the transactions in either the general journal or one of the four special journals—Sales Journal, Purchases Journal, Cash Receipts Journal, or Cash Payments Journal.
6. Print a trial balance ($245,197.60).
7. Print a schedule of accounts receivable ($11,466.60). Compare the total with the Accounts Receivable account in the trial balance. They should be the same. If not, there is an error; reverse the process until you find the error.
8. Print a schedule of accounts payable ($14,107.94). Compare the total with the Accounts Payable account in the trial balance. They should be the same. If not, there is an error; reverse the process until you find the error.

Cumulative Self-Check: Chapters 10–12

PART I: COMPLETION

Complete each of the following statements by writing the appropriate word(s) in the spaces provided:

1. The normal balance of the Purchases Discount account is on the ______ side.
2. Entries in the Accounts Payable Debit column of a cash payments journal are posted daily to the ______.
3. The ______ is the amount a customer may deduct for paying a bill within a specified period of time.
4. The form sent to the supplier of merchandise is called a(n) ______.
5. The ______ account is used to record the buying of merchandise for resale only.
6. If the freight charges are FOB shipping point, the ______ pays the transportation charges.
7. Plans and procedures built into the accounting system to promote efficiency and prevent fraud and waste are called ______.
8. Increases in Sales Returns and Allowances are recorded on the ______ side.
9. The sales journal is used to record all ______.
10. The schedule of accounts receivable lists the balances of all the ______ customers' accounts at the end of the month.

PART II: MATCHING

For each numbered item, choose the appropriate journal, and write the identifying letter.

____ 1. Paid freight bill on merchandise purchased.

____ 2. Bought office equipment for our office on account.

____ 3. Received a credit memo for merchandise we returned.

____ 4. Journalized the adjustment for supplies used.

S Sales journal

P Purchases journal (3 columns)

CR Cash receipts journal

CP Cash payments journal

J General journal

Note: Answers to Cumulative Self-Check begin on page A-1.

____ 5. Sold merchandise on account.

____ 6. Journalized the closing entries.

____ 7. Paid state sales tax to the state revenue department.

____ 8. Bought merchandise for resale on account.

____ 9. Sold merchandise for cash.

____ 10. Bought merchandise for resale for cash.

PART III: TRUE/FALSE

For each question circle T if it is True or circle F if it is False.

T F 1. The Purchases Discount account is classified as a revenue account.

T F 2. The normal balance of the Sales Discount account is on the debit side.

T F 3. Check marks in the Post. Ref. column of the sales journal indicate that the amounts are not to be posted.

T F 4. When you post directly from the purchases invoice, you eliminate the accounts payable ledger.

T F 5. The purchases journal is used for the buying of merchandise for cash and on account.

13 Work Sheet and Adjusting Entries

WINDOWS ON THE WORLD WIDE WEB

How many videos do you watch in a year? Chances are you can find many of them at Blockbuster. Each store carries approximately 7,000 to 10,000 videos. And Blockbuster, Inc., is the only national video chain in the United States with more than 4,000 video stores. You can be sure to find your favorite drama, comedy, or action flick without traveling too far. Imagine taking inventory of all those videos. Would you use a periodic inventory system or a perpetual inventory system? How would you record supplies used, depreciation, and expired insurance for Blockbuster? What would you need to write on the work sheet? How would you make adjustments for unearned revenue? To find out fun stats about Blockbuster, visit **http://www.blockbuster.com/co/trivia.jhtml**.

Performance Objectives

After you have completed this chapter, you will be able to do the following:

1. Prepare an adjustment for merchandise inventory under the periodic inventory system.
2. Prepare an adjustment for unearned revenue.
3. Record the adjustment data in a work sheet (including merchandise inventory, unearned revenue, supplies used, expired insurance, depreciation, and accrued wages or salaries).
4. Complete the work sheet.
5. Journalize the adjusting entries for a merchandising business under the periodic inventory system.
6. Journalize the adjusting entry for merchandise inventory under the perpetual inventory system.

We have talked about the special journals and accounts kept by a merchandising business. Now we take another step toward completing the accounting cycle by presenting the related adjustments and the work sheet. Many of the adjustments made by a service business are also made by a merchandising firm. First, let's briefly review the adjusting entries described so far. To begin, look over the following accounts.

Supplies		Prepaid Insurance		Accumulated Depreciation		Wages Expense	
+	−	+	−	−	+	+	−
Bal. 600		Bal. 300			Bal. 1,000	Bal. 2,600	

Here are the data for the adjustments, along with the related adjusting entries:

Ending supplies inventory, $250. (Remember, subtract the amount left over to get the amount used: $600 − $250 = $350.)

Supplies			
	+	−	
Bal.	600	Adj.	350
Bal.	250		

Supplies Expense			
	+	−	
Adj.	350		

Insurance expired, $260. (The amount expired is the amount used.)

Prepaid Insurance			
	+	−	
Bal.	300	Adj.	260
Bal.	40		

Insurance Expense			
	+	−	
Adj.	260		

Additional depreciation, $280. (Add to both accounts.)

Depreciation Expense			
	+	−	
Adj.	280		

Accumulated Depreciation			
	−	+	
		Bal.	1,000
		Adj.	280
		Bal.	1,280

Accrued wages (owed but not yet paid), $390. (Add to both accounts.)

Wages Expense			
	+	−	
Bal.	2,600		
Adj.	390		
Bal.	2,990		

Wages Payable			
	−	+	
		Adj.	390

In this chapter, we introduce two more adjusting entries. One adjustment is for merchandise inventory, which is used exclusively for a merchandising business. Another adjustment is for unearned revenue, which could apply to either a merchandising or a service business. We also discuss how to handle the specialized accounts of a merchandising business in the work sheet. Finally, we briefly describe the perpetual inventory system and the accompanying adjustment.

ADJUSTMENT FOR MERCHANDISE INVENTORY USING THE PERIODIC INVENTORY SYSTEM

Objective 1

Prepare an adjustment for merchandise inventory under the periodic inventory system.

Under the **periodic inventory system**, we do not make an entry in the Merchandise Inventory account until an actual **physical inventory** or count of the stock of goods on hand has been taken. Instead, we record the purchase of merchandise as a debit to Purchases for the amount of the cost and the sale of the merchandise as a credit to Sales for the amount of the selling price. Finally, after a physical count of merchandise has been taken, one method of adjusting inventory is to make two adjusting entries to record the dollar amount of the inventory. The first adjusting entry is to remove the beginning inventory. The second entry is to enter the ending inventory.

Consider this example. A firm has a Merchandise Inventory balance of $37,000, which represents the cost of the inventory at the beginning of the fiscal period. At the end of the fiscal period, the firm takes an actual count of the stock on hand and determines the cost of the ending inventory to be $42,000. Naturally, in any business, goods are constantly being bought, sold, and replaced. The cost of the ending inventory is larger than the cost of the beginning inventory because the firm bought more than it sold. When we adjust the Merchandise Inventory account, we place the new figure of $42,000 in the account. This method can require two steps.

Step 1 Eliminate the amount of the beginning inventory from the Merchandise Inventory account by closing the account into Income Summary. This transfers the balance into Income Summary. (Remove the beginning inventory.)

Merchandise Inventory				Income Summary			
	+	–					
				Adj.	37,000 ①		
Bal.	37,000	Adj.	37,000 ①				

We handle this just as we handle the closing of any other account, by making the balance equal to zero. We treat the entry as a credit to Merchandise Inventory and then do the opposite to Income Summary, which means that we debit this account.

Remember!

The Income Summary account is the same Income Summary account that we used to record closing entries. Income Summary now has the extra function of being the balancing or offsetting account in the adjustment of Merchandise Inventory.

Step 2 Enter the ending Merchandise Inventory, because you must record on the books the cost of the asset remaining on hand. (Enter the ending inventory.)

Let's repeat the T accounts, showing step 1 and adding step 2.

Merchandise Inventory				Income Summary			
		–		Adj.	37,000 ①	Adj.	42,000 ②
Bal.	37,000	Adj.	37,000 ①				
Adj.	42,000 ②						

In step 2, we debit Merchandise Inventory (recording the asset on the plus side of the account) and do the opposite to Income Summary.

The reason for adjusting the Merchandise Inventory account in these two steps is that both the beginning and the ending amounts appear as distinct figures in the Income Statement columns of a work sheet, and these columns are used as the basis for preparing the income statement.

ADJUSTMENT FOR UNEARNED REVENUE

Objective 2

Prepare an adjustment for unearned revenue.

Now let's introduce another adjusting entry, **unearned revenue**, which is cash received in advance for goods or services to be delivered or performed later. This entry could pertain to a service business as well as to a merchandising business. Frequently, cash is received in advance for services to be performed in the future. For example, a professional sports team sells tickets in advance, a concert association sells season tickets in advance, a magazine publisher sells subscriptions in advance, and an insurance company receives premiums in advance. If the cash amounts received by each of these organi-

College students pay in advance to participate in a meal plan. Until all those meals are consumed, this money represents unearned revenue for the college or university dining hall services.

zations will be earned during the present fiscal period, the amounts should be credited to revenue accounts. On the other hand, if the amounts received will *not* be earned during the present fiscal period, the amounts should be credited to unearned revenue accounts. **An unearned revenue account is classified as a liability,** because an organization is liable for (owes) the amount received in advance until it is earned.

To illustrate, assume that on April 1, Bell Publishing Company receives $82,000 in cash for subscriptions covering two years and records them originally as debits to Cash and credits to Unearned Subscriptions. At the end of the year, Bell finds that $30,750 of the subscriptions have been earned. Accordingly, Bell's accountant makes an adjusting entry, debiting Unearned Subscriptions and crediting Subscriptions Income. In other words, the accountant takes the earned portion out of Unearned Subscriptions and adds it to Subscriptions Income. T accounts show the situation as follows:

Cash

+	−
April 1 82,000	

Unearned Subscriptions

−	+
Dec. 31 Adj. 30,750 (9 months)	April 1 82,000 (24 months)
	Bal. 51,250

Subscriptions Income

−	+
	Dec. 31 Adj. 30,750 (9 months)

FYI

The adjusting entries presented so far are end-of-the-fiscal-year adjustments. There may be other necessary changes or adjustments during the fiscal year.

Now, suppose that Jackson Electric Supply offers a course in wiring for homeowners and apartment managers. On October 1, Jackson Electric Supply receives $1,200 in fees for a four-month course. Because Jackson Electric Supply's present fiscal period ends on December 31, the four months' worth of fees received in advance will not all be earned during this fiscal period. Therefore, Jackson Electric Supply's accountant records the transaction as a debit to Cash of $1,200 and a credit to Unearned Course Fees of $1,200. Unearned Course Fees is a liability account because Jackson Electric Supply must complete the "how-to" course or refund a portion of the money it collected. **Any account beginning with the word *Unearned* is a liability.**

On December 31, because three months' worth of course fees have now been earned, Jackson Electric Supply's accountant makes an adjusting entry to transfer $900 (3/4 of $1,200) from Unearned Course Fees to Course Fees Income. Using T accounts, the situation looks like this:

Cash

+	−
Oct. 1 1,200	

Unearned Course Fees

−	+
Dec. 31 Adj. 900 (3 months)	Oct. 1 1,200 (4 months)
	Bal. 300

Course Fees Income

−	+
	Dec. 31 Adj. 900 (3 months)

ERY PRODUCTS

Under the periodic inventory system, the Merchandise Inventory account is not adjusted until the goods on hand have actually been counted. This is called taking a physical inventory of the stock.

Before we demonstrate how to record adjustments, let's first look at the trial balance section of Jackson Electric Supply's work sheet (Figure 1).

FIGURE 1

Jackson Electric Supply
Work Sheet
For Year Ended December 31, 20—

	Account Name	Trial Balance Debit	Trial Balance Credit	Adjustments Debit	Adjustments Credit
1	Cash	21,154.00			
2	Notes Receivable	4,000.00			
3	Accounts Receivable	29,446.00			
4	Merchandise Inventory	77,000.00			
5	Supplies	1,440.00			
6	Prepaid Insurance	960.00			
7	Land	12,000.00			
8	Building	96,000.00			
9	Accumulated Depreciation, Building		32,000.00		
10	Equipment	33,600.00			
11	Accumulated Depreciation, Equipment		16,400.00		
12	Accounts Payable		36,400.00		
13	Notes Payable		3,000.00		
14	Unearned Course Fees		1,200.00		
15	Mortgage Payable		8,000.00		
16	N. C. Jackson, Capital		140,574.00		
17	N. C. Jackson, Drawing	48,900.00			
18	Sales		235,180.00		
19	Sales Returns and Allowances	840.00			
20	Sales Discount	1,880.00			
21	Interest Income		120.00		
22	Purchases	89,140.00			
23	Purchases Returns and Allowances		2,832.00		
24	Purchases Discount		1,248.00		
25	Freight In	2,460.00			
26	Wages Expense	55,800.00			
27	Taxes Expense	1,960.00			
28	Interest Expense	374.00			
29		476,954.00	476,954.00		

DATA FOR THE ADJUSTMENTS

Objective 3

Record the adjustment data in a work sheet (including merchandise inventory, unearned revenue, supplies used, expired insurance, depreciation, and accrued wages or salaries).

Listing the adjustment data appears to be a relatively minor task. In a business situation, however, you must take actual physical counts of the inventories and match them with the recorded costs. You must check insurance policies to determine the amount of insurance that has expired. Finally, you must systematically write off, or depreciate, the cost of equipment and buildings.

For income tax and accounting purposes, land cannot be depreciated. Even if a building and lot were bought as one package for one price, the buyer must separate the cost of the building from the cost of the land. For real estate taxes, the county assessor appraises the building and the land separately. If there is no other qualified appraisal available, you can use the assessor's ratio or percentage as a basis for separating building cost and land cost.

Here are the adjustment data for Jackson Electric Supply recorded in T accounts.

a–b. Ending merchandise inventory, $64,900

Merchandise Inventory

	+	–	
Bal.	77,000	**(a)** Adj.	77,000
(b) Adj.	64,900		
Bal.	64,900		

Income Summary

(a) Adj.	77,000	**(b)** Adj.	64,900

c. Course fees earned, $900

Unearned Course Fees

	–	+	
(c) Adj.	900	Bal.	1,200
		Bal.	300

Course Fees Income

	–	+	
		(c) Adj.	900

Remember!

The amount of the adjusting entry for supplies used equals the balance of the Supplies account minus the amount of the ending inventory.

d. Ending supplies inventory, $515

Supplies

	+	–	
Bal.	1,440	**(d)** Adj.	925
Bal.	515		

Supplies Expense

	+	–	
(d) Adj.	925		

e. Insurance expired, $380

Prepaid Insurance

	+	–	
Bal.	960	**(e)** Adj.	380
Bal.	580		

Insurance Expense

	+	–	
(e) Adj.	380		

In listing adjustment data, a business must check insurance policies to account for insurance that has expired as well as systematically write off, or depreciate, the cost of equipment.

MING WINTER

f. Additional year's depreciation of building, $5,000

Accumulated Depreciation, Building

−	+	
	Bal.	32,000
	(f)	5,000
	Bal.	37,000

Depreciation Expense, Building

+		−
(f)	5,000	

g. Additional year's depreciation of equipment, $4,000

Accumulated Depreciation, Equipment

−	+	
	Bal.	16,400
	(g) Adj.	4,000
	Bal.	20,400

Depreciation Expense, Equipment

+		−
(g) Adj.	4,000	

h. Wages owed but not paid to employees at end of year, $1,220

Wages Payable

−	+	
	(h)	1,220

Wages Expense

+		−
Bal.	55,800	
(h)	1,220	
Bal.	57,020	

We now record these in the Adjustments columns of the work sheet, using the same letters to identify the adjustments (see Figure 2).

Jackson Electric Supply
Work Sheet
For Year Ended December 31, 20—

		Trial Balance		Adjustments	
	Account Name	Debit	Credit	Debit	Credit
1	Cash	21,154.00			
2	Notes Receivable	4,000.00			
3	Accounts Receivable	29,446.00			
4	Merchandise Inventory	77,000.00		(b) 64,900.00	(a) 77,000.00
5	Supplies	1,440.00			(d) 925.00
6	Prepaid Insurance	960.00			(e) 380.00
7	Land	12,000.00			
8	Building	96,000.00			
9	Accumulated Depreciation, Building		32,000.00		(f) 5,000.00
10	Equipment	33,600.00			
11	Accumulated Depreciation, Equipment		16,400.00		(g) 4,000.00
12	Accounts Payable		36,400.00		
13	Notes Payable		3,000.00		
14	Unearned Course Fees		1,200.00	(c) 900.00	
15	Mortgage Payable		8,000.00		
16	N. C. Jackson, Capital		140,574.00		
17	N. C. Jackson, Drawing	48,900.00			
18	Sales		235,180.00		
19	Sales Returns and Allowances	840.00			
20	Sales Discount	1,880.00			
21	Interest Income		120.00		
22	Purchases	89,140.00			
23	Purchases Returns and Allowances		2,832.00		
24	Purchases Discount		1,248.00		
25	Freight In	2,460.00			
26	Wages Expense	55,800.00		(h) 1,220.00	
27	Taxes Expense	1,960.00			
28	Interest Expense	374.00			
29		476,954.00	476,954.00		
30	Income Summary			(a) 77,000.00	(b) 64,900.00
31	Course Fees Income				(c) 900.00
32	Supplies Expense			(d) 925.00	
33	Insurance Expense			(e) 380.00	
34	Depreciation Expense, Building			(f) 5,000.00	
35	Depreciation Expense, Equipment			(g) 4,000.00	
36	Wages Payable				(h) 1,220.00
37				154,325.00	154,325.00

FIGURE 2

COMPLETION OF THE WORK SHEET

Objective 4

Complete the work sheet.

When we introduced work sheets, we included the Adjusted Trial Balance columns as a means of verifying that the accounts were in balance after recording the adjusting entries. Now, to reduce the number of columns in the work sheet, we eliminate the Adjusted Trial Balance columns. The account balances after the adjusting entries are carried directly into the Income Statement and Balance Sheet columns. The completed work sheet looks like Figure 3 on pages 450–451.

Jackson Electric Supply
Work Sheet
For Year Ended December 31, 20—

Account Name	Trial Balance Debit	Trial Balance Credit
Cash	21,154.00	
Notes Receivable	4,000.00	
Accounts Receivable	29,446.00	
Merchandise Inventory	77,000.00	
Supplies	1,440.00	
Prepaid Insurance	960.00	
Land	12,000.00	
Building	96,000.00	
Accumulated Depreciation, Building		32,000.00
Equipment	33,600.00	
Accumulated Depreciation, Equipment		16,400.00
Accounts Payable		36,400.00
Notes Payable		3,000.00
Unearned Course Fees		1,200.00
Mortgage Payable		8,000.00
N. C. Jackson, Capital		140,574.00
N. C. Jackson, Drawing	48,900.00	
Sales		235,180.00
Sales Returns and Allowances	840.00	
Sales Discount	1,880.00	
Interest Income		120.00
Purchases	89,140.00	
Purchases Returns and Allowances		2,832.00
Purchases Discount		1,248.00
Freight In	2,460.00	
Wages Expense	55,800.00	
Taxes Expense	1,960.00	
Interest Expense	374.00	
	476,954.00	476,954.00
Income Summary		
Course Fees Income		
Supplies Expense		
Insurance Expense		
Depreciation Expense, Building		
Depreciation Expense, Equipment		
Wages Payable		
Net Income		

FIGURE 3

Adjustments Debit	Adjustments Credit	Income Statement Debit	Income Statement Credit	Balance Sheet Debit	Balance Sheet Credit	
				21,154.00		1
				4,000.00		2
				29,446.00		3
(b) 64,900.00	(a) 77,000.00			64,900.00		4
	(d) 925.00			515.00		5
	(e) 380.00			580.00		6
				12,000.00		7
				96,000.00		8
	(f) 5,000.00				37,000.00	9
				33,600.00		10
	(g) 4,000.00				20,400.00	11
					36,400.00	12
					3,000.00	13
(c) 900.00					300.00	14
					8,000.00	15
					140,574.00	16
				48,900.00		17
			235,180.00			18
		840.00				19
		1,880.00				20
			120.00			21
		89,140.00				22
			2,832.00			23
			1,248.00			24
		2,460.00				25
(h) 1,220.00		57,020.00				26
		1,960.00				27
		374.00				28
						29
(a) 77,000.00	(b) 64,900.00	77,000.00	64,900.00			30
	(c) 900.00		900.00			31
(d) 925.00		925.00				32
(e) 380.00		380.00				33
(f) 5,000.00		5,000.00				34
(g) 4,000.00		4,000.00				35
	(h) 1,220.00				1,220.00	36
154,325.00	154,325.00	240,979.00	305,180.00	311,095.00	246,894.00	37
		64,201.00			64,201.00	38
		305,180.00	305,180.00	311,095.00	311,095.00	39
						40
						41
						42

Observe in particular the way we carry forward the figures for Merchandise Inventory and Income Summary. **Income Summary is the only account in which we don't combine the debit and credit figures. Instead, we carry them into the Income Statement columns in Figure 3 as two distinct figures.** As we said, the reason is that we need both figures to complete the income statement. The amount listed as Income Summary in the Income Statement Debit column is the beginning merchandise inventory. The amount listed as Income Summary in the Income Statement Credit column is the ending merchandise inventory.

When developing the work sheet, complete one stage at a time:

1. Record the trial balance, and make sure that the total of the Debit column equals the total of the Credit column.
2. Record the adjustments in the Adjustments columns, and make sure that the totals are equal.
3. Complete the Income Statement and Balance Sheet columns by recording the adjusted balance of each account. Here are the accounts and classifications pertaining to a merchandising business that appear in these columns:

INCOME STATEMENT		BALANCE SHEET	
DEBIT	CREDIT	DEBIT	CREDIT
Sales Returns and Allowances + Sales Discount + Purchases + Freight In + Expenses + Income Summary	Revenues (including Sales) + Purchases Returns and Allowances + Purchases Discount + Income Summary	Assets + Drawing	Accumulated Depreciation + Liabilities + Capital

Study the following example, noting especially the way we treat these special accounts for a merchandising business:

ACCOUNT NAME	INCOME STATEMENT DEBIT	INCOME STATEMENT CREDIT	BALANCE SHEET DEBIT	BALANCE SHEET CREDIT
Merchandise Inventory			64,900.00	
Sales		235,180.00		
Sales Returns and Allowances	840.00			
Sales Discount	1,880.00			
Purchases	89,140.00			
Purchases Returns and Allowances		2,832.00		
Purchases Discount		1,248.00		
Freight In	2,460.00			
Income Summary	77,000.00	64,900.00		

ADJUSTING ENTRIES UNDER THE PERIODIC INVENTORY SYSTEM

Objective 5

Journalize the adjusting entries for a merchandising business under the periodic inventory system.

Figure 4 shows the way the adjusting entries look when they are taken from the Adjustments columns of the work sheet and recorded in the general journal.

FIGURE 4

GENERAL JOURNAL PAGE 96

DATE		DESCRIPTION	POST. REF.	DEBIT	CREDIT
20–		Adjusting Entries			
Dec.	31	Income Summary		77,000.00	
		Merchandise Inventory			77,000.00
	31	Merchandise Inventory		64,900.00	
		Income Summary			64,900.00
	31	Unearned Course Fees		900.00	
		Course Fees Income			900.00
	31	Supplies Expense		925.00	
		Supplies			925.00
	31	Insurance Expense		380.00	
		Prepaid Insurance			380.00
	31	Depreciation Expense, Building		5,000.00	
		Accumulated Depreciation,			
		Building			5,000.00
	31	Depreciation Expense,			
		Equipment		4,000.00	
		Accumulated Depreciation,			
		Equipment			4,000.00
	31	Wages Expense		1,220.00	
		Wages Payable			1,220.00

ADJUSTMENT FOR MERCHANDISE INVENTORY UNDER THE PERPETUAL INVENTORY SYSTEM

Objective 6

Journalize the adjusting entry for merchandise inventory under the perpetual inventory system.

Under the perpetual inventory system, a business continually maintains a record of each item in stock. **Under the perpetual inventory system, when merchandise is purchased, the Merchandise Inventory account (not the Purchases account) is debited for the cost of the merchandise and Accounts Payable or Cash is credited. When merchandise is sold, the Merchandise**

Inventory account is credited for the cost of the merchandise and the Cost of Goods Sold account is debited for the cost of the merchandise.

Many firms use electronic devices to keep track of stock items. For example, when a sale is made at a supermarket checkout counter, as the bar code on each item is scanned, the price and stock number are recorded. The cash register is connected to a computer that updates the inventory record and records the cost of the item. So the business perpetually (always) knows how much inventory it should have on hand.

However, to verify the inventory record, a physical count should be taken from time to time. The amount shown by the physical count may be less than the recorded amount as a result of errors, shrinkage, or shoplifting. If this is the case, an adjusting entry must be made to record the amount of the loss. This entry is a debit to the Cost of Goods Sold account (an expense account) and a credit to the Merchandise Inventory account.

Adjusting Entry Under the Perpetual Inventory System

Here is a comparison of entries in T-account form under both the periodic and the perpetual inventory systems. Assume a beginning inventory of $80,000.

1. Bought merchandise on account, $50,000.

Periodic Inventory

Purchases	
(1) 50,000	

Accounts Payable	
	(1) 50,000

Perpetual Inventory

Merchandise Inventory	
Bal. 80,000	
(1) 50,000	

Accounts Payable	
	(1) 50,000

2. Sold merchandise for $82,000 having a cost of $61,200.

Periodic Inventory

Accounts Receivable	
(2) 82,000	

Sales	
	(2) 82,000

Perpetual Inventory

Accounts Receivable	
(2) 82,000	

Sales	
	(2) 82,000

Cost of Goods Sold	
(2) 61,200	

Merchandise Inventory	
Bal. 80,000	(2) 61,200
(1) 50,000	

Remember!

The ending inventory of one period becomes the beginning inventory of the next period.

3. Adjusting entry for ending inventory by physical count, $68,400. The recorded balance of the perpetual inventory is $68,800 ($80,000 + $50,000 − $61,200).

Periodic Inventory

Income Summary	
(3a) Adj. 80,000	(3b) Adj. 68,400

Merchandise Inventory	
Bal. 80,000	(3a) Adj. 80,000
(3b) Adj. 68,400	

Perpetual Inventory

Cost of Goods Sold	
61,200	
(3) Adj. 400	

Merchandise Inventory	
Bal. 80,000	(2) 61,200
(1) 50,000	(3) Adj. 400

FIGURE 5

GENERAL JOURNAL PAGE 96

	DATE		DESCRIPTION	POST. REF.	DEBIT	CREDIT	
1	20–		Adjusting Entries				1
2	Dec.	31	Cost of Goods Sold		400 00		2
3			Merchandise Inventory			400 00	3
4			or				4
5		31	Merchandise Inventory		500 00		5
6			Cost of Goods Sold			500 00	6

FYI

This entry would have been previously listed in the Adjustments columns of the work sheet.

The difference of $400 ($68,800 − $68,400) is the adjustment amount under the perpetual inventory system (actual physical count versus the accounting records). The adjusting entry required to record the $400 loss is shown in Figure 5.

On the other hand, if the physical count of the stock of merchandise ($65,300) is more than the recorded amount ($64,800), the adjusting entry is to debit Merchandise Inventory and credit Cost of Goods Sold (account) for the difference ($65,300 − $64,800 = $500).

Additional adjusting entries would follow, such as those for supplies used, insurance expired, accrued wages, and other such expenses.

In the income statement, under the periodic inventory system, the Cost of Goods Sold account is listed under one line, rather than there being a Cost of Goods Sold section.

Here is a comparison of income statements under each of the two systems.

Periodic

Sales		$82,000
Cost of Goods Sold:		
Merchandise Inventory (beginning)	$ 80,000	
Purchases (net)	50,000	
Goods Available for Sale	$130,000	
Less Merchandise Inventory (ending)	68,400	
Cost of Goods Sold		61,600
Gross Profit		$20,400

Perpetual

Sales	$82,000
Cost of Goods Sold	61,600
Gross Profit	$20,400

CHAPTER REVIEW

Review of Performance Objectives

1. Prepare an adjustment for merchandise inventory under the periodic inventory system.

   The adjustment for merchandise inventory under the periodic inventory system requires two adjusting entries. In the first adjusting entry (to remove the beginning inventory), debit Income Summary and credit Merchandise Inventory. In the second adjusting entry (to enter the ending inventory), debit Merchandise Inventory and credit Income Summary.

2. Prepare an adjustment for unearned revenue.

   For revenue received in advance, an adjustment is required to separate the portion that has been earned from the portion that is unearned. We assume that the amount of cash received in advance was originally recorded as unearned revenue, which is a liability. In the adjusting entry for the amount actually earned, debit the unearned revenue account (Unearned Course Fees) and credit the revenue account (Course Fees Income).

3. Record the adjustment data in a work sheet (including merchandise inventory, unearned revenue, supplies used, expired insurance, depreciation, and accrued wages or salaries).

   In the Adjustments columns of the work sheet, record the following adjusting entries:

   For merchandise inventory: first, debit Income Summary and credit Merchandise Inventory (to remove the beginning inventory); next, debit Merchandise Inventory and credit Income Summary (to enter the ending inventory).

   For unearned revenue: debit the unearned revenue account and credit the revenue account (to record revenue earned).

   For supplies used: debit Supplies Expense and credit Supplies.

   For expired insurance: debit Insurance Expense and credit Prepaid Insurance.

   For depreciation: debit Depreciation Expense and credit Accumulated Depreciation.

   For accrued salaries or wages: debit Salaries Expense or Wages Expense and credit Salaries Payable or Wages Payable.

4. Complete the work sheet.

   Carry the Income Summary account from the Adjustments columns into the Income Statement columns as two separate figures. For merchandise inventory, record the amount of the ending inventory in the Balance Sheet Debit column. For unearned revenue, record the unearned revenue account in the Balance Sheet Credit column and the revenue account in the Income Statement Credit column.

5. Journalize the adjusting entries for a merchandising business under the periodic inventory system.

   Take the adjusting entries recorded in the journal directly from the Adjustments columns of the work sheet.

6. Journalize the adjusting entry for merchandise inventory under the perpetual inventory system.

   Assuming that the amount of the physical count of the stock of merchandise is less than the recorded amount, the adjusting entry is a debit to Cost of Goods Sold (account) and a credit to Merchandise Inventory for the amount of the difference. On the other hand, if the physical count of the stock of merchandise is more than the recorded amount, the adjusting entry is to debit Merchandise Inventory and credit Cost of Goods Sold (accounts) for the amount of the difference.

Glossary

Periodic inventory system The system under which the buying of merchandise during the year is recorded as a debit to Purchases and a credit to Accounts Payable or Cash. At the end of the year, a physical count of the stock of goods is taken and adjusting entries are made to record the amount of the physical count. (443)

Perpetual inventory system The system under which the buying of merchandise during the year is recorded as a debit to Merchandise Inventory and a credit to Accounts Payable or Cash. When merchandise is sold, the cost of the merchandise is recorded as a debit to the Cost of Goods Sold account and a credit to Merchandise Inventory. At the end of the year, a physical count of the stock of goods is taken and an adjusting entry is made to record the difference between the amount of the count and the amount previously recorded. (453)

Physical inventory An actual count of the stock of goods on hand. (443)

Unearned revenue Revenue received in advance for goods or services to be delivered later; considered to be a liability until the revenue is earned. (444)

QUESTIONS, EXERCISES, AND PROBLEMS

Discussion Questions

1. What is a physical inventory? What does the word *periodic* mean in the term *periodic inventory?*
2. On the Income Summary line of a work sheet, $126,200 appears in the Income Statement Debit column, and $124,100 appears in the Income Statement Credit column. Which figure represents the beginning inventory?
3. Using the perpetual inventory system, what account is debited when a business buys more merchandise?
4. On a work sheet, where will the amount of the ending merchandise inventory be recorded?
5. What is meant by unearned revenue and why is it treated as a liability?
6. Why is it necessary to adjust the Merchandise Inventory account under a system of periodic inventories?
7. If a company begins the fiscal period with a $1,260 balance in Prepaid Insurance, would it be wrong to debit Insurance Expense for the next payment of an insurance premium?
8. When a college receives one semester's dormitory rent in advance, an entry is made debiting Cash and crediting Unearned Rent. At the end of the year, a large portion of the rent has been earned. What adjusting entry would you suggest?

Exercises

P.O. 1

Journalize adjustments for merchandise inventory.

Exercise 13-1 After adjusting entries are posted, the Merchandise Inventory account appears as on page 458. Journalize the complete entries that support these postings. The Income Summary account is numbered 313.

ACCOUNT **Merchandise Inventory** ACCOUNT NO. **114**

DATE		ITEM	POST. REF.	DEBIT	CREDIT	BALANCE DEBIT	BALANCE CREDIT
2004							
Dec.	31	Balance	✓			96,400.00	
2005							
Dec.	31	Adjusting	J112		96,400.00	—	—
	31	Adjusting	J112	97,100.00		97,100.00	

P.O. 2

Journalize the adjustment for unearned revenue.

Exercise 13-2 On October 31, the Igloos Hockey Club received $400,000 in cash in advance for season tickets for eight home games. The transaction was recorded as a debit to Cash and a credit to Unearned Admissions. By December 31, the end of the fiscal year, the team had played three home games and received an additional $50,000 cash admissions income at the gate.

a. Journalize the adjusting entry as of December 31.
b. List the title of the account and the related balance that will appear on the income statement.
c. List the title of the account and the related balance that will appear on the balance sheet.

P.O. 2

Determine the entries in an unearned revenue account.

Exercise 13-3 For the basketball federation's Unearned Season Tickets account, list the debits and credits for each amount posted to the account and briefly describe the transaction.

ACCOUNT **Unearned Season Tickets** ACCOUNT NO. **214**

DATE		ITEM	POST. REF.	DEBIT	CREDIT	BALANCE DEBIT	BALANCE CREDIT
20–							
Jan.	1	Balance	✓				10,200.00
Mar.	6		J71	10,200.00		—	—
Oct.	15		CR42		12,400.00		12,400.00
Nov.	1		CR43		22,100.00		34,500.00
Dec.	31	Adjusting	J99	22,500.00			12,000.00

P.O. 5

Determine entries in the Supplies account.

Exercise 13-4 For the Supplies ledger account on page 459, determine the debits and credits for each amount posted to the account and briefly describe each transaction. The entry of December 9 involved the return of defective goods. The purchases of December 17 involved the Beedle Company.

ACCOUNT **Supplies** ACCOUNT NO. 115

	DATE		ITEM	POST. REF.	DEBIT	CREDIT	BALANCE DEBIT	BALANCE CREDIT	
1	20–								1
2	Jan.	1	Balance	✓			420 00		2
3	Apr.	6		CP42	160 00		580 00		3
4	May	31		CP44	90 00		670 00		4
5	Nov.	21		CP53	225 00		895 00		5
6	Dec.	9		J77		42 00	853 00		6
7		17		J77	141 00		994 00		7
8		31	Adjusting	J78		220 00	774 00		8

P.O. 4

Place account balances in work sheet columns.

Exercise 13-5 Indicate the work sheet columns (Income Statement Debit, Income Statement Credit, Balance Sheet Debit, Balance Sheet Credit) in which the balances of the following accounts should appear:

a. F. Drexel, Drawing
b. Advertising Expense
c. Merchandise Inventory (ending)
d. Purchases Discount
e. Unearned Fees
f. Sales Returns and Allowances
g. Accumulated Depreciation, Building
h. Income Summary
i. Fees Income
j. Prepaid Rent

P.O. 2,3

Journalize adjustments for expired insurance, unearned revenue, and depreciation.

Exercise 13-6 Journalize the required adjusting entries for the year ended December 31 for Malloy Dance Studio. Begin on journal page 42.

a. On June 1 of this year, $600 was paid for a one-year insurance policy.
b. On October 1 of this year, $160 was paid for four months of advertising.
c. As of December 31, the balance of the Unearned Membership Fees account is $12,400. Of this amount, $8,200 has now been earned.
d. Equipment purchased on April 1 of this year for $3,400 is expected to have a useful life of five years and will have a trade-in value of $400. All the other equipment has been fully depreciated. The straight-line method is used.
e. As of December 31, two days' wages of $240 per day had accrued.

P.O. 2,3

Journalize adjusting entries.

Exercise 13-7 On December 31, the end of the year, the accountant for *Family Magazine* was called away suddenly because of an emergency. However, before leaving, the accountant jotted down a few notes pertaining to the adjustments. Record the necessary adjusting entries.

a. Subscriptions received in advance amounting to $136,400 were recorded as Unearned Subscriptions. At the end of the year, $90,200 has been earned.
b. Depreciation of equipment for the year is $18,600.
c. The amount of expired insurance for the year is $916.
d. The balance of Prepaid Rent is $2,800, representing four months' rent. Three months' rent has now expired.
e. Three days' salaries will be unpaid at the end of the year; total weekly (five days') salaries are $3,600.

P.O. 6

Journalize adjustment for merchandise inventory using the perpetual inventory system.

Exercise 13-8 On December 31, Benn Company took a physical count of its merchandise inventory. Benn Company operates under the perpetual inventory system. The physical count amounted to $178,400. The Merchandise Inventory account shows a balance of $180,200. Journalize the adjusting entry to Merchandise Inventory.

WHAT IF . . .

What would happen if a business spent the cash it had received in advance for services it promised to perform at a later date?

CRITICAL THINKING

On November 1, an exterior painting company received $3,420 for a paint job that will not be finished during this fiscal period. The bookkeeper inaccurately credited Painting Income instead of Unearned Painting Income. As of December 31, which is the end of the fiscal period, $1,200 worth of painting will have been completed. The bookkeeper intended to make the following adjustment at the end of the year:

Cash (Debit)	Cash (Credit)	Painting Income (Debit)	Painting Income (Credit)	Unearned Painting Income (Debit)	Unearned Painting Income (Credit)
11/1 3,420		12/31 2,220	11/1 3,420		12/31 2,220

The owner wants to get a bank loan by December 1. The bank requires interim financial statements to be submitted as of December 1. How will the bookkeeper's entries affect the accuracy of the interim balance sheet and statements? What difference will the bookkeeper's methods make in the December 31 balance sheet and income statement?

A MATTER OF ETHICS

The owner of a bicycle shop allows his two sons to take bicycles home to try them out on different types of ground because he believes that they need to be familiar with the products they sell. Sometimes the bicycles are not returned to the store by the time the physical count of inventory takes place. Respond to this practice.

WEB WORK

Using an Internet web browser, type the phrase for the home page of a retail clothing company in the search box. How does it determine cost of goods sold? Discuss or write your findings in a memo to your instructor. Is cost of goods sold calculated or an amount in an account? Can you tell whether the company uses perpetual or periodic inventory?

PROBLEM SET A

For additional help, see the demonstration problem at the beginning of each chapter in your Working Papers.

P.O. 4

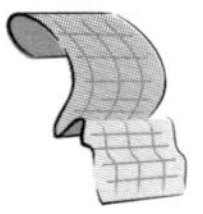

Problem 13-1A The trial balance of Tenson Company as of December 31, the end of its current fiscal year, is as follows:

Tenson Company
Work Sheet
For Year Ended December 31, 20—

	Account Name	Trial Balance Debit	Trial Balance Credit
1	Cash	9,663.92	
2	Merchandise Inventory	63,422.84	
3	Store Supplies	1,541.12	
4	Prepaid Insurance	860.00	
5	Store Equipment	36,380.00	
6	Accumulated Depreciation, Store Equipment		24,220.00
7	Accounts Payable		14,478.80
8	Sales Tax Payable		343.36
9	G. O. Tenson, Capital		54,630.00
10	G. O. Tenson, Drawing	28,440.00	
11	Sales		178,036.74
12	Sales Returns and Allowances	1,343.04	
13	Purchases	76,468.46	
14	Purchases Returns and Allowances		1,778.94
15	Purchases Discount		1,597.90
16	Freight In	4,975.00	
17	Salary Expense	36,558.80	
18	Rent Expense	14,300.00	
19	Miscellaneous Expense	1,132.56	
20		275,085.74	275,085.74
21			

Here are the data for the adjustments.

a–b. Merchandise Inventory at December 31, $65,832.56.
c. Store supplies inventory, $486.40.
d. Insurance expired, $390.
e. Salaries accrued, $592.
f. Depreciation of store equipment, $2,880.

Check Figure
Net income, $44,128.72

Instructions

Complete the work sheet after entering the account names and balances into the work sheet.

P.O. 4,5

Problem 13-2A The balances of the ledger accounts of Tallon Furniture as of December 31, the end of its fiscal year, are as follows:

Tallon Furniture
Work Sheet
For Year Ended December 31, 20—

	Account Name	Trial Balance Debit	Trial Balance Credit
1	Cash	11,692.00	
2	Accounts Receivable	42,862.00	
3	Merchandise Inventory	121,738.00	
4	Store Supplies	1,670.00	
5	Prepaid Insurance	1,528.00	
6	Store Equipment	37,024.00	
7	Accumulated Depreciation, Store Equipment		29,520.00
8	Office Equipment	9,536.00	
9	Accumulated Depreciation, Office Equipment		1,820.00
10	Accounts Payable		29,822.00
11	Unearned Rent		3,100.00
12	Notes Payable		5,000.00
13	P. Tallon, Capital		121,532.00
14	P. Tallon, Drawing	27,500.00	
15	Sales		650,500.00
16	Sales Returns and Allowances	9,648.00	
17	Purchases	518,474.00	
18	Purchases Returns and Allowances		13,340.00
19	Purchases Discount		7,734.00
20	Freight In	24,624.00	
21	Wages Expense	55,300.00	
22	Interest Expense	772.00	
23		862,368.00	862,368.00
24			

Data for the adjustments are as follows:

a–b. Merchandise Inventory at December 31, $102,676.
c. Store supplies inventory at December 31, $832.
d. Insurance expired during the year, $541.
e. Wages accrued at December 31, $1,256.
f. Depreciation of store equipment, $5,664.
g. Depreciation of office equipment, $1,532.
h. Rent earned, $2,200.

Check Figure
Net income, $36,063

Instructions

1. Complete the work sheet after entering the account names and balances into the work sheet.
2. Journalize the adjusting entries.

P.O. 4,5

Problem 13-3A The accounts in the ledger of Monty's Mountain Shop, with the balances as of December 31, the end of its fiscal year, are as follows:

Monty's Mountain Shop
Work Sheet
For Year Ended December 31, 20—

	Account Name	Trial Balance Debit	Trial Balance Credit
1	Cash	12,500.00	
2	Accounts Receivable	2,140.00	
3	Merchandise Inventory	120,500.00	
4	Store Supplies	1,520.00	
5	Prepaid Insurance	3,040.00	
6	Land	48,000.00	
7	Building	108,000.00	
8	Accumulated Depreciation, Building		16,600.00
9	Store Equipment	36,400.00	
10	Accumulated Depreciation, Store Equipment		11,600.00
11	Accounts Payable		14,650.00
12	Sales Tax Payable		4,192.00
13	Notes Payable		5,000.00
14	B. Monty, Capital		216,135.00
15	B. Monty, Drawing	44,200.00	
16	Sales		467,550.00
17	Sales Returns and Allowances	2,634.00	
18	Purchases	284,719.00	
19	Purchases Returns and Allowances		5,560.00
20	Purchases Discount		3,671.00
21	Freight In	7,868.00	
22	Salary Expense	58,673.00	
23	Advertising Expense	7,259.00	
24	Utilities Expense	5,895.00	
25	Miscellaneous Expense	840.00	
26	Interest Expense	770.00	
27		744,958.00	744,958.00

Data for the adjustments are as follows:

a–b. Merchandise Inventory at December 31, $104,682.
c. Store supplies inventory at December 31, $620.
d. Insurance expired during the year, $2,040.
e. Salaries accrued at December 31, $1,865.
f. Depreciation of building, $2,142.
g. Depreciation of store equipment, $2,731.

Check Figure
Net income, $82,627

Instructions

1. Complete the work sheet after entering the account names and balances into the work sheet.
2. Journalize the adjusting entries.

Instructions for General Ledger Software

1. Record the adjusting entries in the general journal.
2. Print the journal.
3. Post the general journal amounts to the general ledger.
4. Print a trial balance.
5. Print the income statement, statement of owner's equity, and balance sheet.

P.O. 4,5

Problem 13-4A A portion of the worksheet of Hurst Oxygen Company for the year ending December 31 is as follows:

	ACCOUNT NAME	INCOME STATEMENT DEBIT	INCOME STATEMENT CREDIT	BALANCE SHEET DEBIT	BALANCE SHEET CREDIT
1	Cash			9,340.00	
2	Merchandise Inventory			76,940.00	
3	Supplies			256.00	
4	Prepaid Insurance			240.00	
5	Store Equipment			39,280.00	
6	Accumulated Depreciation, Store Equipment				26,220.00
7	Accounts Payable				14,600.00
8	P. R. Hurst, Capital				68,940.00
9	P. R. Hurst, Drawing			27,600.00	
10	Sales		173,420.00		
11	Sales Returns and Allowances	1,520.00			
12	Purchases	82,312.00			
13	Purchases Returns and Allowances		940.00		
14	Purchases Discount		1,600.00		
15	Freight In	1,948.00			
16	Salary Expense	37,560.00			
17	Rent Expense	14,800.00			
18	Income Summary	65,680.00	76,940.00		
19	Supplies Expense	944.00			
20	Insurance Expense	760.00			
21	Depreciation Expense, Store Equipment	4,040.00			
22	Salaries Payable				560.00
23		209,564.00	252,900.00	153,656.00	110,320.00
24					

Check Figure
Salaries accrued, $560

Instructions

1. Determine the entries that appeared in the Adjustments columns and present them in general journal form.
2. Determine the net income for the year.
3. What is the amount of the ending capital?

PROBLEM SET B

For additional help, see the demonstration problem at the beginning of each chapter in your Working Papers.

P.O. 4

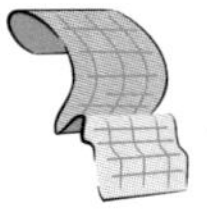

Problem 13-1B The trial balance of Halaka Company as of December 31, the end of its current fiscal year, is as follows:

Halaka Company
Work Sheet
For Year Ended December 31, 20—

	Account Name	Trial Balance Debit	Trial Balance Credit
1	Cash	9,036.54	
2	Merchandise Inventory	62,954.82	
3	Store Supplies	1,366.84	
4	Prepaid Insurance	1,120.00	
5	Store Equipment	37,240.00	
6	Accumulated Depreciation, Store Equipment		24,736.00
7	Accounts Payable		14,186.96
8	Sales Tax Payable		346.98
9	O. G. Halaka, Capital		54,759.00
10	O. G. Halaka, Drawing	28,900.00	
11	Sales		178,966.34
12	Sales Returns and Allowances	1,393.84	
13	Purchases	79,800.84	
14	Purchases Returns and Allowances		1,757.82
15	Purchases Discount		1,603.64
16	Freight In	2,737.00	
17	Salary Expense	36,468.86	
18	Rent Expense	14,300.00	
19	Miscellaneous Expense	1,038.00	
20		276,356.74	276,356.74

Here are the data for the adjustments:

a–b. Merchandise Inventory at December 31, $64,749.80.
c. Store supplies inventory, $504.32.
d. Insurance expired, $636.
e. Salaries accrued, $686.80.
f. Depreciation of store equipment, $3,810.

Check Figure
Net income, $42,388.92

Instructions

Complete the work sheet after entering the account names and balances into the work sheet.

P.O. 4,5

Problem 13-2B The balances of the ledger accounts of Balar Home Center as of June 30, the end of its fiscal year, are as follows:

Balar Home Center
Work Sheet
For Year Ended June 30, 20—

	ACCOUNT NAME	TRIAL BALANCE DEBIT	TRIAL BALANCE CREDIT
1	Cash	14,875.00	
2	Accounts Receivable	51,200.00	
3	Merchandise Inventory	72,800.00	
4	Supplies	1,570.00	
5	Prepaid Insurance	1,180.00	
6	Store Equipment	26,690.00	
7	Accumulated Depreciation, Store Equipment		16,300.00
8	Office Equipment	9,500.00	
9	Accumulated Depreciation, Office Equipment		4,715.00
10	Accounts Payable		29,922.00
11	Unearned Rent		3,100.00
12	Notes Payable		3,500.00
13	F. C. Balar, Capital		121,532.00
14	F. C. Balar, Drawing	25,800.00	
15	Sales		452,886.00
16	Sales Returns and Allowances	3,110.00	
17	Purchases	368,110.00	
18	Purchases Returns and Allowances		7,270.00
19	Purchases Discount		2,180.00
20	Freight In	13,590.00	
21	Salary Expense	52,250.00	
22	Interest Expense	730.00	
23		641,405.00	641,405.00

Here are the data for the adjustments:

a–b. Merchandise Inventory at June 30, $112,326.
c. Supplies inventory at June 30, $374.
d. Insurance expired during the year, $1,012.
e. Salaries accrued at June 30, $2,100.
f. Depreciation of store equipment, $3,645.
g. Depreciation of office equipment, $1,827.
h. Rent earned, $2,125.

Check Figure
Net income, $56,417

Instructions

1. Complete the work sheet after entering the account names and balances into the work sheet.
2. Journalize the adjusting entries.

P.O. 4,5

Problem 13-3B Here are the accounts in the ledger of Pollard's Jewel Box, with the balances as of December 31, the end of its fiscal year.

Pollard's Jewel Box
Work Sheet
For Year Ended December 31, 20—

	ACCOUNT NAME	TRIAL BALANCE DEBIT	TRIAL BALANCE CREDIT
1	Cash	11,380.00	
2	Accounts Receivable	1,454.00	
3	Merchandise Inventory	116,000.00	
4	Store Supplies	1,384.00	
5	Prepaid Insurance	2,186.00	
6	Land	16,000.00	
7	Building	77,000.00	
8	Accumulated Depreciation, Building		29,240.00
9	Store Equipment	77,590.00	
10	Accumulated Depreciation, Store Equipment		17,260.00
11	Accounts Payable		14,170.00
12	Sales Tax Payable		2,684.00
13	Notes Payable		5,000.00
14	L. Pollard, Capital		190,438.00
15	L. Pollard, Drawing	46,400.00	
16	Sales		379,354.00
17	Sales Returns and Allowances	3,788.00	
18	Purchases	250,868.00	
19	Purchases Returns and Allowances		3,161.00
20	Purchases Discount		4,510.00
21	Freight In	12,100.00	
22	Salary Expense	23,500.00	
23	Advertising Expense	2,026.00	
24	Utilities Expense	1,258.00	
25	Miscellaneous Expense	823.00	
26	Interest Expense	2,060.00	
27		645,817.00	645,817.00

Here are the data for the adjustments.

a–b. Merchandise Inventory at December 31, $115,327.
c. Store supplies inventory at December 31, $847.
d. Insurance expired during the year, $890.
e. Salaries accrued at December 31, $1,289.
f. Depreciation of building, $3,860.
g. Depreciation of store equipment, $4,182.

Check Figure
Net income, $79,171

Instructions

1. Complete the work sheet after entering the account names and balances into the work sheet.
2. Journalize the adjusting entries.

Instructions for General Ledger Software

1. Record the adjusting entries in the general journal.
2. Print the journal.
3. Post the general journal amounts to the general ledger.
4. Print a trial balance.
5. Print the income statement, statement of owner's equity, and balance sheet.

P.O. 4,5

Problem 13-4B A portion of the work sheet of Susan's Flowers for the year ending December 31 is as follows:

		INCOME STATEMENT		BALANCE SHEET		
	ACCOUNT NAME	DEBIT	CREDIT	DEBIT	CREDIT	
1	Cash			7736.00		1
2	Merchandise Inventory			74298.00		2
3	Supplies			298.00		3
4	Prepaid Insurance			250.00		4
5	Store Equipment			37960.00		5
6	Accumulated Depreciation, Store Equipment				29440.00	6
7	Accounts Payable				13760.00	7
8	S. R. Hale, Capital				75142.00	8
9	S. R. Hale, Drawing			30800.00		9
10	Sales		171816.00			10
11	Sales Returns and Allowances	1434.00				11
12	Purchases	85934.00				12
13	Purchases Returns and Allowances		964.00			13
14	Purchases Discount		1636.00			14
15	Freight In	2658.00				15
16	Salary Expense	37852.00				16
17	Rent Expense	14400.00				17
18	Income Summary	68228.00	74298.00			18
19	Depreciation Expense, Store Equipment	4360.00				19
20	Insurance Expense	552.00				20
21	Supplies Expense	884.00				21
22	Salaries Payable				588.00	22
23		216302.00	248714.00	151342.00	118930.00	23

Check Figure

Accrued salaries, $588

Instructions

1. Determine the entries that appeared in the Adjustments columns and present them in general journal form.
2. Determine the net income for the year.
3. What is the amount of the ending capital?

14 Financial Statements, Closing Entries, and Reversing Entries

WINDOWS ON THE WORLD WIDE WEB

Apple iMacs, PCs, DVDs, laser printers, CD-ROMs, and software are all examples of the merchandise offered at CompUSA, the computer superstore. The accounting department at CompUSA can calculate working capital to determine if CompUSA has enough capital to stay in business. To determine if the firm has the ability to pay its debts, accounting personnel can calculate the current ratio. Can you determine CompUSA's current ratio based on a peek at its most recent balance sheet? How are CompUSA's liabilities and assets classified on the balance sheet for this past year? What accounts did the accounting department have to close in the income statement? Why would CompUSA need to make a reversing entry on the first day of a new fiscal period for wages payable and wages expense? Find the figures you need to answer some of these questions at **http://www.compusastores.com/about/finance.asp**.

Performance Objectives

After you have completed this chapter, you will be able to do the following:

1. Prepare a classified income statement for a merchandising firm.
2. Prepare a classified balance sheet for any type of business.
3. Compute working capital and current ratio.
4. Journalize the closing entries for a merchandising firm.
5. Determine which adjusting entries can be reversed, and journalize the reversing entries.

This chapter again demonstrates how to prepare financial statements directly from a work sheet. We also explain the functions of closing entries and reversing entries as means of completing the accounting cycle. Finally, we look at the financial statements in their entirety, and explain their various subdivisions.

FYI

Accountants sometimes number contra accounts as subaccounts. For example, Accumulated Depreciation, Building, is 122.1, Sales Returns and Allowances is 411.1, Sales Discount is 411.2, Purchases Returns and Allowances is 511.1, and so on.

First, here is the chart of accounts for Jackson Electric Supply.

Assets (100–199)

111 Cash
112 Notes Receivable
113 Accounts Receivable
114 Merchandise Inventory
115 Supplies
116 Prepaid Insurance
121 Land
122 Building
123 Accumulated Depreciation, Building
124 Equipment
125 Accumulated Depreciation, Equipment

Liabilities (200–299)

211 Wages Payable
213 Notes Payable
217 Unearned Course Fees
221 Accounts Payable
251 Mortgage Payable

Owner's Equity (300–399)

311 N. C. Jackson, Capital
312 N. C. Jackson, Drawing
313 Income Summary

Revenue (400–499)

411 Sales
412 Sales Returns and Allowances
413 Sales Discount
421 Course Fees Income
422 Interest Income

Cost of Goods Sold (500–599)

511 Purchases
512 Purchases Returns and Allowances
513 Purchases Discount
514 Freight In

Expenses (600–699)

621 Wages Expense
622 Depreciation Expense, Building
623 Supplies Expense
631 Depreciation Expense, Equipment
632 Taxes Expense
633 Insurance Expense
634 Interest Expense

THE INCOME STATEMENT

Objective 1

Prepare a classified income statement for a merchandising firm.

As you know, the work sheet is merely a tool used by accountants to prepare the financial statements. In Figure 1, we present the part of the work sheet for Jackson Electric Supply that includes the Income Statement columns. Of course, **each of the amounts that appear in the Income Statement columns of the work sheet will also be used in the income statement.** Notice that the amounts for the beginning and ending merchandise inventory appear separately on the Income Summary line. Figure 2 on page 472 shows the entire income statement. Pause for a while and look it over carefully; then we will break it down into its components.

The income statement follows a logical pattern that is much the same for any type of merchandising business. The ability to interpret the income statement and extract parts from it is very useful when gathering information for decisions. To realize the full value of an income statement, however, you need to know the basic format of an income statement. Let's look at the statement section by section.

Net Sales	$232,460
− Cost of Goods Sold	99,620
Gross Profit	$132,840
− Operating Expenses	69,285
Income from Operations	$ 63,555

Jackson Electric Supply
Work Sheet
For Year Ended December 31, 20—

Account Name	Trial Balance		Adjustments		Income Statement	
	Debit	Credit	Debit	Credit	Debit	Credit
Cash	21,154.00					
Notes Receivable	4,000.00					
Accounts Receivable	29,446.00					
Merchandise Inventory	77,000.00		(b) 64,900.00	(a) 77,000.00		
Supplies	1,440.00			(d) 925.00		
Prepaid Insurance	960.00			(e) 380.00		
Land	12,000.00					
Building	96,000.00					
Accumulated Depr., Building		32,000.00		(f) 5,000.00		
Equipment	33,600.00					
Accumulated Depr., Equipment		16,400.00		(g) 4,000.00		
Unearned Course Fees		1,200.00				
Accounts Payable		36,400.00				
Notes Payable		3,000.00				
Mortgage Payable		8,000.00	(c) 900.00			
N. C. Jackson, Capital		140,574.00				
N. C. Jackson, Drawing	48,900.00					
Sales		235,180.00				235,180.00
Sales Returns and Allowances	840.00				840.00	
Sales Discount	1,880.00				1,880.00	
Interest Income		120.00				120.00
Purchases	89,140.00				89,140.00	
Purchases Returns and Allowances		2,832.00				2,832.00
Purchases Discount		1,248.00				1,248.00
Freight In	2,460.00				2,460.00	
Wages Expense	55,800.00		(h) 1,220.00		57,020.00	
Taxes Expense	1,960.00				1,960.00	
Interest Expense	374.00				374.00	
	476,954.00	476,954.00				
Income Summary			(a) 77,000.00	(b) 64,900.00	77,000.00	64,900.00
Course Fees Income				(c) 900.00		900.00
Supplies Expense			(d) 925.00		925.00	
Insurance Expense			(e) 380.00		380.00	
Depreciation Expense, Building			(f) 5,000.00		5,000.00	
Depreciation Expense, Equipment			(g) 4,000.00		4,000.00	
Wages Payable				(h) 1,220.00		
			154,325.00	154,325.00	240,979.00	305,180.00
Net Income					64,201.00	
					305,180.00	305,180.00

FIGURE 1

To illustrate the concepts of **gross** and **net**, here is an example of a simple single-sale transaction.

Several years ago, Billie Reed bought an antique table at a second-hand store for $90. She decided to sell the table for $140. She advertised in the daily newspaper at a cost of $5. How much did she make as clear profit?

Sale of table	$140
Less cost of table	90
Gross Profit	$ 50
Less Advertising Expense	5
Net Income or Net Profit (gain on the sale)	$ 45

FIGURE 2

Jackson Electric Supply
Income Statement
For Year Ended December 31, 20—

Revenue from Sales:				
Sales			$235,180.00	
Less: Sales Returns and Allowances		$840.00		
Sales Discount		1,880.00	2,720.00	
Net Sales				$232,460.00
Cost of Goods Sold:				
Merchandise Inventory, January 1, 20—			$77,000.00	
Purchases		$89,140.00		
Less: Purchases Returns and				
Allowances	$2,832.00			
Purchases Discount	1,248.00	4,080.00		
Net Purchases		$85,060.00		
Add Freight In		2,460.00		
Delivered Cost of Purchases			87,520.00	
Goods Available for Sale			$164,520.00	
Less Merchandise Inventory, December 31, 20—			64,900.00	
Cost of Goods Sold				99,620.00
Gross Profit				$132,840.00
Operating Expenses:				
Wages Expense			$57,020.00	
Taxes Expense			1,960.00	
Supplies Expense			925.00	
Insurance Expense			380.00	
Depreciation Expense, Building			5,000.00	
Depreciation Expense, Equipment			4,000.00	
Total Operating Expenses				69,285.00
Income from Operations				$63,555.00
Other Income:				
Course Fees Income			$900.00	
Interest Income			120.00	
Total Other Income			$1,020.00	
Other Expenses:				
Interest Expense			374.00	646.00
Net Income				$64,201.00

Gross Profit is the profit on the sale of the table before any expenses have been deducted; in this case, it is $50. **Net Income**, or **Net Profit**, is the final or clear profit after all expenses have been deducted. In a single-sale situation such as this, we refer to the final outcome as the net profit. But for a business that has many sales and expenses, most accountants prefer the term *net income.* Regardless of which word you use, *net* refers to clear profit—after all expenses have been deducted.

Revenue from Sales

Now let's look at the Revenue from Sales section of the income statement for Jackson Electric Supply:

Revenue from Sales:			
Sales		$235,180.00	
Less: Sales Returns and Allowances	$840.00		
Sales Discount	1,880.00	2,720.00	
Net Sales			$232,460.00

When we introduced Sales Returns and Allowances and Sales Discount, we treated them as deductions from Sales. You can see that in the income statement, they are deducted from Sales to give us **Net Sales**. Note that we record these items in the same order in which they appear in the ledger.

Cost of Goods Sold

Remember!

Returns and Allowances (Sales or Purchases) is listed on one line, and Discount (Sales or Purchases) is listed below.

The section of the income statement that requires the greatest amount of concentration is the **Cost of Goods Sold** section, where the cost of the goods we sold is computed. Let's repeat it in its entirety:

Cost of Goods Sold:				
Merchandise Inventory, January 1, 20—			$77,000.00	
Purchases		$89,140.00		
Less: Purchases Returns and				
Allowances	$2,832.00			
Purchases Discount	1,248.00	4,080.00		
Net Purchases		$85,060.00		
Add Freight In		2,460.00		
Delivered Cost of Purchases			87,520.00	
Goods Available for Sale			$164,520.00	
Less Merchandise Inventory, December 31, 20—			64,900.00	
Cost of Goods Sold				$99,620.00

First, look closely at the Purchases section.

Purchases		$89,140.00	
Less: Purchases Returns			
and Allowances	$2,832.00		
Purchases Discount	1,248.00	4,080.00	
Net Purchases		$85,060.00	
Add Freight In		2,460.00	
Delivered Cost of Purchases			$87,520.00

Note the parallel to the Revenue from Sales section. To arrive at **Net Purchases**, we deduct the sum of Purchases Returns and Allowances and Purchases Discount from Purchases. To complete the Purchases section, we add Freight In to Net Purchases to get **Delivered Cost of Purchases**.

Now look at the full Cost of Goods Sold section. You might think of Cost of Goods Sold like this:

Amount we started with (beginning inventory)	$ 77,000
+ Net amount we purchased, including freight charges	87,520
Total amount that could have been sold (available)	$164,520
− Amount left over (ending inventory)	64,900
Cost of the goods that were actually sold	$ 99,620

Here's the Cost of Goods Sold expressed in proper wording.

Merchandise Inventory, January 1, 20—	$ 77,000
+ Delivered Cost of Purchases	87,520
Goods Available for Sale	$164,520
− Merchandise Inventory, December 31, 20—	64,900
Cost of Goods Sold	$ 99,620

The Cost of Goods Sold account begins with current inventory and adjusts for Purchases, Purchases Returns and Allowances, Discounts, and Freight In to arrive at a new inventory figure, from which the actual cost of goods sold can be determined.

Balducci's
MAIN ENTRANCE
MOR GREEN

Operating Expenses

Operating expenses, as the name implies, are the regular expenses of doing business. We list the accounts and their respective balances in the order in which they appear in the ledger.

Many firms use subclassifications of operating expenses, such as the following:

1. **Selling Expenses** Any expenses directly connected with the selling activity, such as
   - Sales Salaries Expense
   - Sales Commissions Expense
   - Advertising Expense
   - Store Supplies Expense
   - Delivery Expense
   - Depreciation Expense, Store Equipment
2. **General Expenses** Any expenses related to the office or administration, or any expense that cannot be directly connected with a selling activity:
   - Office Salaries Expense
   - Taxes Expense
   - Depreciation Expense, Office Equipment
   - Rent Expense
   - Insurance Expense
   - Office Supplies Expense

FYI

In preparing the income statement, classifying expense accounts as selling expenses or general expenses is a matter of judgment. The only reason we're not using this breakdown here is that we're trying to keep the number of accounts to a basic few.

If the Cash Short and Over account has a debit balance (net shortage), the balance is added to and reported as Miscellaneous General Expense. Conversely, if the Cash Short and Over account has a credit balance (net overage), the balance is added to and reported as Miscellaneous Income, which is classified as Other Income.

Income from Operations

Now let's repeat the skeleton outline:

Net Sales
− Cost of Goods Sold

Gross Profit
− Operating Expenses

Income from Operations

If Operating Expenses are the regular, recurring expenses of doing business, then Income from Operations should be the regular or recurring income from normal business operations. When you compare the results of operations over a number of years, Income from Operations is the figure to use as a basis for comparison.

Other Income and Other Expenses

The Other Income classification, as the name implies, includes any revenue account other than Revenue from Sales. What we are trying to do is to isolate Sales at the top of the income statement as the major revenue account, so that the Gross Profit figure represents the profit made on the sale of merchandise *only.* Additional accounts that may appear under the heading of Other Income are Rent Income (the firm is subletting part of its premises),

Jackson Electric Supply
Work Sheet
For Year Ended December 31, 20—

Account Name	Trial Balance Debit	Trial Balance Credit	Adjustments Debit	Adjustments Credit	Balance Sheet Debit	Balance Sheet Credit
Cash	21,154.00				21,154.00	
Notes Receivable	4,000.00				4,000.00	
Accounts Receiv.	29,446.00				29,446.00	
Merchandise Inven.	77,000.00		(b) 64,900.00	(a) 77,000.00	64,900.00	
Supplies	1,440.00			(d) 925.00	515.00	
Prepaid Insurance	960.00			(e) 380.00	580.00	
Land	12,000.00				12,000.00	
Building	96,000.00				96,000.00	
Accum. Depr., Build.		32,000.00		(f) 5,000.00		37,000.00
Equipment	33,600.00				33,600.00	
Accum. Depr., Equip.		16,400.00		(g) 4,000.00		20,400.00
Accounts Payable		36,400.00				36,400.00
Unearn. Course Fees		1,200.00	(c) 900.00			300.00
Notes Payable		3,000.00				3,000.00
Mortgage Payable		8,000.00				8,000.00
N. C. Jackson,						
Capital		140,574.00				140,574.00
N. C. Jackson, Draw.	48,900.00				48,900.00	
Sales		235,180.00				
Sales Returns and						
Allowances	840.00					
Sales Discount	1,880.00					
Interest Income		120.00				
Purchases	89,140.00					
Purchases Returns						
and Allowances		2,832.00				
Purchases Discount		1,248.00				
Freight In	2,460.00					
Wages Expense	55,800.00		(h) 1,220.00			
Taxes Expense	1,960.00					
Interest Expense	374.00					
	476,954.00	476,954.00				
Income Summary			(a) 77,000.00	(b) 64,900.00		
Course Fees Income				(c) 900.00		
Supplies Expense			(d) 925.00			
Insurance Expense			(e) 380.00			
Depr. Expense,						
Building			(f) 5,000.00			
Depr. Expense,						
Equipment			(g) 4,000.00			
Wages Payable				(h) 1,220.00		1,220.00
			154,325.00	154,325.00	311,095.00	246,894.00
Net Income						64,201.00
					311,095.00	311,095.00

FIGURE 3

FIGURE 4

Jackson Electric Supply
Statement of Owner's Equity
For Year Ended December 31, 20—

N. C. Jackson, Capital, January 1, 20—		$ 136 574 00
Additional Investment,		
August 26, 20—		4 000 00
Total Investment		$140 574 00
Net Income for the Year	$ 64 201 00	
Less Withdrawals for the Year	48 900 00	
Increase in Capital		
N. C. Jackson, Capital,		
December 31, 20—		$ 155 875 00

Remember!

The columns *do not* represent debit or credit columns. The columns are for making computations and listing totals.

Interest Income (the firm holds an interest-bearing note or contract), Gain on Disposal of Plant and Equipment (the firm makes a profit on the sale of plant and equipment), and Miscellaneous Income (the firm has an overage recorded in the Cash Short and Over account).

The classification Other Expenses records various nonoperating expenses, such as Interest Expense or Loss on Disposal of Plant and Equipment.

THE STATEMENT OF OWNER'S EQUITY AND THE BALANCE SHEET

Figure 3 is a partial work sheet for Jackson Electric Supply. Here again we find that **every figure in the Balance Sheet columns of the work sheet is used in either the statement of owner's equity or the balance sheet.**

Remember!

Net income appears on both the income statement and the statement of owner's equity.

Preparation of the financial statements follows the same order we presented before: first, the income statement; second, the statement of owner's equity; third, the balance sheet. The statement of owner's equity shows why the balance of the Capital account has changed from the beginning of the fiscal period to the end of it. In preparing the statement of owner's equity, always look into the ledger for the owner's Capital account to find any changes, such as additional investments, made during the year.

In Figure 4, observe that the balance of N. C. Jackson, Capital, listed on the work sheet is $140,574. Also note $4,000 in the completed statement of owner's equity, representing an additional investment. Therefore, the beginning balance of N. C. Jackson, Capital, was $136,574 ($140,574 − $4,000).

BALANCE SHEET CLASSIFICATIONS

Objective 2

Prepare a classified balance sheet for any type of business.

Balance sheet classifications are generally uniform for all types of business enterprises. You are strongly urged to take the time to learn the following definitions of the classifications and the order of accounts within them. As you read, refer to Figure 5 on the following page.

Jackson Electric Supply
Balance Sheet
December 31, 20—

Assets			
Current Assets:			
Cash		$21,154.00	
Notes Receivable		4,000.00	
Accounts Receivable		29,446.00	
Merchandise Inventory		64,900.00	
Supplies		515.00	
Prepaid Insurance		580.00	
Total Current Assets			$120,595.00
Plant and Equipment:			
Land		$12,000.00	
Building	$96,000.00		
Less Accumulated Depreciation	37,000.00	59,000.00	
Equipment	$33,600.00		
Less Accumulated Depreciation	20,400.00	13,200.00	
Total Plant and Equipment			84,200.00
Total Assets			$204,795.00
Liabilities			
Current Liabilities:			
Mortgage Payable (current portion)		$2,000.00	
Accounts Payable		36,400.00	
Notes Payable		3,000.00	
Wages Payable		1,220.00	
Unearned Course Fees		300.00	
Total Current Liabilities			$42,920.00
Long-Term Liabilities:			
Mortgage Payable			6,000.00
Total Liabilities			$48,920.00
Owner's Equity			
N. C. Jackson, Capital			155,875.00
Total Liabilities and Owner's Equity			$204,795.00

FIGURE 5

FYI

Some companies are so successful that they accumulate cash from earnings that is not needed to pay current obligations. Rather than leaving the cash in a bank account, companies may prefer to invest it in short-term government or corporate notes or bonds. These are called marketable securities. On the balance sheet, Marketable Securities is a separate account listed just below Cash.

Current Assets

Current Assets consist of cash and any other assets or resources that are expected to be realized in cash or to be sold or consumed during the normal operating cycle of the business (or one year, if the normal operating cycle is less than twelve months).

Accountants list current assets in the order of their convertibility into cash—in other words, their **liquidity**. (If you've got an asset such as a car or a stereo and you sell it quickly and turn it into cash, you are said to be turning it into a *liquid* state.) If the first four accounts shown under Current Assets in Figure 5 are present, they are always recorded in the same order: (1) Cash, (2) Notes Receivable, (3) Accounts Receivable, and (4) Merchandise Inventory.

Notes Receivable (current) are short-term (one year or less) promissory notes (promise-to-pay notes) held by the firm. A note is generally received from a customer as a substitute for a charge account.

Supplies and Prepaid Insurance are considered prepaid items that will be used up or will expire within the following operating cycle or year. Generally, these prepaid items are not converted into cash and that's why they appear at the bottom of the Current Assets section. There is no particular reason to list Supplies before Prepaid Insurance. Prepaid Insurance could just as easily have preceded Supplies.

The barn, the tractor, and the land this man is working are all classified as fixed assets in the Plant and Equipment account. Only the barn and tractor, however, are subject to depreciation.

Plant and Equipment

Plant and Equipment are relatively long-lived assets that are held for use in the production or sale of other assets or services; some accountants refer to them as *fixed assets.* The three types of accounts that usually appear in this category are Land, Building, and Equipment (refer to Figure 5). Note that the Building and Equipment accounts are followed by their respective Accumulated Depreciation accounts. We list these assets in order of their length of life, with the longest-lived asset placed first.

Current Liabilities

Current liabilities are debts that will become due within the normal operating cycle of the business, usually within one year; they normally will be paid, when due, from current assets. List current liabilities in the order of their expected payment. Mortgage Payable is the payment one makes to reduce the principal of the mortgage in a given year. Accounts Payable are debts owed to creditors. Wages Payable and any other accrued liabilities, such as Commissions Payable and the current portion of unearned revenue accounts, usually fall at the bottom of the list of current liabilities.

Remember!

Since Accumulated Depreciation is a contra account, it is deducted from the appropriate asset.

Long-Term Liabilities

Long-term Liabilities are debts that are payable over a comparatively long period, usually longer than one year. Ordinarily, Mortgage Payable is the only account in this category for a sole-proprietorship (or one-owner) type of business. One single amount in a category can be placed in the column on the extreme right.

Working Capital and Current Ratio

Both the management and the short-term creditors of a firm are vitally interested in two questions:

1. Does the firm have a sufficient amount of capital to operate?
2. Does the firm have the ability to pay its debts?

Objective 3

Compute working capital and current ratio.

Two measures used to answer these questions are a firm's working capital and its current ratio; the necessary data are taken from a classified balance sheet.

Working capital is determined by subtracting current liabilities from current assets; thus,

Working Capital = Current Assets − Current Liabilities

The normal operating cycle for most firms is less than one year. Because current assets equal cash—or items that can be converted into cash or used up within one year—and current liabilities equal the total amount that the company must pay out within one year, working capital is appropriately named. It is the amount of capital the company has available to use or to work with. The working capital for Jackson Electric Supply is as follows:

Working Capital = $120,595 − $42,920 = $77,675

FYI

The current ratio has a weakness. It favors companies with lots of current assets. However, the current ratio does not attempt to measure the overall strength of a company.

The **current ratio** is useful in revealing a firm's ability to pay its bills. It is determined by dividing current assets by current liabilities:

$$\text{Current Ratio} = \frac{\text{Current Assets (amount coming in within one year)}}{\text{Current Liabilities (amount going out within one year)}}$$

CA ÷ CL

The current ratio for Jackson Electric Supply is calculated like this:

$$\text{Current Ratio} = \frac{\$120{,}595}{\$\ 42{,}920} = 2.81 \qquad 42{,}920\overline{)\,120{,}595} = 2.8097$$

(quotient shown above the division: 2.81)

In the case of Jackson Electric Supply, $2.81 in current assets is available to pay every dollar currently due on December 31.

makes SENSE

Chart of Accounts

Remember!

A common organization for the chart of accounts is

Assets	1--
Liabilities	2--
Owner's Equity	3--
Revenue	4--
Cost of Goods Sold	5--
Expenses	6--

When we introduced the chart of accounts and the account number arrangement, we said that the first digit represents the classification of an account. Since you are now acquainted with classified income statements and balance sheets, we can introduce the second digit. The second digit stands for the subclassification.

Assets	1--	Revenue	4--
Current Assets	11-	Revenue from Sales	41-
Plant and Equipment	12-	Other Income	42-
Liabilities	2--	Cost of Goods Sold	5--
Current Liabilities	21-	Purchases	51-
Long-Term Liabilities	22-	Expenses	6--
Owner's Equity	3--	Selling Expenses	61-
Capital	31-	General Expenses	62-
		Other Expenses	63-

The third digit indicates the placement of the account within the subclassification. For example, account number 411 represents Sales, which is the first account listed under Revenue. Account number 512 represents Purchases Returns and Allowances, which is the second account listed under Cost of Goods Sold. Account number 312 represents Drawing, which is the second account listed under Owner's Equity.

CLOSING ENTRIES

Now let's look at closing entries for a merchandising business. You follow the same four steps to close or zero out the revenue, expense, and Drawing accounts as for a service business.

ACCOUNT NAME	TRIAL BALANCE DEBIT	TRIAL BALANCE CREDIT	INCOME STATEMENT DEBIT	INCOME STATEMENT CREDIT
Cash	21,154.00			
Notes Receivable	4,000.00			
Accounts Receivable	29,446.00			
Merchandise Inventory	77,000.00			
Supplies	1,440.00			
Prepaid Insurance	960.00			
Land	12,000.00			
Building	96,000.00			
Accumulated Depreciation, Building		32,000.00		
Equipment	33,600.00			
Accumulated Depreciation, Equipment		16,400.00		
Mortgage Payable		8,000.00		
Accounts Payable		36,400.00		
Notes Payable		3,000.00		
Unearned Course Fees		1,200.00		
N. C. Jackson, Capital		140,574.00		
N. C. Jackson, Drawing	48,900.00			
Sales		235,180.00		235,180.00
Sales Returns and Allowances	840.00		840.00	
Sales Discount	1,880.00		1,880.00	
Interest Income		120.00		120.00
Purchases	89,140.00		89,140.00	
Purchases Returns and Allowances		2,832.00		2,832.00
Purchases Discount		1,248.00		1,248.00
Freight In	2,460.00		2,460.00	
Wages Expense	55,800.00		57,020.00	
Taxes Expense	1,960.00		1,960.00	
Interest Expense	374.00		374.00	
	476,954.00	476,954.00		
Income Summary			77,000.00	64,900.00
Course Fees Income				900.00
Supplies Expense			925.00	
Insurance Expense			380.00	
Depreciation Expense, Building			5,000.00	
Depreciation Expense, Equipment			4,000.00	
Wages Payable				
			240,979.00	305,180.00
Net Income			64,201.00	
			305,180.00	305,180.00

FIGURE 6

Objective 4

Journalize the closing entries for a merchandising firm.

At the end of a fiscal period, you close the revenue and expense accounts so that you can start the next fiscal period with zero balances. You close the Drawing account because it, too, applies to one fiscal period. Recall that these accounts are called **temporary-equity accounts**, or *nominal accounts.*

Figure 6 shows the isolated Income Statement columns. After you have looked them over, let us look at the four steps of the closing procedure.

IMPORTANT AGAIN

1. Close All Temporary Credits

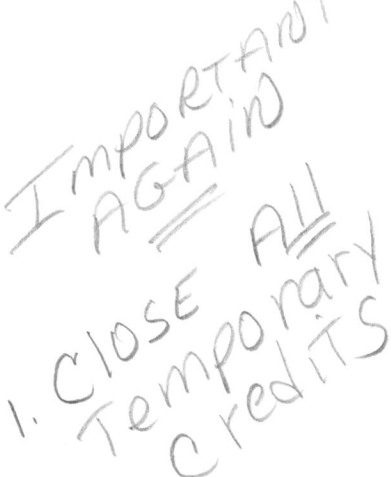

Four Steps in the Closing Procedure

These four steps should be followed when closing:

1. Close the revenue accounts and the other accounts that appear in the income statement and have credit balances (all temporary or nominal accounts with credit balances). **(Debit the figures that are credited in the Income Statement columns of the work sheet, except the figure on the Income Summary line.)** This entry is illustrated as follows:

GENERAL JOURNAL PAGE 97

DATE		DESCRIPTION	POST. REF.	DEBIT	CREDIT
20–		**Closing Entries**			
Dec.	31	Sales		235,180.00	
		Interest Income		120.00	
		Purchases Returns and			
		Allowances		2,832.00	
		Purchases Discount		1,248.00	
		Course Fees Income		900.00	
		Income Summary			240,280.00

2. Close the expense accounts and the other accounts appearing in the income statement that have debit balances (all temporary or nominal accounts with debit balances). **(Credit the figures that are debited in the Income Statement columns of the work sheet, except the figure on the Income Summary line.)**

   Note that you close Purchases Discount and Purchases Returns and Allowances in step 1 along with the revenue accounts. Note also that in step 2 you close Sales Discount and Sales Returns and Allowances along with the expense accounts.

2. Close All Temporary Debits

GENERAL JOURNAL PAGE 97

DATE		DESCRIPTION	POST. REF.	DEBIT	CREDIT
Dec.	31	Income Summary		163,979.00	
		Sales Returns and Allowances			840.00
		Sales Discount			1,880.00
		Purchases			89,140.00
		Freight In			2,460.00
		Wages Expense			57,020.00
		Taxes Expense			1,960.00
		Interest Expense			374.00
		Supplies Expense			925.00
		Insurance Expense			380.00
		Depreciation Expense, Build.			5,000.00
		Depreciation Expense, Equip.			4,000.00

3. Close summary to Capital = NI or NL

3. Close the Income Summary account into N. C. Jackson, Capital. **(Debit Income Summary by the amount of the net income; credit it by the amount of a net loss.)**

GENERAL JOURNAL PAGE 97

	DATE		DESCRIPTION	POST. REF.	DEBIT	CREDIT	
22	Dec.	31	Income Summary		64 2 0 1 00		22
23			N. C. Jackson, Capital			64 2 0 1 00	23
24							24

KNOPFLER
Like service businesses, merchandisers such as this CD store need to close entries to track net income.

Here is what the T accounts look like. Note that the Income Summary account already contains adjusting entries for merchandise inventory.

Income Summary

Adjusting (Beginning Merchandise Inventory)	77,000	Adjusting (Ending Merchandise Inventory)	64,900
(Expenses and other debit balance accounts)	163,979	(Revenue and other credit balance accounts)	240,280
(Net Income)	64,201		

N. C. Jackson, Capital

−		+	
		Balance	140,574
		(Net Income)	64,201

4. Close the Drawing account into the Capital account.

4. Close DRAW to CAPITAL

GENERAL JOURNAL PAGE 97

	DATE		DESCRIPTION	POST. REF.	DEBIT	CREDIT	
25	Dec.	31	N. C. Jackson, Capital		48 9 0 0 00		25
26			N. C. Jackson, Drawing			48 9 0 0 00	26
27							27
28							28
29							29

Here is what the T accounts would look like:

N. C. Jackson, Drawing

	+	−	
Balance	48,900	Closing	48,900

N. C. Jackson, Capital

	−	+	
(Drawing)	48,900	Balance	140,574
		(Net Income)	64,201

REVERSING ENTRIES

FYI

The use of reversing entries is optional.

Reversing entries are general journal entries that are the exact reverse of certain adjusting entries. A reversing entry enables the accountant to record routine transactions in the usual manner, *even though* an adjusting entry affecting one of the accounts involved in the transaction has intervened. We can understand this concept best by looking at an example.

Suppose there is an adjusting entry for accrued wages owed to employees at the end of the fiscal year. Assume that all the employees of a certain firm earn, altogether, $400 per day for a five-day week and that payday occurs every Friday throughout the year. When the employees get their checks at 5:00 P.M. on Friday, the checks include their wages for that day and for the preceding four days. And assume that, one year, the last day of the fiscal year happens to fall on Wednesday, December 31. A diagram of this situation would look like this:

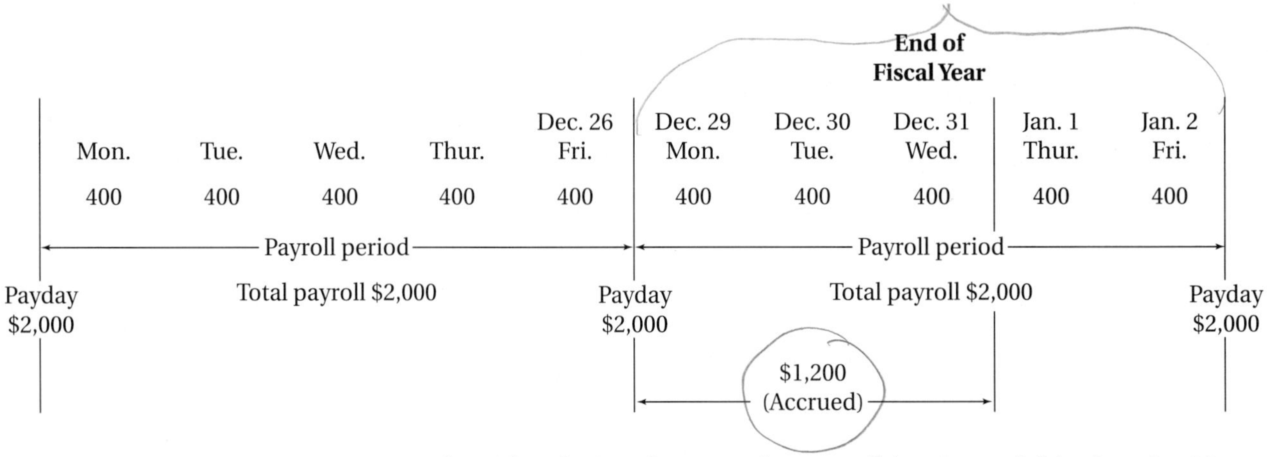
End of Fiscal Year
Mon. 400
Tue. 400
Wed. 400
Thur. 400
Dec. 26 Fri. 400
Dec. 29 Mon. 400
Dec. 30 Tue. 400
Dec. 31 Wed. 400
Jan. 1 Thur. 400
Jan. 2 Fri. 400
Payroll period
Total payroll $2,000
Payroll period
Total payroll $2,000
Payday $2,000
Payday $2,000
Payday $2,000
$1,200 (Accrued)

Each Friday during the year, the payroll has been debited to the Wages Expense account and credited to the Cash account. As a result, Wages Expense has a debit balance of $102,800. Here is the adjusting entry in T account form:

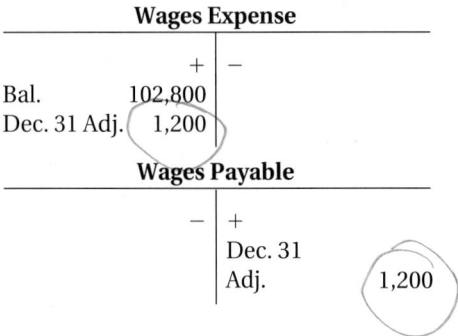

Wages Expense

	+	−
Bal.	102,800	
Dec. 31 Adj.	1,200	

Wages Payable

−	+	
	Dec. 31 Adj.	1,200

must split up This one Payroll Recording

Next, when all the expense accounts are closed, Wages Expense is closed by crediting it for $104,000. However, Wages Payable continues to have a credit balance of $1,200. The $2,000 payroll on January 2 must be split up by debiting Wages Payable $1,200, debiting Wages Expense $800, and crediting Cash $2,000.

The employee who records the payroll not only has to record this particular payroll differently from all other weekly payrolls for the year but also has to refer back to the adjusting entry to determine what portion of the $2,000 is debited to Wages Payable and what portion is debited to Wages Expense. In many companies, however, the employee who records the payroll does not have access to the adjusting entries.

There is a solution to this problem. The need to refer to the earlier entry and divide the debit total between the two accounts is eliminated *if a reversing entry is made on the first day of the following fiscal period.* You make an entry that is the exact reverse of the adjusting entry, as follows:

GENERAL JOURNAL PAGE 118

DATE		DESCRIPTION	POST. REF.	DEBIT	CREDIT
20–		Reversing Entries			
Jan.	1	Wages Payable		1 2 0 0 00	
		Wages Expense			1 2 0 0 00

Now let's bring the T accounts up to date.

Wages Expense

	+	−	
Balance	102,800	Dec. 31 Closing	104,000
Dec. 31 Adjust.	1,200		
		Jan. 1 Reversing	1,200

Wages Payable

	−	+	
Jan. 1 Reversing	1,200	Dec. 31 Adjust.	1,200

The reversing entry has the effect of transferring the $1,200 liability from Wages Payable to the credit side of Wages Expense. Wages Expense will temporarily have a credit balance until the next payroll is recorded in the routine manner. In our example, this occurs on January 2. See the T accounts on the following page.

Wages Expense

+		−	
Balance	102,800	Dec. 31 Closing	104,000
Dec. 31 Adjust.	1,200		
Jan. 2	2,000	Jan. 1 Reversing	1,200

Wages Payable

−		+	
Jan. 1 Reversing	1,200	Dec. 31 Adjust.	1,200

Cash

+		−	
		Jan. 2	2,000

Reverse on Jan 1 odd to have a cr Bal!

There is now a *net debit balance* of $800 in Wages Expense, which is the correct amount ($400 for January 1 and $400 for January 2). To see this, look at the following ledger accounts. December 26 was the last payday of one year, and January 2 is the first payday of the next year.

GENERAL LEDGER

ACCOUNT **Wages Expense** ACCOUNT NO. **521**

DATE		ITEM	POST. REF.	DEBIT	CREDIT	BALANCE DEBIT	BALANCE CREDIT
20–							
Dec.	26		CP16	2,000.00		102,800.00	
	31	Adjusting	J116	1,200.00		104,000.00	
	31	Closing	J117		104,000.00	—	—
20–							
Jan.	1	Reversing	J118		1,200.00		1,200.00
	2		CP17	2,000.00		800.00	

ACCOUNT **Wages Payable** ACCOUNT NO. **213**

DATE		ITEM	POST. REF.	DEBIT	CREDIT	BALANCE DEBIT	BALANCE CREDIT
20–							
Dec.	31	Adjusting	J116		1,200.00		1,200.00
20–							
Jan.	1	Reversing	J118	1,200.00		—	—

Objective 5

Determine which adjusting entries can be reversed, and journalize the reversing entries.

The reversing entry for accrued salaries or wages applies to service as well as merchandising companies. You can see that a reversing entry simply switches around an adjusting entry. The question is: Which adjusting entries should be reversed? Here are two handy rules for reversing. **If an adjusting entry is to be reversed, it must meet both of the following qualifications:**

1. **The adjusting entry increases an asset or liability account.**
2. **The asset or liability account did not have a previous balance.**

With the exception of the first year of operations, Merchandise Inventory and contra accounts—such as Accumulated Depreciation—always have previous balances. Consequently, adjusting entries involving these accounts should never be reversed.

Let's apply these rules to the adjusting entries for Jackson Electric Supply.

Good Review

(Do not reverse; Merchandise Inventory is an asset, but it was decreased. Also, it has a previous balance.)

Merchandise Inventory			
	+	–	
Balance	77,000	Adjust.	77,000

Income Summary			
Adjust.	77,000		

(Do not reverse; Merchandise Inventory is an asset, but it has a previous balance.)

Merchandise Inventory			
	+	–	
Balance	77,000	Adjust.	77,000
Adjust.	64,900		

Income Summary			
Adjust.	77,000	Adjust.	64,900

(Do not reverse; Unearned Course Fees is a liability, but it was decreased. Also, it has a previous balance.)

Course Fees Income			
	–	+	
		Adjust.	900

Unearned Course Fees			
	–	+	
Adjust.	900	Balance	1,200

(Do not reverse; Supplies is an asset account, but it was decreased. Also, it has a previous balance.)

Supplies Expense			
	+	–	
Adjust.	925		

Supplies			
	+	–	
Balance	1,440	Adjust.	925

(Do not reverse; Prepaid Insurance is an asset account, but it was decreased. Also, it has a previous balance.)

Insurance Expense			
	+	–	
Adjust.	380		

Prepaid Insurance			
	+	–	
Balance	960	Adjust.	380

(Do not reverse; Accumulated Depreciation is a contra-asset, and it always has a previous balance after the first year.)

Depreciation Expense, Building			
	+	–	
Adjust.	5,000		

Accumulated Depreciation, Building			
	–	+	
		Balance	32,000
		Adjust.	5,000

(Do not reverse; Accumulated Depreciation is a contra-asset, and it always has a previous balance after the first year.)

Depreciation Expense, Equipment			
	+	–	
Adjust.	4,000		

Accumulated Depreciation, Equipment			
	–	+	
		Balance	16,400
		Adjust.	4,000

(Reverse; Wages Payable is a liability account. It was increased, and it had no previous balance.)

Wages Expense			
	+	–	
Balance	45,800		
Adjust.	1,220		

Wages Payable			
	–	+	
		Adjust.	1,220

Remember!

Reversing entries are optional.

Whenever we introduce additional adjusting entries, we will make it a point to state whether they can be reversed.

CHAPTER REVIEW

Review of Performance Objectives

1. Prepare a classified income statement for a merchandising firm.

   The outline of the income statement looks like this:

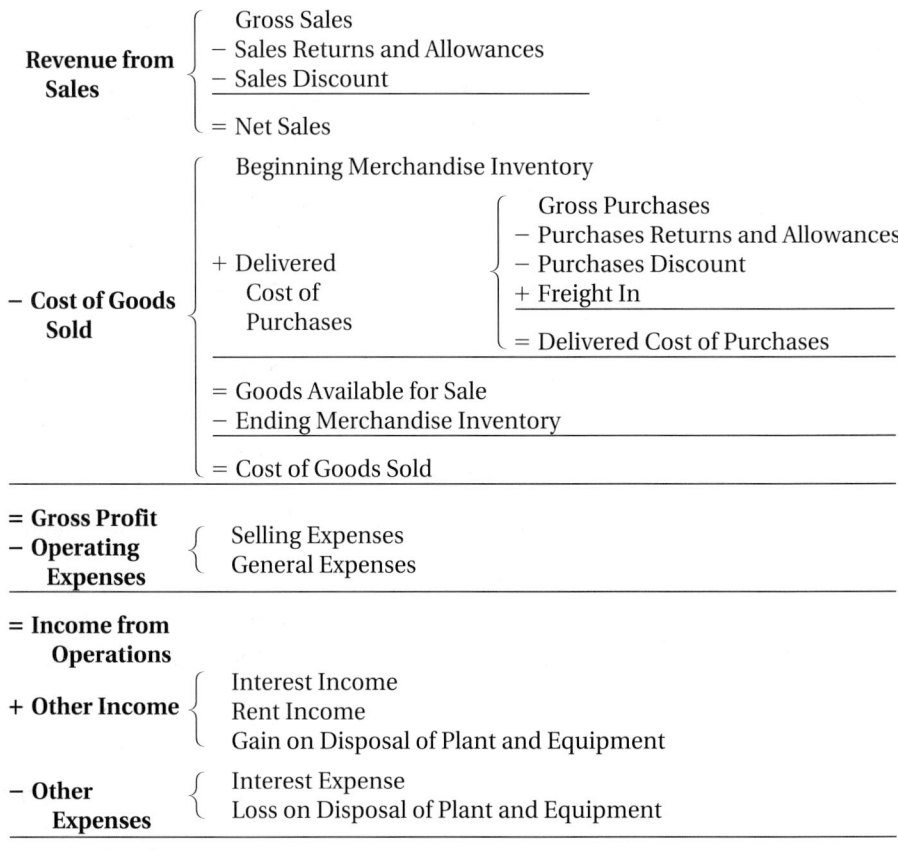

Revenue from Sales
- Gross Sales
- − Sales Returns and Allowances
- − Sales Discount
- = Net Sales

− Cost of Goods Sold
- Beginning Merchandise Inventory
- + Delivered Cost of Purchases
  - Gross Purchases
  - − Purchases Returns and Allowances
  - − Purchases Discount
  - + Freight In
  - = Delivered Cost of Purchases
- = Goods Available for Sale
- − Ending Merchandise Inventory
- = Cost of Goods Sold

= Gross Profit

− Operating Expenses
- Selling Expenses
- General Expenses

= Income from Operations

+ Other Income
- Interest Income
- Rent Income
- Gain on Disposal of Plant and Equipment

− Other Expenses
- Interest Expense
- Loss on Disposal of Plant and Equipment

= Net Income

2. Prepare a classified balance sheet for any type of business.

   The outline of the balance sheet looks like this:

   Assets Current Assets (listed in the order of their convertibility into cash)

   1. Cash
   2. Notes Receivable
   3. Accounts Receivable
   4. Merchandise Inventory
   5. Prepaid items (Supplies; Prepaid Insurance)

   Plant and Equipment (listed in the order of their length of life; the asset with the longest life is placed first)

   1. Land
   2. Buildings
   3. Equipment

Liabilities Current Liabilities (listed in the order of their urgency of payment; the most pressing obligation is placed first)

1. Accounts Payable
2. Notes Payable
3. Accrued liabilities (Wages Payable; Commissions Payable)
4. Unearned Revenue
5. Mortgage Payable or Contracts Payable (current portion)

Long-Term Liabilities (Contracts Payable; Mortgage Payable)

Owner's Equity Capital balance at end of the fiscal year

3. Compute working capital and current ratio.

These two measures help analysts determine whether a firm has enough capital to operate and whether it can pay its debts.

$$\text{Working capital} = \text{Current assets} - \text{Current liabilities}$$

$$\text{Current ratio} = \frac{\text{Current assets}}{\text{Current liabilities}}$$

4. Journalize the closing entries for a merchandising firm.

There are four steps in making closing entries for a merchandising business:

Step 1. Close all revenue accounts, Purchases Returns and Allowances, and Purchases Discount into Income Summary (any accounts listed as credits in the work sheet Income Statement columns except Income Summary).

Step 2. Close all expense accounts, Sales Returns and Allowances, and Sales Discount into Income Summary (any accounts listed as debits in the work sheet Income Statement columns except Income Summary).

Step 3. Close Income Summary into Capital (transfer net income or net loss into the owner's Capital account). The Income Summary balance should now be zero.

Step 4. Close Drawing into Capital.

5. Determine which adjusting entries can be reversed, and journalize the reversing entries. The use of reversing entries is optional.

Reverse the adjusting entries that increase either asset or liability accounts and that do not have previous balances. A contra-account like Accumulated Depreciation should not be reversed. Reversing entries are dated as of the first day of the next fiscal period.

Glossary

Cost of Goods Sold A section of the income statement in which the amount of the cost of the goods we sold is calculated. Terms often used to describe the same thing are *cost of merchandise sold* and *cost of sales*.

Merchandise Inventory (beginning)
Plus Delivered Cost of Purchases

Goods Available for Sale
Less Merchandise Inventory (ending)

Cost of Goods Sold (473)

Current Assets Cash and any other assets or resources that are expected to be realized in cash or to be sold or consumed during the normal operating cycle of the business (or one year, if the normal operating cycle is less than twelve months). (478)

Current liabilities Debts that will become due within the normal operating cycle of a business, usually within one year, and that are normally paid from current assets. (479)

Current ratio A firm's current assets divided by its current liabilities. Portrays a firm's short-term debt-paying ability. (480)

Delivered Cost of Purchases Net Purchases plus Freight In:

Net Purchases
Plus Freight In

Delivered Cost of Purchases (474)

General Expenses Expenses incurred in the administration of a business, including office expenses and any expenses that are not completely classified as Selling Expenses or Other Expenses. (475)

Gross Profit Net Sales minus Cost of Goods Sold, or profit before deducting expenses:

Net Sales
Less Cost of Goods Sold

Gross Profit (473)

Liquidity The ability of an asset to be quickly turned into cash, either by selling it or by putting it up as security for a loan. (478)

Long-term Liabilities Debts payable over a comparatively long period, usually more than one year. (479)

Net Income or **Net Profit** The final figure on an income statement after all expenses have been deducted from revenues. (473)

Net Purchases Purchases minus Purchases Returns and Allowances and minus Purchases Discount:

Purchases
Less Purchases Returns and Allowances
Less Purchases Discount

Net Purchases (474)

Net Sales Sales minus Sales Returns and Allowances and minus Sales Discount:

Sales
Less Sales Returns and Allowances
Less Sales Discount

Net Sales (473)

Notes Receivable (current) Written promises to pay the seller/lender the amount due in a period of less than one year. (479)

Plant and Equipment Long-lived assets that are held for use in the production or sale of other assets or services; also called *fixed assets.* (479)

Reversing entries The reverse of certain adjusting entries, recorded as of the first day of the following fiscal period. The use of reversing entries is optional. (484)

Selling Expenses Expenses directly connected with the selling activity, such as salaries of sales staff, advertising expenses, and delivery expenses. (475)

Temporary-equity accounts Accounts whose balances apply to one fiscal period only, such as revenues, expenses, and the Drawing account. Temporary-equity accounts are also called *nominal accounts.* (481)

Working capital A firm's current assets less its current liabilities. The amount of capital a firm has available to use or to work with during a normal operating cycle. (479)

QUESTIONS, EXERCISES, AND PROBLEMS

Discussion Questions

1. What is the difference between the cost of goods available for sale and the cost of goods sold?
2. What are the basic classifications found on an income statement for a merchandising business?
3. On an income statement, what is the difference between income from operations and net income? Which is more useful in comparing the results of operations over a number of years?
4. Explain the calculation of net sales and net purchases.
5. What is the order for listing accounts in the Current Assets section of the balance sheet?
6. On a balance sheet, what is the difference between Current Liabilities and Long-Term Liabilities? Give an example of an account in each classification.
7. In the closing procedure, what happens to (a) Purchases Discount, (b) Sales Returns and Allowances, (c) Freight In, (d) Gain on Disposal of Plant and Equipment?
8. What is the rule for recognizing whether or not an adjusting entry can be reversed?

Exercises

P.O. 1

Provide missing amounts on an income statement.

Exercise 14-1 Calculate the missing items in the following:

Sales	Sales Returns and Allowances	Net Sales	Beginning Merchandise Inventory	Net Purchases	Goods Available for Sale	Ending Merchandise Inventory	Cost of Goods Sold	Gross Profit
a. $249,000	$ 6,000	243,000	$148,000	$170,000	318,000	$136,000	$182,000	61,000
b. 304,000	8,000	$296,000	144,000	260,000	$404,000	196,000	208,000	88,000
c. 640,000	12,000	628,000	84,000	412,000	496,000	92,000	404,000	224,000

P.O. 1

Prepare Cost of Goods Sold section.

Exercise 14-2 Using the following information, prepare the Cost of Goods Sold section of an income statement.

Purchases Discount	$ 9,000
Merchandise Inventory, December 31	192,000
Purchases	480,000
Merchandise Inventory, January 1	188,000
Purchases Returns and Allowances	16,000
Freight In	27,000

P.O. 1

Classify income statement accounts.

Exercise 14-3 Identify each of the following items relating to sections of an income statement as Revenue from Sales (S), Cost of Goods Sold (CGS), Selling Expenses (SE), General Expenses (GE), Other Income (OI), or Other Expense (OE).

a. Advertising Expense
b. Rent Expense
c. Purchases Discount
d. Sales Returns and Allowances
e. Interest Income
f. Freight In
g. Depreciation Expense, Building
h. Interest Expense
i. Insurance Expense
j. Delivery Expense

P.O. 1

Prepare an income statement.

Exercise 14-4 The partial Income Statement columns of the June 30 (year-end) work sheet for Dahl Company are shown here. From the information given, prepare an income statement for the company. To save time and space, the expenses have been grouped together into two categories.

	ACCOUNT NAME	INCOME STATEMENT DEBIT	INCOME STATEMENT CREDIT
21	Income Summary	27,000.00	25,000.00
22	Sales		291,000.00
23	Sales Returns and Allowances	11,100.00	
24	Sales Discount	4,100.00	
25	Purchases	116,000.00	
26	Purchases Returns and Allowances		1,200.00
27	Purchases Discount		1,000.00
28	Freight In	7,500.00	
29	Selling Expenses	56,000.00	
30	General Expenses	49,000.00	
31		270,700.00	318,200.00
32	Net Income	47,500.00	
		318,200.00	318,200.00

P.O. 2

Classify balance sheet items.

Exercise 14-5 Identify each of the following items relating to sections of a balance sheet dated 2001 as Current Assets (CA), Plant and Equipment (PE), Current Liabilities (CL), Long-Term Liabilities (LTL), or Owner's Equity (OE).

a. Accounts Receivable
b. Building
c. Wages Payable
d. Prepaid Taxes
e. Mortgage Payable (current)
f. Supplies
g. Mortgage Payable (due May 31, 2008)
h. Unearned Fees
i. D. Deal, Capital
j. Notes Payable (due in 3 months)

P.O. 3
Determine working capital and current ratio.

Exercise 14-6 On December 31, 2001, the following selected accounts and amounts appeared in the balance sheet. Determine the amount of the working capital and the current ratio.

Building	$160,000
Prepaid Insurance	600
Merchandise Inventory	76,000
Store Equipment	14,000
Unearned Fees	700
Notes Payable (due within 12 months)	7,000
Accumulated Depreciation, Building	76,000
Accounts Payable	22,000
Land	40,000
Store Supplies	1,000
Cash	9,000
Accumulated Depreciation, Store Equipment	6,000
Notes Receivable (mature within 12 months)	4,000
Mortgage Payable (current portion)	4,400
Salaries Payable	2,000
C. Ray, Capital	101,500
Mortgage Payable (due June 30, 2010)	85,000

P.O. 4
Journalize closing entries.

Exercise 14-7 From the following T accounts, journalize the closing entries dated December 31:

Salary Expense

+	–
68,000	

H. Mann, Drawing

+	–
54,000	

Purchases Returns and Allowances

–	+
	7,600

Purchases

+	–
236,800	

Miscellaneous Expense

+	–
13,200	

Rent Expense

+	–
24,000	

Sales Returns and Allowances

+	–
8,000	

Freight In

+	–
15,200	

Sales

–	+
	504,000

Income Summary

88,000	104,000

H. Mann, Capital

–	+
	336,000

Purchases Discount

–	+
	5,600

P.O. 4

From T accounts, prepare a statement of owner's equity.

Exercise 14-8 From the following information, journalize the last two closing entries, and present a statement of owner's equity for Rea Company:

T. H. Rea, Capital

–		+	
		Jan. 1 Balance	440,000
		Apr. 7	16,000

T. H. Rea, Drawing

+		–
Mar. 1	42,000	
Dec. 9	37,000	

Income Summary

Dec. 31 Adj.	192,000	Dec. 31 Adj.	204,000
Dec. 31 Closing	410,000	Dec. 31 Closing	490,000

WHAT IF . . .

What if the freight charges on a new desk for the owner were journalized and posted to the Freight In account? Would this affect the Cost of Goods Sold section? If so, how?

CRITICAL THINKING

You are an owner/bookkeeper in a country whose economy has been nearly destroyed. Goods are scarce; in fact, you have no goods to sell at the start of each day. You go out early each morning to purchase goods and haul them back to sell. At the end of the day, you have sold everything. Prepare a Cost of Goods Sold section for a day when you purchased $400 in goods and assume you sold everything. What conclusion can you draw?

A MATTER OF ETHICS

Molly is an accountant. Sometimes printouts of financial statements have errors and are not usable. Molly doesn't like to waste anything. She even takes the unusable financial statements to her son's day care center to use as drawing paper. Explain why you think this is or is not unethical behavior.

WEB WORK

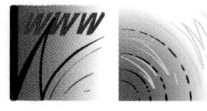

Using an Internet web browser, type the phrase for the home page of a retail organization or association in the search box. Find the balance sheet. Look for Current and Long-Term Assets and Liabilities on the balance sheet. Compute working capital. Compute the current ratio. Discuss your findings or write them in a memo to your instructor.

PROBLEM SET A

For additional help, see the demonstration problem at the beginning of each chapter in your Working Papers.

P.O. 1,4

Problem 14-1A A partial work sheet for Poe Music Store is presented here. The merchandise inventory at the beginning of the fiscal period was $49,584. F. L. Poe, the owner, withdrew $32,000 during the year.

Poe Music Store
Work Sheet
For Year Ended December 31, 20—

	Account Name	Income Statement Debit	Income Statement Credit
21	Sales		326,592.80
22	Sales Returns and Allowances	5,229.20	
23	Sales Discount	1,908.00	
24	Interest Income		324.98
25	Purchases	195,191.00	
26	Purchases Returns and Allowances		1,656.00
27	Freight In	14,265.00	
28	Wages Expense	39,524.00	
29	Rent Expense	9,360.00	
30	Commissions Expense	9,440.00	
31	Interest Expense	656.32	
32	Income Summary	49,584.00	43,972.00
33	Supplies Expense	637.20	
34	Insurance Expense	936.00	
35	Depreciation Expense, Building	4,800.00	
36	Depreciation Expense, Equipment	3,340.00	
37		334,870.72	372,545.78
38	Net Income	37,675.06	
39		372,545.78	372,545.78

Check Figure
Cost of Goods Sold, $213,412

Instructions

1. Prepare an income statement.
2. Journalize the closing entries.

P.O. 2,3

Problem 14-2A Here is the partial work sheet for The Mountain Shop.

The Mountain Shop
Work Sheet
For Year Ended December 31, 20—

ACCOUNT NAME	BALANCE SHEET DEBIT	BALANCE SHEET CREDIT
Cash	9,723.00	
Notes Receivable	3,600.00	
Accounts Receivable	42,879.60	
Merchandise Inventory	56,697.00	
Supplies	474.00	
Prepaid Taxes	613.50	
Prepaid Insurance	630.00	
Land	8,400.00	
Building	63,000.00	
Accumulated Depreciation, Building		21,600.00
Office Equipment	5,424.00	
Accumulated Depreciation, Office Equipment		4,170.00
Store Equipment	6,570.00	
Accumulated Depreciation, Store Equipment		4,995.00
Delivery Equipment	5,565.00	
Accumulated Depreciation, Delivery Equipment		4,305.00
Mortgage Payable		55,713.00
Accounts Payable		29,591.70
Notes Payable		5,430.00
Mortgage Payable (current portion)		2,700.00
N. Olston, Capital		65,058.90
N. Olston, Drawing	25,194.00	
Wages Payable		1,278.00
	228,770.10	194,841.60
Net Income		33,928.50
	228,770.10	228,770.10

Check Figure
Working capital, $75,617.40

Instructions

1. Prepare a statement of owner's equity (no additional investment).
2. Prepare a balance sheet.
3. Determine the amount of the working capital.
4. Determine the current ratio (carry to one decimal place).

P.O. 4,5

Problem 14-3A The following partial work sheet covers the affairs of Koto and Company for the year ending June 30:

Koto and Company
Work Sheet
For Year Ended June 30, 20—

	Account Name	Income Statement Debit	Income Statement Credit	Balance Sheet Debit	Balance Sheet Credit	
1	Cash			32,384.34		1
2	Accounts Receivable			104,634.54		2
3	Merchandise Inventory			119,456.00		3
4	Supplies			1,032.00		4
5	Prepaid Insurance			1,320.00		5
6	Delivery Equipment			12,920.00		6
7	Accumulated Depreciation, Delivery Equipment				6,480.00	7
8	Store Equipment			36,500.00		8
9	Accumulated Depreciation, Store Equipment				10,360.00	9
10	Accounts Payable				67,437.34	10
11	Salaries Payable				852.00	11
12	C. P. Koto, Capital				195,921.14	12
13	C. P. Koto, Drawing			37,440.00		13
14	Income Summary	115,226.00	119,456.00			14
15	Sales		536,352.40			15
16	Purchases	393,930.00				16
17	Purchases Returns and Allowances		7,828.00			17
18	Purchases Discount		5,746.00			18
19	Freight In	23,350.00				19
20	Salary Expense	51,400.00				20
21	Truck Expense	9,342.00				21
22	Supplies Expense	2,564.00				22
23	Insurance Expense	1,920.00				23
24	Depreciation Expense, Delivery Equipment	2,700.00				24
25	Depreciation Expense, Store Equipment	2,896.00				25
26	Miscellaneous Expense	1,418.00				26
27		604,746.00	669,382.40	345,686.88	281,050.48	27
28	Net Income	64,636.40			64,636.40	28
29		669,382.40	669,382.40	345,686.88	345,686.88	29
30						30
31						31
32						32

Check Figure
Reversing entry amount, $852

Instructions

1. Journalize the seven adjusting entries.
2. Journalize the closing entries.
3. Journalize the reversing entry.

P.O. 1,2,4,5

Problem 14-4A The following accounts appear in the ledger of The Short Company on January 31, the end of this fiscal year:

Cash	$ 5,400
Accounts Receivable	14,100
Merchandise Inventory	55,500
Store Supplies	690
Prepaid Insurance	1,080
Store Equipment	27,900
Accumulated Depreciation, Store Equipment	2,700
Accounts Payable	13,800
Wages Payable	—
M. R. Short, Capital	113,620
M. R. Short, Drawing	36,000
Income Summary	—
Sales	224,000
Sales Returns and Allowances	3,000
Purchases	170,000
Purchases Returns and Allowances	3,450
Purchases Discount	2,400
Freight In	7,000
Wages Expense	27,000
Advertising Expense	3,900
Depreciation Expense, Store Equipment	—
Store Supplies Expense	—
Rent Expense	8,400
Insurance Expense	—

The data needed for adjustments on January 31 are as follows:

a–b. Merchandise inventory, January 31, $53,400
c. Store supplies inventory, January 31, $390
d. Insurance expired for the year, $615
e. Depreciation for the year, $6,395
f. Accrued wages on January 31, $1,270

Check Figure
Net loss, $130

Instructions

1. Prepare a work sheet for the fiscal year ended January 31.
2. Prepare an income statement.
3. Prepare a statement of owner's equity. No additional investments were made.
4. Prepare a balance sheet.
5. Journalize the adjusting entries.
6. Journalize the closing entries.
7. Journalize the reversing entry.

Instructions for General Ledger Software

1. Record the adjusting entries in the general journal and print a copy of the entries.
2. Post the general journal amounts to the general ledger.
3. Print an adjusted trial balance and the general ledger after adjustments.
4. Print the income statement, statement of owner's equity, and balance sheet.

5. Record the closing entries in the general journal and print a copy of the entries.
6. Post the general journal amounts to the general ledger.
7. Print a post-closing trial balance.
8. Record the reversing entry in the general journal at the beginning of the next month.

PROBLEM SET B

For additional help, see the demonstration problem at the beginning of each chapter in your Working Papers.

P.O. 1,4

Problem 14-1B A partial work sheet for The Fall Shop is presented here. The merchandise inventory at the beginning of the year was $53,200. C. A. Fall, the owner, withdrew $26,500 during the year.

The Fall Shop
Work Sheet
For Year Ended December 31, 20—

ACCOUNT NAME	INCOME STATEMENT	
	DEBIT	CREDIT
Sales		328,000.00
Sales Returns and Allowances	4,480.00	
Sales Discount	3,707.32	
Interest Income		1,840.00
Purchases	199,490.00	
Purchases Returns and Allowances		2,980.00
Freight In	12,750.00	
Wages Expense	43,200.00	
Rent Expense	9,600.00	
Commissions Expense	10,320.00	
Interest Expense	964.22	
Income Summary	53,200.00	44,360.00
Supplies Expense	832.46	
Insurance Expense	1,040.00	
Depreciation Expense, Building	4,800.00	
Depreciation Expense, Equipment	3,600.00	
	347,984.00	377,180.00
Net Income	29,196.00	
	377,180.00	377,180.00

Check Figure
Cost of Goods Sold, $218,100

Instructions

1. Prepare an income statement.
2. Journalize the closing entries.

P.O. 2,3

Problem 14-2B Here is the partial work sheet for Haven Stereo.

Haven Stereo
Work Sheet
For Year Ended December 31, 20—

	ACCOUNT NAME	BALANCE SHEET DEBIT	BALANCE SHEET CREDIT	
1	Cash	12,915.00		1
2	Notes Receivable	6,300.00		2
3	Accounts Receivable	33,270.00		3
4	Merchandise Inventory	55,344.00		4
5	Supplies	420.00		5
6	Prepaid Taxes	630.00		6
7	Prepaid Insurance	540.00		7
8	Land	7,800.00		8
9	Building	60,000.00		9
10	Accumulated Depreciation, Building		18,900.00	10
11	Store Equipment	4,392.00		11
12	Accumulated Depreciation, Store Equipment		1,674.00	12
13	Testing Equipment	7,230.00		13
14	Accumulated Depreciation, Testing Equipment		5,424.00	14
15	Delivery Equipment	5,400.00		15
16	Accumulated Depreciation, Delivery Equipment		4,470.00	16
17	Mortgage Payable (current portion)		1,800.00	17
18	Accounts Payable		28,140.00	18
19	Notes Payable		4,215.00	19
20	Mortgage Payable		55,200.00	20
21	C. R. Gonza, Capital		67,314.00	21
22	C. R. Gonza, Drawing	22,440.00		22
23	Wages Payable		984.00	23
24		216,681.00	188,121.00	24
25	Net Income		28,560.00	25
26		216,681.00	216,681.00	26
27				27
28				28
29				29
30				30

Check Figure
Working capital, $74,280

Instructions

1. Prepare a statement of owner's equity (no additional investment).
2. Prepare a balance sheet.
3. Determine the amount of the working capital.
4. Determine the current ratio (carry to one decimal place).

P.O. 4,5

Problem 14-3B The following partial work sheet covers the affairs of Bessel and Company for the year ended June 30:

Bessel and Company
Work Sheet
For Year Ended June 30, 20—

ACCOUNT NAME	INCOME STATEMENT		BALANCE SHEET	
	DEBIT	CREDIT	DEBIT	CREDIT
Cash			28,196.61	
Accounts Receivable			92,006.00	
Merchandise Inventory			112,400.00	
Supplies			837.39	
Prepaid Insurance			1,220.00	
Delivery Equipment			12,400.00	
Accumulated Depreciation, Delivery Equipment				5,800.00
Store Equipment			33,400.00	
Accumulated Depreciation, Store Equipment				9,600.00
Accounts Payable				60,200.00
Salaries Payable				1,240.00
L. Bessel, Capital				167,820.00
L. Bessel, Drawing			28,000.00	
Income Summary	109,200.00	112,400.00		
Sales		520,000.00		
Purchases	380,000.00			
Purchases Returns and Allowances		7,600.00		
Purchases Discount		4,800.00		
Freight In	24,000.00			
Salary Expense	48,000.00			
Truck Expense	8,600.00			
Supplies Expense	2,200.48			
Insurance Expense	1,840.00			
Depreciation Expense, Delivery Equipment	2,400.00			
Depreciation Expense, Store Equipment	2,800.00			
Miscellaneous Expense	1,959.52			
	581,000.00	644,800.00	308,460.00	244,660.00
Net Income	63,800.00			63,800.00
	644,800.00	644,800.00	308,460.00	308,460.00

Check Figure

Reversing entry amount, $1,240

Instructions

1. Journalize the seven adjusting entries.
2. Journalize the closing entries.
3. Journalize the reversing entry.

P.O. 1,2,4,5

Problem 14-4B The following accounts appear in the ledger of Clos and Company as of June 30, the end of this fiscal year:

Cash	$ 4,349.76
Accounts Receivable	14,910.00
Merchandise Inventory	51,480.00
Store Supplies	735.52
Prepaid Insurance	975.00
Store Equipment	29,640.00
Accumulated Depreciation, Store Equipment	7,880.00
Accounts Payable	11,085.00
Wages Payable	—
D. E. Clos, Capital	102,195.00
D. E. Clos, Drawing	28,260.00
Income Summary	—
Sales	202,630.00
Sales Returns and Allowances	2,640.00
Purchases	137,050.00
Purchases Returns and Allowances	4,395.00
Purchases Discount	2,565.28
Freight In	9,260.00
Wages Expense	33,100.00
Advertising Expense	8,150.00
Depreciation Expense, Store Equipment	—
Store Supplies Expense	—
Rent Expense	10,200.00
Insurance Expense	—

The data needed for the adjustments on June 30 are as follows:

a–b. Merchandise inventory, June 30, $48,196
c. Store supplies inventory, June 30, $269.20
d. Insurance expired for the year, $640
e. Depreciation for the year, $6,290
f. Accrued wages on June 30, $472

Check Figure
Net loss, $1,962.04

Instructions

1. Prepare a work sheet for the fiscal year ended June 30.
2. Prepare an income statement.
3. Prepare a statement of owner's equity. No additional investments were made during the year.
4. Prepare a balance sheet.
5. Journalize the adjusting entries.
6. Journalize the closing entries.
7. Journalize the reversing entry.

Instructions for General Ledger Software

1. Record the adjusting entries in the general journal and print a copy of the entries.
2. Post the general journal amounts to the general ledger.
3. Print an adjusted trial balance and the general ledger after adjustments.

4. Print the income statement, statement of owner's equity, and balance sheet.
5. Record the closing entries in the general journal and print a copy of the entries.
6. Post the general journal amounts to the general ledger.
7. Print a post-closing trial balance.
8. Record the reversing entry in the general journal at the beginning of the next month.

Cumulative Self-Check: Chapters 13–14

PART I: COMPLETION

Complete each of the following statements by writing the appropriate word(s) in the spaces provided.

1. An actual count of a stock of goods is called a(n) ______.
2. Under the ______ system, entries to record the purchase of merchandise are recorded in the Merchandise Inventory account.
3. Unearned revenue is classified as a(n) ______.
4. Under the periodic inventory system, the first adjustment is to debit ______ for the amount of the beginning inventory.
5. Under the perpetual inventory system, after recording the sale of the goods, the accountant debits the ______ account and credits ______.
6. An increase in Rent Expense results in a(n) ______ to net income.
7. Gross Profit is calculated by subtracting ______ from Net Sales.
8. Current Assets minus Current Liabilities equals ______.
9. Gross Profit minus Total Operating Expenses equals ______.
10. Net Purchases plus ______ equals Delivered Cost of Purchases.

PART II: TRUE/FALSE

T F 1. The second adjustment for Merchandise Inventory under the periodic inventory system is to debit Cost of Goods Sold and credit Merchandise Inventory.

T F 2. Unearned Rental Income is classified as a revenue.

T F 3. The perpetual inventory system requires that each sale of goods has two entries: one to reduce inventory and affix the cost of the goods sold and one to record the sale.

T F 4. The periodic inventory system requires two adjusting entries: one to remove the old inventory amount and one to enter the latest inventory amount.

T F 5. The adjustment to unearned revenue allows the correct amount of liability and revenue to be applied to each fiscal period involved.

T F 6. Freight In is classified in the Operating Expenses section of an income statement.

T F 7. Under the perpetual inventory system, the cost of goods sold is calculated by subtracting ending inventory from goods available for sale.

Note: Answers to Cumulative Self-Check begin on page A-1.

T F 8. Reversing entries are optional, and only some adjusting entries are reversed.

T F 9. Delivery Expense is added to net purchases to arrive at delivered cost of purchases.

T F 10. Purchases Returns and Allowances increases Income from Operations.

PART III: APPLICATION

1. Alphonse Company uses the periodic inventory system. Employees have just taken a physical count of its inventory. This ending inventory has been valued at $136,000. The company's accounting records show the Merchandise Inventory account with a debit balance of $132,000. Journalize the entries on December 31 to adjust the records for this situation.

2. Regletto Company uses the perpetual inventory system. Employees have just taken a physical count of its inventory. This ending inventory has been valued at $146,000. The company's accounting records show the Merchandise Inventory account with a debit balance of $148,000. Journalize the entry on December 31 to adjust the records for this situation.

3. On December 1, Wesley Company collected $20,000 for a remodeling job that will be completed on March 31 of the following year. Wesley Company's fiscal period ends December 31. Make the entries to record the collection of the cash and the year-end adjustment to reflect the amount of revenue earned in December.

4. Yorkland Company has total assets of $250,000, of which non-current assets amount to $140,000. The company also has total liabilities of $130,000, of which $80,000 are long-term liabilities. Calculate (a) working capital and (b) current ratio.

Comprehensive Review Problem

You are to record transactions completed by Fine Fabrics during the month of February of this year. This company is located in Dallas. To gain practice in completing the steps in the accounting cycle, assume that the fiscal period consists of one month.

CHART OF ACCOUNTS

Assets

111 Cash
112 Petty Cash Fund
113 Accounts Receivable
114 Merchandise Inventory
117 Supplies
118 Prepaid Insurance
122 Equipment
123 Accumulated Depreciation, Equipment

Liabilities

221 Accounts Payable
226 Employees' Income Tax Payable
227 FICA Tax Payable
228 State Unemployment Tax Payable
229 Federal Unemployment Tax Payable
230 Salaries Payable

Owner's Equity

311 J. L. Fisher, Capital
312 J. L. Fisher, Drawing
399 Income Summary

Revenue

411 Sales
412 Sales Returns and Allowances

Cost of Goods Sold

511 Purchases
512 Purchases Returns and Allowances
513 Purchases Discount
514 Freight In

Operating Expenses

611 Salary Expense
612 Payroll Tax Expense
613 Rent Expense
614 Utilities Expense
616 Supplies Expense
617 Insurance Expense
618 Depreciation Expense, Equipment
619 Miscellaneous Expense

JOURNALS

Sales Journal, page 56
Purchases Journal, page 62
Cash Receipts Journal, page 69
Cash Payments Journal, page 75
General Journal, pages 89–92

ACCOUNTS RECEIVABLE

Hotel Bentnor
Jerome and Woods
Wilkes Decorators

ACCOUNTS PAYABLE

Byran, Inc.
Keller Textiles
Meldon Fabrics
Taylor Manufacturing Company

TRANSACTIONS

The following transactions were completed during February of this year.

Feb. 1 Reversed the adjusting entry for accrued salaries, $710.

1 Sold merchandise on account to Hotel Bentnor, $13,052.97, invoice no. 5221.

2 Issued Ck. No. 7216, $17,271.62, to Keller Textiles, in payment of its invoice no. D1739 for $17,624.10 less 2 percent discount.

5 Bought merchandise on account from Meldon Fabrics, $4,551.90; invoice no. RE275, dated February 2; terms 1/10, n/30; FOB Orlando; freight prepaid and added to the invoice, $147 (total, $4,698.90).

5 Received an electric bill and paid Regional Power, Ck. No. 7217, $121.

6 Received check from Jerome and Woods for $11,619.50 in payment of account.

7 Issued Ck. No. 7218, $9,519.84, to Meldon Fabrics, in payment of its invoice no. RE64 for $9,616 less 1 percent discount.

9 Cash sales for February 1 through February 9, $7,951.60.

12 **Recorded the payroll in the payroll register** for regular semimonthly salaries for period ended February 12. Salaries: M. B. Corson, $2,730; K. L. Vickers, $2,240. Income tax withholdings are $382.20 for Corson and $313.60 for Vickers. Assume the following tax rates and taxable earnings limits (see payroll register for beginning cumulative earnings):

- Social Security taxable earnings, $68,400, with a rate of 6.2 percent.
- Medicare taxable earnings, all earnings, with a rate of 1.45 percent.

12 Recorded the payroll entry in the general journal, crediting Salaries Payable.

12 Issued Ck. No. 7219, $2,138.95, to M. B. Corson. Issued Ck. No. 7220, $1,755.04, to K. L. Vickers. Use two lines and debit Salaries Payable. (Verify these amounts.)

12 Recorded payroll taxes. Assume the following tax rates and taxable earnings:

- Federal unemployment taxable earnings, $7,000, with a rate of .8 percent.
- State unemployment taxable earnings, $7,000, with a rate of 5.4 percent. *Note:* Corson's taxable earnings for unemployment amount to $1,540 and Vickers's amount to $2,240.

12 Received a credit memo from Meldon Fabrics for defective merchandise, $542, credit memo no. 916.

Feb. 14 Issued Ck. No. 7221, $2,912.44, to State Bank for monthly deposit of January employees' federal income tax withheld, $1,391.60, and FICA taxes, $1,520.84.

14 Sold merchandise on account to Jerome and Woods, $15,692.50, invoice no. 5222.

14 Issued Ck. No. 7222, $4,116.80, to Meldon Fabrics in payment of its invoice no. RE275 less the credit memo for defective merchandise and less the discount ($40.10). *Note:* Debit Accounts Payable, $4,156.90, and credit Purchases Discount, $40.10. Verify these amounts: $4,698.90, less $147 freight, less $542 return, less 1 percent cash discount (cash discounts can't be taken on freight).

18 Bought merchandise on account from Byran, Inc., $20,488.20; invoice no. 164M, dated February 14; terms 2/10, n/30; FOB Miami; freight prepaid and added to the invoice, $1,152 (total, $21,640.20).

18 Cash sales for February 10 through February 18, $7,994.14.

19 Issued Ck. No. 7223 payable to Faster Printing for invoice forms, $327 (not previously recorded). (Debit Supplies.)

19 Received check from Wilkes Decorators for $4,920.14 in payment of account.

22 Issued Ck. No. 7224, $12,710, to Taylor Manufacturing Company, in payment of its invoice no. 9264D.

22 Sold merchandise on account to Wilkes Decorators, $16,721.42, invoice no. 5223.

24 Issued credit memo no. 214 to Wilkes Decorators, $156, for merchandise returned.

24 Bought merchandise on account from Keller Textiles, $16,448.01; invoice no. D1797, dated February 22; terms 2/10, n/30; FOB Memphis.

26 **Recorded the payroll in the payroll register** for regular semimonthly salaries for period ended February 26. Salaries: M. B. Corson, $2,730; K. L. Vickers, $2,240. Income tax withholdings are $382.20 for Corson and $313.60 for Vickers. *Note:* See the entry of February 12 for taxable earnings limits and tax rates. See payroll register for beginning cumulative earnings.

26 Recorded the payroll entry in the general journal, crediting Salaries Payable.

26 Issued Ck. No. 7225, $2,138.95, to M. B. Corson. Issued Ck. No. 7226, $1,755.04, to K. L. Vickers. Use two lines and debit Salaries Payable.

26 Ck. No. 7227 voided.

26 Recorded payroll taxes. *Note:* Vickers's taxable earnings for unemployment amount to $280.

27 Issued Ck. No. 7228, $994, to Greater Freight Line for transportation charge on merchandise purchased from Keller Textiles.

28 Issued Ck. No. 7229, $48.63, payable to Cash to reimburse the petty cash fund. Petty cash payments consist of Supplies, $27.16, and Miscellaneous Expense, $21.47.

28 Cash sales for February 19 through February 28, $7,685.20.

28 Issued Ck. No. 7230, $650, to Grandy Realty for monthly rent.

28 J. L. Fisher (owner) withdrew $3,000 for personal use, Ck. No. 7231.

INSTRUCTIONS

1. Journalize and post the transactions completed during February.
   a. Post the amounts in the Other Accounts columns of the special journals daily.
   b. Post the general journal daily.
   c. Post the totals of the special columns of the special journals at the end of the month.
2. Prepare a schedule of accounts receivable and a schedule of accounts payable.
3. Complete the work sheet for February.
   Data for the month-end adjustments are as follows:
   a–b. Merchandise inventory at February 28, $44,262
   c. Salaries accrued at February 28, $710
   d. Supplies inventory at February 28, $472
   e. Insurance expired during February, $40
   f. Depreciation of equipment during February, $105
4. Journalize and post the adjusting entries.
5. Prepare an income statement.
6. Prepare a statement of owner's equity. (No additional investment was made during the month.)
7. Prepare a balance sheet.
8. Journalize and post the closing entries.
9. Prepare a post-closing trial balance.

INSTRUCTIONS FOR GENERAL LEDGER SOFTWARE

1. Journalize and post the transactions completed during February.
2. Print the journals and the general ledger.
3. Print a trial balance.
4. Print a schedule of accounts receivable and a schedule of accounts payable.
5. Journalize and post the month-end adjustments:
   a–b. Merchandise inventory at February 28, $44,262
   c. Salaries accrued at February 28, $710
   d. Supplies inventory at February 28, $472
   e. Insurance expired during February, $40
   f. Depreciation of equipment during February, $105
6. Print the adjusting entries, an adjusted trial balance, and the general ledger after adjustments.
7. Print the income statement, the statement of owner's equity, and the balance sheet.
8. Journalize and post the closing entries.
9. Print the closing entries.
10. Print a post-closing trial balance.

APPENDIX

C Inventory Methods

Performance Objectives

After you have completed this appendix, you will be able to do the following:

1. Determine the amount of the ending merchandise inventory by the weighted-average-cost method.
2. Determine the amount of the ending merchandise inventory by the first-in, first-out method.
3. Determine the amount of the ending merchandise inventory by the last-in, first-out method.

To determine the dollar amount of the ending merchandise inventory, it is necessary to take a physical count of the various items in stock and match them up with their costs. In other words, the ending inventory consists of the number of units of each type of item on hand multiplied by the cost of each unit.

If each unit were purchased at exactly the same price, the job of determining the total cost of the inventory would be simple. For example, if there are 100 units of Product A on hand, and all 100 units were bought at $15, the total cost of the ending inventory is $1,500 (100 × $15). However, over a period of time, costs of individual purchases of units may differ. Changes in costs of individual units make the different methods of inventory valuation necessary.

We will use Casey Electronics, a distributor of compact disc (CD) players, to illustrate the three methods of inventory valuation. Casey's ending inventory consists of 182 Model M43 CD players acquired through various purchases, as follows:

Specific Purchase	Number of Units	Cost per Unit	Total Cost
Beginning inventory	34	$270	$ 9,180
First purchase	60	282	16,920
Second purchase	256	298	76,288
Third purchase	164	312	51,168
Total units available	514		$153,556

Of the 514 units available for sale, 182 units are still on hand and 332 have been sold (514 − 182).

Casey Electronics may choose any one of the three following methods of recording the total cost of the 182 units in the ending inventory of CD players.

WEIGHTED-AVERAGE-COST METHOD

Objective 1

Determine the amount of the ending merchandise inventory by the weighted-average-cost in Ending Inventory method.

$$\text{Average Cost per Unit} = \frac{\text{Total Cost}}{\text{Total Units Available}} = \frac{\$153{,}556}{514} = \$298.75 \text{ (rounded)}$$

$$\text{Cost of 182 units} = \$298.75 \times 182 \text{ units} = \$54{,}373 \text{ (rounded)}$$

$$\text{Cost of 541 units sold} = 298.75 \times 332 \text{ units} = 99.183 \text{ (rounded)}$$

FIRST-IN, FIRST-OUT METHOD

Objective 2

Determine the amount of the ending merchandise inventory by the first-in, first-out method.

This method is based on the **assumption** that the first units of CD players purchased will be sold first. The costs of the units left will be those of the most recently purchased units. You may think of this as the way a grocery store sells milk. Because milk will sour, the oldest milk is moved to the front of the display shelf and is sold first. Consequently, the cartons of milk remaining on the shelf are the freshest milk.

Relating to our illustration of CD players,

Specific Purchase	Number of Units	Cost per Unit	Total Cost
Beginning inventory	34	$270	$ 9,180
First purchase	60	282	16,920
Second purchase	256	298	76,288
Third purchase	164	312	51,168
Total units available	514		$153,556

The cost of the 182 CD players on hand (most recently purchased) is as follows:

164 units (third purchase)	@ $312 each =	$51,168
18 units (second purchase)	@ $298 each =	5,364
182 units		$56,532

LAST-IN, FIRST-OUT METHOD

Objective 3

Determine the amount of the ending merchandise inventory by the last-in, first-out method.

This method is based on the **assumption** that the last units of CD players purchased will be sold first. The costs of the units left over will be those of the earliest purchased units. You may think of this as the way a coal yard sells coal. When the coal yard sells coal to its customers, it takes coal off the top of the pile. Consequently, the tons of coal in the ending inventory consist of those first few tons at the bottom of the pile.

Relating to our illustration of CD players shown above, the cost of the 182 CD players on hand (earliest purchased) is as follows:

34 units (beginning inventory)	@ $270 each =	$ 9,180
60 units (first purchase)	@ $282 each =	16,920
88 units (second purchase)	@ $298 each =	26,224
182 units		$52,324

Comparison of Three Methods

Method	Ending Inventory (182 units)	Cost of Goods Sold (Goods Available for Sale − Ending Inventory) (332 units = 514 − 182)
Weighted-average-cost	$54,373	$ 99,183 ($153,556 − $54,373)
First-in, first-out	56,532	97,024 ($153,556 − $56,532)
Last-in, first-out	52,324	101,232 ($153,556 − $52,324)

Assume that the CD players were sold for $380 each.

	Weighted-Average-Cost	First-in, First-out	Last-in, First-out
Sales (332 units × $380 each)	$126,160	$126,160	$126,160
Cost of Goods Sold	99,183	97,024	101,232
Gross Profit	$ 26,977	$ 29,136	$ 24,928

PROBLEMS

P.O. 1

Check Figure

Cost of ending inventory, $279.24

Problem C-1 Bermingham Nursery sells bark to its customers at retail. Bermingham buys bark from a plywood mill in bulk and transports the bark in its own trucks. Information relating to the beginning inventory and purchases of bark is as follows:

Beginning inventory	1,500 cubic yards @ $.20 per cubic yard
First purchase	2,100 cubic yards @ $.22 per cubic yard
Second purchase	1,400 cubic yards @ $.26 per cubic yard
Third purchase	1,000 cubic yards @ $.27 per cubic yard

Find the cost of 1,200 cubic yards in the ending inventory by the weighted-average-cost method. Carry average cost per cubic yard to four decimals.

P.O. 2

Check Figure

Cost of ending inventory, $322

Problem C-2 Using the information presented in Problem C-1, find the cost of the ending inventory by the first-in, first-out method.

P.O. 3

Check Figure

Cost of ending inventory, $240

Problem C-3 Using the information presented in Problem C-1, find the cost of the ending inventory by the last-in, first-out method.

APPENDIX

D The Statement of Cash Flows

Performance Objectives

After you have completed this appendix, you will be able to do the following:

1. Classify cash flows as Operating Activities, Investing Activities, and Financing Activities.
2. Prepare a statement of cash flows.

The fourth major financial statement is the statement of cash flows. This statement explains in detail how the balance of Cash has changed between the beginning and the end of the fiscal period. Some accountants refer to the statement as the "where got, where gone" statement of cash.

SECTIONS OF THE STATEMENT OF CASH FLOWS

Objective 1

Classify cash flows as Operating Activities, Investing Activities, and Financing Activities.

The statement has three main sections: Operating Activities, Investing Activities, and Financing Activities. Cash flows are subdivided as cash inflows and cash outflows.

Operating Activities

This section covers cash received and used in carrying out the company's operations.

Cash Inflows

- Cash from selling of services or merchandise
- Miscellaneous income

Cash Outflows

- Payments for purchases of merchandise and supplies from suppliers
- Payments of salaries or wages
- Payments of rent, utilities, insurance
- Payment of interest to creditors

Investing Activities

This section covers cash used in or received from buying or selling of plant and equipment assets and all other noncurrent assets, such as long-term investments.

Cash Inflows

- Cash received from the sale of noncurrent assets

Cash Outflows

- Cash payments to buy noncurrent assets

Financing Activities

This section covers cash related to changes in the owner's equity accounts and long-term liabilities accounts.

Cash Inflows

- Investment of cash by the owner
- Borrowing from creditors

Cash Outflows

- Withdrawals of cash by the owner
- Repayment of loans to creditors

FINANCIAL STATEMENTS NEEDED FOR PREPARING THE STATEMENT OF CASH FLOWS

The financial statements required for preparing the statement of cash flows consist of the income statement and statement of owner's equity for the fiscal period, the balance sheet at the end of the fiscal period, and the balance sheet at the end of the previous fiscal period. Using the two balance sheets, we can prepare a comparative balance sheet for the two fiscal periods, showing the increases and decreases in the various accounts.

ILLUSTRATION OF THE STATEMENT OF CASH FLOWS

Objective 2

Prepare a statement of cash flows.

The financial statements for Morrow Company are shown here. To save space, we present the comparative balance sheet. Based on the comparative balance sheet, the first step is to record the increases and decreases in the accounts.

Morrow Company
Income Statement
For Year Ended December 31, 2001

Revenue from Sales:		
Net Sales	$ 647,000.00	
Less Cost of Goods Sold	500,000.00	
Gross Profit		$ 147,000.00
Operating Expenses:		
Salary Expense	$ 70,000.00	
Rent Expense	10,000.00	
Depreciation Expense, Equipment	6,000.00	
Supplies Expense	1,000.00	
Total Operating Expenses		87,000.00
Net Income		$ 60,000.00

Morrow Company
Statement of Owner's Equity
For Year Ended December 31, 2001

B. Morrow, Capital, January 1, 2001		$ 120 000 00
Additional Investment, March 2, 2001		10 000 00
Total Investment		$ 130 000 00
Net Income for the Year	$60 000 00	
Less Withdrawals	50 000 00	
Increase in Capital		10 000 00
B. Morrow, Capital, Dec. 31, 2001		$ 140 000 00

Morrow Company
Comparative Balance Sheet
December 31, 2001, and December 31, 2000

	2001		2000		Increase or Decrease
Assets					
Cash		$ 12 000 00		$ 7 000 00	$ 5 000 00
Accounts Receivable		70 000 00		66 000 00	4 000 00
Merchandise Inventory		120 000 00		113 000 00	7 000 00
Supplies		3 000 00		4 000 00	(1 000 00)
Equipment	$72 000 00		$60 000 00		12 000 00
Less Accumulated Deprec.	(62 000 00)	10 000 00	(56 000 00)	4 000 00	(6 000 00)
Total Assets		$ 215 000 00		$ 194 000 00	$21 000 00
Liabilities					
Accounts Payable	$71 000 00		$69 000 00		$ 2 000 00
Salaries Payable	4 000 00		5 000 00		(1 000 00)
Total Liabilities		$ 75 000 00		$ 74 000 00	$ 1 000 00
Owner's Equity					
B. Morrow, Capital		140 000 00		120 000 00	20 000 00
Total Liabilities and Owner's Equity		$ 215 000 00		$ 194 000 00	$21 000 00

Note the $5,000 increase in Cash. First let's see how this increase comes about.

- Cash flows related to operating activities involve changes in current asset and current liability accounts.
- Cash flows related to investing activities involve changes in plant and equipment (long-term assets) accounts (with the exception of Accumulated Depreciation).
- Cash flows related to financing activities involve changes in owner's equity accounts and long-term liabilities accounts.

Now let's present the statement of cash flows.

Morrow Company
Statement of Cash Flows
For Year Ended December 31, 2001

Cash Flows from (Used by) Operating Activities		
Net Income	$ 60,000.00	
Add (Deduct) Items to Convert Net Income from Accrual Basis to Cash Basis		
Depreciation Expense	6,000.00	
Increase in Accounts Receivable	(4,000.00)	
Increase in Merchandise Inventory	(7,000.00)	
Decrease in Supplies	1,000.00	
Increase in Accounts Payable	2,000.00	
Decrease in Salaries Payable	(1,000.00)	
Net Cash Flows from Operating Activities		$ 57,000.00
Cash Flows from (Used by) Investing Activities		
Purchase of Equipment	$ (12,000.00)	
Net Cash Flows Used by Investing Activities		(12,000.00)
Cash Flows from (Used by) Financing Activities		
Cash Investment by Owner	$ 10,000.00	
Cash Withdrawals by Owner	(50,000.00)	
Net Cash Flows Used by Financing Activities		(40,000.00)
Net Increase (Decrease) in Cash		$ 5,000.00

EXPLANATION OF ITEMS IN THE STATEMENT OF CASH FLOWS

Cash Flows from Operating Activities

- Net income of $60,000, from the income statement, included such items as sale of services or merchandise, miscellaneous income, and payment of expenses such as salaries or wages, utilities, and interest.
- Depreciation of $6,000 was included as an expense on the income statement, but it did not result in the payment of cash to anyone. Since depreciation expense was deducted on the income statement, we now add $6,000 back in. Depreciation expense is always an addition under Cash Flows from Operating Activities.
- Accounts Receivable increased by $4,000. Of the amount shown as Sales on the income statement, $4,000 was in the form of additional charge account balances and therefore were not cash inflows. So we deduct $4,000 from Cash Flows from Operating Activities.
- Merchandise Inventory increased by $7,000. Because the inventory increased by $7,000 during the year (more merchandise was bought than was sold), we can assume that the change resulted in a $7,000 decrease in Cash Flows from Operating Activities.
- Decrease in Supplies of $1,000 means that the company used up supplies bought in a previous fiscal period and included the entire amount of supplies used as Supplies Expense on the income statement. In other words, the $1,000 of Supplies Expense shown on the income statement did not result in a payment of cash in the current period.
- Increase in Accounts Payable of $2,000 in this case means that $2,000 of the amount listed as Purchases on the income statement (not shown because

we included Purchases in Cost of Goods Sold) did not result in the payment of cash. So we add $2,000 to Cash Flows from Operating Activities.

- Decrease in Salaries Payable of $1,000 means that the amount listed as Salary Expense on the income statement is $1,000 less than the amount of cash spent by the company. So we deduct $1,000 from Cash Flows from Operating Activities.

Cash Flows from Investing Activities

Equipment increased by $12,000. We would have to look at the journal entry to determine how much cash was involved. In this case, we assume that the purchase of equipment resulted in a payment of $12,000 cash. So we deduct $12,000 from Cash Flows from Investing Activities.

Cash Flows from Financing Activities

- The owner's Capital account increased by $10,000 as a result of an additional investment. We would have to look at the journal entry to determine how much cash was involved. In this case, we assume that the investment was in the form of cash. So we add $10,000 to Cash Flows from Financing Activities.
- The owner's Drawing account increased by $50,000. We would have to look at the journal entries to determine how much cash was involved. In this case, we assume that the withdrawals were in the form of cash. So we deduct $50,000 from Cash Flows from Financing Activities.

Here are some handy guidelines for preparing a statement of cash flows.

Add to Net Income	
If Current Assets decrease	Why? If an account like Accounts Receivable decreases, this means that we received more cash than the amount listed as Net Sales.
If Current Liabilities increase	Why? If an account like Accounts Payable increases, this means that we bought more merchandise or supplies than we paid for in cash.
Deduct from Net Income	
If Current Assets increase	Why? If an account like Prepaid Insurance increases, this means that we paid more cash for insurance than the amount listed as Insurance Expense on the income statement.
If Current Liabilities decrease	Why? If an account like Notes Payable decreases, this means that we paid out cash to pay off the note.

PROBLEMS

P.O. 1,2

Problem D-1 Metter Company has the following financial statements for 2000 and 2001. Assume that the withdrawals were in the form of cash.

Check Figure

Net cash flows from operating activities, $44,500

Instructions

Prepare a statement of cash flows for the year ended December 31, 2001.

Metter Company
Income Statement
For Year Ended December 31, 2001

Revenue:		
Income from Services		$ 134,000.00
Expenses:		
Wages Expense	$77,000.00	
Rent Expense	8,000.00	
Depreciation Expense, Equipment	5,000.00	
Supplies Expense	2,000.00	
Total Expenses		92,000.00
Net Income		$ 42,000.00

Metter Company
Statement of Owner's Equity
For Year Ended December 31, 2001

B. N. Metter, Capital, January 1, 2001		$94,000.00
Net Income for the Year	$42,000.00	
Less Withdrawals for the Year	40,000.00	
Increase in Capital		2,000.00
B. N. Metter, Capital, December 31, 2001		$96,000.00

Metter Company
Comparative Balance Sheet
December 31, 2001, and December 31, 2000

	2001		2000		INCREASE (DECREASE)
Assets					
Cash		$ 9,000.00		$ 6,500.00	$2,500.00
Supplies		5,000.00		2,500.00	2,500.00
Equipment	$100,000.00		$98,000.00		2,000.00
Less Accumulated Depreciation	(18,000.00)	82,000.00	(13,000.00)	85,000.00	(5,000.00)
Total Assets		$96,000.00		$94,000.00	$2,000.00
Owner's Equity					
B. N. Metter, Capital		$96,000.00		$94,000.00	$2,000.00
Total Liabilities and					
Owner's Equity		$96,000.00		$94,000.00	$2,000.00

P.O. 1,2

Problem D-2 The financial statements for Arms and Company are presented below. Assume that the additional investment and the withdrawals were both in the form of cash.

Check Figure

Net cash flows from operating activities, $77,000

Instructions

Prepare a statement of cash flows for the year ended December 31, 2001.

Arms and Company
Income Statement
For Year Ended December 31, 2001

Revenue:		
Income from Services		$ 270,000.00
Expenses:		
Wages Expense	$ 161,000.00	
Rent Expense	18,000.00	
Depreciation Expense, Equipment	12,000.00	
Supplies Expense	4,000.00	
Insurance Expense	1,000.00	
Total Expenses		196,000.00
Net Income		$ 74,000.00

Arms and Company
Statement of Owner's Equity
For Year Ended December 31, 2001

S. T. Arms, Capital, January 1, 2001		$ 150,000.00
Additional Investment		2,000.00
Total Investment		$ 152,000.00
Net Income for the Year	$74,000.00	
Less Withdrawals for the Year	70,000.00	
Increase in Capital		4,000.00
S. T. Arms, Capital, December 31, 2001		$ 156,000.00

Arms and Company
Comparative Balance Sheet
December 31, 2001 and December 31, 2000

	2001		2000		INCREASE (DECREASE)
Assets					
Cash		$ 11,800.00		$ 2,800.00	$ 9,000.00
Accounts Receivable		32,000.00		26,000.00	6,000.00
Supplies		10,000.00		9,400.00	600.00
Prepaid Insurance		3,200.00		600.00	2,600.00
Equipment	$145,400.00		$145,400.00		—
Less Accumulated Depreciation	(36,000.00)	109,400.00	(24,000.00)	121,400.00	(12,000.00)
Total Assets		$166,400.00		$160,200.00	$ 6,200.00
Liabilities					
Accounts Payable		$ 10,400.00		$ 10,200.00	$ 200.00
Owner's Equity					
S. T. Arms, Capital		156,000.00		150,000.00	6,000.00
Total Liabilities and Owner's Equity		$166,400.00		$160,200.00	$ 6,200.00

P.O. 1,2

Check Figure

Net cash flows used by financing activities, (70,000)

Problem D-3 The financial statements for Torres Company are presented below. Assume that the withdrawals were in the form of cash.

Instructions

Prepare a statement of cash flows for the year ended December 31, 2001.

Torres Company
Income Statement
For Year Ended December 31, 2001

Revenue from Sales:		
Net Sales	$ 942,000.00	
Less Cost of Goods Sold	753,600.00	
Gross Profit		$ 188,400.00
Operating Expenses:		
Salary Expense	$ 86,900.00	
Rent Expense	18,000.00	
Depreciation Expense, Equipment	10,000.00	
Supplies Expense	4,700.00	
Insurance Expense	2,800.00	
Total Operating Expenses		122,400.00
Net Income		$ 66,000.00

Torres Company
Statement of Owner's Equity
For Year Ended December 31, 2001

C. L. Torres, Capital, January 1, 2001		$ 196 0 0 0 00
Net Income for the Year	$ 66 0 0 0 00	
Less Withdrawals for the Year	70 0 0 0 00	
Decrease in Capital		4 0 0 0 00
C. L. Torres, Capital, December 31, 2001		$ 192 0 0 0 00

Torres Company
Comparative Balance Sheet
December 31, 2001 and December 31, 2000

	2001		2000		INCREASE (DECREASE)
Assets					
Cash		$ 9 4 0 0 00		$ 10 9 0 0 00	$ (1 5 0 0 00)
Accounts Receivable		56 0 0 0 00		48 6 0 0 00	7 4 0 0 00
Merchandise Inventory		104 6 0 0 00		104 4 0 0 00	2 0 0 00
Supplies		8 2 0 0 00		6 0 0 0 00	2 2 0 0 00
Prepaid Insurance		1 6 0 0 00		1 8 0 0 00	(2 0 0 00)
Equipment	$156 0 0 0 00		$156 0 0 0 00		————
Less Accumulated Depreciation	(76 4 0 0 00)	79 6 0 0 00	(66 4 0 0 00)	89 6 0 0 00	(10 0 0 0 00)
Total Assets		$259 4 0 0 00		$261 3 0 0 00	$ (1 9 0 0 00)
Liabilities					
Accounts Payable	$ 62 7 0 0 00		$ 60 4 0 0 00		$ 2 3 0 0 00
Salaries Payable	4 7 0 0 00		4 9 0 0 00		(2 0 0 00)
Total Liabilities		$ 67 4 0 0 00		$ 65 3 0 0 00	$ 2 1 0 0 00
Owner's Equity					
C. L. Torres, Capital		192 0 0 0 00		196 0 0 0 00	(4 0 0 0 00)
Total Liabilities and Owner's Equity		$259 4 0 0 00		$261 3 0 0 00	$ (1 9 0 0 00)

APPENDIX

E Financial Statement Analysis

Performance Objectives

After you have completed this appendix, you will be able to do the following:

1. Determine gross profit percentage.
2. Determine merchandise inventory turnover.
3. Determine accounts receivable turnover.
4. Determine return on investment.

An important function of accounting is to provide tools for interpreting the financial statements or the results of operations. This appendix presents a number of percentages and ratios that are frequently used to analyze financial statements.

GROSS PROFIT PERCENTAGE

Objective 1
Determine gross profit percentage.

DeClerk Card Shop will serve as our example (see the comparative income statement on the next page).

For each year, net sales is the base (100 percent). All other items on the income statement can be expressed as a percentage of net sales for the particular year involved. For example, let's look at the following percentages:

$$\text{Gross Profit \% (2001)} = \frac{\text{Gross Profit for 2001}}{\text{Net Sales for 2001}} = \frac{\$150{,}000}{\$428{,}000} = .35 = 35\%$$

$$\text{Gross Profit \% (2000)} = \frac{\text{Gross Profit for 2000}}{\text{Net Sales for 2000}} = \frac{\$152{,}000}{\$400{,}000} = .38 = 38\%$$

$$\text{Sales Salary Expense \% (2001)} = \frac{\text{Sales Salary Expense for 2001}}{\text{Net Sales for 2001}}$$

$$= \frac{\$\ 63{,}600}{\$428{,}000} = .1486 = 15\%$$

$$\text{Sales Salary Expense \% (2000)} = \frac{\text{Sales Salary Expense for 2000}}{\text{Net Sales for 2000}}$$

$$= \frac{\$\ 58{,}000}{\$400{,}000} = .145 = 15\%$$

DeClerk Card Shop
Comparative Income Statement
For Years Ended January 31, 2001, and January 31, 2000

	2001		2000	
	AMOUNT	PERCENT	AMOUNT	PERCENT
Revenue from Sales:				
Sales	$ 453 6 0 0 00	106	$ 420 0 0 0 00	105
Less Sales Returns and Allowances	25 6 0 0 00	6	20 0 0 0 00	5
Net Sales	$ 428 0 0 0 00	100	$ 400 0 0 0 00	100
Cost of Goods Sold:				
Merchandise Inventory, February 1	$ 116 0 0 0 00	27	$ 64 0 0 0 00	16
Delivered Cost of Purchases	320 0 0 0 00	75	300 0 0 0 00	75
Goods Available for Sale	$ 436 0 0 0 00	102	$ 364 0 0 0 00	91
Less Merchandise Inventory, January 31	158 0 0 0 00	37	116 0 0 0 00	29
Cost of Goods Sold	$ 278 0 0 0 00	65	$ 248 0 0 0 00	62
Gross Profit	$ 150 0 0 0 00	35	$ 152 0 0 0 00	38
Operating Expenses:				
Sales Salary Expense	$ 63 6 0 0 00	15	$ 58 0 0 0 00	15
Rent Expense	24 0 0 0 00	6	24 0 0 0 00	6
Advertising Expense	21 4 0 0 00	5	16 0 0 0 00	4
Depreciation Expense, Equipment	20 0 0 0 00	5	18 0 0 0 00	4.5
Insurance Expense	2 0 0 0 00	—	2 0 0 0 00	.5
Store Supplies Expense	1 0 0 0 00	—	1 0 0 0 00	—
Miscellaneous Expense	1 0 0 0 00	—	1 0 0 0 00	—
Total Operating Expenses	$ 133 0 0 0 00	31	$ 120 0 0 0 00	30
Net Income	$ 17 0 0 0 00	4	$ 32 0 0 0 00	8

Here's how you might interpret a few of the percentages:

2001

- For every $100 in net sales, gross profit amounted to $35.
- For every $100 in net sales, sales salary expense amounted to $15.
- For every $100 in net sales, net income amounted to $4.

2000

- For every $100 in net sales, gross profit amounted to $38.
- For every $100 in net sales, sales salary expense amounted to $15.
- For every $100 in net sales, net income amounted to $8.

The gross profit percentage declined from 38% in 2000 to 35% in 2001 because the Cost of Goods Sold percentage increased from 62% in 2000 to 65% in 2001.

MERCHANDISE INVENTORY TURNOVER

Objective 2

Determine merchandise inventory turnover.

Merchandise inventory turnover is the number of times a firm's average inventory is sold during a given year.

$$\text{Merchandise Inventory Turnover} = \frac{\text{Cost of Goods Sold}}{\text{Average Merchandise Inventory}}$$

$$\text{Average Merchandise Inventory} = \frac{\text{Beginning Merchandise Inventory} + \text{Ending Merchandise Inventory}}{2}$$

	2001	2000
Beginning Merchandise Inventory (from the Cost of Goods Sold section of the income statement)	$116,000	$ 64,000
Ending Merchandise Inventory (from the Cost of Goods Sold section of the income statement or the balance sheet)	$158,000	$116,000

2001

$$\text{Average Merchandise Inventory} = \frac{\$116{,}000 + \$158{,}000}{2} = \frac{\$274{,}000}{2} = \underline{\underline{\$137{,}000}}$$

$$\text{Merchandise Inventory Turnover} = \frac{\$278{,}000}{\$137{,}000} = \underline{\underline{2.03}} \text{ times per year}$$

2000

$$\text{Average Merchandise Inventory} = \frac{\$64{,}000 + \$116{,}000}{2} = \frac{\$180{,}000}{2} = \underline{\underline{\$90{,}000}}$$

$$\text{Merchandise Inventory Turnover} = \frac{\$248{,}000}{\$90{,}000} = \underline{\underline{2.76}} \text{ times per year}$$

With each turnover of merchandise, the company makes a gross profit, so the higher the turnover, the better.

The inventory turnover deteriorated from 2.76 in 2000 to 2.03 in 2001 because the beginning inventory in 2000 of $64,000 nearly doubled to $116,000 at the end of 2000 and increased to $158,000 at the end of 2001. Over the same period net sales increased only 7% from $400,000 in 2000 to $428,000 in 2001.

ACCOUNTS RECEIVABLE TURNOVER

Objective 3

Determine accounts receivable turnover.

Accounts receivable turnover is the number of times charge accounts are turned over (paid off) during a given year. A turnover implies a sale on account followed by the cash collection of the amount owed to us.

$$\text{Accounts Receivable Turnover} = \frac{\text{Net Sales on Account}}{\text{Average Accounts Receivable}}$$

$$\text{Average Accounts Receivable} = \frac{\text{Beginning Accounts Receivable} + \text{Ending Accounts Receivable}}{2}$$

Going back to DeClerk Card Shop, let's assume the following information for 2001 and 2000.

	2001	2000
Net sales on account (from the sales journal)	\$330,000	\$302,000
Beginning accounts receivable (from Accounts Receivable account)	39,680	37,500
Ending accounts receivable (from Accounts Receivable account)	45,840	39,680

2001

$$\text{Average Accounts Receivable} = \frac{\$39{,}680 + \$45{,}840}{2} = \frac{\$85{,}520}{2} = \underline{\underline{\$42{,}760}}$$

$$\text{Accounts Receivable Turnover} = \frac{\$330{,}000}{\$42{,}760} = \underline{\underline{7.72}} \text{ times per year}$$

2000

$$\text{Average Accounts Receivable} = \frac{\$37{,}500 + \$39{,}680}{2} = \frac{\$77{,}180}{2} = \underline{\underline{\$38{,}590}}$$

$$\text{Accounts Receivable Turnover} = \frac{\$302{,}000}{\$38{,}590} = \underline{\underline{7.83}} \text{ times per year}$$

A lower turnover rate indicates that a firm is experiencing greater difficulty in collecting charge accounts. In addition, more investment capital is tied up in accounts receivable.

The receivable turnover deteriorated slightly from 7.83 to 7.72 in 2000, possibly because the seller granted easier credit terms or the buyers incurred cash flow problems because of a declining economy. From the end of 2000 to the end of 2001, the receivables balance increased 16% from \$39,680 to \$45,840. However, over the same period net sales increased only 7%. This provides further evidence of the company's deteriorating financial condition.

RETURN ON INVESTMENT (YIELD)

Objective 4

Determine return on investment.

Return on investment represents the earning power of the owner's investment in the business.

$$\text{Return on Investment} = \frac{\text{Net Income for the Year}}{\text{Average Capital}}$$

$$\text{Average Capital} = \frac{\text{Beginning Capital} + \text{Ending Capital}}{2}$$

Getting back to DeClerk Card Shop, let's assume the following information for 2001 and 2000:

	2001	2000
Beginning balance of owner's Capital account	\$176,920	\$181,440
Ending balance of owner's Capital account	184,780	176,920

2001

$$\text{Average Capital} = \frac{\$176{,}920 + \$184{,}780}{2} = \frac{\$361{,}700}{2} = \underline{\underline{\$180{,}850}}$$

$$\text{Return on Investment} = \frac{\$17{,}000}{\$180{,}850} = .094 = \underline{\underline{9.4\%}}$$

2000

$$\text{Average Capital} = \frac{\$181{,}440 + \$176{,}920}{2} = \frac{\$358{,}360}{2} = \underline{\underline{\$179{,}180}}$$

$$\text{Return on Investment} = \frac{\$32{,}000}{\$179{,}180} = .179 = \underline{\underline{17.9\%}}$$

As a result, we can state the following:

- In 2001, for an average investment of $100, the business earned $9.40.
- In 2000, for an average investment of $100, the business earned $17.90.

The return on investment deteriorated from 17.9% in 2000 to 9.4% in 2001 because net income declined 47% from $32,000 in 2000 to $17,000 in 2001.

PROBLEMS

P.O. 1

Problem E-1 Ross Company's abbreviated comparative income statement for years 2001 and 2000 is as follows:

Ross Company
Comparative Income Statement
For Years Ended December 31, 2001 and December 31, 2000

	2001	2000
Net Sales	$ 487,200.00	$ 462,000.00
Cost of Goods Sold	287,400.00	277,200.00
Gross Profit	$ 199,800.00	$ 184,800.00
Total Operating Expenses	152,240.00	146,160.00
Net Income	$ 47,560.00	$ 38,640.00

Check Figure

Net income % (2000), 8.4%

Instructions

1. For the years 2001 and 2000, determine gross profit as a percentage of net sales.
2. For the years 2001 and 2000, determine net income as a percentage of net sales.

P.O. 2

Problem E-2 Ross Company's merchandise inventory figures are:

	2001	2000
Beginning merchandise inventory (January 1)	$ 88,420	$106,110
Purchases	302,190	259,510
Ending merchandise inventory (December 31)	103,210	88,420

Check Figure

Cost of goods sold (2001), $287,400

Instructions

Determine the merchandise inventory turnover for the years 2001 and 2000.

P.O. 4

Problem E-3 A. L. Ross, Capital, account balances are as follows:

January 1, 2000	$375,670
January 1, 2001	$493,970
December 31, 2001	$526,820

Check Figure

Return on investment (2000), 8.9%

Instructions

Determine the return on investment for the years 2001 and 2000 if net income is $47,560 for 2001 and $38,640 for 2000.

Cumulative Self-Check Solutions

CHAPTERS 1–3

Part I: 1. d; 2. e; 3. d; 4. b; 5. e; 6. a

Part II: 1.

GENERAL JOURNAL — PAGE 31

DATE		DESCRIPTION	POST. REF.	DEBIT	CREDIT
20–					
Dec.	1	Cash	111	10,000.00	
		D. Stanfill, Capital	311		10,000.00
		Invested an additional amount, Deposit Slip No. 41372.			
	4	Rent Expense	513	900.00	
		Cash	111		900.00
		Ck. No. 2331.			
	11	Cash	111	1,860.00	
		Accounts Receivable	112		1,860.00
		Cash on account from customers, Cash Receipt Nos. 1430-1438.			
	19	Accounts Receivable	112	2,150.00	
		Service Income	411		2,150.00
		M. Linares, Sales Inv. No. 2591.			
	22	Utilities Expense	512	197.00	
		Cash	111		197.00
		Ck. No. 2332.			
	23	Supplies	113	248.00	
		Accounts Payable	221		248.00
		Staple Works, Inv. No. 2606.			
	31	Wages Expense	511	1,665.00	
		Cash	111		1,665.00
		Paid month's wages, Ck. No. 2333.			
	31	D. Stanfill, Drawing	312	1,800.00	
		Cash	111		1,800.00
		Ck. No. 2334.			

2, 3, 4.

Assets = Liabilities + Owner's Equity + Revenue − Expenses

Account	+ / −	Debit	Credit
Assets	+ Debit / − Credit		
Liabilities	− Debit / + Credit		
Owner's Equity	− Debit / + Credit		
Revenue	− Debit / + Credit		
Expenses	+ Debit / − Credit		

Cash 111

+ Debit	− Credit
Bal. 18,900	12/4 900
12/1 10,000	12/22 197
12/11 1,860	12/31 1,665
30,760	12/31 1,800
26,198	4,562

Accounts Receivable 112

+ Debit	− Credit
Bal. 6,300	12/11 1,860
12/19 2,150	
8,450	
Bal. 6,590	

Supplies 113

+ Debit	− Credit
Bal. 870	
12/23 248	
Bal. 1,118	

Prepaid Insurance 114

+ Debit	− Credit
Bal. 1,230	

Equipment 124

+ Debit	− Credit
Bal. 31,200	

Accounts Payable 221

− Debit	+ Credit
	Bal. 6,340
	12/23 248
	Bal. 6,588

D. Stanfill, Capital 311

− Debit	+ Credit
	Bal. 49,590
	12/1 10,000
	Bal. 59,590

D. Stanfill, Drawing 312

+ Debit	− Credit
Bal. 11,200	
12/31 1,800	
Bal. 13,000	

Service Income 411

− Debit	+ Credit
	Bal. 39,600
	12/19 2,150
	Bal. 41,750

Wages Expense 511

+ Debit	− Credit
Bal. 10,450	
12/31 1,665	
Bal. 12,115	

Utilities Expense 512

+ Debit	− Credit
Bal. 2,760	
12/22 197	
Bal. 2,957	

Rent Expense 513

+ Debit	− Credit
Bal. 12,620	
12/4 900	
Bal. 13,520	

5.

Stanfill Services
Trial Balance
December 31, 20—

ACCOUNT NAME	DEBIT	CREDIT
Cash	26,198.00	
Accounts Receivable	6,590.00	
Supplies	1,118.00	
Prepaid Insurance	1,230.00	
Equipment	31,200.00	
Accounts Payable		6,588.00
D. Stanfill, Capital		59,590.00
D. Stanfill, Drawing	13,000.00	
Service Income		41,750.00
Wages Expense	12,115.00	
Utilities Expense	2,957.00	
Rent Expense	13,520.00	
	107,928.00	107,928.00

6.

Stanfill Services
Income Statement
For Year Ended December 31, 20—

Revenue:		
Service Income		$41,750.00
Expenses:		
Wages Expense	$12,115.00	
Utilities Expense	2,957.00	
Rent Expense	13,520.00	
Total Expenses		28,592.00
Net Income		$13,158.00

7.

Stanfill Services
Statement of Owner's Equity
For Year Ended December 31, 20—

D. Stanfill, Capital, December 1, 20—	$49,590.00	
Additional Investment	10,000.00	
Total Investment		$59,590.00
Net Income	$13,158.00	
Less Withdrawals	13,000.00	
Increase in Capital		158.00
D. Stanfill, Capital, December 31, 20—		$59,748.00

8.

Stanfill Services
Balance Sheet
December 31, 20—

Assets		
Cash	$26,198.00	
Accounts Receivable	6,590.00	
Supplies	1,118.00	
Prepaid Insurance	1,230.00	
Equipment	31,200.00	
Total Assets		$66,336.00
Liabilities		
Accounts Payable		$6,588.00
Owner's Equity		
D. Stanfill, Capital		59,748.00
Total Liabilities and Owner's Equity		$66,336.00

CHAPTERS 4–5

Part I

1. b; 2. d; 3. d; 4. a; 5. a; 6. b; 7. c; 8. c

Part II

GENERAL JOURNAL PAGE 1

DATE		DESCRIPTION	POST. REF.	DEBIT	CREDIT
20–		Closing Entries			
Dec.	31	Income from Services		25,900 00	
		Income Summary			25,900 00
	31	Income Summary		8,500 00	
		Wages Expense			1,500 00
		Rent Expense			2,400 00
		Utilities Expense			1,000 00
		Depreciation Expense,			
		Equipment			500 00
		Supplies Expense			2,200 00
		Miscellaneous Expense			900 00
	31	Income Summary		17,400 00	
		T. L. Hanley, Capital			17,400 00
	31	T. L. Hanley, Capital		16,400 00	
		T. L. Hanley, Drawing			16,400 00

Part III

1. b; 2. h; 3. m; 4. q; 5. d; 6. k; 7. u; 8. w; 9. o; 10. s; 11. e; 12. f; 13. i; 14. n; 15. a; 16. t; 17. x; 18. p; 19. y; 20. v; 21. j; 22. c; 23. r; 24. l; 25. g

CHAPTERS 7–9

Part I

1. canceled; 2. deposit in transit or late deposit; 3. endorsement; 4. payee; 5. petty cash fund.

Part II

1. \$1,775 per month × 12 months = \$21,300 per year
   \$21,300 per year ÷ 52 weeks = \$409.62 per week
   \$409.62 per week ÷ 40 hours = \$10.24 per regular hour
   \$10.24 per regular hour × 1.5 = \$15.36 per overtime hour

   Earnings for 45 hours:

Forty hours at straight time = 40 × \$10.24 =	\$409.60
Five hours overtime = 5 × \$15.36 =	76.80
Total gross pay	\$486.40

2.

GENERAL JOURNAL PAGE ____

DATE		DESCRIPTION	POST. REF.	DEBIT	CREDIT
20–					
June	30	Cleaning Salaries Expense		9000 00	
		Office Salaries Expense		3000 00	
		Employees' Federal Income Tax Payable			1500 00
		FICA Tax Payable (\$12,000 × .062) + (\$12,000 × .0145)			918 00
		Savings Bonds Payable			500 00
		Medical Insurance Payable			962 00
		Salaries Payable			8120 00

3.

GENERAL JOURNAL PAGE ____

DATE		DESCRIPTION	POST. REF.	DEBIT	CREDIT
20–					
Dec.	31	Payroll Tax Expense		12477 50	
		FICA Tax Payable (\$143,000 × .062) + (\$155,000 × .0145)			11113 50
		State Unemployment Tax Payable (\$22,000 × .054)			1188 00
		Federal Unemployment Tax Payable (\$22,000 × .008)			176 00

Part III

1. T; 2. F; 3. F; 4. T; 5. F

CHAPTERS 10–12

Part I

1. credit; 2. accounts payable ledger; 3. cash discount; 4. purchase order; 5. Purchases; 6. buyer; 7. internal controls; 8. debit; 9. sales of merchandise on account; 10. charge customers.

Part II

1. CP; 2. J; 3. J; 4. J; 5. S; 6. J; 7. CP; 8. P; 9. CR; 10. CP

Part III

1. F; 2. T; 3. F; 4. F; 5. F

CHAPTERS 13–14

Part I

1. physical inventory; 2. perpetual inventory; 3. current liability; 4. Income Summary; 5. Cost of Goods Sold, Merchandise Inventory; 6. decrease; 7. Cost of Goods Sold; 8. working capital; 9. Income from Operations; 10. Freight In.

Part II

1. F; 2. F; 3. T; 4. T; 5. T; 6. F; 7. F; 8. T; 9. F; 10. T

Part III

1.

GENERAL JOURNAL PAGE ____

	DATE		DESCRIPTION	POST. REF.	DEBIT	CREDIT	
1	20–		Adjusting Entries				1
2	Dec.	31	Income Summary		132,000.00		2
3			Merchandise Inventory			132,000.00	3
4							4
5		31	Merchandise Inventory		136,000.00		5
6			Income Summary			136,000.00	6

2.

GENERAL JOURNAL PAGE ____

	DATE		DESCRIPTION	POST. REF.	DEBIT	CREDIT	
1	20–		Adjusting Entries				1
2	Dec.	31	Cost of Goods Sold		2,000.00		2
3			Merchandise Inventory			2,000.00	3

3.

GENERAL JOURNAL — PAGE ____

DATE		DESCRIPTION	POST. REF.	DEBIT	CREDIT
20–					
Dec.	1	Cash		20 000 00	
		Unearned Revenue			20 000 00
		To record collection of cash			
		for a four-month job.			
		Adjusting Entry			
	31	Unearned Revenue		5 000 00	
		Remodeling Revenue			5 000 00
		To record one month's			
		revenue earned.			

4. a. \$250,000 total assets − \$140,000 plant and equipment = \$110,000 current assets
\$130,000 total liabilities − \$80,000 long-term liabilities = \$50,000 current liabilities
\$110,000 current assets − \$50,000 current liabilities = \$60,000 working capital

b. $\frac{\$110{,}000 \text{ current assets}}{\$50{,}000 \text{ current liabilities}} = 2.2{:}1 \text{ current ratio}$

Credits

(credits continued from p. iv)

Chapter 3
p. 72, John Elk/Stock Boston; p. 89, Barbara File/Tony Stone Images.

Chapter 4
p. 112, © Griffin/The Image Works; p. 121, © Brink/The Image Works; p. 127, Joseph Sohm/Stock Boston.

Chapter 5
p. 150, Jeff Greenberg/Photo Edit; p. 157, courtesy of W. B. Mason Truck; p. 159, Bill Aron/Photo Edit.

Chapter 6
p. 193, R. P. Kingston/The Picture Cube; p. 197, Richard Pasley/Stock Boston; p. 199, Brian Hainer/Photo Edit.

Chapter 7
p. 227, Associated Press; p. 235, Tony Freeman/Photo Edit; p. 241, J. Greenberg/The Image Works.

Chapter 8
p. 262, Bruce Forester/Tony Stone Images; p. 263, G. Greenlar/The Image Works; p. 263, J. L. Berlcao/Gamma Liaison.

Chapter 9
p. 290, Stephen Ferry/Gamma Liaison; p. 296, B. Roland/The Image Works; p. 307, Bob Daemmrich/Stock Boston; p. 309, Gregg Mancuso/Stock Boston.

Chapter 10
p. 331, Tony Freeman/Photo Edit; p. 335, Greg Mancuso/Stock Boston; p. 347, Michael Newman/Photo Edit.

Chapter 11
p. 369, David Wells/The Image Works; p. 373, David Young Wolff/Photo Edit; p. 377, Bonnie Kamin/Photo Edit.

Chapter 12
p. 404, Gabe Palmer/The Stock Market; p. 405, Myrleen Ferguson/Photo Edit; p. 409, Bill Aron/Photo Edit.

Chapter 13
p. 445, Bob Mahoney/The Image Works; p. 446, Lawrence Migdale/Stock Boston; p. 448, Bob Daemmrich/The Image Works.

Chapter 14
p. 474, T. Shumsky/The Image Works; p. 479, Joe Sohm/Stock Boston; p. 483, Bob Daemmrich/Stock Boston.

Index

Note: *Boldface* indicates a key term and the page where it is defined.

The Accounting Cycle

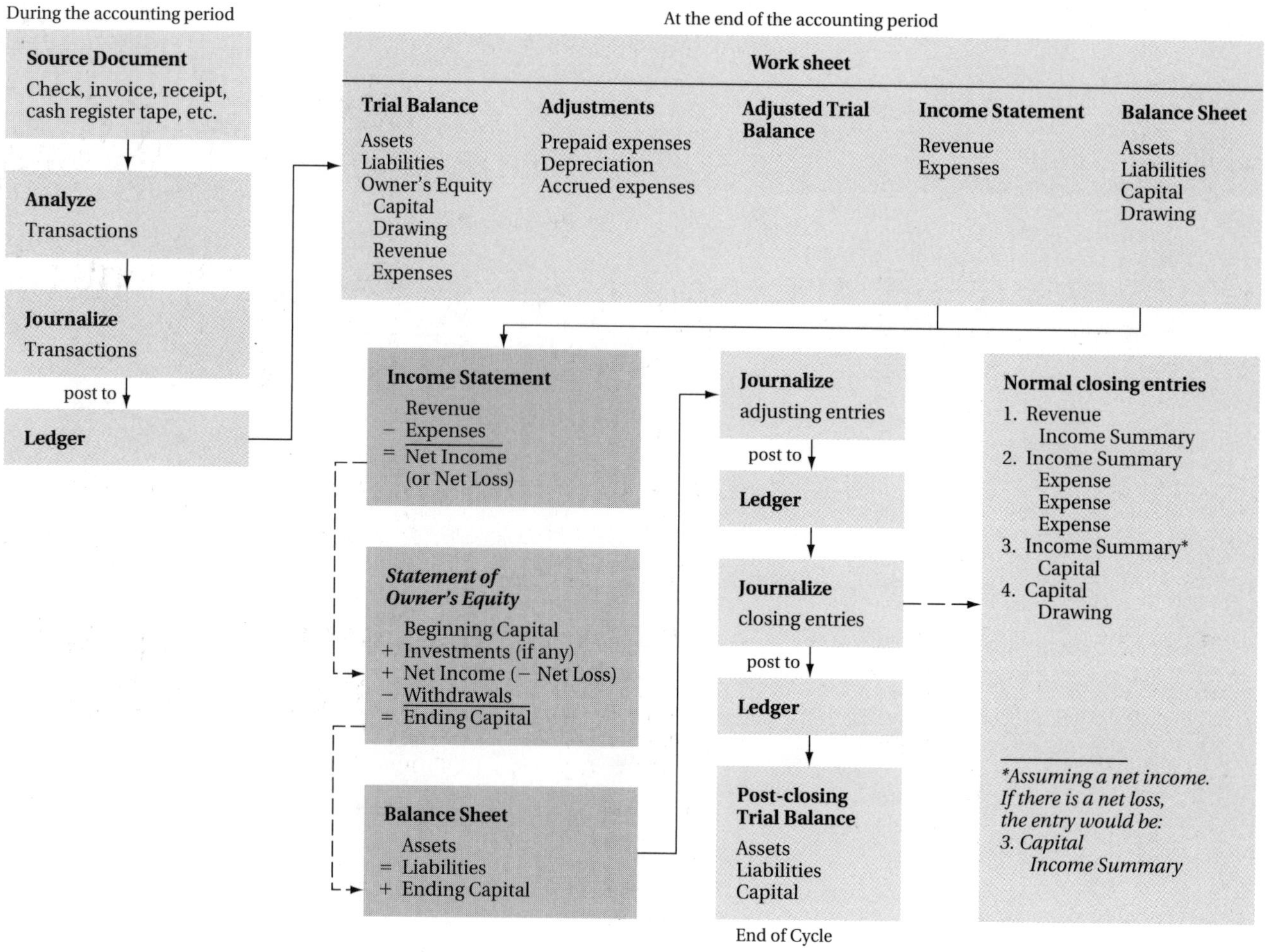

During the accounting period
Source Document
Check, invoice, receipt, cash register tape, etc.
Analyze
Transactions
Journalize
Transactions
post to
Ledger
At the end of the accounting period
Work sheet
Trial Balance
Assets
Liabilities
Owner's Equity
Capital
Drawing
Revenue
Expenses
Adjustments
Prepaid expenses
Depreciation
Accrued expenses
Adjusted Trial Balance
Income Statement
Revenue
Expenses
Balance Sheet
Assets
Liabilities
Capital
Drawing
Income Statement
Revenue
− Expenses
= Net Income
(or Net Loss)
Statement of Owner's Equity
Beginning Capital
+ Investments (if any)
+ Net Income (− Net Loss)
− Withdrawals
= Ending Capital
Balance Sheet
Assets
= Liabilities
+ Ending Capital
Journalize
adjusting entries
post to
Ledger
Journalize
closing entries
post to
Ledger
Post-closing Trial Balance
Assets
Liabilities
Capital
End of Cycle
Normal closing entries
1. Revenue
Income Summary
2. Income Summary
Expense
Expense
Expense
3. Income Summary*
Capital
4. Capital
Drawing
*Assuming a net income. If there is a net loss, the entry would be:
3. Capital
Income Summary